Cumberland and Westmorland Antiquarian and Archaeological Society
Research Series, Volume I

ROMANS IN NORTH-WEST ENGLAND

Excavations at the Roman forts of
Ravenglass, Watercrook and Bowness on Solway

by

T. W. Potter

with sections by

D. Charlesworth, J. Cherry, A. Donaldson, P. Fifield, K. F. Hartley, M. Henig, H. Lockwood, A. C. H. Olivier, D. C. A. Shotter, R. C. Turner, F. Wild and J. H. S. Witherington

ISBN 0 950077 9 1 7
PRINTED BY TITUS WILSON & SON LTD., KENDAL
1979

CONTENTS

                                                                        Page

List of figures vi

List of plates x

Preface xiii

I   THE ROMAN FORT AT RAVENGLASS 1
    Introduction 1
    Sites in the Ravenglass area:
        The settlement evidence .... J. Cherry 6
    The excavations (with R. C. Turner) 12
        The early fortlet, phase 0 14
        The defences of the later fort 19
        The rampart ovens 21
        The *intervallum* road 23
        The interior: phase 1 25
        The interior: phase 2 29
        The interior: phase 3 36
        The interior: phase 4 42
        The internal street 46
        Summary 48
    Bibliography 62

II RAVENGLASS: THE FINDS 65
    Brooches .... A. C. H. Olivier 65
    Other bronzes 69
    Stone discs 72
    Bone 72
    Glass armlets 72
    Beads 73
    Lead 73
    Whetstones 75
    Gaming-counters 75
    Iron 87
    Leather 90
    Wood 92
    Querns .... R. C. Turner 94
    Tile 96
    Gemstones .... Martin Henig 97
    Glass .... Dorothy Charlesworth 99

Flints .... R. C. Turner   100
Graffiti .... D. C. A. Shotter   101
Medallion   102
Coins .... D. C. A. Shotter   102
Coarse pottery .... Helen Lockwood   106
Mortaria stamps .... K. F. Hartley   120
Samian ware .... Felicity Wild   123
Faunal remains .... R. C. Turner   133
Botanical analysis .... Alison Donaldson   133
Bibliography   136

III   THE ROMAN FORT AT WATERCROOK   139
    Introduction   139
    The excavations of 1974-75   148
        The fort defences, rampart walls and fence   150
        The north east gate and road   156
        The east angle of the fort   167
        The ditches and other elements of the outer defences   168
        The military area: chronological discussion and implications ...   176
        The north *vicus*   180
        The east *vicus*   185
        The fluvial history: the results of the January 1975 excavations   195
    Bibliography   203

IV   WATERCROOK: THE FINDS   205
    Silver   205
    Bronze   206
    Brooches .... A. C. H. Olivier   206
    Other bronzes   212
    Lead   217
    Stone and clay   218
    Jet and amber   218
    Bone   218
    Leather   220
    Tile and slate   220
    Iron   220
    Glass, beads, armlets .... Dorothy Charlesworth   230
    Querns .... R. C. Turner   234
    Flints .... R. C. Turner   234
    Epigraphy .... D. C. A. Shotter   236
    Coarse pottery .... Helen Lockwood   237
    Mortarium stamp .... K. F. Hartley   268
    Samian ware .... Felicity Wild   269
    Coins .... D. C. A. Shotter   291
    Animal bones .... P. W. Fifield   299
    Bibliography   312

V   WATERCROOK AND RAVENGLASS:
THE NAMES AND THE GARRISONS .... D. C. A. Shotter   315
Antonine Itinerary 316
Notitia Dignitatum 317
Ravenna Cosmography 319
Bibliography 320

VI   THE ROMAN FORT AT BOWNESS ON SOLWAY 321
Introduction 321
The 1976 excavations .... R. C. Turner and J. H. S. Witherington   324
Description of the phases 327
Chronology of the phases 1-3 333
Interpretation of the building 334
Small objects 336
Roman and medieval pottery .... R. C. Turner and J. H. S. Witherington   337
Samian ware .... Felicity Wild   344
Coins .... D. C. A. Shotter   348
Bibliography 349

VII   SYNTHESIS:
THE ROMAN OCCUPATION OF THE NORTH-WEST 351
Data and method 351
Native settlements 353
Early military occupation 356
Hadrian's Wall and the second century 358
The third and fourth centuries 364
Bibliography 366

INDEX 369

LIST OF FIGURES

Page

1. Map illustrating recently excavated sites and Roman forts in north-west England... xii
2. Sites in the Ravenglass area 2
3. General plan of the fort platform at Ravenglass 4
4. Map showing the contours and trench plan of the site at Ravenglass 11
5. Ravenglass: plan summarizing the main features of each phase 13
6. Ravenglass: plan of the early Hadrianic fortlet 15
7. A reconstruction of a section of the breastwork of the Hadrianic fortlet at Ravenglass 17
8. Plan of the defences of the later fort at Ravenglass 19
9. Ravenglass: plans of successive ovens behind the rampart 22
10. Ravenglass: section through the ovens behind the rampart 23
11. Ravenglass: plan of the interior in phase 1 26
12. Ravenglass: plan of the interior in phase 2 30
13. Ravenglass: diagram showing the chronological distribution of dated finds in the destruction deposits marking the end of phase 2 35
14. Ravenglass: plan of the interior in phase 3 37
15. Ravenglass: plan of the interior in phase 4 43
16. Ravenglass: plans of the medieval grave 48
17. Ravenglass: trench E 51
18. Ravenglass: sections through the ditch and palisade of the Hadrianic fortlet 52
19. Ravenglass: section through the defences of the later fort 54
20. Ravenglass: the west sections of trenches C and B 55
21. Ravenglass: sections of trench D 58
22. Ravenglass: the south section of trench C 60
23. Ravenglass: the north section of trench B 60
24. Ravenglass: section through the rubbish pit of phase 2 61
25. Ravenglass: section across trench F 61
26. Ravenglass: objects of bronze 66
27. Ravenglass: objects of bronze, stone, bone, glass 70
28. Ravenglass: objects of lead, stone 74
29. Ravenglass: bone gaming-counters 80
30. Ravenglass: bone gaming-counters 84
31. Ravenglass: gaming-counters 87
32. Ravenglass: objects of iron 88
33. Ravenglass: objects of leather 91
34. Ravenglass: objects of wood 93

35. Ravenglass: quernstones 95
36. Ravenglass: tile from phase 3 96
37. Ravenglass: vessels of glass 99
38. Ravenglass: flints 101
39. Histogram showing the distribution of coarse-wares at Ravenglass 106
40. Ravenglass: coarse-ware 107
41. Ravenglass: coarse-ware 109
42. Ravenglass: coarse-ware 111
43. Ravenglass: coarse-ware 113
44. Ravenglass: coarse-ware 115
45. Ravenglass: coarse-ware 117
46. Ravenglass: coarse-ware 119
47. Ravenglass: the mortaria stamps and amphora stamp 121
48. Ravenglass: samian 125
49. Ravenglass: samian 127
50. Ravenglass: samian 129
51. Ravenglass: samian 131
52. Map of sites and roads in the Watercrook area 140
53. Plan of the Watercrook peninsula 142
54. The Roman fort at Watercrook showing details from excavation, aerial
    photography and parch-marks 144
55. Defences at the south corner of the fort at Watercrook 145
56. Watercrook: plan of the central range 146
57. Watercrook: general plan of the north-east defences 151
58. Watercrook: detailed plan of the east angle of the fort 153
59. Watercrook: detailed plan of the north-east gate 157
60. Watercrook: plan and section of the east guard-chamber 158
61. Diagram illustrating the distribution of dated objects from the east
    guard-chamber 159
62. Histogram showing the distribution of samian from Watercrook and
    Ravenglass 162
63. Histogram showing the distribution of dated coarse-ware from the military
    areas and north *vicus* at Watercrook 162
64. Plan showing the location of the sections for the military areas and north
    vicus at Watercrook 163
65. Watercrook: sections through the east angle of fort and the north-east
    gateway 165
66. Watercrook: section through the north-east road and fence 166
67. Watercrook: section through the north defences 169
68. Watercrook: section through ditch 1 170
69. Watercrook: section through ditches 1a and 1b 171
70. Watercrook: plan and section of the palisade trench 172
71. Watercrook: sections through ditch 2 173
72. Watercrook: section through ditch 2 174
73. Watercrook: section through ditch 2 175
74. Watercrook: section through ditch 3 176

75. Watercrook: plan of timber buildings in the north *vicus* 181
76. Watercrook: iron-smithing hearth 184
77. Watercrook: east *vicus* (site A) general plan 186
78. Watercrook: east *vicus* section 189
79. Watercrook: east *vicus* section 191
80. Watercrook: east *vicus* section 192
81. Histogram showing distribution of coarse pottery from the east *vicus* 194
82. Watercrook: section of the alluvial deposits 195
83. Watercrook: the remains of kilns in the bank of the River Kent 196
84. Watercrook: objects of silver and bronze 207
85. Watercrook: objects of bronze 213
86. Watercrook: objects of bronze 216
87. Watercrook: objects of lead, stone, clay, jet, amber 219
88. Watercrook: objects of bone and iron 221
89. Watercrook: objects of iron 225
90. Watercrook: objects of iron 227
91. Watercrook: objects of iron 228
92. Watercrook: objects of iron 229
93. Watercrook: vessels of glass 231
94. Watercrook: objects of glass 233
95. Watercrook: quernstones 235
96. Watercrook: flint tools 235
97. Watercrook: coarse-ware 239
98. Watercrook: coarse-ware 240
99. Watercrook: coarse-ware 242
100. Watercrook: coarse-ware 244
101. Watercrook: coarse-ware 245
102. Watercrook: coarse-ware 247
103. Watercrook: coarse-ware 249
104. Watercrook: coarse-ware 251
105. Watercrook: coarse-ware 253
106. Watercrook: coarse-ware 255
107. Watercrook: coarse-ware 256
108. Watercrook: coarse-ware 258
109. Watercrook: coarse-ware 261
110. Watercrook: coarse-ware 263
111. Watercrook: coarse-ware 264
112. Watercrook: coarse-ware 266
113. Watercrook: coarse-ware 267
114. Watercrook: samian 271
115. Watercrook: samian 273
116. Watercrook: samian 275
117. Watercrook: samian 279
118. Watercrook: samian 281
119. Watercrook: samian 283
120. Watercrook: samian 285

121. Watercrook: samian 287
122. Watercrook: samian 288
123. Watercrook: mortarium stamp and illiterate stamp 291
124. Watercrook: histogram of the coins 294
125. Measurements for cattle bones from Watercrook 302
126. Bowness on Solway: plan of the fort 322
127. Bowness on Solway: general plan of the 1973 excavations 323
128. Bowness on Solway: plan showing the excavated areas 324
129. Bowness on Solway: general plan of the excavations 325
130. Bowness on Solway: section through the clay quarry pit 326
131. Bowness on Solway: interpretative plan of the buildings of phases 1-3 327
132. Bowness on Solway: sections 328
133. Bowness on Solway: detailed plan of zone E 329
134. Bowness on Solway: plan of the fourth-century building 331
135. Histograms showing the distribution of datable coarse-ware from the
      1973 and 1976 excavations 333
136. Bowness on Solway: the small objects 336
137. Bowness on Solway: coarse-ware 338
138. Bowness on Solway: coarse-ware 340
139. Bowness on Solway: coarse-ware 341
140. Bowness on Solway: medieval pottery 343
141. Bowness on Solway: samian vessel from the clay quarry pit 345
142. Bowness on Solway: samian vessel and mortaria stamps 346
143. Histogram showing coins from Roman sites in Cumbria 352
144. Map showing the distribution of native sites in Cumbria and northern
      Lancashire 355
145. Map showing successive phases in the Roman military occupation of
      Cumbria 357
146. Biglands milefortlet: the sequence of occupation 361
147. Distribution of dated inscriptions of the later second and early third
      centuries 362
148. Maryport: distribution of dated finds 363
149. Distribution of Roman military sites and coin-finds in Cumbria and
      northern Lancashire in 253-70 and the late fourth century 364

LIST OF PLATES

Ia.   Ravenglass: aerial photograph taken at the end of the 1976 season

Ib.   The fort platform at Ravenglass seen from the estuary

IIa.   Ravenglass: general view of the 1976 excavation

IIb.   Ravenglass: ditch of the early Hadrianic fortlet (phase 0)

IIIa.   Ravenglass: part of a palisade stake in the cleaning-channel of the ditch of the early Hadrianic fortlet

IIIb.   Ravenglass: palisade trench of the early Hadrianic fortlet

IVa.   Ravenglass: the defences of the later fort

IVb.   Ravenglass: the latest of the three ovens at the back of the rampart

Va.   Ravenglass: an earlier tiled oven at the back of the rampart

Vb.   Ravenglass: stone-lined drain of fourth-century date

VIa.   Ravenglass: trench B, phases 1 and 2

VIb.   Ravenglass: wall-trenches towards the end of excavation in trench C

VIIa.   Ravenglass: trench C, phases 3 and 4

VIIb.   Ravenglass: tile hearth in the inner room of barrack-block 7, phase 3

VIIIa. Ravenglass: trench B, *intervallum* road and drain

VIIIb. Ravenglass: bag of gaming-counters, resting on burnt floorboards

IX.   Ravenglass: the gaming-counters

Xa.   Ravenglass: gemstones

Xb.   Ravenglass: the bronze medallion of Admiral Vernon, 1739

XI.   Watercrook: aerial photograph looking south-east

XIIa.   Watercrook: the east corner of the fort

XIIb.   Watercrook: detail of the fort wall

XIIIa. Watercrook: the junction between the incomplete fort wall of phase 2 and the fort wall of phase 3

XIIIb. Watercrook: the east guard-chamber of the north-east gate

XIVa.   Watercrook: detail showing the masonry of the north wall of the east guard-chamber

XIVb.   Watercrook: the north-east gate, blocking wall and drain

XVa.   Watercrook: the north-east road

XVb.   Watercrook: the inner ditch

XVIa.   Watercrook: the inner ditch

XVIb.   Watercrook: palisade-trench on the berm between ditches 1 and 2

XVIIa. Watercrook: tips of iron slag and charcoal filling the lower part of ditch 2

XVIIb. Watercrook: ditch 2

XVIIIa. Watercrook: ditch 3

XVIIIb. Watercrook: lime-kiln set into alluvium beside the River Kent

XIXa.   Watercrook: general view of the north *vicus*

XIXb.   Watercrook: stone-packed post-settings in a wall-trench of the north *vicus* building

XXa.   Watercrook: the service road overlying ditch 1a

XXb.   Watercrook: wall-trench and a line of stakes in the east *vicus*

XXIa.   Watercrook: east *vicus*, section through the floors of the phase 3 building

XXIb.   Watercrook: east *vicus*, section through the floors and occupation deposits

XXIIa. Bowness on Solway: aerial view of the village

XXIIb. Bowness on Solway: at the end of the excavation

XXIIIa. Bowness on Solway: north part of the site

XXIIIb. Bowness on Solway: zone D, showing the east wall of the building of phases 2 and 3

XXIVa. Bowness on Solway: one of the timber sill-beam partitions

XXIVb. Bowness on Solway: zone C, showing postholes of the fourth-century building

BEWCASTLE

Birdoswald

BOWNESS
BIGLANDS
TURRET 4b
SILLOTH
KIRKBRIDE
CARLISLE

Beckfoot

Old Carlisle

OLD PENRITH

Maryport

CROSS HILL FARM

Burrow Walls

Moresby

MAIDEN CASTLE

Hardknott   Ambleside

Low
Borrow
Bridge

RAVENGLASS

■ WATERCROOK

■ HINCASTER

■ BURROW-IN-LONSDALE

■ Lancaster University excavations
Recent excavations
□ military △ native

○ Other major forts

■ LANCASTER

0   10   20   30
                          km

■ RIBCHESTER

R.C.T. 1978

FIG. I. – Map illustrating recently excavated sites and Roman forts in north-west England.

PREFACE

The excavations reported in this volume represent the results of five years' work in the north-west of England. All of the investigations were carried out as rescue projects, conducted for the Department of the Environment by a team from the University of Lancaster. Five principal sites were involved, all of them Roman forts or fortlets: Bowness on Solway on Hadrian's Wall; Biglands House and Ravenglass on the Cumbrian coast; and Watercrook and Lancaster in the hinterland. Minor work was also carried out at Burrow in Lonsdale and Hincaster. Some of the results have already been published either in preliminary or in final form, while discussion of the excavations in Lancaster is to appear in a separate volume. Here, the final reports are set out for Ravenglass and Watercrook and for the 1976 season at Bowness on Solway. In addition, I have included summaries of some other work and have attempted a brief synthesis of the data now available for the Roman occupation of north-west England.

While any attempt at synthesis may well seem premature, it is nevertheless the case that the volume of archaeological work in the region has increased dramatically over the last few years, especially on Roman sites. Not since the days of the Cumberland Excavation Committee (which became effectively moribund in the early 1950s) has there been such a concerted effort to initiate large-scale research. The 1950s and 60s, it is true, saw some important rescue and research excavations, including a major project in 1966 at Maryport to celebrate the centenary of this Society. In addition, Richard Bellhouse was carrying out a brilliant campaign of field-work and small-scale excavation upon sites of the Cumberland coast and elsewhere, based entirely on amateur resources. Even so, the commitment of archaeological expertise and finance was beginning to fall far short of the levels being applied elsewhere in the country. At the same time, chronological models evolved for Hadrian's Wall were being increasingly accepted without the rigorous testing that these ideas demanded.

Early in the 1970s the situation began to change. Not only did the prevalent hypotheses about the archaeological development of the Roman North come under scrutiny, but the much greater resources made available by the Department of the Environment for rescue work meant that the current models could be thoroughly examined through further excavation. In 1973, the creation of archaeology as a teaching subject in Lancaster University afforded the opportunity to build up a new field-work team. Within a few weeks of my own appointment as the University's first lecturer in archaeology, we were exploring a bath-house in Lancaster, brought to light by building work; and within three months the team was in the field at Bowness on Solway, a Hadrian's Wall site that had seen no proper work inside the fort since 1930. It soon became evident that the scale of the rescue problem was a very considerable one, far more than a University team, tied to vacations, could really cope with. Over the five years between 1973 and 1978, there were no less than 18 separate seasons of work in the north-west; in addition, the same team also undertook three rescue excavations in central Italy and one in Algeria. The English projects were funded by the Department of the Environment, backed up handsomely by the University of Lancaster, where all kinds of resources were made available. At the same time, Manchester University, under Barri Jones, began to extend its areas of research and started a programme of systematic aerial survey, combined with carefully chosen excavation projects: rescue work at Ribchester and Lancaster in the early 1970s was followed by survey of parts of Cumbria, and the study both of native sites, such as Crosshill Farm near Penrith, and of military sites on the Cumberland coast. Equally important was the creation in 1974 of an archaeological post in the Planning Department of the Cumbria County Council, where construction threats could be monitored; and in 1976 of a Field Officer for Lancashire, based at the University of Lancaster.

By the mid 1970s, however, it was becoming clear that University rescue teams could only fulfil a limited role in rescue work. The need was increasingly for field teams that could be available throughout the year, to deal with threats as they arose and to undertake long-term excavation. Carlisle, a site of exceptional interest for Roman and medieval studies and with rich organic deposits, was one obvious place to create a permanent unit. The first appointments were made in 1977 and the team has now completed a year-long examination of a fascinating and crucial site in the centre of the city. The Central Excavation Unit has also been at work in the region with a large-scale, long-term project at the fort of Old Penrith, and the basis of a permanent excavation unit for Lancashire and Cumbria is now being established at Lancaster University. As a result we can expect over the next few years both extensive excavations of the highest standards and a wealth of new data.

The 1970s therefore will probably prove to have been a decisive period in the history of archaeological work in the north-west. As long-established ideas come increasingly into question, so has the volume and scale of the field-work seen a dramatic increase. It is an encouraging moment to present some of the first results of this new phase of research, and I am delighted that the Society, one of the oldest in the country, has undertaken to publish our work as the first of a new series of monographs.

Acknowledgements

It is a particularly pleasant duty to record my warmest gratitude to the members of the team that has accomplished so much over the last five years. Through their enthusiasm and hard work, an enormous amount of field-work has been achieved in a very short space of time, often involving the sacrifice of most or all of the vacations and, frequently, spare moments of term-time as well. A great deal of credit goes to those who supervised the sites and made the field records, amongst them Richard Andrews, Tim Appleton, Gerald Dudgeon, Stuart Eastwood, Peter Fisher, Nick Hakiel, Peg Howard, David Longley, Hilary Major, Robert Poulton, Colin Reed, Edmund Southworth, Nick Stylianou, Rick Turner, Elizabeth Tutty and John Witherington; indeed, several have made their own contribution to this volume. I would also like to thank Helen Lockwood who ran the finds department on virtually all of the excavations and, while holding a Research Assistant post at Lancaster University (funded by the Department of the Environment), brought together much of the material into publishable form. The speed with which this volume has been assembled is due in large part to her efforts. Special credit is due, too, to Rick Turner, Graduate Assistant at Lancaster University; he has been very actively concerned in the field-work since 1975 and has produced many of the drawings and substantial sections of text for this report. Similarly, John Witherington has been closely associated with the field-work since the very first project in Lancaster in October 1973 and taken a supervisory role at nearly every site, both in Britain and abroad.

The University of Lancaster has played a very important part in the programme of field-work. Not only have excellent facilities been provided at both the University and at Watercrook, but there has been generous provision both of equipment and finance. To the Vice-Chancellor, Sir Charles Carter, and the many administrative officers (especially those in the Finance Department), who have been involved in the organisation of our work, I offer my warm thanks. I would like to pay special tribute to my colleagues, who have accepted the metamorphosis of the Department of Classics with startling equanimity, and who have helped the growth of archaeological studies at Lancaster in every possible way. I should especially like to thank the Professor of Classics, Malcolm Willcock, for his support, and David Shotter, Senior Lecturer in Classics. David Shotter's contribution to Roman north-west studies is well known and he has provided some vital sections of this volume. He also played a crucial role both in the setting up of archaeology at Lancaster and in the implementation of the programme of field-work.

Outside the University, my principal debt of gratitude is to the Department of the Environment and especially to Miss Dorothy Charlesworth. There has been very substantial government funding for all our projects, both in terms of field-work and at a post-excavation level. That the programme of work has developed so smoothly is due in large measure to Miss Charlesworth's skilful and painstaking direction. The Department of the Environment has also made an extremely generous subvention towards the costs of this book. I would also like to express my thanks to the officers of the Cumberland and Westmorland Antiquarian and Archaeological Society for their help in the work of publication, especially Fred Hughes and Anthony Ellwood (in addition, one of our most dedicated volunteers), and, too, the many people who have aided our research, amongst them Lindsay Allason-Jones (Newcastle University), David Breeze, Tom Clare (Cumbria County Council), Clare Fell, Barri Jones (Manchester University), Michael McCarthy (Director of the Carlisle Unit), Colin Richardson (Tullie House Museum, Carlisle) and Andrew White (formerly of Lancaster Museum). My debt to those who have provided specialist reports will become evident from the chapters of this book, but particular mention should be made to Felicity Wild's studies of the samian, a task made daunting both by the large volume of material and the deadlines that rapid publication has set.

Finally, I should like to thank Professor Sheppard Frere, who read substantial sections of the draft manuscript and made numerous suggestions for improvements; our marvellous secretarial team of Janet Atkins, June Clayton and Pat Kitchen; and all those, too numerous to name individually, who have in one way or another contributed to and supported our work. The five years' teamwork that this volume describes has for me been a particularly rich and rewarding time.

6th June 1978   Timothy Potter
Department of Classics and Archaeology
Lancaster University.

CHAPTER I

THE ROMAN FORT AT RAVENGLASS

INTRODUCTION

THE ROMAN FORT at Ravenglass lies at the foot of a long spur extending south-westwards from the fells and pikes of the Eskdale hills (Fig. 2). The spur is bounded by two rivers, the Mite to the north and the Esk to the south. Of the two, the Esk is by far the larger. It rises high in the fells to the north-east of Hardknott and then runs towards the sea in an increasingly broad valley, forming a prominent natural corridor nearly a kilometre wide. The Mite, on the other hand, is a smaller stream, draining the western slopes of Eskdale; but it belongs to the much larger system whose principal river, the Irt, has carved out a triangular area of flattish ground extending as far as Wast Water. Both the Irt and the Mite drain into an estuary just to the north of Ravenglass, while the Esk joins them to the south, creating a small bay. This is protected from the open sea by sand bars but there is a navigable channel through them, making the site a perfect harbour for boats with a shallow draught (Caine 1922). That this was a factor which influenced the position of the Roman fort seems quite clear, for the site is otherwise remotely located and comparatively difficult of access: land communications, for example, would have been much better served by building the fort towards the mouth of the Mite, where there are easy routes both to the north and to the east (via the trough of low ground at Eskdale Green). In fact, the Roman command chose a site right on the edge of the bay, where shipping could tie up close to the fort. It seems evident, therefore, that Ravenglass was designed to liaise between a naval detachment and the land garrisons, a task that, in a topographical sense, it was well equipped to do.

The land bordering the fort is fertile and easily farmed. Today it is used both for pasture and for cereal cultivation, and would have been well suited to the development of the extensive civilian settlement that there appears to have been at Ravenglass (Birley 1958, 26; Salway 1965, 125-6). The site chosen for the fort lay between two of the numerous stream-gullies that drain westwards into the bay, dividing the land above the shore into a series of low spurs. None of these gullies is particularly large but they do have the effect of restricting the area available for building, so that the fort could have a width no greater than about 150 m. On the other hand, they also provided some measure of defence and appear to have been incorporated into the ditch system. Details of the overall plan are not easy to work out since much of the site is heavily overgrown with a dense plantation of conifers. This extends over the whole of the eastern sector of the fort platform, open ground being confined to a narrow driveway leading down to Walls House. In addition, part of the platform has been completely removed by a massive cutting for the Furness railway. This forms a wide swathe, 60 m across and 15 m deep, which runs diagonally through the site, and has completely obliterated all archaeological features

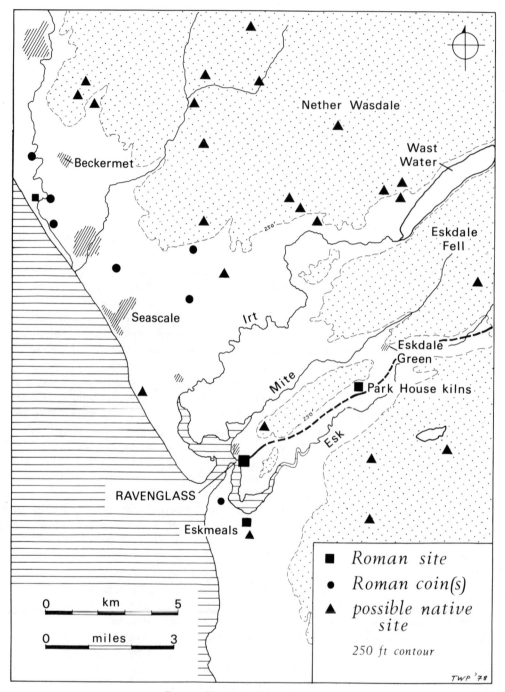

FIG. 2. – Sites in the Ravenglass area.

along its course. Yet, despite, these encumbrances, something of the plan of the fort can be defined (Fig. 3). Its rectangular form is not in doubt, since the line of the ditch and bank can be followed on both the east and north sides (where the natural gully appears to have reinforced the ditch), and meet at right angles. There is no trace, however, of either the rampart or the ditches along the southern side of the platform, so that the limits cannot be precisely ascertained; on the other hand, the ground drops away so steeply beyond the last visible point of the eastern rampart that we can safely assume a return line approximately as indicated on Fig. 3, an observation that closely matches the rather clearer topography of the area to the west of the railway line. If so, when the data from the excavations to the west of the railway are taken into account, we can suggest a size of 3·6 acres for the fort at Ravenglass, a figure closely comparable to that of Watercrook.

There is some corroboration for these measurements in the description provided by R. G. Collingwood (1928). Collingwood did not publish a general plan of the site, but he saw it before it was planted with trees and made a precise record of his observations. Indeed, his figures correspond almost exactly with those of the survey made under far from ideal conditions in 1976 (Fig. 3). In addition, Collingwood noted a number of features that are no longer visible. The east rampart, for example, is described as a "well-defined bank . . . between 3 and 5 feet high", beyond which was a double ditch, partially covered by the drive to the Walls Castle. The north rampart was similarly obvious, lying behind a single ditch that became "deeper as it travels westward and develops into a ravine about 20 ft. deep". On the south side was a "very clear and sharp rampart, falling to a flattish strip of ground beyond which is a little ravine with a stream at the bottom. Surface indications show no ditch".

Collingwood's remarks give confidence that the outline plan (Fig. 3) is reasonably close to the original dimensions of the site: that it was a small fort with space appropriate to a quingenary unit. But despite that fact that the site was first referred to as early as 1600 in Camden's *Britannia,* there has never been much attempt to explore the buildings of the fort. Some discoveries were made in 1850 when the railway was laid across the site, including "three remarkable constructions about 20 yards apart from each other". These apparently consisted of pits some 15 feet deep, with a narrow square mouth and a shape that widened to a diameter of 10-12 feet at the bottom. The floor was flagged and the sides made of big logs, laid horizontally. The fill consisted of "dark, peaty matter which . . . contained many various bones and many human bones and skulls of various sizes. There were two oak clubs found in one of the structures, and a skin covering for the leg, with thongs attached" (Jackson 1876, 18-19). But no dating evidence for these pits is recorded, although the same cutting did yield a gold coin of Vespasian. In the same paper Jackson also mentions that there were no traces of internal buildings, the surviving structures being confined to Walls Castle (the bath-house) (Fig. 3), and the remains of "round towers" at the two eastern angles. His description (Knowles and Jackson 1876) of the bath-house, a finely preserved building situated a short distance from the north-east corner of the fort, does appear to have encouraged some work on the site for, in 1881, he, Chancellor Ferguson and Joseph Robinson of Maryport carried out some excavation upon Walls Castle (Jackson 1883; Ferguson 1888). They uncovered several rooms to the east of the standing remains, although they did not attempt any exploration of the part to the north and south. Nevertheless it became clear from their work that Ravenglass possessed a large and complex bath-house, with at least four ranges of rooms and a total width of nearly 90 feet (27·6 m). Subsequently, in 1885-6, Lord Muncaster carried out some work on the fort itself. A "short length of the western wall showing a bold set-off" was uncovered which, if correctly interpreted, would suggest that cliff erosion has advanced dramatically since that date; but otherwise the gates and angles were found to have been more or less completely robbed of stone and only "trails" of walls were uncovered in the interior (Ferguson 1888). Consequently the programme of excavation was abandoned and, despite the valuable syntheses of Collingwood (1928) and Birley (1958), no further attempts to dig the site have been made.

The only fieldwork to be carried out in the period between the late nineteenth-century excavations and the present programme was a careful study of the surface remains, made by Miss Mary Fair. In 1925, she reported "shattered slates, bricks, floor tesserae, *tegulae*

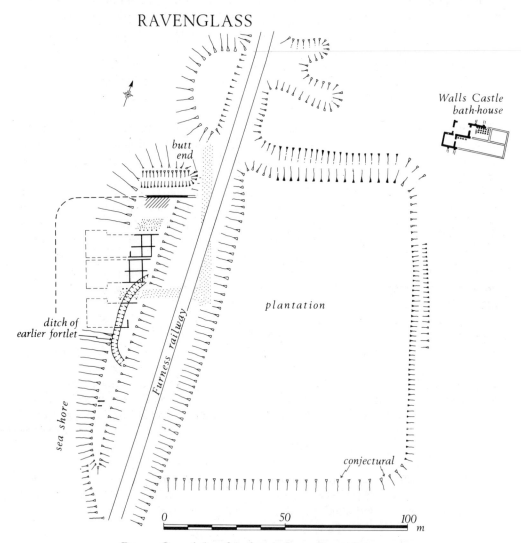

FIG. 3. – General plan of the fort platform at Ravenglass.

scored to hold plaster, box-flue tiles and heavy floor-tiles" from a substantial structure to the north of the fort (Fair 1925). This presumably lay close to the road heading up the coastal plain towards the other forts of the Cumbrian coastal system and was one of the more important buildings of the *vicus*. At the same time she began a careful watch of the rapidly eroding cliff to the west of the railway. Her observations, fully summarised by Birley (1958), showed that there were levels with burnt construction beams (interpreted by Birley as a destruction deposit to be associated with the end of the first period on Hadrian's Wall in A.D. 197) and considerable quantities of pottery and other finds. It was clear, therefore, that this area lay within the fort and that the defences had been eroded away.

It was the rapid acceleration of this coastal erosion that finally prompted a renewal of work upon the site. When described by Collingwood in 1928, this area west of the railway (Fig. 4) consisted of a "slender triangle, 20 yards across at widest, now under grass". Since then the activities of sea, wind and people have combined to reduce the width quite considerably, especially in recent years. Eventually, in 1975, the decision was taken to mount a rescue excavation upon the site, to be undertaken by the University of Lancaster for the Department of the Environment. Two main seasons of work ensued, one a five-week campaign in July-August 1976, followed by a much longer period of excavation between March and May 1977. A few days' work was also carried out in June 1978. Although the site proved to be more damaged by post-Roman ploughing than had been anticipated, we were able to examine the greater part of the surviving area. Only the major east-west baulks between the trenches, a walkway along the edge of the railway cutting and a narrow strip at the south end of the triangle (which was used for dumping as no stratigraphy survived there) were left untouched. As a sample it is not large – just over 600 m² – amounting to less than 5% of the area within the defences. On the other hand, the value of the excavation was considerably enhanced by the fact that the trenches cut across the buildings, thus providing maximum data about the layout of the site. In addition, three of the five trenches yielded a fairly deep stratigraphy, from whose study emerged a comparatively clear idea of the plan and history of these structures. The sum result of this work, therefore, is a detailed understanding of the development of one corner of a significant and, in some respects, unusual fort, gained for a comparatively modest investment of time and resources. Whether other parts of the platform will ever become available for excavation is a matter for conjecture; but, even if they do, it seems likely that the combination of stone robbing, ploughing and tree and root disturbances will have damaged much of the site almost beyond recall. The area studied in 1976-78 thus takes on particular importance since it must represent the best preserved section of the fort.

SITES IN THE RAVENGLASS AREA (Fig. 2)

Our knowledge of the settlement patterns in the vicinity of Ravenglass is due very largely to the intensive field surveys made over a number of years by Mr J. Cherry. He has kindly contributed a discussion of his results, presented below. Only two matters require additional comment; the Ravenglass-Hardknott road and the Park House (or Muncaster) kilns. The road, which provided Ravenglass with a cross-country route through to Ambleside and thus south-eastern Cumbria, has received authoritative study in an article by Richmond (1949), and needs no detailed description here. The magnificently engineered section through the mountains at Hardknott and Wrynose is a well known and still finely preserved example of Roman military work. West of Hardknott, on the other hand, its course is much less certain, since the intensive agriculture of Eskdale has long since removed all obvious traces of its line. Its probable route is indicated by a dashed line on Fig. 2, but the only points where its position is certain is at Ravenglass itself and at the Park House kilns. Clearly, however, it kept as far as possible to the low flat ground bordering the valley, skirting the Muncaster Head ridge.

The Park House kiln site has been known since 1884 but has still to receive the attention it merits. Two kilns have been identified, both of rectanglar form with a long stokehole. They were definitively examined by Mr R. L. Bellhouse in 1959 and 1960 and shown to be concerned with the production of tiles. Second-century pottery was associated with them. Bellhouse (1960, 1961) has also gathered together earlier references to the site, including the comments of Miss Mary Fair, who evidently did some digging there. Her most elusive reference (Fair 1948) is to a "potter's workshop or perhaps the supervisor's house; it had a floor of tiles and walls of timber and wattle and daub". She makes it clear elsewhere that there was pottery manufacture at the site although Bellhouse was unable to locate either the potter's workshop or any pottery wasters. Nevertheless, it seems clear that at Park House we have a small tile and pottery factory, rather like that at Quernmore, which served the fort at Lancaster (Leather *in* Jones and Shotter 1978). In Chap. II we shall attempt to identify the pottery made at Park House in terms of the material recovered from the present excavations.

The Settlement Evidence by J. CHERRY

The narrow coastal plain of west Cumberland has been extensively farmed so that structural remains of pre-medieval occupation no longer exist. Cultivation of the fells has been largely confined to the lower slopes so that much of the land above 500 ft is used only for grazing of sheep, and consequently the destruction of the evidence of habitation in this region has been much less severe. The most common of the fellside remains are the cairns, and until comparatively recently the popular view of these was that they were monuments covering burials of the Bronze Age. The first record of the remains of the west Cumberland fells was made by Ward (1877) and it was noticeable that in his description of groups of cairns he made occasional reference to associated "ancient walls". Later surveys by J. Cherry and J. Bromwich in the Birker Fell and Dunnerdale Fell area (Cherry 1961) showed that many of the groups of cairns lay between the 500 and 800 ft contours, and were often associated with the remains of stone walls and structures which appeared to be of a similar age. They concluded independently that many of the cairns could be the result of field clearance associated with farming activities. It is estimated that there are more than 3000 cairns on Ulpha Fell, Birker Fell, Corney Fell and Thwaites Fell, which lie to the east of the mouth of the Esk. There was clearly considerable activity by man on these uplands.

Little work has been done to date the fellside remains. In 1963, an excavation was carried out at Brantrake Moss, which lies in an upland hollow between Eskdale and Birker Fell. This yielded pollen evidence of agriculture between the lower and upper limits of A.D. 200 and 580 (Pearsall and Pennington 1973). The samples were obtained from an old soil level below the remains of a field bank which was associated with enclosures and cairns. The pollen indicated the cultivation of barley, rye and possibly wheat in the cleared areas round the enclosures.

A detailed survey of one of the sites at Crosbythwaite, at the southern edge of Ulpha Fell, revealed a complete field system with terracing on a south-west-facing slope. At the north-western corner of the system were the remains of buildings or enclosures. The field walls bordered a clearly defined lane which approached the structural remains from the east and north. An aerial photograph of this site was taken by Professor J. K. St Joseph. Efforts were made by Dr W. Pennington to obtain pollen evidence from the soil levels beneath the stone walls of the enclosures, but these were unsuccessful.

There is an enclosure at High Stainton on an area of flat ground between Whitrow Beck and Samgarth Beck. This is roughly circular, with a smaller structure inside. To the east can be detected the outlines of small rectangular fields and to the north and west are a large number of associated cairns. A bronze penannular brooch was reported from here (Fell 1972), and flakes of flint were found under an adjacent cairn. The mouth of the Esk is clearly visible from this site. There is a less well defined enclosure associated with cairns lower down the fellside, about a quarter of a mile to the west.

The settlement at Barnscar (Dymond 1892; Walker 1965) is well known, but the date of the occupation has not been determined, although a Bronze Age date has been suggested for at least part of its occupation. Here there is a clearly defined field system of rectangular fields together with about 300 cairns, and at the south-western edge of this are the remains of what appears to have been the farmhouse and associated buildings. Although there is no evidence for a Roman date, it appears to be too crudely constructed to fit the pattern of medieval farming.

On Corney Fell above Buckbarrow Bridge there are the remains of a group of enclosures on the banks of Buckbarrow Beck. A little further down the fellside towards the sea is a circular enclosure. The whole fellside in this area is covered with dozens of cairns, and the excavation of two of these in 1972 revealed no satisfactory evidence of burials (Ward 1977). To the north, in the direction of Whitrow Beck, are more cairns and traces of other stone structures, so that the whole of the fellside must have been extensively farmed.

To the south of Black Combe, on Thwaites Fell, there are further signs of extensive farming. Cairns and remains of grass-covered stone walls extend to the east towards Biggert Mire and Ulpha Fell. Further exploration is needed in this area to ascertain the full extent of the settlement, but it seems likely that it will link up with the settlements in the Birker Fell area, thus almost completely encircling the uplands of Ulpha Fell, Waberthwaite Fell, Corney Fell and Thwaites Fell, the circle broken only in the south-west by the steep sides of Black Combe.

At Whitehow Head, Haile, the presence of an oval enclosure was revealed by a crop-mark, and away to the south on the higher fells, at Tongue How, in an angle formed by the River Calder and Worm Gill, is a circular enclosure of stones, well covered with vegetation, with smaller stone structures inside. Round the enclosure are further structures and cairns. To the east of Tongue How are several small groups of cairns and to the south, above Worm Gill, are a few cairns and the remains of stone walls and enclosures.

On the west side of Worm Gill, and lying similarly on high ground between the River Calder and Worm Gill, above Thornholme farm, is an irregularly shaped, stone-banked enclosure, within which are the remains of a number of clearly defined structures, one of which is almost circular, about 25 ft in diameter; it has a single entrance on the west. The amount of stone visible would suggest that the walls of the internal structures had not been more than a foot or so in height, or that there has been a great deal of robbing. The enclosure has its own water-supply from a spring on its southern side. There are only a few cairns associated with this farmstead, although there are numerous cairns on Stockdale Moor to the south. About a mile to the south of Thornholme is the site of Prior Scales. Here there is evidence of a circular ditched enclosure, together with cairns and small "hut circles", which are only 12 ft or so in diameter, and could possibly be excavated cairns.

At Infell, in Ponsonby parish, is a rectangular earthwork, described respectively by J. C. Ward and W. G. Collingwood as a Roman camp and a medieval garth (Ward 1877; Parker 1905). To the west of the earthwork is a group of small ill-defined cairns. Excavation of one of these yielded the oxidised remains of a blade-like object, which was examined by Dr R. F. Tylecote of the Department of Metallurgy of the University of Newcastle. Although the object was too oxidised for metallurgical analysis, it was considered by Dr Tylecote to be a sword blade of the La Tène type. It is at present preserved at Cambridge University. Also found in the roots of uprooted trees at the enclosure was a rough whetstone and a fragment of the base of a vessel, made of a hard grey fabric. Though it is not possible to date the sherd at all closely, it was thought by Mr J. P. Gillam to be part of a Roman cooking-pot. At Hurlbarrow, south-east of Infell (Pearsall and Pennington 1973), the farmer reported the dismantling of a circular structure to the south of the present farm. During later draining operations a jet cloak-fastener with an asymmetric hole was found close by.

As is to be expected, evidence of habitation in the coastal plain is very scarce. Stone would not be so readily available as it would be on the lower slopes of the hills, and traces of other building materials such as wood and turf would soon have been destroyed by later agricultural activities. The present-day cluster of small farmsteads in the low land between the mountains and the sea is due in large part to an efficient system of drainage. Much of the land, therefore, would be denied to early farmers, who would mostly be confined to self-drained areas on the sands and gravels which occur mainly near the coast.

Fragments of Roman pottery and the upper stone of a bee-hive quern were found during the excavation of the Neolithic site at Ehenside Tarn (Darbishire 1874). A number of potsherds were found in a river erosion at Warborough Nook, close to the mouth of the River Ehen (Fair 1948). These were examined by Mr J. P. Gillam, and included fragments of cooking-pot and a mortarium of second-century date, although one fragment of a mortarium was considered to belong to the early years of the fourth century. It has been suggested that this was the site of a tower, but the map reference given for this site would place it well below the crest of the hill, away from the sea on the landward edge of an escarpment overlooking the River Ehen. This does not seem the likeliest place to have a tower. To the west of this site, about a hundred yards away, is Lantern Tarn. Close by Warborough Nook, at Braystones, a hoard of Roman coins was said to have been found, while at Starling Castle, which lies below Warborough Nook to the south, a *sestertius* of Antoninus Pius was found (Fair 1948). This was in the Whitehaven Museum. A silver coin of Nerva was reported in 1905 from Hallsenna, near Gosforth (Parker 1906).

A fine example of the upper stone of a bee-hive quern was found at Holmrook during the removal of a hedge bank on land belonging to Hill Green farm. The quern showed no signs of wear, and the hole in the side was rectangular in shape, suggesting the use of an iron handle. During ploughing of the adjoining field a large flat misshapen piece of stone of the same material as the quern was found. Apart from this, a careful search revealed nothing further.

A number of slag heaps has been found in the sand-dunes at Eskmeals (Cherry 1966); these represent the waste from the bloomery process used in the manufacture of iron. Although there is no way in which the slag can be dated, it is obvious that the process used in the sand-dunes was primitive. There was no sign of tap-slag and, from the size of the furnace bottoms, it was possible to deduce that the furnaces could only have been about 13 ins in diameter. The process would also require the destruction of the furnace in order to remove the smelted blooms. Associated with two of these slag heaps were a number of artifacts of Roman date, including fragments of cooking-pot dated to the second half of the fourth century and two melon-shaped, blue faience beads (Fair 1936). On the second site was a fragment of cooking-pot and a blue glass bead, described as Iron Age by Dr D. B. Harden (Cherry 1963).

On a gravel bed on the banks of the River Irt are the remains of more iron smelting (Cherry and Cherry 1968). Associated with this site were fragments of cooking-pot, a fragment of a glass bangle, a jet finger-ring, several spindle whorls, two "cresset" stones, and two pebbles carved in the shaped of human heads. The latter were considered by Dr Anne Ross to be second-century sculptures of a native deity; they are now in Carlisle Museum.

Signs of temporary occupation were discovered in 1971 in the sand-dunes a quarter of a mile south of the road from Drigg to the beach. Excavation by J. Cherry and J. E. Ward revealed a hearth and fragments of pottery said to be of the first century A.D. A further fragment of cooking-pot (undated) was found in a bed of gravel at a point where the low sandy cliff was eroded by the sea.

To the south of Ravenglass, between the Rivers Esk and Annas, the land is generally low-lying and gently undulating, with a thin soil overlying boulder clay. South of the Annas, between the bottom of Black Combe and the sea, there is a ridge of sand and gravels which drains naturally to the east and west. In 1977 a crop-mark in the form of an oval enclosure was reported on this naturally drained ridge from an aerial photograph by Professor St Joseph, in a field to the south-east of a deserted farm known as New Buildings. A number of struck flints has been recovered from this field in recent years after ploughing, but no other evidence of early occupation was found. Roman coins were reported to have been found in a field which lies on the raised beach to the north-west of Eskmeals House, but there was no structural evidence of occupation.

In compiling this list of early habitation sites it is appreciated that further investigation might show that not all of them can be contained within the period of Roman occupation. Nevertheless, it is significant that there are many points of similarity in the remains and in their relative positions on the fellsides. Although little work has been done to obtain dates for these agricultural activities all the evidence so far obtained would suggest that most of them took place in the Roman period.

The topography of the site (Fig. 4, Pls Ia, b, II)

The triangular platform which formed the site of the present excavations rests upon bedded deposits of red clay, silt and gravel, laid by marine action. The edges of this platform stand at a height of 6 m above the cobble beach that marks the level of the high tides; but the ground gradually rises towards the south and east so that the southern **part**

List of sites

Name of site	Map Reference	Height OD in feet	Evidence
Birker Fell:			
Hall Beck	3163 4967	825	Cairns
Water Crag	3154 4974	900	Cairns
Rough Crag	3187 4965	1000	Cairns and wall
The Seat	3174 4973	815	Cairns and walls
Brown Rigg	3181 4961	780	Cairns
Crosbythwaite	3188 4956	800	Cairns and enclosures
Crosby Gill	3185 4949	870	Cairns and enclosures
Brantrake	3154 4980	650	Cairns and enclosures
Whitrowbeck	3134 4939	650	Cairns and enclosures, bronze brooch
Barnscar	3133 4959	600	Cairns and enclosures
Buckbarrow bridge	3134 4905	850	Cairns and enclosures
Thwaites Fell	3166 4906	850	Cairns and enclosures
Whitehow Head	3027 5093	450	Crop mark
Tongue How	3070 5099	750	Cairns and enclosures
Thornholme	3073 5087	750	Enclosures
Prior Scales	3068 5074	650	Cairns and enclosures
Infell	3060 5061	550	Cairns and enclosure, La Tène blade, potsherd and whetstone
Hurlbarrow	3072 5057	625	Jet cloak-fastener, Site of enclosure and cairns
Guards Head	3095 5055	625	Cairns
Stockdale Moor	3108 5083	900	Cairns and enclosures
Ehenside	3003 5071	50	Potsherds, beehive quern
Warborough Nook	3008 5053	75	Potsherds
Braystones	3007 5063	50	Roman coins
Starling Castle	3013 5045	25	Roman coins, beehive quern
Holmrook	3080 5000	75	Beehive quern
Drigg sand dunes	3067 4966	25	Iron slag, potsherds, spindle whorls, fragments of jet finger-ring and glass bangle, two carved pebble heads, two hollowed-out stones
Drigg sand dunes	3050 4984	35	Hearth, potsherds
Eskmeals sand dunes	3081 4943	25	Iron slag, potsherds, melon beads, potsherds
Eskmeals sand dunes	3080 4938	25	Blue glass bead
New Buildings	3116 4831	80	Crop mark

of the triangle (where no intact archaeological stratigraphy has survived, as the cliff exposure makes clear: Fig. 25) is as much as 1·5 m above the rest of the site. Flooding cannot, however, have presented any problem: even though the fort lay in an uncomfortably exposed position, its platform still remains well above the level of the highest winter tides. Indeed there are many military sites along the Cumbrian coast, such as Cardurnock (Simpson and Hodgson 1947) and Biglands (Potter 1977), which were located on much lower ground, in the dunes and salt marsh bordering the Solway Firth and Irish sea, and must have been much more directly vulnerable to marine incursions.

To the north of the site is a second flat-topped spur, some 30 m in width. This is separated from the main platform by a steep-sided gully, 20 m across. The gully appears to be a natural feature which, to the east of the railway, is nearly 3 m in depth and progressively deepens and widens towards the sea. As will be shown below, this gully was incorporated into the defensive system of the fort.

RAVENGLASS   *CONTOUR PLAN*

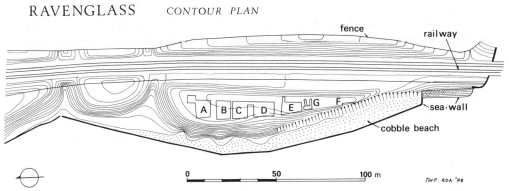

FIG. 4. – Map showing the contours and trench plan of the site at Ravenglass. Contour interval: 60 cm.

At the southern end of the site the platform gradually tapers to a point from which the ground falls away quite steeply into a shallow trough. Exposures in the cliff edge show that the fort buildings extended right up to the point of the platform and it would appear, therefore, that the southern section of the defences has been lost partly to erosion and partly to construction work for the Furness railway: the trough is, therefore, a recent feature. On the far side of the railway the situation is, on the other hand, rather clearer: here the fort platform continues for another 25 m before dropping away into a second wide gully, 5 m in depth. This must mark the line of the fort's southern defences, all traces of which have been obliterated on the seaward side by a modern sea wall and a railway underpass.

The foreshore below the site comprises a gently sloping cobble beach, with extensive mussel beds and a salmon garth. The estuary of the Esk here reaches a width of a little over 200 m, its western limits being formed by a long promontory of high sand dunes, which provide some protection from the open sea. Surface finds of prehistoric material from these dunes (Cherry 1963) show that they were in position long before Roman times, creating a sheltered anchorage in Ravenglass bay. The channel of the Esk between the dunes and the site is, however, navigable only at high tide and even then passage is restricted to vessels of shallow draught. Yet in the Roman period conditions may have been rather different. Erosion of the foreshore has substantially widened the estuary at this point as Fig. 3 makes clear. Originally, therefore, the Esk must have flowed through much narrower straits and this could well have created a deeper river channel, enabling shipping to tie up close to the fort site; certainly, this is an inference that would do much to explain why the fort does not lie more towards the present-day settlement of Ravenglass. Shipping charts show that the channel was significantly deeper even as recently as the early nineteenth century when Ravenglass was a flourishing port (Caine 1922), and Collingwood (1929) has shown that the maritime importance extends back as far as the thirteenth century.

THE EXCAVATIONS (with R. C. TURNER)

A number of practical considerations dictated the form of the excavations, the principal difficulty arising from the absence of suitable areas for the soil dumps. As a result the platform had to be investigated by a series of hand-cut trenches of limited extent rather than the more appropriate technique of total area excavation. The numerous trench sections did, however, prove something of a boon, since it emerged both that the buildings on the site had been constructed throughout its history in timber and that the same basic layout was retained from the reign of Hadrian to the end of the fourth century. This meant that most of these construction-trenches had been recut on a great many occasions to carry out repairs or rebuilding of the barrack-blocks; without a number of sections, it would probably have been impossible to achieve a full understanding of the sequences. In the event, it emerged that four principal phases could be identified, together with a number of minor periods that in most cases reflected activity applicable only to part of the site. This phase scheme forms the basis of the presentation of the results. In addition, the western defences of an earlier fortlet, on a different alignment, was also identified; this is referred to as phase 0.

In the sections that follow we consider first the fortlet of phase 0, then the defences of the later fort, and finally the history of the interior, phase by phase. The evidence is summarised in a concluding section and in Fig. 5. The dating evidence is set out under each phase and the principal finds are discussed either in the main text or under a special sub-heading. A detailed inventory of the finds will be found in Chap. II, whose catalogue numbers (e.g.: inv. 41) are cited in parenthesis as appropriate. It should be noted that the small objects and the pottery are listed separately, each with their own series of serial numbers. Reference is occasionally made to the trench plan (Fig. 4), each trench being identified by a letter, A-G. There are also separate notes with a detailed description and interpretation of the units in the drawn sections. A bibliography is provided at the end of the chapter.

Summary of the dating.
Phase 0: *c.* 120-130
Phase 1: *c.* 130
Phase 2: *c.*130-190/210
Phase 3: *c.* 190/210-350/370
Phase 4: *c.* 350/370-400+

Acknowledgements

The composition of the team and the debt that is owed to the many people who contributed to this project has already been acknowledged in the general preface. Here we would like to thank British Rail, the landowners, who gave us permission to excavate; Mr Robert Orrell, the tenant, who very kindly gave up his grazing land between 1976 and 1978; and Sir William Pennington-Ramsden, who allowed us to carry out the survey of the eastern part of the fort, in the Muncaster estates. It is also a pleasure to offer our thanks to the villagers of Ravenglass, and especially the Rev. and Mrs Murray Hodges, for their help and hospitality.

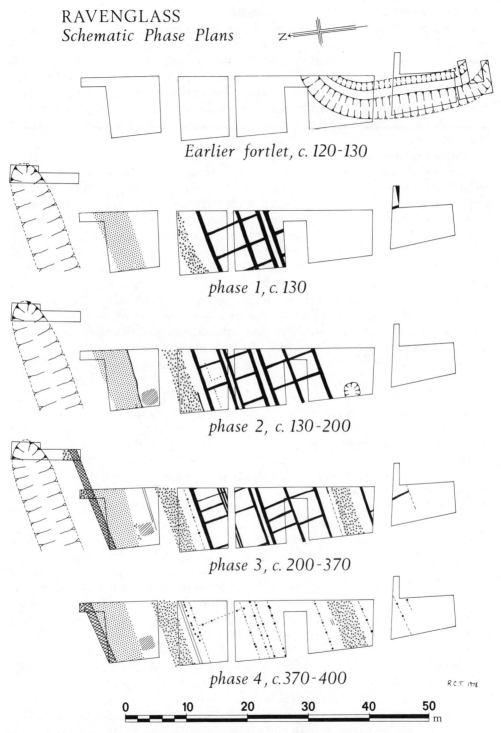

RAVENGLASS
Schematic Phase Plans

Earlier fortlet, c. 120-130

phase 1, c. 130

phase 2, c. 130-200

phase 3, c. 200-370

phase 4, c.370-400

R.C.T. 1978

0   10   20   30   40   50
                                    m

FIG. 5. – Ravenglass: plan summarizing the main features of each phase.

The Early Fortlet, Phase o (Fig. 6, Pls IIb, III)

It was especially fortuitous that within the small area excavated should lie part of the western defences of a fortlet that preceded the late Hadrianic fort. The presence of these features initially became evident in trench D where cleaning of the later road-surfaces revealed several areas of slumping. The removal of the road make-up showed that this had been caused by the existence beneath the road of two ditches which ran diagonally across the trench. Further work demonstrated that the ditches then continued southwards on an alignment that made it clear that trench D contained part of the north-west corner of these defences.

In June 1978 an attempt was made by means of limited trial-trenching to establish the full north-south extent of these ditches. The south-western corner of the fortlet was easily located as a prominent area of slumping in trench G. Although the ditches were not emptied, it is clear that the overall width of the fortlet, measured over the outer ditch, cannot have been more than 34 m. Within the inner ditch (which, as we shall see below, was a palisade-trench, revetting a rampart) the width must have been less than 24m. It is evident, therefore, that the primary military settlement on the site took the form of a small fortlet, whose dimensions closely parallel those of the Hadrianic milefortlets of the north Cumbrian coast and, indeed, those of the milecastles on Hadrian's Wall (Potter 1977, fig. 16). Given that the dating evidence from Ravenglass (set out below) does not imply occupation before Hadrian's reign, there is a good case for suggesting an extension of the Cumbrian coastal *limes* down to Ravenglass and indeed beyond. We shall consider this hypothesis in greater detail in the concluding part of this section.

Of the two components of the defences, the outer ditch was by far the larger. It varied in width between 2.80 and 3.30 m and on average was 1.60 m in depth (Figs 17, 18; Pl. IIb). It was cut through layers of marine clay, which should have provided the basis for smooth and stable sides; but its profile was in fact rough and irregular, particularly along the outer side, where there were a number of overhangs and ledges. Indeed, in places the ditch gave the impression of a job that was only finished in part, although elsewhere there appear to have been attempts to recut the side. In profile the ditch was V-shaped, but with a steep outer scarp; this suggests that it is mostly appropriately described as a *fossa punica* (Hyginus, *de munitionibus castrorum*, 49), a defensive arrangement often found in outer ditches so that their attackers might find difficulty in escaping (Richmond 1955, 3; Jones 1975, 112-3). There was no rectangular channel at the bottom of the ditch (a feature often thought to derive from regular cleaning of the ditch silt: Jones 1975, 36) but there were a number of large cobbles, which may have been intended to aid drainage.

The inner trench (Pl. IIIb) was much smaller. It ranged in width from 1 to 1.40 m and was only 60 cm in depth. Over much of its length its profile consisted of a wide shallow V-shaped form (Figs 18, 19, 21); however, at the north-west corner of the fortlet its shape became that of a deep, nearly rectangular trench with steep sides. This section disclosed a number of stake-impressions along the base of the trench. They consisted of small circular marks, some 10 cm in diameter, where the stakes had been driven into the subsoil. Subsequently these uprights had been withdrawn. Some of these stakes were fairly regularly set, at intervals of about 60 cm; but other impressions occurred much closer together as if the position of the upright had been altered.

These post-settings make it quite clear that this trench had originally held a wooden palisade. It could have constituted an obstacle, such as a line of sharpened stakes, an

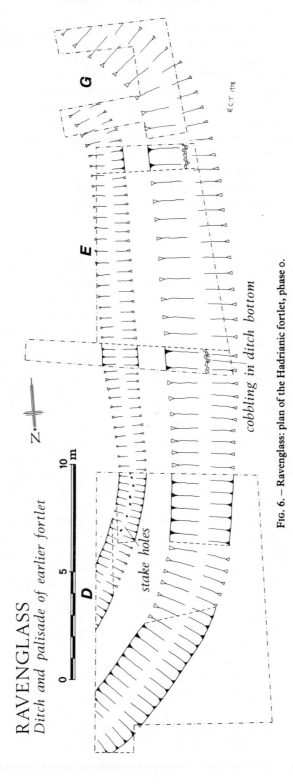

RAVENGLASS

Ditch and palisade of earlier forlet

G

E

D

stake holes

cobbling in ditch bottom

R.C.T. 1978

0   5   10
m

N

FIG. 6. — Ravenglass: plan of the Hadrianic fortlet, phase o.

example of which was found at Watercrook (cf. Chap. III; also Jones 1975, 113-4); but, given the fortlet plan, it is much more likely that it revetted the front of a rampart. It should be said at once that no trace of any rampart was found. A trench was cut to test this possibility (Fig. 17) but it revealed nothing more than construction features belonging to the later fort. However, the fills of the ditches provided much more positive evidence. Every section that was made through the ditches showed that they had been levelled to the top with tips of grey humic clay and black peat. These deposits were either interleaved or (as at the fortlet corner: Pl. IIb) divided into thick, separate layers. At first, the peat was taken to be a natural accumulation but subsequent study (cf. Chap. II) suggests that it had not grown *in situ* but represents (as does the clay) the remains of a rampart, made with turves cut from a nearby marsh deposit, the dominant plants being sedges and rushes. We can assume, therefore, that the rampart lay close to the line of the ditch and was levelled either when the fortlet was abandoned or more probably when the late Hadrianic fort was laid out.

The rampart deposit was both damp and interleaved with clay seals and it was not, therefore, surprising when well-preserved organic material began to emerge. This included a great deal of wood, together with leather objects, a hazel-nut and a number of mussel shells. With the exception of the shells (which were found in the middle of the peat fill) all the finds came either from the scarp of the ditch or from the lowest silt, showing that they had been thrown in before the rampart was pulled down. The leather objects were not numerous, comprising the remains of three shoes and a cover, perhaps from a tent (Fig. 33); wood, on the other hand, occurred in fairly prolific quantities and in an exceptional state of preservation (Fig. 34). The bulk of the pieces consisted of twigs and small branches, sawn or lopped from various types of tree, principally oak, (cf. Chap. II), and then immediately discarded; most retained their cover of bark. We might assume that these fragments were the result of the initial clearance of the site, but, on reflection, it is obvious that this cannot be the case. Although they were only found in the primary silt at the bottom of the ditch, it is inconceivable that such discards would have been thrown into a newly-cut feature. They must represent, therefore, the trimmings from a subsequent phase of construction, presumably the building of the late Hadrianic fort. This implies that the phase 0 fortlet was still standing when the decision was taken to build the new fort (and, if the absence of any significant quantities of primary silt is meaningful, it must still have been either fully garrisoned or regularly maintained). The structures were then demolished while, at the same time, new timbers were being prepared. The discards were thrown into the ditch and the rampart material was then used to level the ground.

Not all the wood represented the trimmings from tree-cutting, however. In addition, there was a number of objects that had been used in the construction of the fortlet (Fig. 34). The largest of these were the remains for four oak stakes, one of which measured 1·32 m in length (Pl. IIIa). The lower part of the stakes was left rough and had clearly stood in the ground: they would have fitted the dimensions of the posts in the palisade-trench exactly. These were not large timbers – none was more than 8×8 cm – and it is clear that they were not major structural elements, for which dimensions approaching 30×30 cm were normal. We can probably assume that they came directly from the palisade revetting the front of the rampart. There were also a number of pieces of planking (some with peg-holes); at least one peg; a section of a substantial beam retaining traces of a nail hole, and some other thick planks which bore evidence of joinery. The most interesting piece (Fig. 34, inv. 94) consisted of a thick plank with a rebate and flange designed to hold a section of panelling, and a rebate for a lap joint with a substantial upright. The arrangement is such that a small aperture, 20 cm wide, was left between the panelling and the upright and, at this point, the plank was very worn (unlike the underside, which retained a small area of bark). Given the proximity of the rampart, it is possible, though conjectural, that the plank, together with another identical fragment, belonged to a part of the breastwork along the top of the rampart. Unfortunately we know virtually nothing of such arrangements, our sources being limited to the reliefs on Trajan's Column; no known sections of breastwork survive. It is clear, however, that merlons were provided and it is possible that our pieces come from the lower part of a crenellated breastwork. Fig. 7 is a very tentative reconstruction of this.

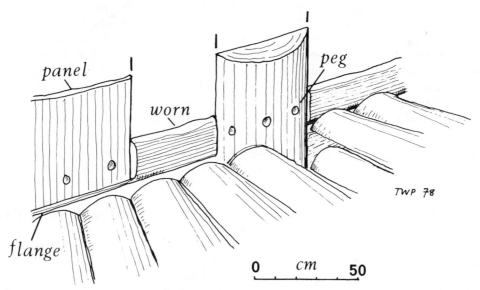

FIG. 7. – A possible reconstruction of a section of the breastwork of the Hadrianic fortlet (phase 0) at Ravenglass.

The phase 0 fortlet: chronology and discussion

As we have seen, it appears that the primary fortlet at Ravenglass was still under maintenance when its late Hadrianic successor was constructed (probably in the 130s). The ditch was kept clean of silt and no rubbish was allowed to accumulate in it. Clearly there must have been a garrison at the site (though, given the very small width of the fortlet, it cannot have been of any size). Unfortunately there is no direct evidence for its date of construction. The ditches contained no pottery at all and the associated occupation deposits must have been completely destroyed with the building of the Furness Railway. However, the overall range of artifacts from these excavations do provide some sort of guide. Of the 600 samian vessels, only nine were in South Gaulish fabrics (all of Flavian-Trajanic date), while the assemblage as a whole best fits a Hadrianic start for the occupation (providing a clear contrast with Watercrook: Fig. 62). Similarly the coarse pottery (Fig. 39) shows little or no emphasis upon first-century types but instead an overwhelming preponderance of Hadrianic and later shapes. The coin evidence also conforms to this picture, the series beginning with two coins of Trajan and five of Hadrian. The cumulative impression therefore is that occupation on this site can hardly have begun before 120 and most probably falls within the bracket 120-30.

The plan of the fortlet also supports this dating. Trajanic fortlets such as Throp, Haltwhistle Burn or Pen Llystyn near Caernarvon (Simpson 1913; Hogg 1968) were generally very large, averaging some 60×90 m within the ditches. Hadrianic fortlets, typified by sites on the Wall and Cumberland coast (Potter 1977), are usually much smaller, being between 200-400 m² within the defences (although there are exceptions like Cardurnock (Simpson and Hodgson 1947), where a century was the likely unit). The fortlet at Ravenglass, therefore, best fits the normal type of Hadrianic fortlet. If so, there seems little doubt that it represents a continuation of the chain of fortlets and turrets now well documented along the north Cumbrian coast. It is usually assumed that this system terminated at St Bees Head, the most prominent topographic feature along the western shore of Cumbria. But it is impossible to envisage the Ravenglass fortlet as an isolated site and it now seems much more likely that the chain continued past St Bees and down the low-lying dunes of south-west Cumbria. This area has yet to be fully studied either by aerial photography or by field-work but there is one interesting entry in the Cumbria County Council records for this region. At Eskmeals, almost exactly 1620 yards (=1 Roman mile) to the south of the Ravenglass fortlet, there is a note of 'traces of a Roman camp' and 'remains of a rectangular earthwork' (T. Clare, *pers. comm.*). Whilst there is no proof of the date of this site, it seems a fair conjecture that the next fortlet of the system lies at this point; and that there was a regular chain of milefortlets along this stretch of coast.

This important conclusion adds a new dimension to our understanding of the Hadrianic *limes*. Clearly much more extensive and elaborate provision was made for the protection of the western flank of the Wall than has been realised. We may legitimately wonder where the system stopped. Certainly there are strong hints of other military activity in the region in the form of stray finds both of coins and pottery. In the Beckermet area, for example, a coin hoard with an issue of Commodus, a *sestertius* of Antoninus Pius, and a group of second- and fourth-century sherds (Fair 1948), may relate to a military site, just as persistent finds of Roman material from the Furness and Cartmel peninsulae are unlikely to be due entirely to civilian settlement. We can reasonably suppose that further work may well demonstrate the presence of other south-western fortlets and forts, protecting this exposed and vulnerable coastline.

One other point is of relevance here. In Chap. VII we shall see how the Cumbrian region as a whole appears to have been brought under formal Roman control after the withdrawal from Scotland on the late 80s. Despite the fact that no late Flavian sites are yet attested in the south-west part of this area, it would be surprising were an enclave to remain without any military presence. Apart from Hardknott (apparently a Trajanic or Hadrianic foundation), the only known fort site is that of Ravenglass, also a Hadrianic site. On the other hand, it should be remembered that, as at Corbridge, the Flavian pattern may well diverge from that of later periods. It is by no means unlikely that eventually a Flavian or Flavian-Trajanic fort will be found in the Ravenglass region (and in other parts of south-west Cumbria).

The Defences of the Later Fort (Figs 8, 19, Pl. IVa)

The building of the latter fort belongs, as will be demonstrated below, to the latter part of Hadrian's reign. It involved the complete demolition of the earlier fortlet and the construction of a new defensive system, enclosing a much greater area. We were able to examine these defences at only one point, on the north side of the site, immediately above the natural gully. Rather surprisingly, the remains of a substantial inner ditch came to light, running parallel with the gully along the edge of the spur. This ditch had a V-shaped profile, much eroded on the north side because of the looseness of the gravel and sand forming the subsoil in this area. It was as much as 6·60 m in width (enlarged, no doubt, by the unstable nature of the sides) and 1·70 m in depth. In the bottom was a cleaning channel, filled over most of its length with cobbles. By a fortunate chance, the small area that was excavated also included the rounded butt end of the ditch, an important discovery since this break in the defences most probably marks the position of the north entrance into the fort. This would place the gate somewhere in the area of the present railway cutting and provides some basis for determining the area lost to the sea and thus the approximate positioning of the western defences. Assuming that the barrack-blocks (which were orientated east-west) were between 45 and 50 m in length (Jarrett 1969, 163) this would imply that a minimum of 30 m has disappeared through coastal erosion. This calculation is of course subject to a wide margin of error – we do not know, for example, how many *contubernia* there were in the barrack-blocks – but it does give a rough idea of the original dimensions of the fort, suggesting a total area within the defences of c. 3·6 acres.

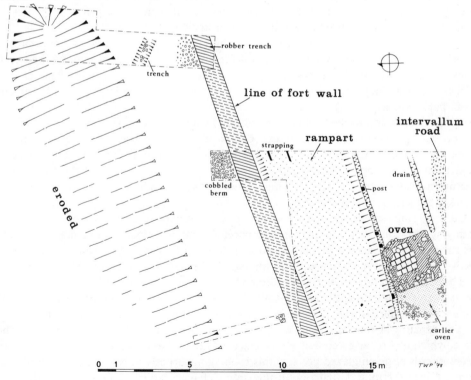

FIG. 8. – Plan of the defences of the later fort at Ravenglass.

The fill of the ditch divided into two parts. The lower fill comprised a tip of grey silt-clay material (Fig. 19, unit 14), thrown in from the south side of the ditch. The turf-like consistency of this layer suggests that it represents the demolished remains of the rampart. Above this were numerous tips of sand (Fig. 19, unit 13), gravel and silt, displaying the characteristic pattern of a deliberate infill. This was cut by a large pit containing a good deal of rubble (unit 11). The upper fill of the ditch yielded a small quantity of pottery (c. 40 sherds) and four coins (coin inventory, nos 14-17). Few of the sherds were closely datable but it is significant that no examples of calcite-gritted ware were found, a type otherwise very common in later fourth-century deposits on the site. The coins included an issue of Severus Alexander (222-8) and a radiate (c. 270) from the middle of the ditch fill, as well as a *Gloria Exercitus* (330-335) in fresh condition, and an illegible coin probably of fourth-century date. The illegible coin came from the intrusive pit (Fig. 19, unit 11) and the coin of Constantine from the latest tip in the ditch. The cumulative picture from this evidence points, therefore, to a deliberate infill of the ditch in the period between c. 335-370, an event which most probably relates to the rebuilding of the barrack-blocks at the beginning of phase 4, possibly after the Great Picts' War of 367-8 (Tomlin 1974).

Behind the ditch was a wide berm with a width of just under 4 m. This was cut by a small flat-bottomed trench, 90 cm wide and 45 cm deep, placed diagonally across the berm and pointing towards the probable position of the gate. No evidence existed to show either its date or function but its shape would be consistent with an interpretation either as a drain or as an obstacle-trench (perhaps holding a palisade), flanking the west side of the entrance to the fort. Behind this trench was a narrow strip of large beach-cobbles, forming an apron in front of the mural defences. These divided into two principal phases; a primary rampart made of turf, later fronted by a stone wall.

The turf rampart was 3·70 m across, widening a little towards the east as it approached the site of the gate. It survived to a height of nearly 50 cm in places although it had been considerably disturbed by intrusive pits. Revetting its inner edge was a cheek of turf blocks, still standing four courses high. These turves were 40 cm long and had been cut from dark brown peat. The intervening space was filled with marsh turf, laid in small irregular blocks and packed round with soil and clay. Whilst no trace was noted of any timber lacing, there were signs at two points of transverse beams at the base of the rampart, set into the grey silt that forms the old ground surface. This wooden underpinning appears to have been confined, however, to the front of the rampart, a feature already noted from other sites (Jones 1975, 74). There may also have been a marker-bank (Fig. 19, unit 9).

At some stage subsequent to the building of the rampart, a section of timber revetting, 7 m long, was constructed along the inner cheek. The timbers were set in a narrow trench, 25 cm wide, with large uprights spaced at intervals of roughly 3 m and smaller stakes between. Presumably the back of the rampart had begun to slip along this line, though the building of the timber work may also have been influenced by the decision to put in an oven at this point. Probably at the same time, other turves were laid at the front of the inner cheek at the east side of the excavation, to bolster up this section of the rampart.

The remains of the stone wall were confined to a robber-trench, 1·10 m wide at the base, which had removed completely all traces of the wall and its footings. To judge from a few sherds of green-glazed pottery, this robbing apparently took place in late medieval times. Given the total destruction of the stone defences, we can only note that the wall must have been comparatively narrow – at Maryport, for example, it was 2 m wide over the footings (Jarrett 1976, 31) – and that the foundations were correspondingly shallow. However, there is no reason to doubt that the wall existed, for there were traces of red clay and cobbles from the footings in the robber-trench fill. The date of its construction is similarly conjectural. The principal clue comes from a deposit between the *intervallum* road and the back of the rampart (Fig. 19, unit 7). This shows a spread of demolished turf-work, charcoal and dark flecks which, in the west section of trench B (Fig. 20, unit 19), was found to seal the *intervallum* road of phases 1 and 2 and was in turn stratified beneath the roads of phases 3 and 4. It looks therefore, as though the upper part of the turf rampart was pulled down in the general rebuilding that followed the destruction of the phase 2 structures late in the second or early in the third century – a reconstruction of the fort which would provide the most obvious context for the insertion of a stone wall. It should, however, be emphasised that this is conjecture, with little direct proof. Indeed, analogies from other sites would suggest a far earlier date. Carvoran, for example, was rebuilt in stone between 136 and 138 (*RIB* 1816, 1818, 1820), while in Wales most auxiliary forts received stone defences between 140 and 160 (Jarrett 1969, 154). On the other hand, it should be remembered that Ravenglass, unlike most other forts in England, was continuously occupied through the second century, so that the opportunity for a major reconstruction following a temporary evacuation was not available. It may be, therefore, that turf defences (which, after all, were widely used along the Cumbrian coast for most of the second century: Potter 1977) were considered adequate.

One further point should be mentioned. Overlying the demolished turf work in the lee of the rampart were tips of gravel and silt which imply a heightening and refacing of the bank. This need occasion no surprise since the evidence from some other sites is for constant refurbishing of the banks throughout the Roman period, the latest rampart at Maryport (possibly datable to the late fourth century: Jarrett 1976, 32) being as much as 8 m wide.

The Rampart Ovens (Figs 8-10, Pls IVb, Va)

At the back of the rampart was a large oven, resting upon a massive platform, 2·75×2·50 m, made of clay and limestone fragments and revetted by large pieces of limestone. The oven was constructed towards the north-east corner of this platform and was rectangular in form, measuring 1·50×1·40 m. Its floor was made up of 20 square tiles, averaging 29×29×6 cm, laid in five rows. There was a small flue at the south end and the footings for a clay, cobble and limestone wall, extending round the edge of the tiles; this wall had right-angled corners at the south end but the north wall appears to have been curved.

The removal of this tile surface disclosed a second floor, belonging to an earlier oven (Pl. Va). This was made of identical tiles (one retaining the impression of a dog's paw) but was orientated at 45° to the axis of the later oven. It was also much smaller, consisting of seven whole and four half tiles, arranged to form a roughly circular shape, with a maximum diameter of just over a metre. All but three of the tiles were heavily cracked through burning. This surface rested on a layer of limestone rubble set into a thin bed of stiff yellow and red clay.

Excavation below the foundations for the platform demonstrated the presence of one other phase of oven, consisting of a ring of stones, resting upon a thick layer of gravel.

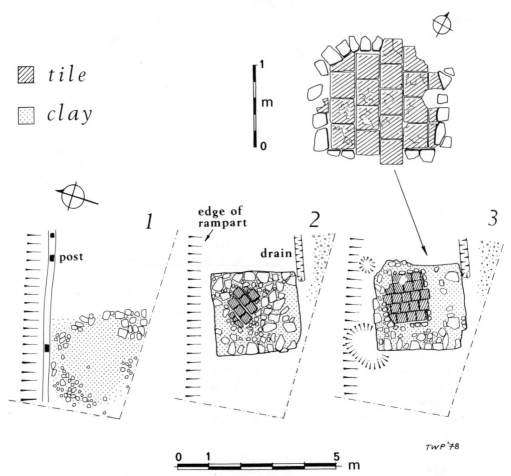

tile

clay

1 m 0

edge of rampart

post

drain

1 2 3

0 1 5 m

TWP '78

FIG. 9. – Ravenglass: plans of successive ovens behind the rampart. 1: phase 2.2, 3: phase 3.

This in turn had been laid over a bed of turf. There was little evidence either of burning or for oven structure and it is clear that most tangible traces of this period were swept away when the new oven platform was built. It seems likely, however, that a circular oven of conventional pattern is represented by the surviving remains.

The only significant quantity of datable pottery came from layers related to the latest of the three ovens. Overlying the oven floor was a deposit with abundant sherds of the latter part of the fourth century, referable to the latest period of the site, phase 4; this material implies that the oven had gone out of use by this time. At the north-east and north-west corners of the platform were two shallow pits, one small and the other rather larger. Both pits contained a good deal of pottery including a bottle or flagon with all but the neck intact (Fig. 42, no. 46). Apart from some sherds of late fourth-century pottery in the top fill, the finds consisted exclusively of second- and third-century material: there were no diagnostic types of the late third or early fourth centuries. To the south of the oven was a further deposit, containing some hearth sweepings and a few sherds. This also dated to the second and third centuries.

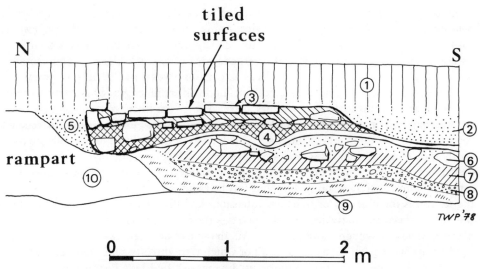

FIG. 10. – Ravenglass: section through the ovens behind the rampart.

It seems clear, therefore, that the latest oven, together with its immediate predecessor, was in use for part and possibly all of phase 3 (early third century-350/370). Whether the platform was constructed at the beginning of phase 3 or at some point during phase 2 is on the other hand much less clear: the second-century material from around the oven could be explained either as rubbish-survival or as normal refuse. On the face of it, it seems most logical to assume that the earliest oven belongs to phase 2 and that the platform with its two successive ovens was a feature built with the reconstruction of the fort in the early third century; but we cannot be certain. One additional pointer is perhaps provided by the size of the tiles, which cannot be matched amongst the known material from Park House, a nearby tilery (Fig. 2) operating until the late second century (Birley 1958, 30; Bellhouse 1960, 1961); similarly it is noteworthy that the large rectangular platform ovens are not normal features of second-century forts, where the circular model was generally preferred; on balance, therefore, we are inclined to see these two later ovens as third-century features, whilst recognising that they could have been built during the latter part of phase 2.

The *Intervallum* Road (Fig. 20, Pls Vb, VIIIa)

A total of five *intervallum* road-surfaces were identified, representing a vertical stratigraphic build-up of just over 60 cm. The sequence was best preserved at the north-west corner of area B (Fig. 20); by contrast the north-east section (Fig. 23) of the same trench retained only the lowest road-surfaces, demonstrating very clearly the destructive nature of post-Roman ploughing and disturbance over parts of the site. The detailed interpretation of this sequence poses, therefore, a good many problems, especially where an attempt is made to relate the road-surfaces with the history of the internal buildings.

Some initial disturbance to the ground seems to have taken place before any of the roads were constructed. A thin layer of charcoal-flecked grey silt (closely resembling the old ground surface on other parts of the site) lay beneath the earliest road, filling a shallow wide scoop in the subsoil (**Fig.** 20, unit 33). Probably by coincidence, this lay directly beneath a series of later ditches and drains, lining the southern edge of the *intervallum* road. The earliest road-surface (Fig. 20, unit 28) appears to have been only 2·20 m wide, its gravel metalling extending into the veranda area of barrack-block 1. This metalling was unusually thick – in places, as much as 20 cm – and was provided at some points with a surface of small flat fragments of sandstone, up to 10 cm in length, which may represent repairs. Covering this surface was a dark layer some 10 cm thick, containing a great deal of charcoal; this in turn was capped by a spread of daub, burnt to a bright red, and confined to the southern end of the road. The daub evidently related to the collapse of the north wall of barrack-block 4 and this layer as a whole presumably derives from the destruction of the internal buildings at the end of phase 2, in the late second or early third century. Unfortunately at no point could this be established beyond doubt – a feature of the section is the ubiquity of trenches, intrusions and discontinuities – but, unless there was some otherwise unattested fire in phase 2 – then the correlation seems sound. It did however yield one samian stamp, Balbini. M., datable to between 125 and 140.

The four subsequent road-surfaces, all of which were directly superimposed, represent a minor replanning of the *via sagularis*: its line was shifted by a distance of just over a metre to the north. The reason for this is explained by the cutting of a shallow drainage ditch between the southern edge of the road and the veranda of the barrack-block. This was matched by a trench, 25 cm wide, along the north side of the road, which may have been designed to hold a timber gutter (Fig. 8). The stratigraphic position of the southern ditch is not without its interpretative problems, however: although the ditch was certainly cut from the level of the second roadway, there was along its southern lip a small deposit of daub (Fig. 20, unit 25) which appeared to overlie the primary silt. Since this daub relates to the destruction at the end of phase 2, we take it that the section is misleading and that the daub was washed into the ditch fill some considerable time after its original deposition; even so, there exists some element of ambiguity. The road itself was made up of a ballast core, founded on a bed of clay and surfaced with rammed gravel. There were also areas of broken roof-slate and fragments of red sandstone blocks which could well represent dumps of material from the demolished remains of the central range of buildings. Its width was narrow – only just over 2 m – but even so it was steeply cambered to facilitate drainage. But subsequently, the road was resurfaced and considerably extended to a width of nearly 4 m. The ground was levelled up with a thick deposit of brown silt and clay (Fig. 20, unit 15), covered with a thin skin of rammed gravel (unit 14). It is possible that the southern ditch (which by this time had acquired a considerable depth of silt) was also recut: but the evidence was not explicit.

The date of the road extension could not be properly established but apparently occurred at some time in phase 3. Similarly, there was no close dating for the two final surfaces (Fig. 23, units 10-12), which could have been laid either towards the end of phase 3 or in phase 4. What is clear is that they represent a major reconstruction of the *intervallum* road, including the provision of a completely new drainage system (Pl. Vb). A thick layer of brown clay was laid over the old surface and a thin skin of gravel rammed into the top. Subsequently the level to the north was built up with red clay taken directly from the subsoil, and surfaced with gravel. There were indications in places of some later repairs to this final surface but these seem not to have been particularly extensive. The drain was built of roughly cut pieces of limestone, forming a channel 25 cm wide internally and some 20 cm in depth. It was set in a bed of red clay and showed signs of repair at several points. A comparable stone-lined drain was also found to line the east-west street between barrack-blocks 10 and 11.

It should be noted that throughout the history of the *intervallum* road there was no accumulation of rubbish upon its surfaces; the site was obviously kept scrupulously clean, despite the proximity of the cooking oven at the back of the rampart. Nor were any traces of wheel-ruts observed, although an insufficient area was uncovered to make their definition easy.

THE INTERIOR OF THE LATER FORT

In this section we shall discuss in chronological order the history of the barrack-blocks and of the minor street that divided buildings 7 and 8 and then 10 and 11 in the third and fourth centuries. The dating evidence for each phase is also set out in the appropriate section, as well as some of the more significant finds.

The Interior: Phase 1 (Fig. 11, Pl. VI)

As in succeeding phases, the structures that lay within the excavated area belonged exclusively to timber-framed barrack-block accommodation. Parts of three buildings were identified, each of them orientated west-east so that it was the narrow end that faced the sea. *Barrack-block 1* yielded the fullest plan, there being two complete and two partially exposed *contubernia* within the excavated area. The foundations of the main longitudinal walls consisted of substantial trenches set up to 70 cm into the subsoil. The partition walls were rather less massive but still averaged 45-55 cm in depth. Dissection of these trenches failed, however, to identify the position of any of the timber uprights; the fill consisted for the most part of a uniform mixture of red clay and grey silt, the latter evidently deriving from the old ground surface. The only hint of any constructional feature came from the foundation-trench for the south wall: here there appeared a clear distinction between packing material on one side and a small trench on the other, possibly cut to remove the uprights. Alternatively the trench may have held a sill-beam, which was subsequently removed.

The overall plan of the barrack-block incorporated two unusual features. In the first place, the central wall that divided each *contubernium* into two rooms, one for baggage and the other for sleeping accommodation, was set well to the south so that there was a small room at the back of the barrack-block and a much larger one at the front. This unequal division of space is by no means uncommon but the arrangement at Ravenglass is the reverse of normal practice in that the smaller room was usually placed at the front of the building (e.g. Jarrett 1969, 164). This rare feature of the design is matched by the exceptional size of the *contubernia*. The individual rooms measure internally $2.60 \times 3.40/3.50$ m and $5.60 \times 3.40/3.50$ m, giving a total internal area of about 28.5 m². By way of comparison we can take the figures presented by Breeze (1974) for the *contubernia* at Fendoch, Housesteads, Carzield and Barburgh Mill: at these sites, the areas vary between 20 and 25.5 m², a range that seems to be widely representative of barracks on British forts and fortlets. The *contubernia* at Ravenglass appear, therefore, to have been unusually large. This, however, is not so much a product of their length – 3.50 m is a figure that can be matched very widely – as of their width. The full measurement across the walls of the barrack-block is 10.10 m (8.80 m internally), a figure that is much closer to the average

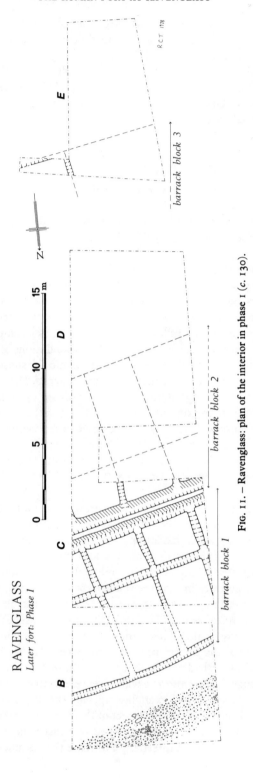

FIG. 11. – Ravenglass: plan of the interior in phase I (c. 130).

width of the officer's quarters than to that of the men's accommodation. However, we can rule out the possibility that we are dealing with the officer's suite of rooms since these were conventionally placed at the rampart end of the barrack-block. As the general plan (Fig. 3) shows, the excavated rooms were situated in the middle of the block and must, therefore, have provided accommodation for the men.

The only standard feature of the layout (apart from the division into *contubernia*) is the length of each individual unit, 3·50 m. As noted above, this figure can be widely paralleled, as at Pen Llystyn (Hogg 1968) or Cardean (Robertson 1975, 86). The barrack-blocks of both these forts have ten *contubernia* in all, room for a century of 80 men, probably forming part of a *cohors quingenaria peditata*. Cavalry in Britain, on the other hand, were normally housed in eight *contubernia* (Breeze and Dobson 1969), the accommodation being for two *turmae* with 60-64 men in all. On the face of it, therefore, we might conclude that the Ravenglass barrack-block was planned for a unit of infantry rather than for cavalry. Corbridge, for example, might be cited as an analogy. Here barrack-blocks of the initial fort, 1A, were provided with eight *contubernia*, each 4.27 m in length, designed presumably for cavalry. Then, in fort 1B the blocks were apparently altered so that they had ten *contubernia*, each 3·55 m in length, which probably indicates a change in the type of unit (Gillam 1977). Unfortunately, however, the assumption that cavalry *contubernia* were normally larger than those of infantry does not always seem to hold good. This much is clear from a survey of the evidence from Hadrian's Wall (Breeze and Dobson 1969), where cavalry and infantry appear to have used much the same size of room. Consequently it would be rash to assume that infantry were housed in the Ravenglass block without knowing the full number of *contubernia* – something that can never now be established.

We may now briefly summarise the evidence from *barrack-blocks 2 and 3*. Only the northern part of block 2 was located, the identifiable sections including the north wall and three of the internal cross-walls. It is clear, however, that blocks 1 and 2 were laid out as a pair, built back to back with a gap of less than 0·50 m between them. The constructional techniques were also identical, the long wall of block 2 containing the same sort of packing material down the south side as its neighbour to the north. The southern part of the building presented some puzzling aspects. Part of the structure lay beneath a massive dump of red clay laid in phase 2; not all of this clay was stripped off since at the time of excavation it was taken to be undisturbed subsoil. Consequently the full extent of the partition-walls was never established. However, the line of the main south wall should have been quite apparent since this must have been cut into the ditch of the earlier fortlet. In fact, no trace of a wall-trench was noted either in plan or in any of the several sections that were left in area D. There is a possibility, therefore, that the wall-trench was never dug, a matter that we shall discuss further below.

To the south of barrack-block 2, we know little of this phase. The only wall-trenches that might be assigned to the initial period are two footings in area E which appear on slight stratigraphic evidence to be primary in the sequence (Fig. 17, unit 15). Both were filled with material taken from the old ground surface and contained no trace either of burnt daub or other archaeological material. This strongly suggests a primary position in the sequence. If so this is best interpreted as the central wall and internal partition of a third barrack-block; this would leave a space of about 8 m between blocks 2 and 3, sufficient for a small street (although there was no evidence for any road-metalling either in this period or in phase 2).

The evidence for phase 1 suggests, therefore, three timber-framed barrack-blocks, probably forming part of a series of paired blocks extending along the west side of the fort. However, there are a number of factors which indicate that the buildings were never used and probably not completed. In the first place we may note that there was a total absence of any occupation deposits or debris. With the exception of a lead lamp-holder (Fig. 28, no. 70), a fragment of amphora and a black-burnished sherd, the wall-trenches were barren of finds and there was no stratigraphic accumulation at all within the rooms: the phase 2 layers were directly superimposed upon the subsoil into which the phase 1 trenches were cut. Secondly, as we have already shown, there was no evidence for timber uprights in any of the wall-trenches: only the adjoining walls of blocks 1 and 2 yielded any sign of use, whereas the other foundations appear to have been dug and then immediately backfilled. Indeed, the southern wall-trenches of barrack-block 2 may never have been completed, as we have seen. Thirdly, no evidence was found either for floors or for verandas, traces of which must surely have survived had they been constructed. The cumulative impression, therefore, is that the initial layout was changed before the barrack-blocks were finished and a new arrangement implemented.

What motives lay behind this change of plan must necessarily remain obscure. It could be explained by a decision to bring in another garrison, perhaps of different composition: for example, a change from a *cohors quingenaria peditata* to a *cohors quingenaria equitata* might well have entailed a drastic alteration in the building programme. But it could also be that the barrack-blocks were replanned for much less major reasons. The new blocks of phase 2 were, as we shall see, moved a short distance to the north, while measures were also taken to build up the level of the ground in barrack-block 2. It is possible, therefore, that the backfilled ditch and palisade trench of the earlier fortlet were seen as less than ideal ground for the southern foundations of barrack-block 2 and thus the decision was taken to re-align the buildings. At the same time the more unconventional aspects of barrack-block 1 could be corrected. The Red House fortress near Corbridge would offer a close parallel in that at least one building was redesigned on a new alignment before the initial structure was completed.

Phase 1: dating evidence

There was no properly stratified datable material from the deposits of phase 1 and we have, therefore, to rely on the overall distribution of finds to provide a date for this period. There are three groups of evidence, the coins, the samian and the coarse pottery. The coin evidence is not especially helpful. Apart from a *denarius* of Mark Antony (a common find on second-century sites), the series begins with two issues of Trajan and five of Hadrian. One of the Hadrianic coins was stratified in phase 2 deposits but the others all come from later deposits. The total sample of samian is on the other hand much larger, even though much of it derives from late Roman or unstratified contexts. Detailed qualification is not easy to achieve since individual types have widely differing life-spans; but we can make a rough chronological breakdown which is sufficient to demonstrate the main overall trends:

Flavian/Trajanic:	9
Trajanic/Hadrianic:	15
Hadrianic:	11
Hadrianic/Antonine:	162
Antonine	347
Late Antonine:	42
Third century:	2
	588

Apart from the scarcity of pre-Hadrianic samian, the most notable feature to emerge from this table is the shortage of typical Hadrianic material. Only about 5% of the samian from Ravenglass appears to have reached the site before late Hadrianic or early Antonine times. Even allowing for the much increased production of samian in the Antonine period there is a clear implication in these figures that the later fort was not in garrison before the later part of Hadrian's reign. This is very largely borne out by the distribution of datable coarse-ware (Fig. 39). These show a pronounced peak for the decade between 140 and 150, and considerable strength for the previous twenty years. When due allowance is made for a period of use, the pattern is most consistent with a sharp rise in levels of activity on the site in the 130s.

We are safe in concluding, therefore, that the construction of the later fort at Ravenglass belongs to the reign of Hadrian and very likely to the later part of that period. This is a date which fits well into what we know of the programme of fort-building in the frontier region at this time. Once the decision had been taken to add forts to Hadrian's Wall, priority seems to have been given to building along the curtain itself: thus the majority of these forts were started during the governorship of Platorius Nepos (122-c. 126) and two (Benwell and Haltonchesters) seem more or less to have been finished by the time he departed in about 126. On the Cumbrian coast, on the other hand, the construction of new forts seems to have been delayed until building on the main frontier line was well advanced. Maryport may already have been in garrison (cf. Chap. VII) but Moresby, as a well known Hadrianic building-inscription attests (*RIB* 801), was being completed sometime after 128. Beckfoot unfortunately is not closely dated but the evidence from Moresby and Ravenglass suggests that the decision to reinforce the coastal defences (Jones 1976) with forts was not implemented until the 130s when the main frontier line must largely have been completed (Breeze and Dobson 1976, 68-72).

The Interior: Phase 2 (Fig. 12, Pl. VIa, b)

The excavated area cut across parts of two timber-framed barrack-blocks belonging to this phase. As in phase 1 they had been constructed back to back, with the narrow end facing the sea. *Barrack-block 4* (the more northerly of the two) was a narrower building than its predecessor, barrack-block 1, being 9·40 m in width instead of 10·10 m. Its position was also shifted so that its south wall lay more than a metre to the north of the original line, although the orientation remained identical. The walls were set in substantial trenches which, though shallower than those of phase 1, still averaged 50 cm in depth. The long walls appear to have held sill-beams some 25 cm in width, packed either with red clay or brown silt-clay (Fig. 20, trench 6, units 29, 30). The internal

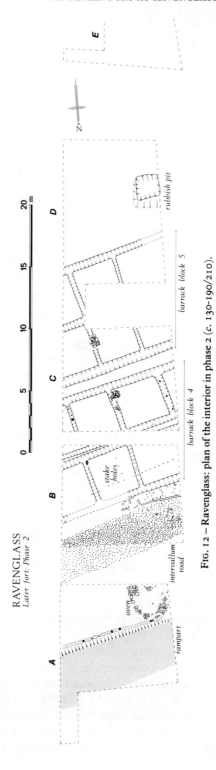

FIG. 12 – Ravenglass: plan of the interior in phase 2 (c. 130–190/210).

partitions, on the other hand, yielded evidence for separate timber uprights bedded directly into the trench. All this timber-work had been demolished at the end of phase 2 but in some trenches the emplacements both for main posts, *c.* 10×10 cm, and for small wands were quite apparent. One wall consisted exclusively of very thin uprights while others consisted of major posts at intervals of about a metre, with a filling of five or six wands between them. The walls were then covered with daub, abundant traces of which were found in the destruction deposits.

Only two complete *contubernia* were uncovered, each consisting of the customary two rooms. These had different lengths, one being 3·30 m and the other 3·60 m; this would give an average internal area of about 23·50 m², well within the normal range (Breeze 1974). Each room was more-or-less square, an arrangement that differs sharply from the far from standard design of phase 1. There is, however, one unusual feature about the layout of the barrack-block in that the rooms were divided by a double median wall rather than the customary single partition. The contemporaneity of these two walls is not in doubt since it was quite clear that none of the *contubernium* partitions crossed either wall-trench; the sections (Figs 20, 23) also confirmed this conclusion. Both trenches appear to have held substantial sill-beams, each 25 cm in width, and set 35 cm apart. This arrangement is closely paralleled at Cardean (Robertson 1975, 85-6) where a timber-framed barrack of Flavian date was also provided with a double central wall. Robertson (1975) suggests that this "median double-rib had been a constructional technique designed to provide extra strong support for penthouse roofs sloping down to either side", a convincing explanation which she also uses to interpret the otherwise curiously narrow buildings of the Antonine fort at Birrens. It is, however, worth noting that at Ravenglass the ground slopes quite sharply from east to west so that the level of the floor of the barrack-block varies by as much as 25 cm in a horizontal distance of less than ten metres; it may be therefore that proper stability was difficult to achieve on such uneven ground with the result that this unusual building technique was adopted. At Birrens too the surface of the ground sloped quite considerably, creating problems for the builders, and perhaps explaining the curious plan of the barracks.

Within the barrack some details were recorded of the internal arrangements. The northern rooms retained traces of a thin layer of gravel make-up which appeared to have been covered with wooden floor-boards. These were preserved as a thin line of charcoal (Fig. 20, trench B, unit 23), immediately underlying the collapsed daub from the walls. Similar flooring was also identified in the southern rooms, resting on a deposit of silt. The floor-boards appeared most clearly beneath a bag of gaming-counters sealed by the layer of collapsed daub (Pl. VIIIb); whilst not sharply defined, they gave the impression of narrow planks, probably not more than 10 cm across, resting upon a thin joist. No other features were found in this part of the barrack but in two of the front rooms there were rows of stakeholes which probably supported benches or beds along the wall. The western front room had only one row of stakes, running parallel with and a metre distant from the main long wall; but in the adjacent room to the east there were benches along both the north and west sides of the room, supported by small stakes, 5 cm in diameter, placed at intervals of 40-50 cm. The puzzling feature of this arrangement is that these benches would have undoubtedly hindered access from the veranda, since there must have been a door leading into each *contubernium*. This could imply an alternative interpretation as screens (in which a door could be more readily set) although it seems unlikely that so small a room should be further subdivided.

Before discussing the other barrack-block, it should be noted that there is some evidence for subsequent maintenance and reconstruction of barrack-block 4. At least one section of cross-wall was replaced, the new partition being placed in a trench running parallel with the old footing. This implies that these partitions carried a sufficient load to necessitate the insertion of the new wall-supports before the old structure could be demolished. Similarly other partitions were in places shored up by the introduction of new uprights, packed around with large cobbles. This reminds us that the Roman engineers did not season their timber and the onset of decay must have been a rapid process, as Richmond (1968, 119-20) demonstrated at Hod Hill. Even so, as we shall see when the dating evidence is set out, these barracks survived without any major rebuild for a period of some 60-70 years, a considerable timespan for wooden buildings in a coastal environment.

Barrack-block 5 was separated from its neighbour by a gap of just under a metre, the intervening space presumably acting as an open drain. The second barrack was 9·25 m in width, its narrower dimension being explained by the use of a single median wall. Its *contubernia* were more or less identical in size, having a total internal area within the wall-trenches of 23·80 m². Careful preparations were made to offset the difficulties caused by the presence of the ditch and palisade-trench of the earlier fortlet: apart from shifting the wall positions a short way to the north, the ground was covered with a layer, 25 cm thick, of red or brown clay. This created a firm platform so that the barrack-block stood well above the level of its neighbour, on comparatively solid ground. This appears to have been a satiafactory solution since, apart from shoring up one of the internal partitions with a separate post, none of the walls required any major repair during the lifetime of the barrack.

No traces of a veranda were found outside the barrack-block although there was a rubbish pit just beyond the area appropriate to a veranda. The contents of the pit will be discussed below but we may note here that it was rectangular in shape, measuring 2·60 by at least 2 m. The overall depth was just over 60 cm but a shelf was left along the north side, to facilitate access from the barrack-block (Fig. 24). Such pits were a common provision in many forts, with comparable examples from sites like Fendoch (Richmond and McIntyre 1938-9). Otherwise this area was left open, there being no evidence for any stratigraphic build-up before the laying out of a small street at the beginning of phase 3.

On the south side of the site, we have a much less clear picture of the situation in this period. No definite evidence for any buildings was found in the south part of trench D nor was there any conclusive proof of structures in trenches E or G. However, as the north section of trench E demonstrates (Fig. 17), there was a make-up layer of orange clay-silt (unit 12) laid over the palisade-trench of the primary fortlet and a thick dump of burnt daub, dating to the end of phase 2, in the top of the ditch of the earlier fortlet. There were also traces of one possible construction-trench in a context appropriate to phase 2. The volume of burnt daub implies that there were buildings in close proximity to this area, even though their exact position cannot be identified. Thus we cannot be certain if the barrack-blocks continued in a regular series of pairs, as seems probable, or whether this was an area of vacant ground in phase 2.

The destruction of the phase 2 buildings

In stratigraphic terms, the destruction of the phase 2 buildings constituted the most closely defined event on the site. This is partly explained by the fact that this level was buried sufficiently deeply to escape any major damage from ploughing; in consequence, the destruction-layers were preserved almost entire throughout the building area. But they were also extremely distinctive in appearance, consisting of a deep layer of bright red daub, resulting from the burning and collapse of the walls. The deepest deposit of daub lay in the top of the primary fortlet ditch (whose fill by this time had slumped very considerably), where it was over 50 cm in depth (Fig. 17, unit 14); but there were also thick deposits, 20 cm deep, all along the west side of barrack-blocks 4 and 5 (Fig. 20, trench C, units 21, 25; trench B, unit 22), and a thinner spread that covered all the east side of these buildings. In addition, immediately beneath the daub was a thin line of charcoal, recognisable at some points as the remains of burnt floor-boards.

The date of this widespread destruction by fire of the barrack-blocks is likely, as we shall see below, to have been towards the end of the second or early in the third century. This was of course a particularly unsettled period, with a sustained war ("the greatest of Commodus' reign": Dio 73, 8) between 180 and 184; the imperial ambition of Clodius Albinus who in 196 took the army to fight in Gaul, leaving the province more or less wide open to enemy attack; the difficulties experienced by Severus' first governor, Virius Lupus (197-201/2), who was forced to buy off the dangerous native confederation of the Maeatae (Dio 76, 5, 4); and the campaigns into northern Scotland led by Severus himself between 208 and 211, who came to Britain because "the barbarians had risen and were overrunning the country, carrying off booty and causing great destruction" (Herodian 3, 14, 1). Damage attributed to enemy attack has been identified at a number of sites – for example Rudchester, Haltonchesters and Corbridge (Frere 1974, 187) – but debate continues both as to the extent and the date of these destruction-deposits. As Breeze and Dobson (1972, 200-6) have emphasised, burnt buildings could just as likely result from accidental firing as from hostile action, a difference that may not always be explicit in the archaeological record. Similarly, there is little agreement about the date of many of the destruction-deposits, that at Corbridge, for example, provoking a protracted and still inconclusive discussion (e.g. Hartley 1972; Simpson 1974; Frere 1974, 217; Gillam *in* Frere 1977, 372).

Thus we have to decide whether the destruction-deposit that defines the end of phase 2 at Ravenglass was the result of enemy action or if we should explain it in any other way. The arguments in favour of destruction at the hands of an enemy are simple: that there are several appropriate historical contexts and that the barrack-blocks were destroyed by fire, before being pulled down. Certainly quite large numbers of objects were left in the building and suffered damage in the fire. There was a considerable quantity of burnt samian and coarse-ware; a rectangular bronze object (inv. 42); and also a bag of 126 gaming-counters, found on the floor and sealed beneath the layer of burnt daub (Pls VIIIb, IX); the bag may well have been hanging on the wall. These objects only prove, however, that the building was not cleared before being set alight and was thus not intentionally demolished.

Other debris from the burnt building was collected up and dumped in a pit immediately outside the barrack. It contained a considerable quantity of organic material, amongst which were several objects of leather (inv. 90-91) and some wood. The wood including a number of unburnt planks (possibly from a door) and part of a heavily charred beam with a rebated joint. There was also a large quantity of samian, some of it burnt, and some coarse-ware vessels, at least three of which were burnt. The pottery was largely Antonine in date but pieces in the group (Fig. 13) show that the pit was finally filled late in the second or early in the third century. A botanical study (Chap. II) was also made of the contents of the fill, which demonstrated the presence of both burnt and unburnt grain as well as the uncarbonised remains of other plants.

Whether we should attribute this fire to enemy attack or to accident is nevertheless a matter for conjecture. Certainly, it must have been easy to set alight timber buildings of this sort, especially as the rampart ovens were close by. On the other hand, due weight should probably be given to the fact that the years between 190-210 were particularly troubled ones and that a fort like Ravenglass could have been an obvious target for a sea-borne attack from Galloway, the Isle of Man or elsewhere. An accidental conflagration at this time is perfectly possible: but this might seem to stretch coincidence too far. On balance we would probably favour an explanation that takes account of the political upheavals of the period.

Phase 2: dating evidence

The very large collection of mid second-century material from Ravenglass suggests that this fort, unlike most others on Hadrian's Wall and in the hinterland, was not abandoned with the shift to the Antonine frontier in the early 140s. Instead it appears to have been continuously occupied from its construction in the 130s (discussed under phase 1, *supra*) to its destruction between *c.* 190-210. Only one stratified coin was found, an *as* of Hadrian, but from later levels came one coin of 148-9, another of 140-61, four issued during the reign of Marcus Aurelius (161-180) and one of Septimius Severus, a *denarius* dated 197-8. To this group of second-century coins should be added a very large collection of samian, mainly of Antonine date. It includes a number of stamps attested on the Antonine Wall (e.g. Cinnamus, Cucalus, Cadgatus, Divixtus: cf. Hartley 1972) as well as much material of the late Antonine period. This distribution suggests that Ravenglass was unaffected by the troop deployments which accompanied the war of 180-185, under Ulpius Marcellus. Interestingly, the coarse-wares show a decline in number at this time (Fig. 39), but this may be connected with a fall in supply rather than with a reduction of the garrison.

The evidence for the latest occupation in phase 2 is set out diagrammatically in Fig. 13. One group of material comes from the collapsed remains of the barrack walls and the other from the rubbish pit beside barrack-block 5. The samian goes right down to the end of the second century, while the coarse-ware includes a few forms which either persist into the third century or in one case does not, on Gillam's chronology (Gillam 1970), appear before 200. The volume of possible third-century material is, however, so small in proportion to that of the second century, that we are probably safe in concluding a date within a decade either side of 200 for these groups. Thus, if we are to favour a destruction at the hands of the enemy, we might argue for a date of 197 for the deposit. Alternatively, and perhaps more plausibly, we might follow Birley (1972) and suggest that Ravenglass was damaged in *c.* 207, a date that takes account of Herodian's reference to trouble in the province (3, 14, 1) and could explain why Severus himself came to Britain in 208. Hartley (1966, 18-20) would, on the other hand, prefer a date of *c.* 205. The reconstruction of the fort would thus form part of the widespread rebuilding programme attested on Hadrian's Wall from *c.* 205, when Alfenus Senecio became governor, and rather earlier in the hinterland under Virius Lupus (Frere 1974, 197-9). But the available evidence cannot give precision of this order.

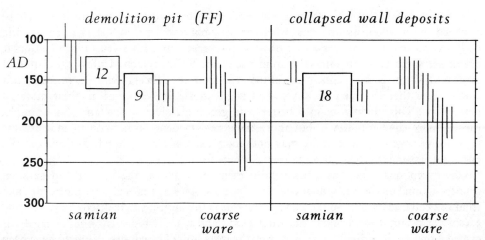

FIG. 13. – Ravenglass: diagram showing the chronological distribution of dated finds in the destruction deposits marking the end of phase 2.

Phase 2: summary of the finds

The most notable objects dating to the second century are a group of brooches, many of them handsomely decorated with enamelling. Only one was found in context (inv. 2), the others coming from deposits of phase 3 (inv. 6, 8) and phase 4 (inv. 3, 5, 7, 9); but all are types which are thought to go out of manufacture c. 200. The most favoured form was the enamelled disc brooch whose popularity at Ravenglass contrasts with its comparative rarity at Watercrook (Fig. 84). The less elaborate trumpet brooch, on the other hand, while represented by only one example (inv. 9) at Ravenglass, is much more frequent at Watercrook, with no less than 7 examples from the present excavations. Personal ornament is otherwise represented by an enamelled pendant (inv. 18), one bead (59), and an armlet (55). There is little obvious military equipment: a spearhead (75), a strap end (22), a belt-plate (13) and a "dress-fastener" (24) which may in fact have been used as a harness-fitting (Wild 1970). There were also two spindle-whorls (53, 54), made of bone, which suggest some domestic activity.

Building-fittings were confined to very large numbers of iron nails, one piece of window-glass and a lock bolt. Tile was sparsely represented, suggesting that the roofs were covered with timber or thatch, a curious conclusion in that there was a second-century tile-kiln three miles up the Esk valley at Park House (Bellhouse 1960, 1961). Park House does, on the other hand, seem to have supplied a good deal of the kitchen-ware in this period, the forms ranging from burnished jars to crudely made gritted fabrics (cf. p. 118). Although the Park House kilns appear to have distributed their wares quite widely through the north-west, the emphasis upon local suppliers for military sites does seem to be pronounced in the second century. In the north-west of England, for example, there are well attested examples of small kiln sites at Quernmore near Lancaster (Jones and Shotter 1978), at Brampton near Carlisle (Hogg 1965) and at Scalesceugh, which lies six miles to the south-east of Carlisle (Bellhouse 1971; Richardson 1973). Presumably Park House was sited so as to supply both Hardknott and Ravenglass. It is notable, however, that samian ware occurs in enormous abundance at Ravenglass, the total vessel count amounting to nearly 600 examples. Bearing in mind that it was the men's quarters that were under excavation, this seems an exceptionally high figure, although it is perhaps matched by the quantity and quality of the personal jewellery. Similarly late first- and early second-century glass vessels were also well represented, with at least nine identifiable examples, some of them imported from the Seine/Rhine region. Unless the range of artifacts is distorted by the inclusion of material from the officers' quarters in the fort, it would seem that the men at Ravenglass were unusually well-to-do in their material possessions. This might hint at a better paid group of soldiers – cavalry, for example, earned more than infantry – but there is no real evidence otherwise to indicate the presence of cavalry. However we may note four items of horse-equipment (inv. 19, 28), one a harness-mount from phase 2 and the others from phase 4.

One exceptional find has already been mentioned above: the bag of 126 gaming-counters, found on the burnt floor boards of barrack block 4, and sealed by the burnt daub from the collapsed walls. So far as we know this is the largest single discovery of its kind except for a burial in Perugia (Carattoli 1887) and it must represent one or more sets owned either by an individual soldier or by the mess unit. The counters seem to have been used in two ways: first in the game *ludus latrunculorum*, using the face of the counters; and second in gambling, employing the numbers and letters scratched onto the underside of 84 of the counters. A full discussion of these aspects will be found in the catalogue in Chap. II.

The Interior: Phase 3 (Fig. 14, Pls VIIa, b, VIIIa)

The deposits of the third and fourth centuries proved to have been badly damaged by later disturbance and, as a result, were extremely difficult to interpret. Fortunately, the phase 4 buildings were built in a comparatively idiosyncratic style and could, therefore, be readily distinguished from their immediate predecessors; but the phase 3 structures, which represent several periods of timber building, were much less easy to sort out stratigraphically. Consequently, we have decided to classify them as one phase, whilst recognising that there are important sub-divisions. The timespan is in fact a very long one – about 150 years – and, since the barracks continued to be constructed in wood, they show extensive evidence of reconstruction and repair. There seems also to have been at least one major conflagration during this period which damaged or destroyed both barrack-blocks to the north of the minor street. This event cannot, however, be closely dated on internal evidence and is not well enough documented stratigraphically to divide the period into two separate phases.

Barrack-block 6 was superimposed directly upon block 4 of the previous phase, 2. Its width over the wall-trenches measured 9.50 m (as compared with 9.40 m for phase 2) and its method of construction also appears to have been very similar to its second-century predecessor. This might be seen, therefore, as a fairly compelling argument for garrison continuity between the two phases. Reconstruction of the blocks seems in fact to have followed more or less immediately. First the wooden uprights were withdrawn, as is clear from the complete absence of charred stumps *in situ*. Then, with the obstructions removed, the new foundation-trenches were dug. These do not appear to have been particularly substantial – 30 cm was the average depth of the wall-trench for the long wall (Fig. 20, trench C, unit 16/30) – which may betoken haste in construction. They were cut from the top of the daub (e.g. Fig. 20, trench C, unit 14), without any preparation of the surface (except perhaps for some levelling) or deposition of any layer of make-up. Indeed,

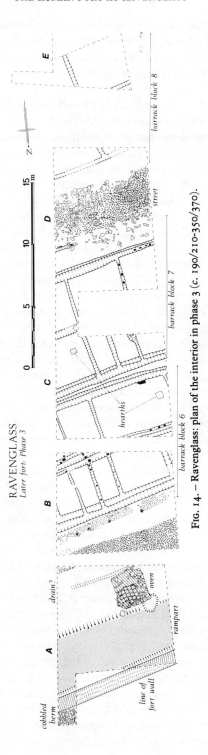

FIG. 14. – Ravenglass: plan of the interior in phase 3 (c. 190/210–350/370).

the only internal feature that was found was a hearth in the inner room at the west end of the block. It was made of a flat slab of stone, some 50 cm square, resting in a bed of clay. Another hearth, made of a piece of tile, was found in the inner room of the adjoining block, 7, suggesting that it was the outer rooms of each *contubernium* that were devoted to storage.

At some later date most of the barrack-block was demolished and completely rebuilt. With the apparent exception of the most northerly wall (which was studied under the very dry and unfavourable conditions that prevailed in July and August 1976), the east-west walls were shifted by some 30 cm to the south and the foundation trenches recut. At the same time the position of the cross-walls dividing the *contubernia* was altered, apparently creating rather smaller rooms. However, we should note here that a combination of unsuitable conditions for excavation and extensive later disturbance effectively prevent us from offering a secure interpretation for the size of the *contubernia*; thus we cannot really establish with confidence the position of the partitions in any sub-phase of this period. It should be noted that the level of the floor was raised by the deposition of a layer of grey silt-clay. This was laid to a depth of 12 cm over the rather lower ground at the south-west part of the building (Fig. 20, trench C, units 14, 24) and it thinned out rapidly towards the north and east, where the ground was higher. A veranda was also constructed outside the north wall. This was indicated by a series of separate posts, packed around with lumps of limestone, demarcating a narrow gravelled strip, 80 cm wide. Beyond the veranda was the shallow ditch bordering the *intervallum* road and then the *via sagularis* itself.

The fate of this barrack-block cannot be demonstrated as effectively as that of earlier buildings on the site: later disturbance has made quite certain of that. However we can be sure that it shared in a general conflagration that destroyed barracks 6 and 7 and probably 8 as well. Overall the evidence was stratigraphically patchy but in the more deeply buried deposits on the western side of the site the layers were still largely intact. They consisted of a deposit of charcoal, overlain by areas of burnt daub (Fig. 20, trench C, units 11, 8, 19; trench B, unit 20). These layers were not as thick as those covering the phase 2 buildings but it is quite evident that the two barrack-blocks were destroyed in the same way. There were also pieces of burnt wood, including part of a plank, 65×35 cm, beside the south wall of the block. This raises again the question of the nature of the destruction: whether it is best seen as the result of an accident or if it can be attributed to enemy attack. Once again we cannot be certain. There is a historical context for enemy attacks towards the end of the third century (discussed further below), but there is no close dating evidence nor any specific indication of attack. What is not in doubt is that the barrack-block was again immediately rebuilt. All the major east-west wall-trenches were recut, the lines of the central and north footings being shifted a short distance to the north. The trenches contained large quantities of burnt daub and charcoal, deriving from the destruction-deposit. Some of the *contubernia* partitions are also likely to belong to this period, although the evidence was less explicit. Unfortunately no floor-levels of this period survived so we cannot determine the nature of the internal arrangements in any detail: but it would seem that this rebuild represents the last constructional activity of phase 3.

It remains to comment upon the building techniques employed in this period. Demolition had been thorough in all sub-phases and we cannot, therefore, document the structural elements in any great detail. However, it is worth emphasising that there was clear evidence from the central wall-trenches (where there was less intercutting than in

THE ROMAN FORT AT RAVENGLASS

the main walls) that a technique of separate uprights, *c.* 25 cm square, was used. These were spaced at intervals of between 60 and 90 cm. Some of the cross-walls also employed this technique, with wattles between the main uprights; but other partitions seem to have comprised only light wattle screens. Unfortunately we cannot with any certainty offer an interpretation of individual *contubernium* sizes, so it is impossible to say whether the type of partition wall changed during phase 3.

Barrack-block 7 formed a pair with block 6, the two buildings lying back to back in exactly the same manner as in phase 2. Block 7 was 9·50 m over the wall-trenches, a width that is identical to that of block 6. Constructionally, too, it is very similar with separate uprights in both the long walls and in the internal partitions. There was also a hearth, made of a tile (Pl. VIIb), in one of the inner rooms as in block 7. The two blocks thus share a close overall similarity of design. The structural history is likewise more or less parallel, except that we cannot demonstrate with certainty the presence of two periods of construction before the conflagration described above. All the wall-trenches show only two definite periods of construction, the later of which represents the reconstruction of the block after the fire. It is, however, possible that the pre-fire recut was either not observed or had destroyed all trace of the earlier trench. The sequence was best preserved in the north-east corner of trench B, where the levels had slumped into the ditch of the primary fortlet (Fig. 21). Here the phase 2 layers were buried beneath a deposit of brown clay-silt make-up 30 cm in depth, laid to fill up the quite considerable depression along the line of the ditch. The south wall-trench of the barrack (Fig. 21, unit 9) was cut to a depth of 65 cm, an unusually deep footing for this period that reflects the quantity of made ground in this area. Sealing this level was a thin layer of charcoal, possibly the remains of floorboards, and a spread of burnt daub from the walls. This layer extended patchily over most of the barrack and lay in a stratigraphic position equivalent to the daub deposits already described for block 6. There is no doubt, therefore, that both barrack-blocks were burnt down in this fire. As with block 6, block 7 was then immediately reconstructed, the trenches cutting down through the burnt level (e.g. Fig. 21, unit 5). Details of this last period of phase 3 were, however, badly damaged by later disturbance and few structural observations could be made.

Barrack-block 8 was the least well understood building of this phase and cannot be documented in any detail. The remains as they survive are those of a block some 10 m wide over the wall-trenches with a central wall (Fig. 17, unit 13) and partitions laid out in the conventional way. There is some evidence to suggest that the northern side of the building was raised on a layer of make-up (Fig. 21, unit 19), possibly deposited not at the beginning of the phase but during it; but the evidence was not explicit. As the section at the north end of trench E shows (Fig. 17), there were several phases of reconstruction. These cannot be related to the periods described for blocks 6 and 7 although it is worth noting that there were sufficient quantities of daub in deposits of this phase to imply that the building shared in the fire that destroyed the neighbouring blocks. But none of this daub survived as anything but small patches and its stratigraphic relationship could not, therefore, be properly established.

Phase 3: dating evidence

It is unfortunate that we cannot provide any detailed chronological breakdown of the events during phase 3: the discontinuities in the stratigraphy were sufficiently pronounced to exclude the recovery of all but a very few properly sealed groups, and none of these yielded an adequate body of data. Indeed the groups of this phase were notable for the large quantities of residual pottery, incorporated into these later layers as a result of the extensive disturbances caused by the construction-trenches. The overall body of data makes it quite clear, however, that occupation never ceased through phase 3. The distribution of dated pottery types (Fig. 39), whilst reflecting a greater dearth of material (probably more an indication of our state of knowledge than of the actual situation), shows a sequence unbroken by any periods of abandonment, a conclusion also borne out, as we have seen, by the stratigraphic evidence.

The beginning of phase 3, as already suggested, is datable to the period between 200 and 210. The barracks were immediately rebuilt, following their destruction in the fire that marks the end of phase 2. Barrack-block 6 was subsequently reconstructed, before being destroyed in a conflagration that also destroyed block 7 and probably block 8. The date of this fire cannot be fixed at all closely on internal evidence: there were no stratified coins or significant groups of pottery in association with this event. The most extensive area of burnt daub came from trench D where there were two areas covering altogether about 3 m²; but the groups from beneath this layer only imply a *terminus ante quem* somewhere in the mid-third – mid-fourth centuries. Similarly we have been unable to establish the cause of the fire, which might have been the result of an accidental conflagration or of an enemy attack. If it was the latter, then there are appropriate historical contexts in the events of the late third century. Although Britain was largely unaffected by the Germanic invasions of Gaul, there is good evidence to show that attacks by sea-raiders did become increasingly common in the period 268-82, principally by Saxons (Frere 1974, 215). In 286 Carausius, a Menapian from Belgium, was put in charge of a naval squadron with orders to suppress this piracy. However, it appears that he attempted to profit personally by seizing for himself the booty of the raiders; and, when the emperor, Maximian, learnt of this, Carausius's execution was ordered. Carausius's response was to take refuge in Britain where he set himself up as emperor, a reign that lasted until his murder by Allectus, his finance minister, in 293. Three years later, the emperor Constantius mounted an expedition against Allectus, who was conclusively defeated in a battle perhaps near Silchester.

It is generally assumed that Allectus stripped the frontier of troops for this battle and that, in consequence, the tribes beyond the Wall took the opportunity to ravage the northern part of the province: 296 is thus often quoted as an important watershed in the history of the frontier. In fact the evidence for destruction on the Wall and in the hinterland is nowhere well documented (Breeze and Dobson 1972, 1976). All that we know for certain is that there was an extensive programme of rebuilding early in the fourth century (Frere 1974, 384-7; Wilkes 1965), followed by a punitive campaign into Scotland by Constantius and his son Constantine, in 306.

The conflagration within phase 3 at Ravenglass might well be seen as reflecting these events. The buildings could well have been burnt down in the course of an enemy attack in 296 or by a seaborne raid at some other time in this troubled period. Alternatively the fire could have been accidental and completely unrelated to these events. On the evidence available we cannot really decide with certainty.

Whatever the truth behind this event, it is clear that the barrack-blocks were immediately rebuilt. Occupation extended on into the fourth century, as pottery and coins make clear. The terminal date of the phase is, however, once again difficult to decide. We know that there were attacks by the Scots and Picts in 360, further raids in 364 and then in 367-9, a concerted war upon the province by a confederation of Picts, Scots, Saxons, Franks, and Attacotti (Frere 1974, 390-2). The danger posed by the *barbarica conspiratio* is underlined by the fact that it took Theodosius a year to recover the province and a much longer period to rectify the damage (Tomlin 1974). Theodosian restoration has now been widely recognised in the frontier region (Breeze and Dobson 1976, 221-9) although Hadrian's Wall itself does seem to have escaped serious damage. This is normally explained by suggesting that the tribal forces sailed past the Wall and landed further south.

At Ravenglass there is some evidence for the end of phase 3. In the first place there is a group of coins which represents a small hoard. Three, found corroded together (inv. 24-6), included two issues of Constans (datable to 346-50) and one of Magnentius (350-1). None of these coins shows much wear. Secondly, there were two areas where patches of burnt daub were found to overlie the latest buildings of phase 3. This is slight evidence but it should imply that the buildings were burnt down at the end of this period. Thirdly, there was a very small but useful group of material from in and under one of these daub patches. This included a vessel of the period 290-370 (Fig. 44, 93), another of 350-400 (Fig. 44, 94) and a sherd of calcite-gritted ware. Most importantly, however, there was a coin in the burnt daub: this was a fairly unworn issue of Magnentius, datable to 350-1.

This *terminus post quem* of 350 takes us very close, therefore, to the events of 360-369, especially if we allow some time for circulation of the coins of Magnentius and attach due significance to the pot of 350-400. The hoard is also a clear indication of the troubles of the period. Thus it is quite possible that Ravenglass was involved in the wars of the 360s and that it was attacked from the sea. If so, we can probably date the rebuilding of the fort in phase 4 to the Theodosian restoration of the frontier region, although we advance this hypothesis with considerable caution.

Phase 3: summary of the finds

Apart from the pottery, the commonest site-find in deposits of this phase (as in phase 2 and 4) was the iron nail, with 629 recognizable examples. Only 19 other iron objects were identifiable, most of them pieces of blade or strapping. There were 41 fragments of bronze, including two second-century enamelled disc or plate brooches (inv. 6, 8) which may have been carefully safeguarded as heirlooms: one (inv. 6) is very handsomely decorated with an enamelled fish, a motif found on two other objects from the site (inv. 3, 4). There were also three brooches of third- or early fourth-century date (inv. 1, 10, 11). The other bronzes were mostly very small and fragmentary, the identifiable objects including a scabbard-chape and several studs.

Window-glass was abundantly represented in this phase, indicating for the first time in the history of the barrack-blocks that panes were provided rather than iron grills. In conjunction with the hearths in blocks 6 and 7, they show that some attempt was made in this period to make the barracks more comfortable in winter: as the excavation team found, the site was particularly vulnerable to westerly gales and the barracks must have been cold and draughty buildings without inside heating.

The most exceptional discovery from deposits of this phase was a lead sealing (inv. 71), bearing the stamp of the *Cohors I Aelia Classica*. This unit is attested in 146 at Chesters

(*CIL*, XVI, 93) and is placed in the *Notitia* at *Tunnocelum*, usually identified as Moresby, although a case can also be made for Burrow Walls. The discovery of the sealing at Ravenglass does not of course imply that it was based here; such sealings were attached to official consignments and must thus have been widely distributed. It is interesting to note that Hind (1974) has suggested that the *cohortes classicae*, normally thought of as units raised from the fleet which then became conventional land cohorts, did in fact still retain some naval functions; the presence of this sealing at Ravenglass, the natural harbour for south-west Cumbria, may hint at liaison with naval forces.

The Interior: Phase 4 (Fig. 15, Pl. VIIa)

The latest buildings on the site, while still made of timber, represent a clear change in constructional techniques from previous periods. Whereas the barracks of phases 1-3 had generally used timbers set in foundation-trenches, the structures of the last period employed separate postholes, with massive stone packing. Thus, even though the associated floor-levels have largely been ploughed away, the building-plans of this phase were still quite easily distinguishable. Rather surprisingly, the basic layout of the site remained much the same as before, the major difference being that the barrack-blocks were turned round, so that the verandas faced each other. The internal divisions seem also to have been largely abandoned, although it could be that they were much less solidly constructed and have left little trace.

Barrack-block 9 was the most northerly of the three buildings. It measured 7·80 m in width, with an additional 1·5 m for a veranda along the south side. The line of the south wall (like the north wall of barrack 10) had been marked out by a very shallow trench but this contained no recognizable structural elements and may only have been a slight recess for the base of the wall infilling. The posts used in the building were on average about 15 cm square and solidly packed with fragments of limestone and clay. They tended to be spaced at intervals of 1·5-2 m but there appeared to be only limited consistency in their layout, as well as several gaps where there must once have been uprights. Inside, the building lacked any central partition but there were three posts, which can best be interpreted as a cross-wall, and two others which seemingly do not belong to any partition-line.

One rather puzzling group of posts was found outside and parallel with the north wall of the barrack-block. With the exception of two posts, they formed a line a metre beyond the block and immediately bordering the stone-lined drain beside the *intervallum* road. The posts, which appeared to be contemporary with the drain, were mostly stone-packed but were much more closely spaced than those used for the barrack-block walls. Thus one group had five posts within a stretch of 2 m and another four, separated by a gap of just over 1 m. The uprights were also substantial: one posthole (which may be taken as typical) was over 40 cm in depth and contained a timber 15 cm square. At first sight this line might be taken as the north wall of the barrack-block, but the line could not be shown to continue in the western part of the excavated area and the density of the posts (if they are all contemporary) is uncharacteristic of building techniques on the site at this time. Similarly, the construction seems excessive for a veranda, unless it had a special load-bearing function. We cannot therefore offer any very convincing explanation for this feature.

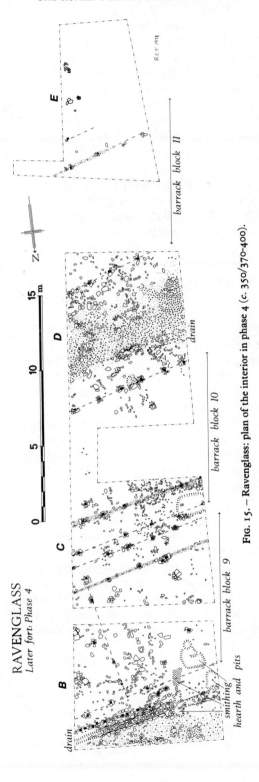

FIG. 15. — Ravenglass: plan of the interior in phase 4 (*c.* 350/370–400).

As we noted above the floors of this phase had mostly disappeared through ploughing. All that was found was a scatter of cobbles, limestone fragments and one piece of quern, presumably from a make-up layer. One very small area, 60 cm across, was paved with flat pieces of stone which appeared to have been deliberately laid: but this could equally well have been a post-pad. One feature, however, that does call for comment was a small pit, 40 cm in diameter and 10 cm in depth, filled with iron slag and charcoal. Beside it was a larger depression and nearby a spread of slag. Nothing but late fourth-century (and residual) pottery was found with these features and it is possible that some smithing took place within this building, an activity well attested elsewhere in the Ravenglass area (e.g. Cherry 1966, 1968).

Barrack-block 10 faced block 9 across a very narrow passage less than a metre in width. This presumably acted as an eaves-drip. The veranda of block 10 was 1·70 m in width – a little wider than that of block 9 – and the building was between 7·25 and 7·50 m wide; it seems to have tapered somewhat towards the east. A shallow marker-trench was employed in the north wall, the construction overall being similar to that of block 9, except that the posts of the south wall were quite regularly spaced at intervals of just over 1·50 m. One internal post was found, possibly forming part of a cross-wall that extended east of the excavated area. Otherwise there were no internal features of note, beyond a scatter of rubble as in block 9.

A small street (discussed in detail in a subsequent section) separated blocks 10 and 11. The street was *c.* 3·5 m in width and had a stone-lined drain (resembling that beside the *intervallum* road) along its north edge. Both sides of the street were also flanked by narrow open spaces, between one and two metres wide, surfaced with some rough cobbling. The total distance between blocks 10 and 11 thus amounted to 7·40 m; but there was no evidence for any front veranda.

Barrack-block 11 was 7.50 m in width, with seemingly a veranda on the south side. The evidence from trench E was, however, far from clear since this area had suffered very considerable plough damage. Only two posts from the south wall could be identified with any certainty and only one from the veranda wall. The north wall was, on the other hand, much better preserved with regularly spaced posts, 15×15 cm in size, set in stone-packed postholes.

To the south of barrack-block 11, it is probable that there had been another building. The ground over the ditch of the earlier fortlet (phase 0) had been levelled with a dump of stones, containing calcite-gritted wares and other characteristic late fourth-century pottery. Curiously, these stones rested directly on the upper ditch-fill, as if the deposits of phases 1-3 had been shovelled off in order to prepare the ground. Three stone-packed postholes were also found, in a position appropriate to the veranda and north wall of a fourth barrack-block, forming a pair with block 11. But no other post-settings were identified and it is possible to assume either that the building was never finished or that it has now largely been destroyed.

The interesting feature of the phase 4 layout – which, as we have seen, dates to after 350 – is the way in which the plan of the buildings duplicates the wall-lines and orientation of the earlier barracks. This is not, moreover, only evidence for continuity: it also evinces a degree of order and regularity which is unusual in this period. At Wallsend (Frere 1977, 372), Haltonchesters and Rudchester (Breeze and Dobson 1976, 222-3), for example, the late fourth-century buildings tend to be free-standing and dispersed. Many of them are built entirely in wood despite the fact that earlier barracks had stone foundations. Similarly at Bowness-on-Solway (cf. Chap. VI) a small wooden building, only 5 m in width, overlay the second-century barrack-block. This timber structure, like analogous features elsewhere in the fort (Potter 1975, 39-40), was apparently constructed sometime during the fourth century, probably in the latter decades. At Housesteads, Greatchesters and High Rochester, on the other hand, the fourth-century barrack-blocks consisted of a series of separate "chalets", which replaced the *contubernia* of previous barrack-blocks. These have been most closely studied at Housesteads (Wilkes 1961; Frere 1977, 372-3) where they date from the early fourth century, with modifications and repairs in the period after 367. These chalets all have stone footings, but the superstructure appears to have consisted of a timber frame, filled with daub.

Ravenglass, therefore, is unusual in that the latest barracks do adhere quite closely to older models on the site. What unifies this group of late buildings in northern England, however, is the emphasis upon timber for the superstructure and, in many cases, the foundations too. Maryport might be cited as an additional example (Jarrett 1976, 37-40), with stone-packed postholes in the later phases, while very recent excavations at both Ribchester and Chester demonstrate a similar pattern. What lies behind these architectural changes is at present hard to assess: but the phenomenon is now well documented (though without sufficient complete building-plans) and it is interesting that Ravenglass adds a slight variant to the theme.

The eventual fate of the phase 4 buildings is not explicitly known. None of the post-sockets yielded any of the dark humic matter that commonly marks the position of a rotted post; this suggests that the structures were eventually demolished. But who was responsible for this work and under what circumstances the fort was abandoned is unclear. The buildings themselves were covered by a layer of dark soil, rich in pottery and small objects (many of them residual). This was not, however, a stratified occupation deposit – it had been ploughed in late medieval times – and, as noted above, no floors were preserved. Thus the last Roman episode in the history of the site cannot be documented in any way.

Phase 4: dating evidence

As Fig. 39 shows, the latest period of occupation on the fort is represented by an enormous abundance of late fourth-century pottery. This includes typical Crambeck mortaria and bowls, as well as hundreds of rims from calcite-gritted jars. The assemblage as a whole is typical, therefore, of classes of pottery in use in the frontier region in the last three or four decades of the fourth century. Unfortunately, the pottery cannot be used to give any more precise date than this; it does not tell us, for example, whether occupation extended after Magnus Maximus's abortive attempt to claim imperial power in 383, with an army recruited from Britain.

The initial date for phase 4, as we showed above, came after 350 and could well belong to Count Theodosius's restoration of the frontier region in 369. The terminal date is less easily established. The latest coin from the excavations is an issue of Valens (364-7), although a *solidus* of Theodosius (379-395) was found in *c.* 1800 in the foundations of the 14th-century pele tower at Muncaster Castle (Fair 1948, 219). The absence of coins later than Valens is unusual for a site occupied in the late fourth-century and might well imply an evacuation in or before 383. On the other hand the volume of late fourth-century pottery is exceptionally large – probably several hundred vessels – which could equally well be taken to imply occupation until the end of the fourth century or beyond. As so often the archaeological evidence is ambiguous. By way of comparison, we might note that Maryport (Jarrett 1976) has yielded coins both of the House of Valentinian (364-392) and of Theodosius (three coins); Beckfoot (Collingwood 1936) a coin of Constantius II (324-361); and Burrow Walls (Bellhouse 1955) late fourth-century pottery but no numismatic evidence. The high proportion of late fourth-century coins from Maryport is very striking, but we may note that the total sample is large (129) whereas that from Ravenglass is small (37 in all). On balance, therefore, we might argue that the forts along the Cumberland coast were kept in garrison after 383 and that Ravenglass should be numbered with this group.

Phase 4: summary of the finds

These deposits yielded the largest sample of finds from the whole site; but many of the objects are typologically old and it is probable that a good proportion occur as rubbish-survival. For example, there were four brooches (inv. 3, 5, 7, 9) of second-century form, and a helmet-carrier (inv. 4), datable to the late second or early third centuries. Some objects, on the other hand, may have been carefully looked after, like the two second-century gemstones (inv. 111, 112) found in late fourth-century layers: both must have been prized objects which could well have been handed down over several generations. A finely decorated belt-fitting (inv. 13) is also likely to belong to a second-century context, as are some of the mounts (inv. 12, 15, 16, 17); but unfortunately we cannot assign a firm date to four items of horse-equipment, a rein-bearing trace (inv. 19) and three identical harness-mounts (inv. 28: 1 is from phase 2). The harness-mounts find their best parallels in early Roman contexts, but there are no exact analogies and it would be unwise to draw conclusions from them. Horse-equipment is on the whole notable for its rarity.

Otherwise the finds are a fairly miscellaneous collection: a variety of studs (inv. 31, 34-8), a bronze bracelet (inv. 39), a spoon (inv. 47), a glass armlet (inv. 57), a scabbard-chape (inv. 27), a lock bolt (inv. 26), and a small group of slate gaming-counters, roughly chipped from local stone (inv. 49-51). Weaponry, as in all periods, is scarce and there are no items of armour.

The Internal Street (Figs 14, 15, 21; Pl. IIb)

Immediately beyond the first pair of barrack-blocks was a small internal street. It lay 24 m to the south of the *intervallum* road and had a width of some 3·5 m. Its original construction could be securely dated since the earliest surface sealed the pit containing debris from the destruction of the phase 2 barracks (Fig. 24). The street must, therefore, have been constructed in phase 3, probably at the beginning of the period: *i.e.* in the early third century. It was also repaired and resurfaced on a number of subsequent occasions, partly because it had slumped badly where it crossed the ditch of the earlier fortlet (phase 0) and the pit of phase 2. The average depth of the metalling was about 30 cm which in places (for example, over the pit) extended to as much as 45 cm.

Sections through the street indicated two main phases of construction. The earlier comprised a layer of cobble and gravel, 10 cm thick, forming a cambered surface some 3·5 m wide. This was later covered by a make-up of heavy cobbles and large pieces of limestone and then surfaced with a thin skin of rammed gravel and small cobbles. This event is not closely dated and could fall either in the later part of phase 3 or at the beginning of phase 4. At the same time, the line of the street was shifted very marginally towards the south and a stone-lined drain inserted along the north edge (Fig. 15). Only a small part of the drain survived the medieval disturbance to the site but sufficient was preserved to show that it resembled closely the form of the drain beside the *intervallum* road. Some heavy kerb-stones (which could have formed one side of a second drain) were also placed along the southern edge of the street.

Stripping of the street in plan revealed, however, a more complex picture of the sequence. At least three surfaces were identified above the layer of heavy make-up suggesting that the street was maintained right up to the final evacuation of the fort. All these surfaces were very localised in extent so that they are best interpreted as repairs rather than a complete rebuild of the road. One distinctive surface comprised a layer of small flat pieces of sandstone, rammed firmly into place; but the other work was carried out with cobbles and gravel, collected presumably from the beach.

It is interesting to note that there was no evidence at all for any street earlier than the beginning of phase 3. This area was apparently open ground before that time, disturbed only by the rubbish pit of phase 2.

TRENCH F (Fig. 25)

A short section of the cliff edge was cleaned up at the southern end of the plateau, 38 m beyond the end of trench E. It emerged that the stratigraphy had been completely destroyed at this point, the plough soil resting directly upon the red-clay subsoil. Three wall-trenches, whose bases had penetrated the subsoil, were, however, located, together with a scatter of burnt daub or charcoal. No attempt was made to examine these trenches in plan, but they do establish that buildings extended to this part of the site and that they probably shared in one or more of the conflagrations described above.

POST ROMAN EVIDENCE

There was a scatter of post-Roman pottery from the site, including pieces of green-glazed ware and some post-medieval sherds. One green-glazed sherd was found in the robber-trench that followed the line of the fort wall, indicating a late medieval date for the removal of the masonry. There was also a fine medallion (inv. 139), struck to commemorate Admiral Vernon's victory at Porto Bello in 1739. The only structural feature of medieval date was a masonry grave, set into the Roman levels at the north east corner of trench C (Fig. 16). It was made of undressed and irregular slabs of limestone, placed so as to form a cist, measuring internally 1·34×29 cm. Six fairly large and two small pieces of stone made up the floor while other lumps of limestone formed the sides and cover. The cist was shallow, 29 cm in depth and contained only an earth fill; but there is no doubt that it was intended as a grave. There are many parallels for this form of coffin, including a great many post-Conquest examples found in the recent excavations at St Patrick's Chapel, Heysham. As at Heysham, the Ravenglass coffin is orientated east-west. The bones of the corpse have presumably perished in the highly acidic soil developed in the Ravenglass area.

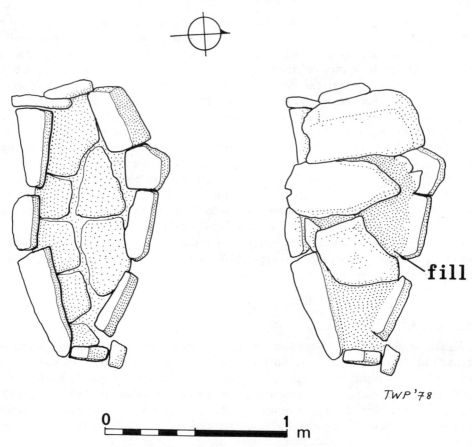

TWP '78

0   1
                                 m

FIG. 16. – Ravenglass: plans of the medieval grave.

Summary

In this section, a summary is given of the principal features of each phase. A discussion of the wider significance of the results will be found in Chap. VII.

The early fortlet (phase 0)

The features include: (1) the ditch (2·80-3·30 m wide by 1·60 m deep) and (2) palisade of a small fortlet, with a maximum width within the defences of *c.* 18-20 m. The fortlet appears to have been demolished when the later fort was build *c.* 130. Rampart material and some wooden elements, probably from the defences, filled the ditch. A period of occupation between *c.* 120-130 is indicated; it was almost certainly built as part of the Hadrianic coastal *limes*.

The later fort

Phase 1 The new fort was larger, probably approaching 3·60 acres in size, and differently orientated. The *defences* comprised a turf rampart, 3·70 m wide; a ditch, 6.60 m wide × 1·70 m deep; and a natural gully. There was a narrow *intervallum* road, 2·20 m wide. Traces of three timber-framed barrack-blocks were found. *Block 1* was 10·10 m wide, with *contubernia* 28·5 m² in area. *Block 2* was similar in plan but may never have been completed. *Block 3* was only partially explored. It is probable that these buildings were never completely finished and certainly were not used. A date of *c.* 130 is indicated.

Phase 2 During this period the site remained continuously occupied from *c.* 130-190/210. The *defences* remained unaltered, although there are some indications of repair during the period. Traces of a circular rampart-oven were found. There were two barrack-blocks, both timber-framed; they were constructed in slightly different positions and with design modifications from those of phase 1. *Block 4* was 9·40 m wide and possessed *contubernia* with an average area of 23·50 m². It was provided with a double median wall (paralleled at Cardean and Birrens) and internal trenches or screens in the outer rooms. *Block 5* was 9·25 m in width and had *contubernia* with an average area of 23·80 m. Only these two barrack blocks were identified.

Block 4 appears to have been partially or totally rebuilt once during this period but both buildings were burnt down *in situ* at the end of the period. A date between 190-210 is indicated on internal evidence for this event.

The quantity of fine table-ware and small objects is especially notable, given that these were the quarters of ordinary soldiers. A very large group of gaming-counters was also found in the destruction deposit.

Phase 3 Rebuilding of the fort appears to have followed on immediately after the destruction at the end of phase 2. The *defences* were remodelled by the insertion of a narrow stone wall in front of the rampart and a new and very elaborate tiled oven was constructed in the lea of the defences. This oven was rebuilt once during phase 3. The *intervallum* road was also widened and resurfaced.

Within the fort three barrack-blocks, all timber-framed, were identified. A complex history of repair and reconstruction prevented any detailed understanding of their internal layout, however. *Block 6* was 9·50 m in width with a veranda along the north side. It lay back to back with *block 7*, which was also 9·50 m wide. Block 6 was reconstructed once before a fire destroyed both it and its neighbour. This event cannot be closely dated but could have occurred in the late third century. Both buildings were subsequently reconstructed on lines similar to their predecessors. *Block 8* was apparently as wide as 10 m but little is known of its layout and history. It was separated from the other barrack-blocks by a small *street*, 3·5 m in width, laid out at the beginning of phase 3.

Occupation seems to have been continuous through the period, terminating between 350 and 370. Very slight indications suggest the blocks 6 and 7 were finally destroyed by fire and it is possible that their destruction was connected with the tumultuous events of the 360s. A small coin-hoard also points to the insecurity of the period.

The most notable find was a lead sealing bearing a stamp of the *Cohors I Aelia Classica*.

Phase 4 The last Roman period in the history of the site saw a slight modification to the *defences* in that the inner ditch was filled in, but there were no other identifiable alterations. The *intervallum* road, on the other hand, was resurfaced and the buildings within the fort completely redesigned. Three barrack-blocks were identified, each built using a technique of separate postholes with heavy stone packing. The blocks were also turned round so that the verandas faced each other. *Block 9* was 7·80 m wide, with an additional 1·50 m for the veranda. One cross-wall was found and there was also evidence for iron-smithing within the building. *Block 10* was between 7·25 and 7·50 m in width with a veranda, 1·70 m wide. *Block 11* was 7·50 m wide; it was separated from the other blocks by the small street, which had been resurfaced several times since its construction in the early third century.

The latest coin from the excavations was an issue of Valens (364-7) but enormous quantities of late fourth-century pottery were found and it seems certain that the fort remained in garrison until *c*. 400 or later. There were no indications, however, of the nature of the final evacuation.

Medieval

Apart from a single medieval grave, post-Roman activity was attested only by a scatter of sherds. One sherd came from the robber-trench along the line of the fort wall, suggesting a late medieval date for the removal of the masonry.

NOTES ON THE SECTIONS

Fig. 10: Section across successive ovens in the lee of the rampart

 1. Ploughsoil.
 2. Dark fill containing some hearth sweepings and pottery of second and third-century date.
 3. Two successive tiled ovens, phase 3.
 4. Bed of red and yellow clay, overlying a thin band of clay, sealing earlier levels.
 5. Trench for a timber revetment placed along the back of the turf rampart.
 6. Remains of a demolished circular oven, phase 2; limestone fragments and brown silt and clay.
 7. Bed of grey-brown clay.
 8. Cobble and gravel make-up layer.
 9. Yellow-grey layer of turf, presumably building up the ground for the oven of phase 2.
10. Turf rampart.

Fig. 17: Trench E, north section through the ditch and palisade of the earlier fortlet (phase 0) and later levels

 1. Topsoil.
 2. Medieval ploughsoil.
 3. *Contubernium* division, phase 3. Brown silt fill with lumps of burnt daub.
 4. *Contubernium* division, phase 3. Dark fill with much burnt daub: possibly post-dating the conflagration in phase 3.
 5. Dark fill with burnt daub overlying a layer of burnt daub and charcoal, probably representing the fire at the end of phase 2. The deposits have slumped into the earlier palisade-trench.
 6. Loose silt fill, probably a later intrusion.
 7. Brown deposit, probably disturbed by medieval ploughing. Beneath is natural orange clay.
 8. Dark deposit, flecked with charcoal and daub. Much later fourth-century pottery.
 9. Central wall of barrack-block 8. Dark fill.
10-11. *Contubernium* walls, possibly phase 2. Dark fill.
12. An extensive layer of pale orange silt laid over the palisade-trench and the berm to the west. Probably a make-up deposit of phase 2.

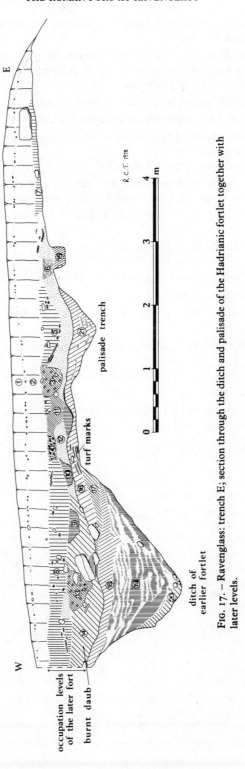

FIG. 17. – Ravenglass: trench E; section through the ditch and palisade of the Hadrianic fortlet together with later levels.

13. Central wall of barrack-block 8, probably preceding 11. It is filled with the brown soil and burnt daub into which it is cut.

14. A very deep deposit of burnt daub and some brown soil, filling the top of the ditch. It is likely to represent a dump of material from one of the buildings burnt down at the end of phase 2; it was presumably intended to level up a subsidence over the ditch.

15. Cross wall-trench, filled with clean grey silt. Probably phase 1.

16. Grey silt, with some turves, especially on the lip of the ditch. Top filling of the ditch, end of phase 1.

17. Tip of brown silt, upper fill of ditch.

18. A pale grey turf-like deposit, upper fill of ditch.

19. A peat deposit interleaved with thin layers and lenses of grey clay. Botanical analysis shows that the peat represents turves cut from nearby marsh, composed mostly of sedge.

20. Tip of brown clay, with heavy cobbles at the bottom of the ditch. Much wood came from this layer.

21. Palisade-trench, phase 0. Filled with rampart turves.

Fig. 18: Sections through the ditch and palisade of the early fortlet

(a) Section towards the corner of the ditch, trench D.

  1. Gravel road-metalling of the minor street, phases 3-4. At least three separate phases of deposition are apparent.

  2. Layer of grey clay, sealing the fill of the ditch of the earlier fortlet. The date of the clay was not established.

  3. Peat fill consisting of turves from the rampart of the fortlet. The layer is remarkable for its lack of internal stratification.

  4. Grey clay with a few black peat turves, grading into a pale silt-sand.

  5. A mixed deposit of grey clay and pale silt. Numerous heavy cobbles in the cleaning-channel at the bottom of the ditch.

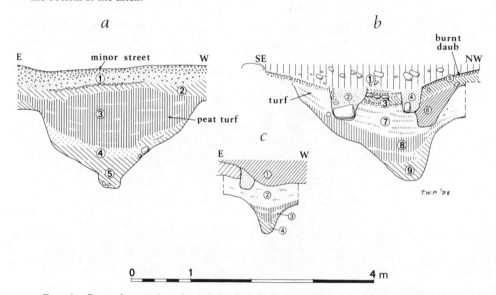

FIG. 18. – Ravenglass: sections through the ditch (a, b) and palisade (c) of the Hadrianic fortlet.

(b) Section across the ditch, trench D, 4 m to the north of (a)

1. Dark deposit, with much late fourth-century pottery. Probably partly disturbed by medieval ploughing.

2. Stone-packed posthole, phase 4.

3. Two layers of gravel, separated by a deposit of brown clay; a spread from the minor street of phases 3 and 4.

4. South wall-trench, barrack-block 7, phase 3. The trench belongs to the rebuild of the block that followed the fire in phase 3. Brown fill, with fragments of burnt daub.

5. Layer of burnt daub forming a smoothly surfaced deposit, overlying a deposit of brown, daub-flecked silt. The daub represents the collapsed walls of the block destroyed by fire within phase 3.

6. South wall-trench, barrack-block 7, phase 3: the predecessor of 4. Brown fill, flecked with burnt daub.

7. A light grey deposit made up of turves and clay from the rampart of the earlier fortlet (phase 0).

8. Two tips of peat turves, without much internal stratification.

9. Grey-brown clay with a good deal of wood, principally discards from the building of the later fort, phase 1.

(c) Section across the palisade-trench, earlier fortlet

1. Later deposits of phases 2-3, including a *contubernium* wall.

2. Grey clay and turf fill. Phase 0.

3. Black peat, consisting of marsh turves. Phase 0.

4. Grey clay.

Fig. 19: Section across the north defences

Note: This drawing represents a combination of two separate sections and the ground level has had, consequently, to have been slightly adjusted, so as to provide a coherent section.

1. Topsoil, overlying a brown loam soil with many pebbles; the loam represents a medieval ploughsoil.

2. Robber-trench following the line of the fort wall. No *in situ* masonry was found but numerous fragments of limestone, cobbles and red clay indicate that there had been a solid clay-and-cobble footing. Medieval green-glazed wares were found in the trench, indicating a fifteenth-century context for the removal of the fort wall.

3. Two intrusive pits, perhaps of medieval date. Brown fill.

4. Brown loam with many pebbles; probably a medieval ploughsoil.

5. Small flat-bottomed trench, orientated NW-SE. Filled with a brown soil and many cobbles. Possibly a palisade-trench or an "ankle-breaker"; alternatively it could have been a drain.

6. Flat-bottomed pit, cut into the turf rampart; homogenous brown fill. Perhaps associated with the insertion of the stone wall into the front of the turf rampart.

7. Demolished turf-work and burnt material in the lea of the turf rampart. This is overlain by tips of gravel and soil, probably associated with a reconstruction of the rampart in phase 3.

8. Rampart made with turves cut from marsh silt and clay. The front of the rampart was removed when the stone wall was inserted, probably in phase 3.

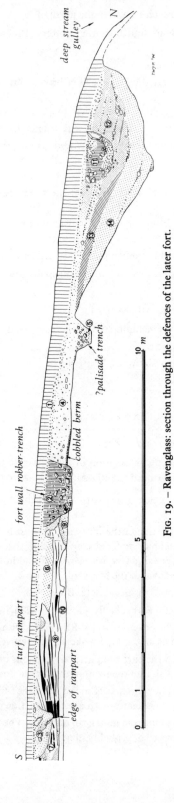

RAVENGLASS 1976 SECTION ACROSS THE NORTH DEFENCES

FIG. 19. – Ravenglass: section through the defences of the later fort.

9. A mound of brown pebbly soil, perhaps resulting from the construction of a level platform at the front of the turf rampart. Alternatively it may have been a marker bank. The layer precedes the building of the turf rampart.

10. A grey leached old ground surface, from which the surface turf has been stripped. The layer rests upon red clay.

11. Pit, cut into the fill of the ditch. Filled with tips of gravel, brown loam and rubble.

12. A series of brown loam, gravel and sand tips, filling the upper part of the ditch. A deliberate fill (with 13 and 14), probably dating to the third quarter of the fourth century.

13. Red-brown sand layer with a few pebbles.

14. A comparatively homogeneous layer of light grey soil, closely resembling the turf of the rampart, and filling the lower part of the ditch.

Fig. 20: West sections of trenches C and B

(a) Trench C

1, 2. Recent and medieval ploughsoil, separated by a distinct pebble horizon.

1a. Recent intrusion.

3. Stone-packed posthole, phase 4: north wall, barrack-block 10.

4. North wall-trench, barrack-block 7; later part of phase 3. Brown fill with pieces of daub.

5. South wall, barrack-block 6, phase 3. The trench was clearly cut after the phase 3 fire (unit 11). Dark brown fill with burnt daub.

6. Barrack-block 6, central wall-trench, phase 3. Dark fill with burnt daub.

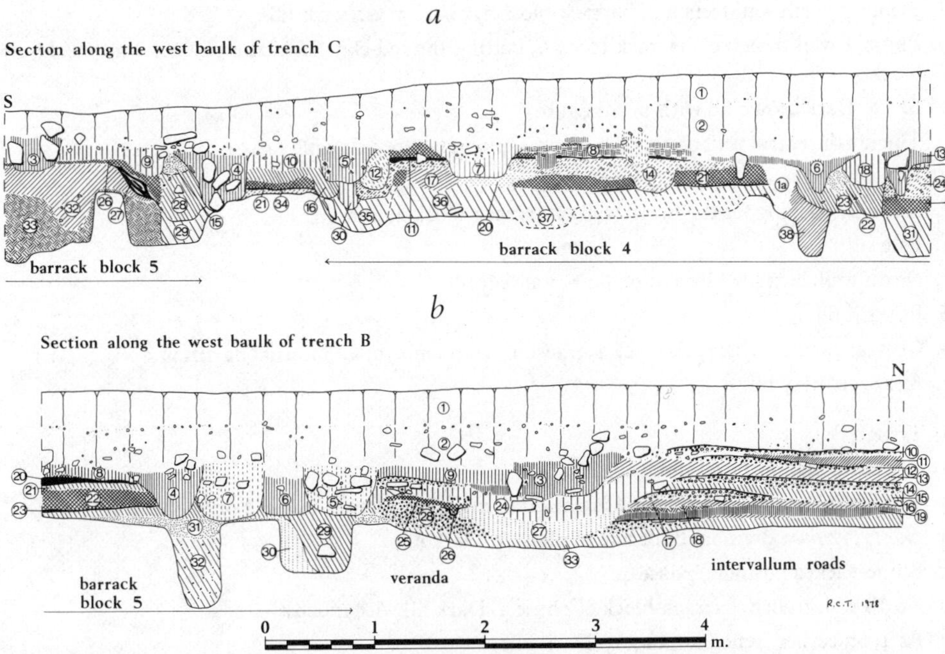

a

Section along the west baulk of trench C

Section along the west baulk of trench B

b

FIG. 20. – Ravenglass: the west sections of trenches C and B.

7. Pit, possibly phase 4. Grey-brown fill with gravel tips.

8. Two layers of burnt daub (the lower sealing a line of charcoal), separated by dark soil. The product of the burning of barrack-block 6 during phase 3. Cf. units 11, 19.

9, 10. Dark brown soil flecked with daub. Phase 3.

11. As 8, 19. A much thicker layer of daub.

12. As 5.

13. Possibly a stone-packed posthole of phase 4.

14. Layer of brown silt, forming a make-up deposit, laid at the beginning of phase 3.

15. Hard brown clay.

16. With unit 30, primary south wall-trench of barrack-block 6, phase 3. Grey clay, flecked with burnt daub.

17. Soft brown soil.

18. As 6, an earlier trench of phase 3. Light brown fill.

19. Burnt daub, marking the fire during phase 3. Cf. units 8, 11.

20. Pale fill of a *contubernium* wall, phase 3.

21. Burnt daub overlying a thin charcoal line, end of phase 2. As 25, 26.

22. Brown silt.

23. Grey clay fill of the primary centre wall of barrack-block 6, phase 3.

24. Clay make-up layer for barrack-block 6, beginning of phase 3.

25. As 21. Note the difference in level between the two units, perhaps explaining the double median wall in phase 2.

26. As 21, 25, but daub from block 7, which was built at a higher level than block 6.

27. Charcoal. End of phase 2.

28. Primary north wall-trench of barrack-block 7, phase 3. Grey silt fill.

29. Phase 2 wall-trench of barrack-block 6, cutting the red-clay fill of the phase 1 wall-trench of block 1.

30. As 16. Dark brown fill with burnt daub.

31. The north central wall of barrack-block 4, phase 2. Grey-clay fill.

32. Red-clay make-up layer, block 5 phase 2.

33. Red-clay packing for the north wall of barrack-block 2, phase 1.

34. Pale silt.

35. North wall, barrack-block 4, phase 2. Pale silt fill.

36. Pale silt fill.

37. Central partition, barrack-block 1, phase 1. To the north, an internal partition.

38. As 28, red-clay fill.

(b) Trench B

1, 2. Recent and medieval ploughsoil.

3. Cut for stone-lined drain beside *intervallum* road, built late in phase 3 or in phase 4.

4. *Contubernium* division, built late in phase 3. Dark fill.

5. Stone-packed posthole, phase 4.

6. North wall-trench, barrack-block 6, phase 3. Dark fill with much charcoal.

7. As 4, an earlier trench in phase 3. Dark fill.

8. Dark silt.

9. As 8: an accumulation on the veranda of phase 3.

10. Latest *intervallum* surface.

11. Red-clay make-up.

12. *Intervallum* road surface.

13. Brown silt-clay make-up.

14. As 12.

15. Grey silt-clay make-up.

16. *Intervallum* road surface, beginning of phase 3.

17. Dump of silt, tiles and fragments of sandstone blocks.

18. Burnt daub and clay: end of phase 2.

19. Thick layer of charcoal and dark soil: end of phase 2.

20. Burnt daub and charcoal, the result of the burning-down of barrack-block 6 during phase 3.

21. Grey silt.

22. Thick layer of burnt daub, resulting from the destruction of block 4 at the end of phase 2.

23. Charcoal, as 22.

24. Dark silt in the ditch beside the *intervallum* road, phase 3.

25. As 22, 18. Overlying *intervallum* road.

26. Small timber slot.

27. As 24, phase 2.

28. *Intervallum* road, phases 1, 2.

29, 30. North wall-trench, barrack-block 4, phase 2. The packing consists of brown silt, while the socket is filled with grey silt.

31. A layer of pebbles and clay forming a make-up for the phase 2 barrack-block.

32. Phase 1 wall-trench, barrack-block 1. Grey silt fill.

33. Grey silt.

Fig. 21. East section of trench D, together with the east part of the north section of trench D

(a) East section

1. Topsoil and medieval ploughsoil.

2. A thin spread of dark soil flecked with charcoal, together with a lens of burnt daub. It is this deposit that marks the final destruction of the phase 3 barrack-block no. 7.

3. Dark soil with fourth-century pottery.

4. Layer of charcoal and some burnt daub, marking the destruction of barrack-block 7 during phase 3.

5. South wall-trench, block 7, phase 3: recut after the fire during phase 3. Brown fill with charcoal.

6. Dark brown fill with cobbles and gravel. Possibly a ploughed road-surface.

7. Minor street, successive road-surfaces, made of gravel cobbles and large lumps of limestone as make up material. Phases 3-4.

8. Northern part of the street make-up, resting on a thin layer of red clay.

9. Wall-trench of barrack-block 7, early part of phase 3. Brown fill, flecked with burnt daub.

10. Wall-trench of barrack-block 5, phase 2. Light brown fill, without burnt daub.

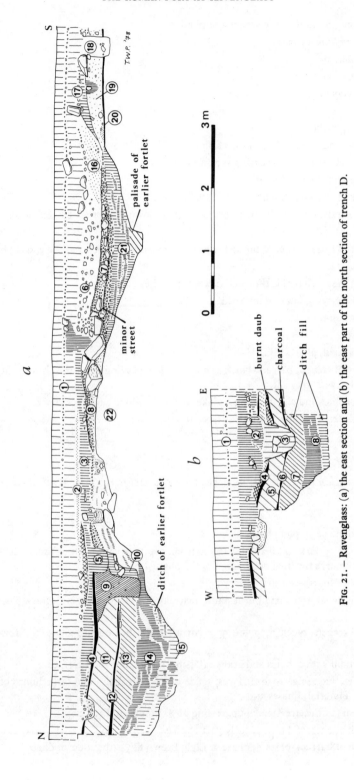

FIG. 21. — Ravenglass: (a) the east section and (b) the east part of the north section of trench D.

11. Brown clay, a make-up deposit for the phase 3 barrack-block.

12. Layer of charcoal and some burnt daub, resting on a few pieces of tile. Destruction-deposit at the end of phase 2.

13. Light grey clay, a make-up deposit for the phase 2 barrack-block.

14. Peat turf fill of the ditch of the earlier fortlet, phase 0.

15. Light-grey clay deposit. The bottom of the ditch was not found at the point of section.

16. Tip of dark brown soil over the street surface.

17. Dark brown accumulation, possibly belonging to phase 4.

18. North wall of barrack-block 8, phase 3; dark brown fill.

19. Make-up deposit of grey-brown silt with patches of gravel; phase 3.

20. Thin layer of charcoal; destruction of phase 2 buildings.

21. Turf fill of the palisade-trench of the earlier fortlet. the section gives an exaggerated width to the trench since it is cut diagonally.

22. Yellow clay-silt. It is possible that this represents a bank between the ditch and palisade, but the point was not firmly established.

(b) East part of north section, trench D.

1. Recent and medieval ploughsoil.

2. Dark soil with much late fourth-century pottery, probably disturbed by medieval ploughing. the pebble horizon at the ease end of the section is probably equivalent to unit 2 in the north section.

3. *Contubernium* division, marking the rebuild of the phase 3 barrack-block, no. 7, in phase 3; dark fill with charcoal and daub.

4. Burnt daub and charcoal, slumped into the earlier ditch; indicates a fire during phase 3. Equivalent to unit 4, east section.

5. Brown silt-clay deposit. Phase 3 make-up.

6. Charcoal and burnt daub; fire that destroyed barrack-block 5 at the end of phase 2.

7. Grey silt-clay; phase 2 make-up.

8. Black peat turves from the rampart of the earlier fortlet, filling the ditch.

9. Grey clay; the full profile of the ditch was not exposed.

Fig. 22. South section, trench C.

1. Recent and medieval ploughsoil.

2. Successive wall-trenches of a *contubernium* division; one of phase 2, the other of phase 3.

3. *Contubernium* division of phase 3.

4. *Contubernium* divisions of phases 2 and 3.

5. Brown fill with later intrusions and a lens of charcoal (possibly marking the fire within phase 3).

6. Burnt daub; fire at the end of phase 2. The lower level of this deposit suggests that the *contubernium* at the wall end of the barrack-block may have been placed on a series of terraces, to compensate for the sloping ground.

7. Make-up of red clay for barrack-block 5, phase 2.

8, 9, 10. Wall-trenches of phase 1. Clean red clay and grey silt.

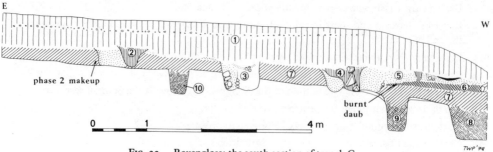

FIG. 22. – Ravenglass: the south section of trench C.

Fig. 23: The north section of trench B

1. Recent and medieval ploughsoil.

2. Dark soil with much later fourth-century pottery; probably a ploughsoil of post-Roman date. The depth of this layer demonstrates the extent of medieval damage to the higher parts of the site.

3. Stone-packed posthole of phase 4; the socket is clearly differentiated from the stone and red-clay packing.

4. Stone-lined drain of phase 4 (or late in phase 3). The drain has been projected on to the section and may in consequence be slightly too low in the stratigraphic sequence.

5, 6. Two successive layers of *intervallum* road, separated by a layer of grey silt.

7. Silt-filled gutter beside the *intervallum* road.

8. North wall of barrack-block 6, later part of phase 3. Dark fill with burnt daub.

9. Burnt daub, clay and, beneath, a line of charcoal, representing the destruction of the phase 2 barrack-block.

10. A complex sequence with the bases of three successive central walls of barrack-block 6, phase 3.

11. North wall of barrack-block 6, phase 3, early part of the period.

12. North wall-trench, barrack-block 4, phase 2; grey silt fill.

13. North wall-trench, barrack-block 1, phase 1; clean fill of red clay and grey silt, sealed by a thick deposit of red clay.

14. Grey silt and a gravel spread, resting on natural red clay. Phase 2 floor make-up.

15. Central wall-trenches of barrack-block 4, phase 2. The sockets are filled with red clay, grey silt and burnt daub, while the packing consists of red clay.

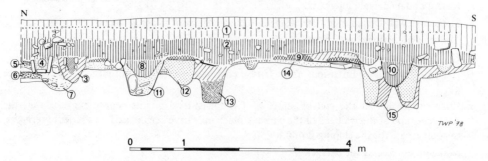

FIG. 23. – Ravenglass: the north section of trench B.

Fig. 24: Rubbish pit of phase 2, trench D

1. Topsoil.
2. Road-surface of the minor street of phases 3 and 4.
3. Dark fill with much organic material, including demolition debris from the barrack-blocks of phase 2.
4. Grey silt.

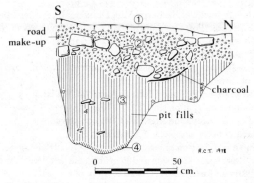

FIG. 24. – Ravenglass: section through the rubbish pit of phase 2, containing demolition debris. It is sealed by the street of phases 3 and 4.

Fig. 25: Section across trench F at the south end of the site

1. Adjacent wall-trenches filled with grey silt, flecked with charcoal and including fragments of burnt daub. Measurement suggests that these could be the end walls of two barrack-blocks, placed back to back.
2. Wall-trench with a fill of grey silt and burnt daub. Possibly a *contubernium* wall, entering the section at an angle.

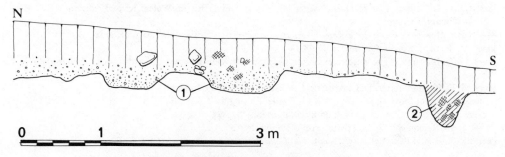

FIG. 25. – Ravenglass: section across trench F.

BIBLIOGRAPHY

Bellhouse, R. L., 1955. "The Roman fort at Burrow Walls near Workington". CW2 lv, 30-45.

—— 1960. "Excavations in Ēskdale, the Muncaster Roman kilns". CW2 lx, 1-12.

—— 1961. "Excavations in Eskdale, the Muncaster Roman kilns". CW2 lxi, 47-58.

—— 1971. "The Roman tileries at Scalesceugh and Brampton". CW2 lxxi, 35-44.

Birley, A. R., 1972, "Virius Lupus". AA4 l, 179-89.

Birley, E., 1958. "The Roman fort at Ravenglass". CW2 lviii, 14-30.

Breeze, D. J., 1974. "The Roman fortlet at Barburgh Mill, Dumfriesshire". *Britannia* V, 130-62.

Breeze, D. J. and Dobson, B., 1969. "Fort types on Hadrian's Wall". AA4 xxxxvii, 15-32.

—— 1972. "Hadrian's Wall: some problems". *Britannia* III, 182-208.

—— 1976. *Hadrian's Wall*. Allen Lane, London.

Carattoli, L., 1887. "Perugia. Tombe etrusche scoperte nel Cimitero". *Notizie degli Scavi* 1887, 391-398.

Caine, C., 1922. "The port of Ravenglass". CW2 xxii, 101-7.

Cherry, J., 1961. "Cairns in the Birker Fell and Ulpha Fell area". CW2 lxi, 7-15.

—— 1963. "Eskmeals sand-dunes occupation sites, I". CW2 lxiii, 31-52.

—— 1966. "Eskmeals sand-dunes occupation sites, II". CW2 lxiii, 46-56.

—— 1969. "Early Neolithic sites at Eskmeals". CW2 lxix, 40-53.

Cherry, J. and Cherry, P. J., 1968. "An iron bloomery at Drigg". CW2 lxviii, 27-30.

Collingwood, W. G., 1929. "Ravenglass, Coniston and Penrith in ancient deeds". CW2 xxix, 39-48.

Collingwood, R. G., 1928. "Roman Ravenglass". CW2 xxviii, 353-66.

—— 1936. "The Roman fort at Beckfoot". CW2 xxxvi, 76-84.

Darbishire, R. D., 1874. "Notes on discoveries in Ehenside Tarn, Cumberland". *Archaeologia* 44, 273-92.

Dymond, C. W., 1892. "Barnscar; an ancient settlement in Cumberland". CW1 xii, 179-87.

Fair, M. C., 1925. *In* Proceedings of the Society. CW2 xxv, 374-5.

—— 1936. "A sandhill site at Eskmeals, West Cumberland". CW2 xxxvi, 20-3.

—— 1948. "Roman finds on the Cumberland Coast". CW2 xxxxviii. 218-21.

Fell, C. I., 1972. *Early settlement in the Lake Counties*. Dalesman.

Ferguson, C., 1888. "The Roman camp at Muncaster". CW1 ix, 296-7.

Frere, S. S., 1974. *Britannia. A history of Roman Britain*. Cardinal.

—— 1977. Roman Britain in 1976. *Britannia* VIII, 356-425.

Gillam, J. P., 1970. *Types of Roman coarse pottery in northern Britain*. Newcastle.

—— 1977. "The Roman forts at Corbridge". AA5 v, 47-74.

Hartley, B. R., 1966. "Some problems of the military occupation of the north of England". *Northern History* 1, 7-20.

—— 1972. "The Roman occupations of Scotland: the evidence of Samian ware". *Britannia* III, 1-55.

Higham, N. J. and Jones, G. D. B., 1975. "Frontiers, forts and farmers: Cumbrian aerial survey 1974-5". *Arch. J.* 132, 16-53.

Hind, J. G. F., 1974. "Agricola's fleet at Portus Trucculensis". *Britannia* V, 285-8.

Hogg, R., 1965. "Excavations of the Roman auxiliary tilery, Brampton". CW2 lxv, 133-68.

Hogg, A. H. A., 1968. "Pen Llystyn: a Roman fort and other remains". *Arch. J.* 125, 101-92.

Jackson, W., 1876. "The camp at Muncaster and certain Roman discoveries there". CW1 iii, 17-22.

—— 1883. "An account of some excavations made at Walls Castle in 1881". CW1 vi, 216-24.

Jarrett, M. G., 1969. *The Roman frontier in Wales*. University of Wales. revised edition of V. E. Nash-Williams's volume.

—— 1976. *Maryport, Cumbria: a Roman fort and its garrison*. CW Extra Series 22. Kendal.

Jones, M. J., 1975. *Roman fort defences to A.D. 117*. BAR 21.

Jones, G. D. B., 1976. "The western extension of Hadrian's Wall: Bowness to Cardurnock". *Britannia* VII, 236-43.

Jones, G. D. B. and Shotter, D. C. A. 1978. *Lancaster Excavations*. In press.

Knowles, Rev. and Jackson, W., 1876. "Walls Castle, Ravenglass". CW1 iii, 23-8.

Parker, C. A., 1905. "The Earthwork on Infell, Ponsonby". CW2 v, 145-9.

—— 1906. "Roman coin found at Gosforth". CW2 vi, 151-2.

Pearsall, W. H. and Pennington, W., 1973. *The Lake District, a landscape history*. Collins.

Potter, T. W., 1975. "Excavations at Bowness-on-Solway 1973". CW2 lxxv, 29-57.

—— 1977. "The Biglands milefortlet and the Cumberland coast defences". *Britannia* VIII, 149-83.

—— 1978. Review of Jarrett 1976. *Britannia* IX, in press.

Richardson, G. G. S., 1973. "The Roman tilery, Scalesceugh, 1970-71". CW2 lxxiii, 79-89.

Richmond, I. A. and McIntyre, J., 1938-9. "The Agricolan Fort at Fendoch". *PSAS* 73, 110-54.

Richmond, I. A., 1949. "The Roman road from Ambleside to Ravenglass". CW2 xxxxix, 15-31.

—— 1955. "Roman Britain and Roman military antiquities". *Proc. British Academy* 41, 297-315.

—— 1968. *Hod Hill. Excavations carried out between 1951 and 1958. Volume 2.* British Museum.

Robertson, A. S., 1975. *Birrens (Blatobulgium).* Constable, Edinburgh.

Salway, P., 1965. *The Frontier people of Roman Britain.* C.U.P.

Simpson, F. G. and Hodgson, K. S., 1947. "The coastal mile-fortlet at Cardurnock". CW2 xxxxvii, 78-127.

Simpson, F. G., 1913. "The fort on the Stanegate at Throp". CW2 xiii, 363-81.

Simpson, G., 1974. "Haltwhistle Burn, Corstopitum and the Antonine Wall: a reconsideration". *Britannia* V, 317-39.

Tomlin, R. S. O., 1974. The date of the "Barbarian Conspiracy". *Britannia* V, 303-9.

Walker, D., 1965. "Excavations at Barnscar, 1957-8". CW2 lxv, 53-65.

Ward, J. C., 1877. "Notes on archaeological remains in the Lake District". CW1 iii, 241-65.

Ward, J. E., 1977. "Cairns on Corney Fell, West Cumberland". CW2 lxxvii, 1-5.

Wild, J. P., 1970. "Button and loop fasteners in the Roman provinces". *Britannia* I, 137-55.

Wilkes, J. J., 1961. "Excavations in Housesteads Fort 1960". AA4 xxxix, 279-300.

—— 1965. "Early fourth-century rebuilding in Hadrian's Wall forts". *In* (eds) Jarrett, M. G. and Dobson, B., *Britain and Rome,* Kendal, 114-38.

CHAPTER II

RAVENGLASS: THE FINDS

ALL THE FINDS from the excavation are discussed in this chapter. The "small finds" are numbered consecutively (except for a unique group of gaming-counters), but the coins, samian ware and coarse pottery are each numbered within their own section. Every catalogue entry includes the original site reference, listed in parenthesis, as well as the phase assigned to the layer in which the object was found. A consolidated bibliography is to be found at the end of the chapter.

OBJECTS OF BRONZE (Figs 26, 27)

Excluding the coins, a total of 159 bronze objects was found. More than half consist of tiny scraps of metal which were probably insignificant when lost or discarded and have suffered still further from the damaging acidity of the soil developed upon the Ravenglass site. Some important items have, however, survived, including a fine series of enamelled brooches, mounts and pendants, discussed in the inventory below. The overall distribution of bronze objects is as follows:

phase	date	brooches	helmet carrier	mounts	locks keys	chapes	studs	rings	bangles	sheet	pins	spoon	nails	misc.	total
0	c. 120-130														
1	c. 130														
2	c. 130-200	1		2			7			4	3			11	28
3	c. 200-360	3	1			1	6	3		4	5			18	41
4	c. 360-400	4	1	5	1	1	4	3	1	4	1	1	5	29	60
Unstratified		2		2			4	6	1		2		2	11	30

In addition, there are also nine lumps of bronze, some of which appear to indicate metal-working. These were concentrated in deposits of phase 4.

BROOCHES by A. C. H. Olivier

1. (SF 11) An unusual P-shaped brooch. The bow is short and strongly arched, D-shaped in cross-section. There are three shallow ornamental grooves running down the length of the bow; the middle groove is plain, whilst the lateral grooves each seem to possess three small decorative knobs. Each lateral groove is also flanked on the outside edge of the bow by a narrow engraved line. It is possible that the grooves may have been filled with enamel, although no trace of such work survives. The head of the bow is drawn into a flat plate, and a small portion of what appears to be a cast head-loop survives. A small band of knurled ornament runs across the plate at the point of junction with the bow. The head is broken, the pin is missing, and the surviving fragment of pin mechanism is heavily corroded, so that it is

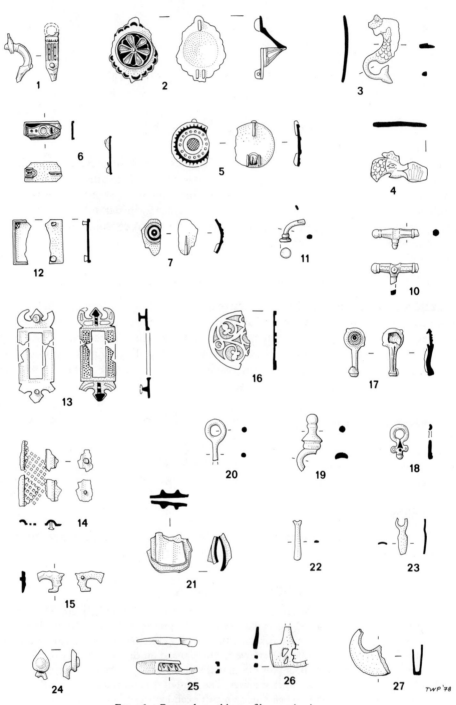

FIG. 26. – Ravenglass: objects of bronze (1:3).

not possible to ascertain the means by which the pin was originally attached to the brooch. The junction at the base of the bow and the foot of the brooch is decorated by an ornamental knob. Most of the foot and catchplate is missing.

Bronze. Corroded and broken. Unstratified.

In general, P-shaped brooches may be dated to the third century.

2. (SF 278)   Disc brooch with conical centre and hinged pin. The raised boss has one ring of long triangular cells with convex bases; alternate cells contain blue enamel, and there are slight traces of green enamel in the remaining cells. A continuous ring of blue enamel surrounds the lower circumference of the boss. The flat plate of the brooch is roughly rhomboidal in shape, with a scalloped outer edge, and has a small projecting lug at either end, one over the catchplate, and one over the pin housing. The scalloped edge is ornamented with a single ring of crescentic cells filled with blue enamel, and the lug over the catchplate possesses an additional crescentic cell at its forward edge, also containing blue enamel. The pin (missing) was hinged between two lugs, and the catchplate is broken.

Bronze. Phase 2.

A rather unusual example of the type, although broadly similar forms are known from London (Wheeler 1930, 96, Fig. 29.7), Leicester (Butcher 1977, 51, Fig. 5, 6) and Richborough (Bushe-Fox, 1932, 78, Pl. X.14). The type in general occurs commonly during the second century.

3. (SF 99)   Plate brooch in the form of a sea creature. The main body of the creature is decorated with engraved scales, although the tail portion appears to have been plain. The head is broken and corroded, and it is not possible to ascertain any details of form or decoration. The pin is missing.

Bronze. Corroded and broken. Phase 4.

The general group of Dragonesque S-shaped plate brooches to which this rather unusual example presumably belongs, is a North British type in use from the mid first century to the second half of the second century. Cf. 4, *infra*.

4. (SF 153)   A bronze helmet-carrier, which is listed in this section because of its close stylistic similarity with no. 3 above. Although their function is different and this piece is perhaps rather more crudely drawn it is possible that the two objects were products of the same workshop. The helmet-carrier bears the head and part of the body of a sea creature; the body is decorated with engraved scales. The head possesses an engraved eye and gills, and a forward fin and barble are also represented in the moulding. The creature has a gaping snout that opens on what appears to be an oval plate with engraved reeding. Both the oval plate and the head and body of the creature are cast in one piece.

Bronze. Slightly corroded and broken. Phase 4.

Robinson (1975, 92) suggests a date range between the late second and early third centuries for this class of helmet-carrier.

5. (SF 90)   Simple enamelled disc brooch. The central circle of the brooch is surrounded by a fairly broad ring in relief, and both these features retain fragmentary traces of red enamel. The outer circumference of the brooch is decorated by a fine scalloped band filled with blue enamel, and is defined on its inner edge by a narrow bronze wall. The band between this wall and the inner ring appears to have been ornamented with a ring of small circular depressions; no trace of enamelling survives in these depressions. The underside of the plate is concave in profile. The pin (missing) was sprung, and both the spring and spring housing survive; the catchplate is broken. There are no apparent traces of lugs projecting from the plate over the positions of either the spring or the catchplate.

Bronze. Badly corroded and broken. Phase 4.

The general form of this brooch is close to similar examples from Portchester (Webster 1975, 199, Fig. 109.3) and Newstead (Curle 1911, Pl. LXXXIX.6). Second century.

6.   (SF 200)   Enamelled rectangular plate brooch. The plate is decorated with the figure of a fish, described in outline by a narrow bronze wall. The head of the fish (overlying the catchplate) is surrounded by a field of green enamel, whilst the body is surrounded by blue enamel; the crescentic portion of the plate between the tail and the edge of the brooch is filled with green enamel. The outline of the head is emphasised by a band of blue enamel; however, it is not now possible to ascertain how the main part of the head may have been decorated, although there appear to be faint traces, in bronze, of the outline of an eye. The central segment of the body is ornamented with a circular depression edged by a bronze band, and this recess would presumably have originally held some form of ornamental stud or "stone". The tail is decorated by two small bronze circlets in relief. There appear to be very faint traces of yellow enamel on the main part of the body and tail. The edge of the plate is defined by a narrow bronze margin. The catchplate is broken, and the pin (now missing) is sprung with an internal chord, attached to the body of the brooch by means of an axial bar threaded through the centre of the spring and hinged between two small lugs projecting from the underside of the brooch.
Bronze. Corroded. Phase 3.
A fairly unusual example of a plate brooch. Second century.

7.   (SF 160)   Moulded disc brooch. This example has two rings of blue enamel separated by a raised bronze ring, with an outer rim of bronze falling sharply to the edge of the plate. The inner ring of enamel has a small central bronze stud. At least one lug, with no apparent traces of ornament, survives, projecting over the catchplate. The catchplate is broken, the pin is missing, and it is not possible to ascertain the means by which the pin was attached to the brooch.
Bronze. Badly corroded and broken. Phase 4.
A simple form current during the second century.

8.   (SF 128)   *Not illustrated.* Fragment, probably of a disc brooch with a conical centre. Only a portion of the outer rim survives. The rim is small, and retains two of the original six small lugs. There is no trace of an enamelled band around the edge; however, part of a double engraved circle survives at the lower point of the disc. The pin is hinged between two lugs; the pin and catchplate are both missing. The centre of the brooch would originally have risen in a curved cone to a cupped stud and nipple.
Bronze. Broken. Phase 3.
A standard form, probably current during the second century (Hull 1967, 56, Fig. 22.207).

9.   (SF 51) *Not illustrated.* Spring and loop only. Part of a Collingwood Type R trumpet brooch (Collingwood and Richmond 1969, 296-7, fig. 104.46-60). The spring is of six turns, and has an internal chord. The loop is formed from a separate piece of bronze wire, with the free ends inserted through the centre of the spring, overlapping each other for the entire length of the spring. The clip of the head-loop is not continuous at the back, and is ornamented on the upper face by two engraved lines forming a central ridge moulding. The spring would originally have been attached to the head of the brooch by the threading of the axial bar, formed by the head-loop ends, through a central pierced lug projecting from the head of the brooch. This example does not possess the more usual rolled sheet bronze tube for the head-loop ends to seat into.
Bronze. Fragmentary. Phase 4.
The type in general may be dated between the mid first century and the mid second century. (Boon and Savory 1975, 50-57).

10. (SF 24) Crossbow brooch (head only). The small surviving segment of bow is plain, and is of rectangular section. The spring case is long, and decorated with simple bulbous endings, each having a narrow basal moulding. The knob at the head of the brooch is slightly onion-shaped, also with a basal moulding. Most of the bow, and the foot, pin and catchplate are missing.
Bronze. Broken. Unstratified.
A fairly common form of crossbow brooch, dated by the style of the rather simple knobs to the late third/early fourth centuries.

11. (SF 185) Part of a pennanular brooch akin to Fowler's types A3/A4 (1960, 151, Fig. 1). The terminal is formed by a large, apparently unmilled, flattened knob, with one additional "collar" moulding. Most of the bow, the pin and second terminal are missing. A comparable example is known from Newstead (Curle 1911, Pl. LXXXVIII. 15).
Bronze. Slightly corroded and broken. Phase 3.
The type A3/A4 variations on the basic penannular type A theme are fairly common on northern British military sites, and are found in contexts ranging from the first to the third century (Fowler 1960, 169-171).

OTHER BRONZES

12. (SF 207) Part of a small rectangular bronze mount, with an inlay. Only a very tiny area of inlay is preserved, consisting of black and yellow millefiori squares. Two attachment rivets survive on the back. Phase 4.

13. (SF 208) A fragmentary rectangular belt-plate open in the centre, and with a triangular knob at each end, flanked by horns. The frame is made of bronze, inset with an elaborate inlay. In the knobs are blue glass tesserae with yellow inlay on either side. The main bars of the mount are filled with black and yellow millefiori-type inlay. There are two attachments rivets on the back. A common type; cf. for example the close parallels from South Shields (Bruce 1885, 262), and Lydney (Wheeler 1932, Fig. 20, No. 97). Phase 4, but they normally occur in early Roman contexts.

14. (SF 169) Several fragments of a badly damaged fretwork mount, probably rectangular in form. It has a centre with regular square perforations and a semi-circular raised rim. The full extent of the object is not preserved but there are the bases of two attachments rivets. Phase 3.

15. (SF 143) Part of a small bronze mount, decorated in relief. The base of one attachment rivet survives. Phase 4.

16. (SF 201) Part of a thin bronze disc decorated with repeating floral motives. It is likely that the deep spaces between the elements of the design were filled with enamel but no obvious traces survive. There are no certain fittings on the back and it is possible that the disc derives either from a brooch or from a mount. Unstratified.

17. (SF 131) An enamelled mount with a knob foot and a round hollow top, with traces of two lugs. The circular part of the mount is inlaid with an inner ring of blue enamel and a larger outer ring of yellow enamel. Phase 4.

18. (SF 222) Bronze pendant, inlaid with a triangle and a blob in blue enamel. There may also have been small circles of yellow enamel on the side knobs. Phase 2.

19. (SF 219) Knob and ring, probably from a bearing-rein trace. Phase 4.

20. (SF 237) Upper part of a rod, terminating in a ring. Phase 2.

21. (SF 140) A heavy piece of folded bronze, bearing two distinct ridges. Phase 4.

22. (SF 238) Part of the ring and shaft from a section of a strap end. Phase 2.

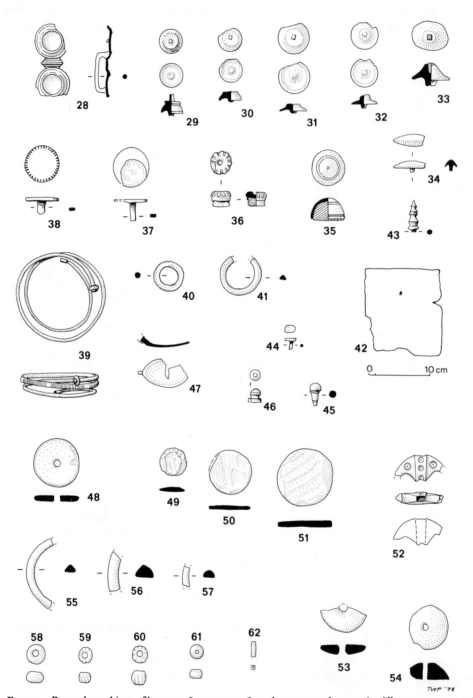

FIG. 27. – Ravenglass: objects of bronze, 28-47; stone, 48-51; bone, 52-4; glass, 55-62. All 1:3, except 42, 1:6.

23. (SF 142)   A fragment of a small bronze object retaining part of a ring and a spatulate dished bowl. Its function may be similar to that of a *ligula* or a scoop. Alternatively and more probably it comes from a strap-end. Phase 4, from whose deposits come one similar object.

24. (SF 272)   The head of what is conventionally known as a dress- or cloak-fastener. It belongs to Wild's class III for which a second-century date is suggested; this example comes from deposits of Phase 2, *i.e.* a second-century context. They are common finds on military sites in Britain and may have been used as harness-fittings rather than for clothing (Wild 1970).

25. (SF 242)   A bronze lock bolt of common form. Phase 2.

26. (SF 116)   A bronze lock bolt, with many parallels (e.g. Fishbourne, Cunliffe 1971, Fig. 50, No. 139). Phase 4.

27. (SF 21)   Part of bronze scabbard-chape, of common type. Phase 4. One other example from an unstratified context.

28. (SF 93)   A bronze harness-mount consisting of two discs with concave centres, joined by a narrow bar. There is a rectangular fitting on the back through which a leather strap must have passed. Phase 4.
    There are two other examples of identical form and size, one from deposits of phase 4 and another from a second-century context, extensively disturbed by phase 4 intrusions. Frere (1974, Fig. 30, No. 57) provides a distant parallel from Longthorpe.

Studs

A considerable number and variety of bronze studs were found. They divide into three main groups: (1) a class with a concave face, a central boss and a shank of bronze or iron (29-33), (2) a series of flat-topped studs (37, 38) with large circular heads, sometimes with decoration (examples of which also occur in iron: Fig. 32, 80) and (3) a group of studs with domed heads, round or oval in form (e.g. 34) The first two types were presumably used mainly as decoration for wooden furniture, doors or other fittings; but the third form was most probably employed to decorate leather work. There are six stratified examples of type 1, all from deposits of the third and fourth centuries; seven examples of type 2, mainly from second-century contexts; and six examples of type 3, from deposits of phases 2-4.

29. (SF 174)   A heavy bronze stud with a square-sectioned shank. Phase 3.

30. (SF 149)   Bronze stud with traces of a shank. Phase 3.

31. (SF 45)   Bronze stud with the stump of a square iron shank. Phase 4.

32. (SF 13)   A flat stud of bronze apparently with a very large shank. Unstratified.

33. (SF 1)   A bronze stud with a square iron shank. Unstratified.

34. (SF 91)   A small oval stud with a hollow head and circular shank. Phase 4. For a parallel from Verulamium, cf. Frere 1972, Fig. 38, no. 101.

35. (SF 137)   A semicircular bronze cap, with lightly incised turning marks, round an iron core. Phase 4.

36. (SF 250)   A small decorative terminal filled with a bronze matrix. Phase 3.

37. (SF 115)   A flat-topped stud. Phase 4.

38. (SF 211)   A flat-topped stud with lightly incised notches round the rim. Phase 4.

39. (SF 134) A bronze bracelet with three coils. The upper and lower coils have a round cross-section, while the middle ring is rectangular in shape, and is decorated with groups of vertical lines. The terminals of the bracelet were provided with a simple green glass paste bead, one of which survives. Phase 4.

40. (SF 71) A small bronze ring. Unstratified.
A total of 12 rings were found, all but three with a round or triangular cross-section, like the examples illustrated; the other types were made with thin wire. Only one ring had a diameter of more than 3 cm., this specimen measuring 6·5 cm. in diameter. No stratified example was recovered from deposits earlier than those of phase 3. Such rings could have served a very wide variety of functions.

41. (SF 164) Part of a bronze ring. Phase 3.

42. (SF 249) A rectangular bronze sheet, found in the destruction-deposit of phase 2, close to the bag of gaming-counters.

43. (SF 288) The head of a comparatively elaborate bronze pin. Phase 3.
Fragments of eleven pins were found, examples occurring in deposits of phases 2, 3 and 4. Six retained traces of the head which, with the exception of the type illustrated, consisted of a very simple knob.

44. (SF 227) A small flat-topped nail, probably from a shoe. Phase 2.

45. (SF 276) A small bronze nail with a domed head. Phase 3.

46. (SF 218) A small bronze knob. Unstratified.

47. (SF 159) The bowl of a spoon in silvered bronze. Phase 4.

STONE DISCS (Fig. 27)

48. (SF 38) A worn pierced disc of brown slate; presumably a spindle-whorl. Unstratified.
Two other spindle-whorls of this type were found. Both were made of samian and derived from phase 4 contexts.

49-51. (SF 78, 132, 41) Three discs made from grey slate. Altogether seven discs of this sort were found, four from the topsoil and three others from deposits of phase 4. They belong, therefore, exclusively to the latest period of occupation on the site. Their function is unclear but it is quite possible that they were used as gaming-counters.

BONE (Fig. 27)

Bone was largely destroyed by the acidic character of the soil: only a few objects survived. Apart from those illustrated, only the tip of an awl and two tiny fragments (possibly from a dice box) were found.

52. (SF 66) Bone toggle or buckle, highly polished on the side decorated with compass-drawn circles. Burnt. Phase 4.

53. (SF 256) Pierced bone disc made from a metapodial; presumably a spindle-whorl. Phase 2.

54. (SF 279) Pierced bone disc. Spindle-whorl. Phase 2.

GLASS ARMLETS (Fig. 27)

55. (SF 254) Pale green-grey paste. Phase 2. This, like 56 and 57, belongs to Kilbride-Jones's (1938) type 3A.

56. (SF 130) Dull white paste. Phase 3.

57. (SF 74) Green-white paste. Phase 4.

BEADS (Fig. 27)

Only eight beads were found: four melon beads (all from deposits of phases 2 and 3), and one of bronze, one of plain glass, a cylindrical blue glass bead and one of jet.

58.   (SF 15)   Pale green-white paste. Unstratified.

59.   (SF 236)   Bright blue-green paste. Phase 2.

60.   (SF 177)   Green paste. Phase 3.

61.   (SF 163)   Highly polished jet bead. Unstratified.

62.   (SF 210)   A thin cylinder of dull blue glass. Rectangular cross-section. Unstratified.

LEAD (Fig. 28)

Only 22 pieces of lead were found, the majority consisting of shapeless scraps, presumably from the buildings. Overall, the objects of lead are more or less evenly distributed between deposits of phases 2, 3 and 4.

63.   (SF 76)   A folded piece of sheet, retaining traces of a rebate along one side. Possibly a pipe-join. Unstratified.

64.   (SF 240)   A solid brick of lead, roughly triangular in form. Both flat surfaces are covered with deep circular recesses, together with a number of much smaller and shallower punch marks. It may well have been used as a working surface. Phase 4.

65.   (SF 235)   Part of a rectangular weight with carefully moulded edges and a deep cut across the centre. Phase 3.

66.   (SF 139)   Pierced lead weight, possibly used as a spindle-whorl. Phase 4.

67.   (SF 281)   Pierced lead weight. Phase 2.

68.   (SF 22)   Disc of lead retaining traces of concentric grooves. Unstratified.

69.   (SF 113)   Fragment of lead; possibly a cramp for mending pottery. Phase 4.

70.   (SF 280)   The greater part of a lead lamp-holder of common form. Found in a construction-trench for the fort-buildings of phase 1, one of the four finds from this context.

71.   (SF 229)   Oval lead sealing, from deposits of phase 3. Deeply stamped on the reverse but only the left hand part of the obverse is properly stamped.

        Obv.   CIAE
                 CL
        Rev.   FLOR
                 T ⋆ D

Discussion by D. C. A. Shotter

Obverse: there can be little doubt that the unit referred to is *Cohors I Aelia Classica*. This cohort is recorded in the *Notitia Dignitatum* (*OCC* XL 51) as in garrison at TVNNOCELVM, which is usually identified with Moresby, the next known auxiliary fort northwards from Ravenglass on the Cumberland coast. I have, however, argued elsewhere in the present volume (Chap. V) that we cannot as yet accept *Notitia* identifications in the north-west as secure: in any case, if Moresby is the correct identification, Birley (1961, 224) has shown that this cohort must have been posted to the site comparatively late in the garrison sequence. There is indeed no reason why it may not have been stationed at Ravenglass itself; for whilst this might appear unlikely, it should be recalled that the Lancaster fort has produced a sealing of the *Ala Sebosiana*, the unit in garrison at the fort

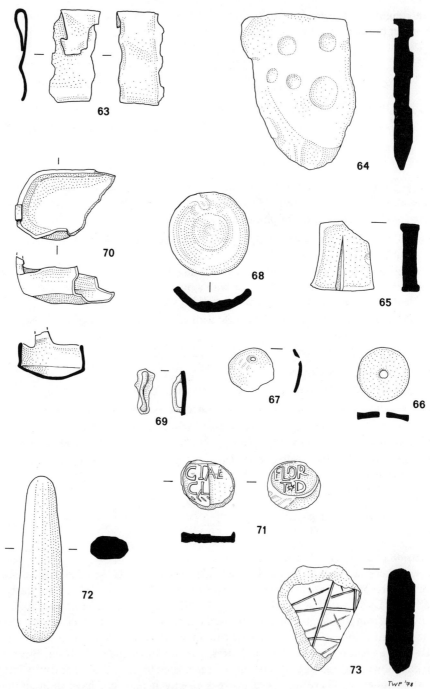

FIG. 28. – Ravenglass: objects of lead, 63-71; stone, 72-3. All 1:3, except 71, 2:3.

in the third century (*RIB* 605; Jones and Shotter 1978). It is certainly attractive to see the *Cohors I Aelia Classica* in garrison at a coastal site, and retaining some kind of naval capacity (Hind 1974, 287).

The only record of the cohort in the second century is on the Chesters diploma of 146 (*CIL* XVI, 93), on which it is mentioned with ten other cohorts and three *alae*.

Reverse: although no example of the Ravenglass sealing was contained in the collection from Brough-under-Stainmore (Richmond 1936, 104-25), elements of the reverse do bear comparison with some of those from Brough. The upper line, which is the least distinct of the sealing, appears to contain the letters FLOR, which are most likely to conceal a personal name. Alternatively, if "F" were "Γ" it could conceivably be a centurial sign.

The lower line (T*D) bears a closer resemblance to a line which appears on a number of the Brough sealings, reading T V D or T$\overset{\text{V}}{\text{Y}}$D, and which Richmond interpreted as an official abbreviation; it seems at least reasonably likely that the T*D of the present sealing has a similar significance. Whilst certainty as to its meaning is unlikely, it is possible that it might be an abbreviation for T(VSSVM)/TV(SSVM) D(ATVM) – "stamped and consigned".

WHETSTONES (Fig. 28)

72. (SF 232)   One of three examples found, from contexts of phases 2 and 4.

GAMING-BOARD (Fig. 28)

73. (SF 210)   Fragment of a gaming-board in a reddish sandstone. The major divisions are deeply scored and there are also traces of crosses in the squares. Unstratified.

GAMING-COUNTERS

Apart from the slate discs discussed above (49-51), there were three counters of black glass paste that were found as loose finds in deposits of phases 2 and 3, and a bag of counters, described below.

The bag of gaming-counters: general observations

The group of bone and glass counters was recovered beneath a thick layer of daub that covered the floor of barrack-block 4 (Pl. VIIIb). The daub derived from the burning and collapse of the buildings of phase 2 and can be dated to the late second or early third century, thus providing a firm *terminus ante quem* for the counters. Beneath the group were the charred boards of the barrack-block floor, implying that the counters may have been hanging on the wall when the building was burnt down.

The tight clustering of the counters makes it clear that they must have been in a container of some sort: it was presumably made of cloth or possibly leather, but no traces survived. Many of the bone counters are warped by heat and show burn marks (Pl. IX), while the glass pieces are fire-crackled and, in some cases, pitted and misshapen. As a result many counters are in a very friable condition and suffered some slight damage both while under excavation and during cleaning. There seems no doubt however that the counters were largely perfect when they were lost and represent a set that should be complete.

The counters divide typologically into four main groups: (a) those with concentric grooves, circles or rings on the front (76 examples) (b) a group with a single drilled spot on the front (42 examples) (c) one counter bearing three drilled spots on the front and (d) a group of seven glass counters. Most of the bone counters are well made and carefully polished, with bevelled edges and, in some examples, a lip on the underside of the rim, so that the piece could readily be turned over. The 'grooved set' show considerable typological variation, in the sense that some have circles which have been drawn with a compass, some have been turned on a lathe, while others seem largely to have been carved by hand. Both the width and depth of the rings and circles also vary, as do the number of rings, which range from two to five; but the difference between one counter and another is often so slight as to imply that these variations probably had no significance in terms of the game played. There are also considerable differences in size and shape, the width of individual pieces ranging between 1.4 and 2.1 cm.; but once again it is hard to believe that these are typologically meaningful.

On the back of the counters there are, however, numerous numbers, letters and symbols forming a remarkable collection of graffiti. Whilst many of the graffiti are quite clear, few are scored to any depth and many are very lightly drawn: indeed, it is hard to see how some can ever have been at all visible, for it required a hard raking light and a hand-lens to identify many of the characters. This process was also complicated by the fact that one number or letter is often superimposed upon another, creating a complex palimpsest of graffiti. In some cases, the graffito has merely been strengthened by re-scoring the line; but in many other instances the value has been changed completely. Consequently, many of the identifications have to be very tentative, especially for the earlier graffiti.

The breakdown of the graffiti is as follows:
Grooved set: 71 with graffiti, 5 blank.
Single spot set: 13 with graffiti, 5 possibly with graffiti, 24 blank.
Three-spot counter: graffito.

The identifications of the graffiti are suggested in the inventory, while the possible nature of the game is discussed in the following section.

The identification of the game by R. C. TURNER

To survey the possibilities we must turn to the classical sources to see what references are made to board games and what can be deduced about the way they are played. Austin (1934) and Balsdon (1969, 156-9) give summaries of the references that survive and it is worth listing their conclusions.

Four games, which are played with counters on a board, are mentioned and in the first two of these the moves are controlled by the throwing of dice. *Duodecim scripta* was played on a board marked out with 24 squares, sometimes numbered, arranged in two rows. The two players are thought to have had 15 counters each and the game follows much the same principle as backgammon, of which it may have been the precursor. The players moved their pieces in opposite directions around the board and the moves were controlled by the throw of three dice. The idea was to move to safe squares, i.e. those on which one had two pieces or more, or to "knock off" isolated pieces of one's opponent, forcing him to start again. The winner was the player to move his pieces round the board first. We do not have an exact idea of the Roman game as most of the rules derive from medieval versions or "improvements", so such details as the number of counters or dice involved may have been changed.

The second game, for which we have no definite name, was played on a board with six, six-letter words, arranged in two columns of three, often forming a rhyme or statement when read consecutively. No direct references survive and Austin (1934) believes that the boards known archaeologically are merely versions on which *duodecim scripta* could be played. Other authorities see it as a different game but can throw no light on how it is played.

The third game, *terni lapilli*, would seem to be a Roman version of noughts and crosses. It was played on a square board with three vertical and three horizontal lines, and with the diagonals also drawn in. These boards are common finds. Presumably, some rule existed to prevent the first player taking the middle square on his first move and thus never losing.

Finally we have the game of *ludus latrunculorum*. This is a "war game" played by two players each with a set of counters on a board marked out in squares. The aim was for one player to surround a piece of his opponent with two of his, either in rank or file, and so capture it; the winner was the player to have taken most pieces in a certain time or number of moves. The pieces were of two or more different types and were allowed to move in different ways, each piece being permitted to move either forwards or backwards.

The rules as stated so far seem to be generally agreed both by the classical authors and by scholars who have studied the sources. However, the Roman sources for this game are not manuals for playing the game but are often passages in which the game is used allegorically or as a descriptive device. The author assumed that the reader is more than familiar with the way in which the game operates. The most elaborate of these passages comes from an anonymous panegyric of the mid first century A.D., *Laus Pisonis*, in which the hero is praised for his skill at the game. The following translation (by D. C. A. Shotter) gives the feel of the play, while being kept as literal as possible.

> The pieces are moved on the open board with superior skill, and wars are conducted with soldiers of glass, to the end that white may trap black, and black white. But is there a piece that does not retreat before you? Is there a piece that yields when you direct it? Or is there any piece which does not risk being lost and in the process break its enemy? Four battle-line fights with infinite tactical variations; whilst one piece retreats before an attacker, it still makes a capture; another, which stood on guard, appears from a distant part of the board; another risks itself in the thick of the battle and cuts out its enemy as the latter advances to a capture; another waits whilst it is attacked on two fronts, and, by pretending to be caught, itself catches two pieces; yet another is moved towards higher objectives so that with swift movement it overthrows the *mandra* (fence?) and breaks in amongst the enemy's forces, ravaging the protected stronghold when the rampart has been thrown down. Meanwhile although fierce battles break out with cut-off soldiers, you yourself are victorious, with your battle-line complete, or even despoiled of a few soldiers; and both of your hands clatter with the mass of captured men.

Analysing this passage and comparing details from other sources, the details of the game become clearer. In the first place, it would appear that each player could decide on his opening position. In the poem each player has his own colour but no indication is given how the types of piece are differentiated. Passages from Ovid (*AA*.ii 208, *Trist*.ii, 477) state that each type of piece was in a different colour of glass, so the status of each piece was known to both players. Some pieces are allowed to move many squares at one time, presumably in much the same way as the rook in chess. Each player defends a central position or *mandra* which may be defined by special pieces (*mandrae* or *viciti*) that are not allowed to move. Martial and others use the expression *ad vicitas redactus* (reduced to immovable pieces), which suggests another tactic, other than capture, for gaining an advantage. Before going any further with this analysis a short review of the archaeological evidence for *ludus latrunculorum* would be of use.

Bone and glass gaming-counters are very common site finds, showing how widespread these games were. In the Roman sewer at Church Street, York (Macgregor 1976) they are the commonest small find, 102 in number, made of bone, glass, stone and pottery. However, complete sets are very much rarer and they usually occur with burials. The largest number came from a grave at Perugia in Italy (Carattoli 1887, 396) where there were 816 glass counters of three different colours and 16 rectangular bone counters, each with a graffito. Romano-British sets are smaller. Groups of 24 come from burials at Ospringe (Whiting, Hawley and May 1931, plate LVI) and Chichester (Down and Rule 1971, 83), but both are accompanied by dice. A set of 30 glass counters came from a coffin at Lullingstone, 15 white and 15 brown (Liversidge 1973, 350). All these three sets suggest *duodecim scripta*. The *ludus latrunculorum* board from Richborough was found with 18 counters (Bushe-Fox 1949, 124-5) and a small set of nine bone counters comes from a burial at Ewell (Frere 1977, 445). The lack of uniformity in the numbers of counters in these sets is reflected in the different sizes and styles of the boards known to us. Complete examples are rare but their size may vary from one 8×7 squares from Corbridge (Austin 1934, 27) to 14×13 squares from Milecastle 79 (Richmond and Gillam 1952, 21). In some cases the diagonals of each square are marked in, as at Richborough and from this site (inv. 73).

When we come to fit our set into the rules of the games as outlined above we face a series of problems. Even though no board was found with the counters, their large numbers and absence of dice would indicate that it is *ludus latrunculorum* that is being played. The set would seem to divide into three basic types, the "grooved set", the "single spot set" and the glass counters, which could form the three types of piece that are apparently used in *ludus latrunculorum*. However a game with 126 pieces a side would seem to be excessively complicated and even a board the size of that from Milecastle 79 would not be large enough to accommodate them. It would seem more sensible to suggest that the "single spot set", 42 in number, represents one player's pieces and that the "grooved set", 76 in number, represents a group of 42 and the remains of a previous set some of which were lost or damaged, making up the remainder. This solution raises the problem of how the different types of piece were differentiated. The glass counters, which are of two types, white and coloured, and the enigmatic "three-spot counter" could have been used. The other alternative is that the graffiti play some part in the game.

Graffiti on the back of the bone gaming-counters occur frequently and many variations are possible. Most commonly numbers are represented, frequently an X or V or combinations of the two, though others are also found; sometimes there are letters and shortened words too. The two hoards from St Pancras cemetery, Chichester (Down and Rule 1971, 83-4) show a wide range of Xs and Vs, as well as other numbers and letters on the back and numbers cut into the edge of the counters. All of the set from Ewell have graffiti, and the letters REMI occur on six of the nine counters. The Ravenglass set shows similarities to the above and even shares some symbols, but it is worth re-emphasising some points about them. In the first place, of the "grooved set", 71 out of 76 have graffiti, whilst of the "single-spot set" only a maximum of 18 out of 42 are marked. Secondly, some counters have several graffiti superimposed and in others the graffiti are difficult to decipher. Thirdly, if the graffiti played a part in the game, they would have been of the same standard as the working on the upper side of the counters. Therefore one must conclude that the graffiti are not directly related to the playing of *ludus latrunculorum*.

Now to summarise the conclusions that can be made about this unique find. The set must represent the complete collection of one man or group of men. The numbers of counters would enable all the Roman board games known to us to have been played and indeed the make-up of this set, two types of bone counters and two colours of glass counters, all in different numbers, would suggest they had not been made as a single group. It is more likely that the collection was made over a period of time and represents a group of sets which it has not been possible fully to differentiate. Further, if *ludus latrunculorum* was played with these counters, it was of a simpler form than that described in the classical sources and played with pieces of one or two types only; the game could be compared in complexity to draughts rather than chess. It is worth remembering that the people using these counters were auxiliary soldiers from a frontier province, not the sophisticated classes of Rome. This leaves the problem of the graffiti, for they do not seem to fit into the rules of any board games known to us. They suggest another use of the counters, as gambling tokens, for example, whilst some may just be doodles. There is clearly room for further study of the graffiti as they remain more mysterious than the games themselves.

74.   *The bag of gaming-counters: inventory* (Figs 29-31; Pl. IX)
Note: every counter is drawn but in most cases only the back is shown. For the front of the pieces, cf. Pl. IX. The thickness of each piece is recorded in the inventory below.

(a) Set with concentric grooves or circles on the front (1-76)

1.   Four-ring bone counter, carefully turned. T (= thickness): 2·5 mm.
     An X, heavily scored, apparently overlies IIIV

2.   Five-ring bone counter, a well turned piece. T: 3 mm. There is a complex series of graffiti: X (heavily scored), overlies X or XIII; in addition there are earlier graffiti representing V and X

3.   Small oval bone counter, with a deeply countersunk central hole and three rings. T: 2 mm. The graffiti could be variously interpreted as either X replacing a V or as I, overlying $\frac{I}{X}$

4.   A thin bone counter with three rings, lightly turned. T: 1·5 mm. A very clear example where two phases of graffiti are represented:
     X overlying $\overline{V}$ (very lightly scored)

5.   A rather crudely made bone counter with rough and unpolished surfaces. Slightly dished profile, and three rings. T: 2 mm.
     X

6.   Small bone counter with two sharply defined rings and a dished shape. T: 1 mm.
     III (lightly scored)

7.   A well turned bone counter with three rings. T: 2·5 mm.
     V overlies X or X̵; there may be traces of a still earlier graffito beneath X

8.   An oval counter, quite carefully turned, with three rings. T: 3 mm.
     X, overlying X. There is also a symbol, faintly preserved, which could represent either X or P or R.

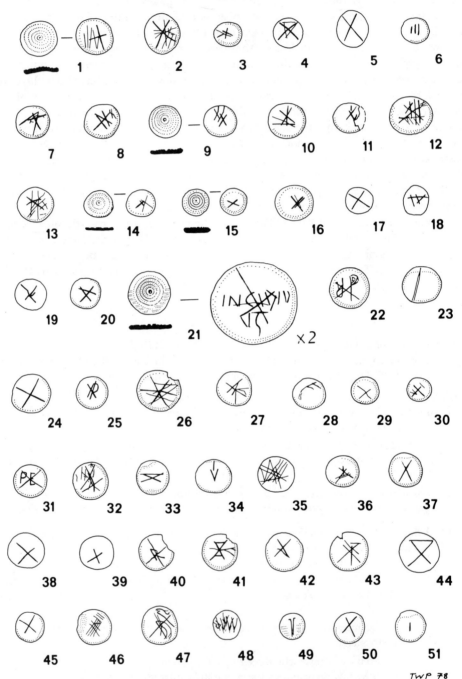

Fig. 29 – Ravenglass: hoard of bone gaming-counters. All 1:2, except 21, 1:1.

9. Bone counter with a deep countersunk hole in the centre and four rings. T: 3 mm. A very lightly scored series of graffiti, of which the latest is quite certainly:

    X

    The earlier series may include X/ and II

10. Oval bone counter with three rings. T: 2·5 mm.

    X, overlying X

11. A thin, damaged bone counter with a rough, unpolished upper surface. Three rings in low relief. T: 1·5 mm.

    X is likely but there are earlier graffiti, not wholly preserved.

12. Carefully turned bone counter with three rings. T: 2·5 mm. The latest graffito is quite certainly XII, which overlies $\overline{X}$. But there are also other earlier scratchings, amongst which may be V and VII (although both readings are conjectural).

13. Well made bone counter, but in low relief, with four rings. T: 2 mm. The graffiti are very lightly drawn, but an X appears to be the latest mark, overlying a (?) II, as well as other lines.

14. Small rather crudely turned bone counter with two rings, in low relief. T: 1 mm.

    X, overlying X

15. A small well polished bone counter, with three compass-drawn circles rather than the normal rings. T: 2·5 mm.

    X

16. Well polished, partially burnt, bone counter, carefully made. It has a pronounced convex profile, and three rings. T: 3 mm.

    X (which has been drawn lightly once and then more strongly)

17. Small dished bone counter with two lightly drawn rings. T: 1·5 mm.

    X

18. Small, quite well turned bone counter, with three rings in low relief. T: 2 mm. Very lightly drawn graffito, with a very conjectural reading: it may be $\overline{IV}$ but, by reversing the piece, XII becomes a possibility.

19. Carefully made bone counter with three rings in low relief. T: 2 mm.

    X (very crudely drawn)

20. A crudely fashioned bone counter with three lines roughly drawn out with a compass and then by hand. T: 1·5 mm.

    $\overline{X}$ (very lightly drawn but quite clear)

21. Lightly turned, well polished bone counter, with three rings. Part of the upper surface is still covered with natural striations, so that the piece must have been instantly recognizable. There is some lipping along the underside, probably to facilitate turning of the counter. T: 2 mm.

    X, which overlies:
      INCIDID
        VS (or VT)
    (cf. 61, *infra*)

22. Well made bone counter with three rings. T: 2·5 mm.

    ꓤP, overlying an (?) X

23. Roughly finished bone counter with three rings in low relief. Pronounced lipping along one part of the lower rim. T: 1·5 mm. The two lines of the graffito are so close together that they are likely to represent an attempt to strengthen the drawing of a single line.

    I

24. Bone counter with very deeply drawn rings, three in number. T: 3 mm.
     X

25. Small bone counter with two rings. T: 2 mm.
     P, overlying X

26. Large bone counter with five lightly turned rings. T: 3 mm.
     X̶, overlying X which, in turn, appears to replace X

27. Oval bone counter with three lightly turned rings. T: 2 mm. A complex series of scratches, of which X appears to replace X, which may overlie a V.

28. Small bone counter with rings in low relief. T: 2 mm. V is the most plausible interpretation of the graffito but is very uncertain.

29. Small two-ring bone counter in low relief. T: 2 mm.
     X

30. Small bone counter, roughly finished, with two rings in low relief. T: 2 mm.
     X, replacing (?) VI

31. Carefully made bone counter, with three rings in low relief. T: 1·5 mm.
     X, overlying PE (cf. no. 77, *infra*)

32. Large counter with only a light polish and some roughness left on the upper surface. The two rings are very lightly turned. T: 2 mm. There is a complex series of graffiti which include an X; a possible P; and perhaps IX. The X appears to have been redrawn at least once.

33. Bone counter with three rings. There is some lipping and wear on part of the lower lip. T: 3 mm.
     X̄

34. Oval bone counter with a deep central hole and three rings. Pronounced lip on part of the lower rim. T: 2 mm.
     ↓ (presumably IV)

35. Bone counter with a deep central hole and six compass-drawn concentric circles. There are a number of scratch marks around the central hole but they make no obvious pattern. Lipping on part of the lower rim. T: 3 mm. The graffito includes a great many very lightly drawn lines, amongst which X̄ and X may with certainty be discerned.

36. Oval bone counter with three lightly turned rings. T: 1·5 mm. A very faintly drawn graffito, probably including X̶

37. A well turned bone counter with three rings. Lip on the lower rim. T: 2 mm.
     X

38. A roughly made bone counter where much of the bone surface has been left unsmoothed. Three prominently turned rings. T: 1·5 mm.
     X

39. A crudely made bone counter with three concentric circles. T: 1·5 mm.
     X

40. Oval bone counter with a deep central hole and three rings. T: 2 mm.
     X overlying R

41. A well made and highly polished bone counter with three lightly turned rings. T: 3 mm.
     X̄ (very deeply incised) replacing a Y-shaped line; or, alternatively, X̲̄

42. A well turned and highly polished bone counter with three rings. T: 3 mm.
     X

43. Bone counter with four rings, quite deeply turned. T: 2 mm. A complex graffito, possibly to be interpreted as
    I (deeply scored), overlying X and $\overline{\mathrm{X}}$ (lightly drawn)

44. Large bone counter with three rings. T: 3 mm.
    $\overline{\mathrm{X}}$

45. Small rather dished bone counter with two rings, roughly drawn and shown in light relief. T: 1·5 mm.
    X

46. Bone counter with four rings. T: 2 mm. A very lightly drawn graffito (on a roughly smoothed back) for which no positive interpretation can be offered.

47. Bone counter with three lightly drawn rings. T: 2·5 mm. A complex series of graffiti, of which an R or P is the most deeply scored. In addition there appears to be an X, overlying what may be successive attempts to draw a D.

48. Small oval bone counter with three rings. T: 1·5 mm. On the back of the counter are a series of feathery graffiti which could be interpreted either as M or VVV. Rather more clearly drawn is a P or R (the diagonal bar of the R is, however, drawn rather more strongly than the rest of the letter and may belong to another graffito).

49. Small bone counter with two rings, shown in light relief. T: 1·5 mm. The back is left fairly rough.
    $\overline{\mathrm{I}}$ or $\overline{\overline{\mathrm{II}}}$

50. Well polished bone counter with four shallow compass-drawn circles. T: 1·5 mm.
    X

51. Rather crudely made bone counter with two rings. T: 2 mm. There is clear lipping on part of the lower rim.
    I

52. A thin and markedly convex bone counter with five carefully drawn concentric rings. T: 1 mm. The lines, all of which are very lightly drawn, may represent successive attempts to draw:
    $\overline{\mathrm{X}}$

53. Roughly finished bone counter with four lightly drawn rings. T: 1·5 mm.
    X

54. Small carefully made bone counter with three rings. T: 2·5 mm.
    X, overlaid by a curved sign with feathery ends.

55. Crudely made bone counter with three rings in light relief. T: 1·5 mm. Some very lightly drawn graffiti, apparently including at least two successive X.

56. A large bone counter with a roughly finished upper surface, decorated with four rings in low relief. T: 1·5 mm. On the back are some thinly drawn lines, including an X.

57. Bone counter with four thinly drawn rings. T: 2 mm.
    X̶

58. Well made bone counter with three rings. T: 3 mm. A complex series of graffiti, of which a Y-shaped sign is the most deeply scored: it partially overlies a P. Another lightly drawn sign comprised a Y with a double cross-bar.

59. A small dish-shaped bone counter with three lightly drawn rings. T: 1·5 mm.
    X

60. A small damaged bone counter with three lightly drawn rings. T: 2 mm. On the back there is a single hole, drilled into the centre, so that the piece resembles the "single spot" series, discussed below (77-118). In addition, there is a faint Y-shaped graffito.

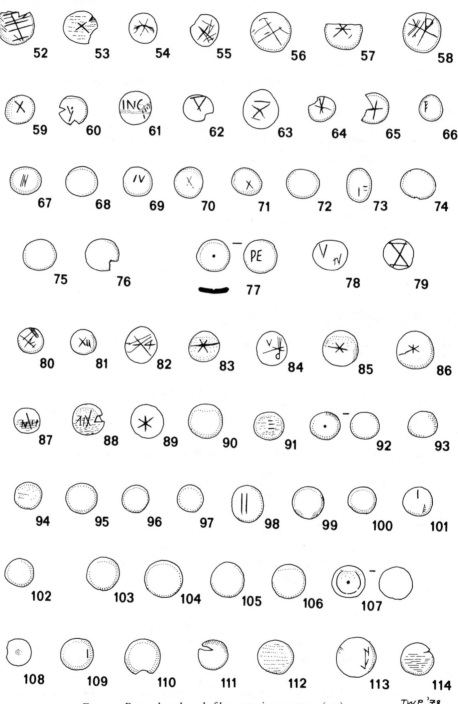

FIG. 30 – Ravenglass: hoard of bone gaming-counters. (1:2).

TWP '78

61. Roughly finished bone counter with two lightly drawn rings. T: 1·5 mm. The back is damaged by two breaks in the counter but the main letters, although very lightly drawn, are still quite clear.

   INC.. (cf. 21 *supra*).

62. Small oval bone counter with three rings in low relief. T: 1 mm.

   $\overline{X}$

63. Oval bone counter with three rings, drawn very precisely. T: 2 mm.

   $\underline{\overline{X}}$

64. Small oval bone counter with three concentric circles. T: 1 mm. $\bar{X}$: or, since one bar is much more deeply scored than the other lines, the sequence may be X and then I.

65. Small badly damaged bone counter with three concentric circles, lightly drawn. T: 1·5 mm.

   X

66. Very small but well made bone counter, with a convex profile. Three well drawn rings. T: 1·5 mm.

   I (?)

67. Small oval bone counter with a slightly dished form. Two rings, shown in quite high relief. T: 1·5 mm. The back is rather roughly finished but the faint scratches of a graffito can just be made out: (?) IV or IIV.

68. Well polished bone counter with three rings. T: 1 mm. The back is blank.

69. Small bone counter, whose front is so worn that the traces of compass-drawn circles can only just be discerned. T: 1·5 mm.

   IV

70. Small oval bone counter with two crudely drawn circles. T: 2 mm. There is certainly a graffito on the back but its identification as X is very tentative.

71. Small oval bone counter with two rings. T: 2 mm.

   X (very faint)

72. Small oval counter with two rings. T: 1·5 mm. The back is blank.

73. Oval bone counter with two fairly crudely drawn rings. T: 1·5 mm.

   I

74. Crudely made oval bone counter with three rings in very low relief. T: 1·5 mm. The back is blank.

75. Roughly made bone counter with rough surfaces and two rings. T: 2 mm. The back is blank.

76. Oval bone counter with three lightly drawn rings. T: 1·5 mm. The back, although slightly damaged, does appear to be blank.

(b) Set with a single spot on the front (42 pieces, 77-118)

77. Well made bone counter, dished in form. T: 2 mm.

   PE (cf. 31, *supra*)

78. A well polished bone counter. T: 1·5 mm.

   V and $\overline{IV}$

79. A polished bone counter. T: 1·5 mm.

   $\underline{\overline{X}}$

80. Small polished bone counter. T: 2 mm. On the back, apart from a natural foramen, are lightly drawn graffiti. These certainly include an X (or possibly $\overline{X}$) as well as VI.

81. Very small polished bone counter. T: 1·5 mm.
    XII (of which the II has been redrawn once)

82. Well polished bone counter. T: 2 mm. A complex series of thinly drawn lines apparently include two $\overline{X}$, one large and one very small.

83. Bone counter with a dished form. There is a break across the centre of the piece. T: 1 mm.
    X

84. Polished bone counter. T: 2·5 mm. The several lightly drawn graffiti would seem to include: P (with a feathered vertical bar); X; and V.

85. Polished bone counter with pronounced lipping on the lower rim. T: 2 mm.
    X

86. Rather roughly finished bone counter. T: 2·5 mm.
    X and, possibly, I (as a separate graffito).

87. Well polished bone counter. T: 1·5 mm. A complex series of graffiti, which appear to include:
    IV; I; and II. The I is more deeply scored than the other graffiti.

88. Lightly polished bone counter. T: 2 mm. The graffiti include IV and what appears to be an X; but one bar of the X is much more deeply scored than the other and it may not be contemporary.

89. Polished bone counter. T: 2 mm.
    X

90. Polished bone counter with some lipping on the underside of the rim. The back is blank.

91. Oval dished bone counter. T: 1·5 mm. There are extremely faint traces of a graffito on the back, probably representing:
    III

92. Oval counter, with traces of tooling on part of the front rim. The back is blank. T: 1·5 mm.

93-97. Small polished bone counters, all with blank backs.

98. Oval bone counter with a dished form and polished surfaces. T: 2 mm. There are extremely faint traces of II on the back which are probably, but not certainly, deliberate.

99. Thin burnt bone counter with chipped edges. T: 1 mm.

100. Small lightly polished bone counter, with a blank back. T: 2 mm.

101. Small polished counter, with a slightly dished form. T: 2 mm.
    I

102-6. Polished bone counters, with blank backs.

107. Polished bone counter with pronounced lipping on one part of the back rim, created by a diagonal knife cut across the rim: the piece clearly shows that such lipping was deliberate. A compass-drawn circle upon the front suggests that the counter was originally intended to belong to the "grooved series". T: 2 mm.

108. Small polished bone counter, with a blank back. T: 2 mm.

109. Polished bone counter with a very light line along one side of the back; but, whilst this is technically a graffito, it seems more likely to be an accidental scratch than a number. T: 2 mm.

110-12. Bone counters with blank backs.

113. Polished bone counter. T: 2 mm. Faint scratching on the back may well not represent a deliberate graffito.

114-7. Bone counters, two of them only roughly finished, with blank backs.

118. Small oval polished bone counter, with a roughly finished back, on which many natural striations are visible. One deeper striation may represent a graffito, I, but it seems unlikely, since it is orientated with the other natural marks. T: 1·5 mm.

(c) Counter with three spots on the front

119. Polished bone counter. T: 2 mm. Very faintly incised graffito.
X̄, redrawn once (?)

(d) Glass counters (120-126)

120. Dull black glass counter, badly mis-shaped by heat.

121. Dark blue glass counter, damaged by heat.

122. Several small fragments of turquoise glass, that can be safely assumed to come from a counter. The original size is *not* known.

123-5. Counters of varying size in cream-coloured glass, all badly heat-shattered.

126. A further cream-coloured counter, the first encountered in excavation of the group of counters. The heat-shattered fragments were mistaken for decayed limestone and none was collected; but the counter clearly belonged to this group. The original size of the counter is *not* known.

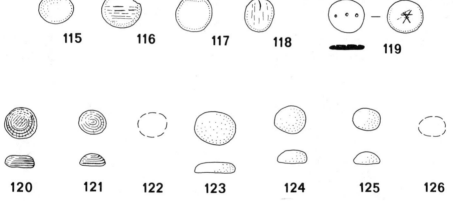

FIG. 31. – Ravenglass: hoard of gaming-counters. 115-9, bone; 120-6, glass. *TWP 78*

OBJECTS OF IRON (Fig. 32)

In the main, the iron objects are notable more for their bulk than for their range and variety: even though nothing more than superficial cleaning has been attempted, it is clear that the sample is dominated by an enormous quantity of nails. Of the 1657 iron objects recovered from stratified levels, all but 65 consist of nails, clearly reflecting the fact that the buildings on the site were, throughout its history, constructed of wood. The nails themselves belong to the categories standard on Romano-British sites, with round or rectangular heads and a square or rectangular shank, of different lengths. A variant that sometimes occurs in Roman Britain and elsewhere, where the head takes a triangular form, does not appear to represented at Ravenglass, matching its general rarity on military sites (Manning 1976, 41-2). No attempt has been made here, however, to offer a

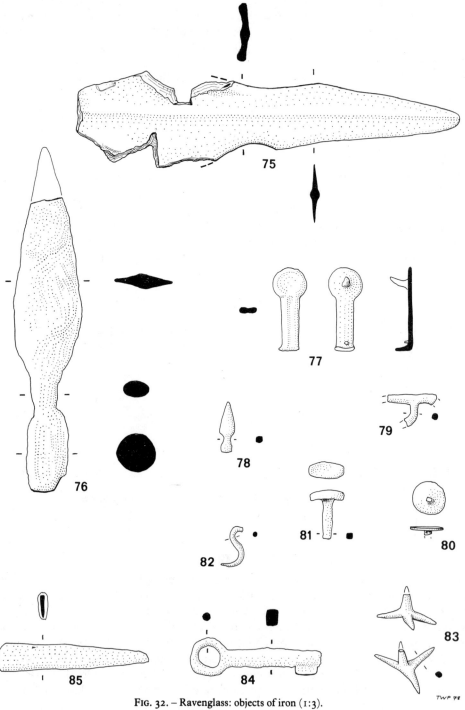

FIG. 32. – Ravenglass: objects of iron (1:3).

detailed classification of the nails: this must await the laborious task of cleaning the objects. It is, on the other hand, worth noting that the percentages of bent nails are consistently small, underlining the falsity of the assumption that bent nails may be equated with the demolition of a structure.

Amongst the other objects, the majority belong to corroded lengths of blade or strapping. Cleaning will probably show that some represent knife blades, while most consist of fittings from the buildings or portable objects. Specific military equipment is particularly rare, a feature of fort sites, noted by Manning (1976, 7): it is confined to two spearheads, one recovered not in the present excavation but as a casual find made in 1962; a small bolt-head and a calthrop. There are also at least four chisel blades, three rings, and a hook which may have been used for fishing.

There is some evidence for the manufacture or repair of iron objects on the site. There were a number of pieces of slag from deposits of phase 2, all of them located within the area of barrack-block 4, although none formed any very localised concentration. The phase 3 deposits included a general scatter of slag across the site, many pieces occurring in make-up deposits for the buildings and roads. In phase 4, there was a similar spread of slag over the whole of the excavated area, but in barrack-block 9 there was also a small circular pit, some 40 cm in diameter and 10 cm in depth. It was filled with charcoal and slag and may have been used for smithing.

phase	date	small nails	large nails	% bent nails	blade/ strapping	chisels	rings	other
0	c. 120-130	1		—				
1	c. 130	2	1	—				
2	c. 130-200	208	63	6·03	8	—	1	4
3	c. 200-350	512	117	7·11	13	2	—	4
4	c. 350-400	487	200	12·82	22	2	2	8

Distribution of iron objects from Ravenglass.

75. (EQ) Part of a long iron spearhead with a constriction towards the centre of the blade. There is a heavy rim along the edge of this constriction. The lower part of the spearhead is badly damaged and the original edges lost. Phase 2.

76. Iron spearhead, recovered from the cliff-face in 1962 by Miss M. Steele and kindly made available to us by courtesy of the Rev. and Mrs M. Hodges. Although the object has been consolidated, there are still areas of heavy corrosion, especially around the socket. Spearheads are relatively common finds along the Cumberland coast (Richmond 1956; Potter 1975) and in the frontier region (Manning 1976, 18-21).

77. (SF 133) Mount with a circular end and a nail attachment. Possibly from a furniture fitting. Phase 4.

78. Small arrow head or artillery bolt-head. The head has a rectangular cross-section but details of the shaft are obscured by corrosion; it probably has a square section. Phase 3. Manning (1976, 21-3) provides a very useful discussion concerning such objects.

79. T-shaped staple, broken at all ends. Phase 4.

80. (SF 220) Flat-topped stud, one of three recognizable examples. For comparable examples in bronze cf. Fig. 27, Nos 37, 38. Phase 2.

81. Nail with an elongated oval head, an unusual item amongst the nails from the site. Phase 4.

82. Small iron hook, quite possibly used for fishing. Unstratified.

83. Iron calthrop, the only recognizable example. One prong has broken away. Unstratified.

84. Iron key. This example comes from post-Roman deposits.

85. (SF 141)   Simple iron knife-blade, apparently with a single cutting edge. Phase 4. One of a number of recognizable examples.

THE LEATHER (Fig. 33)

Ditch of earlier fortlet, phase 0

86. A boat-shaped cover made from a single piece of leather. Two triangular areas have been cut out at each end and stitched together with fine thong, one tiny fragment of which has survived at the left hand side. The edges of the cover have been roughly cut with a knife. Note: unlike the other pieces of leather, this object was drawn while damp: within a few hours, it had shrunk from a maximum length of 20·8 cm to 18·5 cm; 10% shrinkage has been estimated for leather objects from the Saalburg (Busch 1965, 160-1).

87. An approximately rectangular object, measuring 10·5×14·5 cm after consolidation. It is made of a double thickness of leather. Possibly a check-piece lining from a helmet.

88. Sole of a small shoe which measured 15·5 cm in length when excavated. It has now shrunk to 13·4 cm in length. The sole is made up of three separate layers, joined by numerous hobnails. A small fragment consisting of several strips from the upper part of the shoe was also found. The sole presumably derives from a *calceus*, the commonest form of shoe at Bar Hill (Robertson, Scott and Keppie 1975, 68-78) and a type well represented at Hardknott (Charlesworth and Thornton 1973); this was a sandal with a heavily studded sole, and an open-work upper.

89. Sole of a shoe with three layers. Although only the heel is at all well preserved, it is clear that it was heavily studded with hobnails. Probably from a *calceus*.

Pit (FF), later fort, phase 2 (late second or early third century)

90. A substantial part of a bag or pocket, made from a single piece of leather, folded double along one side and joined by a back stitch. The width of the bag after conservation is 18 cm; originally it was some 3 cm wider.
    There was one other identical object made in exactly the same way. It appears to have been a little narrower – 17 cm after conservation – and , although fragmentary, has a surviving depth of nearly 15 cm. The lower part of the object appears to narrow a little in width, so that it begins to resemble the pocket from Newstead (Curle 1911, Pl. XIX, 4); but neither of the two bags retains any trace of stitching holes along the top. In addition there is one fragment from the body of a similar object, which also possesses the same fold-over join; it may belong to one of the other two bags or could derive from a third example.

91. A folded piece of leather with a simple hem, fastened by a back stitch. It is possible that this represents a variation of the bag discussed above but it is much more likely that it was folded up only when discarded and belongs to part of a tent-panel (McIntyre and Richmond 1934). Unfolded, the fragment would have a surviving length (after conservation) of *c*. 36 cm. The largest panels from such tents measure 65×50 cm (McIntyre and Richmond 1934; Groenman-van Waateringe 1967; Robertson, Scott and Keppie 1975) and appear to be quite common finds in auxiliary forts of the second century.
    One other folded fragment, with a hem 2·5 cm in height, was found in this pit.

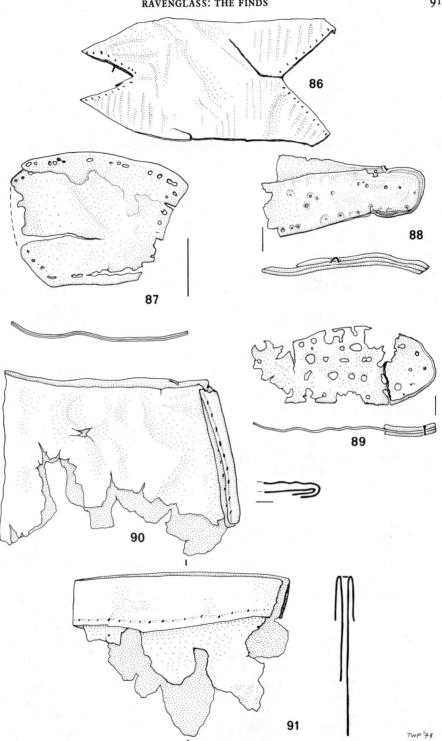

FIG. 33. – Ravenglass: objects of leather (1:3).

WOOD (Fig. 34; Pl. IIIa)

Note: We are indebted to Mr S. H. Turner for identifying the species of wood represented here.

Ditch of the primary fortlet, phase 0

The lower silt of the ditch yielded very large quantities of organic material, mostly consisting of pieces of wood. The great majority comprised twigs and branches, lopped or sawn from the trunks of trees, mainly ring-porous hardwoods, particularly oak (*Quercus sp.*). Most of these fragments (all of which are heavily impregnated with salt) were quite small, the largest piece being under 40 cm in length and 5 cm in diameter; and in nearly every case the bark was still preserved. They represent the discards that resulted from the trimming of tree-trunks and large branches used in the construction of the late Hadrianic fort.

In addition there were some pieces that had belonged to structural elements of the primary fortlet. As well as the items discussed in the inventory below, there was a fragment of thin planking, retaining traces of a peg hole; a circular peg, sawn at both ends and measuring 2 cm in diameter and 7 cm in length; a rather larger piece of planking, 46 cm in length and 14 cm in width; a section from a substantial beam 4·5 × 2·5 cm in cross-section, with traces of a nail-hole; and a few other small fragments with sawn edges, possibly carpentry discards.

92. The lower part of a stake, 1·32 m in length. It is made of oak. The upper 30 cm has been roughly squared off to dimensions of 5 × 8 cm but the lower section has been crudely shaped with an adze to give an approximately triangular cross-section, which tapers towards a point. The stake has been sawn off at the top. This stake is the best preserved of four examples recovered from the ditch. They are also made of oak. They are likely to have been used in the palisade-trench immediately behind the ditch (Fig. 6; Pl. IIIa) where, as excavation clearly showed, the wooden uprights had been completely removed during demolition. The other stakes consist of one piece, 1·10 m in length, with a square cross-section, 8 × 8 cm; the spatulate end of a stake with a rectangular cross-section measuring 8 × 4·5 cm and a surviving length of 52 cm; and the spatulate end of a third stake with a cross-section of 5 × 4 cm.

93. A peg made of oak. It measures 33 cm in length and has an approximately rectangular cross-section, 2 × 3·5 cm. The top has been carefully sawn across, but it is unclear whether the peg represents the lowest part of a larger stake or if it is a complete object in itself. To some extent it resembles a tent peg, but there are no traces of wear from ropes and it is not shaped as are the examples from Newstead (Curle 1911, Pl. LXXXIII, 6, 13).

94. Part of a thick plank made of oak, inset with two partially preserved rebates. The left-hand rebate was evidently designed to hold some sort of panelling, since part of a grooved flange is preserved along the lower edge; but there is no such flange on the right-hand side and it is therefore likely that this formed a lap joint with a major upright. There are peg holes, 2 cm in diameter (the size of the peg mentioned above), drilled through each rebated part. The lower edge of the central part of the plank retains a small area of bark, but the upper edge seems to be quite worn, as if there had been an aperture above it. This suggests (as does the panel flange) that this plank may have been used in a wall rather than on a floor or in a ceiling and, given its recovery-position in a ditch of the defences, it seems possible that it may have formed part of the breastwork along the rampart of the fortlet (Fig. 7).

One other piece of planking, of near-identical dimensions and inset with a similar rebate was found in the ditch.

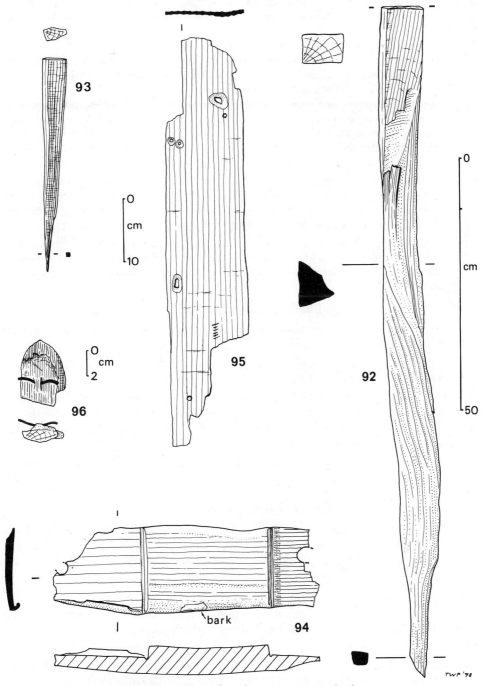

FIG. 34. – Ravenglass: objects of wood. 92, 1:7·5; 93-5, 1:6; 96, 1:3.

Note: with future researchers in mind, it should be reported that while the plank was under study, the drying out of the wood caused the flange to shrink and eventually become detached. It was however drawn as soon as it was taken from its protective air-tight wrappings.

Pit (FF), later fort, phase 2, late second or early third century

95. A section of thin planking, from a board some 13 cm in width. The surfaces, as preserved, are comparatively rough, but it is likely that originally they were dressed fairly level. There are several small nail-holes in the planking.

   The example illustrated is the best preserved of at least three such planks, all approximately of the same width. In addition there were a number of very small fragments of similar boarding. The thickness of these planks – 2-4 mm – shows that they were too thin to have been floor-boards and, given that the walls of the barrack-blocks were plastered with daub, it seems likely that this planking may have come from a door.

96. A small fragment of wood made of oak, with one sawn edge and badly damaged surfaces. The object is pierced by a hole, still retaining a thin thong of leather, 1·5 mm in width. There are many possible explanations for this object but, given the proximity of the site to the sea, one plausible possibility is that it represents part of a float for a fishing net.

97. *(Not illustrated)*. The only other object amongst the quite large collection of wood recovered from this pit was part of a beam with a rectangular rebate. The beam, which has a minimum dimension of 6×8 cm, is heavily burnt. It may well have been a corner-post of a section of the barrack-block.

QUERNS (Fig. 35) by R. C. TURNER

We are indebted to Dr R. Macdonald for his assistance in the identification of the types and origins of the following examples:

98. (FF) Part of a lower quernstone in Niedermendig lava. It is grooved radially on the upper surface and vertically round the edge. Phase 2/3 interface.

99. (FF) Part of an upper quernstone in Niedermendig lava. It is grooved radially on its lower surface and has a circular hole in its centre. It may belong to No. 98. Phase 2/3 interface.

100. (FF) Fragment of an upper quernstone in Niedermendig lava, radially grooved on its lower surface. Phase 2/3 interface.

101. (FF) Part of an upper quernstone in Niedermendig lava. It has radial grooves underneath, vertical grooves round the edge and shows shallow parallel tooling on the upper surface. Phase 2/3 interface.

102. (NF) Fragment of an upper quernstone in Millstone Grit of Pennine origin. Phase 4.

103. (AT) Part of an upper quernstone in a fine Carboniferous sandstone, probably of local origin. Phase 4.

104. (AU) Part of an upper quernstone in Niedermendig lava. The grinding surface is very worn but the upper surface shows radial tooling. Phase 4.

105. (AU) Part of an upper quernstone in a Carboniferous sandstone. Phase 4.

106. (AM) Part of an upper quernstone in a coarse granite of south-west Scottish origin. It has a peg-hole, 3 cm in diameter and 6 cm in depth, in the side. Unstratified.

107. (NA) Part of an upper quernstone in Niedermendig lava. Unstratified.

108. (NA) Part of an upper quernstone in a Permatriassic sandstone as found at St Bees Head and elsewhere in west Cumbria. The lower surface is marked with concentric grooves. Unstratified.

109. (NA) Part of a lower quernstone in Carboniferous sandstone. Unstratified.

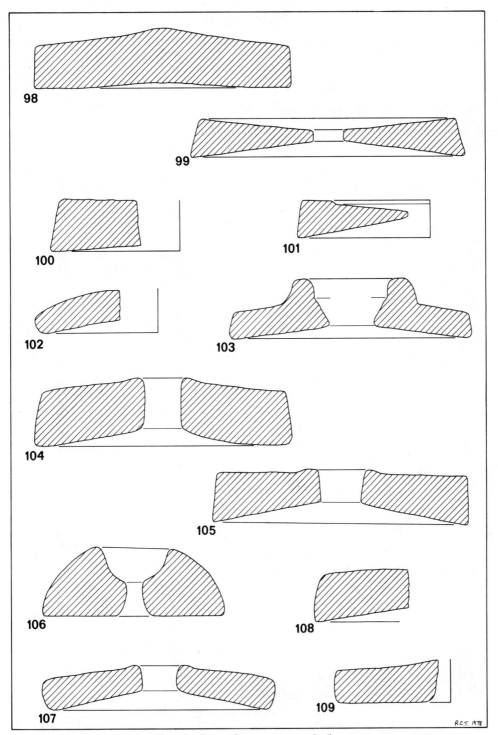

FIG. 35. – Ravenglass: quernstones (1:6).

TILE (Fig. 36)

Only small quantities of tile were found. Apart from the tiles used in the rampart ovens (which measured individually 29 × 29 × 6 cm), the best preserved was a *tegula* employed as a hearth in an inner room of barrack-block 7. It belongs to phase 3. Like the tiles used in the rampart ovens, it is made of a hard red gritty fabric.

110.   Tile from barrack-block 7, used as a hearth.

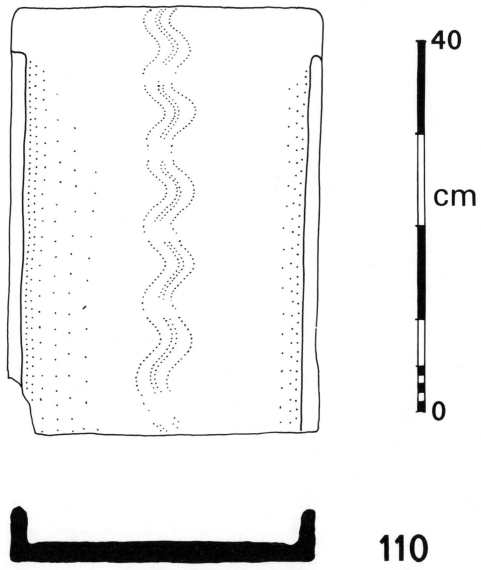

FIG. 36. – Ravenglass: tile from phase 3.

GEMSTONES (Pl. Xa) by MARTIN ḦENIG

Note: the footnotes are to be found at the end of this section.

III. (SF 92) From deposits of phase 4.

The gem is a red jasper, oval in shape, with a flat upper face (14 mm× 10·5 mm) and slides which bevel inwards. It is 3 mm thick. The underside is slightly convex and also roughly cut without the highly polished finish of the rest of the stone: perhaps it was recut in order to affix it more securely into its ring.[1] With the exception of a chip at the top of the gem which has resulted in slight damage to the intaglio, the piece is in excellent condition.

It bears an image of a youth, nude apart from the chlamys hanging from his shoulders, standing in profile to the right (*impression described*). His left leg is flexed and the weight of his body is taken by his right leg, a stance derived from a statue by Polycleitus, and frequently employed for images of young men on gems.[2] He holds two ears of corn in his right hand, and a wreath in his left hand. The former attribute identifies the youth as *Bonus Eventus*, and, indeed, similar representations of this personification are recorded both on British sites and elsewhere. They may reflect a lost statue by Euphranor.[3] The wreath is a remarkable variant on the usual dish of fruit, and it associates the figure with Victoria whose symbol it is.[4] An analogous use of the wreath is to be seen on an onyx from Cirencester showing Roma, who holds one instead of the usual victoriola.[5] Doubtless this alludes to the successes won by the Roman army, just as the intaglio from Ravenglass – presumably a soldier's signet – invokes the powers of future prosperity and abundance for its owner both in the context of his everyday life and on the field of battle.

The standard of cutting is high, with the modelling of the body executed both in relatively bold relief and with anatomical assurance. Thus the torso narrows at the waist and the buttocks obtrude with a convincing naturalism seldom seen on gems of this type from provincial sites. An attempt has also been made at rendering the physiognomy and hair, although unfortunately the detail of the latter has been lost, at least in part, by the damage to the gem mentioned above. Red jaspers can seldom be dated earlier than the second century, but the careful, classicising style seen here is suggestive of a time before the impressionistic "patterned" manner of late Antonine times became widespread.[6] Indeed, both in style and in subject matter the signet expresses the quiet confidence and assurance of the reigns of Hadrian and of Antoninus Pius.

112. (SF 247) From deposits of phase 4.

Intaglio of orange cornelian, oval, convex upper face (11 mm× 10·5 mm). Sides bevel inwards, underside slightly convex.[7] Thickness 3 mm.

The device is a satyr standing on the base-line in profile to the right (*impression described*). His body is slightly bent, his right arm is outstretched and in his left, which is close to his side, he holds his hunting spear as well as a leash which restrains the hound prancing by his side. The satyr appears to be nude apart from the mantle hanging down from his shoulders.

It is apparent that the gem was cut in a hasty and very slapdash manner. The face is composed of three or four strokes of the lap-wheel, the figure's body is entirely lacking in detail and the hind-quarters of the hound are not shown. No attempt has been made at giving a finished appearance to the work by, for instance, polishing the area of cutting. Stylistically it is perhaps related to intaglios belonging to Sena Chiesa's "Officina dei

Dioscuri" which – if it is really one workshop at all – is said to have commenced operations as early as the middle of the first century A.D.[8] A recent writer would like to assign all these coarsely cut stones to the second and third centuries.[9] However, these signs of hasty manufacture are surely to be connected with mass production rather than with general artistic trends within the Empire. The position is perhaps comparable with that of second-century samian ware in central Gaul, whose figured devices become ever more debased, as a result of market pressures.

Both type and style are closely matched by a cornelian found at Newstead which differs only in the angle at which the spear is held and the mistaken extra groove cut parallel to it.[10] Amongst other gems from northern Britain one from Chesters (also a cornelian) portraying a satyr with a bunch of grapes, has an especial stylistic likeness to the Ravenglass stone.[11] While at present caution should be exercised about assigning many of the gems found in Britain to common workshops – especially when the distinguishing style is one of purely negative qualities as here – the possibility of such stones being the work of local gem cutters should not be overlooked.

Footnotes

[1] M. Henig, *A Corpus of Roman Engraved Gemstones from British Sites*, BAR 8 (1974), part i, fig. 1, shape F 6.

[2] *Ibid.*, part ii, 27 and Pl. V, Nos 153-55 (Bacchus or Satyr); 65 and Pl. XIV, No. 454 (Meleager); Nos 455f. (Thesus); 66 and Pl. XV, Nos 457-460 (Achilles); 68 and Pl. XV, Nos 471f. (Ganymede). Note also the Achilles gem from the fort at Watercrook (chap. IV, *infra*).

[3] M. Henig, *Corpus* part ii, 31f. and Pl. vii. Nos 190-99 are especially appropriate as are the gems in P. Gercke, *Antike Gemmen in Deutschen Sammlungen* III, Wiesbaden (1970), 88 and Pl. XXXVII, No. 99 in the gem collection of the Archäologischen Institut, Göttingen) and P. Steiner, *Xanten. Sammlung des Niederrheinischen Altertums-Vereins*, Frankfurt a.m. (1911), 142 and Pl. XV, No. 36. For a general discussion of the Bonus Eventus types *cf.* M. Henig, "Success as personified on a Roman intaglio", *Glasgow Archaeological Journal* III (1974), 71-3.

[4] M. Henig, *Corpus*, part ii, 43-5 and Pl. X, Nos 295-311; 114 and Pl. XXV, No. App 57.

[5] *Britannia* VI (1975), 273 and Pl. XXI, C.

[6] On a group of gems in this later style from Britain, M. Henig, "The Huntsman Intaglio from South Shields", AA4 xlix (1971), 215-30.

[7] M. Henig, *Corpus, BAR* part i, fig. 1, shape B 5.

[8] G. Sena Chiesa, *Gemme del Museo Nazionale di Aquileia*, Aquileia (1966), 60-2, Pls XCII and XCIII.

[9] M. Maaskant-Kleibrink, *Classification of Ancient Engraved Gems. A Study based on the collection in the Royal Coin Cabinet, The Hague*, Leiden (1975), 225ff.

[10] M. Henig, *Corpus* part ii, 19 and Pls VI and XXXIX, No. 171. Parallels are cited in Aquileia (Sena Chiesa *op. cit.*, 305 and Pl. XLIII, No. 847f.) which are said to have been cut by the first-century "Officina della Sfinge".

[11] M. Henig, *Corpus*, part ii, 29 and Pl. VI, No. 174.

GLASS (Fig. 37) by DOROTHY CHARLESWORTH

It is impossible to estimate the number of vessels represented by the fragments submitted because a surprisingly high proportion of the fragments are melted in a fire, making their shape unrecognisable, crackled or completely shattered by a sudden change of temperature. For example, it is probable that all the deep blue glass (117) is from a single, or at most two, vessels although found in contexts of phases 2, 3 and 4. It is completely shattered. Only one vessel can be partially restored, a beaker (119) in good colourless glass decorated with 3 groups of faint wheel-abraded lines. No fragments of rim or base remain. Its probable shape is Isings 29, a form with a convex decorated side, no base ring and an unworked or ground rim; this is a development of the mid first-century beaker (Isings form 12). Its date would be late first or early second century. Most of the fragments which can be identified are from square or other angular-bodied bottles dating to between *c.* 60-130 (Isings form 50). Three moulded bases were found but retain only the edge of the moulded pattern, together with either one or two circles (118). Two flagons belong to the same period: there is a vessel with the rim, part of the neck and the upper sticking part of the handle in amber glass (120); and a fragment of the lower sticking part, a horizontally ridged tail in green glass (121). Most of these flagons were made in the Seine/Rhine area. In general the coloured examples are first century.

Eight pieces of moulded window-panes were identified. There are also two pieces that are probably blown window-glass (Harden 1961). Two fragments came from deposits of phase 2 but the rest derived exclusively from phase 3 contexts. No piece has any indication of how it was fixed in place.

For the glass armlets and beads, cf. 55-62, *supra.*

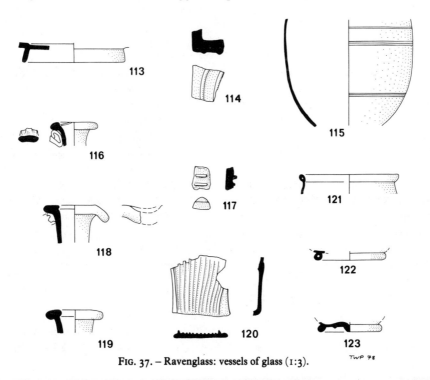

FIG. 37. – Ravenglass: vessels of glass (1:3).

113.   (SF 204)   Fragment of a base, possibly from a plate. A high ring, probably an added true ring. Blue glass with brown enamel-like weathering. First century. Phase 2.

114.   (NW)   Fragment of a square bottle base with two concentric rings. Green glass, crackled. Phase 2.

115.   (NC)   Part of a beaker in good colourless glass decorated with three groups of wheel-abraded lines. Close to Isings 29. Late first or early second century. Unstratified.

116.   (SF 282)   A flagon with an infolded and flattened rim, part of the neck and the upper sticking part of the handle. Amber glass. c. 70-150. Phase 4.

117.   (BW)   Fragment of the ridged tail from the lower sticking part of the handle of a flagon. Blue-green glass. c. 70-150. Phase 3.

118.   (SF 104)   Infolded and flattened rim and neck from a square bottle. Green glass. Phase 4.

119.   (SF 286)   Similar to 122, though this may not be a square bottle. Unstratified.

120.   (SF 283)   Handle in green glass. The lower sticking part up to the angle from a multi-ribbed square bottle. Phase 2.

121.   (SF 85)   Infolded hollow tubular rim and part of the side of a beaker, in poor quality blue-green glass. Second century? Phase 4.

122.   (SF 117)   Fragment of a base ring and flat base in blue-green glass. First-third centuries. Phase 4.

123.   (SF 35)   Base in a good colourless glass with a coiled base ring and trail round the underside of the concave base, with a domed centre. Probably second century. Phase 4.

FLINTS (Fig. 38) by R. C. Turner

Prehistoric activity in the vicinity of the site is represented by a total of nine flints. They are all of very poor quality and derive from small cobbles washed up from the sea bed. Whilst none of the forms is especially diagnostic, Mr Jim Cherry tells us that the Mesolithic industries can be crudely distinguished from those of the Bronze Age by the appearance of the patination: the former tend towards greyish colours and the latter are generally patinated brown. More than 60 sites with flint scatters are known from this stretch of the Cumbrian coast (Cherry 1963, 1969). Characteristic Neolithic industries are very rare, but both Mesolithic and Bronze Age forms are well represented. One Mesolithic chipping floor lies some 400 m to the south of the site, while Bronze Age settlement is attested at several points on the sand-dunes across the estuary.

124.   (SF 8)   Scraper, made on a broad flake of brown flint. The original flake was larger and was shortened, leaving a bend fracture along one edge. The remaining edges have been retouched at least once. The ventral surface has several thinning flakes to improve the angle of the cutting edge.

125.   (SF 182)   Waste flake in a rich brown flint.

126.   (SF 226)   Cortex lump in a poor-quality whitish grey flint. Its surfaces are formed by fracture along faults in the cobble but one surface shows a degree of secondary working.

127.   (SF 202)   Waste flake in a high-quality black igneous rock. The striking platform has broken off.

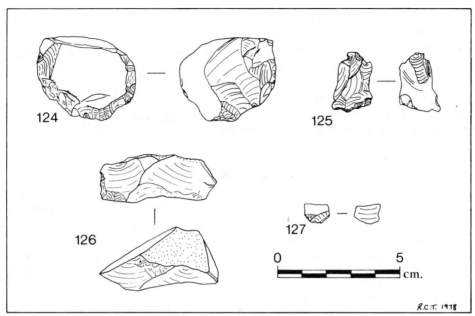

FIG. 38. – Ravenglass: flints (2:3).

GRAFFITI by D. C. A. SHOTTER

No inscriptions were found in the excavations; indeed only one is on record from Ravenglass (*RIB* 795). This stone, which was recovered during excavations at the site in 1881 (Collingwood 1928, 357), was discarded before a record had been made. Birley (1958, 14) refers to the discovery of other now untraceable inscriptions.

For a lead sealing, cf. 71, *supra*.

Graffiti (not illustrated)

128. (S 467)   On the base of a samian vessel, a complete graffito in capital letters. Phase 4.
TITVS

129. (FF 33)   On a rim of grey-ware; a part-graffito in cursive letters –]II C N[. From the pit, (FF) end of phase 2.

130. (AR 4)   On a rim of black-burnished ware; a part-graffito in large cursive letters –]XII[. Phase 3.

131. (NF 1)   On a rim of a pie-dish; a part-graffito (? possibly a batch-number) in capital letters – IV. Phase 4.

132. (OM 9)   On a rim of black-burnished ware; two separate graffiti:
(i) in capital letter, complete – M.
(ii) in cursive script, part –]I II[(possibly simply three strokes). Phase 2.

133. (OM)   On a rim of black-burnished ware; graffito, probably consisting of three strokes. Phase 2.

134. (FF 37)   On a base of black-burnished ware; two phases of graffiti, the primary one a lightly scored X, the secondary a deeply incised X. Pit (FF), end of phase 2.

135. (AA 313) On a wall-sherd of black-burnished ware; a part-graffito in capital letters BO[. Unstratified.

136. (AA 20) On the external surface of a wall-sherd of samian ware (?) in capital letters, a part-graffito]SΛN[. Unstratified.

137. (AA 1) On the internal surface of the base of a black-burnished bowl: in large cursive letters, a part-graffito]VII[. Unstratified.

138. (AA 11) On the internal surface of the base of a black-burnished vessel, in large capital letters, a part-graffito]VI[. Unstratified.

MEDALLION (Pl. Xb)

139. (SF 23) A fine eighteenth-century bronze medallion, 3·8 cm in diameter, was recovered from the topsoil. It commemorates Admiral Vernon's famous victory at Porto Bello in the War of Jenkin's Ear. His success in taking the town and destroying its fleet of *guarda costas* (shown on the reverse of the medallion) was celebrated by the striking of no less than 46 different varieties of medallions, as well as by the issue of decorated mugs, buttons and even the renaming of inns (Hawkins 1885). The recovery of one of these medallions is probably a matter of coincidence but Ravenglass was a small but flourishing port (Caine 1922) and it is possible that one of Vernon's sailors came from the area.
Obv. THE. BRITISH. GLORY REVIV.D. BY. ADMIRAL VERNON.
Rev. HE. TOOK. PORTO. BELLO. WITH. SIX. SHIPS. ONLY.
            NOV 22 1739

Hawkins has provided a classification, listed reign by reign, for medallions of this sort; this example belongs to his type 107, issued during the reign of George II (Hawkins 1885, 535).

COINS by D. C. A. SHOTTER

The excavations produced 32 Roman coins as follows:

Phase 2 (1 coin)

1. (SF 203) AE *as*, Hadrian   A.D. 136
   Obv. HADRIANVS AVG COS III P P
   Rev. AEGYPTOS S C
   Moderate wear   (*RIC* 839)

Phase 3 (4 coins)

2. (SF 150) AR *denarius*, M. Antonius   32–1 B.C.
   Obv. ANT AVG III VIR R P C
   Rev. Illegible
   Very worn   (Crawford 544)

3. (SF 112) AE *dupondius*, Hadrian   A.D. 117–138
   Worn and fragmentary

4. (SF 114) AE *as*, Hadrian   A.D. 117–138
   Very worn

5. (SF 186) AE, Magnentius   A.D. 350–1
   Obv. D N MAGNENTIVS P F AVG
   Rev. FELICITAS REPVBLICE mm. illegible
   Fragmentary, but little wear   (as *LRBC* ii.49)

Phase 4 (7 coins)

6. (SF 69) AR *denarius*, Trajan   A.D. 98-9
      Obv. IMP CAES NERVA TRAIAN AVG GERM
      Rev. PONT MAX TR POT COS II (Abundantia)
      Little wear   (*RIC* 1)

7. (SF 29) AE *sestertius*, Hadrian   A.D. 117-138
      Very worn

8. (SF 97) AE *sestertius*, M. Aurelius   A.D. 168-9
      Obv. M ANTONINVS AVG TR P XXIII
      Rev. SALVTI AVG COS III S C
      Worn   (*RIC* 964)

9. (SF 111) AE *sestertius*, Faustina II   A.D. 176-80
      Obv. DIVA FAVSTINA PIA
      Rev. Illegible
      Worn

10. (SF 46) AE *as*, Faustina II (?)   A.D. 145-80
      Fragmentary and very worn

11. (SF 94) AE *antoninianus*, Tetricus II   A.D. 271-3
      Fragmentary, worn

12. (SF 175) AE, Constantine I   A.D. 323-4
      Obv. CONSTANTINVS IVN NOB C
      Rev. CAESARVM NOSTRORVM VOT X
      Fragmentary, moderate wear   mm. illegible (as *RIC* VII. 433)

13. (SF 63) AE   A.D. 335-41
      Obv. Illegible
      Rev. GLORIA EXERCITVS, 1 standard
      Very fragmentary, but not very worn   mm. illegible

Ditch of the later fort (4 coins)

14. (SF 54) AR *denarius*, Alexander Severus   A.D. 222-8
      Obv. IMP C M AVR SEV ALEXAND AVG
      Rev. IOVI VLTORI
      Fragmentary, but with little wear   (*RIC* 143)

15. (SF 30) AE, probably a radiate   A.D. 270
      Fragmentary, worn

16. (SF 25) AE, Constantine I   A.D. 330-5
      Obv. CONSTANTINVS IVN NOB C
      Rev. GLORIA EXERCITVS T̄R̄P
      Little wear   (*LRBC* I.49)

17. (SF 26) AE ?   probably 4th century
      Fragmentary

Unstratified (12 coins)

18. (SF 47) AE *sestertius*, Trajan   A.D. 103-111
      Obv. IMP CAES NERVAE TRAIANO AVG GER DAC P M TR P COS V P P
      Rev. S P Q R OPTIMO PRINCIPI S C (Dacia)
      Fragmentary and worn   (*RIC* 560)

19. (SF 289)   AR *denarius*, Hadrian   A.D. 134-8
    Obv. HADRIANVS AVGVSTVS
    Rev. SALVS AVG
    Little wear   (*RIC* 268)

20. (SF 4)   AR *denarius*, Antoninus Pius for M. Aurelius   A.D. 148-9
    Obv. AVRELIVS CAESAR AVG PII F
    Rev. TR POT III COS II
    Moderate wear   (*RIC* (Antoninus) 447)

21. (SF 290)   AE *dupondius*, Antoninus Pius for M. Aurelius   A.D. 140-161
    Legends illegible, very worn

22. (SF 57)   AE *sestertius*, Faustina II   A.D. 176-180
    Obv. DIVA FAVSTINA PIA
    Rev. CONSECRATIO (Altar)
    Moderate wear   (*RIC* (Marcus) 1706)

23. (SF 9)   AR *denarius*, Septimius Severus   A.D. 197-8
    Obv. L SEPT SEV PERT AVG IMP X
    Rev. PACI AETERNAE
    Moderate wear   (*RIC* 118)

24. (SF 2)   AE *antoninianus*, Postumus (?)   A.D. 260-8
    Worn

25. (SF 80)   AE *antoninianus*, Postumus (?)   A.D. 260-8
    Fragmentary and worn

26. (SF 68)   AE, Constans   A.D. 346-50
    Obv. D N CONSTANS P F AVG
    Rev. FEL TEMP REPARATIO
    Little wear   *$\overline{PLG}$ (*LRBC* II.180)

27. (SF 3 (i))   AE, Constans   A.D. 346-50
    Obv. D N CONSTANS P F AVG
    Rev. FEL TEMP REPARATIO
    Little wear $\overline{PLG}$*   (*LRBC* II.196)

28. (SF 3 (ii))   AE, Magnentius   A.D. 350-1
    Obv. D N MAGNENTIVS P F AVG
    Rev. FELICITAS REIPVBLICE
    Little wear $\overline{TRP}$ (*LRBC* II.49)

29. (SF 3 (iii))   AE, Magnentius   A.D. 350-1
    Obv. D N MAGNENTIVS P F AVG
    Rev. FELICITAS REIPVBLICE
    Little wear   mm. illegible   (as *LRBC* II.49)

The three coins Nos 26-28 were found corroded together: this and the fact that other coins of Constans and Magnentius of similar type and condition were found in the excavations suggest the possibility of a disturbed hoard.

30. (SF 64)   AE, Magnentius   A.D. 351-3
    Obv. D N MAGNENTIVS P F AVG
    Rev. VICTORIAE D D N N AVG ET CAE VOT V MVLT X
    Little wear $\overline{AMB}$ (*LRBC* II.7)

31. (SF 7)   AE, Valens   A.D. 364-7
    Obv. D N VALENS P F AVG
    Rev. SECVRITAS REIPVBLICAE
    Fragmentary, little wear   OF|I
                               LVG
                        (*LRBC* II.276)

Possible coin

32. (SF 270)   Some crumbled fragments of corroded silver, which may have been a coin. Phase 2.

The group of coins was in general in a very poor condition: the *aes* coins in particular were in a very crumbled and fragmentary state.

The latest coin from the excavations was a bronze of Valens, issued in the period 364-367; although its condition would suggest that its loss should be placed at a point after 370, we should recall that a *solidus* of Theodosius is recorded from Muncaster Castle (Fair 1948; Birley 1958).

To the group excavated in 1976-78, we should add a small number previously reported (Birley 1958, 20; Jackson 1876, 21) making 39 in all, of which two were illegible.

		1976-78	Other finds	Total
I	(–A.D. 41)	I	I	2
II	(41-54)			—
III	(54-68)			—
IV	(69-96)		I	I
V	(96-117)	2	2	4
VI	(117-138)	5		5
VII	(138-161)	2		2
VIII	(161-180)	4		4
IX	(180-192)			—
X	(192-222)	I		I
XI	(222-235)	I		I
XII	(235-259)			—
XIII	(259-275)	4		4
XIV	(275-294)			—
XV	(294-317)			—
XVI	(317-330)	I	I	2
XVII	(330-346)	2	2	4
XVIII	(346-364)	6		6
XIX	(364-378)	I		I
XX	(378-388)			—
XXI	(388-)			—
Illegible		2		2

Comment should be restricted to a few observations: the relationship of periods IV, V and VI does not suggest occupation from the Flavian period; it would fit a date of initial occupation in the first half of the second century. An unusual feature is the relatively strong showing of period VIII (the reign of M. Aurelius), which normally on sites in north-west England displays a marked decline on earlier periods. The third century is poorly represented: even period XIII, which provides on average 20% of the coin sample of north-western sites, is low. The fourth century provides a not untypical picture, though it is possible that the peak in period XVIII, the best represented period on the site, is contaminated by hoard material.

THE COARSE POTTERY (Figs 40-6) by HELEN LOCKWOOD AND R. C. TURNER

The discussion of the coarse-wares follows the arrangement of the main body of text, so that the pottery is considered phase by phase. Some groups of material from contexts within a phase are listed separately. At the end of this section there is also a short note concerning the products and distribution of the nearby Park House kilns. For the mortaria and amphora stamps, cf. p. 120 and for the graffiti, p. 101. Park House products are noted in the main catalogue.

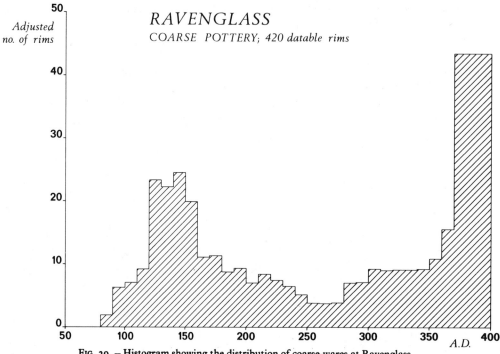

FIG. 39. – Histogram showing the distribution of coarse-wares at Ravenglass.

Phase 1 (c. 130)

Only a few sherds were recovered in the building-trenches of this period. None is closely datable (although there were two sherds of black burnished ware) or merits illustration.

Phase 2 (c. 130-190/210: Fig. 40)

The sample from the structural features of the buildings of phase 2 was small and few sherds worthy of illustration were found. Nos 125 and 126 were used as packing for the very narrow timber-trench in the north veranda of barrack-block 4.

1. (QH 2) Mortarium in a pinkish fabric with a grey core; traces of a cream slip and white grits. Similar to fabrics of Austinus and Docilis. 130-170.

2. (OG 5) Beaker with a cornice rim in a soft, buff fabric.

3. (RA 1) Crudely made, small beaker in a light grey fabric with a buff-coloured exterior.

4. (QE1/QG3) Segmental bowl in an orange, gritty fabric (Park House product). Gillam 294. 120-150.

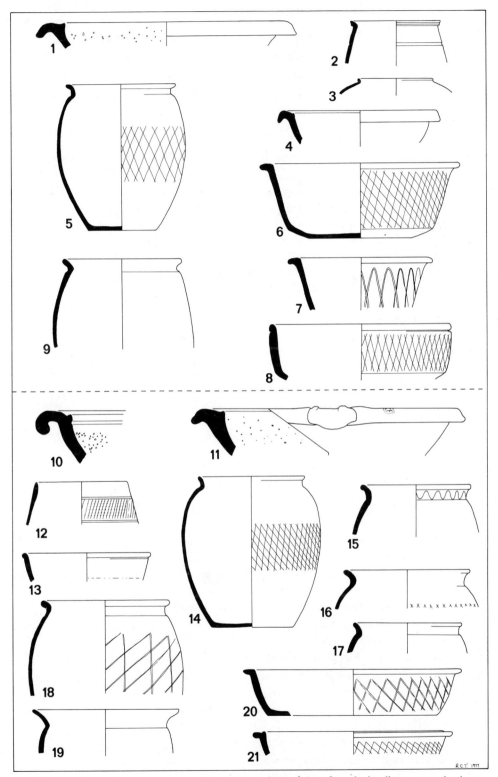

FIG. 40. – Ravenglass: coarse-ware of phase 2, 1-9; phase 2/3 interface, daub collapse, 10-21 (1:4).

5. (QO 11)   Jar in a BB1 fabric with acute lattice decoration. Gillam 122. 120-160.

6. (QO 7)   Bowl in a BB1 fabric with acute lattice decoration. Gillam 220. 120-160.

7. (EL 1)   Bowl in a BB1 fabric with acute looped decoration. Gillam 220. 120-160.

8. (QG 4)   Dish in a BB1 fabric with acute lattice decoration. Gillam 318. 160-200.

9. (PX 1)   Jar in a very coarse, gritty fabric (Park House product). The jar is burnt and it is difficult to say if the true colour is dark grey or orange-red. Imitates second-century black-burnished forms.

Phase 2/3 interface (c. 190/210: Figs 40-2)

This is the most closely datable event on the site, for which there are two major groups of finds: first, a group from the burning and collapse of the daub walls of barrack-blocks 4 and 5 and the finds lying on the wooden floor beneath (groups DS, EQ, NM, NW and OM); second, from the rubbish and demolition pit (feature 137, group FF). Stratigraphically, there seems to be little or no time separating these two phases, so the groups can be considered to be contemporary. Cf. also Fig. 13.

Pottery from the daub collapse of barrack-blocks 4 and 5:

10. (DS 3)   Mortarium in an orange fabric, burnt grey inside, with traces of a cream slip and white and grey grits. Fragmentary stamp (no. 135).

11. (OM 21)   In shape Gillam 254. 140-180. Mortarium in an orange fabric with a grey core and white and grey grits. Stamped DOCF (no. 136).

12. (OM 24)   Colour-coat beaker in a hard, buff fabric with darker grey-brown slip. Decorated with a band of rouletting. Similar to Gillam 78/81. 190-260.

13. (OM 14)   Cup reminiscent of Drag. 27 in a smooth, buff-orange fabric with some mica dusting.

14. (NW 6)   Jar in a BB1 fabric burnt to orange, with acute lattice decoration. Closest to Gillam 121. 120-160.

15. (NW 7)   Jar in a BB1 fabric, burnt to orange, with a wavy line decoration under the rim. Gillam 125. 120-160.

16. (OM 27)   Jar in a BB1 fabric. Gillam 122. 120-160.

17. (EQ 1)   Jar in a BB1 fabric. Gillam 133. 160-220.

18. (OM 7)   Jar in a soft, light-grey fabric with a very gritty surface (Park House product). Lightly applied, acute lattice decoration.

19. (NM 2)   Jar in an orange, gritty fabric (Park House product) imitating black-burnished forms.

20. (OM 18)   Dish in a BB1 fabric with acute lattice decoration. Gillam 309. 160-200.

21. (OM 25)   Dish with a flanged rim in a BB1 fabric, burnt to orange, with acute lattice decoration. Gillam 226. 200-240.

22. (OM 8)   Bowl in a BB1 fabric with acute lattice decoration. Gillam 220. 120-160.

23. (OM 9)   Bowl in a smooth, mid-grey fabric with white, sandy inclusions. It has a graffito on the rim (No. 132). Gillam 225. 200-250.

24. (NW 5)   Bowl in a light grey, gritty fabric (Park House product) decorated with a shallow groove round the body.

25. (OM 23)   Tiny bowl or cup in a smooth, hard, grey fabric.

26. (OM 22)   Bowl or dish in an orange-red, gritty fabric (Park House product).

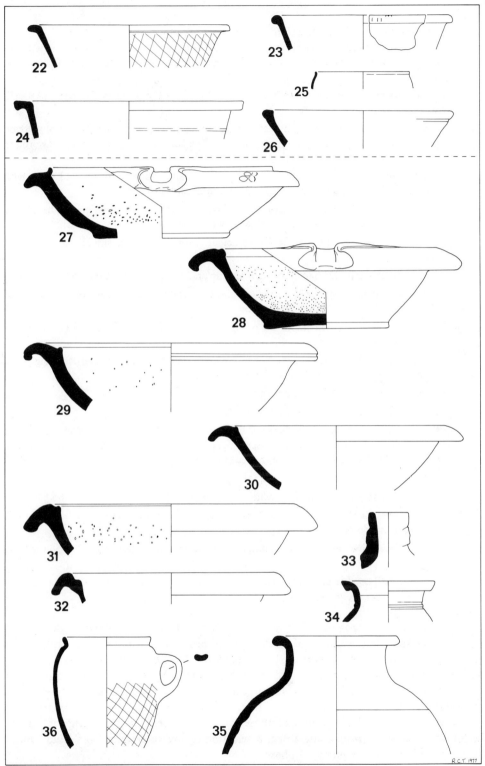

FIG. 41. – Ravenglass: coarse-ware from phase 2/3 interface. Daub collapse, 22-6; rubbish pit, 27-35 (1:4).

Pottery from the pit (FF) on the south side of barrack-block 5:

27. (FF 22) Mortarium in a hard, buff fabric with large variegated grits. It is stamped with four hand-drawn circles on either side of the spout (No. 139). In shape closest to Gillam 254. 140-165.

28. (FF 23) Mortarium in a smooth, hard, white fabric with reddish grits. Stamped SARRUS (No. 141). Gillam 254. 140-180.

29. (FF 3) Mortarium that has been heavily burnt to a purple-grey colour. Traces of a cream slip remain as do black and white grits. In shape like Gillam 257, but with a groove round the rim. 160-200.

30. (FF 17) Mortarium in a flaky, buff fabric. The inside is heavily burnt and thick with charcoal, as if used for a special purpose. Mid second-century type.

31. (FF 12) Mortarium in a hard, red-brown fabric with white and brown grits. The outside and the rim have a rich brown gloss (Wilderspool product). Gillam 269. 180-220.

32. (FF 6) Mortarium burnt to a light grey colour throughout. Very similar to No. 31 but smaller in size.

33. (FF 36) Double-handled flagon with a plain rim and neck, in a gritty, buff fabric.

34. (FF 7) Narrow-mouthed jar in a hard, grey, sandy fabric with a darker grey exterior. The neck is decorated with two shallow grooves.

35. (FF 32) Narrow-mouthed jar in an orange-red, sandy fabric with a groove round the shoulder and the lower body.

36. (FF 21) Tankard in a grey-burnished fabric decorated with an acute lattice design. See Gillam 1976, 65, Fig. 2, No. 25. Mid second century.

37. (FF 1) Jar in a BB1 fabric. Gillam 135. 170-250.

38. (FF 18) Large jar in a BB1 fabric. Gillam 135. 170-250.

39. (FF 14) Jar in a hard, grey, sandy fabric burnished on the outside to a metallic sheen (Park House product). A band of very lightly scribed, acute lattice decoration covers the body. The form imitates black-burnished jars of the second century.

40. (FF 10) Dish in a BB1 fabric. Gillam 306. 120-160.

41. (FF 38) Dish in a BB1 fabric with acute lattice decoration. Gillam 316. 125-160.

42. (FF 28) Small dish or lamp in a BB1 fabric, grooved under the rim to give a beaded effect, with a wavy line decoration.

43. (FF 33) Small bowl or dish in a smooth, hard, light-grey fabric with a graffito on the body (No. 129).

44. (FF 39) Small bowl or dish in an orange, gritty fabric (Park House product).

Phase 3 (Figs. 42-4)

This phase covers a long period, *c*. 190/210-350/370, in which the basic building plan remained the same but recutting of the main structural features and the changing of the internal arrangements of the barrack-blocks could be detected. The buildings were also destroyed by fire during this period. However the stratigraphy was such that the groups of finds of this phase were difficult to relate to each other. As a result it has been decided to represent the pottery in three main units: first, pots from the pits round the rampart ovens that seem to belong to the beginning of phase 3; second, a selection of the range of types to be found in phase 3 groups; and third, a selection of fourth-century pots from groups known to be late in the sequence of phase 3.

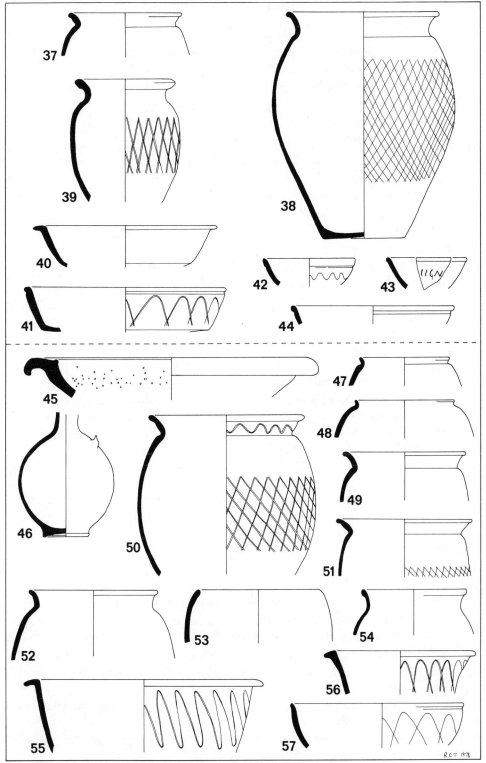

FIG. 42. – Ravenglass: coarse-ware from phase 2/3 interface. Rubbish pit, 37-44; phase 3, 45-57 (1:4).

Phase 3 groups from pits round the rampart ovens:

45. (AK 22)   Mortarium in an orange, gritty fabric with multi-coloured grits (Park House product). Slight groove on the outside of the rim. Gillam 257. 160-200.

46. (AN 7)   One-handled flagon in a soft, orange, sandy-textured fabric. Gillam 13. 80-130.

47. (AK 32)   Beaker in a BB1 fabric. Gillam 170. 130-180.

48. (AK 30)   Small jar in a BB1 fabric. Gillam 118. 120-160.

49. (AK 13)   Jar in a BB1 fabric. Gillam 135. 170-250.

50. (AK 28)   Jar in a BB1 fabric with acute lattice decoration. Gillam 135. 170-250.

51. (AK 29)   Jar in a BB1 fabric. Gillam 138. 150-250.

52. (AK 19)   Jar in a BB1 fabric. Mid second-century type.

53. (AR 3)   Rimless jar in a BB1 fabric.

54. (AK 23)   Jar in a gritty, grey fabric (Park House product), imitating black-burnished forms of the later second century.

55. (AN 1)   Bowl in a BB1 fabric with acute looped decoration. Gillam 221. 140-180.

56. (AK 30)   Bowl in a BB1 fabric with acute looped decoration. Gillam 220/221. 140-180.

57. (AN 2)   Dish with a suggestion of a beaded rim in a BB1 fabric. Widely spaced looped decoration.

A representative selection of phase 3 forms:

58. (DC 1)   Mortarium in a hard, orange, gritty fabric with multi-coloured grits (Park House product) and a groove round the outside of the flange. Shape as Gillam 246. 120-160.

59. (BN 5)   Mortarium in an orange fabric with a grey core and traces of a cream slip. The grits are grey and white. This is the fabric of Austinus and Docilis. 130-170.

60. (DO 1)   Mortarium in an orange-red, gritty fabric with a red gloss on the rim (Wilderspool product). Gillam 269/270. 180-220.

61. (OZ 2)   Very similar to No. 60 but burnt to a light grey colour. This is a small vessel of a type common in phase 3.

62. (CV 6)   Mortarium in a hard, cream fabric with a sandy texture. A third-century type.

63. (BO 1)   Mortarium in a white, pipe-clay fabric with black grits. Gillam 284. 280-360.

64. (PO 1)   Mortarium in a hard, white fabric with pink and white grits. A late second to early third-century type.

65. (BY 2)   A small ring-necked flagon in a soft, white fabric. Closest to Gillam 8. 140-180.

66. (BH 4)   Base of a cup in a hard, grey fabric with smooth, black exterior (London Ware). It is decorated with a band of rouletting between two pairs of horizontal grooves.

67. (NH 1)   Rim of a colour-coat beaker in a soft, white fabric with a near black slip (Nene Valley product). Traces of decoration with barbotine dots exist. Gillam 84/85. 180-220.

68. (ND 1)   Jar in an orange, sandy-textured fabric with a pie-crust rim.

69. (OZ 3)   Narrow-mouthed jar in an orange, gritty fabric (Park House product) with a groove on the inside of the rim.

70. (CV 5)   Narrow-mouthed jar in a smooth, hard, light-grey fabric with two horizontal bands of wavy line decoration.

71. (CF 3)   Jar in a BB1 fabric. Gillam 118. 120-160.

72. (BV 2)   Jar in a BB1 fabric. Gillam 130. 140-180.

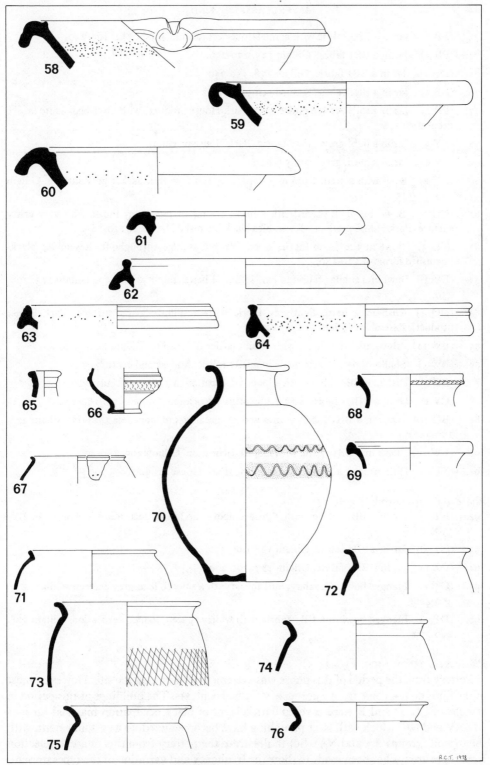

FIG. 43. – Ravenglass: coarse-ware from phase 3 (1:4).

73. (PP 1)   Jar in a BB1 fabric with acute lattice decoration. Gillam 134. 160-230.

74. (PR 3)   Jar in a BB1 fabric. Gillam 135. 170-250.

75. (DE 1)   Jar in a BB1 fabric. Gillam 138. 150-250.

76. (BF 3)   Jar in a BB1 fabric. A third-century type.

77. (PP 2)   Jar in a soft, orange-pink fabric (Park House product) with inscribed, acute lattice decoration.

78. (EY 3)   Jar in a light grey, gritty fabric (Park House product).

79. (PR 2)   Jar in a hard, grey, sandy fabric.

80. (EY 2)   Bowl with a reeded rim in a hard, grey fabric with a darker grey surface. Gillam 214. 80-125.

81. (CU 2)   Bowl, burnt in places, either in an orange or light grey fabric with very gritty surface (Park House product). Resembles black-burnished bowls of 120-180.

82. (NL 3)   Bowl in the same fabric as No. 81 but orange throughout. Resembles black-burnished forms of 120-180.

83. (BV 3)   Bowl in a similar fabric to No. 81 but of better quality. In shape Gillam 225. 200-250.

84. (DO 4)   Dish in a hard, light-grey fabric with a slightly gritty surface (Park House product). Resembles Gillam 328. 150-200.

85. (BW 11)   Bowl in a BB1 fabric with a faint lattice decoration. Gillam 221. 140-180.

86. (BW 5)   Shallow bowl, poorly made in a BB1 fabric. Mid second century.

87. (BG 4)   Dish in a BB1 fabric with a looped decoration. Mid second century.

88. (CV 1)   Dish in a BB1 fabric with acute lattice decoration. Gillam 318. 160-200.

89. (BG 10)   Dish in a BB1 fabric with a widely spread acute looped decoration. Gillam 329. 190-340.

90. (BW 10)   Dish in a BB1 fabric with looped decoration. Gillam 309. 160-200.

91. (NL 7)   Dish or lid in a gritty, orange fabric (Park House product).

Phase 3 groups with late pottery:

92. (BY 5)   Jar in a BB1 fabric, with a groove above the lattice decoration. Gillam 146. 280-350.

93. (CT 3)   Jar in a BB1 fabric. Gillam 148. 290-370.

94. (OZ 1)   Jar in a BB1 fabric. Gillam 147. 290-370.

95. (CT 2)   Flanged bowl in a sandy, buff fabric with a smooth lead-grey exterior. Gillam 229. 350-400.

96. (DP 1)   Flanged bowl in a BB1 fabric with widely spaced, looped decoration. Gillam 228. 290-370.

Phase 4 (c. 350-70/400: Figs 44-5)

Pottery from the period of this phase was extremely common on the site. However, most of the finds do not come from rigorously stratified contexts. The buildings of this period in trenches B, C, D and E were covered with a layer of black occupation material (groups AL, AV and NF) which with later ploughing have become mixed, to a certain extent, with the topsoil (groups AA and NA). So, to illustrate the pottery from this phase, a selection from these groups has been made to show the frequency and variation of the types present.

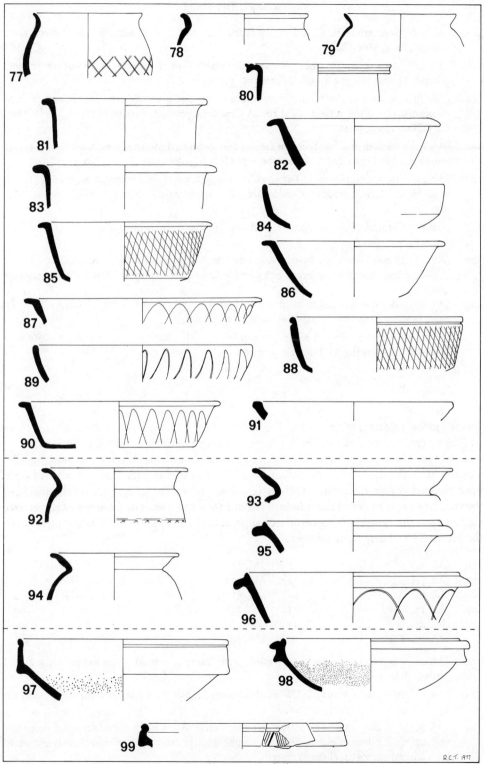

FIG. 44. – Ravenglass: coarse-ware from phase 3, 77-91; late deposits of phase 3, 92-6; phase 4, 97-99 (1:4).

97.   (AL 11)   Mortarium in a hard cream fabric with traces of a buff slip. Large black grits. Gillam 287-9, 360-400.

98.   (AV 48)   Mortarium in a hard, cream fabric with tiny black grits. A Crambeck product (Corder 1937, 403, type 8). Cf. Gillam 290. 370-400.

99.   (AA 40)   Mortarium in a hard, cream fabric burnt to grey in parts. Red-brown painted decoration round the outside of the rim. A Crambeck product (Corder 1928, Pl. V, No. 130). Cf. Gillam 289. 370-400.

100.   (AA 42)   Platter in a hard, cream fabric. It is decorated internally with bands of varying motifs in a red-brown paint. A Crambeck product (Corder 1928, Pl. III, No. 60).

101.   (AA 41)   Bowl reminiscent of Drag. 38 in a soapy, cream fabric with sparse, orange grits. A probable Crambeck product (Corder 1928, Pl. II, Nos 24-29). Similar to Gillam 204. 360-400.

102.   (OB 1)   Flanged bowl in a light grey fabric, sandy in texture, burnished internally. Gillam 231/232. 370-400.

103.   (AV 4)   Flanged bowl in a hard, cream fabric with a burnished, light grey exterior. Traces of a wavy line decoration internally. A possible Crambeck product; cf. Gillam 231/242. 370-400.

104.   (AV 27)   A small flanged bowl in a soft, light grey fabric with a grey exterior. It has an extra beading round the junction of the flange and rim.

105.   (AL 189)   Flanged bowl in a hard, cream fabric with a dark grey core and a surface with traces of mica dusting. Gillam 229. 350-400.

Jars in calcite-gritted fabrics:

There were hundreds of rims in this ware, showing a number of minor variations of two main classes, Gillam 160/1 and 163. No. 106 is a rather unusual rim for which no parallel was found. Nos 107-110 are of Gillam 160/161, dated 300-370. Nos 111 and 112 are hook-rimmed vessels resembling Gillam 163, but missing the groove round the inside of the rim. Nos 113-121 are of the standard Gillam 163, 370-400. The presence of the groove seems to put the vessel later in this date range than those without. The following list is of the inventory and catalogue numbers:

106.	(AK 34)	113.	(AL 6)	119.	(AV 39)
107.	(AA 34)	114.	(AA 37)	120.	(AA 36)
108.	(AL 20)	115.	(AL 8)	121.	(DF 2)
109.	(AV 46)	116.	(AV 25)		
110.	(NG 4)	117.	(AA 32)		
111.	(AA 29)	118.	(AE 10)		

122.   (AA 26)   Bowl in a calcite-gritted fabric with traces of a beaded rim formed by a line of pitting under the rim.

123.   (AR 6)   Bowl, or possibly a lid, in a calcite-gritted fabric with a marked thinning below the rim.

124.   (AA 400)   A body sherd in a brown, laminar fabric with a black core. It is hand-made and the surface is pitted in places, giving a resemblance to calcite-gritted wares. It is decorated with a lightly grooved, chevron design.

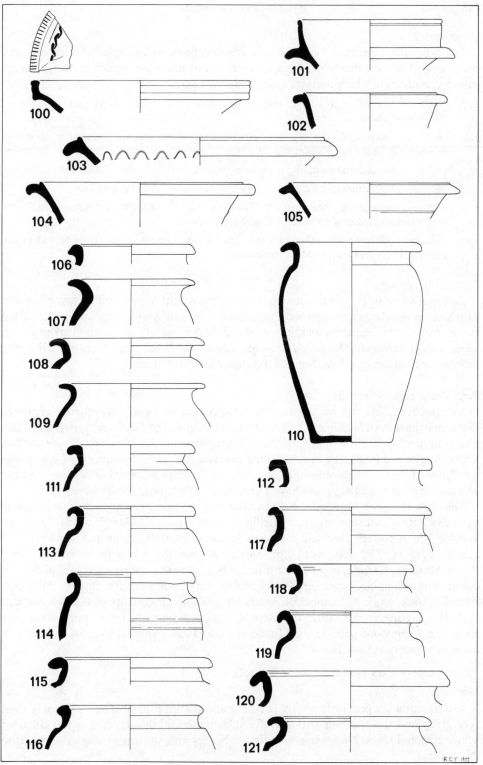

FIG. 45. – Ravenglass: coarse-ware from phase 4, 100-5; calcite-gritted wares, 106-21 (1:4).

Other vessels:

The following examples, Nos 125-130, are illustrated as examples of mortaria and colour-coated beakers that are present in layers of this phase but do not appear in earlier stratified contexts to which they are more likely to belong.

125. (AU 11) Mortarium in a hard, white, pipe-clay fabric with large black and reddish grits. Resembles Gillam 284. 280-340.

126. (AL 229) Mortarium in a soft, white fabric with small black grits. There are traces of red-brown paint on the rim. Gillam 284. 280-360.

127. (AA 43) Mortarium in a hard, cream fabric with large, black grits. Gillam 278. 210-320.

128. (AU 18) Mortarium in a hard, white pipe-clay fabric. Gillam 280. 210-320.

129. (AA 401) Colour-coat beaker in a buff fabric with near black slip. Decorated in barbotine with a running frieze of dolphins. Gillam 85. 180-220.

130. (AL 400) Colour-coat beaker in a soft, pink fabric with an orange interior and brown exterior. Decorated with bands of rouletting.

Post-Roman pottery

This was surprisingly uncommon considering the extent of the area excavated. A few sherds of the usual modern types were represented. Two sherds of Cistercian ware, dating to the 16th or 17th centuries, and thirteen sherds of the typical late medieval green-glazed ware, were discovered. The only stratified piece of the latter came from the fill of the robber-trench of the fort wall. None of this material is illustrated.

Park House pottery (Fig. 46)

A distinctive fabric was recognised among the coarse-ware and its frequency suggested that it may have been locally produced. The fabric is quite hard and very gritty, including a large proportion of black and white sandy filler, giving the pottery a very coarse texture. This is heightened in the case of some of the mortaria and jars where the vessel apparently was rolled in the sand before firing. The colour varies from brick-red or orange to a light grey and in some cases the vessels have a grey wash. The vessels are wheel-made.

The Park House or Muncaster Roman kilns (Fig. 2) have been known since 1884 and our knowledge is well summarized by Bellhouse (1960, 1961). Although primarily known as a tile kiln, a potter's shed and a potter's kiln were partially excavated by Miss M. C. Fair in 1922-23. The only sherd from this excavation that could be located in Tullie House Museum, Carlisle, is a base of a jar. It is in the same fabric as above, pinkish in colour with a light-grey exterior. In describing stray finds from Ravenglass, Miss Fair remarks (1925, 374): "a number of coarse, grey-washed fragments of ware as made at Park House pottery (the Muncaster Roman kiln), a fragment of very hard silver-grey ware, like Wedgewood (similar ware found at Park House pottery); a rim of a pie dish as made in numbers at Park House".

The range of Park House products is as follows:

Mortaria

The mortaria are primarily orange in colour and are not slipped. Their surface is often very gritty and the grinding grits are of similar material but larger; they are coloured white, grey and black. No stamps were found. Nos 45 and 58 (*supra*) may be assigned to this group.

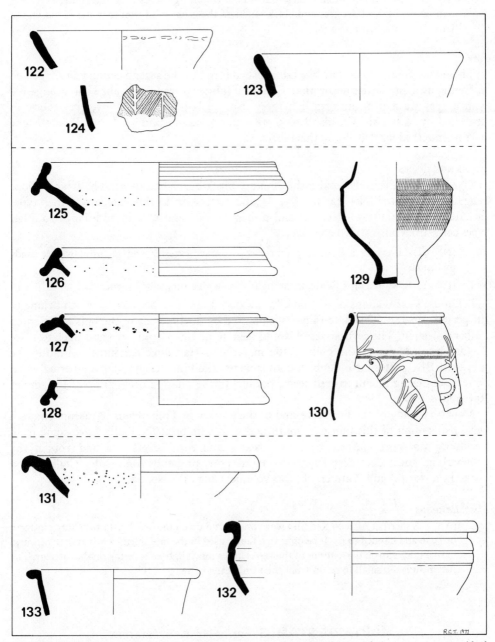

FIG. 46. – Ravenglass: coarse-ware from phase 4. 122-4: calcite-gritted ware of phase 4; 125-30, residual pottery in phase 4 contexts; 131-3, products of the Park House kilns (1:4).

131. (NF 92) Mortarium in an orange-buff fabric with a light-grey core. The outer surface is tempered with a white, grey and black sand and the grits are of similar material but larger. Gillam 242 in shape. 90-130.

Jars

These vessels tend to imitate black-burnished forms of the second century in shape and in having an acute lattice decoration. Colour of fabric varies from orange and orange-red with a grey wash to a uniform light grey. No. 39 is in a hard, shiny, grey fabric as described by Miss Fair. Cf. also Nos 9, 18, 19, 39, 54, 77 and 78, *supra*. There is one narrow-mouthed jar, No. 69, in this fabric.

Bowls and dishes

Like the jars, the bowls and dishes imitate black-burnished types. The whole colour range is represented. Nos 44, 81, 82, 83 and 84 belong to this category. Other types include a segmental bowl (No. 24) and dishes (Nos 26 and 91). In addition, two other types come from unstratified contexts.

132. (NF 93) Bowl in a light-grey fabric with darker exterior and plentiful white, sandy inclusions.

133. (PZ 2) Bowl in a pink fabric, burnt light grey, with a very sandy surface.

Bellhouse's excavations of the tile kilns produced four datable sherds, which belong to the period 120-180. This date-range is supported by the typology of the pots represented in this collection. The earliest vessel would seem to be No. 31 (90-130) and the latest No. 83 (200-250). However the bulk of the material is Hadrianic-Antonine, imitating the prevalent BB1 pottery. No doubt the kilns were of military origin and the period when pottery was being manufactured seems parallel to the phase 2 occupation of the fort at Ravenglass.

A cursory study of the literature and of the pottery in Tullie House Museum shows a wide distribution of this fabric in south and west Cumbria. Examples have come from Beckfoot, Maryport (Jarrett 1976, 59, Nos 4 and 8); Turrets 15a and 16b of the Cumberland coast defences; Papcastle; Hardknott; probably Ambleside (Collingwood 1914, 456, No. 42) and Watercrook (this volume, Chap. IV, No. 230).

Miscellaneous

134. (AA) A sherd of African Red Slip ware was picked up on the beach below the fort-platform in 1976 and handed to us. It belongs to a fabric used in the late third – early fourth century, with a thick slip on the exterior of the vessel and a much lighter covering on the interior. The fragment is too small to reconstruct the form of the vessel.

MORTARIA STAMPS (Fig. 47) by K. F. HARTLEY

135. (DS 3) Two small, joining fragments from a mortarium which has been overfired to an abnormally hard texture; some warping is indicated and the vessel is technically a waster though it may have been saleable as a second. The fabric is red-brown, fired to black on the inside, with thin buff slip and abundant white and transparent quartz trituration grit with some indeterminate grey particles. The fragmentary stamp is from a die which reads DOCIF when complete. Phase 2.

FIG. 47. – Ravenglass: the mortaria stamps, 135-41, and amphora stamp, 142 (1:2).

136. (OM 21) A fragment from a mortarium in self-coloured, pinkish brown fabric with thick bluish grey core; it is unusually heavily tempered with grey, white and red-brown gritty material and there are no signs of any additional trituration grit on this fragment. The stamp which is almost complete reads DOC.F.

These stamps are from two of at least eight dies giving readings like DOCIF, DOCIFE and DOCCIFE, which are attributable to one potter. The name intended is perhaps most likely to be Docius, Doccius or Docilis; there are several instances in mortarium stamps of variations like the doubling of consonants occurring in the dies of one potter.

Forty of his stamps are now known, all from north western Britain, in an area from Wilderspool to the Antonine Wall, with a heavy concentration on Hadrian's Wall and in the Cumberland coast forts. His activity probably fell within the period 120-155 and his products and their distribution points to manufacture in north western England, probably in the Eden valley not far from Carlisle, though it is possible that he started his career at Wilderspool (Hartley and Webster 1973, 91, Fig. 9, 95 & 96). The two Ravenglass examples are unlikely to be among his late products. Phase 2/3 interface.

137. (NF 99)   A mortarium in soft, fine-textured fabric with bluish grey core, tempered with fine grit including some quartz; slight traces of a cream slip survive under the flange. This trademark has also been recorded from Ambleside; Hardknott; Lancaster, and Watercrook. The fabric and form are typical of mortaria made at Wilderspool (*ibid.* 92, fig. 8, o. and 95-97 for a discussion of possible links with Austinus). Mortaria were being produced at Wilderspool in the period 100-165, and the rim-forms associated with stamps from the same die as this example indicate pre-Antonine activity. Phase 4.

138. (OC 2)   A mortarium in slightly abrasive cream fabric with some pink in the core and in patches at the surface. The clay has been quite heavily tempered with quartz, grey and red-brown (some of it haematite) particles and the trituration grit is similar. The incomplete stamp can be restored from other examples to DIICΛ, from one of the six dies of Decanius.

Fifty-five of his stamps are now known from sites in the west midlands, south-west England, Wales and north-west England. Thirty-two of these are from Wroxeter where he undoubtedly worked along with a number of other potters whose products and markets are identical. Their workshops were active within the period 110-160, and their mortaria (though not Decanius' to date), are occasionally recorded from forts on the western half of the Antonine Wall. Phase 3.

139. (FF 22)   Diameter *c.* 27 cm. Two joining pieces giving almost half of a burnt mortarium in hard, greyish buff fabric with thick blue-black core and probably a buff slip; there is abundant red-brown, dark-grey and white quartz trituration grit. The potter has used an almost circular, hollowed object to imitate potter's stamps by impressing it four times together in complementary positions to each side of the spout. This implies an illiterate potter. This mortarium was not made in any of the major potteries in Britain and it seems likely to be the work of a potter working on a small scale. The fabric is unusual and is unlikely to have been produced in north-western England. The profile clearly indicates an Antonine date. Phase 2/3 interface.

140. (AL 221)   A mortarium in fine, creamy white fabric, tempered with red-brown, grey and quartz grit; no certain trituration grit survives. The broken, retrograde stamp is from one of the sixteen dies of Iunius who had kilns at Mancetter and Hartshill. He shared one kiln at Hartshill with Bruscius, and one at Mancetter probably with Sarrius, both potters whose products are found on the Antonine Wall. More than eighty stamps of Iunius are known excluding those from kiln sites. His work is widespread but its virtual absence from Antonine forts in Scotland (one example only) contrasts so sharply with the distribution for most Warwickshire potters of any importance that one may reasonably assume that most of his activity coincided with a period when the Antonine Wall was not in use. His rim-forms also fit with a mid- or late Antonine date, *c.* 155/160-185. Phase 4.

141. (FF 23; FF 24; FF 26)   Diameter 28 cm. Three joining pieces forming about three quarters of a worn mortarium which was burnt before fracture. It is in creamy white fabric with orange-brown trituration grit. The incompletely impressed stamp is from one of the six dies of Sarrius who had kilns at Mancetter and probably also at Hartshill. A second workshop of his has also been discovered at Rossington Bridge near Doncaster but this example was made in Warwickshire. Over a hundred mortaria of his are known, excluding those from kiln sites, and more than twenty of these are from Antonine deposits in Scotland. A stamp from Verulamium occurred in a deposit dated to 155/160 (Frere 1972, 378, No. 35). Production within the period 135/140-165 is indicated by the total evidence. Phase 2/3 interface.

Amphora Stamp (Fig. 47)

142. (AA 2)   A fragmentary amphora stamp reading MR. It can be reconstructed as QMR (Callender 1965, 229, No. 1481). The fabric of the handle is buff-orange on the exterior, and the core is buff. The amphora originated in southern Spain and can be dated to *c.* 140-80. Examples are known from the north-western sites of Ambleside and Papcastle.

SAMIAN WARE (Figs 48-51) by FELICITY WILD

Note: I wish to thank Mr B. R. Hartley of Leeds University for discussing a number of the decorated pieces with me, and his assistant, Miss Brenda Dickinson, for providing the report on the stamps. I have retained her system of footnotes throughout the stamp report:

1. The stamp has been recorded at the pottery in question.
2. Other stamps of the same potter, but not that particular one, have been recorded from the pottery.
3. Assigned to the pottery on form and fabric.

Abbreviations: The figure types are quoted from F. Oswald, *Index of Figure Types on Terra Sigillata* (O.); Rheinzabern ovolos and types from Ricken-Fischer 1963. S&S=Stanfield & Simpson 1958.

The excavation produced about fifteen hundred sherds of samian ware. On the whole they tended to be in a poor state of preservation, and the high proportion of burnt pieces was remarkable. In all, almost 75% of the sherds showed some degree of burning.

The earliest phases of the site produced little dating evidence, apart from a single rim sherd of form 18/31 (PY S1439), of Hadrianic date, from deposits of phase 1.

The samian as a whole showed scant evidence of occupation before the Hadrianic period. There were sherds from only nine vessels of South Gaulish origin; a single example of forms 18 and 27, three of Curle 11, three of form 37 (two of rim only) and a beaker fragment. None of these are likely to have been made earlier than the Flavian-Trajanic period. There was only one decorated sherd (28 below, from an unstratified context), which was stylistically among their latest products. Few pieces can definitely be attributed to Les Martres-de-Veyre, the main exporter between the end of import from South Gaul, *c.* 110, and the start of large-scale export from Lezoux, *c.* 120. Curiously, no decorated pieces appear to have come from this source. The present assemblage suggests that if there were any earlier occupation on the site, it did not long antedate the construction of the main Hadrianic fort.

Import on a significant scale started during the Hadrianic period, and appears to have continued without notable intermission until the end of the Central Gaulish industry at the end of the second century. The proportion of East Gaulish products reaching the site was low, as is to be expected, but some appear to have been arriving from the Hadrianic period. Five decorated pieces from East Gaul have been included here (22, 23, 31-33), all of Hadrianic or Antonine date, and including wares from La Madeleine and Lavoye as well as Rheinzabern. No examples of the work of the later Rheinzabern potters occur, though this may be fortuitous. It has not been possible to assess the exact proportion of East Gaulish wares, or of those from Les Martres-de-Veyre, owing to the number of burnt sherds, which made precise fabric identification impossible.

All the significant decorated ware from phase 2, and from the phase 2/3 destruction deposit and demolition pit have been published, and a representative selection from phase 3. That from phase 4 has been treated as unstratified. All identifiable stamps have been published in full, under the period from which they come.

Phase 2

The stratified material from phase 2 included two sherds of South Gaulish origin, of form 18 and 27 (both from PE). Several sherds of form Curle 11 in South Gaulish fabric, burnt, and presumably all from the same bowl, came from the barrack destruction deposit (phase 2/3 below). Four examples of form 18/31, including those stamped by Balbinus and Reginus (A and B below), can be assigned to Les Martres-de-Veyre. The scarcity of wares from Les Martres, and total absence of decorated ware, suggests that the foundation of the site took place later in Hadrian's reign.

The end of the phase hinges on the date of the destruction deposits of phase 2/3, detailed below. The latest sherd from the layers included here is the piece with Cinnamus' ovolo 1 (7), which must be later than c. 155.

Stamps

A. I:ALBINVS.I: (PE S1317) Form 18/31, Central Gaulish. Die 1a of Balbinus of Les Martres-de-Veyre[2]. The initial letter was cut in such a way as to resemble an F, but this stamp certainly belongs to Balbinus and not to Flo(rius?) Albinus. It is much less common than one of Balbinus' other stamps (frequently misread II/IBINI.M) and, unlike it, does not appear in groups from the London second fire. It may therefore be slightly later, perhaps belonging to the period c. 125-140.

B. [REGIN]VS.F (QN S1504) Form 18/31, Central Gaulish. Die 2a of Reginus ii of Les Martres-de-Veyre[1]. The earlier of Reginus' stamps, it occurs in deposits from the London second fire, while his later stamp occurs at Mumrills. c. 110-130.

C. VERTECISSA.F (PL S1463, 1466) Form 18/31, Central Gaulish burnt. Die 1a of Vertecissa of Lezoux[1]. There is no site dating for the stamp, but it was used on forms 18/31 and 27. Other stamps of this potter appear at Chester-le-Street and on form 79. c. 140-170.

Decorated Ware

1. (EG S900) Form 37, Central Gaulish. All the motifs are common in the style attributed to X.6. The ovolo is his ovolo 4 (S&S, Fig. 18,4); the Hercules with lion (0.796) and border with trefoil occur on a bowl in this style from Middlewich (S&S, Pl. 75,19); the medallions on other bowls (S&S, Pl. 75,13,17). c. 125-150.

2. (NC S1085, 1113, QB S1436-8, OA S1261, OW S1305-6) Form 37, Central Gaulish, Eight sherds, three joining, of which four are burnt, two heavily. The ovolo, borders and wreath motif were used by X.6. Panel decoration shows the Diana with hind (0.106), panther (0.1542) and pigmy (0.691).

3. (QG S1484) Form 37, Central Gaulish, slightly burnt. The ovolo, vine-scroll, stag (0.1697) and other details occur on a bowl from Heronbridge (S&S, Pl. 89,12) showing the cursive signature of Drusus ii of Lezoux. c. 125-150.

4. (QG S1468) Form 37, Central Gaulish, heavily burnt. The ovolo and bear (0.1588) were used by the Sacer group. The other type may be a hound (0.2005?). c. 125-150.

5. (QC S1479) Form 37, Central Gaulish, showing saltire motif with fleur-de-lys (Rogers 1974, G88) inside chevron (G344). The ovolo is probably that of X.5 (ibid., B31), who used the fleur-de-lys and similar borders. However, this is not one of his more typical products, and precise attribution remains in doubt, although a date in the Hadrianic-early Antonine period is clear.

6. (QW S1489) Form 37, Central Gaulish?, slightly burnt. No precise parallels to the ovolo are forthcoming, either from Central Gaul or from Lavoye, to the wares of which the decoration shows affinities. The general style suggests a date in the Hadrianic or early Antonine period.

7. (NC S1084) Form 37, Central Gaulish, showing Cinnamus ovolo 1. Both leaves were used by him (S&S, pl. 161,53). c. 155-175.

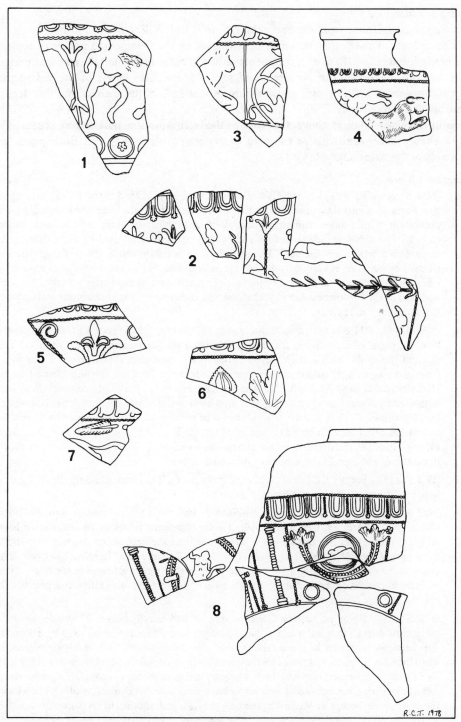

FIG. 48. – Ravenglass: the samian (1:2).

Phase 2/3 Interface
The destruction deposit from the barracks (DS, EQ, NM, NW, OM)
   The violence of the destruction may be witnessed by the fragmented nature of some of
the bowls listed below (8, 9, 11), fragments of which came from many layers and periods
over the site. However, the occurrence of sherds from these bowls in the destruction
deposit appears to justify their inclusion here. About 80% of the sherds from this deposit
were burnt, many heavily.
   As in the phase 2 layers above, the work of the later Antonine potters was absent. The
latest sherds were, again, those showing Cinnamus' ovolo 1 (11, 12). Both pieces are
probably of the date-range *c*. 155-180.

Decorated Ware
   8.   (NM S1337, QC S1475, 1477, BW S1325, 1352, 1354, OA S1259, PT S1381, 1386-
        8)   Form 37, Central Gaulish, burnt. Eleven fragments from the same bowl, showing panel
        decoration with festoon containing medallion with bird; column; arcade with dancer
        (0.348). The ovolo, arcade, acanthus and beaded circle were all used by Secundinus i. An
        unpublished bowl from Carzield, Dumfriesshire, in his style shows the ovolo, arcade and
        circle. The signature is known from a bowl from Nursling, Hants., very similar in style to the
        Carzield bowl (Rogers and Laing 1966, 59). The occurrence of this potter's work at Carzield
        and also in the Birdoswald Alley (Richmond and Birley 1930, Fig. 3) suggests a Hadrianic-
        Antonine date. *c*. 125-145.

   9.   (NM S1168, OM S1234, 1279, 1280, 1419, PK S1375, QL S1460)   Form 37, Central
        Gaulish, slightly burnt. Seven fragments, showing a smaller version of the Triton (0.25) in
        place of the ovolo, with a thick, roped border. The decoration shows arcades. The figure
        types are fragmentary and uncertain, but may show the Bacchus (0.566), Diana (0.109),
        Hercules (0.782) and Apollo (0.78). The leaf (Rogers 1974, J22) and acanthus (K.6) were
        both used by Sissus ii, and occur together on a bowl in the Musée des Antiquités Nationales,
        St. Germain-en-Laye. The general style cannot be parallelled on a bowl signed by Sissus, but
        clearly has affinities with bowls attributed to the Medetus-Ranto group (Rogers' X.9, S&S,
        Pl. 30). However, the details here are clearly those of Sissus. The work of this potter occurs
        in Scotland, and he is likely to be early Antonine in date.

  10.   (OM S1277)   Form 37, Central Gaulish, slightly burnt. The festoon and Apollo (0.84) were
        used by Cinnamus and his associates. *c*. 150-175.

  11.   (NM S1429, NC S1090, QL S1456: EF S902-4, 898, NB S1104, By s839, 840, BN S673,
        OW S1304)   Form 37, Central Gaulish. Twelve fragments probably from the same bowl,
        all burnt except one, two from phase 2 layers, one from the destruction deposit. Two sherds
        show part of the CINNAMI (ret.) stamp (die 5b) of Cinnamus ii of Lezoux. The ovolo is his
        ovolo 1, the decoration a freestyle hunting scene with his corn-stook as space-filler. Types
        include: horseman (0.245), deer (0.1743), male figure (0.644), a panther and possibly the
        boar (0.1641). *c*. 155-175.

  12.   (NW S1356)   Form 37, Central Gaulish, abraded and heavily burnt. The ovolo, similar if
        not identical to Cinnamus' ovolo 1, has a straight line underlying it as used by Secundus.
        The beadrow junctions lack a masking motif, another characteristic of his style, and the
        worn motif in the corner of the panel may possibly be his dolphin, ill-impressed (*c.f.* S&S, Pl.
        154,14, now attributed to Secundus). The caryatid is probably 0.1201. This potter shows
        clear links with Cinnamus, and appears to have used both his ovolos 1 and 3. A bowl with
        the latter ovolo occurs at Mumrills (Hartley 1961,4), and another in an Antonine I context
        at Birrens (Wild 1975, 20). The copy of Cinnamus' ovolo 1, if so it be, is unlikely to be
        earlier than its original, *c*. A.D. 155. *c*. 150-180.

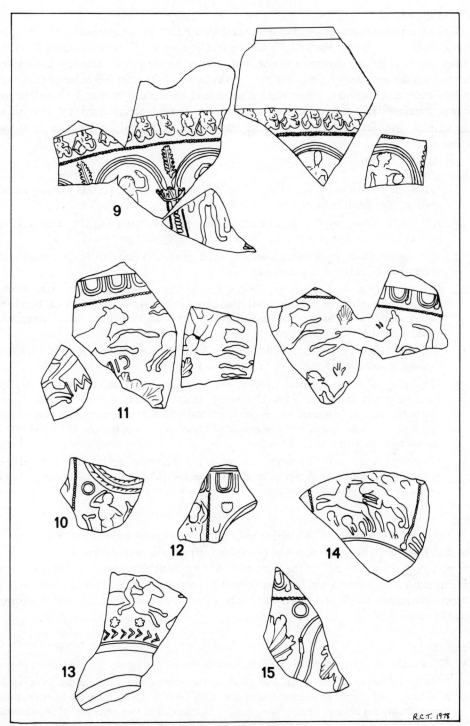

FIG. 49. – Ravenglass: the samian (1:2).

The rubbish pit (FF)

While most of the samian sherds from the pit were burnt, the proportion of burnt pieces was slightly lower than in the phase 2 and destruction layers. The earliest sherd from the group was (13) below, dating to the second quarter of the second century. Unlike the destruction deposit, the pit contained pieces in the style of the later Antonine potters such as Advocisus and Paternus, whose work is not found on Scottish sites and whose starting date is therefore likely to have been after *c.* A.D. 160. The Advocisus sherd (17) and that in the style of Paternus' associates (18) were burnt; that in the style of Paternus (19) was unburnt.

Decorated Ware

13. (FF S988)   Form 37, Central Gaulish, burnt. The Amazon (0.241) and chevron wreath both occur on bowls in the style of X. 6 (S&S, Pl. 75,18,15,). *c.* 125-50.

14. (FF S1007)   Form 37, Central Gaulish, showing panel with stag (0.1781), bear (0.1627) and leaftip filling ornament used by Cinnamus and the Paullus group. *c.* 145-175.

15. (FF S993)   Form 37, Central Gaulish. Small bowl, showing the ovolo 2 and scroll decoration of Cinnamus. *c.* A.D. 150-170.

16. (EY S940, FF S1013)   Form 37, Central Gaulish, burnt. Two fragments, with similar burning, probably from the same bowl. One shows the mould-stamp [DI]VIX.F below the decoration, die 9d of Divixtus i of Lezoux, and the feet of his warrior (0.213), which appears on the other sherd along with his erotic group O.H. *c.* 150-180.

17. (FF S992) Form 37, Central Gaulish, slightly burnt. One sherd in the style of Advocisus, showing his ovolo 1 and Minerva (0.126). *c.* 160-190.

18. (FF S987)   Form 37, Central Gaulish, heavily burnt. The rams' horns were used by Censorinus and Mammius (S&S, Pl. 102,15, 103,2), although neither of these potters commonly used the coarse astragalus for the vertical border, as did Paternus and Laxtucissa. However, the piece is certainly to be associated with this group of potters. The figure type is uncertain. *c.* 150-190.

19. (FF S1054, 1017, 1018)   Form 37, Central Gaulish. Three joining fragments of scroll bowl in the style of Paternus. A signed bowl from London (S&S, Pl. 107,26) shows the same ovolo, scroll and leaves. *c.* 160-190.

Phase 3

Although the samian from this phase must all to some extent be residual, a selection of the decorated ware has been published to show the range of wares present. The work of the potters of the second half of the second century was well represented, particularly that of Cinnamus and Paternus and his associates. The proportion of decorated to plain vessels was comparatively small, and much was badly abraded. About 71% of the sherds showed signs of burning.

Stamps

D. AP>RILISFC   (AN)   Form 18/31, East Gaulish, burnt.

E.]P>RIL (AK S173)   Form 18/31, East Gaulish. Two stamps from the same die, 1a of Aprilis iii of East Gaul[3]. Although another stamp of an East Gaulish Aprilis is known from Pont-des-Remes, it may not belong to this potter, and the distribution of this particular stamp does not suggest origin in the Argonne. There is no very satisfactory dating evidence for it, but as it consistently occurs on form 18/31 and appears at Corbridge, a date *c.* 130-160 is likely.

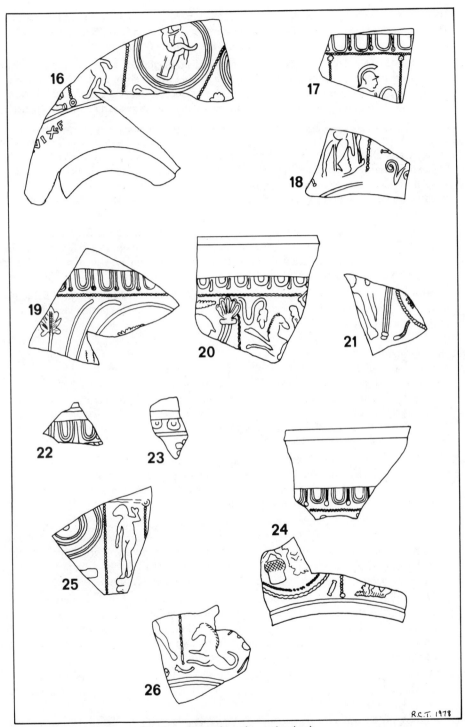

FIG. 50. – Ravenglass: the samian (1:2).

F. BRICCI.M (AJ S80) Form 33, Central Gaulish, burnt, Die 3a of Briccus of Lezoux[2]. Most
    of the examples of this stamp are on form 38, and one comes from Corbridge. Some of his other
    stamps appear on forms 27 and 80, and there is one example from Mumrills. c. 150-180.

G. CVCΛLI[M] (AN S497) Form 80, Central Gaulish, burnt. Die 2d of Cucalus of Lezoux[1].
    This stamp appears at Corbridge. It has been recorded once on form 27, but is more common
    on forms 79 and 80. It is therefore likely to be one of Cucalus' latest stamps, since many of his
    others appear frequently on form 27. His site record includes Newstead and Old Kilpatrick. c.
    150-170.

H. PAΛLIM (CT S826) Form 33, Central Gaulish. Die 5b of Paullus iv of Lezoux[2]. This
    stamp nearly always has a faint stroke between the A and V, presumably a scratch on the die.
    There is no dating evidence for it, but it belongs to the potter who made decorated ware in the
    style of the Cerialis ii – Cinnamus ii group at Lezoux. His plain ware appears in dated groups
    from Castleford (the Pottery Shop of 140-150), Verulamium (the second fire) and Wroxeter
    (the Gutter). c. 140-170.

I. REGALIS.F (AK S238) Form 33, Central Gaulish, burnt. Die 4a of Regalis i of Lezoux[2].
    This stamp was used on forms 18/31R, 31R and 79R, and occurs at Benwell and Corbridge.
    Regalis also used forms 80, Ludowici Tg and (occasionally) form 27. One of his other stamps
    appears at Newstead. c. 150-180.

J. SABI[NIOF] (AK S243) Form 31, Central Gaulish, burnt. Probably die 5a of Sabinus viii
    of Lezoux[1]. Sabinus' record includes forms 31, 31R, 79 and 80. This particular stamp occurs
    at Bainbridge. c. 150-180.

Decorated Ware

20. (AK S342) Form 37, Central Gaulish, showing panel decoration with hare (0.2115) in
     festoon, and horseman (0.258). The bush motif is probably Rogers' G20, used by
     Quintilianus, and the bud, his G150. The bud occurs on a bowl attributed to one of the
     Ranto group, Rogers' X.9 (S&S, Pl. 34,411), which shows certain similarities in style to this
     bowl. However, the bowl is in a Lezoux fabric, and the ovolo is known from Lezoux. A
     Hadrianic date seems probable.

21. (BW S905) Form 37, Central Gaulish. One fragment showing figure type (probably
     0.341), column and festoon. The column, although incomplete, is probably that on a bowl
     from Birdoswald (Richmond and Birley 1930, 183, Fig. 9). The potter is uncertain, but a
     Hadrianic or early Antonine date is probable.

22. (AK S836) Form 37, East Gaulish. Fragment showing Ricken's ovolo E.39b, used by
     Ianus i of Rheinzabern, possibly from the same bowl as (32) below, although in a better state
     of preservation. Ianus was one of the earliest Rheinzabern potters. Work in his style occurs
     in the Birdoswald Alley (Richmond and Birley 1930, 182, Fig. 7,5), indicating that he
     started work during the Hadrianic period. Hadrianic or early Antonine.

23. (NH S1173) Form 37, East Gaulish. Small fragment showing frieze of rosettes in place of
     the ovolo. The sherd is closely paralleled by a bowl from Zugmantel attributed by Ricken to
     the style of ovolo D at Lavoye (Ricken 1934, Taf.XIII,47). The rosette motif is that
     illustrated (*ibid.*, Taf.XII,2), and the motif at the edge of this sherd may be the same trefoil,
     associated with ovolo D ware from Lavoye. Antonine.

24. (AK S200, 216, 218, 483) Form 30, Central Gaulish, slightly burnt. Four fragments
     showing Cinnamus' ovolo 2 and festoon with dolphins (S&S, Fig. 47,18) and Pan Mask
     (0.1214). c. 150-170.

25. (OP S1230) Form 37, Central Gaulish, burnt. One sherd in the style of Divixtus, showing
     his Venus (0.305) and concentric circles. c. 150-180.

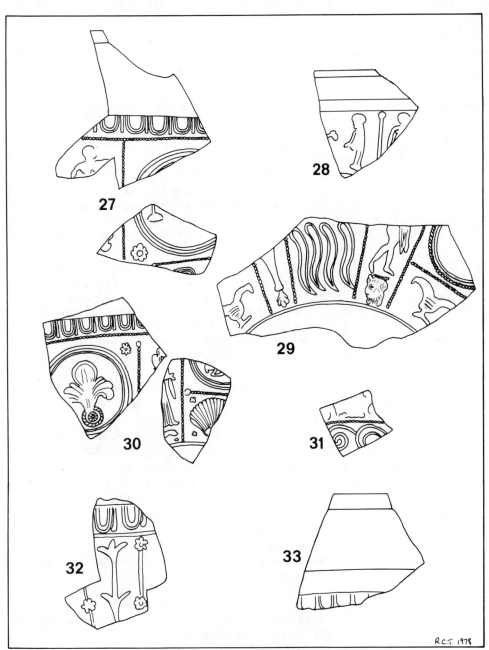

FIG. 51. – Ravenglass: the samian (1:2).

26. (CB S731-6) Form 37, Central Gaulish. Five joining fragments showing the characteristic leaf and astragalus border of Paternus and his associates, with the seahorse (0.31). *c.* 160-190.

27. (BF S616, 625, BW S1302) Form 37, Central Gaulish. Three fragments showing the ovolo 1 of Iullinus, his rosette (Rogers 1974, C179) and cup (S&S, Fig. 36,10). *c.* 160-190.

Unstratified

Stamps

K. ALBVC.I (NF S1126) Form 31, Central Gaulish, burnt. Die 6a of Albucius ii of Lezoux[1]. This stamp has been recorded from Birrens and Corbridge, and is in the group from the Wroxeter Fire. It was used on forms 79 and 80. *c.* 150-180.

L. [C]ADGAT[I:MA] (NF S1371) Form 31, Central Gaulish, burnt. Die 1a of Cadgatis of Lezoux[1]. This stamp occurs at Newstead and Benwell and was used on forms 31R and 38. Cadgatis also made form 27. One of his stamps is on the rim of a bowl from Bregenz in the style of Albucius ii. His site record includes Camelon, Castlecary, Catterick and Corbridge. *c.* 150-170.

M. DOMITIANVSF (AL S439) Flat base, possibly 79, East Gaulish, burnt. Die 3b of Domitianus of Kräherwald[1], Rheinzabern[1], Heiligenberg[2] and Waiblingen-Beinstein[2]. Domitianus seems to have been a migratory potter and it is possible that the die for this stamp was used at all four centres (though the record for Waiblingen is decorated ware). However, the distribution of the stamp suggests mainly Kräherwald and Rheinzabern, and the Ravenglass piece almost certainly comes from the latter. The stamp occurs on form 27 (on vessels from Kräherwald and at Rheinzabern is on the rim of a bowl with an ovolo by Ianus ii. *c.* 155-185.

N. MAIN[CNI] (AU S570) Form 33, Central Gaulish. Die 2a of Mainacnus of Lezoux[1]. The stamp, which was used on form 79, occurs at South Shields, and there are at least six examples from it at Pudding Pan Rock. *c.* 160-190.

O. MV[XTVLLI.M] (AA S47) Form 31, Central Gaulish, heavily burnt. Die 1a of Muxtullus of Lezoux[2]. This is one of Muxtullus' later stamps, which occurs on sites founded or reoccupied *c.* A.D. 160, and in the destruction deposit of the Wroxeter Forum. *c.* 150-180.

P. NICEPHOR.[F] (NA S1071) Form 18/31R, Central Gaulish. Die 2a of Nicephor ii of Lezoux[1]. The presence of this stamp in Lower Germany, the frequency of its use on forms 18/31, 18/31R and 27, and the one example of it on form 80, suggest a date *c.* 140-160.

Q. SATVRNINI (AL S467) Form 31, Central Gaulish. Die 8c of Saturninus ii of Lezoux[1]. There is no satisfactory dating evidence for this particular stamp, but Saturninus' vessels are in the cargoes from the Pudding Pan Rock wreck, and appear at Bainbridge and Binchester. His forms include 31R, 79R and 80. *c.* 160-190.

Decorated Ware

28. (FL S1031) Form 37, South Gaulish. One fragment showing panel decoration typical of the latest products of La Graufesenque, with gladiators (0·1041, 1042). The ovolo has been removed during the bowl-finishing process. *c.* 90-110.

29. (CE S747) Form 37, Central Gaulish, burnt, and containing rivet-hole. One fragment showing panel decoration in the style of Casurius. Panels show his vase with acanthus (S&S, Pl. 135,35), herm or caryatid, gadroons, figure (0·638) over Pan mask (0·1214), festoon over vase. *c.* 160-190.

30. (NE S1109, NN S1316)   Form 37, Central Gaulish. Two fragments, almost joining, in the style of Doeccus. The ovolo is his ovolo 2, and panels show the leaf (S&S, Pl. 151,59) in medallion, draped woman (0·926), festoon over his fan. c. 160-190.

31. (AL S112)   Form 37, East Gaulish. Small fragment showing basal wreath of spirals bordered with square beads. The spiral is probably one used at La Madeleine (Ricken 1934, Taf. VII, 34). A close parallel to wreath and beads is illustrated by Fölzer (Fölzer 1913, Taf. I,42). Wares from La Madeleine have been found at the Saalburg Earth-fort, suggesting that production started during the Hadrianic period. Hadrianic or early Antonine.

32. (AA S47, 18)   Form 37, East Gaulish. Two worn sherds in the style of Ianus i of Rheinzabern. The ovolo (Ricken's E.39b), trefoil (P.125) and dot rosette (0·42) occur together on a bowl in his style from Rheinzabern (Ricken 1948, Taf. 3,15). Hadrianic or early Antonine.

33. (AU S759)   Form 37, East Gaulish, showing abraded ovolo without tongue, probably Ricken's E.69 or 70. Both ovolos were used by Ianus, and a date in the Antonine period seems likely.

FAUNAL REMAINS by R. C. TURNER

Bone was very poorly preserved and only survived if burnt or in well sealed deposits. The rubbish pit of phase 2 yielded the largest sample: horse was represented by a scapula; cow by a scapula and four teeth; and sheep/goat by a complete mature skull and atlas vertebra, and mandibular fragment, two horn cores and a scapula. It is worth remarking that only skulls and scapulae are represented in this group.

The remainder of the site produced very few diagnostic pieces, these consisting mainly of fragments of long bone or rib. Ten bones could be assigned to sheep/goat, one to cow, one to horse, one to pig, and one to rabbit/hare.

BOTANICAL ANALYSIS by ALISON DONALDSON

The ditch of the fortlet of phase 0.

A column was collected from the fill of the ditch of the earlier fortlet, occupied c. 120-30. The fill of the ditch showed no clear stratification but the deposit was very heterogeneous with sand, clay and silt throughout and areas of darker, more organic material in "lumps". These "lumps" were not distinct enough to be separately sampled but did suggest deliberate infilling of the ditch. Horizontal layering, as would be expected from natural silting-up were not much in evidence. The column was divided into nine 10 cm samples, and 2·5 kg of each was washed, sieved, subjected to paraffin flotation and sorted microscopically, whilst checking residues. Identifications are shown in the attached table (Bryophyte identifications by Mrs A. Elmaghrabi).

The components of the species list may include *in situ* plant material and remains from elsewhere in the area brought in deliberately, as well as those incorporated by normal means. The list is dominated by plants of wet and damp areas. There are none which grow exclusively in open water so it is unlikely that the ditch contained standing or flowing water. Most are plants of fens and marshes and they are represented in such quantity that they must have been growing in the ditch or have been removed as whole plants or peaty turf from a damp area and used as infill. A number of weeds of waste ground were found and presumably represent the vegetation within the fortlet where instability of soils, trampling and midden encouraged the growth of plants so often associated with habitation sites. Although no crop plants were represented, the presence of a few weeds of arable land indicate cultivation in the region. The corn spurrey grows in cereal and flax fields with sandy, acid soils.

The only exclusively maritime species is a moss, *Mnium cuspidatum*, which grows on dune slacks. However, many plants, especially in the heathland and grassland groups, are frequent on dunes and similar maritime, sandy habitats. The presence of shoots of heather probably means that it was used as infill because it is unlikely to have been growing in a damp ditch. Seeds alone could have been blown into the ditch from a considerable distance. Any woodland in the area is likely to have been of a fairly open type.

There was very little difference between the samples in terms of the vegetation they represent. Three of them (3c, 3a and 2b) contained abundant monocotyledenous stems, lending weight to the idea of turf/peat infill. Mosses occur only on the basal samples and may be *in situ*, growing before there was much infill or accumulation. Indicators of cultivation are more frequent in the basal samples but, as only low numbers are involved, this may not be significant.

Both botanically and stratigraphically it is evident that this early ditch did not fill up entirely through the natural accumulation of silt and remains of *in situ* and local plants. This natural element, although probably present, is obscured by the obvious importation of lumps of vegetation, turf, peat or soil from elsewhere. Plant remains include species of fen, heath, grassland, arable and wasteland and dune areas.

Key to the following table

Habitats
W   wasteland
A   arable
G   grassland
H   heathland
F   fen/marsh
B   acid bog
Wa waterside (banks or margins of open water)
Aq aquatic (open water)
Wo woodland or scrub
M   maritime
ac acid soil

Nomenclature is according to Clapham, Tutin and Warburg, *Flora of the British Isles* (1962), for flowering plants, and Watson, *British Mosses and Liverworts* (1969), for Bryophytes.

Figures are the number of fruits or seeds recovered. (The *Juncus* figures are approximate). It must be stressed that the number of fruits or seeds of a species cannot be interpreted as representing a particular number of plants in the local vegetation.

Botanical remains from the ditch of phase 0

Flowering Plants	Part	Habitat	Distance in Centimetres along Column								
			90-80	80-70	70-60	60-50	50-40	40-30	30-20	20-10	10-0
Alphanes arvensis (Parsley Piert)	achene	A G		1	2	3		10			
Atriplex patula/ hastata (Orache)	seed	W A M							1		
Calluna vulgaris (Heather)	seed	H B Wo ac	15								
	shoots()		+	+			3	+	+		
Carex c.f. *pilulifera* (Pill-headed Sedge)	nutlet	H G Wo ac	6	5	35	50	4	2	55	12	1
Carex spp. (Sedges)	nutlets		39	14	5	140	18	17	50	35	5
Chenopodium album (Fat Hen)	seeds	W A			1		2	1	8	1	1
Galeopsis tetrahit/ speciosa (Hemp Nettle)	nutlet	A	1	5		3		3			
Gramineae (Grasses)	caryopsis		2		5	2	2			6	
Hydrocotyle vulgaris (pennywort)	fruit	B F			15	6	11	6	1		
Isolepis sectacea (Bristle Scirpus)	nutlet	F Wa	4	2	13	29	1	2	87	26	8
Juncus articulatus/ acuriflorus (Rushes)	seed	F H	2								
Juncus bufonius (Toad Rush)	seed	W A Wa		80	20	50	10	50	100	100	200
Juncus effusus/ conglomeratus (Rushes)	seed	B F Wo	4	70	100	1200	500	100	300	300	1000
Juncus squarrosus (Heath Rush)	seed	H B ac	14		12		28	5	3	8	
Montia fontana ssp. *chondrosperma*	seed	F Wa ac			41	3					
Polygonum aviculare (Knotgrass)	fruit	W	1	5							
Polygonum convolvulus (Black Bindweed)	fruit	W A		2	1	1					
Polygonum persicaria/ lapathifolium (Persicaria)	fruit	W A Wa	11	28		3	1	1	6	1	1
Potentilla anserina (Silverweed)	achene	W G M			1						
Potentilla erecta (Tormentil)	achene	G H B F	123	6	15	9	25	6	53	10	1
Prunella vulgaris (Self-Heal)	nutlet	G W Wo			1	4	5		8	5	
Ranunculus flammula (Lesser Spearwort)	achene	Wa Aq			2	1	2	1			
Ranunculus sect. *Ranunculus* (Buttercups)	achene	G W Wo	2	4		1					
Rubus fruticosus agg. (Blackberry)	achene	Wo H W					2		1		
Rumex acetosella (Sheep's Sorrel)	nutlet	H G A ac									
Rumex crispus (Curled Dock)	fruit	W A G M	3								
Sonchus asper (Spiny Milk Thistle)	achene	W A			1	1		1			
Spergula arvensis (Corn Spurrey)	seed	A ac	1	2							
Stellaria graminea (Lesser Stitchwort)	seed	Wo H G	2				1				
Stellaria media (Chickweed)	seed	W A	6	12	3	3		1			
Bryophytes											
c.f. *Campylopus atrovirens*	shoots	H B	+								
Ceratodon purpureus	shoots	M H Wo A		+							
Hypnum cupressiforme	shoots	Wo G H N	+	+							
Mnium cuspidatum	shoots	M		+							
Mnium undulatum	shoots	M F Wo	+								
Scorpidium scorpioides	shoots	F			+						
Sphagnum s.p.	leaf	B H Wo	+								

+ indicates the presence of shoots and/or leaves of a species.

The rubbish pit beside barrack-block 5, end of phase 2 (c. 190-210)
Two 2½ kg samples were examined.

Sample 1 (Grey fill)

Carex sp. (Sedge)	5 nutlets
Cruciferae (Cress family)	1 piece of seed
Galeopsis tetrahit L./*speciosa* Mill. (Hemp nettle)	1 nutlet
Gramineae (Grasses)	2 caryopses
Hordeum (Barley)	3 carbonised grains
Polygonum lapathifolium L./*persicaria* L. (Persicaria)	1 fruit
Potentilla erecta (L) Räusch (Tormentil)	1 achene
Ranunculus sect. Ranunculus (Buttercup)	2 achenes
Triticum aestivum s.1. (Wheat)	30 carbonised grains
Triticum dicoccum (Emmer)	2 carbonised grains
Urtica dioica L. (Nettle)	2 achenes

Sample 2

Carex sp. (Sedge)	2 nutlets
Chenopodium album L. (Fat Hen)	1 seed
Gramineae (Grasses)	1 caryopsis
Hordeum (Barley)	1 carbonised grain
Polygonum lapathifolium L./*persicaria* L. (Persicaria)	1 piece of fruit
Ranunculua sect. Ranunculus (Buttercup)	1 achene
Triticum aestivum s. l. (Wheat)	1 carbonised grain

Both samples contain a mixture of carbonised and uncarbonised grain and uncarbonised remains of other plants. The grain was probably carbonised accidentally during drying and discarded, hence its incorporation in rubbish. Most of the wheat is of hexaploid "modern" type but the occurrence of 2 grains of emmer is interesting. It is a primitive, diploid variety of wheat which was widely cultivated in prehistoric times and often in Roman times, its use continuing even later in some areas. The barley is a hulled variety. The uncarbonised seeds probably represent the plants growing within the fort, in waste places, beside paths and on rubbish dumps.

BIBLIOGRAPHY

Austin, R. G., 1934. "Roman board games". *Greece and Rome* iv, 24-34; 76-83.

Balsdon, J. P. V. D., 1969. *Life and Leisure in Ancient Rome*. London.

Bellhouse, R. L., 1960. "Excavations in Eskdale, the Muncaster Roman kilns". CW2 lx, 1-12.

——, 1961. "Excavations in Eskdale, the Muncaster Roman kilns". CW2 lxi, 47-58.

Birley, E., 1958. "The Roman fort at Ravenglass". CW2 lviii, 14-30.

——, 1961. *Research on Hadrian's Wall*. Kendal.

Boon, G. C. and Savory, H. N., 1975. "A silver trumpet brooch with relief decoration, parcel-gilt, from Carmarthen, and a note on the development of the type". *Ant. J.* lv, 41-61.

Bruce, Collingwood J., 1885. "The recent discoveries on the Lawe, South Shields". AA2 x, 223-318.

Bulmer, W., 1938. "Dragonesque brooches and their development". *Ant. J.* xviii, 146-53.

Busch, A. L., 1965. "Die römerzeitlichen Schuh- und Lederfunde der Kastelle Saalburg, Zugmantel and Kleiner Feldberg". *Saalburg Jahrbuch* xxii, 158-210.

Bushe-Fox, J. P., 1932. *Third report on the excavations of the Roman fort at Richborough, Kent*. London, Society of Antiquaries, 10.

——, 1949. *Fourth report on the excavations of the Roman fort at Richborough, Kent*. London, Society of Antiquaries, 16.

Butcher, S. A., 1977. "Enamels from Roman Britain". *In* (eds) Apted, M. R. *et al.*, *Ancient monuments and their Interpretations*. Chichester, Phillimore.

Caine, C., 1922. "The port of Ravenglass". CW2 xxii, 101-7.

Carattoli, L., 1887. "Perugia. Tombe etrusche scoperte nel Cimitero". *Notizie degli Scavi* 1887, 391-98.

Callender, M. H., 1965. *Roman Amphorae*. OUP.

Charlesworth, D. and Thornton, J. H., 1973. "Leather found in Mediobogdum, the Roman fort of Hardknott". *Britannia* iv, 141-52.

Cherry, J., 1963. "Eskmeals sand-dunes occupation sites". CW2 lxiii, 31-52.

——, 1969. Early Neolithic sites at Eskmeals. CW2 lxix, 40-53.

Collingwood, R. G., 1914. (With Haverfield, F. and Freeston, L. B.). "Report on the exploration of the Roman fort at Ambleside, 1903, with a preliminary report of exploration in March and April 1914". CW2 xiv, 433-65.

Collingwood, R. G., 1928. "Roman Ravenglass". CW2 xxviii, 353-66.

Collingwood, R. G. and Richmond, I. A., 1969. *The Archaeology of Roman Britain*. Methuen.

Corder, P., 1928. *The Roman pottery at Crambeck, Castle Howard*.

——, 1937. "A pair of fourth-century Romano-British kilns near Crambeck". *Antiq. J.* xvii, 393-413.

Cunliffe, B., 1971. *Excavations at Fishbourne, 1961-1969*. London, Society of Antiquaries.

——, 1975. *Excavations at Portchester Castle. Vol. I, Roman*. London, Society of Antiquaries.

Curle, J., 1911. *A Roman frontier post and its People. The Fort of Newstead*. Glasgow.

Down, A. and Rule, M., 1971. *Chichester Excavations, volume I*. Oxford.

Fair, M. C., 1925. *In* Proceedings of the Society. CW2 xxv, 374-5.

——, 1948. "Roman finds on the Cumberland Coast". CW2 xxxxviii, 218-21.

Fölzer, E., 1913. *Die Bilderschüsseln der Ostgallischen Sigillata Manufakturen*.

Fowler, E., 1960. "The origins and development of the penannular brooch in Europe". *PPS* xxvi, 149-77.

Frere, S. S., 1972. *Verulamium excavations, vol. I*. London, Society of Antiquaries.

——, 1977. "Roman Britain in 1976". *Britannia* viii, 356-425.

Frere, S. S. (with St Joseph, J. K.), 1974. "The Roman fortress at Longthorpe". *Britannia* v, 1-129.

Gillam, J. P., 1970. *Types of Roman coarse pottery in northern Britain*. Newcastle.

Groenman-van Waateringe, W., 1967. *Romeins Lederwerk uit Valkenberg Z. M. Groningen*. Nederlands Oudheden 2.

Harden, D. B., 1961. "Domestic window glass, Roman, Saxon and medieval." *In* (ed.) Jope, E. M., *Studies in building history*, London, 39-63.

——, 1967. The glass jug. *In* Biddle, M., "Two Flavian burials from Grange Road, Winchester". *Ant. J.* xxxxvii, 238-40.

Hartley, B. R., 1961. The Samian ware. *In* Steer, K. A., "Excavations at Mumrills Roman Fort, 1958-60". *Proceedings of the Society of Antiquaries of Scotland*. lxxxxiv, 100-10.

——, 1972. "The Roman Occupation of Scotland: the evidence of samian ware". *Britannia* iii, 1-55.

Hartley, K. F. and Webster, P. V., 1973. "Romano-British Pottery Kilns near Wilderspool". *Archaeol. J.* cxxx, 77-103.

Hawkins, 1885. *Medallion illustrations of the history of Great Britain and Ireland vol. II* (1969 reprint, eds. Franks, A. W. and Grueber, H. A.).

Hind, J. G. F., 1974. "Agricola's fleet and the Portus Trucculensis". *Britannia* v, 285-88.

Hull, M. R., 1967. The Nor'nour brooches. *In* Dudley, D., "Excavations at Nor'nour in the Isles of Scilly, 1962-6". *Arch. J.* cxxiv, 1-64.

Isings, C., 1957. *Roman Glass from dated finds*. Groningen.

Jackson, W., 1876. "The camp at Muncaster and certain Roman discoveries there". CW1 iii, 17-22.

Jarrett, M. G., 1976. *Maryport, Cumbria: Roman fort and its garrison*. CW Extra Series xxii. Kendal.

Jones, G. D. B. and Shotter, D. C. A., 1978. *Roman Lancaster*. In press.

Kilbride-Jones, H. E., 1938. "Glass armlets in Britain". *PSAS* lv, 366-95.

Liversidge, J., 1973. *Britain in the Roman Empire*. Cardinal.

Macgregor, A., 1976. *Finds from a Roman sewer system and an adjacent building in Church Street*. Archaeology of York, series 17.

Manning, W. H., 1976. *Catalogue of Romano-British ironwork in the Museum of Antiquities, Newcastle upon Tyne*. University of Newcastle upon Tyne.

McIntyre, J. and Richmond, I. A., 1934. "Tents of the Roman Army and leather from Birdoswald". CW2 xxxiv, 62-90.

Potter, T. W., 1975. "Excavations at Bowness-on-Solway 1973". CW2 lxxv, 29-57.

Richmond, I. A., 1936. "Roman leaden sealings from Brough-under-Stainmore". CW2 xxxvi, 104-25.

——, 1956. "Cote How Tower (16a) on the Cumberland coast". CW2 lvi, 62-6.

Richmond, I. A. and Birley, E. B., 1930. "Excavations on Hadrian's Wall in the Birdoswald – Pike Hill Sector, 1929". CW2 xxx, 169-205.

Richmond, I. A. and Gillam, J. P., 1952. "Milecastle 79 (Solway)". CW2 lii, 17-40.

Ricken, H., 1934. "Die Bilderschüsseln der Kastelle Saalburg und Zugmantel". *Saalburg Jahrbuch* viii, 130ff.

——, 1948. *Die Bilderschüsseln der römischen Töpfer von Rheinzabern* (Tafelband).

Ricken, H. and Fischer, C., 1963. *Die Bilderschüsseln der römischen Töpfer von Rheinzabern* (Textband).

Robertson, A., Scott, M. and Keppie, L., 1975. *Bar Hill: a Roman fort and its finds*. BAR 16.

Robinson, H. Russell, 1975. *The armour of Imperial Rome*. London.

Rogers, G. B., 1974. *Poteries Sigillées de la Gaule Centrale* I (Gallia Supplement 28).

Rogers, G. and Laing, L. R., 1966. *Gallo-Roman Pottery from Southampton*. Southampton City Museums Publications 6.

Webster, G., 1969. *The Roman Imperial Army*. London.

Webster, J., 1975. Objects of bronze and silver. *In* Cunliffe, B., 1975, 198-214.

Wheeler, R. E. M., 1930. *London in Roman Times*. London Museum Catalogue 3.

———. 1932. (With Wheeler, T. V.) *Report on the excavation of the prehistoric, Roman and post-Roman site at Lydney Park, Gloucestershire*. London, Society of Antiquaries, 9.

Whiting, W., Hawley, W. and May, T., 1931. *Report on the excavation of the Roman cemetery at Ospringe, Kent*. London, Society of Antiquaries.

Wild, F., 1975. The samian ware. *In* Robertson, A. S., *Birrens (Blatobulgium)*, 141-76.

Wild, J. P., 1970. "Button and loop fasteners in the Roman provinces". *Britannia* i, 137-55.

CHAPTER III

THE ROMAN FORT AT WATERCROOK

INTRODUCTION

THE FORT AT WATERCROOK lies on the southern edge of Kendal, in the central reaches of the Kent valley. It is overlooked by ridges of high ground on both the east and west sides, and occupies a low and apparently vulnerable promontory of gravel and alluvium in the valley bottom (Fig. 53). In fact, its position was well chosen. A sharp loop in the river affords protection on three sides of the fort (the only ox-bow curve of this sort between the estuary and the tributaries to the north of Kendal) and the natural communications are good in nearly every direction. The fort was thus well placed to control the native population along the coastal lowlands of southern Cumbria and northern Lancashire and to counter the possibility of sea-borne attack from Morecambe Bay. Indeed, it is likely to have been just one of a series of military installations, indicated by numerous finds of coins and other material, along the southern coast of Cumbria: a fort at Watercrook, in conjunction with others on the Cartmel and Furness peninsula, would have made good strategic sense in what is likely to have been a densely settled region.

The full extent of the Roman road network (Fig. 52) is still far from clear. The principal route northwards passed well to the east of Watercrook, heading from Lancaster via the Lune valley to Burrow in Lonsdale and Low Borrow Bridge, and then down the Eden valley to Carlisle (Margary 1973, road 7c). The Middleton milestone (*RIB* 2283; Fig. 52) records a distance of 53 miles, which is best interpreted as a measurement from Carlisle, emphasising the northern connections of this route. It was a carefully constructed trunk road, between 6 and 7 m in width, and in places founded upon a corduroy of brushwood (Ewbank 1960; Macadam 1964). At least two *diverticula* left it, to connect with Watercrook and the south-western Lake District. One road began at Low Borrow Bridge in the Tebay gorge and followed an upland course over Whinfell before descending towards Kendal along the valley of the river Mint (Wilson 1884). Its precise route in the vicinity of the Kent valley is not known but it is generally assumed to have passed to the east of Kendal Castle on its way to Watercrook. The other *diverticulum* (Villy 1937) probably provided a link road between the fort at Burrow in Lonsdale and Watercrook. Its course is established only as far as Lupton, a distance of some five miles; but it is reasonably certain that its objective was the fort at Watercrook, choosing a route through Hincaster (where a Roman site, probably of military origin, is attested: Potter 1975) and then up the Kent valley.

The only other road associated with Watercrook is indicated by the slight traces of an *agger* that follows a course north-westwards from the fort. It has been traced along the side of the valley to the west of Kendal (J. Marsh, *pers. comm.*), after which it swings with

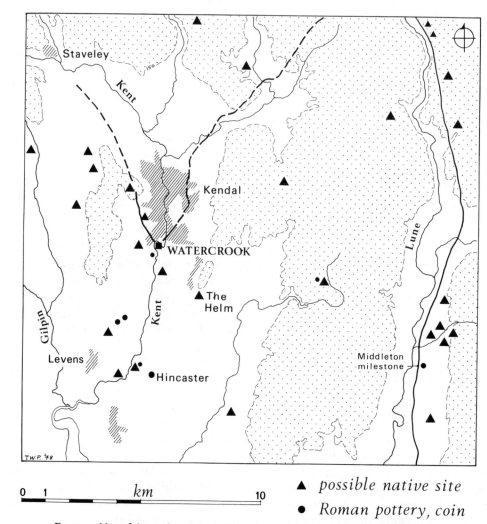

FIG. 52. – Map of sites and roads in the Watercrook area. Land above 150 m is stippled.

the low ground towards Staveley. The road then presumably headed for Ambleside, but details of its course have yet to be identified.

The surviving elements of the road network indicate, therefore, that Watercrook, if peripheral to the main trunk roads, was nevertheless the centre of a comprehensive system of local communications; there was ready access in nearly every direction. Unfortunately, we cannot yet comment in equivalent detail about the distribution of settlement in the Watercrook region: the data are still sparse and haphazardly collected. That this region of fertile lowland was densely inhabited in the Roman period is the clear implication from surveys in the adjacent areas both of Dalton (6 km north of Carnforth) and of Kirkby Lonsdale. Fieldwork in these parishes has revealed a pattern of small homesteads, distributed along the sides of the valleys where farmers could exploit both the alluvial fill laid down by the rivers and the adjacent upland pasture. East of Kirkby Lonsdale, Lowndes (1963) identified six such farmsteads within an area of 150 acres: we cannot assume that all were occupied at the same time but they do indicate a high density of settlement. One site, at Eller Beck, was tested by excavation and proved to consist of a rectangular enclosure, measuring some 100×38 m; there were two phases of building and pottery of the third and fourth centuries (Lowndes 1964). Other comparable sites have been identified all the way up the Lune valley, with a marked cluster in the region of Middleton (Fig. 52). Similarly there is a scatter of farms within the vicinity of Watercrook, again mostly located at the junction between the lowland and upland. That the known distribution is far from representative seems clear enough but it is worth emphasising that the majority of these sites are on the whole quite small and should mostly be interpreted as farms. The principal exception is the Helm (alternatively called Castlesteads), a complex of earthworks which straddle a low but steep-sided hill, 2 km to the south-east of Watercrook (Fig. 52). There is a double ditch and rampart system to the north (the most accessible side the hill) and a single rampart to the south. The east and west sides lack any obvious signs of defences. The area enclosed is small – about 1100 m² – but there is no reason to doubt that this was a hillfort, one of the few examples to be found in north-west England. There is, however, no dating evidence and either a pre- or a post-Roman context is possible (Collingwood 1908; RCHM 1936, 181-2).

Roman material, particularly pottery and coins, is represented on these sites in only a very meagre way, so that an abundance of Roman finds would tend to suggest rather different processes at work. In the Hincaster/Levens area, 4-5 km to the south of Watercrook, considerable quantities of Roman finds have been made. Just to the north of Hincaster (whose name is suggestive of Roman activity), motorway construction brought to light large quantities of second-century samian, ranging in date from Hadrian to c. 200 (Potter 1975). There are also finds of coins from Levens (J. Marsh, *pers. comm.*) and, in Levens Park, a complex sequence of features of prehistoric, Roman or early medieval date (Sturdy 1972, 1973). The long-lived tradition that Levens was the site of a circular temple to Diana appears to have little factual evidence to support it: but there is Roman material from the area (much of it from still unpublished excavations by Sturdy), including a very fine carved jet figure, seated and in a pose of mourning. This is supposed to have been found with a coin of c. 330 (Munby 1975). Taken together, the volume of Roman finds from the Hincaster/Levens region certainly is hard to explain purely in terms of native settlement: this concentration is much more likely to reflect Roman activity. What form this activity took – religious or military, or probably both – is impossible to decide without further data. In a strategic sense, Hincaster would have been as appropriate a setting for a fort as Watercrook itself, and it is not unlikely that a fortlet or signal station was placed there. What is certain is that we should not see the fort and *vicus* at Watercrook in isolation from these other sites, for its *territorium* was without doubt thickly settled.

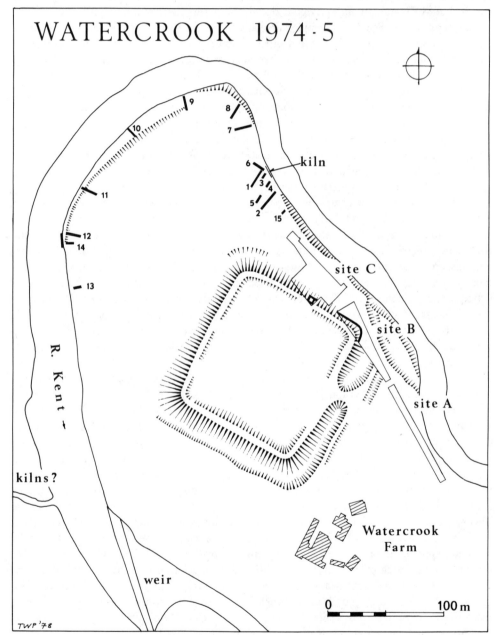

FIG. 53. – Plan of the Watercrook peninsula showing the areas excavated 1974-5. Based on a new survey by RCHM.

We may now turn to the site of Watercrook itself and examine briefly the previous discoveries made there. The antiquarian references, which extend as far back as the seventeenth century, have been gathered in three valuable syntheses, those of W. G. Collingwood (1908), R. G. Collingwood (1930) and Eric Birley (1957). All these quote the account of Horsley (1732) who observed that "the ramparts of the fort are very discernible, and there is a faint appearance of the ditch, though now much levelled." He adds that the site was under cultivation, which revealed "stones and pieces of Roman brick . . . in abundance", and later goes on to say that "the town, I believe, has chiefly stood between the fort and the water on the west side; for here they still plow up cement and stones" – an important observation in that it still constitutes our only evidence for occupation (presumably civilian buildings) on this side of the fort. A much fuller description of the site is, however, to be found in the notebooks of Thomas Machell (1647-98), who was rector of Kirkby Thore and a keen historian. Machell's writings have never been fully published but they contain much of interest. For Watercrook he provides a detailed description of two buildings. One is the bath house, a structure with a stokehole, *tepidarium, caldarium, frigidarium* and cold plunge, as well as a semicircular *laconicum* placed on one side of the range. The precise location of the bath house is unfortunately not given, but W. G. Collingwood (1908, 105) tells us that the farmer at Watercrook had seen "underground cavities and the summits of arches appearing above the level of the ground" in the "shippon" (cowshed) and "at the corner of (Watercrook) House", and identifies these as the remains of the bath house. R. G. Collingwood (1930, 103) could not find these remains and there is no trace of them today; but it seems a very fair inference that Watercrook farm does cover the footings of the regimental bath house. The other building described by Machell consisted of three rooms, each 5 yards square, with a stokehole for a hypocaust at the north-east end. Machell locates this structure as being "near the N. Corner (of the fort) at 70 yards distance . . . , fronting and flanking with the N. East side of the great Romane fort." The difficulty with this measurement is that it places the building in the river, unless we assume that the traverse is orientated well to the north-west. Nor does this provide any very satisfactory solution, for the area to the north and north-west of the fort was thoroughly explored in 1974-5 and yielded no trace of Machell's building. The only structure which did come to light was the apsidal wall of what is probably a fairly recent lime-kiln (Fig. 83, Pl. XVIIIb), set into alluvial deposits by the river bank. Thus we must take it either that the building has been destroyed by the river (a very remote possibility) or that it lay much more to the west of the fort, reading "N. West" for "N. East" in Machell's description.

Apart from the record of three inscriptions (*RIB* 752-4) and various finds, the principal value of the antiquarian observations concerns the traces of what was probably a tilery, situated across the river to the south-west of the fort. The remains of a kiln are described both by Machell and later by Nicholson in the second edition of his *Annals of Kendal* (1861). There is no clue as to the date of the kilns but it is probably safe to assume that they belong to the Roman period.

The excavations of 1931 and 1944

The only two excavations to have taken place at Watercrook before the present work were two seasons by Colonel O. H. North, the second in conjunction with Mr E. J. W. Hildyard. In 1931, North (1932) cleared the north-west gate and traced parts of the wall, including the north corner of the fort. He also excavated a section across the ditch which he found to contain much building stone. The fort wall had been extensively robbed but its original width appeared to have been about 1·5 m, with a moulded plinth at the foot of the front face. The gate consisted of two square side-chambers, built of good-quality masonry blocks which, in the photographs, seem to measure *c.* 30×30 or 30×40 cm. The rooms were 3·15 m square internally and were separated by a roadway, 7·32 m wide. The central *spina* had been robbed out but is recorded as being just over a metre in width. The finds are collected together in a subsequent article (North 1934); they include a belt-plate of second-century type and a simple gold ring. There are no proper stratigraphic details but two sherds of the first half of the fourth century are recorded from the south guard-chamber, "under gravel, above stones". Whether the gravel represents a floor is uncertain, although the caption to one of the photographs (North 1932, Fig. 3) makes it clear that three floor-levels were identified. The question of fourth-century occupation at Watercrook is considered further on p. 180 below.

WATERCROOK

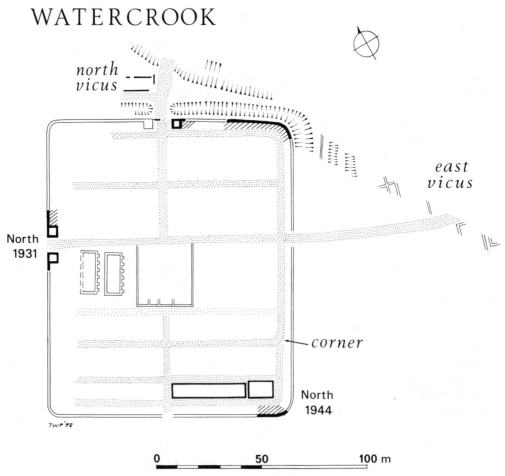

FIG. 54. – The Roman fort at Watercrook showing details from excavation, aerial photography and parch-marks.

The 1944 excavations (North and Hildyard 1945) focussed on the area at the southern angle of the fort (Fig. 54). Two sections were cut through the defences and a drawing was made of one of them: it is reproduced in a modified form in Fig. 55. The remains of a turf and clay rampart were found, with an *intervallum* road-surface behind. The *intervallum* road was sealed with a layer of black soil with Flavian-Trajanic material in it. Flavian pottery also came from the ditch in front of the rampart: this ditch was 6 m wide and had been deliberately filled with clean gravel. It was concluded, therefore, that Watercrook was initially occupied under Agricola, a view that had held the field until the present work demonstrated a rather later date in the Flavian period for the first fort.

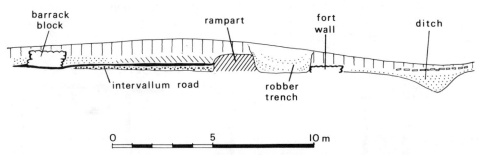

FIG. 55. – Defences at the south corner of the fort at Watercrook. After North and Hildyard (1945).

Subsequently the front of the rampart was cut back for a stone wall. Two phases were identified. One was represented by a clay and cobble footing from which all dressed masonry had been removed. That was later replaced by a wall set immediately behind the footing; this survived only as a robber-trench, full of discarded stone, closely paralleling the situation on the north-east defences (Fig. 67). There was no dating evidence for either wall.

One barrack-block was also partially explored. It was provided with separate quarters for the centurion, measuring 13·1×8·84 m; the block itself measured 35·8×8·23 m. The total length was 49·7 m. This is well within the normal range (Jarrett 1969, 163) and would imply an arrangement with ten *contubernia*, each 3·58 m in length, suitable for a unit of infantry. The walls were stone-built, but the footings, which stood three courses high, were set in yellow clay and substantially offset. It is possible, therefore, that two periods of construction are represented. No stratified pottery is mentioned, but both late Flavian and fourth-century pottery was found in the centurion's quarters. One jar is of Gillam's type 163, and has an internal groove: it should belong between 360 and 400. The building was also shown to overlie the layer of black soil that sealed the earliest *intervallum* road and must therefore post-date the Flavian-Trajanic period.

The fort plan

In 1887 a summer of exceptional drought brought up distinct parch marks in the grass covering the fort platform. A survey was made of these by Arthur Hoggarth and the plan published by W. G. Collingwood in 1908. They revealed the main elements of the street plan, together with traces of a road heading north-westwards out of the gate excavated by North in 1931 (the *porta principalis sinistra*). In 1975, similar drought conditions prevailed and for more than two weeks during the month of July the layout of the fort was visible as strongly defined yellow parch-marks. In addition to the streets, the two granaries and much of the *principia* were plainly shown, affording the opportunity for a detailed plan (Fig. 54). This has been supplemented in two ways: first, by features shown on a magnificent aerial photograph by Professor J. K. St Joseph (Pl. XI), taken in 1949 when the site was under cultivation; and second, by the results of geophysical survey, carried out over the area of the *principia, praetorium* and range of buildings immediately to the south (Blundell, Garside and Wilton 1974). An interpretation of the geophysical survey is shown in Fig. 56.

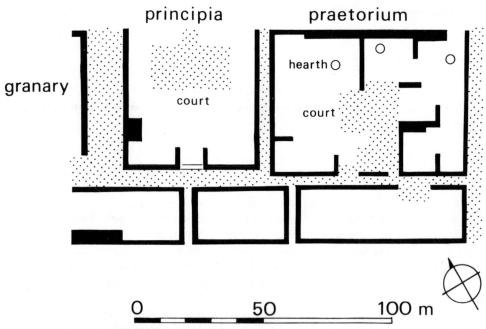

FIG. 56. – Watercrook: plan of the central range, based on geophysical survey. After Blundell, Garside and Wilton (1974). The stippling indicates gravelled or paved areas.

The fort was close to being square in shape, measuring 136×117 m (446×384 ft.) over the stone walls; this figure includes the turf ramparts of the first phase, whose fort was, therefore, marginally smaller, *c.* 130×111 m (426×364 ft.) inside the bank. The area of the stone fort over the walls is 1·57 hectares or 3·87 acres. This size is normally considered appropriate to a *cohors quingenaria peditata* (Jones 1975, 49-65), a unit of 500 infantry. By way of comparison, it is useful to list the sizes of other forts in north-west England:

Ambleside:	1·9	acres
Beckfoot:	2·75	,,
Burrow in Lonsdale:	4·75	,,
Caermote:	3·6	,,
Hardknott:	2·4	,,
Low Borrow Bridge:	3·0	,,
Maryport:	6·5	,,
Moresby:	3·5	,,
Old Carlisle:	4·5	,,
Papcastle:	6·0	,,
Watercrook:	3·87	,,

The great majority of these forts is clearly designed for 500 infantry, the smallness of their size excluding any larger units. Watercrook is closely comparable with Caermote and Moresby, although at neither of these sites have we details of the garrison history. The larger forts include Burrow in Lonsdale, Maryport, Old Carlisle and Papcastle, two of which (Maryport and Old Carlisle) have yielded evidence suggesting that they were designed for cavalry units (Jarrett 1976; Birley 1951).

The street pattern at Watercrook is fairly obviously the product of more than one phase. There is a distinct corner (most apparent on the aerial photographs) to the south of the main range of administrative buildings, leaving space for only one row of buildings in the *retentura* (Fig. 54). Since North and Hildyard (1945) identified the turf rampart in the south angle of the fort, as well as stratified Flavian-Trajanic levels, it seems likely that the corner incorporated in the street plan represents a contraction of the fort (or possibly a turn through 90 degrees, though this seems less plausible) at some point during its history. An Antonine remodelling of the *castellum* is a probability, given that there was extensive rebuilding during that period. If, however, we exclude the street associated with the corner, it will be seen that the *retentura* divides into two wide *insulae*, separated by the *via decumana*, together with two much narrower blocks, one of which has been shown to hold barrack accommodation. The wide *insulae* could have been employed either for two pairs of barrack-blocks or for workshops, storehouses or other buildings. The geophysical survey (Fig. 56) in fact indicates a row of three structures, fronting onto the *via quintana*, which resemble workshops. The *praetentura*, on the other hand, was divided simply into four *insulae*, averaging 21×50 m, spaces appropriate to four pairs of barrack-blocks, orientated *per scamna* as in the *retentura*. No trace of these buildings has been found either by aerial photography or by parch-marks.

The central range included two granaries, side by side; the *principia*, and what was presumably the *praetorium*. The granaries seem to have been laid out at a slight angle to the general orientation of the streets, and one is marginally in front of the other. Their plan was quite clear on the ground in July 1975, showing them to be *c.* 21×8 m. There were six buttresses along the south-east wall of both buildings but, unusually, none was apparent on the north-west sides, a feature unique in Britain (Gentry 1976). When allowance is made for the walls (about 1 m thick), the internal floor area would have been *c.* 230 m², a figure almost identical to those of Ambleside and Gelligaer. The *principia* measured about 28×26 m, only its north-east wall eluding identification. Its area of *c.* 730 m² is large for a fort with 500 infantry – Jarrett (1969, 159-60) suggests an average of *c.* 800-1000 m² for cavalry, *c.* 600 for milliary cohorts and 500 for quingenary cohorts – but it should be emphasised that our measurements are very approximate. There was little indication of any exceptional feature in the plan; the paving in the courtyard was plain both as a parch-mark and as a geophysical anomaly; the tribunal showed very clearly at the north-west end of the cross-hall; and the *sacellum* was also well marked. The *praetorium*, on the other hand, appeared neither on the air photographs nor as parch-marks: it may well be heavily robbed of masonry. Something of the plan was, however, recovered by geophysical means (Fig. 56). The indications are of an exceptionally large building, *c.* 39×26 m, with a paved court and several hearths; but we cannot assume that this structure consists solely of the commandant's house and it may be that it should be considered as two separate buildings.

To sum up, the broad outlines of the fort are reasonably clear, even though little excavation has taken place. It is unfortunate, however, that there is as yet no indication of the total barrack accommodation, which would tell us the sort of unit that was stationed at Watercrook. It is possible that there were as many as twelve buildings, in addition to the central range, in which case the fort could have held a *cohors quingenaria equitata* (Breeze and Dobson 1969): this view might be supported by the quite large quantities of horse-equipment from the present excavations. But the overall size of the fort is small for this type of unit and a quingenary cohort of infantry would have been a much better fit. It is a question that badly needs to be answered by future work.

The topography of the site (Fig. 53)

The fort at Watercrook lies on a small alluvial peninsula, surrounded on three sides by the River Kent. At its narrowest point, a line through Watercrook farm, the peninsula is 220 m across. To the north-west stretch some 9 hectares (22·2 acres) of low-lying meadows used today as high-quality grazing. To the south and east the ground begins to rise towards the side of the valley, where the village of Natland is to be found. There is, however, comparatively little change in elevation over the peninsula. The fort is still prominent as a rectangular platform, between 1 and 1·5 m above the level of the surrounding ground; and there is also a ridge of higher land immediately to the north-west. Otherwise the peninsula is relatively flat. Until the recent work by the Lancashire River Unit, there were traces of two older river beds, one to the east of the fort and another to the north-west: as we shall see in the section devoted to the fluvial history, much of the ground immediately bordering the river is composed of alluvial deposits laid down in the late and post-Roman times.

THE EXCAVATIONS OF 1974-5

It was originally intended that Lancaster University should conduct an annual training excavation at Watercrook to complement the teaching of archaeology as a degree subject. In 1973 a lease was taken on the land and one of the barns was converted into storage and office accommodation. Early in 1974, however, it was learnt that the Lancashire River Unit was planning an extensive programme to widen the course of the River Kent in the Watercrook area. This operation, already then under way in the upper reaches of the river, was intended to relieve flooding in the low-lying parts of Kendal, where disastrous inundations had occurred in 1954 and 1964 and on several previous occasions. The research excavation which had been intended for the summer of 1974 had, therefore, to be set aside in favour of a massive rescue campaign, funded by the Department of the

Environment. July and August 1974 saw the exploration of more than 250 m of the river bank on the east and north-east side of the fort. Nearly 3000 m² was examined, revealing a great deal of information about the eastern defences and the history of the *vicus* buildings beside the road that headed eastwards out of the fort. The following January this work was followed up with the excavation of 15 machine-cut trenches round the northern loop of the river. It was anticipated that this area would be largely barren of finds, and fortunately this proved to be the case. However, there was much of value to be learnt about the history of the river and the results were also useful in establishing the limits of the settlement.

Soon afterwards, it became clear that the River Unit's programme was well behind schedule and that there would be one more opportunity for a summer season. We elected to re-open the area round the north-east gate (site C) where many problems had been incompletely resolved in 1974. Four weeks in July 1975 were devoted to this work, enabling much better definition of the *vicus* building facing the north-east road and clearance of part of the fort gate. Time did not allow a complete examination of the gate but all the threatened levels were thoroughly studied and important new evidence for the history of the fort was recovered. Shortly afterwards, the River Unit began their work of widening the channel of the River Kent. They very kindly agreed to alter details of their intended scheme and to leave intact the east corner of the fort, but large parts of the other excavated areas have now been completely destroyed.

The publication of these results presented something of a problem. It was intended to follow the rescue work with a systematically planned programme of research-excavation upon the interior of the fort; consequently we decided to publish an interim report of the 1974 season, deferring a definitive account until later. The report (Potter 1976) was perhaps more thorough than we had originally envisaged but, with the 1975 interim (Potter 1977), provided a provisional interpretation of the results and made available some of the more important data. However, by late 1975, it was becoming rapidly clear that the research-excavation would have to be postponed. This was partly due to the fact that there were pressing rescue problems at other sites like Bowness on Solway and Ravenglass, and that the Lancaster team (now effectively a part-time rescue unit) was the only group available to deal with them. It was unquestionably wrong to continue with research work as other important sites were being destroyed. The other significant consideration was a financial one. The economic recession meant that there was little money available for research work and we could envisage only a season of two to three weeks a year with few funds to cover the overheads. Clearly it was impracticable to continue at Watercrook under these circumstances and the project was shelved. This made the full publication of the rescue work a high priority and in 1977 work began on the finds. The thorough nature of sections of the 1974 interim inevitably means a duplication of some of the data and a summary treatment of other categories of finds. Thus, the full details of the coins from 1974, and of the mortaria and amphora-stamps will only be found in the interim. Moreover, some of the general interpretations put forward in the interim reports have been modified in the light of full study of the finds.

The future of the research project at Watercrook remains undecided. Work in the interior is badly needed to supplement the observations made from study of the peripheral parts of the fort and to test some of the hypotheses. The matter is largely outside the writer's hands since he has now moved from Lancaster University. But the volume of rescue projects is presently declining and other teams are now available to carry out this work. We may hope that before long the Watercrook project will be revived and that the University of Lancaster will begin excavations within the defences.

The 1974-5 excavations: general remarks

The report is divided into four main sections. In the first the military features are considered, as far as possible by phase. This section includes sites B and C, and is followed by sections on the north *vicus* (site C) and the east *vicus* (site A). Finally the results of the January 1975 season are presented, the discussion focussing on the history of the river. The main site areas are shown on Fig. 53. Notes on the sections are gathered at the end of this chapter, together with a bibliography. References to finds, discussed in the next chapter, are quoted by inventory number.

Acknowledgements

The composition of the team and the general acknowledgements have already been covered in the preface to this volume. Here I should like to thank the landowners, K Shoes, for their generous cooperation; the officers of the Lancashire River Unit, particularly Mr R. V. Williams, Mr V. Harrison and Mr C. Stringer, who did all they could to facilitate the archaeological work; Mr R. A. H. Farrar, who produced a new survey of Watercrook; and our many friends in the Kendal group of this Society, many of whom worked as volunteers on the site.

The Fort Defences: Rampart, Walls and Fence

Phase 1: the turf and clay ramparts (Figs. 57, 65, 67)

The fort was initially provided with a turf and clay rampart, varying in width between at least 3·60m and 4·40 m. The full dimensions remain unknown since the front cheek was subsequently removed by the insertion of a stone wall. The turves, many of which corresponded with the Vegetian model of 1 × 1·5 ft., were made up either of a dark humic soil or of turf with a considerable admixture of clay. Both were readily available in the river valley. The rampart survived to a height of about 50 cm, made up of four or five courses of turves. The rear cheek was especially well preserved in the east angle (Fig. 65) where rather larger turves were used to revet the edge of the rampart. But, despite the larger area of rampart that was stripped down to the underlying subsoil (which, it may be noted, retained no evidence for an old ground surface), no real evidence emerged for an underlying wooden corduroy. The only indication of any timber elements were two widely spaced uprights in the east angle of the fort (Fig. 58, nos 1, 2), which may have served to provide some lateral stability. Within the body of the rampart, however, some slight traces of horizontal strapping were identified at one point in the long section through the defences at the west corner of site B. Here there were faint signs of parallel beams, some 20 cm in width or less, aligned longitudinally; but we could find no other evidence for strapping elsewhere in the rampart and it may be that these beams represent a very localised consolidation.

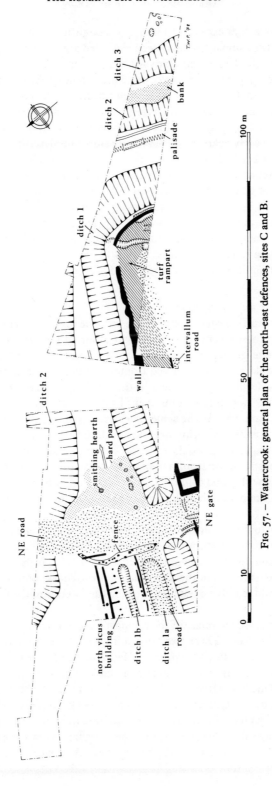

FIG. 57. – Watercrook: general plan of the north-east defences, sites C and B.

As well as the stretches excavated in 1974-5 along the north-east and east sides of the fort, the course of the rampart has also been identified at the north-west gate (North 1932) and in the south angle (North and Hildyard 1945). The description and section (Fig. 55) suggest that the rampart at these points was closely comparable to that on the north-east side and we can probably assume that its circuit mirrored the course of the stone wall. If so, it will have enclosed an area measuring c. 130×111 m. North and Hildyard (1945) were inclined to think that the rampart was of Agricolan date, the fort being founded in 79 or 80 during the early years of the northern campaigns described by Tacitus. Now that we have a much larger body of material from the site, it is clear that this cannot be so. Despite the fact that there is no stratified material from the rampart, it is evident from the samian (a sample of nearly 1600 vessels) and the coins (which total 100) that the initial period of occupation began in the decade 90-100. There were only two fragments of form 29, a type that went out of manufacture in c. 85, and a pattern of coin loss that is quite inconsistent with known Agricolan sites like Ribchester and Manchester. Unless the sample is exceptionally biased by its recovery from a peripheral position in the fort's topography, we can quite safely exclude a period of Agricolan occupation.

Phase 2: the heightening of the rampart

Throughout the north-eastern sector of the fort, the turf rampart had been reduced to a height of no more than 50 cm and subsequently buried beneath a dump of brown soil, with an admixture of gravel and cobbles (Fig. 65a, units 10, 11; Fig. 67, unit 11). This material, which could well have derived from a cleaning of the ditches, was in places as much as 60 cm in height. It was sealed in the south-west corner of site B by a layer of yellow clay, in which was placed a number of slabs of sandstone, forming a platform or walkway (Fig. 67, unit 10). At the same time the back of the rampart was extended by a distance of about a metre, covering over and sealing the primary *intervallum* road. The only significant variation was disclosed in the south-east side of site B where this dump divided into two parts: to the front a deposit of sandy soil (Fig. 65a, unit 10) and to the back a layer of yellow clay and cobbles (unit 11). There was no evidence for any revetment to the back of the rampart although this loose material must have been retained in some way.

It is interesting to note that the old rampart had been levelled to a height of 50 cm before this work of reconstruction was put in hand. Whether this levelling might reflect a short period of abandonment between phases 1 and 2 is unclear: but there is some slight evidence to support this idea in the distribution of the coarse pottery (Fig. 63) and it is a hypothesis that could readily be tested by work in the interior of the fort, and is considered further below.

The finds from the second phase of the rampart were not numerous overall but included some closely dated objects. There were two coins, one a *sestertius* of Trajan, dated after 103, and the other a fresh *dupondius* of Hadrian, minted between 134 and 138. In addition there was a group with 44 pieces of samian, most of them Hadrianic or early Antonine forms. One decorated sherd is dated 125-50, and there were two stamps, of Dagomarus (125-40) and Quintilianus (125-50). The Dagomarus bowl was found resting directly on top of the phase 1 rampart. There was no later Antonine samian in the deposit and we can probably assume, therefore, that the rampart was raised either right at the end of Hadrian's reign or in very early Antonine times. A *terminus ante quem* of the early

140s is likely since Watercrook was very probably evacuated when the move to the Antonine Wall took place, a matter which is discussed more fully in the chronological summary below.

The stone walls (Figs 57, 58, 65, Pls XII, XIIIa)

The fort wall turned out to have been very throughly robbed so that in places all that remained was a scatter of mortar and rubble. Even so it was obvious that more than one phase of construction was represented. The least well preserved section lay between the guard-chamber of the north-east gate and the east angle of the fort. All but two of the facing stones had been robbed out, but the course of the wall was quite plain as a spread of rubble and crumbling yellow mortar, bonded with a light aggregate. The one section where the facing stones (both of which were of yellow sandstone) remained *in situ* showed the wall to have been 1·20 m in width. Elsewhere the make-up of the footings was dispersed in a haphazard and random way, illustrating the thoroughness with which the stone robbers had done their job. All that did survive was a kerb of irregular pieces of limestone, laid along the inner lip of ditch 1, in two rows. This must have been intended to bolster up the front of the wall which was sited dangerously close to the ditch in soft and unstable ground.

At the east angle of the fort, both the wall footings and the kerb stones petered out. The point where they terminated (which lay directly beneath the corner) was marked by a shallow scarp, perhaps indicating the end of the construction-trench. This was seen to be turning through 90 degrees, as though for a sharp corner, but was then lost beneath the

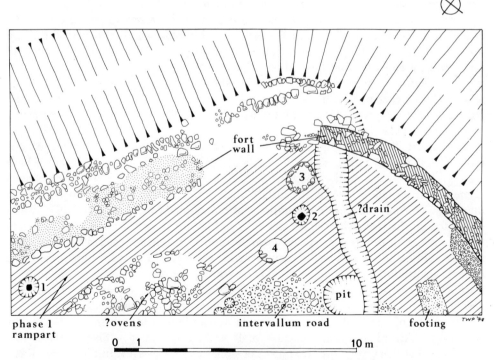

FIG. 58. – Watercrook: detailed plan of the east angle of the fort.

remains of a later fort wall and did not appear again. Similarly there was no trace of this type of footing further to the south. Instead the line was taken up by a wall of quite different construction, much better preserved. The surviving remains consisted of a concrete and rubble core, standing some 60 cm in height and 70-75 cm in width. The facing comprised four courses of very roughly dressed masonry, made up largely of small and irregular blocks and other filling material (Pl. XIIb). The stone was bonded in a hard grey-white concrete with a heavy aggregate, a quite different mortar from the one used for the north-east wall. At the corner of the fort this core terminated quite abruptly, but was demonstrably later than both the other wall footing and a drain (discussed in detail below). The drain seems to have been filled by the early Antonine period, thus providing a *terminus post quem* for the wall. This date is corroborated by the evidence from the north-east gate where the guard-chamber, described below, was built with an identical type of mortar and in a masonry technique similar to the later fort wall. As we shall see, the construction of the guard-chamber can be dated to the mid-late second century. We may conclude, therefore, that substantial new sections of the fort defences were built at this time, although this work did not extend to the stretch between the north-east gate and the east corner. Similarly, the north-west gate and the adjacent parts of the fort wall were also left untouched, for here North (1932) found well preserved footings with an external plinth; there is not much doubt that this good-quality masonry belongs to the first period of the fort wall.

This still leaves unresolved a number of questions. We described the later fort wall as a wall core since it lacks any proper facing and, as it survives, comprises only a very narrow footing for a major defensive feature. Unfortunately the sections across the wall were in some respects ambiguous (Fig. 65a). On either side of the wall was a trench (Fig. 65a, unit 14), certainly cut through the primary rampart and probably through its later heightening. The bottom of the trench was filled with cobbles and rubble, as if forming a platform for an ashlar facing. However, this cobbling only extended along part of the wall core, terminating 6 m before the end of the wall itself. This trench was cut by a second intrusion (unit 8), whose date could not be established with any certainty. It may have been a robber trench or have been dug in the Roman period. Thus we cannot demonstrate the presence of any proper facing, nor are we able to explain properly the half-completed cobble footing flanking the wall.

Another equally puzzling question concerns the southern course of the primary stone wall. Since the surviving core is demonstrably a later feature, it follows that it should have been preceded by an earlier footing. As we have shown, the north-eastern stretch terminated in a shallow scarp at the eastern angle and could not be traced any further to the south. The only possible continuation was represented by a short length of clay and cobble footing, located inside the fort corner, 2 m from the later wall core. The footing, as Fig. 65a makes clear, was constructed when the rampart was heightened in late Hadrianic and early Antonine times. It would require further excavation to test the hypothesis but it remains a possibility. Alternatively it could be argued that the later wall has cut away all traces of its predecessor, an equally plausible possibility, or that the earliest fort wall was never completed. That this last is the likeliest explanation will become clear below.

The results of one further excavation need now to be considered, the section cut by North and Hildyard (1945) at the south angle of the fort (Fig. 55). They inferred from their work that there were also two phases of stone wall in this area. Initially there was a clay and cobble foundation, just under 1·60 m in width. Behind it was a robber-trench whose position implied a second wall, abutting on to the first. This arrangement is unique on the site – there are no other instances of two walls built one behind the other – and indicates yet another variation in the sequence of events. What explanation can we find, therefore, to account for these differences from one area to another? The key may well lie in the fact that, as we noted above, the fort does seem to have been reduced in size during its history (Fig. 54); a corner preserved in the road system is one of the clearest features on the aerial photographs and was equally obvious as a parch-mark. We might then suggest the following sequence of events:

Phase 1: turf rampart built c. 90-95.

Phase 2: construction of a stone wall in good-quality ashlar, c. 135-45. Probably never finished.

Phase 3: reduction in the size of the fort. Rebuilding of the north-east gate and part of the south-east wall. c. 150-170.

Phase 4: enlargement of the fort and rebuilding of the south-west wall. ? c. 270.

The only event in the sequence which has no direct dating evidence is the suggested rebuild of phase 4. However, it is worth noting that the bulk of North and Hildyard's finds (1945) belong to the period between c. 85-140 and the fourth century, and that Antonine and especially late Antonine material is rare, which supports the interpretation.

The fence lining the north-east road (Figs 57, 66)

An unusual feature of the phase 1 defences was the provision of a curved timber wall or fence along one side of the north-east road. In some respects it resembles the *clavicula*, a device widely employed in first-century marching camps to channel the attacker into an oblique approach towards the gate, so that his shield afforded little protection; an example is shown upon Trajan's Column (Webster 1969, Pl. XXIVb). Such *claviculae* always consist, however, of a rampart and ditch curved either inwards or outwards from the gate and, given the absence of these features at Watercrook, we must assume that the fence was designed more to demarcate the road from the ditch system.

The foundations for this wall began just beyond the outer edge of ditch 1 and extended for a distance of 17 m. For much of its course it ran straight, bordering the north-east road; then, 5 m from the end, it began to turn in a gradual curve towards the north-east. The detail of the construction of the timber wall was to some extent confused by the thorough nature of its demolition and by intrusive post-pits for the north *vicus* buildings. Nevertheless it was clear that it was mainly solid timbers, c. 30×30 cm, that were used, together with a few rather smaller uprights. These were bedded in a trench that varied in width between 40 and 80 cm, tapering towards the north-west. Its profile showed that it had been cut in two stages: first as a fairly wide trench with a depth of 50-60 cm and then as a narrower bedding channel for the uprights. In places the total depth was as much as 1·35 m (Fig. 66, unit 7). In the better preserved section, the post-footings in the channel were spaced at very frequent intervals, often with a gap of only some 30 cm between them; presumably the intervening space was then filled in with boarding above ground level.

Given the presence of this long timber wall down one side of the road, we might wonder if the eastern flank was left entirely open. It is certain that there was no timber wall along this side of the road, the only possible structural feature being a line of pits or postholes parallel with the outer edge of the inner ditch. There was, however, a strongly defined area of red-brown soil covered by a hard pan, with a distinct curved edge. This began some 10 m out from the road and then turned towards the junction between the road and ditch 2. It is possible that this distinction reflects no more than a coincidental variation in the subsoil between the silts and the gravel (which covered the area beyond the hard pan), but we cannot exclude the possibility that it formed the base of a turf rampart, flanking the south-east side of the road. Chemical action would then account for the formation of the hard pan. It is impossible to test this conjecture since, if the rampart existed, it was completely demolished before the construction of the smithing hearth and other features in this area: but it remains a possibility which would make good sense, given the alignment of the wooden fence on the other side of the road.

Turning to the dating evidence, we have a quite large sample of finds from the trench. Two coins, both issues of the period 268-73, were discovered in the top fill, but are to be discounted as strays, dropped during the occupation of the north *vicus* buildings. This much is clear from the fact that the pottery from the trench forms a tightly knit group of Flavian-Trajanic date. The samian was all South Gaulish except for a single fragment of Les Martres-de-Veyre, implying a date after 100. The coarse-ware consisted of types with parallels in the period 70-130. There was one piece of black-burnished ware, but this could well be a stray in a feature with certain later disturbance. We can assume, therefore, that this group of material (which included a complete cup: 198) was deposited in the early second century, probably in the first ten or possibly 20 years. Moreover, it is important to note that the material from the trench derives not only from the period of construction but also from the period of demolition: the complete cup, for example, was found in one of the post-sockets where it presumably slipped after the timber had been withdrawn. This implies therefore that there was a phase of structural alterations in the Trajanic period, long before the fort was converted to stone-built defences. Indeed, it might well support the case for a period of abandonment in late Trajanic/early Hadrianic times (see chronological discussion below).

The North-East Gate and Road

Only part of the gate lay within the area threatened by the river-widening activity and it was just the upper levels that were likely to suffer damage. Consequently, we could not examine the whole gate complex and were unable to complete the strippage of the road down to subsoil. Our information about this area is confined very largely, therefore, to details of the east guard-chamber in its stone phase, together with some information concerning the carriageway.

The guard-chamber (Figs 59, 60, Pls XIIIb, XIVa)

The guard-chamber was considerably smaller than those excavated by North (1932), measuring 2·45 m square internally, as against 3·15 m at the north-west gate. The walls were especially thick, varying from 1·10-1·40 m, so that the total width was some 5 m. This brings the figure much more into line with the external size of the chambers on the north-west gate and is also close to the common standard of 15 Roman feet for these rooms (Jarrett 1969, 157). Nevertheless, the masonry technique used in the north-east gate is totally different from that of the north-west gate. As North's photographs make clear (1932, Figs 1-3), his gateway was built with good-quality ashlar, competently dressed and laid. The masonry of the north-east gate is in complete contrast to this. A few dressed facing stones were used in the north wall (Pl. XIVa) but they all clearly represent re-used material. Elsewhere the walls consisted of limestone rubble, set in a hard grey-white cement. There was no foundation-trench except for a bed of chippings and little attempt at an orderly arrangement of the stones: the only real exceptions were the back and east walls where the rubble was slightly pitched, in an arrangement reminiscent of herring-bone designs. Mistakes were also made in the layout of the guard-chamber, so that there were two lengths of footing in the east wall (evidently begun as separate building operations from each end) which did not quite meet (Fig. 60). This then was building work at its shoddiest, comparable in terms of technique and materials with the rebuild of the fort wall at the east corner, and reminiscent of the slovenly standard of construction on many of the Antonine Wall forts occupied in period II (which, following Hartley (1972), we should regard as dating to between c. 159 and 163). This late building on the Antonine Wall is normally attributed to auxiliaries rather than legionaries (Steer 1964), thus explaining its indifferent quality. It is interesting to note, therefore, that this rebuild at Watercrook is, as we shall see below, datable in general terms to the second period of the Antonine Wall and may well have been carried out by soldiers regarrisoning the fort after the final withdrawal from that frontier line.

The walls of the guard-chamber still stood to an overall height of 50 cm, and inside them was a valuable stratigraphic sequence, with a varied range of finds. A full inventory of the coins, pottery and objects is given below. There was no trace of any plastering on

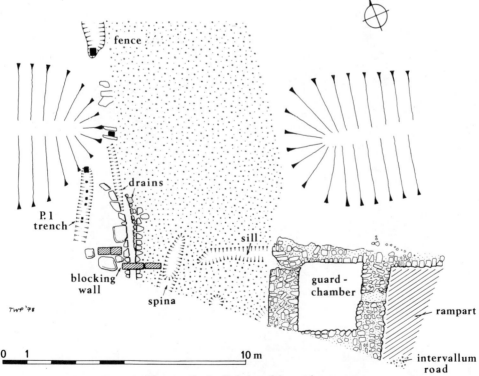

FIG. 59. – Watercrook: detailed plan of the north-east gate.

the inside of the walls, either over the upper courses or at foundation level. The original floor lay at the level of the subsoil (a red-brown silt), where there was a spread of yellow sand over one side of the room and three flat stones towards the centre (Pl. XIIIb). The stones could have formed part of a flagged floor or may have been intended as a hearth, though there were few signs of burning. There was no evidence for a doorway but, given the build-up of road-surfaces outside the room (Fig. 65b), it is probable that it was situated at a higher level so that one stepped down into the interior.

The subsoil was covered with 15-20 cm of grey-brown silt, flecked with some charcoal. In this layer and overlying the hearth stones was a slight depression, filled with white lime-like material. Behind it, to the south-west, was a spread of mortar. Presumably this represents an area where the cement was mixed for the pointing of the masonry. There was also another small depression, about 40 cm across, beside the lime basin: this contained a small quantity of slag, indicating some smithing activity. Except for four

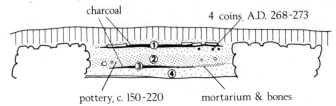

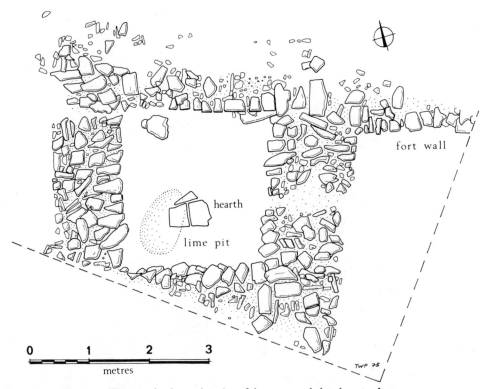

FIG. 60. – Watercrook: plan and section of the east guard-chamber, north-east gate.

groups of chain-mail, finds were not especially plentiful in this layer and it may well have formed more as a construction level than as an occupation deposit. Overlying it, however, was a spread of refuse (unit 3) which without any doubt had built up *in situ*. It comprised a layer of tread, rich in charcoal, and containing numerous objects. Amongst them in one corner of the room, was a smashed mortarium, surrounded by animal bones, as well as a horse-bit and one of three calthrops from the guard-chamber. This deposit was in turn sealed by a layer of brown silt (unit 2) which was fairly rich in charcoal on the west side of the room, but without any internal stratification over its 20 cm of depth. It is unlikely, therefore, to represent a gradual build-up of refuse on the floor, and may have been dumped or comprise a natural accumulation. Finds were notably less prolific in this deposit. The latest accumulation (unit 1) was quite different. The lower part of the unit consisted of a dark soil with much charcoal and a large quantity of objects. This was sealed by a thick spread of charcoal, over which was a haphazard scatter of small flat stones. These did not give the appearance of forming part of a floor, however, and may have derived from a collapsed roof. Structural evidence was otherwise confined to two vertical stones, possibly part of a hearth emplacement, and patches of gravel and rubble, laid to form a rough floor at the base of the level.

The overall collection of finds, listed in detail below, comprises a curious miscellany. They range from military objects (including scale- and chain-armour, arrowheads, a snaffle-bit and calthrops) to building fittings (a key and door strap) and kitchen equipment: cooking was evidently customary practice in the guard-chamber. A finger-ring, brooches, beads, a pin and buckles all belong in the category of personal apparel. Pottery was not especially abundant but, with the five coins that were found, gives a fairly clear idea of the chronology of the occupation deposits. The data are set out in Fig. 61. That the guard-chamber belongs to the partial reconstruction of the defences that took place in phase 3 is clear enough from the style of the masonry. As our discussion of the fort wall showed, this has a *terminus post quem* in the late Hadrianic or early Antonine period

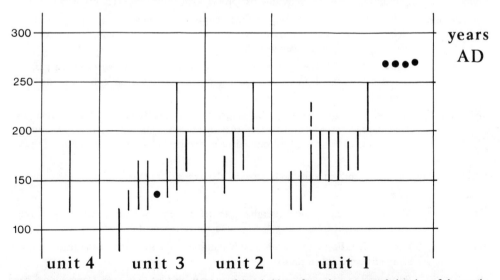

FIG. 61. – Diagram illustrating the distribution of dated objects from the east guard-chamber of the north-east gate at Watercrook. For the units, see Fig. 60. Circles: coins; vertical lines: pots.

and is most likely to have occurred at the end of Antonine Wall I or II. The bulk of the pottery from the guard-chamber supports this dating; it belongs predominantly to the second half of the second century, there being a distinct paucity of pre-Antonine forms. It suggests an initial date on internal evidence of *c.* 150-60, a figure that also would correspond well with the period of withdrawal from the Antonine Wall. Occupation evidently then persisted for the rest of the second century and probably into the early third century, unit 2 representing this period of activity. The difficulty comes in allocating a time span for unit 4. The four coins of 268-73 establish a clear fixed point and the separation of the guard-room stratigraphy into two distinct occupation levels might be taken to imply two periods of use, with a phase of abandonment between. Unfortunately the second and third quarters of the third century are notably sparse in closely dated artifacts. There are few vessels that are diagnostic of this period and the coin diagrams normally display a low rate of loss at this time. It is possible, therefore, that there was continuous occupation between units 2 and 4, which is not made apparent in the artifact record. On balance, we would be inclined to think that the layer of silt (unit 3) between the refuse deposits does indicate a period of abandonment; but we would hesitate to affirm this categorically.

The question of fourth-century occupation is discussed in the chronological summary below. We may note here that there is no evidence for levels of that century nor any fourth-century pottery from the area round the guard-chamber.

North-east gate, east guard-chamber: inventory of finds

Cf. Fig. 60 for the section. Illustrated objects include their inventory number in parenthesis.

UNIT 1: layer of dense charcoal and occupation debris

Coins: Claudius II (168-70); two radiate copies of Victorinus (269-71); Tetricus I (271-3)

Coarse-ware: Dish (220) of 160-200; beaker (221) closest to Gillam 170 (130-80), although variants on this form extend in date down to the mid third century; two scraps of colour-coat; amphora; grey-ware base.

Samian: Stamp of MARTIVS iv, *c.* 160-90. sherds of an East Gaulish Form 37 (12); cf. unit 2, below. Five sherds in Central Gaulish fabrics: two Hadrianic or Antonine, three Antonine.

Objects: Surgical probe (54); small bronze finger-ring (63); rectangular bronze staple (69); triple-barbed arrowhead; two calthrops; iron chain-links (142); T-shaped tumbler lock key (149); strip of iron from a door with a keyhole and pin for a hinge (132).

UNIT 2: layer of brown soil with much charcoal on the west side of the chamber

Coins: None.

Coarse-ware: Mortarium (224) closely resembling that from unit 3, below; dish (225), joining with a fragment from unit 3, below; scrap of colour-coat.

Samian: East Gaulish Form 37 (12), probably datable to the first half of the third century; scrap of East Gaulish samian, Antonine.

Objects: Bone pin (98); iron split-pin (134); two iron buckles (144, 147); green glass bead (182).

UNIT 3:   layer of charcoal and refuse

Coin: Sestertius of Hadrian (134-8).

Coarse-ware: Mortarium found in fragments but largely complete. Stamped LOCCI.PRO, a
              Mancetter potter whose work is best dated by the occurrence of his vessels on the
              Antonine Wall. c. 135-65 (226); jar (222) joining with a fragment from the rubble
              over the guard-chamber (150-250); dish (225) which joins with another fragment
              in unit 2 (160-200); sherds of black-burnished ware.

Samian: Form 37, Hadrianic or Antonine; Form 18/31, Hadrianic or Antonine; Form
              18/31, probably Hadrianic; Form 35 (?), Flavian or Trajanic.

Objects: Enamelled disc brooch (15); bronze (?) crest-holder (42); lead weight (77); amber
              bead (89); bone spindle-whorl (90); arrowhead; calthrop (119); two-link snaffle-bit
              (121); split-spike loop (125); iron handle probably used for suspending a cauldron
              over a fire (140).

UNIT 4:   grey-brown silt, flecked with charcoal

Coins: None.

Coarse-ware: Grey-ware jar (227); grey-ware cooking pot with a lattice design; amphora handle;
              nine small sherds, six in grey-ware, three in orange fabrics.

Samian: None.

Objects: Small T-shaped brooch (11); a catchplate of a brooch; thin bronze boss (49); blue
              glass bangle (186); plate from scale armour (34). There were also large quantities of
              chain-mail: one group of 77 rings (126), as well as three other smaller groups (126,
              127).

The gate (Figs 59, 65b)

As we indicated above, not all of the gate was excavated and the subsoil was only
located within the guard-chamber. We know little, therefore, of the wooden gate for the
fort of phase 1. The only feature of this period that was identified was a trench, some
45 cm in depth, at the west side of the gate. It ran between the inner lip of the ditch and
the turf rampart and held one substantial timber and a number of smaller uprights. Other
post-settings, packed with stone, were also located round the butt end of ditch 1 and
belong to the same period. Taken in conjunction with the wooden fence whose
foundation-trench began just beyond the main ditch, it would seem that the timber
elements were intended to provide a screen that continued right up to the gate itself.

Within the gateway, a total of four road-surfaces were identified, forming a wide
metalled carriageway. The section (Fig. 65b) suggests that only one more surface
remained to be uncovered before the subsoil was reached. There was little or no
constructional difference between the roadways, each of which was surfaced with a skin of
rammed gravel and cobbles. The central spina had been robbed out but its location was
quite clearly marked as a foundation-trench (Fig. 65b, unit 4), set into the gravel. Its
position indicates a width for each carriageway of c. 3·50 m. Late in the history of the
gateway, however, the spina was removed and the western side of the passage blocked off
by a wall (Pl. XIVb). The masonry used for this construction consisted of several large
blocks, all of them re-used, as well as other lumps of undressed stone. At the same time
posts were set into the centre of the reduced roadway and at the south-west corner of the
guard-chamber; they must have supported the new gate. There had also been a sill across
the gate, parallel with the front wall of the guard-chamber. Its position was marked by a

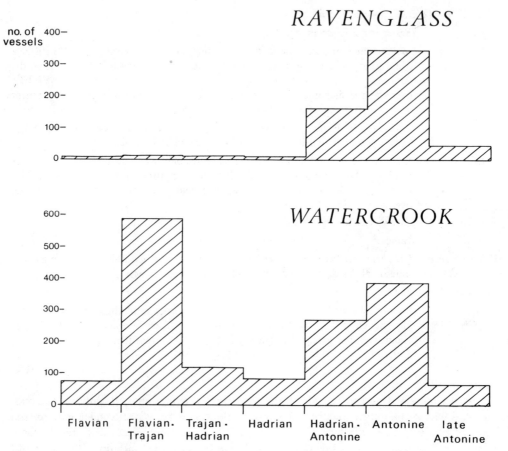

FIG. 62. – Histogram showing the distribution of samian from Watercrook and Ravenglass.

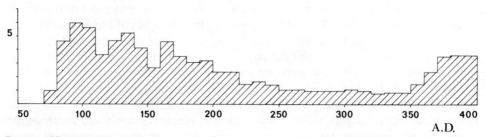

FIG. 63. – Histogram showing the distribution of dated coarse-ware from the military areas and north *vicus* at Watercrook.

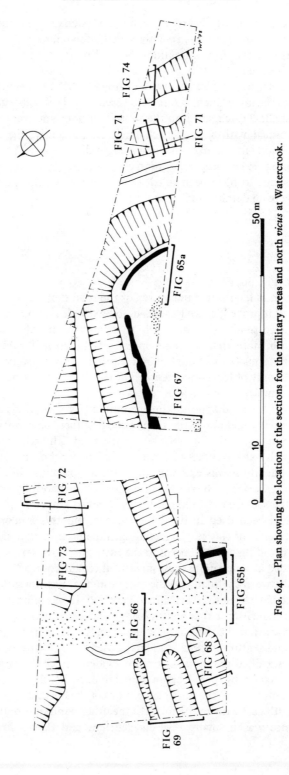

FIG. 64. — Plan showing the location of the sections for the military areas and north *vicus* at Watercrook.

shallow trench, some 20 cm in depth, from which the wooden or stone door stop had been removed (probably when the gate was re-designed). Unfortunately we cannot provide a date on internal evidence for these alterations, beyond noting that it was the last major building activity in this area.

The only other feature in the gateway was a drain (PL. XIVb), which ran beneath the west carriageway into the inner ditch. It disclosed three periods of construction. Initially it took the form of a shallow ditch, cut into the subsoil without any trace of lining: it may well have been furnished with a wooden channel. Subsequently, the drain was twice rebuilt in stone, the successive courses showing a slight divergence. The later and better-preserved drain was 65-60 cm deep and 20-30 cm wide, its stone facing resting on the natural subsoil. It seems to have been filled with rubble when the gateway was partly blocked, but there were no datable finds from its fill.

The north-east road (Fig. 66, Pl. XVa)

A stretch some 30 m in length was uncovered of the road that led out of the north-east gate. At the gate itself it proved, as we have seen, to have at least four surfaces. Fifteen m to the north these were reduced to three (Pl. XVa) and by the edge of ditch 2, it was difficult to distinguish more than a single spread of rubble and cobbling. The road, therefore, declined in terms both of quality and depth as it travelled northwards, which may imply that it was only of local importance. The carefully maintained road in the east *vicus* provides, for example, a considerable contrast.

The section through the road opposite the one building of the north *vicus* showed that the road had been initially laid out at the time of the first fort. This much was clear from its stratigraphic association with the fence beside the road. The road was nearly 4 m in width and built up with a sharp camber by means of a heavy rubble make-up, resting on a layer of clay. Subsequently it was extended in width to about 5 m by the addition of a second surface on the east side of the road. The extension was carefully built with a rubble underpinning, and the surface rendered hard with rammed gravel. In places, it appeared as though mortar had been used to bond the surface, but this is more likely to have resulted from the presence of clay in the metalling. Finally, a further skin of gravel was added to the road, spreading over the berm to the east: this, however, was a poor surface and cannot be regarded as much more than superficial repair work.

The relationship between the road and the outer ditch, 2, posed a number of problems and cannot be said to have been satisfactorily understood. It was quite clear that the ditch cut across the road, indicating either that a bridge was used to cross it (of which there were no traces at all) or that the road did not continue further north. Once the ditch was filled, in the late second century, passage can have posed no problems: but the existence of a route across the back-filled ditch was not really evident, since the stratigraphy at this point was badly damaged by post-Roman alluvial deposits. It was our impression, therefore, that the main route to the north lay not out of the north-east gate but via either the north-west or south-east exits to the fort. On the other hand, it is only proper to point out that the evidence was in many respects deficient and that a firm conclusion is excluded.

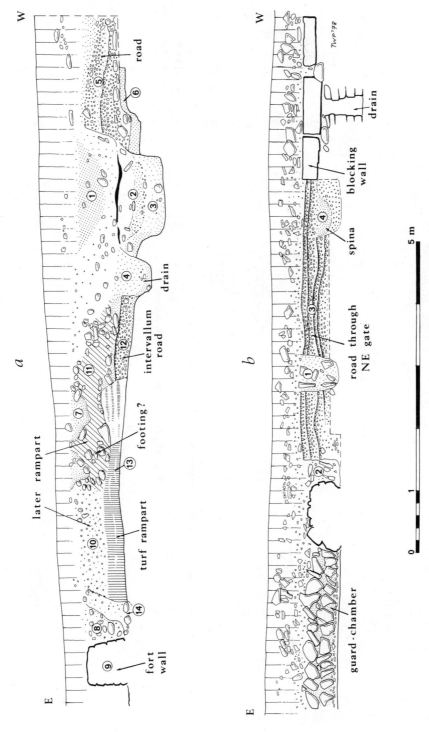

FIG. 65. — Watercrook: sections through (a) the east angle of fort; (b) the north-east gateway.

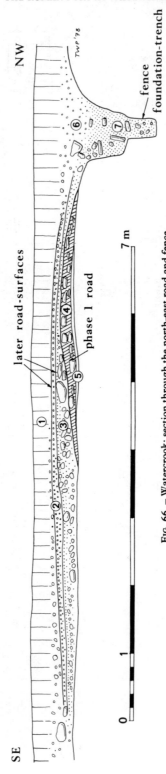

FIG. 66. — Watercrook: section through the north-east road and fence.

Intervallum *road*

The perimeter road of the fort was partially sectioned at the south-west corner of site B (Fig. 67) and was also examined at the east corner (Fig. 65a). It proved to have four main phases. The earliest road (unit 16) was founded on a thick layer of rubble and cobbles and surfaced with rammed gravel: it is contemporary with the phase 1 fort and was laid out in the lee of the rampart. This was partially sealed by the extension of the rampart, built in phase 2, which overlay a layer of grey silt, 20 cm thick. This deposit yielded a little late Hadrianic/early Antonine samian. Only the edge of the next road-surface (unit 14) lay within the excavated area and, as preserved, comprised just a very thin skin of rammed gravel and cobbles. This was succeeded by two more surfaces, both resting on thick beds of gravel. The latest road was bordered by a wall made of irregular lumps of stone, set in a deep trench (unit 9). It is possible that it formed part of a building but it is much more likely to have been a kerb, revetting the side of the road.

The East Angle of the Fort (Figs. 58, 65a, Pl. XIIa)

We have already summarized the details of the turf rampart and successive phases of stone wall at the east corner of the fort, and may now describe briefly the other features of this area. The most surprising divergence from the normal pattern was the absence of any convincing evidence for a turret in the corner of the fort, either in timber or in stone. This anomaly is apparently matched at the north corner where trenching also failed to locate any trace of a turret (North 1932). The features that were identified in the east angle included two postholes (Fig. 58, 1, 2) that preceded the primary rampart and may have been intended to tie strapping within the turf make-up. In addition, there were two later postholes (3, 4) cut through the deposits of the second phase of the rampart. These later postholes were both packed with cobbles and held substantial uprights, *c.* 25 cm square. They would thus have been large enough to have supported an angle turret (and appropriately situated in relation to the corner of the fort) but, in the absence of any matching pair, they cannot be regarded as evidence for such a tower.

The most prominent feature in this area was a long channel which began under the fort wall and followed a rather sinuous course towards the south-west, out of the excavated area. It was cut through the primary rampart and first *intervallum* road and appears to have preceded the extension of the primary rampart. It also cut through a rubbish pit (Fig. 65a, units 2, 3), filled with animal bone. There was one scrap of samian in this pit, dated *c.* 90-110. The purpose of the channel was not established with certainty. It contained no traces of timber uprights and was filled with mixed deposits of silt of varying colours, some rubble and a little clay. There was a considerable quantity of animal bone and some pottery, including four pieces of samian, the latest sherds being of late Hadrianic/early Antonine type. Its profile varied but over most of its course it consisted of a flat-bottomed, U-shaped trench. Its purpose could probably only be worked out by defining its full limits but, in default of full evidence, we may suggest it to have been a drain, perhaps cut as a preliminary to building work on this corner of the fort.

The only other feature requiring mention is a rather haphazard collection of rubble, tile and burnt clay, set into the back of the rampart, just to the north of the east corner. The feature had been very thoroughly demolished but traces of a stone revetment wall, creating a semicircular space, were observed, as well as distinct clusters of burnt clay and tile. There can be no doubt that these represent the remains of circular cooking ovens, of familiar type. There was some stratified material from this complex, including a poorly preserved coin of the first half of the second century, and samian of comparable date. The coarse-ware also comprised second-century forms, with a number of types in the bracket 120-180. Given the absence of mid-late Antonine samian, we can probably assume that these ovens went out of use by c. 140-50.

The Ditches and Other Elements of the Outer Defences (Fig. 57)

The north-east defences extended for a distance of 36 m beyond the fort wall, just beyond the effective range of spears and javelins. They included three main ranks of ditches (1, 2 and 3) as well as two smaller ones (1a, 1b), situated on the wide berm between ditches 1 and 2 on the north side of site C. In addition there was at least one palisade trench. In combination, these features make an impressive defensive arrangement which underlines the limited advantages of the peninsula position occupied by the fort. However, the defences also represent a complicated history of filling and recutting which is best demonstrated by discussion of each feature individually.

Ditch 1 (Figs 67, 68, Pls XVb, XVIa)

The inner ditch was separated from the fort wall by a narrow berm, only a metre or so in width. The ditch was presumably designed originally to accompany the turf rampart, but with regular cleaning of the loose gravel sides and the insertion of the fort wall at the front of the rampart, the berm became much reduced in width. Eventually it became necessary to support the wall by the insertion of a stone kerb along the lip of the ditch (Pl. XIIa). The ditch itself varied in width between 6 and 8 m and in depth between 1·60 and 1·90 m. Its profile was weathered and in places very irregular; but it still retained a well defined cleaning-channel over much of its length and an outer scarp that was marginally steeper than the inner slope. It is possible, therefore, that the original design was that of the *fossa punica*, where escape was impeded by the steeper angle of the outer edge of the ditch.

The ditch yielded a complex series of deposits. North and Hildyard (1945) had established that the inner ditch at the south angle of the fort was deliberately filled at the end of the first period of occupation (Fig. 55); but, on both the north-west (North 1932) and north-east sides, the sequence is different. Here the ditch appears to have been kept in use until the fort was finally abandoned and the ditch filled up with debris from the walls. To the east of the north-east gate the ditch section yielded a consistent picture, with a primary silt fill (Fig. 67, unit 6), cut by a second phase of ditch (unit 5). The later ditch was rather narrower – about 5 m in width – but its profile closely duplicates that of its predecessor (although it lacks a cleaning channel) and must have been dug while the line of the earlier ditch was still visible. The later ditch was filled with a dark silt containing a large quantity of pottery, animal bone (including numerous bones of red deer) and many objects of metal and other materials. This deposit cannot have accumulated while the fort was under maintenance and presumably represents a wash deposit that formed after the fort was abandoned. Similarly, the upper fill – a thick layer of gravel and rubble – is also best interpreted as a levelling-out of the ground at some period after the final evacuation.

The finds from the primary ditch were not numerous but included samian of the late Antonine period, as well as third-century coarse-wares (e.g. 246). There was also a coin of Gallienus from the side of the ditch. We can probably assume, therefore, that the

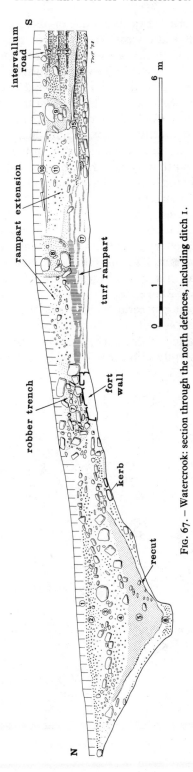

Fig. 67. – Watercrook: section through the north defences, including ditch 1.

recutting of the ditch took place at the beginning of phase 4, in the third quarter of the third century. The dark silt yielded second- and third-century material only, but the top fill contained pottery of the fourth century, including forms datable to 360-400 (e.g. 233): we can probably take it that the ditch was completely filled by c. 400.

To the west of the north-east gate, the ditch sections indicated two phases of recut. The first (Fig. 68, unit 5) was offset by about a metre from the original centre of the ditch, while the second (unit 4), which would seem from its dark fill to correspond with the recut described above, was centred directly over the original ditch. The upper fill was identical in its form to that on the east side of the gate and, to judge from North's description (1932), to that outside the north-west gate. It is interesting to note that North's section also yielded many red deer bones from the ditch fill, paralleling the finds from ditch 1. No red deer bones were found elsewhere on the site and they may indicate hunting activity that postdates the military occupation.

The west section of the ditch contained two sherds of Hadrianic/Antonine samian in the silt of the first recut and pottery and coins of the late third-early fourth centuries from the primary fill of the later recut. The coins included issues of Victorinus (269-71) and Tetricus II (271-3), implying that the silt began to form during or immediately after the brief occupation of phase 4. Above this silt was a layer with fourth-century pottery, extending down into the post-367 period. There was also a coin in fresh condition of Constantine I, datable to 320, as well as a coin of Claudius II (268-70) and a radiate copy of c. 270. As in the east stretch of this ditch, the rubble layer was, therefore, a fourth-century accumulation, apparently with a long period of formation.

fort →

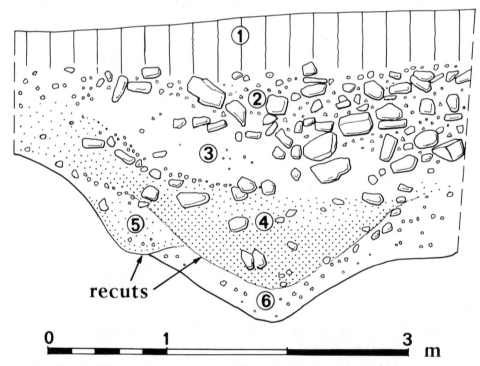

FIG. 68. – Watercrook: section through ditch 1 on the west side of the north-east road.

Ditches 1a and 1b (Figs 57, 69)

An exceptionally wide berm, 24 m across, was left between the inner and outer ditches (1 and 2) on the west side of the north-east gate and various steps were taken to protect this exposed flank. As we have seen, in phase 1 a curved trench holding timber uprights was constructed along one side of the road and there may have been a rampart on the other side. This arrangement was swept away with the remodelling of the defences in phase 2 and replaced by two small parallel ditches. These were laid out in line with the inner ditch (1), from which they were separated by a berm only 2 m wide. Ditch 1a was the larger of the two, being nearly 4 m across and a metre in depth. It had a shallow rounded profile, quite unlike the normal V-shaped military ditch. Ditch 1b was much smaller, varying in width between 1·50 and 2 m and between 0·50 and 0·70 m in depth. Its profile was also rounded rather than V-shaped. Neither ditch can have afforded much measure of protection unless it held some sort of obstacle such as thorn bushes or a series of stakes. No trace of any such feature was found beyond one or two possible post-settings in the north scarp of ditch 1a (shown on the section). But the proximity of the gate would have made such additions to the defences highly desirable and there was in fact certain evidence for an obstacle near the east angle of the fort, discussed below.

Dating evidence from these ditches was sparse. Ditch 1a was filled with two layers of silt and then sealed over by the metalling of a street (Pl. XXa), serving the buildings of the north *vicus*. In the silt were three scraps of Flavian-Trajanic samian and coarse-ware of the second century. One piece is of Gillam type 135, dated to *c.* 170-250, and should imply that the ditch was not filled up and covered by the road before the late second century. Ditch 1b was extensively disturbed by the post-pits of later *vicus* buildings which may have introduced some intrusive material. The bulk of the pottery was second-century in date, but two sherds of third-century type were also found (254, 257). These cannot, however, be regarded as securely stratified, and it is likely that both ditches went out of use towards the end of the second century.

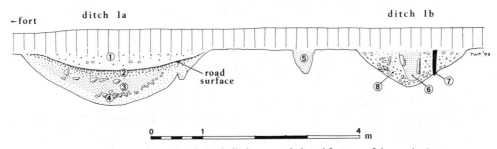

FIG. 69. – Watercrook: section through ditches 1a and 1b and features of the north *vicus*.

The palisade (Figs 57, 70, Pl. XVIb)

On the east side of the inner fort ditch there was a berm 8 m wide between ditches 1 and 2. This consisted of a flat gravel surface, cut by two narrow trenches. One was a very slight affair, 35 cm wide, and with little depth. No features were observed in its fill. The other (which lay more or less centrally on the berm) was altogether larger and more substantial, being 90 cm in width and 30 cm in depth. On the bottom of this trench, differential drying brought to light a series of stake- and post-sockets, distributed in two lines along either side of the trench. These features were only visible along part of the trench, and even here they had only just penetrated the subsoil; but there is no doubt that they formed some sort of obstacle, supplementing the main defences of the fort. The uprights were disposed so that larger timbers, up to 20 cm in diameter, were interspersed with smaller stakes of about half the size. Whether these two lines were contemporary or represent a replacement was unclear; but it seems most likely that they were built at the same time, forming two lines of hurdles, bound together at the top. This would have provided both stability and a more effective fence, with uprights projecting outwards at an angle.

Slight traces of a palisade trench were also observed on parts of the berm between ditches 1 and 2, along the north-east side of the fort. The trench was very narrow and survived only in short stretches where it had been cut into the subsoil. We can take it, however, that the palisade was not confined to the eastern angle of the fort. Unfortunately dating evidence was very slight, stratified pottery being confined to a few scraps of second-century coarse-ware and a mortarium, datable to 180-250 (258).

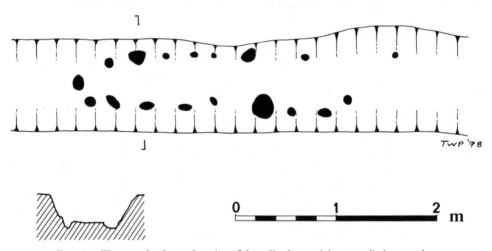

FIG. 70. – Watercrook: plan and section of the palisade trench between ditches 1 and 2.

Ditch 2 (Figs 57, 71-3, Pl. XVIII)

The second ditch of the defences was represented in the excavated areas by a short stretch on the east side of the corner of the fort and by a much larger length to the north. The join between these two sections of ditch was not examined and had probably been lost to river erosion. This is a more important *lacuna* in the evidence than at first sight might appear, since the two sections of ditch differed very remarkably in character. The more conventional length was that to the east where it had the usual V-shaped profile and, for most of its course, a square cleaning-channel. It approached 6 m in width and was about 1·50 m in depth. Its fill suggested two main phases in its history. The ditch was initially filled with a series of tips of gravel and brown loam (Fig. 71, units 7, 8) bearing all the hallmarks of a deliberate levelling. This deposit contained a scrap of Flavian-Trajanic samian and a few sherds of coarse-ware but a quite insufficient body of material to date the layer. It was subsequently dug to a V-shaped profile, without a cleaning-channel. The primary deposit in this ditch comprised a grey-blue clay, indicative of standing water, covered by a tip of gravel, an extensive layer of brown loam and then tips of gravel and stones. It would appear, therefore, that the ditch, once maintenance had lapsed, was left open for a time before being deliberately back-filled. The finds from these layers (Fig. 71, units 6-8) were again meagre, but there were eleven fragments of late Antonine samian

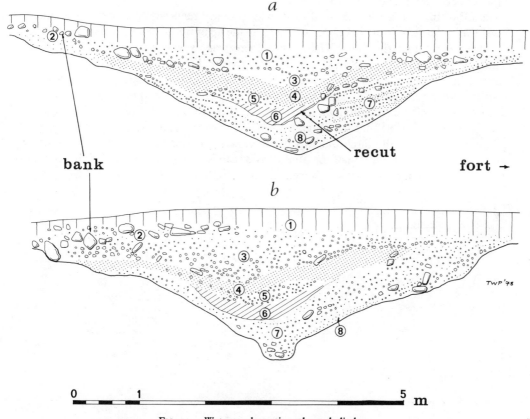

FIG. 71. – Watercrook: sections through ditch 2.

and coarse-ware of the same general period, implying a *terminus post quem* of at least the early third century for the ditch fill. That it had gone out of use by the late third century is evident from the fact that a pile of debris on the berm between ditches 2 and 3 had spilled over the top fill of ditch 2. This debris, derived from the recutting of ditch 3, contained a third-century mortarium. The recutting of the ditch 3 can probably be placed in the third quarter of the third century, at the beginning of phase 4.

The ditch on the north-east side of the fort was, as we indicated above, quite different in form. Its overall dimensions were never fully established but a long section at the north-east corner of site C (Fig. 72) showed it to be at least 11 m in width and more than 3 m in depth. It was cut down through the beds of gravel that underlie this part of the site, creating a shallow profile with, over much of its length, a steep (and, in places, near vertical) edge along the south side of the ditch. Only close to the north-east road did the sides become less steep. We can only guess at the purpose of this enormous excavation but the most plausible suggestion is that it was intended as a quarry for the large quantities of gravel needed in the construction of the fort. There were, for example, more than 1200 m of road which, at a rough calculation, would have required some 3000 m³ of make-up. Many of the floors must also have been laid on ballast, for which the ditches were the most expedient source. It is unlikely that a pair of conventionally designed ditches would have yielded all the building material that was needed and we can assume, therefore, that parts of the outer ditch were enlarged to provide the extra gravel.

The fill of the north-east part of ditch 2 was similarly remarkable. Apart from some gravel wash, the bulk of the lower deposits were made up of tips of charcoal, ash, iron slag and other burnt material (Pl. XVIIa). That there was extensive iron working in the vicinity is quite plain, a conclusion corroborated by the discovery of a nearby smithing hearth (Fig. 76) on the berm between ditches 1 and 2 (cf. north *vicus, infra*). These deposits were in turn sealed by more tips of gravel and brown soil and the top of the ditch filled with water-deposited alluvium, formed in post-Roman times on the floodplain of the River Kent. It is possible that the roughly V-shaped channel apparent on Fig. 72, unit 3, represents a recut of the ditch but this question was not resolved. It is worth noting, however, that there was a line of massive slabs of sandstone along the top of the ditch, parallel with this channel; they may have been intended to revet the edge of this feature.

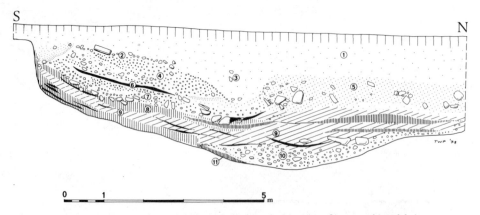

FIG. 72. – Watercrook: section through ditch 2, showing tips of iron-working debris.

The dating evidence for the infill of the ditch, especially in terms of the coarse-ware, is not full. A coin of Vespasian (wrongly provenanced in Potter 1976, 61, no. 46) was found on the bottom of the ditch and there was an issue of Hadrian (*idem.*, no. 45) in the middle fill. The coarse-ware consists in the main of second-century types, although a few forms are third century (e.g. 264). These later forms came, however, exclusively from the top fill and not from the tips of charcoal and iron-working debris. The samian is more informative. There were three useful groups from a section dug in 1975 (Fig. 73): one, from the upper part of unit 4, contained some 20 pieces, ranging in date from Flavian to late Hadrianic (one piece may be Antonine); the lower part of the unit had eight fragments, all Flavian-Trajanic; while the lowest unit (5) contained a Hadrianic sherd and 11 Flavian or Flavian-Trajanic sherds. These tips must therefore have been made within or at the end of the Hadrianic period, and included much rubbish from the phase 1 fort. This situation was more or less mirrored in the main section (Fig. 72) excavated in 1974. The gravel tip (unit 4) sealing the layers derived from industrial activity contained late Antonine material, while the deposits below yielded quite significant quantities of Flavian and Flavian-Trajanic pottery, as well as Hadrianic and Hadrianic/Antonine types. We can conclude, therefore, that the iron-working was primarily a late Hadrianic activity, and that the ditch was then left partially open until the ground was levelled in the first half of the third century.

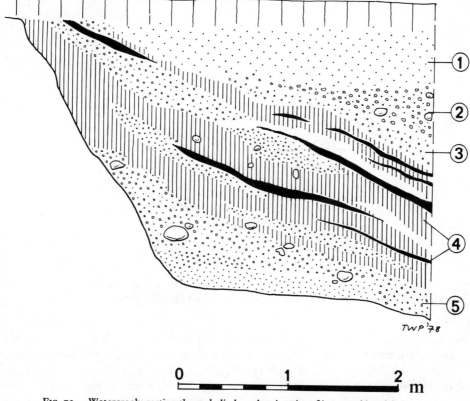

FIG. 73. – Watercrook: section through ditch 2, showing tips of iron-working debris.

Ditch 3 (Figs 57, 74, Pl. XVIIIa)

Only a short length, 8 m in extent, was uncovered of this ditch. It was separated from ditch 2 by a berm, 4 m in width, and was close to a complex of postholes belonging to the east *vicus*. The ditch represented two phases of construction. In the earlier period there was a shallow cut with a rounded profile: it was *c.* 4·5 m in width and 1·20 m in depth. It had been filled with gravel silts, separated by a layer of grey-brown silt. These deposits yielded a coin of Trajan; samian that included late Antonine pieces and East Gaulish wares of the early third century; and coarse-ware (276-280) of the second and third centuries. The latest coarse-ware forms included examples of Gillam 280 (210-320) and 226 (200-240). The fill suggests a gradual accumulation of deposits and we can probably assume, therefore, that the ditch was left open when the fort is likely to have been evacuated in the early third century and began slowly to silt up. A tip of charcoal (Fig. 74, unit 9) suggests some activity during this period, however.

Subsequently the ditch was recut. Its replacement was a much slighter obstacle, being only 3·20 m in width and 1 m in depth. It was V-shaped in profile and aligned along the western edge of its predecessor. The spoil from this excavation was heaped up on the berm between ditches 2 and 3, spilling out over the back-fill of ditch 2. This bank yielded a fragment of a third-century mortarium, suggesting that this recut belongs to the regarrisoning of the fort in phase 4, the later third century.

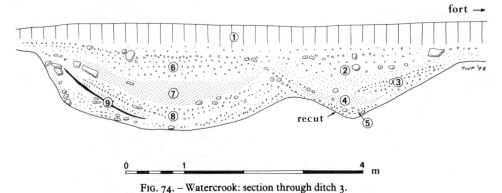

FIG. 74. – Watercrook: section through ditch 3.

The Military Area: Chronological Discussion and Implications

Phase 1

That the earliest fort at Watercrook was founded in the last decade of the first century seems clear enough: it is a conclusion based on a sample of more than 1500 samian vessels, 100 coins and a large quantity of coarse pottery. Both the pattern of coin loss – a modest volume of Flavian issues, followed by a very strong showing under Trajan – and the near-absence of samian form 29 (there are only two fragments) point to a post-Agricolan foundation, as does the coarse-ware. Thus Watercrook falls into line with other Lake District forts, at none of which can we demonstrate occupation much before 90-100. We can probably assume therefore that most of Cumbria was unoccupied by the Roman Army during the northern advance of Agricola, with the exception of the Lune and Eden valleys (cf. Chap. VII). Indeed, Tacitus (*Agricola* 20) implies that a treaty was made with the tribes of this region: "And when he (Agricola) had achieved sufficient by striking terror into the enemy, he turned to clemency and held out allurements of peace." Not until the retreat from Scotland in the late 80s was the region brought under formal Roman control with a regular garrison.

The duration of the first fort is more difficult to decide. It is perfectly possible to argue that occupation continued without interruption into the Hadrianic period, when the defences were remodelled in stone. The coins would support this case and there is a quite large volume of pottery dating to *c.* 100-130. On the other hand, there are hints of an interruption. The fence beside the north-east road, for example, was demolished and its trench filled, at a date closer to 100 than 120. Similarly, the inner ditch may have been allowed to silt up at this time, since it was demonstrably recut over part of its course and there was Hadrianic/early Antonine samian in the primary silt of the new ditch. Ditch 2 may also have been deliberately filled, while at the south corner of the fort North (1932) found that the inner ditch had been completely back-filled with a dump of gravel and loam that contained nothing later than the Flavian period. In addition the first *intervallum* road was also allowed to accumulate a layer of dark silt over its surface and the turf rampart was at some point demolished to a height of only 50 cm. This quite extensive catalogue can be further supplemented by the statistics for the samian (Fig. 62), which show a pronounced low in the Trajanic-Hadrianic period, and by a less conspicuous but noticeable fall in the breakage of coarse-ware (Fig. 63). The cumulative evidence is such, therefore, that we might well postulate a substantial reduction in the garrison (perhaps to a caretaker force) or even a break in occupation (preceded by a deliberate demolition) for perhaps a couple of decades in the early part of the second century. Such a view would not be inconsistent with what we know of the history of other neighbouring sites. At Ambleside, for example, the late Flavian fort (probably founded about the same time as Watercrook: Hartley 1966, 12) was completely redesigned in the Trajanic/Hadrianic period (Collingwood 1915, 1916, 1921), probably after a break in occupation. At Lancaster too, recent work has indicated a brief evacuation at the end of the first phase (Potter *in* Jones and Shotter 1978), followed by Trajanic rebuilding (*RIB* 604). Similarly at Maryport (Jarrett 1976) the finds of this period seem to fall into two groups, one of the late first century and the other of the reign of Hadrian, while there may be a similar sequence at Kirkby Thore (Charlesworth 1964). It is unfortunate both that these inferred fluctuations in the garrisons are so imprecisely defined and that the broader history of Roman Britain at this time is equivalently ill-documented. Frere (1974, 143) cites evidence for a "serious setback" about 105 and we know that there was fighting at the beginning of Hadrian's reign. But overall we have only a very patchy idea of the events of the period. Certainly it was attended by troop redeployments, as Birley (1953a) and others have made clear, in part consequent upon the final phases of the withdrawal from Scotland, datable to the early years of the second century (Hartley 1972). It would not, therefore, be surprising to find these reflected in the history of some of the north-western forts, although on what scale is very much a matter of conjecture.

Phase 2

The events of phase 2 can on the whole be quite closely dated and reveal a remarkable consistency in the evidence. Only for the earliest fort wall is there a scarcity of data, although there is no doubt that it belongs to this period since its partial rebuild is quite firmly dated to phase 3. The other structural modifications belonging to phase 2 include the refurbishing of the rampart, the laying of a new *intervallum* road, the construction and filling of a drain in the east corner of the fort and the recutting of at least one stretch of the inner ditch and probably ditch 2. There was also a considerable amount of iron working (conceivably associated with the new phase of building activity) whose debris was dumped into part of the quarry ditch outside the north-eastern gate. As we have seen, all these events in the history of the site yielded groups of samian (and in some cases coins) which terminate in the late Hadrianic and early Antonine period. The reconstruction of the rampart, for example, sealed samian stamps of Dagomarus (125-140) and Quintilianus (125-150) as well as a fresh coin minted between 134 and 138. The destroyed remains of some rampart ovens may also be associated with this building activity since the datable finds terminate in the bracket 140-50.

We may assume, therefore, that the first stone fort was being built *c.* 140, about the time that Lollius Urbicus was conducting the campaigns in Scotland that led to the building of the Antonine Wall. It is satisfactory to note that both the samian and coarse-ware histograms show appropriate peaks at this time (Figs 62, 63). Similarly the coin data would also not be inconsistent with increased activity at the beginning of Antoninus Pius's reign (Fig. 124). What then were the consequences of the victories of Lollius Urbicus in 142-3, when commemorative coins were issued? In the discussion of the fort wall, we observed that it is possible that the south-eastern stretch may never have been completed. Equally, there is no evidence at all to show that the gate of phase 3 was ever preceded by an earlier stone-built structure and we might well assume that it had never been started. In sum, there are pointers towards a conclusion that the first stone fort at Watercrook was only partially completed. We might very reasonably infer, therefore, that the unit was called away to share in garrison duties in the new frontier zone.

There is some evidence to support this conjecture in the distribution of samian stamps. Hartley (1972) has used this approach very effectively to demonstrate that Hadrian's Wall was largely abandoned while the Antonine frontier was in existence: the same is true for many of the hinterland forts, south of Hadrian's Wall. That Watercrook should be numbered amongst the forts that were evacuated seems clear from the fact that, of the 21 stamps from the site, only one (Quintilianus) occurs on the Antonine Wall. Ravenglass, on the other hand, was demonstrably still held at this time, as we saw in Chap. I. By way of further corroboration, we may also note the relative differences between the Hadrianic/Antonine and Antonine columns in the samian histograms for Watercrook and Ravenglass: in a comparative sense, Watercrook has yielded far less Antonine samian than Ravenglass (Fig. 62), a feature that would be readily explained by a twenty-year gap in the occupation. Similarly, there is a comparable drop in the volume of early Antonine coarse-ware (Fig. 63). In short, all these factors in combination would seem to provide a good case for arguing a partial or total evacuation of Watercrook during the period of the Antonine Wall, a matter that now requires testing by excavation of the interior of the fort.

Phase 3

The principal building event of this period involved the completion and reconstruction of the fort wall at the east angle and along the south-east side, together with the building of the north-east gate. We may also suggest that it is to this period that the reduction in the fort's area should be assigned, although this is not yet capable of proof. The best dating evidence for the beginning of phase 3 came from the east guard-chamber of the north-east gate. The bulk of the pottery from successive layers belonged to the second half of the second century, with a few forms of third-century date. There was also a shattered mortarium from the lowest occupation deposit of a type found on the Antonine Wall, and dated *c.* 135-65. Late Hadrianic and early Antonine material was, on the other hand, very poorly represented. Thus, there is nothing inconsistent with a date in the range 150-170 for the beginning of this period.

The chronology of the later occupation of the Antonine Wall has seen an extensive debate in recent years (Frere 1974, 179-81). But it is now generally agreed that there was an initial withdrawal between *c.* 155-9, conventionally explained by a Brigantian revolt, followed by a brief regarrisoning of some of the forts on the Antonine Wall and in lowland Scotland between *c.* 159-65 (Hartley 1972). The final abandonment of the Antonine frontier probably came in the governorship of Calpurnius Agricola (*c.* 163-6) whose building inscriptions indicate considerable activity at forts on and to the south of Hadrian's Wall (Fig. 147) including Hardknott (*RIB* 793) and Ribchester (*RIB* 589). We can probably assume, therefore, that Watercrook was re-occupied in *c.* 155 or in *c.* 165, either being possible on the evidence available.

What is much less easy to determine is the history of the garrison in the later second and first half of the third century. This is principally because no results are yet available from the interior of the fort, but it is a situation exacerbated by a shortage both of closely dated pottery forms and of coinage in the period *c.* 220-60. The only useful sequence from inside the fort comes from the east guard-chamber of the north-east gate, where occupation appears to have continued unbroken down to at least 220. There may then have been a break although we cannot really be certain. The ditches on the other hand imply a rather more drastic level of interruption. Both the inner and outer ditches (1 and 3) appear to have been allowed to silt up from early in the third century so that recutting became necessary at the beginning of phase 4 (*c.* 270). By contrast, ditches 1a, 1b and 2 were completely back-filled, to make way for the building of the north *vicus*. A late second or, more probably, early third-century context is indicated for this activity. In short, the defences of the fort appear to have fallen into a total state of disrepair by about 220. Significantly, the east *vicus* also entered a decline at this time (Fig. 81), although the north *vicus* apparently continued in occupation.

We should perhaps be cautious in assuming a total lack of a garrison after 220. The quantity of third-century pottery (Fig. 63) from the military areas of the site is sufficiently high to imply some activity and it would be ill advised to attribute this entirely to a civilian presence without further excavation within the fort's interior. Indeed, given the well known difficulties of interpreting the results of ditch sections (where there is always liable to be a pronounced admixture of finds), it would be appropriate to test our hypothesis on other sides of the fort. But the evidence as it stands is consistent in implying a break in occupation about the end of Caracalla's reign, and might well be seen as a consequence of the highly successful Severan campaigns and the period of peace that ensued in Britain (Frere 1974, 213-4).

Phase 4 and the problem of the fourth century

The renewal of activity at Watercrook is represented by a further occupation level in the guard-chamber of the north-east gate and the refurbishing of the ditch system. The re-use of the guard-chamber is dated by four coins of 268-73, sealed in a layer of charcoal and refuse. The recutting of ditches 1 and 3 (ditch 2 was apparently left untouched) can be similarly dated, a coin of Gallienus (dating to 257-68) apparently preceding the recut, while the primary silt of the new ditch contained coins of 269-73. The fort may also have been enlarged in this period, explaining the two adjacent fort-wall footings located by North and Hildyard (1945) at the south angle.

We shall review the overall evidence for occupation at this time in the north-west of England in Chap. VII. Here it will suffice to say that many forts show evidence of increased activity in this period which cannot be wholly explained by the frequency of radiate coins or their copies. Indeed, the abundance of hoards of this period very clearly implies something of the uncertainties which brought about an increase of garrison strengths at this time. Watercrook very readily fits this pattern.

What is less clear is the duration of occupation at Watercrook. When preparing the interim statements concerning the results of the excavation, we were impressed by the absence of fourth-century finds from stratified contexts and by the astonishing rarity of fourth-century coins. Only one coin was found in the present work, an issue of Constantine, dated to 320, from the top fill of the inner ditch. In addition, Kendal Museum records a Constantine (now lost) from North's excavation, while a Valens and a Gratian were reportedly recovered from the site during the River Board's work in 1975-6. It should be emphasised that this rarity of fourth-century coins is totally at variance with the normal pattern of loss from both military and civilian sites in this period (Reece 1973; Casey 1974) and must imply either very limited occupation or unusual factors at work.

The volume of fourth-century pottery is, on the other hand, much greater than we had realised in 1974-5. There are considerable quantities from the top fill of the ditches and from the unstratified levels over the military area. The sherds are quite sufficiently numerous to demonstrate activity through the fourth century and form a peak in the years 360-400 (Fig. 63). It should, however, be remembered that late fourth-century pottery is both very distinctive and, as Ravenglass shows, extremely common. Whether the presence of this fourth-century pottery on the site is best explained by military occupation is a question that can only be settled by further excavation. The rarity of coins and the absence of fourth-century levels in the guard-chamber might well be taken to imply that the pottery derives from native settlement. Moreover, there is a good deal of evidence from the ditches to suggest that they had been entirely filled by about 400. In 1976 it was suggested that Watercrook may have been liable to flooding in the fourth century (Potter 1976), an argument whose main points are reiterated elsewhere in this chapter and whose conclusions are not substantially altered. It is perhaps superfluous to take the debate any further at this point since the question can very readily be solved by future excavations. But the tentative conclusion would be that the fourth-century finds are best explained by factors other than military occupation of the known fort.

The North *Vicus* (Figs 57, 75, Pl. XIX)

The presence of extra-mural buildings beyond the north-east side of the fort was attested by the remains of two superimposed timber-framed structures beside the north-east road. They occupied the berm between ditches 1 and 2, the intervening ditches, 1a and 1b, being filled in to accommodate the new buildings. The surviving remains were not especially impressive. Much damaged by ploughing, the foundation-trenches and postholes existed mainly as shallow depressions in the gravel subsoil, seldom attaining more than 30 cm in depth. The floor-levels had also been destroyed, their traces being confined to a layer of disturbed red gravel, spread over the area of the buildings. Consequently there were no properly stratified deposits associated with the buildings and a number of puzzling and unexplained features were found.

That there were two main phases of construction was obvious from the fact that the side-walls were duplicated, the two pairs being separated by a gap of a metre in the case of the northern walls and 50 cm for the southern pair. On the evidence of the few intersecting features the later walls would seem to comprise W1 and W3, showing that the building was moved a little to the north, away from the fort, when it was reconstructed. This would give a width of 6·10 m for the building of first phase and 6·75 m for the second. The full length was not established, since the western end of the building lay beyond the excavated area: but the walls did stretch for at least 13 m, showing that we are dealing with the remains of a long strip house, familiar from many extramural areas of northern military sites. The walls themselves consisted principally of square timber

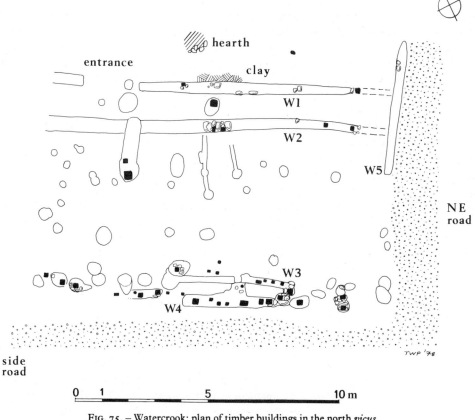

FIG. 75. – Watercrook: plan of timber buildings in the north *vicus*.

uprights, up to 40×40 cm; many were packed around with stones (pl. XIXb). They were set either in trenches or in separate postholes, the continuous footings being much better represented along the northern side of the building than on the southern. Long stretches of these northern walls yielded no evidence for uprights and it is possible that here a sill-beam was used; but there was no clear indication of this type of footing and it may equally be that demolition work had been much more thorough in this area. The southern walls on the other hand provided much clearer signs of the timbers, showing that major posts occurred at intervals of between one and two metres, while the intervening space was filled with smaller uprights, averaging 10×10 cm. Daub was presumably applied to the superstructure, explaining the spread of clay found on the north side of wall W1. This wall also yielded the only indications of a side entrance, consisting of a gap in the foundation-trench, 2 m in width, with a post at one side on which to hang the door.

Inside the building there was a complex pattern of postholes and small partitions. The most striking feature is the apparent division of the interior into three aisles, by two rows of posts laid out approximately parallel with the side walls. Many of the postholes proved to be of quite considerable size and, while spaced irregularly, nevertheless are sufficiently numerous to imply a fairly substantial, load-bearing wall. However, given that the side-walls show two phases of construction, it seems unlikely that we can regard the two rows of internal posts as contemporary. Only one upright appeared to have been replaced and the arrangement in two lines would be consistent with an interpretation involving a reconstruction of the building a short distance to the north. We should infer therefore that the building was designed in both periods with a main room, some 4 m in width, and a rather narrower side-aisle, c. 2·75 m in width. This side-aisle appears to have been divided up into several separate chambers. There were traces of three partition-trenches on the north side of the building and the beginning of at least one on the south side. These rooms do not appear to have been very large but it is impossible to reconstruct their sizes in detail without knowing more of the relative sequence of individual features.

The frontage of the building evidently lay on the main north-east road leaving the fort. The surviving structural evidence consisted of a stretch of wall-trench, 5 m in extent, and several postholes. The arrangement of the posts suggests that in both periods there was an entrance 2 m wide, giving access to the central part of the building. The wall-trench, which appeared to represent only one phase, extended beyond the north side-wall by a distance of 2 m, as if intended to support a veranda. Except for one possible socket, there was no trace of any veranda posts but it is quite possible that they were set in shallow pits which have been ploughed away. The only surviving feature in the veranda area was a badly disturbed hearth, marked by a half-circle of stones and a surface of baked clay and tile.

Along the south side of the building, a road (Pl. XXa) was laid over the filled-in course of ditch 1a. Its line was quite apparent since the deposits in the ditch had subsided and the road was thus preserved as a layer in the top fill. It was substantially made with a make-up of heavy rubble, surfaced with cobbles and gravel. It was also exceptionally wide for a minor street – over 4 m – but this is probably explained by the presence of the earlier ditch. It is interesting that a road and civilian building should have been allowed so close to the inner ditch of the fort: proper maintenance of the defences had clearly been permitted to lapse. Similar encroachment is in fact widely attested in the later Roman period; at Old Penrith, for example, the current excavations (1978) outside the south gate have revealed masonry strip-houses extending right up to the inner ditch of the fort, while the ditch itself was filled in and covered with a road. At Old Carlisle (Higham and Jones 1975, 18) the situation also appears to have been similar, underlining the close relationship between fort and *vicus* at this time. The Watercrook buildings certainly seem to have been constructed quite late in the history of the fort. The best guide to their date of construction comes from the contents of ditches 1a and 1b, discussed above: there we concluded that they had been filled towards the end of the second century, the latest object from a sealed deposit being a jar with parallels in the period 170-250. Otherwise stratified material is meagre. Only nine of the features yielded any potsherds, and there were no large groups. Amongst these sherds were two pieces of colour-coat and a scrap of a mortarium, probably of third-century date. In addition, ditch 1b contained two third-century vessels (254, 257), both of which probably were introduced into the fill by later postholes. The unstratified pottery from the area was also predominantly third century, with a marked absence of Antonine samian. It looks therefore as though the first timber building may have been constructed in the last part of the second century and that occupation persisted for much of the third century. The coin evidence, such as it is, would also support this conclusion, there being one radiate copy from the topsoil over the building and two intrusive coins in the uppermost fill of the phase 1 fence foundation-trench, of the period 268-273.

The scarcity of pottery in this area was matched by the rarity of other finds. The few objects from the building and its vicinity included only two querns, a glass armlet, a clay weight, a knife blade and a cheese-press or strainer. There was no tile and no accumulation of rubbish, as there was in the east *vicus*. Despite the damaging effect of ploughing, it is hard to imagine that occupation deposits had been so completely dispersed as to leave little or no trace: it seems much more probable that these buildings were never used as domestic habitations. Industrial activity is also excluded since, apart from a scatter of slag (derived from earlier metal-working, discussed further below), there was no appropriate debris or structures. The one explanation which seems consistent with the evidence is that the building may have been used to stall cattle or horses. This would explain the small compartments found on one side of the interior and account for the paucity of domestic refuse. Peter Fifield's analysis of the animal bones (Chap. IV) shows that a small number of horses was kept in the fort (attested also by equestrian equipment such as snaffle-bits) and that cattle are well represented in the faunal sample. He infers from the mortality data that most of the cattle were brought to the site when mature; but even so we may assume that some were kept for dairy purposes and a cow-shed on an otherwise unused side of the fort would have been a convenient arrangement, with water very close at hand.

The small area available for buildings on the east side of the road appears to have been left vacant for most of the period. There were a few shallow depressions, perhaps the lowest part of postholes, in line with the inner ditch of the fort (Fig. 57), but they do not appear to have formed part of a building. The one significant feature in this area was a small metal-working hearth, situated a short distance from the edge of the road in the centre of the berm. It was rectangular in plan, measuring 1·10×0·70 m, and had been set in a shallow depression in the subsoil (Fig. 76). The bottom of the hearth was lined with clay, burnt red, over which was a deposit of iron slag. In addition there were a series of small perforations around the edge of the hearth. This type of hearth can be readily paralleled by numerous examples from Manchester, Wilderspool, Middlewich, Northwich and elsewhere. Bestwick and Cleland (1974) have provided a detailed discussion of their function, arguing that they were used for iron smithing. They suggest that the perforations either formed part of a structure covering the hearth or were designed to ventilate the area beneath the floor. It is also possible that they represent the seating for portable bellows that were moved round the hearth as necessary. The Watercrook hearth does not throw any further light on the interpretation of the perforations, but it does contribute to the impression that metal-working is to be expected in any military *vicus*. Whether there was smelting as well as smithing is uncertain but it is worth recalling the very large quantity of slag found in the fill of ditch 2, near to the hearth. Dating mainly to the Hadrianic period, this slag implies large-scale metal-working activity, far more than the presence of a single hearth indicates. Given that the surviving hearth was itself only a few cm deep, it may be that others have been completely destroyed by ploughing and other factors. The source of the ores remains unclear however. Haematite ores are quite common in the south and west Lake District (and were extensively exploited in the Ravenglass area) and would have proved a ready supply. In that case, it may well have been easier to transport the smelted blooms to Watercrook: only full analysis of the slag, not yet attempted, will establish whether they represent the product of both smelting and smithing.

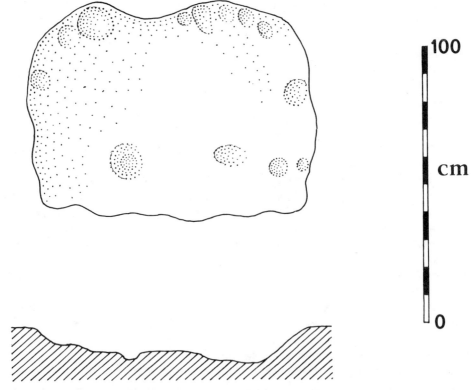

FIG. 76. – Watercrook: iron-smithing hearth on the berm between ditches 1 and 2, near to the north-east road.

The East *Vicus* (Figs. 53, 77-80, Pls XXb, XXI)

Rescue priorities were such that the exploration of the area to the east of the fort was confined to a single long trench, measuring some 90×5-6 m (site A). It was laid out immediately behind the river bank so that the main east road out of the fort passed through the middle of the trench. That this road was a focus of extra-mural settlement was clear from exposures in the river bank, where deep stratified occupation-deposits could be seen. We did not anticipate the recovery of any very meaningful building plans in so narrow an excavation; but we did hope to learn something of the history of these occupation deposits, together with an indication of the extent and character of the structures. In the event, it emerged that there was about a metre of stratified layers, representing an accumulation of just over a century. The earliest buildings dated to the Flavian-Trajanic period, coinciding with the initial garrison of the fort, and occupation lasted into the early third century. During this time, the buildings became increasingly substantial, those of the Antonine period having mortared floors and stone footings. However, apart from sporadic activity in the late third century, represented by four coins and a small quantity of pottery, the east *vicus* seems to have been abandoned by about 220, corresponding with the evacuation of the fort proposed above (Fig. 81). As Hartley (1972, 25) has pointed out, civilian settlement is likely to have reflected closely the vicissitudes of the garrison history, an observation that finds confirmation from the east *vicus* at Watercrook.

Pre-vicus activity

There was no trace anywhere in site A of an old turf line over the clay-silt subsoil. Instead, the base of the Roman layers rested upon a layer some 5-20 cm thick of charcoal-flecked grey-red silt, with all the appearance of a ploughing horizon. No plough marks as such were observed but there seems little doubt that this part of the valley was under cultivation before the army arrived.

The road

The east road out of the fort left the south-east gate some 70 m from the site of the excavation and then swung in a gradual curve towards the river. Its approximate onward course up the east side of the Kent valley is indicated on Fig. 52, with its ultimate destination the fort in the Tebay gorge at Low Borrow Bridge. The road was laid out early in the fort's history, in the Flavian-Trajanic period. It had a width of over 5 m and a steeply cambered surface of gravel and cobbles, resting upon nearly 40 cm of rubble make-up. Its profile was thus not dissimilar to that of the north-east road but its greater width and more solid construction underline its function as a route with long-distance objectives. There was also a low bank to the north of the *agger* (Fig. 79) which may have been intended to demarcate the area of the highway, as well as to channel storm-water towards the river.

The relationship of the road to the river poses a number of problems. The position of the road is such that it heads directly for the loop in the river, as if intending to cross it; indeed traces of paving suggestive of a ford have been reported in the bed of the Kent at this point. It does, however, seem unlikely that the road should have crossed the river when, with a small diversion, it could have skirted the loop. In fact, as we shall see in the next section, the course of the river has undoubtedly altered a number of times since the

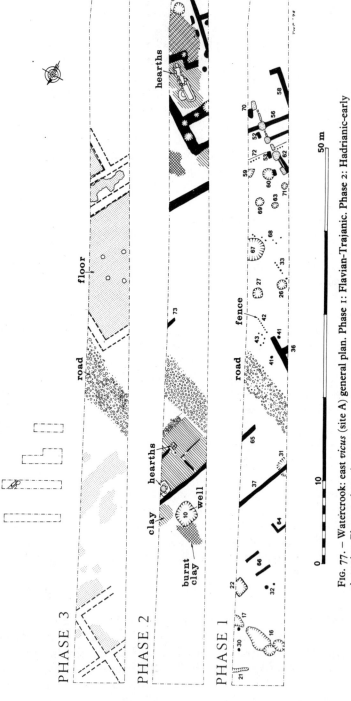

FIG. 77. – Watercrook: east *vicus* (site A) general plan. Phase 1: Flavian-Trajanic. Phase 2: Hadrianic-early Antonine. Phase 3: Antonine–c. 220.

Roman period and we can probably suppose that the ox-bow lay some distance to the north of its present channel in the early Roman period. The "ford" is thus either illusory or, more probably, the remains of some much more recent feature.

In the Hadrianic-early Antonine period, the road was rebuilt by the addition of nearly 4 m of make-up and surfacing on the north side of the original *agger*. This was partly to compensate for the rise in level of the occupation-deposits beside the road and partly because of the encroachment of buildings and debris from the south. The new surface was flat and without any proper provision for drainage. The surface was subsequently raised in the Antonine period by the addition of 15 cm of ballast and small rubble on top of the road of phase 2.

The buildings of phase 1 (Flavian-Trajanic)

A full description of the features belonging to the earliest occupation beside the road is listed below. Whilst the overall pattern is fragmentary, the quantity of Flavian-Trajanic material and the very considerable extent of the structural remains show that the east *vicus* developed very rapidly after the foundation of the first fort. Even though the site of the excavation lay over 70 m from the south-east gate, both sides of the road had been built up by the early second century and finds extended for a distance of more than 30 m on either side. To the north of the road there were traces of a timber-framed house with a length of at least 14 m. It had one room 5·5 m in width and a second, smaller room to the west, with a width of 4·5 m and a cross-wall. There may have been a veranda or corridor beyond that. No traces were found either of a floor or of individual post-settings but the building as a whole was poorly preserved and had been thoroughly demolished. Beyond the building were a well, various rubbish pits and a few miscellaneous postholes. There were also five pits at the south end of site B, some of which may belong to this period. There was presumably a backyard behind the house, possibly with some structural features, but used mainly for rubbish disposal.

To the south of the road there was a complex series of timber-framed structures. Too little was uncovered to provide any definitive interpretation but there appear to have been two separate buildings, divided by an area of pits and fences. Close to the road, in the centre of the excavated area, was a substantial wall-trench, in the form of a T in plan (A36). It may have comprised part of a building with a veranda on the east side. Beyond this and on the same alignment were two rows of stakeholes (Pl. XXb) which, in the absence of any major uprights, are best interpreted as the remains of low fences. They could well have marked the division between different properties or belonged to pens for animals. There was also a semicircle of stakes, perhaps a wicker-lined basket-setting, and other stake-settings on a different alignment. Pits and a well confirm the impression that this area was given over to rubbish-disposal and to yards in a space between houses. To the south-east was a second building-complex which, given the alignment of the road, must have extended at least 20 m back from it. The plan of the structure is not easily disentangled from the large number of features in this area, which include a line of stakes, wall-trenches and a row of postholes, joined by a narrow slot. There was also some reconstruction, as the replacement of the post and slot wall by a line of rectangular postholes makes clear. The overall impression is of a long strip-house, divided into a number of small rooms; but the posthole settings imply a special load-bearing function and it may be that they form the central wall of a rectangular building, with the long axis parallel with rather than perpendicular to the road. There were no traces of any floor material or of internal features.

The dating of these buildings rests upon the evidence of pottery from the features and the layer of refuse that accumulated round them. The bulk of the material was of Flavian-Trajanic date although some features also yielded a few fragments that are probably Hadrianic. These could well have derived from demolition work or from foundation-trenches cut when later buildings were under contruction. It is of note that finds were generally sparse, there being only one coin, a *denarius* of Julius Caesar (46 B.C.), and very few objects of metal (inv. 62, 76): initially, therefore, the *vicani* may have been fairly impoverished, although this situation was soon to change.

The features of phase 1 (Fig. 77)
North of the road:

A21.   Shallow wall-trench, petering out to the west.

A30.   Two stone-packed postholes, 50 cm in diameter and 50 cm in depth.

A17.   Shallow pit, 30 cm in depth. Flavian samian.

A16.   A complex of three intersecting pits, two fairly clearly post-pits, the other perhaps a rubbish pit. Depth 1·20-1·30 m. Coarse-ware 15, 25; samian: Flavian (4), Flavian-Trajanic (7), Trajanic/Hadrianic (3).

A22.   A square well with sides 1·20 × 1·20 m; apparently without any revetting. The feature (which had caused drastic slumping) had gravel in the lower fill above which was a deposit of white clay and charcoal. The bottom was not reached. Samian: Flavian-Trajanic (11), Trajanic (1), Trajanic-Hadrianic (1).

A32.   Posthole, 50 cm diameter, with stone packing; and an adjacent stakehole.

A66.   Two parallel wall-trenches, set to a very shallow depth into the subsoil.

A64.   A shallow wall-trench, which turns through a right angle. 35 cm wide. It is cut by A10.

A10.   A square well, cut through wall-trench A64. It may have been dug late in phase 1. There were traces of a yellow clay lining on one side. It was filled with layers of gravel and rubble and excavated to a depth of 1·80 m. Bottom was not reached. The lower fill contained Flavian-Trajanic coarse-ware (17-22) and samian, amongst which were Flavian (1), Flavian-Trajanic (6), Trajanic-Hadrianic (3) and ?Hadrianic (1). There was a coin of Vitellius. The top fill yielded one sherd of Antonine pottery.

A37.   Wall-trench with two periods of construction, the later belonging to phase 2 (though the finds have been classified under phase 1). 40 cm wide, 30 cm deep. The trench was prolific of pottery, including much coarse-ware (1-14), mainly of Flavian-Trajanic date. The samian includes Flavian (4); Flavian-Trajanic (12) and one fragment in the fabric of Les Martres-de-Veyre (Trajanic-Hadrianic).

A31.   Shallow pit, lined with yellow clay and pebbles. Max. depth 30 cm. Samian: Flavian-Trajanic (1), Trajanic-Hadrianic (1).

A65.   Shallow trench, 40 cm wide, 20 cm deep.

South of the road:

A36.   Wall-trench with a return to the south-west on a projecting end, perhaps for a veranda. A U-shaped slot, 55 cm in depth, with a clay fill. A samian stamp of Lucundus ii (c. 75-95) and Flavian-Trajanic samian (4). One Hadrianic/Antonine piece is presumably intrusive.

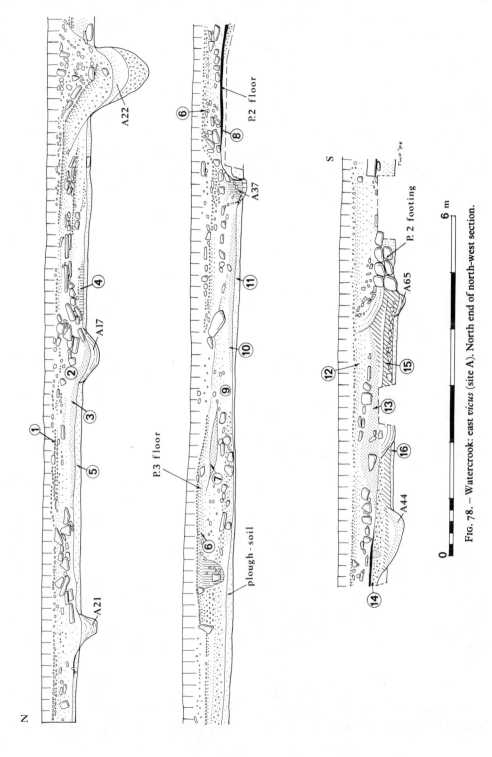

Fig. 78. — Watercrook: east *vicus* (site A). North end of north-west section.

A42.   A line of seven stakeholes, averaging 7 cm in diameter and 12 cm in depth. They continue the outside line of A36.

A43.   A half-ring of stakeholes, of similar dimensions to A42. Possibly the lining for a wickerwork basket.

A40, 41.   Two small postholes, 25-30 cm in diameter, 20 cm deep.

A27, 26.   Two flat-bottomed pits with undercut sides. They are both 1-1·10 m in diameter and some 50 cm in depth. A loose, fairly sterile fill. Samian: Flavian-Trajanic (1), Trajanic-Hadrianic (1).

A33.   A line of six stakeholes, parallel with A42. 8-10 cm in diameter, 10 cm average depth.

A68.   A further group of stakeholes, comparable in size to A33 and disposed mainly in pairs.

A67.   A large pit or well, cut from the old ground surface. It was not excavated.

A59, 60, 63, 69, 71.   A group of postholes, none of them particularly large (average depth 30 cm) and all more or less barren of finds.

A72.   A line of stakeholes, some 8 cm in diameter and 12-15 cm in depth. A slight ridge on the south-east side of the line may mark the base of a shallow slot.

A70, 52, 53, 60.   A line of rectangular postholes, averaging 80×40 cm in plan and 50 cm in depth. They replace a similar line immediately to the south.

A70, 62.   A line of posts connected by a very narrow wall-slot which, from the evidence of A70, replaces the line described *supra*. The slot has a depth of some 25 cm while the postholes are rather deeper.

A54, 56.   Two north-south wall-trenches, of which 54 stops at the line of the cross wall. The trenches are *c.* 40 cm in depth. A56 yielded two sherds of Flavian-Trajanic samian.

A58.   Wall-trench with a right-angled turn, similar to A54, 56. This presumably marks the back of the building as well as the furthest extent of occupation south of the road.

The buildings of phase 2 (Hadrianic-early Antonine)

The second period in the history of the east *vicus* saw both a sharp increase in material prosperity and the conversion of the buildings into much more solid and elaborate constructions. The structures still continued to be timber-framed but extensive use was made of stone packing and thick clay floors were laid down. To the north of the road the new building largely duplicated the wall-lines of its predecessor, although the more westerly rooms were abandoned. There was a frontage 7 m wide along the road and the building extended back at least 10 m, beyond the excavated area. No trace of a front wall was found but both the side walls and internal partitions of wattle and daub were clearly defined. There was a small front room 2·5×3·5 m, a rather larger front room and one partition dividing the back into two. One of the front rooms was provided with a small hearth, 60×70 cm, made of four tiles, and there was an elaborate oven at the back of the house. This consisted of a clay platform 1·30 m square, with a circular oven in the centre; it was 55 cm in diameter and edged with pieces of limestone. The whole building was floored with yellow clay.

To the north of this house there were further areas of clay make-up, one of them burnt, but no other obvious indications of a building. There was, however, a well (A10) which, while probably cut towards the end of phase 1, was almost certainly in use during phase 2. Beyond this area there was nothing more than a scatter of refuse, sealing the features of the first period.

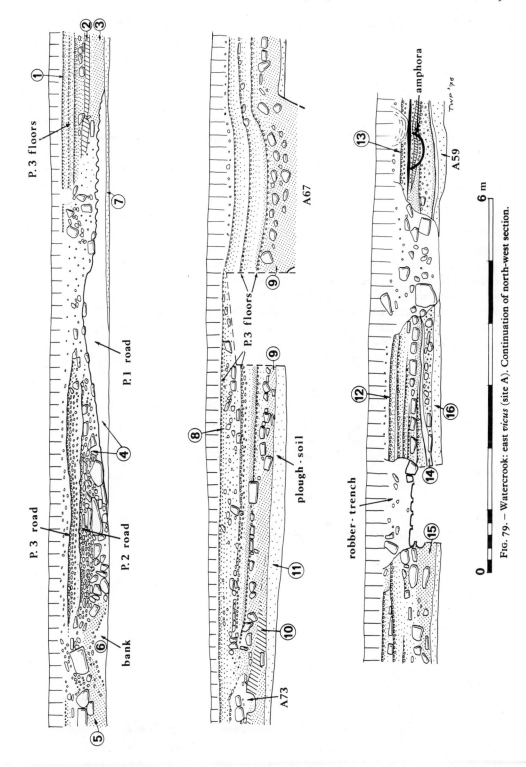

FIG. 79. — Watercrook: east *vicus* (site A). Continuation of north-west section.

Immediately to the south of the road, the evidence for structures was confined to a single short length of trench (A73) which petered out in the middle of the excavated area. There were a few patches of clay make-up but no indications of a properly laid floor. We can probably assume that this was vacant ground, perhaps devoted to gardening, at this time. Twenty metres beyond the road, however, there were the remains of a substantial building, which extended throughout the remaining part of site A. With the exception of one rather slight wooden partition (A46), the walls were strongly constructed of large wooden uprights set in a rubble-filled trench *c.* 1 m in width. Measurable timbers appeared to average *c.* 50 cm square. No complete dimensions were obtained for any of rooms but one had a width of only 2·5 m, while another had a width of 7 m and a minimum length of 13 m. This larger room which, with other parts of the building, retained traces of a yellow clay floor, was provided with a series of clay hearths or ovens. Three phases of construction were represented. The earliest consisted of a circular platform of clay with a small oven in the centre, 50 cm in diameter. It was replaced by a long rectangular hearth, over 2 m in length and nearly a metre in width. This in turn was superseded by a third hearth, measuring 2·80 × 1·00 m; here the edges were revetted with stone and the interior, which was 60 cm in width and 40 cm in depth, lined with clay. Filling the interior were layer upon layer of burnt and unburnt clay, indicating that the base of the hearth had been resurfaced on at least eight or nine occasions. There was nothing in the finds from this area to indicate any special usage, however, and we can probably assume that it was employed solely for domestic purposes.

The pottery both from this house and from the other building north of the road belongs mainly to the Trajanic-Hadrianic periods, although a few pieces may be early Antonine in date. There is also a large group of coins, 14 in all; eight are issues of Trajan while the rest belong to the first century or before. The growth in material wealth indicated by these coins is notable, a feature matched by the increased number of small objects compared with phase 1. The objects include a ring with an intaglio (102), another finger-ring (101), a stylus (151), a strap-end (23), a spoon (51), two pieces of mirror (61) and various other fittings.

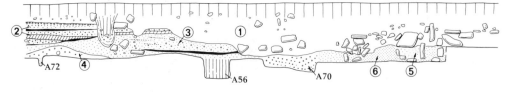

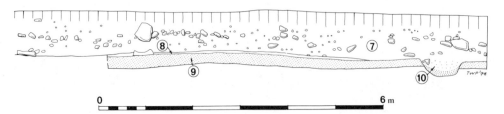

0   6 m

FIG. 80. – Watercrook: east *vicus* (site A). Continuation of north-west section.

The buildings of phase 3 (Antonine-early third century)

The last building phase on the site can be dated to the Antonine period, and may possibly coincide with the regarrisoning of the fort in the 150s or 160s. The road was given its final surface and a layer of rubble spread over the structures of phase 2. Floors made of pebbles and mortar were then laid on the rubble, creating the most solidly constructed buildings in the history of the east *vicus*. The remains were not, however, easy to interpret. In the area to the north of the road only isolated patches of floor-surfaces were preserved and the wall-lines were virtually impossible to distinguish from the general spread of rubble forming the make-up of the floors. The dashed lines on Fig. 77 show the possible position of some of the walls but we should emphasise that there is a strong element of conjecture. To the south of the road the floors were much better preserved and indicate a long history of repair work and resurfacing. Over much of this area they were as much as 45 cm in thickness (Pl. XXIb), with at least three major rebuilds. Indeed excavation in places within the house immediately beside the road disclosed no less than nine different surfaces (Pl. XXIa), although of course some of these floors may represent separate stages in the laying of a single surface. The accumulation of rubbish on the floors was on the whole fairly sparse. There were a few centimetres of dark soil (though with little refuse) over the lowest floor (Fig. 79) but the upper surfaces were generally much cleaner. The main exception was the area round part of an amphora (Fig. 80) which had been set into the second floor as a hearth. Nearby was an extensive spread of charcoal and ash.

The main problem in the area south of the road came in defining the walls. The building-levels at the south end of the site had been completely destroyed in recent centuries and the position of the walls elsewhere was indicated only by irregular and indistinct robber-trenches. The presence of these trenches is in themselves a good indication that stone was employed in this period for the wall footings; but no single block of dressed masonry survived, either *in situ* or in the fill of the robber-trenches. It is nevertheless clear that there was a rectangular building, c. 13·5 m in width, beside the road and a second house to the south. An alleyway, 2·30 m in width, separated the two buildings; it had been surfaced on five separate occasions with cobbles and mortar, once with a layer of heavy rubble make-up (Fig. 79, unit 12). Four post-seatings in the front building may indicate partitions, while the second house was very clearly divided internally by a masonry wall. There is no reason to doubt that these were strip-houses of conventional plan, as attested outside numerous military sites in northern England.

The large quantity of finds both from the building-levels and from the disturbed deposits overlying the structures show that these buildings were occupied by prosperous *vicani*. There were eight coins, some military equipment (including arrowheads and chain-mail) and numerous objects of bronze, iron and bone. The pottery suggests, however, that there was a decline in the scale of occupation from the beginning of the third century and that the buildings were largely abandoned c. 220 (Fig. 81). There was a thin scatter of third- and fourth-century sherds, together with coins of Gallienus, Tetricus, Claudius II and two radiate copies; but none of this material came from stratified deposits and no building-activity can be associated with it. It would appear then that the east *vicus* and the military area show a similar pattern in the third century, perhaps explicable in terms of an evacuation of the garrison for much of the period.

If this early demise of the *vicus* is repeated on the west and south sides of the fort (where we may assume civilian activity although it remains to be proved), then Watercrook is to

be numbered amongst several sites where the extra-mural occupation comes to an end
surprisingly early. The most curious example is Ribchester where, despite considerable
evidence for a third-century garrison (*RIB* 583, 587, 590, 591), the civilian settlement
seems from the results of several recent excavations to have been levelled in the early third
century. This in fact contradicts the evidence of two of the inscriptions which must refer
to monuments outside the fort (*RIB* 583, 587). It is also at odds with the name of
Ribchester in the Ravenna Cosmography, *Bresnetenaci Veteranorum*, a description
which, as Richmond (1945) pointed out, must indicate that land was allocated to retired
soldiers. The garrison was in fact a unit (*numerus*) of Sarmatian cavalry (*RIB* 583) who
had been brought to Britain in 175 (Cassius Dio 71.16), and it may be that it was their
arrival at Ribchester (perhaps as a consequence of Severan reorganisation) that resulted
in the drastic treatment of the existing *vicus*. But where the *veterani* may have lived is
unknown, for there is no evidence from work on the west, north or east sides of the fort to

WATERCROOK
COARSE POTTERY FROM THE EAST VICUS

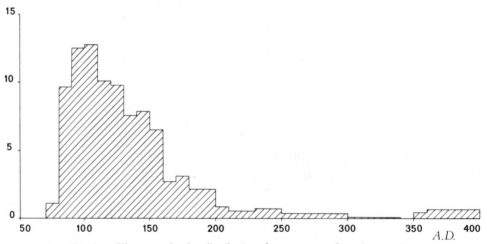

FIG. 81. – Histogram showing distribution of coarse pottery from the east *vicus*.

indicate third- or fourth-century buildings. It could well be that there was a dispersed
vicus with settlement based upon centuriated land-plots as at *Diana Veteranorum* in
present-day Algeria. Equally at Manchester (Jones and Grealey 1974), the Deansgate
excavations north of the fort failed to reveal any evidence for extra-mural settlement after
the early- to mid-third century (though the fort was undoubtedly in garrison during the
later third and fourth centuries). At Lancaster, too, the present evidence is for an
extensive *vicus* in the second century, but drastically curtailed occupation after the early
third century. Evidence from Brough under Stainmore also hints at a similar pattern
(Jones 1977). This picture should be balanced with sites where civilian settlement
undoubtedly persisted much later, such as Old Carlisle and Old Penrith (Salway 1965),
both of which possessed large *vici*. Indeed at Old Carlisle, where there was a complex
street pattern and dense housing (Higham and Jones 1975, 18) there is epigraphic
evidence for *vicani*, dated to 238-44 (*RIB* 899). All that we can safely conclude in our

present state of knowledge is that most forts attracted civilian settlement (Hardknott is a notable exception), which show strong development in the second century but a much more varied history thereafter. It was certainly not automatic that the presence of a third-century garrison should result in continued growth of the *vicus* (even if it had flourished during the previous century) and it may be that the situation was influenced by administrative decisions, such as the creation by the *civitas Carvetiorum*. This is attested epigraphically by tombstones at Old Penrith (*RIB* 933) and Brougham (Wright 1965, 224), the latter dated to the reign of Postumus (258-68). Its centre may have been at Carlisle but it is reasonable to suppose the *territorium* was an extensive one, perhaps stretching as far as the Middleton milestone near Kirkby Lonsdale (Birley 1953). If so, Watercrook may well have come within its orbit and been affected directly or indirectly by the changes in the civil administration of the region.

Fluvial History: The results of the January 1975 excavation

The decision of the River Board to widen the Kent over the whole length of the Watercrook loop provided a valuable opportunity to cut machine trenches round the periphery of the site. It was not expected that much of archaeological interest would be found, although there were hopes that the bath-house described by Machell (cf. Collingwood 1930) as being "near the N. Corner (of the fort) at 70 yards' distance" might be located. Consequently the relevant area was very thoroughly explored (Fig. 53, trenches 1-6, 15), but with no success. The only feature to be found was a semicircular structure, built of roughly dressed limestone (Fig. 83, Pl. XVIIIb). It was set into alluvium at the edge of the river and stood four to six courses high. It had apparently replaced an earlier curved wall and was associated with a line of stones to the south, probably the remains of a retaining wall.

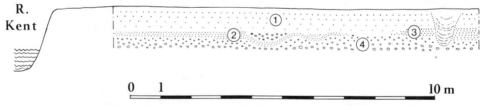

FIG. 82. – Watercrook: section of the alluvial deposits in trench 1.

Many of the stones within the semicircular apse had been burnt to a blue colour, so that we can probably assume that it was built as a lime-kiln, perhaps dating to the period when the wall of the fort was robbed. That it was a post-Roman feature was perfectly clear from its insertion into silts which, as we shall see below, are demonstrably later than the fort.

The other trenches excavated during January 1975 yielded only alluvial deposits. This was not in itself surprising since traces of older river channels could be detected both on the east side of the fort platform, beyond site B (Fig. 53) and, less distinctly, in the pasture bordering the northern curve of the Kent. We were, however, hopeful that something could be learnt of the extent and history of the river deposits. In the event, the stratigraphy proved remarkably unintricate (Fig. 82). Reduced to essentials, they showed that there was an older bed of the River Kent which lay beneath the ground bordering the present channel, overlaid by between one and two metres of unlaminated flood-plain silt.

The flood-plain deposits occasionally revealed thin lenses of fine gravel and pebbles where the Kent had topped its bank in a winter flood but interfaces of this sort were by no means common. There was, however, some archaeological material in both the silts and the gravel beds beneath. It included a considerable volume of abraded Roman pottery, ranging in date from the second to the fourth centuries, giving a firm *terminus post quem* for this fluvial activity.

Some evidence for the deposition of flood-plain silt was also recorded from the excavation in site C. The deposits were confined to the upper fill of the massive quarry ditch, 2, where upwards of a metre of alluvium sealed (and in places had cut away) the Roman fill (Fig. 72). There was abraded pottery of the third and fourth centuries in these layers. The silt did not extend into the inner ditch and we should assume therefore that it was only the peripheral parts of the site that were directly liable to flooding.

In recent years considerable attention has been paid to the post-glacial geological history of river valleys. It is now clear that the behaviour of rivers is subject to fluctuations of very marked character. Thus in some periods they may flow in comparatively shallow channels and are especially liable to flood, while at others (including the present day) they tend to cut very deeply into the valley floor, inundating the flood plain only at very sporadic intervals. Such variations in vertical movement can also be matched by a significant degree of lateral change. In a Mediterranean valley to the north of Rome, for example, the river was found to have traversed the valley no less than four times in the last 2000 years (Potter 1976a, Cherkauer 1976). We can assume, therefore, that the River Kent may well have changed its course and height quite considerably since the foundation of the Roman fort, a conclusion borne out by the results of the trenching described above. The channel has certainly altered both its position and its height relative to the present river bed in recent times, and the low-lying meadows have been subject to heavy inundation, resulting in the deposition of over a metre of silt.

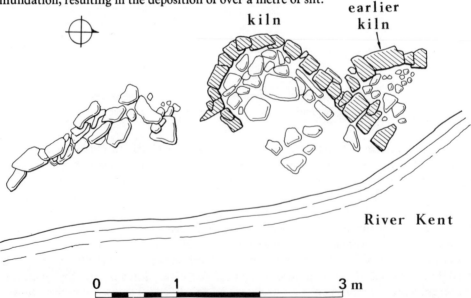

FIG. 83. – Watercrook: the probable remains of kilns in the bank of the River Kent near to trenches 6, 3, 4. The kilns appear to be of recent date.

The chronology of these changes is less easy to determine. Roman pottery occurred in the silts and gravels as deep as the excavation penetrated, about 2 m below ground level; but this emphasises only that the deposits were laid at or after the date of the latest sherd. The silts could in theory have been deposited at any time in the last 1500 years. There is, however, a growing body of evidence to show that the tendency for rivers to alluviate falls within quite well defined chronological limits. The case is best documented in the Mediterranean where (leaving aside the problems of the pre-Roman pattern) the river valleys show a widespread pattern of heavy silt formation from the mid to late Roman period to late medieval times (Vita-Finzi 1969, Potter 1976a). Many sites are in fact deeply buried beneath several metres of alluvium, one of the latest being a building of A.D. 209 in the Fosso della Crescenza near to Rome. In Britain, there are an increasing number of comparably dated examples. At Braughing in Hertfordshire, for instance, a bath-house constructed on the valley floor of the River Rib was found to be choked in flood silt and had been abandoned as early as the first part of the third century (Partridge 1975), although other parts of the site continued in occupation until the end of the Roman period. Flood deposits that sealed late Roman levels were also identified at Braughing, indicating an increased scale of inundation in the early medieval period. Similarly, at York (Ramm 1971, 181-3) and Brough-on-Humber (Wacher 1969, 78-81), there is evidence for a rise in the water-table in the late Roman period, while in the Cambridge-shire Fenland inundations are attested both in the mid-third century and after c. 400 (Phillips 1970).

The causes of this flooding have been variously assigned, some favouring local factors and others a more general explanation, such as climatic change; but, whatever the reasons, there can be no doubt of the ubiquity of riverine alluviation in the late Roman period. It is reasonable to assume, therefore, that Watercrook was probably no exception to this pattern and the formation of flood-plain silts may well have begun during the third or fourth centuries. In our discussion of this phase of the site's history, we have drawn attention to the strong possibility that there was only a limited military presence in the third century and no garrison in the fourth century (when, however, there was certainly some occupation). In a strategic sense, the exclusion of Watercrook from the list of forts garrisoned in the fourth century would certainly be a curious anomaly. If, however, the site had become liable to occasional inundation, it might well explain why the decision was taken to evacuate the fort. This would presumably leave a substantial body of civilian settlers whose presence would account for the abundance of fourth-century pottery, and whose investment in the area was sufficient for them to maintain their homes and fields. Whether it was the collapse of the Roman authority or a further deterioration in the local environment that finally caused them to move is unknown: but it is noteworthy that not one medieval find was made during the present large-scale excavations, a clear pointer towards the disadvantages of the Watercrook peninsula in the Middle Ages.

Stratigraphic details of the trenches cut in January 1975 (Fig. 52 for locations)

The measurements recorded below are all taken from the present-day ground surface at each trench. There is an overall drop in the ground level from the area of trenches 1-6 to that of trenches 11-14 of about 1 m. The water table in January 1975 lay on average at 1.5 m below the present surface on the east side of the peninsula. It was correspondingly higher on the east side of the peninsula.

1. (Fig. 82). Unit 1: unlaminated brown silt. 2: grey-orange silt with some laminae. 3: laminated grey silt. 4: fine gravel with average grit size of 0·1 cm, giving way to pebbles and cobbles, up to 30 cm in size. Unit 4 represents an old river bed.

2. Excavated to 1·60 m. 0·12-0·6 m: fine gravel and small cobbles. 0·6-1·2 m: laminae of silt with two prominent thin bands of fine gravel, each 5-10 cm thick. 1·2 m to water-table: coarse gravel, an old river bed.

3. Unlaminated silt to 1·5 m, resting on a coarse gravel.

4. Unlaminated silt to 1·10 m. 1·10-1·70 m: layer of large cobbles, representing an old river bed. 1·70 m to water-table (20 cm): coarse gravel.

5. Unlaminated silt to 1·12 m. 1·12-1·2 m: grey-white silt. 1·2 m onwards: coarse gravel and cobbles.

6. Unlaminated silt to 1·5 m with, beneath, a coarse gravel.

7. 0-0·5 m silt and fine gravel layer. 0·5-0·86 m: unlaminated silt. 0·86-0·96 m coarse gravel, small cobbles and a lens of fine gravel. 0·96-7 m fine silt band, with cobbles and gravel beneath.

8. A thin lens of gravel at 0·85 m, with a deposit of unlaminated silt, between 1·10 m (south-west end) and 2·00 m (north-east end, nearer river) thick. This silt rested upon a band of gravel, 0·50 m thick at the south-west end, beneath which was a further deposit of silt, flecked with (?) charcoal.

9. 0-1·20. Silt with a few pebbles. 1·20-1·40 m: fine gravel. 1·40 and below: large cobbles at the level of the water table.

10. Unlaminated silts to an unrecorded depth.

11. Unlaminated silts, extending in depth to between 0·6-0·8 m; they rested upon a coarse gravel.

12. Unlaminated silts to the water table at 1·35 m.

13. Unlaminated silts to a variable depth of between 0·85 and 1·20 m, resting on a fine gravel.

14. As trench 12.

15. Trench cut near to trenches 1-6. The sequence is more or less identical to that of trench 2.

NOTES ON THE SECTIONS

For the location of the sections in sites B and C, cf. Fig. 64.

Fig. 65a: Section at the east angle of the fort, looking west.

1. Grey silt fill in an extensive feature, cutting down through both the rampart extension and the *intervallum* road. There is a spread of charcoal at the base of the pit. Probably post-Roman.

2. Rubbish-pit dating to phase 1 or early in phase 2. Tips of refuse with dark soil and a thin lens of yellow clay.

3. Lower fill of 2; dark silt fill.

4. Drain of phase 2. Dark silt at the bottom, red-brown silt above.

5. Two phases of *intervallum* road, separated by a dark silt layer. The earlier period of road dates to phase 1.

6. Grey-brown silt, perhaps representing a turf levelling of uneven ground.

7. Intrusive post-Roman pit.

8. Trench filled with rubble. Probably a robber-trench.

9. Fort wall of phase 3, built of rubble and hard white-grey cement.

10. Front part of rampart, rebuild of phase 2; mixed dark brown fill.

11. Back part of rampart rebuild, a deposit of yellow clay and cobbles. The concentration of rubble and clay at the junction between unit 10 and 11 may represent a wall-footing.

12. Primary *intervallum* road.

13. Primary rampart. Dark turf with a heavy admixture of clay towards the edge of the rampart. The cheek consists of four courses of turves.

14. Trench cut through the primary rampart and probably through the rampart rebuild. It is filled with a dark silt, and has many cobbles at the base: these may have been intended as the basis for an ashlar facing to the fort wall.

Fig. 65b: Section across part of the north-east gate

1. Post-pit cut from the latest road surface; it may mark the centre of the narrowed gateway of phase 4.

2. Intrusive pit, perhaps for a post, cut down against the corner of the guard-chamber.

3. Four successive carriageways in the north-east gate, consisting of rammed gravel and small cobbles. The earliest surface rests upon a layer of yellow sand, but the subsoil was not reached.

4. Two successive trenches, the later filled with brown-orange clay, the earlier with grey silt and pebbles. Probably the foundation trench for the central wall in the gateway.

Fig. 66: Section across the north-east road

1. Topsoil.

2. Latest road-surface, made up of small cobbles and gravel.

3. Second phase of road, representing an extension to the east. Heavy rubble make-up and a hard, well metalled surface.

4. Primary road, steeply cambered. Heavy rubble make-up.

5. A thin layer of grey-brown clay, laid as a foundation for the earliest road.

6. Brown gravel fill in a depression along the west side of the road.

7. Foundation-trench for the fence of phase 1; filled with brown silt, rubble and pebbles.

Fig. 67: Section through the north defences, site B

1. Ploughsoil.

2. Brown fill with numerous pebbles, covering ditch 1.

3. Layer of large rubble, including some pieces of dressed masonry from the fort wall, and brown soil.

4. Brown fill with pebbles, covering a tip of large rubble on the south side of the ditch.

5. Dark fill flecked with charcoal and comparatively few pebbles. There is a sharp interface with 6, indicating a recut.

6. Dark brown silt with much gravel in the cleaning-channel and along the sides of the ditch.

7. Robber-trench, filled with heavy rubble, cutting down to the fort wall. The lowest course of the wall survives *in situ*, with three dressed blocks, bonded with a soft yellow mortar.

8. Pit with a dark fill and much rubble, cut from the ploughsoil.

9. Pit or trench, cut from the level of the latest *intervallum* surface. The upper part of the pit contained a rough line of heavy stone, perhaps intended to revet the *intervallum* road. Alternatively, it could have been a wall-footing.

10. Thin layer of clay, capped by slabs of limestone, sealing the second phase of rampart. This layer extended over part of the trench only.

11. The second phase of rampart, belonging to phase 2. A light-**brown pebb**le fill with, at the base, small dumps of gravel, turf and dark soil.

12, 13. *Intervallum* road surfaces, made of gravel on a bed of cobbles and larger rubble.

14. *Intervallum* road surface, resting on a layer of grey fill.

15. A thin spread of yellow-white clay, underlying both 14 and the late rampart, 11.

16. Phase 1 *intervallum* road, a carefully made feature with a gravel and cobble surface, resting on a thick layer of heavy rubble.

17. Turf and clay rampart of phase 1. It rests on a layer of orange clay from which the original turf has been stripped. A *sondage* showed that this layer of clay was 40 cm thick; beneath was fine gravel from an old river bed.

Fig. 68: Ditch 1, site C, west of north-east gate

1. Ploughsoil.

2. A thick layer, but thinning to the north, of heavy rubble and brown soil.

3. Brown fill, fairly free of pebbles.

4. A tip of brown charcoal-flecked soil, grading into a dark brown fill. The sharp interface at the base of the unit indicates a recut.

5. A U-shaped recut, filled with a grey silt and pebbles. This recut was identified only along this stretch of ditch 1: it was not identified at any point to the east of the north-east gate.

6. Silt with gravel, charcoal, bone and iron slag.

Fig. 69: Site C, section across ditches 1a and b and part of the north 'vicus'

1. Ploughsoil and brown fill with pebbles.

2. Gravel and rubble make-up and surface of road running between the inner ditch (1) of the fort and the buildings of the north *vicus*. The road has slumped into the ditch fill.

3. Dark brown silt fill.

4. Tip of small rubble, overlying a dark silt with pebbles.

5. Post-pit belonging to the south wall of one of the two north *vicus* buildings.

6. Post-pit, *vicus* building.

7. Stake-pipe, *vicus* building.

8. Yellow-brown fill with pebbles, in ditch 1b.

Fig. 71: Sections across ditch 2, site B

(a) South section

1. Topsoil, grading into a brown upper fill of the ditch, with many pebbles.

2. Tail of a bank with third-century pottery, constructed between ditches 2 and 3.

3. Light-brown fill with pebbles.

4. Dark brown silt fill, fairly pebble-free.

5. Tip of brown soil with pebbles.

6. Stiff grey-blue clay, filling what appears to be a recut.

7. Brown fill with gravel and pebbles, forming a series of tips from the inner lip of the ditch.

8. Brown silt fill with gravel lenses.

(b) North section (mirror image)

1-6. As (a).

7. Brown silt fill with pebbles and some charcoal.

8. A thin layer on the side of the ditch of yellow-brown silt.

Fig. 72: Section across ditch 2, site C

1. Pale brown alluvial silt, fairly pebble-free. Presumably flood-plain deposits, of late- or post-Roman date.

2. Tip of rubble including a line, running parallel with the lip of the ditch, of heavy dressed sandstone slabs.

3. Channel or ditch, filled with alluvial silt, cut into the top fill of the ditch.

4. Tips of gravel and brown loam.

5. Dark brown silt, stratigraphically earlier than unit 4.

6. Tip of charcoal and iron slag.

7. Gravel and sand.

8. Tip of charcoal, dark brown loam and iron slag with lenses of grey ash.

9. Tips of grey ash, charcoal and iron slag.

10. Brown silt with gravel and pebbles.

11. Tip of ash, charcoal and iron slag.

Fig. 73: Ditch 2, site C, section beside north-east road

1. Alluvial silt fill with water-worn pottery of the third and fourth centuries.

2. Gravel and brown silt.

3. Very fine gravel, possibly water-laid.

4. A series of tips comprising lenses of charcoal, some burnt clay, grey soil with charcoal, gravel and yellow silt.

5. Tips or wash material of fine and coarse gravel.

Fig. 74: Ditch 3, site B, south section

1. Ploughsoil.

2-5. Fill of a recut of the ditch.

2. Brown silt with some small rubble and pebbles.

3. Unit of dark brown silt with pebbles, washed in from the inner edge of the ditch.

4. Dark brown silt: in other parts of the ditch this rested upon the bottom.

5. Brown silt.

6-9. Fill of the original ditch.

6. Brown silt with pebbles.

7. Homogeneous grey-brown silt with few pebbles.

8. Dark brown silt with pebbles, including several distinct wash lenses.

9. Lens of charcoal.

Fig. 78: Site A, east 'vicus', *western part of the east section*

Note: for the features denoted A21 etc., cf. discussion under phase 1 of the east *vicus*. The sections shown in Figs 78-80 represent a continuous record of the east section of site A, from north-south.

1. Poorly preserved remains of mortared gravel floors of phase 3.
2. Brown fill, phase 2.
3. Spread of occupation debris, phase 1.
4. Yellow sand and gravel, spoil from the cutting of A17.
5. Charcoal-flecked red soil, a pre-*vicus* ploughing horizon.
6. As 1.
7. Lens of brown clay. Textured soil.
8. Burnt clay from the hearth within the building of phase 2.
9. Brown fill with tips of rubble and gravel. Phase 2.
10. Spread of dark occupation debris, phase 1.
11. As 5.
12. As 1. There is a robber-trench cut from this level down to the stone footing of phase 2.
13. Dump of dark soil sealing the phase 2 building.
14. Burnt clay overlying the gravel make-up for the floor of the phase 2 building.
15. Layers of yellow clay, forming the floor of the phase 2 building.
16. As 5.

Fig. 79: Site A, east 'vicus', *central part of east section*

A continuation of Fig. 78.

1. Successive gravel and mortar floors of phase 3.
2. Yellow clay, overlying a thin layer of fine gravel.
3. Occupation debris of phase 1.
4. Successive roads of phases 1-3, made up of gravel and heavy rubble.
5. As 3.
6. A bank of brown silt, possibly demarcating the road of phase 1.
7. Charcoal-flecked red soil a pre-*vicus* ploughing horizon.
8. Three distinct mortar and gravel floor-surfaces with numerous minor surfaces. The lowest surface is covered by a thin layer of occupation material. Phase 3.
9. Occupation debris, partly resting upon the pre-*vicus* plough-soil. Phases 1-2.
10. Yellow clay, phase 2.
11. As 7.
12. Successive gravel and mortar surfaces in an alley between the phase 3 buildings.
13. A succession of mortar and gravel floor-surfaces, interspersed by levels of burnt clay, charcoal and occupation debris. A part of an amphora forms a basin and hearth, beneath which is a layer of gravel make-up. Phase 3.
14. Layer of red clay and cobbles, resting upon a make-up deposit of gravel and rubble.
15. Occupation debris, phases 1-2.
16. As 7.

Fig. 80: Site A, east 'vicus', eastern part of east section

A continuation of Fig. 79.

1. A deep and extensive disturbed deposit with pottery of the nineteenth century.

2. Two gravel and mortar floors, separated by occupation debris with charcoal. Beneath, there is a deposit of burnt clay (hatched diagonally), a lens of charcoal and a further gravel and mortar floor. Phase 3.

3. Dark brown fill with a prominent layer of charcoal. Phase 2.

4. A low bank of grey-brown silt, sealing a line of stake-holes (A72) of phase 1.

5. Wall-trench, phase 2.

6. Brown silt-clay, overlying the undisturbed subsoil.

7. As 1.

8. Spread of burnt and unburnt clay, deriving from the phase 2 hearth.

9. Occupation debris of phase 1.

10. Pit of phase 2. Dark fill with some charcoal.

BIBLIOGRAPHY

Bestwick, J. D. and Cleland, J. H., 1974. "Metal working in the North-West". *In* Jones, G. D. B. and Grealey, S., 1974, 143-57.

Birley, E., 1951. "The Roman fort and settlement at Old Carlisle". CW2 li, 16-39.

—— 1953. "The Roman milestone at Middleton in Lonsdale". CW2 liii, 52-62.

—— 1953a. *Britain and the Roman Army*. Kendal.

—— 1955. "A Roman inscription from Watercrook". CW2 lv, 46-53.

—— 1957. "The Roman fort at Watercrook". CW2 lvii, 13-17.

Blundell, D. J., Garside, A. W. and Wilton, T. J., 1974. "Geophysical surveys across the centre of the Roman fort at Watercrook, Kendal". *Prospezioni Archeologiche* ix, 35-45.

Breeze, D. J. and Dobson, B., 1969. "Fort types on Hadrian's Wall". AA4 xxxxvii, 15-32.

Casey, P. J., 1974. "The interpretation of Romano-British site finds". *In* Casey, P. J. and Reece, R., *Coins and the Archaeologist*. BAR iv, 37-51.

Charlesworth, D., 1964. "Recent work at Kirkby Thore". CW2 lxiv, 63-75.

Cherkauer, D., 1976. "The stratigraphy and chronology of the River Treia alluvial deposits". *In* Potter T. W., *A Faliscan Town in South Etruria*. British School at Rome, 106-20.

Collingwood, R. G., 1915 (with Haverfield F. and Freeston, L. B.). "Report on the exploration of the Roman fort at Ambleside, 1903, with a preliminary report of exploration in March and April 1914". CW2 xiv, 433-65.

—— 1916. "The exploration of the Roman fort at Ambleside: report on the third year's work (1915)". CW2 xvi, 57-90.

—— 1921. "Explorations in the Roman fort at Ambleside (fourth year, 1920) and at other sites on the Tenth Iter". CW2 xxi, 2-42.

—— 1930. "The Roman fort at Watercrook, Kendal". CW2 xxx, 96-107.

Collingwood, W. G., 1908. "Three more ancient castles of Kendal". CW2 viii, 97-112.

Ewbank, J. M., 1960. "A cross-section of the Roman road in Casterton". CW2 lx, 28-31.

Frere, S. S., 1974. *Britannia. A history of Roman Britain*. Cardinal.

Gentry, A. P., 1976. *Roman military stone-built granaries in Britain*. BAR xxxii.

Hartley, B. R., 1966. "Some problems of the military occupation of the north of England". *Northern History* i, 7-20.

—— 1972. "The Roman occupations of Scotland: the evidence of the samian ware". *Britannia* iii, 1-55.

Higham, N. J. and Jones, G. D. B., 1975. "Frontiers, forts and farmers: Cumbrian aerial survey 1974-5". *Arch. J.* cxxxii, 16-53.

Horsley, J., 1732. *Britannia Romana*.

Jarrett, M. G., 1969. *The Roman Frontier in Wales*. University of Wales. Revised edition of V. E. Nash-Williams's volume.

—— 1976. *Maryport, Cumbria: a Roman fort and its garrison*. CW Extra Series xxii. Kendal.

Jones, G. D. B. and Grealey, S., 1974. *Roman Manchester*. Altrincham.

Jones, G. D. B. and Shotter, D. C. A., 1978. *Lancaster Excavations*. In press.

Jones, M. J., 1975. *Roman fort-defences to AD 117*. BAR xxi.

—— 1977. "Archaeological work at Brough under Stainmore 1971-72: I The Roman discoveries". CW2 lxxvii, 17-48.

Lowndes, R. A. L., 1963. " 'Celtic' fields, farmsteads and burial-mounds in the Lune Valley". CW2 lxiii, 77-95.

—— 1964. "Excavation of a Romano-British farmstead at Eller Beck". CW2 lxiv, 6-13.

Macadam, E. M. L., 1964. "A section of the Roman road south of Low Borrow Bridge". CW2 lxiv, 76-80.

Margary, I. D., 1973. *Roman roads in Britain*. 3rd edition, London.

Munby, J., 1975. "A figure of jet from Westmorland". *Britannia* vi, 216-18.

Nicholson, C., 1861. *Annals of Kendal*. 2nd edition.

North, O. H., 1932. "The Roman station at Watercrook". CW2 xxxii, 116-23.

—— 1934. "Finds from the Roman station at Watercrook". CW2 xxxiv, 35-40.

—— 1943. "A Roman altar found at Watercrook". CW2 xxxxiii, 161.

—— 1944. "Samian ware from Watercrook". CW2 xxxxiv, 146.

North, O. H. and Hildyard, E. J. W. 1945. "Excavations at the Roman fort of Watercrook 1944". CW2 xxxxv, 148-62.

Partridge, C. R., 1975. "Braughing". *In* Rodwell, W. and Rowley, T. (eds), *Small Towns of Roman Britain*. BAR xv, 139-57.

Phillips, C. W., 1970. *The Fenland in Roman Times*. Royal Geographical Research Memoir, no. 5.

Potter, T. W., 1975. "A Roman site at Hincaster, Westmorland". CW2 lxxv, 376-7.

—— 1976. "Excavations at Watercrook 1974: an interim report". CW2 lxxvi, 6-66.

—— 1976a. "Valleys and settlement: some new evidence". *World Archaeology* viii, no. 2, 207-19.

—— 1977. "Excavations at the Roman fort of Watercrook, 1975; a second interim report". CW2 lxxvii., 49-52.

RCHM 1936. *An inventory of the historical monuments in Westmorland*. London, HMSO.

Ramm, H. G., 1971. "The end of Roman York". *In* Butler, R. M. (ed.), *Soldier and Civilian in Roman Yorkshire*, 179-200.

Reece, R., 1973. "Roman Coinage in Britain and the Western Empire". *Britannia* iv, 227-51.

Richmond, I. A., 1945. "The Sarmatae, *Bremetennacum Veteranorum* and the *Regio Bremetennacensis*." JRS xxxv, 15-29.

Salway, P., 1965. *The Frontier People of Roman Britain*. CUP.

Steer, K. A., 1964. "John Horsley and the Antonine Wall". AA4 xxxii, 1-40.

Sturdy, D., 1972. "A ring-cairn in Levens Park, Westmorland". *Scottish Archaeological Forum* iv, 52-5.

—— 1973. "The temple of Diana and the Devil's Quoits". *In* Strong, D. E. (ed.), *Archaeological Theory and Practice*. Seminar Press, 27-43.

Vita-Finzi, C., 1969. *The Mediterranean Valleys*. CUP.

Villy, F., 1937. "A Roman road north-west from Overborough". CW2 xxxvii, 49-51.

Wacher, J. S., 1969. *Excavations at Brough-on-Humber 1958-1961*. Society of Antiquaries of London Research Report 25.

Wilson, T., 1884. "The Roman road over Whinfell". CW1 vii, 90-5.

Wright, R. P., 1965. "Roman Britain in 1964. The Inscriptions". JRS lv, 220-8.

CHAPTER IV

WATERCROOK: THE FINDS

THE ARRANGEMENT of this chapter broadly follows that of Chapter II; objects of metal, leather, glass, clay and stone are dealt with first, followed by sections discussing the pottery and the coins. There is also a full report on the important sample of animal bones, which includes all but some supplementary metrical data: these have been filed in the library of Lancaster University. As in Chapter II, the full catalogue references are cited in parenthesis. The contexts of the finds follows the arrangement of Chapter III; it will be useful, however, to repeat again the phases and their approximate dates.

East *vicus*:
 phase 1: Flavian-Trajanic.
 phase 2: Hadrianic-early Antonine.
 phase 3: Antonine-early third century.

Fort:
 phase 1: Flavian-Trajanic.
 phase 2: Late Hadrianic-early Antonine.
 phase 3: *c.* 155/165-220.
 phase 4: *c.* 265-290.

Guard-chamber, north-east gate:
 Unit 1: *c.* 270.
 Unit 2: *c.* 160-220.
 Unit 3: *c.* 150-160.
 Unit 4: *c.* 150-160.

SILVER (Fig. 84)

1. (SF 17)   A silver ring, resembling a ring-key (Kenyon 1948, Fig. 86, No. 12); but it is hard to imagine that this finely decorated ring was used in that way. The hoop is thin and flat and tapers towards the back. The plaque (which is fairly worn) shows in relief and openwork two opposed feline animals. They appear to be sitting on stools and are drinking from an urn. Charlesworth (1961, Pl. IV, No. 12 and Pl. IX, No. 1) illustrates two comparable examples, one in gold and the other in silver, from Corbridge. These examples have stone settings below the plaque. She quotes analogies from Rhenish sites and suggests a third to fourth-century context for these types (Charlesworth 1961, 16-17). Cf. also Henig 1977, 355. East *vicus*, phase 3.

2. (SF 298)   A twisted silver ring made up of four separate threads. These expand at one end, possibly to accommodate the bezel. The bezel itself may be represented as a small sub-rectangular piece of silver, found with the ring. East *vicus*, phase 2.

BRONZE (Figs 84-6)

Only 165 objects of bronze were found, a total that seems modest in proportion to the large extent of the excavated area. On the other hand, we should bear in mind that much of the investigation was concerned with the defences of the fort, which are not likely to have been used much for the dumping of rubbish. Of the finds, nearly one half consisted of small unidentifiable scraps of bronze; but the remainder provide a very useful cross-section of military and domestic objects. The overall distribution is shown in the table below, which demonstrates fairly clearly the absence of any obvious typological difference between finds from the *vicus* and fort. Domestic objects occur in both areas, just as military equipment is by no means confined to the fort.

Two lumps of bronze slag, both from the east *vicus*, suggest that some bronze working took place on the site.

	Vicus	Fort
Armour, weapons	1	6
Mounts	2	2
Fittings	0	6
Lock-bolts	2	0
Handles	2	2
Tweezers	3	0
Surgical instruments	0	3
Votive plaque	0	1
Studs	1	7
Brooches	8	11
Mirrors	2	0
Finger-rings	1	2
Other rings	2	2
Bracelets	0	3
Spoons	0	2
Needles/pins	3	7
Buttons	2	1
Strips	0	9
Scraps	12	49
Miscellaneous	6	5
	47	118

BROOCHES by A. C. H. OLIVIER

3. (SF 279)   An unusual T-shaped brooch. The bow has a fairly straight profile, with a flattened cross-section and a sharp angle at the head of the brooch. The centre of the bow is raised slightly between two shallow lateral grooves, and the bow tapers to a point at the foot, which is ornamented by a vestigial foot-knob. The head of the brooch forms a semi-cylindrical spring-cover with the ends closed by pierced half discs; each lateral edge of the spring-cover is decorated with a shallow incised line. The nine-turn spring has an external chord caught under the forward edge of the spring-cover, and is attached to the brooch by means of an axial bar threaded through the centre of the spring and seated in the pierced half discs of the spring-cover. Polden Hill brooches, to which this example is probably related, invariably possess either a hook or a pierced plate projecting from the head of the brooch, through which the chord of the spring is threaded; however, there is no trace of any such mechanism on this example.

Bronze. Slightly corroded. End of pin broken. East *vicus*, phase 1. Mid first century to mid second century.

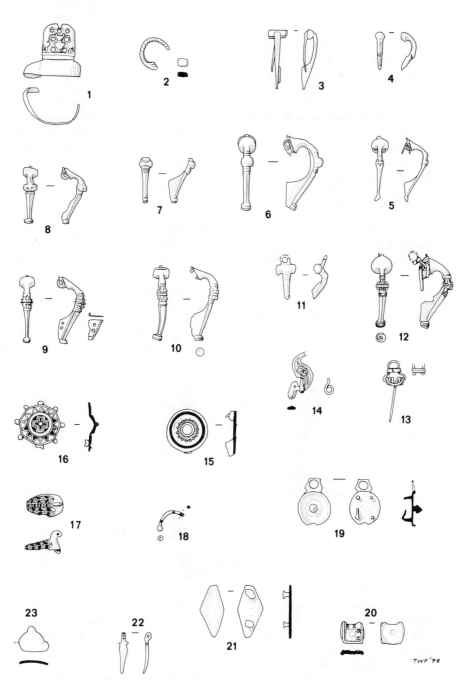

FIG. 84. – Watercrook: objects of silver, 1, 2; and bronze, 3-23. All 1:3 except 1, 2:3.

4. (SF 59) A small trumpet brooch; Collingwood type Riii (Collingwood and Richmond 1969, 297-6, Fig. 104. 54-6). The lower portion of the bow is V-shaped in cross-section, with a slightly raised central spine emphasised by two incised grooves running down its length. Each flank of the lower bow is also ornamented by a shallow incised groove. The foot and catchplate are missing. The mouldings at the crest of the bow are badly corroded, but appear to have consisted of a pair of opposed chevrons or leaves, outlined by a slight raised ridge; these mouldings do not continue around the back of the bow. There are extremely faint traces of decoration on the upper portion of the bow, although it is not now possible to ascertain the precise form of the ornamentation. The head of the brooch is trumpet-shaped, with part of a small lug projecting from its underside. The spring and pin are both missing, and the forward edge of the trumpet is broken, so it is not possible to ascertain whether there may have been a head-loop originally cast in one piece with the brooch.
Bronze. Badly corroded and broken. Fort, unstratified.
Riii Trumpet brooches generally occur during the late first century A.D., and the early second century (Boon and Savory 1975, 54).

5. (SF 340) Trumpet brooch. The lower portion of the bow is undecorated and slightly D-shaped in cross-section, tapering to a point which is ornamented with a foot-knob. The mouldings just below the crest of the bow are rather corroded, and it is difficult to ascertain the precise details of the decorative motifs employed, and it is therefore not possible to classify this example as a Collingwood Ri or Rii Trumpet brooch (Collingwood and Richmond 1969, 297). The fairly simple central moulding completely encircles the bow and is set between two transverse ridges in a rather similar fashion to an Ri Trumpet brooch from Stanwick (Wheeler 1954, 50. Fig. 15.2). Although no traces of acanthus leaves survive, this could merely be the result of corrosive activity. The head of the brooch is trumpet-shaped with a perforated plate projecting from its underside; the spring is of six turns with an internal chord, attached to the brooch by means of an axial bar threaded through the perforated lug. The axial bar is formed from a separate piece of bronze wire with the free ends inserted through the spring and lug, overlapping each other for the length of the spring; the ends of the axial bar would originally have formed a head-loop and collar, although this feature is now missing. The small projection on the head of the trumpet would have prevented the loop and collar from falling over the head of the brooch. The pin is broken and missing.
Bronze. Corroded and broken. East *vicus,* phase 3.
Ri and Rii Trumpet brooches may be dated between the first century and the mid second century.

6. (SF 300) Trumpet brooch; Collingwood Riv (Collingwood and Richmond 1969, 297). The lower portion of the bow is undecorated and D-shaped in cross-section, with an elaborate knob at the foot, consisting of three large cross-mouldings. The moulding just below the crest of the bow is somewhat corroded, but appears to consist of a waist-knob, with faint traces of opposed acanthus leaves; above and below this central embellishment are three simple and shallow cross-mouldings. None of this moulding has been carried round the bow, and the back has been left plain. The head of the brooch is trumpet-shaped, with a perforated projecting plate; this plate has a small notch at the rear edge, to house the internal chord of the spring (the spring of this brooch has been incorrectly conserved, and originally would have faced the opposite direction, so that the chord was internal). The spring, originally of six turns, is now broken, and the pin is missing. The spring is attached to the brooch in the same fashion as no. 6, although the head-loop and collar are also missing from this example; similarly the trumpet head has a small projection to prevent the loop and collar from falling over the head of the brooch.

Bronze. Corroded and slightly broken. East *vicus*, phase 2.

Riv Trumpet brooches develop as a simplification of the Rii form, and in general may be dated between the late first century and the mid second century.

7. (SF 42)   The lower half of a Collingwood Riv Trumpet brooch. The lower portion of the bow is undecorated and D-shaped in cross-section, with a knob at the foot. The moulding is just below the crest of the bow, and consists of a waist-knob set between opposed cusps of rather crudely represented acanthus leaves; below this ornament are three simple transverse mouldings. None of the moulding has been carried round the bow, and the back is plain. The head and upper portion of the bow is missing.
Bronze. Slightly corroded and broken. East *vicus*, unstratified.
Late first century to mid second century.

8. (SF 275)   Collingwood Rii Trumpet brooch. The lower portion of the bow is undecorated and V-shaped in cross-section with a sharply defined central spine. The ornamental foot-knob is formed by three fairly large circular mouldings. The moulding just below the crest of the bow consists of a very narrow central button set between opposed cusps of acanthus leaves, and this ornament is carried all round the bow. On either side of this central ornament are two narrow cross-mouldings, although the upper pair is badly corroded. The head of the brooch forms a rather flat trumpet, with a large perforated lug. The spring is broken, but was originally of six turns, attached to the brooch by means of an axial bar which would have formed a head-loop and clasp (now missing). The trumpet head retains the small forward projection. The pin is missing. A very similar example is known from Newstead (Collingwood and Richmond 1969, Fig. 104.52).
Bronze. Corroded and slightly broken. Fort, foundation trench for the fence beside north-east road, phase 1.

Rii Trumpet brooches are now generally dated to the second half of the first century and the first half of the second century (Boon and Savory 1975, 50-7).

9. (SF 276)   Collingwood Rii Trumpet brooch. The lower portion of the bow is V-shaped in cross-section with a sharply raised central spine, and each flank of the lower bow is also defined by a shallow longitudinal groove. The bow tapers to a point, ornamented by a large foot-knob. The catchplate is somewhat unusual in that it possesses two small circular perforations, one of which retains a small bronze rivet. A separate matching catchplate, cut out of sheet bronze, with two corresponding perforations, was found in association with this brooch; the original catch must have broken in antiquity, and the brooch repaired by the addition of this new catchplate. The moulding below the crest of the bow consists of a thin central button set between opposed cusps of acanthus leaves. Below this ornament there is a pair of cross-mouldings at the junction of the upper and lower bow, whilst there is a single cross-moulding at the crest of the bow. The head of the brooch forms a fairly flat trumpet shape, with the normal forward projection, and a pierced lug underneath. The spring is broken, but was originally of six turns, attached to the brooch by means of an axial bar threaded through the perforated lug. The pin and the head-loop and clasp are now missing.
Bronze. Slightly corroded and broken. East *vicus*, phase 3.
Second half of the first century to the first half of the second century.

10. (SF 350)   Collingwood Rii Trumpet brooch. The lower half of the bow is V-shaped in cross-section with a slightly raised central spine. The outline of this portion of the brooch is emphasised by a raised ridge and corresponding shallow groove on its inner edge. The ornamental knob at the foot of the bow is formed by four circular mouldings. The catchplate is broken. The moulding below the crest of the bow consists of a narrow central button set between opposed cusps of acanthus leaves. There is a single cross-moulding on either side of this ornament, although the lower one is the slightly broader of the two. All the mouldings

are carried round the bow. The trumpet head is fairly flat, decorated by a circumferential groove; both the lug for the axial bar and the forward projection are broken. The spring, pin, head-loop and clasp are missing.

Bronze. Slightly broken. Ditch 1.

Second half of the first century to the first half of the second century.

11. (SF 447) A T-shaped brooch. The bow is D-shaped in cross-section and the foot and most of the catchplate are missing. The forward portion of the bow is badly corroded, but there are no apparent traces of a head-stud. The head-loop is cast in one piece with the bow, and the head-plate is ornamented with two shallow grooves. The head of the brooch is also heavily corroded, and it is not possible to ascertain the precise means by which the pin was attached to the brooch, although there are faint traces of a surviving hinge or axial bar. The wings appear to have been decorated with cross-mouldings, and there are also faint traces of pierced plates at the end of the wings. The pin is missing.

Bronze. Broken and badly corroded. Guard-chamber, unit 4.

Late first and second centuries.

12. (AIP) Trumpet brooch, very similar to No. 10. The lower portion of the bow is V-shaped in cross-section with a raised central spine. The outline of this part of the brooch is emphasised by a slightly raised ridge and shallow groove. The ornamental foot-knob is formed by three circular mouldings, the central moulding being slightly wider than the other two, and retains faint traces of milled decoration. The moulding below the crest of the bow consists of a narrow central button set between opposed cusps of acanthus leaves. On either side of this central ornament, there is a pair of double cross-mouldings, and on the lower pair, there are traces of milled decoration similar to that employed on the foot-knob. All these mouldings (with the exception of the acanthus leaves), are carried round the bow, although on the underside they have been flattened to conform to the basic line of the brooch profile. Typologically, therefore, this brooch would appear to stand at the point of divergence between Collingwood Rii and Riv types (Collingwood and Richmond 1969, 297). The head of the brooch is trumpet-shaped with a perforated lug and a forward projection. The spring was originally of six turns with an internal chord, attached to the brooch by means of an axial bar threaded through the perforated lug. The head-loop is broken, but the free ends are inserted through the centre of the spring, and seated in a rolled sheet-bronze tube which forms the axial bar. The clip of the head-loop is not continuous at the back, and is ornamented on the upper face by two engraved lines forming a central ridge moulding; this central ridge possesses milled decoration. The pin has been broken in antiquity, and apparently replaced by the addition of an iron pin and coil to the spring.

Bronze and iron. Slightly corroded and broken. Construction trench for fort wall, phase 3.

Late first century to mid second century.

13. (SF 351) Spring, pin and head-loop only. Part of a trumpet brooch. The spring is of six turns with an internal chord. The free ends of the head-loop that would have formed an axial bar to attach the spring to the brooch are broken and missing. There is no trace of a rolled tube of sheet-bronze for these ends to seat into. The clip of the head-loop is not continuous at the back and is ornamented on the upper face by two engraved lines forming a central ridge moulding; this moulding possesses milled decoration.

Bronze. Broken. Ditch 1, upper fill.

Mid first century to mid second century.

14. (SF 261) Bulmer H1 Dragonesque brooch (Bulmer 1938, 148-9, Fig. 4). An S-shaped plate brooch in the form of a sea creature, in which a circular motif has been substituted for the central square that is the more common form of embellishment on Dragonesque brooches. The circumference of the circle is outlined by a small raised ring of bronze, and the

circle itself contains a relief bronze quatrefoil ornament; the crescentic cells between the petals would originally have been filled with enamel, although no traces of this work now survives. On either side of this ornament are two curvilinear V-shaped cells outlined by a narrow raised bronze band; originally these cells were filled alternately with blue and green enamel, of which only faint traces now survive. The head of the brooch is missing, although part of the projecting stay that would have connected the chin of the creature to its chest survives. The tail is broken, but the surviving fragment possesses a small circular cell that would have been filled with enamel, which is now absent. Part of the pin also survives. Bronze. Corroded and broken. East *vicus*, phase 2.

A very close parallel to this example has been found at Margidunum (Feachem 1951, 37. Fig. 2.32). This class of Dragonesque brooch may be dated between the late first century and the mid second century.

15. (SF 403) Simple flat enamelled disc brooch ornamented by two concentric rings of enamel surrounding a central circle; each ring of enamel is outlined, in relief, by a band of bronze. The central circle, which has lost its original setting, is surrounded by a broad ring of bronze. The inner ring is filled with green enamel decorated on its outer edge by a series of small circular cells, filled with what appears to be yellow or cream enamel. The outer ring is of plain blue enamel. Two pierced lugs project from the underside of the plate. The spring is of three turns with an internal chord, attached to the brooch by means of an axial bar seated in the lug perforations. The pin is missing.
Bronze. Corroded. Guard-chamber, unit 3.
Second century.

16. (SF 333) Elaborate enamelled disc brooch. A deep circular groove surrounds the central conical boss, which ends in a small raised knob. The central raised boss bears a quatrefoil design, with the individual petal cells filled alternately with blue and green enamel; the field of the quatrefoil is composed of four flattened triangular cells, each filled with blue enamel. The broad ring of the disc surrounding the boss is ornamented with fourteen roughly triangular-shaped cells of which at least six have been filled with blue enamel; these cells are set in a field of green enamel. The outer circumference of the disc is defined by a narrow wall of bronze. There are six small plain, and two larger lugs round the circumference of the disc; one of the larger lugs (over the hinge-housing) is broken, but would originally have formed a loop. The large lug over the position of the catchplate is also broken, and it is not now possible to ascertain its original appearance. The pin, now missing, was originally hinged between two perforated lugs projecting from the underside of the disc; the catchplate is also missing.
Bronze. Slightly corroded and broken. East *vicus*, phase 2.
Broadly similar forms are known from Richborough (Bushe-Fox 1932, 78. Pl. X.14; Hull 1968, 88. Pl. XXXI.66) and Leicester (Butcher 1977, 51. Fig. 5.6). The type in general occurs commonly during the second century.

17. (SF 252) Brooch in the form of a swimming duck. Each wing is represented by a series of large, split, and alternately green and blue enamel crescents; the points of the crescents face the tail of the bird. The back and tail of the bird are decorated by a series of small, alternately blue and green crescents, facing the opposite direction. The neck and front portion of the brooch is plain, whilst the eyes are represented by a small bead of blue enamel. The surface of the brooch has been silvered. The pin and hinge mechanism, originally under the tail of the bird, are missing, and the catchplate is broken.
Bronze and silver. Slightly corroded and broken. From the latest surface of the north-east road.
Second century (?).

18. (SF 6)   Part of a penannular brooch of class A3 (Fowler 1960, 151, Fig. 1). The terminal is formed by a fairly large knob, with one additional collar-moulding. The knob is too heavily corroded to ascertain whether originally it may have been milled. Most of the ring, the pin and the second terminal are missing.
Bronze. Badly corroded and broken. Fort, unstratified.
The type is common on northern British military sites, and is current from the first to the third century.

Not illustrated

(SF 299)   Spring and pin only. Part of a trumpet brooch. Similar to No. 13, except that the central moulding of the clip does not possess any milled decoration.
Bronze. Badly corroded and broken. East *vicus*, phase 2.
Mid first century to the mid second century.

Other brooches include a piece of a catchplate and a possible fragment of a penannular brooch (not illustrated).

OTHER BRONZES

19. (SF 159)   Circular harness-mount for attachment to a strap. The ring is provided for the suspension of a pendant (Webster 1969, Pl. XVIII). The mount is deeply recessed for enamel decoration, placed round a central knob: but no trace of any decoration survives. Ditch 2, upper fill.

20. (SF 321)   A small rectangular plaque with a shallow recess, filled with squares of black and yellow millefiori and green enamel. The bottom of a circular attachment survives on the back, suggesting that the plaque was set on a boss. Ditch 2, lower fill.

21. (SF 32)   A diamond-shaped mount with two studs on the back. The surface is very worn but could well have been decorated with enamelling. East *vicus*, unstratified.

22. (SF 319)   Small but complete bronze object, consisting of an eye with incised decoration and a tapered, slightly curved tongue below. Possibly a tongue from a buckle (Brailsford 1962, Fig. 15, 016) or a type of mount (Frere 1972, Fig. 33, No. 48). East *vicus*, unstratified.

23. (SF 313)   A thin decorative bronze plate, broken at the bottom. Slightly curved. Possibly from a strap-end. East *vicus*, phase 2.

24. (SF 154)   Heavy bronze object with damage both to the rim of the disc and to the socket. The end is also broken. The rim is inset with a circle formed by a prominent lip: this contains traces of red enamel. The lower end consists of bronze, wrapped around an iron core. Possibly a chariot fitting. Ditch 2, upper fill.

25, 26. (SF 197)   Two closely similar bronze fittings, found together. They are hollow and possess a prominent flange, together with rings of bead and groove decoration. The Corbridge hoard provides quite close analogies for these objects; they are interpreted as decorative elements for folding stools (Daniels 1968, 120), following Liversidge (1955, 28-37, Pls 17, 39-41). Other stools have been found in Britain in the Bartlow and Holborough burials and there are similar fittings from Newstead (Curle 1911, Pl. LXIV). Jacobsthal (1944, Pl. 902, No. 153a) would, on the other hand, interpret such objects as axle-bushes. Ditch 2, upper fill.

27. (SF 36)   Cylindrical bronze object, broken at the narrow end. There is a flanged rim at the top. The tube is ridged to give a firm grip. Since the cylinder is hollow, the temptation is to interpret this object as a musical instrument, as from Lydney (Wheeler 1932, Fig. 16, No. 47). but the "mouthpiece" does not appear to be pierced. East *vicus*, unstratified.

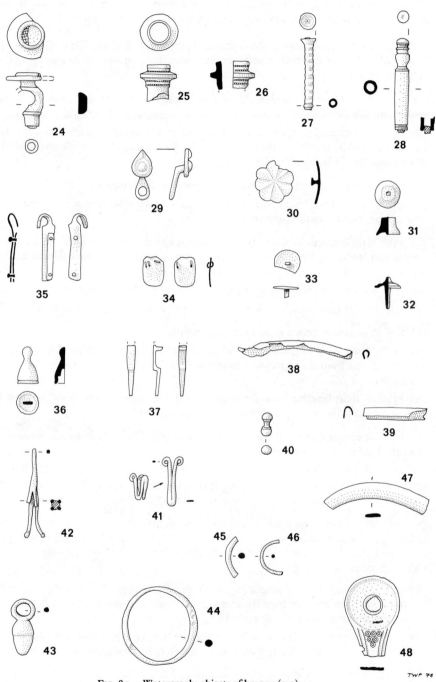

FIG. 85. — Watercrook: objects of bronze (1:3).

28. (SF 66)   Bronze handle with carefully turned decoration. The tube is hollow and there is a plug of iron set into it, presumably the tang of a blade. East *vicus*, unstratified.

29. (SF 273)   Bronze petal-headed "dress-fastener", belonging to Wild's Class III (Wild 1970). He considers that some of these objects are more plausibly identified as harness-fittings. East *vicus*, phase 3.

30. (SF 117)   Silvered bronze stud in the form of a rosette, with an attachment on the back. Ditch 1, middle fill.

31. (SF 253)   Bronze stud with a concave head and an iron shank in the back. This type of stud was represented by only two other examples: the form is therefore much less common at Watercrook than at Ravenglass (Fig. 27). Fort, phase 3.

32. (SF 7)   A stud with a domed head and a bronze shank. Fort, unstratified.

33. (SF 442)   A flat-topped stud with a bronze shank. Two other comparable examples in bronze were found. Guard-chamber, unit 4.

34. (SF 438)   One segment of scale-armour *(lorica squamata)* with some of the bronze wire used to join the scales. For chain-mail *(lorica hamata)*, cf. 126, 127 *infra*. Guard-chamber, unit 4.

35. (SF 15)   A bronze cuirass hook (cf. Robinson 1975, 180). Fort, unstratified.

36. (SF 55)   Bronze knob-handle with a recess for a rectangular tang. Fort, unstratified.

37. (SF 16)   A bronze scabbard-slide. Fort, unstratified.

38. (SF 453)   A section of bronze shield-binding. Ditch 1, top fill. Two other similar fragments were found, one from the east *vicus* (unstratified) and the other from close to the fort wall (unstratified).

39. (SF 171)   A short length of straight binding, retaining one rivet-hole. This may well have been used to bind the edge of a scabbard. Ditch 2, bottom fill.

40. (SF 269)   A bronze dumb-bell button, of common form. There is a fragment of one similar example. East *vicus*, robber-trench.

41. (SF 215)   A bronze hook with two eyes, shown both as found and unfolded. This was almost certainly used in costume, being a type with a long ancestry in the Mediterranean Iron Age (Potter 1976a, Fig. 46, No. 73). East *vicus*, unstratified.

42. (SF 405)   A curious object made of thin bronze wire, with four prongs (two broken) ending in knobs, and an iron shank in the middle. We can suggest no good analogy but it may have been some sort of crest-holder, although Robinson (1975, 46-7) can provide no parallel. Guard-chamber, unit 3.

43. (SF 452)   A heavy bronze weight in the shape of an acorn. Wt: 36 g. A weight for a steelyard. For close parallels from Richborough, cf. Cunliffe 1968, Pl. XLVII, Nos 215, 216. Road through north-east gate, top make-up.

44. (SF 260)   Bronze ring with two marked constrictions and one heavy area of wear. The ring seems small for a bracelet and may have been a bit-ring. East *vicus*, phase 3.

45. (SF 225)   Bronze bracelet, one of two examples. Fort, trench for fence beside north-east road, phase 1.

46. (SF 13)   Small bronze wire ring. Fort, unstratified.

47. (SF 218)   Heavy bronze ring with a flattened profile and bevelled edges. Ditch 2, top fill.

48. (SF 284) Bronze *patera* handle with decoration comprising six interlocking concentric circles. The disc-handle has a raised rim and is pierced by a hole. Cleaning revealed faint traces of a stamp on the handle, which was then submitted to Dr R. S. O. Tomlin (University of Durham). He writes:

I would like to read the surviving letters as ANDID, from the CANDIDVS F stamped on a handle excavated at Stockstadt (*ORL* B iii (1914), No. 33, p. 53 and Pl. VII, 54). So far as I know, close dating of these skillets is not yet possible; the handle which ends in a disc pierced by a round hole seems to be current in the later first century and the second century, but any attempt at dating would be hazardous.

East *vicus,* phase 3.

49. (SF 439) A hemispherical thin bronze boss apparently with the edges mostly complete. No trace of any attachment-rivet or pin survives. Guard-chamber, unit 4.

50. (SF 362) Fragment from the bowl of a large spoon in silvered bronze. Apart from 51 *infra,* one other fragment of a spoon was found. Fort, unstratified.

51. (SF 262) Part of a small spoon whose rim is mainly lost, as is the end of the handle. East *vicus,* phase 2.

52. (SF 22) Small bronze drop-handle, retained in place by a loop of wire. Fort, unstratified.

53. (SF 5) A severely distorted wire fragment from a bracelet, decorated by incised lines. Fort, unstratified.

54. (SF 450) Part of a surgical probe. Its central point is demarcated by incised rings and is square in cross-section and inset with grooves. Guard-chamber, unit 1.

55. (SF 229) A medical chatelaine with a flattened head and part of a ring for carrying other implements. The end is lost. Ditch 2, top fill.

56. (SF 122) A small bronze scoop, whose end has been hammered flat. This may well have been used for medical purposes. Ditch 1, middle fill.

57. (SF 402) The head of a bronze pin, decorated with incised rings and cross-hatching. Found on the surface of the north-east road.

58. (SF 314) Bronze pin with a knob-head. Ditch 1, upper fill.

59. (SF 86) Bronze tongs with widely expanded ends, now partly broken. Such tongs have surgical purposes. Fort, phase 3. One other similar pair was found, from an unstratified context in the east *vicus.*

60. (SF 212) Pair of bronze tweezers. East *vicus* phase 3.

61. (SF 207, 334) Two pieces from rectangular bronze mirrors with polished faces, giving the appearance of silvering. Both came from the east *vicus,* phase 2. Cf. Lloyd-Morgan (1977) for a general discussion of mirrors in Britain.

62. (SF 329) A very small finger-ring, whose bezel is inset with blue-green enamel. East *vicus,* phase 1.

63. (SF 361) Small finger-ring. The surface of the bezel is slightly recessed and retains traces of four prongs to hold the setting. Guard-chamber, unit 1.

64. (SF 74) Finger-ring with a decorated ribbon-hoop and a circular bezel. This is filled with green enamel, leaving a space in the middle for another type of enamel or some other setting, now missing. Fort, unstratified.

65. (SF 150) Bronze lock-bolt of common type: east *vicus,* phase 3. One other example in bronze from the east *vicus,* phase 3; and also one in iron, from the primary silt of ditch 1.

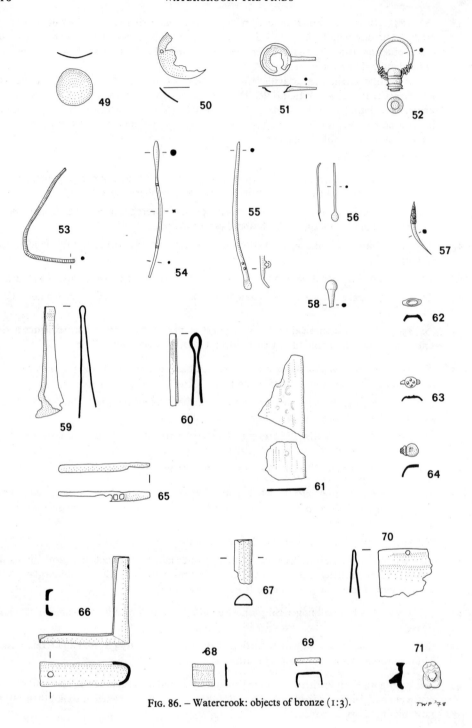

FIG. 86. – Watercrook: objects of bronze (1:3).

TWP '78

66. (SF 149)   A complete bronze bracket with a square cross-section along one side and semi-circular cross-section along the other. Both sides are pierced by nail holes towards the end. The bracket could have been used to bind the edges of a variety of objects, such as slate palettes (e.g. Frere 1972, Fig. 58, 229) which have bevelled edges to enable them to slide into grooved containers; alternatively, it could have been employed as shield-binding. Fort, phase 3.

67. (SF 297)   A short fragment of hemispherical tubing with lightly facetted surfaces. Fort, unstratified.

68. (SF 251)   Small rectangular plaque with two raised parallel lines. East *vicus*, phase 2.

69. (SF 388)   Small strip of bronze, bent to form a rectangular staple. Guard-chamber, unit 1.

70. (SF 238)   A folded piece of bronze sheet, pierced by one small nail hole on each side. Fort, unstratified.

71. (SF 2)   A miniature votive plaque depicting the male genitals together with pubic hairs. The back of the plaque is recessed and only roughly finished and clearly was not intended to be seen. The origin of this type of votive may be found in the great collections of Republican votive offerings made at sanctuaries over much of the Mediterranean world. The heyday of these sanctuaries was the fourth-second centuries B.C., after which the use of votives went into decline (although the practice never ceased). The vast majority of the Republican votives were made of terracotta and generally were modelled at life-size; otherwise, exact parallels can be found for the Watercrook example (e.g. Fenelli 1975a, Fig. 354; cf. also Potter *in press* and Fenelli 1975b). They do not appear to be common on military sites in Britain, although there is what seems to be an unusual variant from Birrens (Robertson 1975, Fig. 33, No. 6, identified as a vessel mounting). From on top of the turf rampart but not a sealed context.

LEAD (Fig. 87)

Thirty pieces of lead were found, evenly distributed over the site. The great majority consisted of folded fragments of thick sheet, many retaining nail holes; these were presumably gathered after demolition for reworking. One piece was in fact a melted-down lump. Objects were confined to a large nail, three circular pierced weights (probably spindle-whorls), a cramp for mending pottery and a weight with the value of 1 *libra* (12 oz.).

72. (SF 174)   A short strip of lead, folded in several places. It is pierced by a single nail hole. Ditch 2, upper fill.

73. (SF 130)   Part of a lead sheet, the only intact edge being along the top. It is pierced by two nail holes; one nail evidently had a wide flat top, perhaps resembling a stud like 33 *supra*. East *vicus*, phase 2.

74. (SF 84)   A lead nail with a rectangular head. Fort, unstratified.

75. (SF 336)   A circular lead weight. It weighs 12 oz. = 1 *libra*, but there is no stamp to indicate its value. East *vicus*, unstratified.

76. (SF 317)   A strip of lead with two rivets. It is probably a cramp for mending pottery. East *vicus*, phase 1.

77. (SF 404)   A circular lead weight, pierced by a hole. Guard-chamber, unit 3.

78. (SF 106)   As 77, but smaller. East *vicus*, phase 3.

79. (SF 19)   A small lead weight, pierced by a hole, and with a domed head. Fort, unstratified.

80. (SF 322)   A circular collar made of lead sheet, folded over several times. Perhaps from a pipe. East *vicus*, phase 2.

STONE AND CLAY (Fig. 87)

For quernstones, tiles and other large pieces of stone, cf. *infra*.

81. (SF 246)   An oculist's stamp made of stiff white clay. X-ray diffraction analysis by the Department of Geological Sciences at Durham University suggests that the clay is kaolinite with an admixture of quartz: in Britain this occurs only in Cornwall, although it is common enough on the Continent. The stamp, which is retrograde, reads P. CLODI. However, it is clear that it has been cut down from a larger original since three of the sides are bevelled while the fourth (immediately before the P) is straight. Dr. Tomlin (*Britannia* VI (1975), 289) compares it with a stamp in green steatite, probably from Britain, which reads COLLYR. P. CLOD (*CIL* vii 1317; xiii 10021, 143). This suggests that the full text of the Watercrook stamp may have been COLLYR. P. CLODI.

   Collyria are eye-salves which were made up either in liquid form or more commonly as small sticks to be dissolved by the patient. The side of the stick was stamped with the name of the doctor (or inventor of the remedy), very often with a list of instructions as to its use (Liversidge 1973, 334-7; Scarborough 1969, Pl. 45-7). Oculists' stamps are well attested in Britain with many examples from military and civilian sites. East *vicus*, phase 3.

82. (SF 335)   Weight made from a local limestone. East *vicus*, phase 2.

83. (SF 41)   Spindle-whorl made from a grey stone. East *vicus,* unstratified.

84. (SF 370)   Baked clay weight made in a gritty orange fabric. North *vicus*, unstratified.

85. (SF 386)   Baked clay weight in a hard reddish fabric. Ditch 1, middle fill.

86. (SF 3)   The lower part of a worn terracotta figurine in a rather gritty pale cream fabric made on a mould; the figurine may show Venus leaning against a rock. Unstratified, from the eastern corner of the fort.

JET AND AMBER (Fig. 87)

87. (SF 87)   The shaft of a highly polished jet hairpin. For a useful survey of the jet industry, which concentrated in the York area, cf. *RCHM* 1961. Ditch 1, middle fill.

88. (SF 8)   Part of a jet ring with a plano-convex cross-section. An example from South Shields has a clear wear mark, showing that these rings were sometimes worn as pendants, though they have also been interpreted as hair-rings and dress-fasteners. Ditch 1, fill.

89. (SF 409)   Bead made of amber. For other beads, cf. the section describing the glass. From the guard-chamber, unit 3.

BONE (Figs 87, 88)

There were comparatively few objects of bone, despite the fact that the soil at Watercrook is well suited to its preservation. All the objects found are in fact illustrated. However, it should be noted that the ditch fills yielded a number of antler fragments which were sawn and cut, implying that these bones were used for the manufacture of objects. North (1932) records a similar discovery in the inner ditch along the north-west side of the fort.

90. (SF 427)   Spindle-whorl. Guard-chamber, unit 3.

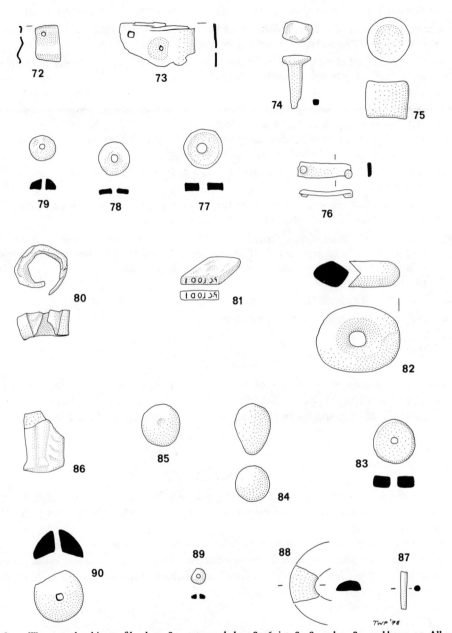

FIG. 87. – Watercrook: objects of lead, 72-80; stone and clay, 81-6; jet, 87-8; amber, 89; and bone, 90. All 1:3 except 81, 2:3.

91. (SF 151)   Two parts of a bone object, polished on the face and left rough on the back. Possibly to be interpreted as a device for tightening tent guys. Ditch 1, primary silt.

92. (SF 478)   Part of a highly polished bone handle. It is carefully decorated with incised lines and compass-drawn circles. Trench within east angle of fort, phase 2.

93. (SF 112)   Part of bone cylinder, decorated with two groups of parallel lines and pierced by a hole. Lightly polished. Probably a hinge used for a box or cupboard (Frere 1972, 149-50), East angle of fort, phase 3.

94. (SF 34)   A finely polished and precisely decorated bone object, pierced medianly by a rectangular socket, as well as by a hole drilled from the end. In this hole was a bone peg with a domed head. It is impossible to interpret this as a hinge and it may well have been intended to hold a strap, held in place by the peg. East *vicus*, phase 3.

95. (SF 65)   Polished bone toggle, carefully carved. It resembles a dumb-bell button. Fort, unstratified.

96. (SF 324)   Bone gaming-counter with compass-drawn circles on the face and a plain back. Two lines have been scratched on the side. East *vicus*, phase 2.

97. (SF 105)   The head of an elaborately carved hair pin, showing a woman wearing a very high feathered head-dress. Dr Wild has suggested a Severan date for this style while Dr Henig would identify the lady as Minerva, with a plumed helmet (Henig 1977, 359 and note 71). Ditch 1, middle fill.

98. (SF 378)   Bone pin with part of a grooved head. Guard-chamber, unit 2.

99. (SF 135)   Bone needle. Ditch 1, middle fill.

LEATHER

Although the decayed fragments of several shoes were found, represented by several clusters of hob-nails (cf. 153), the only piece of leather was one small fragment of a sole. It came from the old ground surface within the east corner of the fort, beneath the turf rampart.

TILE AND SLATE

One complete slate roofing tile was found in phase 3 deposits in the east *vicus*. In shape it is roughly sub-rectangular, measuring 31×29.5 cm. It is perforated by a single nail hole towards the top edge.

Most of the tile consisted of square bricks used in hearths. No example survived complete but none seems to have been more than 28 cm square and 5.5-6 cm deep. In addition there were a few pieces of box tile, some with scoring on the surface. None came from stratified deposits.

IRON (Figs 88-92)

Rather more than 10,000 iron objects were found, evenly distributed throughout the whole site. As the table shows, the vast majority consisted of fragments of nails, belonging mainly to the common type with a flat, round head and a shank with a square cross-section; but there was also a good range of other objects, from weapons and armour to personal items and structural fittings. The most notable discovery was that of a number of

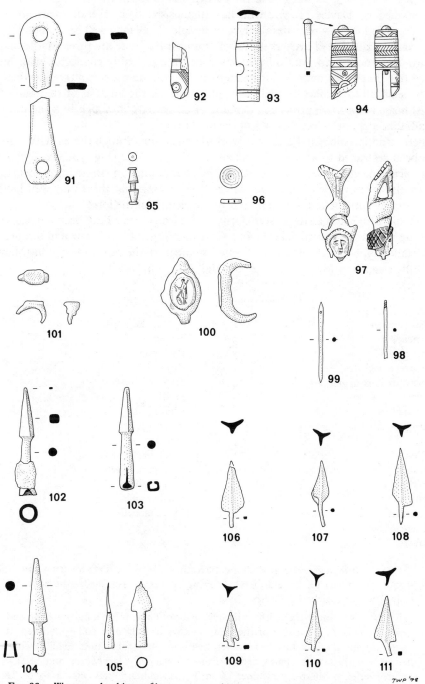

FIG. 88. – Watercrook: objects of bone, 91-9; and iron, 100-111. All 1:3, except 97, 100, 2:3.

arrowheads (105-11), all but one of the barbed and tanged variety. These have recently been studied by Davies (1977), who has emphasised their overall rarity in Britain: Watercrook in fact now provides the largest sample. They may well be an indication that there was a vexillation of archers in the garrison. Also of note are three snaffle-bits (121-3), two horseshoes (120) and other items which are probably connected with harness-fittings (e.g. 124): they underline the equestrian element on the site, although whether the horses belonged to soldiers or civilians is unknown. As the analysis of the fauna (infra) shows, horse bones were present in deposits of all periods, although in small quantities: overall, they amount to less than 1% of the total sample.

There is no question that iron was worked on the site, though the activity is likely to have been restricted to smithing. A small smithing furnace (Fig. 76) was found in the north *vicus* and there were tips of slag in the nearby ditch, 2. In addition, nearly every deposit elsewhere yielded some slag material, suggesting that there may well have been quite extensive production of iron objects in the vicinity of the fort.

It should be noted that the vast majority of the iron objects have been studied without anything more than superficial cleaning. Corrosion is generally heavy and has prevented any detailed typology of the nails. A small number of the other objects has, however, been fully cleaned by Mr J. Anstee (Abbot Hall Museum, Kendal).

Distribution of iron objects by type

Dagger pommel	1	Split-spike loops	6
Spearheads	3	T-staples	2
Artillery bolts	5	Lock-bolt	1
Arrowheads, socketed	1	Keys	2
Arrowheads, barbed and tanged	14	Socketed chisel	1
Ferrules	2	Styli	4
Chain-mail	6	Chain-links	1
Calthrops	3	Rings	12
Knives	7	Hooks	5
Snaffle-bits	3	Blade-like objects	50
Horseshoes	2	Strapping-binding	96
Shoes (hobnails)	5	Large nails	821
Buckles	4	Smaller nails	9,387
Finger-rings	2	Miscellaneous	41
Ring-headed bars	2		
Holdfast	2		10,491

100.   (SF 315)   Iron finger-ring, resembling the form of 101, *infra*. Thin hoop with an oval cross-section, and a near-rectangular bezel. The ring has not been cleaned, so details of the setting cannot be seen clearly. East *vicus*, phase 2.

101.   (SF 316)   Iron finger-ring with an intaglio made of onyx. It has a narrow hoop and an oval bezel. Dr Henig's discussion of the gemstone has already been fully published (in Potter 1976, 36) and it will suffice here to note that the impression shows Achilles with a spear, helmet and shield. The motif derives from Polykleitos' *Doryphoros* and belongs to the notable series of "heroic gemstones" from British military sites (Henig 1970). Dr Henig would like to point out, however, that the gem falls in the group that Kleibrink (1975) describes as the "Plain Grooves Style", dating between the first and third centuries. East *vicus*, phase 2.

102. (SF 291) Artillery bolt-head with a rectangular head and a split socket. One of five bolt-heads, including 103, 104 *infra*. Cf. Brailsford 1962, 6 and Pl. VI; Manning 1976, 21-2. The group as a whole belongs in Brailsford's group of "lighter bolt-heads". From trench in the eastern angle of the fort, phase 2. Other examples (not illustrated) from the fort defences (1) and the east *vicus*, unstratified (1).

103. (SF 357) Artillery bolt-head with a split socket. Ditch 1, lower fill.

104. (SF 70) Artillery bolt-head. The shaft is damaged but it is unlikely that the socket was split. Fort, unstratified.

105. (SF 80) Small socketed arrowhead. This is the only arrowhead of this type from this site, the others all being triple barbed. Cf. Manning 1976, 22-3, No. 37. East *vicus*, phase 3.

106-111. An important group of six triple-barbed arrowheads. In addition there are another eight examples. Davies (1977) has made a survey of this type of arrowhead, suggesting that it may identify special units of *sagittarii*, largely recruited in the eastern provinces. His list of find-spots in Britain includes Ham Hill (1), Hod Hill (1), Kingsholm, Gloucester (1), Richborough (1), Margidunum (1), Wall (2), Wilderspool (1), Corbridge (3), Caerleon (1), Turret 25b (1), Housesteads (1), Newstead (7), Bar Hill (7), Dinorben (2). The sample from Watercrook is thus the largest yet found. Davies argues for a first- and second-century date for these types, which were then superseded by new socketed forms. It may well be, therefore, that there was a unit of archers at Watercrook, although it is clear from the ancient sources that all soldiers were expected to use the bow.

    The type of arrowhead does not vary in anything more than size. All have three barbs and simple tangs. None is socketed. The contexts are as follows;

106. (SF 274) In front of fort wall, phase 2.

107. (SF 381) Ditch 1, top fill.

108. (SF 475) Fort-wall collapse.

109. (SF 72) Fort, unstratified.

110. (SF 20) Fort, phase 3.

111. (SF 26) Heightening of rampart, phase 2.

Not illustrated;

    (SF 21) Fill of ditch 1.

    (SF 111) East *vicus*, phase 3.

    (SF 161) Ditch 1, middle fill.

    (SF 401) Guard-chamber, unit 3.

    (SF 428) Guard-chamber, unit 1.

    (SF 432) Ditch 1, fill.

    (APA) Fort, unstratified.

    (ACG) East *vicus*, phase 3.

112. (SF 193) Iron spearhead, of common form. Brailsford (1962) provides the best general survey of spearheads. Ditch 2. Only two other examples were identified, but it is likely that others exist, disguised by corrosion.

113. (SF 263) Socketed object with a long shaft, tapering towards the end where there is the beginning of a blade. The base of the socket retains traces of the wooden shaft. It is best explained as a socketed chisel, as from Newstead (Curle 1911, Pl. LIX, No. 7), and Brampton (Manning 1966, 14-5, No. 8). Fort, trench for fence beside north-east road, phase 1.

114. (SF 114) Ferrule with a split socket and one rivet hole. This could have been used for a variety of purposes but it may have been used to tip the butt-end of a spear-shaft. East *vicus*, phase 3.

At least one other similar ferrule was found, in the trench for the fence beside the northeast road, phase 1.

115. (SF 83) Iron knife with a flat tang. Fort, unstratified.

116. (SF 127) Iron knife with a tang set along the mid-point of the blade. The commonest form of Romano-British knife. Make-up for latest *intervallum* road.

117. (SF 14) Knife with a long tang and a small rectangular hilt. Romano-British knives are not normally provided with hilts and this may be post-Roman in date. Fort, unstratified.

118. (SF 11) Iron knife, badly damaged by corrosion. Ditch 1.

Other knives

To the illustrated examples (cf. also 163) should be added at least two others: one is socketed and might best be described as a chopper.

119. (SF 423) Four-pronged iron calthrop from the guard-chamber, unit 3. Two other examples were found, both from unit 1 in the guard-chamber.

120. (SF 60) Iron horseshoe, badly damaged by corrosion. From the bank between ditches 2 and 3, a fairly securely stratified deposit with third-century pottery. The outline is smooth and there is no trace of a calkin at the surviving end of the shoe. The exact position of the nail-holes is not clear but sunken areas imply that they existed. Manning (1976, 31) provides a valuable discussion of horseshoes. Although rarely found in stratified contexts, they appear at Camulodunum in deposits that immediately precede the Roman Conquest (Hawkes and Hall 1947, 342-3). There is also a well known collection from late Roman deposits at Maiden Castle (Wheeler 1943, 290).

One other horseshoe was found, in an unstratified context.

121. (SF 393) A two-link snaffle-bit, with one side ring. The commonest form of Romano-British bit. Guard-chamber, unit 3.

122. (SF 30) A ring and an attached bar. Probably from a snaffle-bit, though the bar is light for the task. East *vicus*, unstratified.

123. (SF 136) Side-ring and bar from a one-link snaffle-bit. Ditch 1, middle fill.

124. (SF 265) Iron object consisting of an eye and rectangular loop. Probably for carrying harness straps. Fort, unstratified.

125. (SF 414) A split-spike loop with a ring passing through the loop. Guard-chamber, unit 3.

126. (SF 431) Chain-mail from unit 4 in the guard-chamber. There are 77 rings in all. One ring has a piece of bone attached to it (detail) while others were found overlapping, as if they had been sewn together. None of the rings was linked to another: cf. Manning 1976, 23. Other examples include 127 *infra*; two other small groups of rings from the guard-chamber, unit 4; and two groups from unstratified deposits overlying the phase 3 buildings in the east *vicus*.

127. (SF 426) Eleven links from chain-mail; guard-chamber, unit 4. A different size of mail from 126, *supra*, although both sets were found in the same deposit, together with two other groups of rings.

128. (SF 34) Corrosion obscures some details of this object. It appears to have an iron back and tang and a bronze rim. The tang has a lump of corrosion at the junction with the plate which may indicate a rivet. It has a broad resemblance to a crescentic-shaped linch-pin (although it lacks a loop) but it is more likely to be the pommel of a dagger. Fort, unstratified.

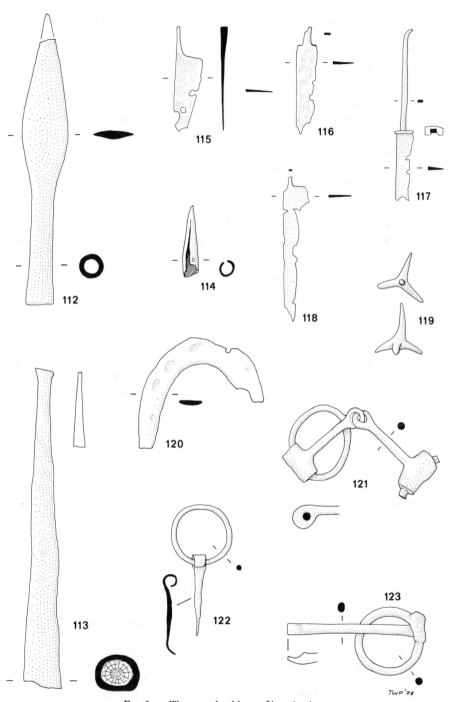

FIG. 89. – Watercrook: objects of iron (1:3).

129. (SF 162)   A "holdfast" with a semicircular head, made in one piece. The head tapers towards a point at each side. The object is probably designed to join a piece of wood with a semicircular cross-section to another. There are close parallels from Brampton (Manning 1966, 33-4). Ditch 1, middle fill.

130. (SF 380)   A bracket with a ring loop. There are no obvious signs of nail holes. North *vicus*, unstratified.

131. (SF 147)   A U-shaped fitting with ring loops at each end. Ditch 2.

132. (SF 392)   A decorative strip of iron with what seems to be a key hole at one end and a split pin (serving as a hinge) at the other. The object was probably used on a door or large box. Guard-chamber, unit 1.

133. (SF 175)   Rake prong (as Curle 1911, Pl. LXI, No. 7). It is made in two parts with a very distinct forked weld at the junction between the tang and blade. Fort, phase 2.

134. (SF 377)   Split pin. The pins were driven through the wooden plank or beam and then hammered over. Guard-chamber, unit 2.

135. (SF 192)   Eyelet spike, as from Portchester (Cunliffe 1975, Fig. 129 No. 225). East *vicus*, phase 3.

136. (SF 295)   Pair of split pins, probably used as a hinge. Top fill of ditch 2.

137. (SF 115)   A thin iron bar, tapering towards one end. East *vicus*, phase 3.

138. (SF 126)   A U-shaped object with a prong welded to it. Possibly a pair of tongs. fort, phase 2.

139. (SF 201)   An iron blade with a hook. East *vicus*, phase 3.

140. (SF 415)   A rectangular handle, with a central loop to hold a rope or chain in place. It is probably not a bucket-handle: these were usually round and the angle of the hook is inappropriate (Neal 1974, 187). A more likely explanation is that it was used to suspend vessels over a fire (Jacobi 1897, 242, Fig. 36). Guard-chamber, unit 3.

141. (SF 379)   Chain-links. Fort, unstratified.

142. (SF 459)   Links of a chain, in the shape of a figure of eight. Possibly a pot chain: Manning 1966, 19-20. Guard-chamber, unit 1.

143. (SF 93)   Figure of eight chain-links. Cf. 142. Ditch 1, middle fill.

144. (SF 369)   Part of a buckle with a small portion of the tongue adhering to the main frame. Guard-chamber, unit 2.

145. (SF 27)   A complete buckle. East *vicus*, unstratified.

146. (SF 50)   A ring or buckle. Fort, unstratified. Iron rings were represented by 12 other examples, ranging in diameter from 2·2-5 cm.

147. (SF 371)   Part of a buckle. Guard-chamber, unit 2.

148. (SF 277)   An L-shaped tumbler-lock lift-key with two teeth. Cf. Manning in Frere 1972, 181, and Manning 1976, 38-9 for general discussion. East *vicus*, phase 2.

149. (SF 434)   A T-shaped tumbler-lock lift-key. Cf. 148. Guard-chamber, unit 1.

150. (SF 440)   Iron *stylus* belonging to Manning's type II (Manning 1976, 34-5). Including No. 150 below, there were four examples altogether from the site. From the make-up for the latest road-surface through the north-east gate.

151. (SF 257)   Iron *stylus*. East *vicus*, phase 2.

152. (SF 433)   Rivet head. Ditch 1.

153. (SF 204)   The sole of a shoe, studded with hobnails. The leather has completely perished. Ditch 2.

A number of hobnails were found, including one group of 20 from a decayed shoe, found in ditch 1.

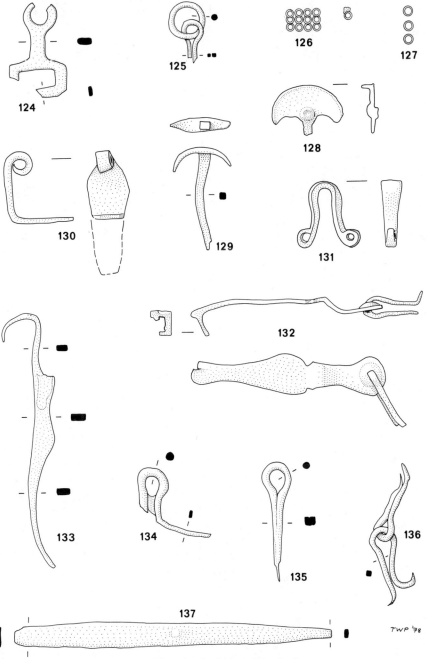

FIG. 90. – Watercrook: objects of iron (1:3).

154. (SF 91) Nail with a triangular head; Manning's Type II (in Frere 1972, 186). There were only three examples of this type of nail (cf. 156, *infra*). Fort, unstratified.

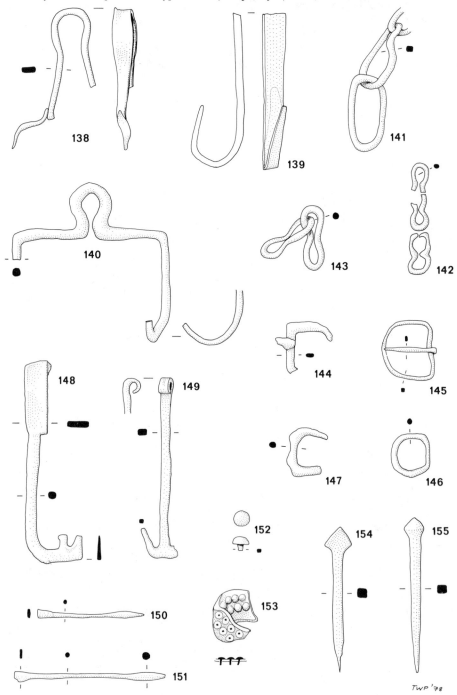

FIG. 91. – Watercrook: objects of iron (1:3).

155. (SF 18) Nail with a domed head. East *vicus*, phase 3.

156. (BAA) Large nail with a triangular head. Cf. 154. Fort, unstratified.

157. (AJK) Nail with a flat top. Fort, phase 2.

158. (AEQ) Nail with a large flat top. There were only four other nails recognisably of this form. East *vicus*, phase 2.

159. (AHI) A long double-headed rivet. Fort, unstratified.

160. (BAA) T-shaped staple. Fort, unstratified.

161. (AHB) A ring-headed bar. Manning (1966, 35, No. 58) notes that the possible uses for such objects range from linch-pins to fixing rings to walls. Fort, unstratified.

162. (AHQ) An iron hook. Fort, unstratified.

163. (BAA) A knife with a ring at the top of the tang. For other knives see 115-18, *supra*. Fort, unstratified.

164. (AHL) Iron binding. Fort, phase 2.

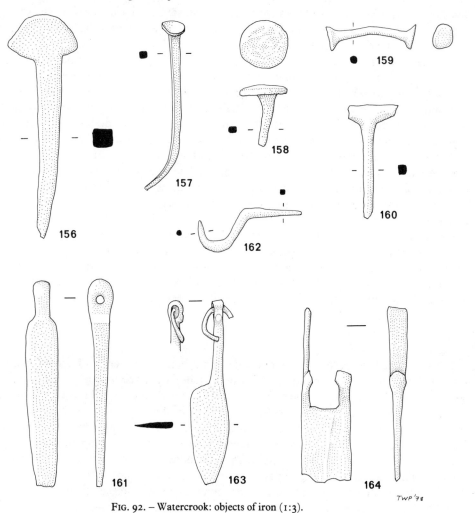

FIG. 92. – Watercrook: objects of iron (1:3).

GLASS, BEADS, ARMLETS By Dorothy Charlesworth

A large quantity of small fragments was found, ranging in date from *c.* 70 to the present day, but mainly falling between *c.* 70-*c.* 250. Most of the fragments are of natural green glass, used for vessels of many shapes and therefore unidentifiable in most cases. Those which can be identified include fragments of at least 17 angular-bodied, probably square, bottles, dating to between *c.* 70-130 (Charlesworth 1966). Of these three moulded square bases have three concentric circles (e.g. 172), another four preserve parts of two circles and one has part of one circle only. Another has a square outline moulded on it; probably there was some device in the centre, now broken off. Six cylindrical bottles of roughly the same date can be distinguished among the fragments.

There is the base of a small unguent flask of first-second century date (167) as well as some fragments from flagons. These date to between the second half of the first century to the middle of the second century, but in no case can the precise type be distinguished from the fragment. Two lower ends of handles with horizontally ridged tails are from conical bodied vessels (168). A range of possible types is illustrated in Charlesworth 1959 (52, Fig. 8, 5-8). There is also a piece of hollow tubular rim (171), which must be from a globular jar, *c.* 70-130. Faider-Feytmans (1952, 71-81) provides discussion of the jar and flagons. There are a few pieces of better quality glass. The only coloured fragments are from flagons, including two pieces of amber colour glass and one in yellowish-green glass: this is a deliberate colour, not the natural green of the bottle glass (169). One piece is outstanding (165); it comprises part of a small bowl, in good-quality colourless glass. Its base-ring is formed by cutting and its surface is rotary-polished. Such products are generally dated between the middle and the end of the first century but, being valuable, can have a long life; thus examples have been found in Scotland on sites of Antonine date, most recently at Cramond (Maxwell 1974, 198-9). The general problem of dating vessels in this metal and technique is discussed by Harden and Price (1971, 330-6).

An unusual vessel or lid (in poor-quality colourless glass, slightly tinged with green) has an outsplayed rim, rounded at the tip, and a small convex body with either a hollow tube or a knob at its centre base; the fragment is broken short of the critical point (170). Either it is a funnel or it is a dome-shaped lid. The funnel-shaped vessel is not common but an example from Mala Mitrovika and, conveniently, a dome-shaped lid from Bribir in Croatia, is illustrated by Dameski (1976: Bribir: Pl. V, 2; Mala Mitrovika: Pl. VIII, 3). There is also a complete funnel at Köln (Doppelfeld 1966, 50, T.89).

Window Glass

Both moulded glass, rough on one side, glossy on the other, and blown cylinder ("muff") glass panes were found. The first dates generally to the first-second century, the second to the third-fourth century. The techniques are discussed by Harden (1959) and Boon (1966). No pane can be restored and no fragment shows evidence of how it was fixed in place. The pane measuring not less than 60×60 cm from the first-century bath house at Red House, Corbridge, is a large size (Charlesworth 1959a, 166). Small quarries also seem to have been used (as in later stained-glass windows) and some at least were fixed at the edge with mortar. One triangular fragment from Watercrook seems to be a quarry, not merely a chance break. It can be compared with pieces from Gadebridge (Charlesworth 1974, 203).

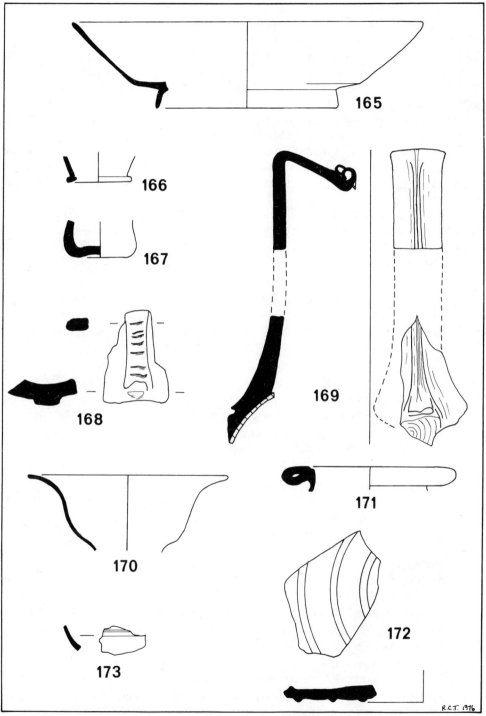

FIG. 93. – Watercrook: vessels of glass (1:2).

Beads, armlets and counters.

A surprisingly large number of melon beads were found, some in very worn condition. All but one are made of frit in varying shades of turquoise, some more blue than others. One half-bead is in clear deep blue glass flashed on poor-quality colourless glass (176). This must have been done to preserve the limited supplies of blue glass and suggests the re-use of material. The same technique is used for some glass bangles (Stevenson 1956, 215). A small cylindrical five-sided roughly made bead in emerald green was also found (174).

Fragments of four armlets were found, two (183, 4) of opaque white glass (Kilbride-Jones 1938, type 3), one of natural blue-green glass with a trail of twisted clear blue and white along the centre (type 2; 185), and one in blue glass with white lines (186). These armlets are best known in the area between Hadrian's Wall and the Antonine Wall in the second century, but they are widely scattered both north and south of this area (Kilbride-Jones 1938; Stevenson 1956). Two plano-convex gaming-counters were found, one in white glass and the other in opaque black glass (188). A drip of glass (187) is difficult to explain; taken in isolation it cannot be seen as evidence for manufacture.

Glass: illustrated Pieces.

Vessels (Fig. 93)

165. (SF 390)   Bowl in good-quality colourless glass, polished. The base-ring is formed by cutting, and the side is slightly convex, expanding upwards. Mid-late first century. Ditch 1.

166. (ADO)   Nearly colourless pushed-in base-ring, centre broken and part of straight side expanding upwards; small vessel in poor-quality glass. Probably Roman. East *vicus*, phase 2.

167. (AES)   Base of small unguent bottle in blue-green glass. East *vicus*, unstratified.

168. (APF)   Horizontally ridged tail of the lower sticking part of a flagon handle, in blue-green glass, *c.* 70-150. Fort, unstratified.

169. (AIH)   Two fragments of a flagon-handle in yellowish-green glass. Fort, unstratified.

170. (ACG)   Unusual vessel or lid with outsplayed rim, rounded at tip, convex side, in thin greenish glass with bubbles. East *vicus*, phase 3.

171. (ACG)   Hollow tubular rim from a globular jar. *c.* 70-130. East *vicus*, phase 3.

172. (AJO)   Fragment of the base of a bottle with three moulded concentric circles. *c.* 70-130. Fort, phase 2.

173. (ABJ)   Convex fragment of good-quality colourless glass with three faint cut lines on it. First-second centuries. East *vicus*, phase 3.

Beads (Fig. 94)

174. (SF 323)   Cylindrical five-sided roughly made bead, in emerald green, cut off from a rod of glass. East *vicus*, phase 1.

175. (SF 228)   As above, but with thicker and larger central hole. East *vicus*, phase 2.

176. (SF 356)   Nearly half of a melon bead; deep blue glass flashed on poor-quality colourless glass. Fort, unstratified.

177. (SF 259)   Complete melon-shaped bead in opaque turquoise paste or frit. Foundation trench for the fence beside the north-east road, phase 1.

178. (SF 325)   Complete very worn melon bead; the outer surface of blue has disappeared. East *vicus*, phase 2.

179. (SF 90)   Complete melon bead in deep blue glass. Fort, unstratified.

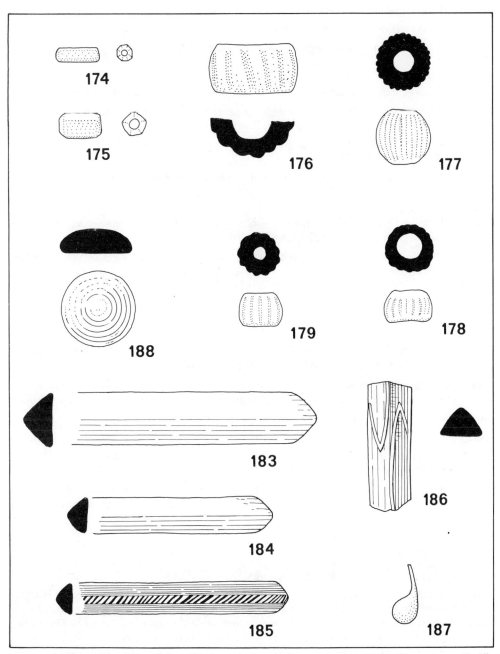

FIG. 94. – Watercrook: objects of glass. Beads, 174-9; bangles, 183-6; droplet, 187; gaming counter, 188. All 1:1.

Not illustrated

180. (SF 248)   Small green bead. East *vicus*, unstratified.

181. (SF 462)   Half a blue glass bead with white blobs. Fort, unstratified.

182. (SF 375)   Cylindrical green glass bead. Guard-chamber, unit 2.

Armlets (Fig. 94)

183. (SF 293)   Part of a armlet, opaque white, rather sharp D-shaped section. East *vicus*, phase 3.

184. (SF 341)   As above, but much smaller. East *vicus*, unstratified.

185. (SF 110) Small armlet in blue-green glass with a marvered trail of twisted opaque white and clear blue. East *vicus*, phase 3.

186. (SF 437)   Blue glass armlet with white lines. Guard-chamber, unit 4.

Miscellaneous (Fig. 94)

187. (SF 353)   Drip of glass. In quantity this would be evidence for manufacture, but not in isolation. Dirty green colour. Fort, unstratified.

188. (SF 198)   Gaming-counter in opaque white glass. East *vicus*, phase 3. One similar counter in black glass, also from phase 3 deposits in the east *vicus*.

QUERNS (Fig. 95) By R. C. TURNER

We are indebted to Dr Macdonald (University of Lancaster) for his assistance in the identification of the types and origins of the following examples.

189. (SF 454)   Part of an upper quernstone in Niedermendig lava. It is decorated with a concentric groove round the upper surface and radial tooling underneath. Fort, unstratified.

190. (SF 433)   Part of an upper quernstone in Niedermendig lava. Ditch 1, middle fill.

191. (SF 400, 478)   Part of an upper quernstone in a Carboniferous sandstone. North *vicus*.

192. (SF 412)   Fragment of an upper quernstone in a Carboniferous gritstone, probably from the Pennines. Fort, unstratified.

193. (SF 394)   Part of an upper quernstone in a Carboniferous sandstone. It has a shallow, circular hole, 40 cm in diameter and 5 cm deep, bored into the upper surface. Fort, unstratified.

FLINTS (Fig. 96) By R. C. TURNER

194. (SF 478)   A rod microlith in translucent, light-grey flint, found on the old ground surface beneath the guard-chamber. It is made by steeply backing one edge which, with 195 below, is paralleled by finds from a series of Pennine sites, typified by Dunford Bridge Site B (Radley et al., 1974). There is also a waste flake with a similar patina (SF 44).

195. (SF 339)   A blank blade made on a dark grey chert speckled with black. Both edges show signs of utilisation.

196. (SF 249)   A thumb-nail end scraper on a translucent, dark grey flint. Along one edge and on part of the dorsal surface the cortex of the pebble is showing. A tool typical of the late Neolithic and Bronze Ages. A fragment of AOC Beaker was also found.

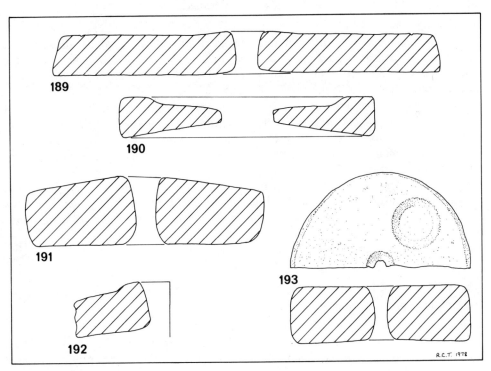

FIG. 95. – Watercrook: quernstones (1:6).

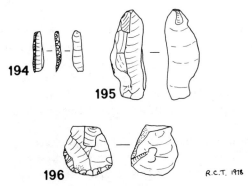

FIG. 96. – Watercrook: flint tools (1:2).

EPIGRAPHY By D. C. A. Shotter

This section will include a summary report of the epigraphic material from the recent excavations, and a discussion of the known inscriptions from Watercrook.

Recent epigraphic material

Most of the epigraphic material from the excavations of 1974 has already been published (Potter 1976, 40-2), and now requires only a brief summary: whilst no inscriptions were recovered, one fragment of *tegula* bore what may have been a very abraded stamp of Legio XX; the possible reading was X V V.

There were fifteen sherds of pottery bearing graffiti; six of these were symbols of various kinds, one was evidently a batch-number incised on to the foot-ring of a samian vessel, whilst the other eight were probably parts of names; most of these consisted of single letters or monosyllables in various types of script, whilst only one gave two syllables (later scratched out) of what was evidently the name, *Candidus*.

From the east *vicus* and presumably indicative of manufacturing activity, was a thin rectangular fragment of china clay and quartz bearing at one end the inverse oculist's stamp P. CLODI (inv. 81, *supra*); R. S. O. Tomlin suggests that the full reading may have been COLLYR P. CLODI and points to a possible parallel in *CIL* VII. 1317.

Subsequent to the interim publication, two further graffiti have been noted:

1. (ADO 714) On the internal surface of a rim of a black cooking-pot, a complete graffito, IV.

2. (ABR 147) On a wall sherd of buff fabric in cursive letters, RV

For a stamped patera handle, cf. inv. 48, *supra*.

The known inscriptions from Watercrook

RIB contains three inscriptions which have been recovered from Watercrook (752-4). Two are inscribed on altars which are now lost, and both are insufficiently recorded to provide information which is particularly useful for reconstructing the history of the site. Professor Eric Birley, however, has pointed out (*pers. comm.*) that he doubts whether the dedicator of *RIB* 752 was a *Procurator Augusti*; he prefers a reading which would give a reference to a centurion of Legio II Augusta.

The third inscription, which is now in the British Museum, is from a large funerary monument, to which Birley (1955, 51) assigned an early third-century date. The stone commemorates P. Aelius Bassus, an ex-centurion of *Legio* XX, and was set up by Bassus' freedmen and heirs through the good offices of Aelius Surinus, centurion of *Legio* VI, who, Birley suggests, may have been at Watercrook as *Praepositus Cohortis*. This recalls apparently similar arrangements at Ribchester (*RIB* 583) and possibly at Manchester also (*RIB* 575: Jones and Grealey 1974, 19). The Ribchester inscription is dated to 238-44, and the Manchester altar, on grounds of letter forms, would also appear to come early in the third century.

The context in which an ex-centurion of *Legio* XX came to be buried at Watercrook remains elusive, although he may have been a predecessor of Surinus as *Praepositus Cohortis*. On the other hand, it might be that, taken in conjunction with the possible brick-stamp of *Legio* XX, it is an indication of the presence at Watercrook for a time, presumably very early in the third century, of a *vexillatio* of the legion.

It is curious to note that, if Birley's observations on *RIB* 752 is correct, two of the three surviving Watercrook inscriptions would carry references to centurions of all three British legions.

COARSE POTTERY By HELEN LOCKWOOD

The coarse pottery from the military areas and the east *vicus* has been catalogued separately. Stratified sherds are listed phase by phase, unstratified sherds are grouped by type of vessel. A quite large quantity of unstratified material has been illustrated, partly to provide documentation for the histograms (Figs 63, 81) and partly to show a range of vessels unrepresented in stratified deposits. Each sherd is identified by a three-letter code (of which the first refers to the year of excavatio, A for 1974, B for 1975; and the second two to the group indicating the area and layer in which the sherd was found) and a number, which was given to each significant piece when excavated. Most of the parallels are taken from J. P. Gillam's *Roman Coarse Pottery in Northern England* (1970), cited as Gillam.

EAST VICUS: STRATIFIED GROUPS

Phase 1 (Figs 97, 98)

The samian and coarse-wares imply a Flavian-Trajanic context for the group: however, there are a few intrusive pieces (e.g. 11).

1. (ADA 315)   Jar in smooth soft grey fabric. Gillam 106. 80-120.
2. (ADA 351)   Jar in grey smooth fabric. Gillam 107. 80-130.
3. (ADA 251)   Jar in grey fabric with darker, sandy-textured surface.
4. (ADA 711)   Jar in smooth grey fabric with two grooves round body.
5. (ACS 707)   Jar in grey fabric with black surface and groove round shoulder.
6. (ADA 349)   Jar in grey fabric with darker grey smooth surface.
7. (ADA 712)   Dish in black-burnished fabric with beaded rim and wavy line on the inside.
8. (ADA 710)   Bowl in grey fabric with darker grey surface and two grooves on rim.
9. (ADA 709)   Bowl with flat rim in grey fabric with black rough surface, grooves round rim and body.
10. (ADA 296)   Bowl in grey smooth fabric with uneven incised line below large rim.
11. (ADA 708)   Bowl in grey fabric with darker grey surface. Similar types dated to 140-200 by Gillam.
12. (ADA 354)   Bowl in grey fabric with darker grey surface and beaded rim. Rouletted decoration round body.
13. (ADA 246)   Flagon with one handle in orange sandy fabric. Three rings round neck.
14. (ADA 323)   Colour-coat cup in buff fabric with grey-black slip on outside and brown on inside.
15. (ADF 436)   Ring-necked flagon in orange sandy fabric with one handle. Closest to Gillam 2. 70-110.
16. (ADR 713)   Ring-necked flagon in buff smooth fabric.
17. (ADX 360)   Jar in soft grey fabric with darker smooth surface. Two grooves on shoulder and barbotine decoration consisting of dots arranged in circles. Shape is the same as Gillam 68. 80-130.
18. (ADX 362)   Jar in soft light grey fabric, with two grooves round shoulder. Gillam 105. 80-120.

19. (ADX 364)   Reeded-rim bowl in light grey fabric with darker grey sandy-textured surface. 80-130.

20. (ADX 361)   Reeded-rim bowl in grey fabric with darker grey surface on rim and outside. 80-130.

21. (ADX 359)   Bowl in grey sandy-textured fabric with groove round outside and top of rim. 80-120.

22. (ADX 363)   Reeded-rim bowl in grey fabric with dark grey smooth surface. Gillam 215. 80-125.

23. (ADY 370)   Rustic-ware jar in light-grey gritty fabric. 80-130.

24. (ADY 369)   Reeded-rim dish in orange fabric with grey core.

25. (AEE 420)   Jar in light-grey gritty fabric.

26. (AEQ 342)   Bowl in grey fabric with smooth darker grey surface. Closest to Gillam 291. 80-120.

27. (AEE 450)   Mortarium in hard buff fabric with no grits remaining. Cf. Gillam 240. 80-120.

28. (AFA 734)   Jar in gritty grey fabric with darker grey surface on exterior. Gillam 111. 110-130

29. (AFR 444)   Jar in light grey fabric with dark grey smooth surface and two grooves round shoulder. Gillam 105. 80-120.

30. (AFR 345)   Jar in grey fabric with darker grey surface. First half second century.

31. (AFR 433)   Bowl in buff fabric burnt to black on the exterior. Similar to Gillam 191. 80-130.

32. (AFR 470)   Mortarium in gritty orange fabric with grey core. White grits. Gillam 249. 130-160.

Phase 2 (Figs 98-100)

A Hadrianic/early Antonine context is implied by the samian, a large group of coins (the latest being eight issues of Trajan) and many Hadrianic/Antonine coarse-ware forms. Again there is intrusive material: e.g. 59, 85, 89, 94.

33. (ABR 147)   Jar in slightly gritty buff fabric with grey core. Graffito on one fragment.

34. (ABR 704)   Jar in grey sandy-textured fabric with darker surface.

35. (ABR 82)   Rustic-ware jar in sandy-textured fabric with darker surface.

36. (ABR 135)   Rustic-ware jar in sandy-textured pale grey fabric. 80-130.

37. (ABR 77)   Rustic-ware jar in a grey fabric.

38. (ABR 741)   Carinated bowl in thick gritty grey fabric with darker surface and decorative line in relief above shoulder.

39. (ABR 729)   Bowl in orange fabric burnt to grey in places with reeded rim and groove round body.

40. (ABR 81)   Bowl in grey fabric with darker grey surface.

41. (ABR 753)   Beaker in red-orange hard mica-dusted fabric.

42. (ABR 754)   Beaker in dull orange hard mica-dusted fabric.

43. (ABR 728)   Mortarium in cream-yellow gritty fabric with hole drilled in the rim. Gillam 238. 70-110.

44. (ABR 79)   Bowl in grey fabric.

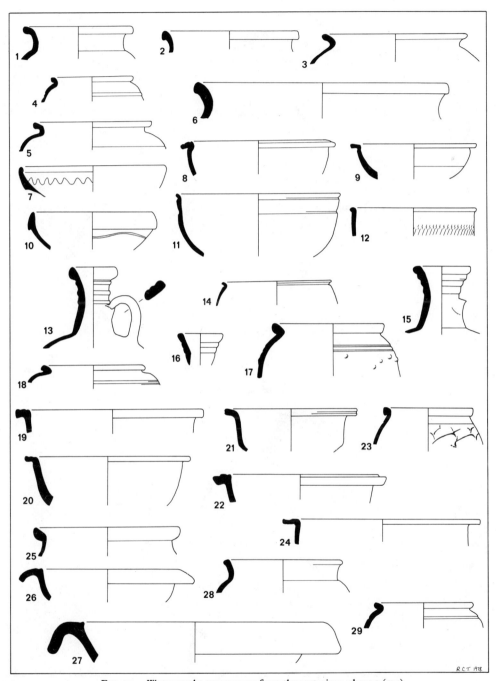

FIG. 97. – Watercrook: coarse-ware from the east *vicus*, phase I (1:4).

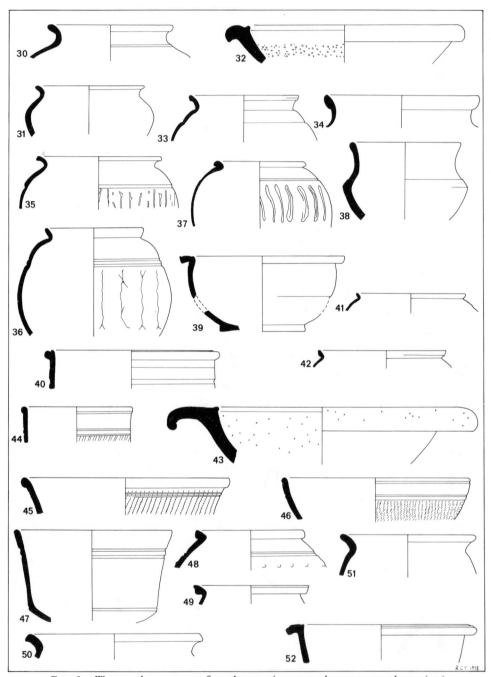

FIG. 98. – Watercrook: coarse-ware from the east *vicus*. 30-2, phase 1; 33-52, phase 2 (1:4).

45. (ABR 195)   Bowl in grey fabric with darker surface.

46. (ABR 168)   Bowl in grey fabric with black surface.

47. (ABR 742)   Bowl in grey fabric with black smooth surface.

48. (ABU 129)   Jar in grey soft fabric with barbotine decoration. Similar to Gillam 68. 80-130.

49. (ABU 143)   Jar in smooth hard grey fabric.

50. (ABU 169)   Jar in hard grey fabric.

51. (ABU 106)   Jar in black-burnished fabric. Cf. Gillam 122. 120-60.

52. (ABU 167)   Reeded-rim bowl in grey fabric burnt to orange in places. Cf. Gillam 215. 80-125.

53. (ABU 730)   Bowl in pink smooth fabric. Gillam 197. 140-200.

54. (ACA 172)   Flat-rimmed bowl in black-burnished fabric. Gillam 219. 120-50.

55. (ACA 180)   Flat-rimmed dish in black-burnished fabric with acute angle lattice. Gillam 306. 120-160.

56. (ACA 182)   Dish with flat rim in smooth orange fabric with grey core. Burnt.

57. (ACA 186)   Jar in grey sandy-textured fabric with darker grey surface. Gillam 111. 110-130.

58. (ADA 142)   Jar in black-burnished fabric. Gillam 125. 120-180.

59. (ADA 184)   Jar in black-burnished fabric. Gillam 135. 170-250.

60. (ACH 204)   Jar in soft grey fabric. First half of second century.

61. (ACH 212)   Bowl in grey smooth fabric with two grooves round body.

62. (ACH 706)   Flat-rimmed bowl in grey fabric with darker grey surface. Similar types dated 80-125.

63. (ACM 751)   Cup in pale grey sandy-textured fabric. For same shape cf. Gillam 102. 80-120.

64. (ACM 285) Mortarium in buff fabric with light-coloured grits. For similar shape cf. Gillam 249. 130-160.

The grey-ware jars listed below (66-72) are all dated to the period before 150.

66. (ACX 480)   Grey sandy-textured fabric. Gillam 103. 80-120.

67. (ACX 301)   Grey fabric with darker grey smooth surface.

68. (ACX 720)   Grey fabric with dark grey hard smooth surface.

69. (ACX 248)   Hard grey fabric with darker surface.

70. (ACX 721)   Soft buff fabric with grey exterior.

71. (ACX 3801)   Soft grey fabric with darker surface.

72. (ACX 3802)   Rustic-ware jar in gritty orange fabric with grey surface. 80-130.

73. (ACX 757)   Dish in grey fabric with dark grey smooth surface. Closest to Gillam 291. 80-120.

74. (ACX 755)   Flat-rimmed bowl in light grey smooth hard fabric.

75. (ACX 286)   Dish in grey fabric in black-burnished style, with flat rim and lattice design incised with broad strokes.

76. (ACX 381)   Bowl in grey smooth fabric with darker surface. Rouletted decoration round body.

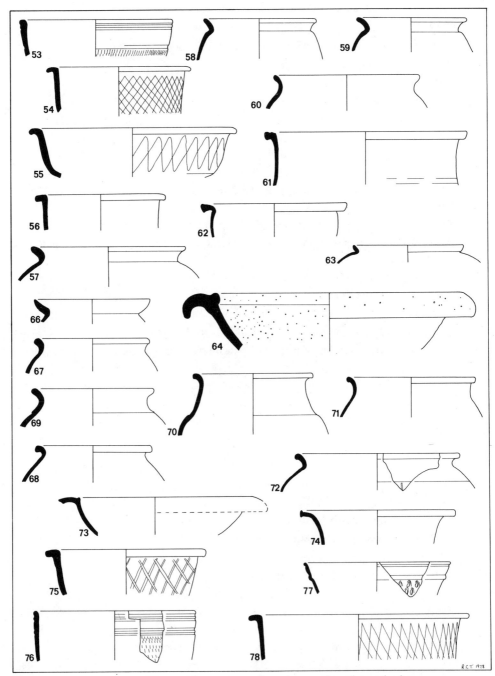

FIG. 99. – Watercrook: coarse-ware from the east *vicus*, phase 2 (1:4).

77. (ACX 735) Bowl in buff-pink smooth hard fabric with rouletted or impressed leaf design.

78. (ACX 275) Dish in black-burnished ware, with flat rim and small acute lattice design. Gillam 306. 120-160.

79. (ACX 294) Lid in grey fabric with darker surface, gritty on the outside but smooth on the inside.

80. (ACY 448) Rustic-ware jar in hard grey sandy-textured fabric. 80-130.

81. (ACY 466) Mortarium in orange-red fabric with white grits. Cf. Gillam 239. 80-110.

82. (ACY 722) Lid in hard buff fabric with grey surface.

83. (ACY 718) Sherd in grey fabric with dark grey smooth surface, possibly base of triple vase. Gillam 343. 80-120.

84. (ADM 746) Bowl in grey gritty fabric with wide reeded rim and groove round body.

85. (ADO 451) Jar in black calcite-gritted fabric. Fourth century type, intrusive.

86. (ADO 714) Jar in black-burnished fabric with lattice design and chevron under rim. Graffito on rim, reading IV. Cf. Gillam 125. 120-180.

87. (AED 416) Jar in a black-burnished fabric with narrow neck having grooves round it.

88. (AEF 422) Reeded-rim bowl in grey fabric with internal and external groove.

89. (AEH 736) Jar in black-burnished fabric. Gillam 135. 170-250.

90. (AEH 752) Flat-rimmed dish in black-burnished fabric. Gillam 308. 130-180.

91. (AEH 409) Flat-rimmed dish in black-burnished fabric. Gillam 306. 120-160.

92. (AEH 408) Dish in black-burnished fabric.

93. (AEH 758) Rough-cast beaker in hard orange fabric with slight traces of brown-grey slip. Late first-early second century.

94. (AEH 703) Beaker in black-burnished fabric. Gillam 172. 250-340. Intrusive.

Phase 3 (Figs 100-103)

These deposits were extensively disturbed but the samian, coins and coarse-ware indicate that the buildings were first laid out in the early to mid Antonine period. A *terminus ante quem* of c. 220 is implied both by the coarse-wares and the coins. However, there is a small group of later pots (102, 127, 141 and, clearly intrusive, 113) and four coins of the third quarter of the third century, which may represent later disturbance or possibly some occupation.

95. (AAH 42) Jar in black-burnished fabric. Cf. Gillam 118. 120-160.

96. (AAH 39) Jar in black-burnished fabric. Cf. Gillam 135. 170-250.

97. (AAH 705) Plain-rim dish in black-burnished fabric.

98. (AAR 27) Flat-rim dish in black-burnished fabric.

99. (ABD 702) Jar in hard grey sandy fabric.

100. (ABD 52) Rusticated-ware jar in grey soft fabric with darker surfae. 80-130.

101. (ABD 702) Jar in black-burnished fabric with small rim. Gillam 117. 130-150.

102. (ABD 717) Jar in black-burnished fabric. Cf. Gillam 145. 230-300.

103. (ABD 74) Fragment of bowl or platter in smooth dark grey fabric with rouletted decoration.

104. (ABD 51) Bowl in buff gritty fabric burnt to grey in places with reeded rim and two grooves round angle. Similar to Gillam 215. 80-125.

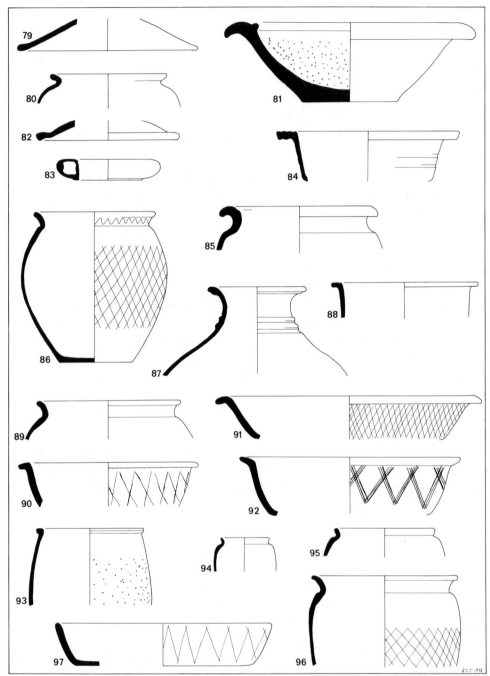

FIG. 100. — Watercrook: coarse-ware from the east *vicus*. 79-94, phase 2; 95-7, phase 3.

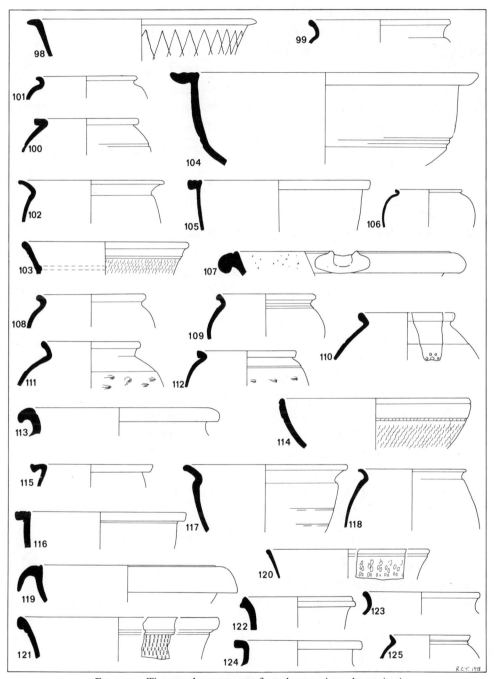

FIG. 101. – Watercrook: coarse-ware from the east *vicus*, phase 3 (1:4).

105.   (ABD 164)   Reeded-rim bowl in smooth grey fabric.

106.   (ABD 756)   Cup in smooth buff fabric. Cf. Gillam 167. 80-120.

107.   (ABD 53)   Mortarium in brick-red fabric. Gillam 248. 130-160.

108.   (ABE 706)   Jar in dark grey gritty fabric with impressed line round shoulder.

109.   (ABE 83)   Waster-jar in grey gritty fabric with two grooves under rim. Burnt.

110.   (ABE 103)   Jar in sandy fabric with barbotine decoration in flower pattern. 70-130.

111.   (ABE 65)   Rustic-ware jar in grey sandy fabric. 80-130.

112.   (ABE 67)   Rustic-ware jar in grey sandy fabric. Gillam 98. 80-130.

113.   (ABE 232)   Jar in black calcite-gritted fabric with groove round inside of rim. Gillam 163. 360-400. Intrusive.

114.   (ABE 69)   Bowl in grey fabric with traces of a black surface. Rouletted design round lower part of body and in groove.

115.   (ABE 84)   Flat-rim bowl in grey smooth fabric.

116.   (ABE 66)   Reeded-rim bowl in coarse red gritty fabric.

117.   (ABP 60)   Jar in grey-black gritty fabric.

118.   (ABP 723)   Jar in black-burnished fabric. Abraded. Gillam 120. 120-160.

119.   (ABP 731)   Bowl with hooked rim in soft pale grey fabric. Similar types dated first half of second century.

120.   (ACC 215)   Bowl in smooth dark grey fabric with rouletted decoration.

121.   (ACC 216)   Bowl in grey fabric with darker surface. Unevenly applied impressed decoration.

122.   (ACD 210)   Jar in sandy orange fabric.

123.   (ACD 376)   Jar in gritty buff fabric with black surface.

124.   (ACD 377)   Jar in hard grey fairly smooth fabric with red core.

125.   (ACD 209)   Beaker in red-brown mica-dusted fabric with grooves under the rim.

126.   (ACD 307)   Bowl in black-burnished fabric. Gillam 306. 120-160.

127.   (ACD 176)   Bowl with flange in black-burnished fabric. Gillam 227. 210-300.

128.   (ACG 276)   Jar in black-burnished fabric. Gillam 117. 130-150.

129.   (ACG 719)   Jar in black-burnished fabric. Gillam 121. 120-160.

130.   (ACG 224)   Beaker in buff sandy fabric.

131.   (ACG 229)   Dish in black-burnished fabric.

132.   (ACG 237)   Dish in black-burnished fabric.

133.   (ACG 235)   Dish in black-burnished fabric. Gillam 308. 130-180.

134.   (ACG 747)   Flat-rimmed dish in black-burnished fabric. Gillam 308. 130-180.

135.   (ACG 24)   Bowl in sandy grey fabric with groove but no decoration.

136.   (ACG 266)   Flanged bowl in black-burnished fabric.

137.   (ACG 234)   Bowl in orange sandy-textured fabric.

138.   (ACG 476)   Mortarium in smooth orange fabric with traces of cream slip and grey grits.

139.   (ACG 715)   Small flagon in hard orange sandy fabric with cream slip.

140.   (ACJ 376)   Jar in buff fabric with black gritty surface.

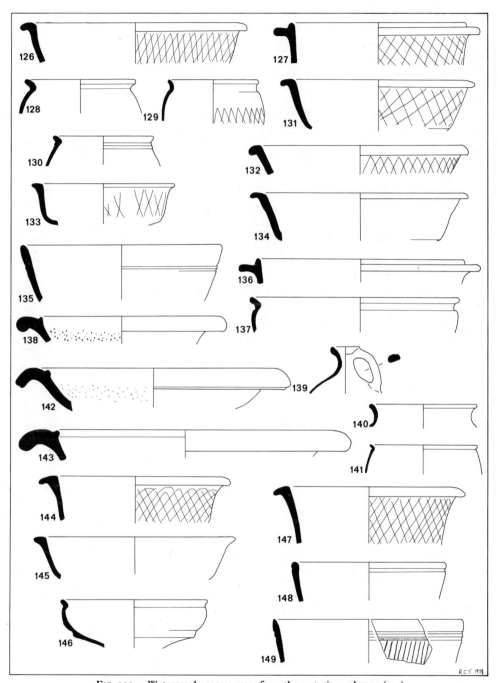

FIG. 102. – Watercrook: coarse-ware from the east *vicus*, phase 3 (1:4).

141. (ACJ 250)   Cup in colour-coat ware; orange fabric with black-brown slip. Third or fourth century.

142. (ACJ 278, ACX 247)   Mortarium in orange-buff fabric with grey core and cream slip. Gillam 245. 110-160.

143. (ACJ 429)   Mortarium in a cream fabric with red, brown and white grits.

144. (ADJ 307)   Flat-rimmed black-burnished dish with small lattice. Gillam 306, 120-160.

145. (ADJ 401)   Flat-rimmed black-burnished dish.

146. (ADJ 435)   Bowl in sandy-textured hard orange fabric.

147. (ADJ 402)   Bowl in uneven flat rim. Gillam 220. 120-160.

148. (ADJ 308)   Beaded-rim dish in black-burnished fabric. Burnt to orange on the outside. Gillam 318. 160-200.

149. (ADJ 310)   Bowl in grey fabric with dark grey core and surface. Rouletted decoration.

150. (ADJ 733)   Bowl in orange sandy fabric with grey core. Traces of decoration painted in cream.

151. (ADJ 310)   Mortarium in buff gritty fabric. No grits remaining. Gillam 240. 80-110.

152. (ADJ 750)   Sherd of bowl or lid in buff-orange smooth mica-dusted fabric. Mica-dusting is thicker on the inside.

153. (ADJ 407)   Sherd of a peculiar vessel in white coarse gritty fabric with curled-over rim. Hemispherical in shape; it has no base. Perhaps a crucible?

154. (ADK 716)   Jar in black-burnished fabric. Gillam 138. 150-250.

155. (AEA 419)   Wide-mouthed jar or bowl in buff fabric with hard grey sandy-textured surface.

156. (AEA 737)   Reeded-rim bowl in grey fabric with darker exterior surface with a sandy texture. 80-125.

157. (AEG 417)   Mortarium in orange smooth fabric with buff slip and greyish grits. Gillam 247. 130-160.

EAST VICUS: MATERIAL FROM DEPOSITS OVERLYING AND CUTTING THE STRATIFIED DEPOSITS (Figs 103, 104)

158. (AAF 725)   Soft grey fabric with two grooves round shoulder. Similar shape to Gillam 102. 80-120.

159. (AAT 31)   Smooth light-grey fabric with groove round shoulder. Cf. Gillam 105. 80-120.

160. (AEW 397)   Grey fabric with darker grey sandy-textured surface. Gillam 109. 90-130.

161. (ADU 302)   Soft buff fabric with grey core and grey exterior surface. Gillam 110. 100-140.

162. (AAB 21)   Grey-buff gritty fabric with darker surface. For similar shape, Gillam 111. 110-130.

163. (ABM 739)   Smooth hard orange fabric.

164. (AAB 19)   Orange sandy-textured fabric. Gillam 30 (160-210) is the same shape and size, but in a different fabric.

165. (ABX 740)   Dark grey smooth fabric with barbotine decoration. 70-150.

166. (ACB 173)   Rusticated jar in a sandy fabric. 80-130.

167. (ADU 304)   Pale grey gritty fabric.

168. (ADU 303)   Pale grey gritty fabric.

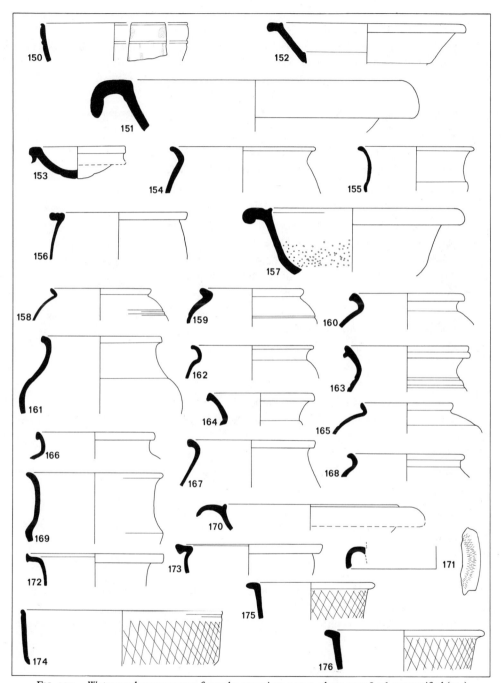

FIG. 103. – Watercrook: coarse-ware from the east *vicus*. 150-7, phase 3; 158-76, unstratified (1:4).

169. (AEW 418)   Wide-mouthed jar in grey gritty fabric.

170. (AEM 749)   Bowl with hooked rim in grey fabric with smooth darker grey surface on outside and light-grey core.

171. (ABF 759)   Flanged bowl in grey fabric with dark grey smooth surface. Rouletting on body and flange. Reminiscent of Drag. form 38.

172. (ADU 306)   Bowl in smooth sandy grey fabric. First half of second century.

173. (AFC 464)   Bowl in soft light grey fabric with darker surface.

174. (AFI 738)   Dish with plain rim and chamfered base in black-burnished fabric. Cf. Gillam 318. 160-200.

175. (AEW 439)   Flat-rimmed dish in black-burnished fabric.

176. (AEW 395)   Flat-rimmed bowl in black-burnished fabric. Cf. Gillam 221. 140-180.

177. (AFD 466)   Dish with flat rim in black burnished fabric, burnt to grey.

178. (AAB 18)   Flat-rimmed bowl in black-burnished fabric. Gillam 306. 120-160.

179. (AAB 20)   Flat-rimmed dish in black-burnished fabric.

180. (AAF 25)   Dish with plain rim in black-burnished fabric. Cf. Gillam 316. 125-160.

181. (ACF 205)   Carinated bowl in buff fabric with black gritty surface, glossy on the exterior. Similar to Gillam 212 (160-200) but in a different fabric.

182. (AAU 726)   Grey sandy fabric with grooves and stippled decoration.

183. (ACQ 724)   Bowl in grey-buff fabric with grey core and hard shiny black surface on the outside. Decorated with impressed leaf shapes.

184. (AEW 727)   Buff fabric with black exterior surface.

185. (AEW 396)   Black fabric, smooth on the outside and gritty on the inside.

186. (ADU 744)   Cup in rough-cast ware. Buff fabric with purplish-brown slip. 80-150.

187. (ABL 49)   Cup in pale grey smooth fabric.

188. (AFC 460)   One-handed flagon in orange sandy-textured fabric. Closest to Gillam 30. 160-210.

189. (ACK 255)   Two-handed flagon in black sandy-textured fabric.

190. (AAF 743)   Sherd of grey soft fabric with rouletted decoration, probably a lid. Fabric and rouletting suggest a mid second-century date.

191. (AAF 748)   Grey smooth fabric, probably a lid.

192. (AEW 394)   Mortarium in red fabric with patchy grey surface and core. Very gritty fabric. Gillam 249. 130-160.

193. (AEW 459)   Mortarium in buff fabric with pink core. No grits remaining. Gillam 238. 70-110.

194. (AAF 751)   Flanged mortarium in orange fabric with orange-brown slip and small black grits. 350-400.

195. (AAB 17)   Possibly a tazza, or incense bowl, in hard sandy orange-buff fabric. Incised decoration on piecrust rim. 140-200.

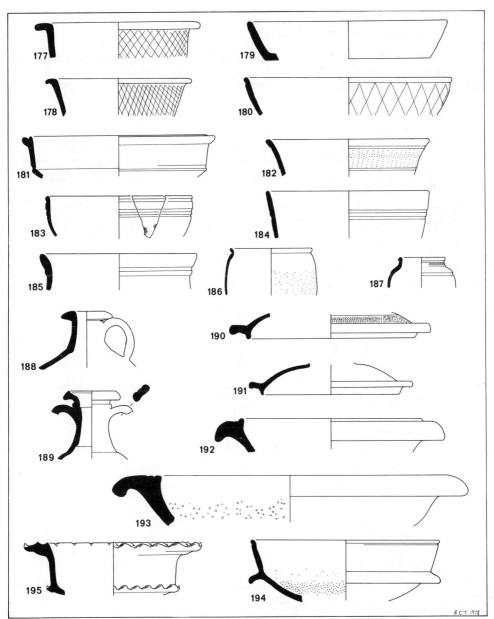

FIG. 104. – Watercrook: coarse-ware from the east *vicus*, unstratified (1:4).

THE FORT: STRATIFIED GROUPS

PHASE 1

The fence beside the north-east road (Fig. 105)

Both the samian and coarse-ware point generally to a Flavian-Trajanic date for the group. However, there is one piece of later samian (an 18/31 from Les Martres-de-Veyre) and some coarse-ware forms which take the date of deposition past 100.

196. (APH 148)   Jar in smooth dark buff fabric.

197. (APH 326)   Wide-mouthed jar in smooth grey fabric.

198. (APH 509)   Complete cup in smooth cream fabric. Single groove on shoulder and two grooves round body. Two of these are emphasised with red paint and there are three wavy lines in red paint. For similar type of the same size, cf. Gillam 167; for similar profile cf. Gillam 68. 80-130.

199 (ARC 287)   Jar in smooth grey fabric.

200. (ARC 288)   Shallow dish in black burnished fabric. Gillam 337 for general type. 70-110.

201. (ARC 279)   Bowl in dark grey sandy fabric. Flavian-Trajanic.

202. (ARC 289)   Bowl in buff fabric with reeded rim. Gillam 215. 70-110.

203. (ARC 222)   Ring-necked flagon in buff fabric with grey and red slip on the inside and red slip on the outside. Gillam 2. 70-110.

204. (BCF 871)   Dish in hard grey sandy-textured fabric with reeded rim.

205. (BCF 872)   Bowl in soft grey fabric with reeded rim.

206. (BCF 811)   Cup exactly the same as 198, *supra*, except that it has a slightly smaller diameter.

207. (ARC 293) Mortarium in red fabric with pink-cream slip. Paralleled by an example from Carrawburgh, dated 100-40.

The following three mortaria are all paralleled by Gillam 239, 80-110:

208. (ARC 292)   Yellow-buff fabric with multi-coloured grits on interior and rim.

209. (ARC 291)   Buff fabric with multi-coloured grits on interior and rim.

210. (APH 152)   Buff fabric with traces of orange slip. Multi-coloured grits on interior and rim.

PHASE 2

Rampart oven (Fig. 106)

A second-century group, probably not extending after *c.* 150. The samian ranges from Flavian to early Antonine types but is mainly Hadrianic. The one coin found is not later than the first half of the second century.

211. (AJA 63)   Jar in black burnished fabric. Gillam 116. 130-150.

212. (AJK 605)   Jar in black burnished fabric.

213. (AJK 604)   Jar in black burnished fabric. Gillam 125. 125-80.

214. (AJK 603)   Beaker in grey fabric with darker surfaces; it has a small lattice design.

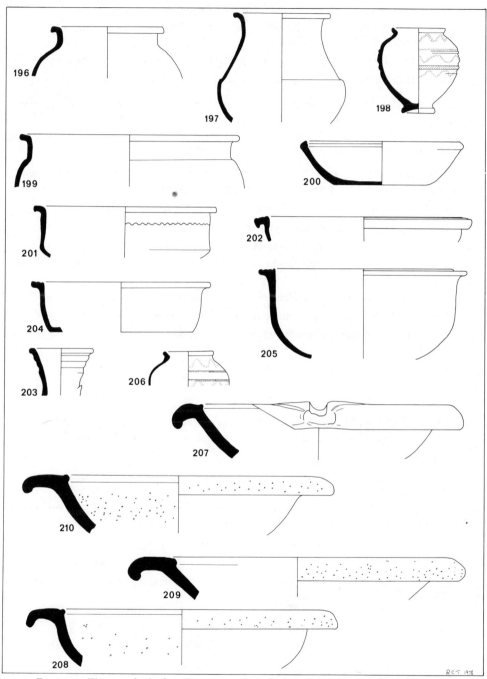

FIG. 105. – Watercrook: the fort. Coarse-ware from the fence lining the north-east road (1:4).

215. (AJK 260)   Jar in grey gritty fabric with everted rim.

216. (AKD 189)   Dish in dark-grey sandy fabric with flat rim and two grooves round body.

217. (AKH 200)   Pie-dish in black burnished fabric with flat rim and tiny acute angle lattice design. Closest to Gillam 306. 120-160.

218. (AKH 490)   Dish in orange-buff fabric with black surface. Two grooves round body.

219. (AKU 481)   Mortarium in gritty yellowish fabric with white grits. Gillam 238. 70-110.

Phases 3 and 4

The east guard-chamber, north-east gate (Figs 106, 107)

The bulk of the coarse ware comes from the lower fill (Fig. 60, units 2-4) and is sealed by a layer (unit 1) with four coins dating between 268 and 273.

220. (BAE 17)   Dish in black burnished fabric. Gillam 309. 160-200.

221. (BAE 16)   Beaker in black burnished fabric. Gillam 170. 130-180.

222. (BAZ 20)   Jar in black burnished fabric. Gillam 138. 150-250.

223. (BAZ 14)   Jar or flagon with handle(s) in smooth grey-buff fabric. Close to Gillam 174. 120-160.

224. (BBL)   *Not illustrated.* Mortarium closely resembling 226, below.

225. (BBL 18)   Dish in grey fabric with beaded rim and groove below rim.

226. (BCT 13)   Cream mortarium with red/brown grits. Stamped, LOCCI. PRO. (cf. p. 107 and Fig. 123). 135-165.

227. (BDB 15)   Jar in grey gritty fabric. Two lines in relief on hollow part of rim.

Ditch 1 (Figs 107, 108)

The material in the ditch fill ranges from Flavian-Trajanic types to fourth century forms. For a detailed analysis of the phases, cf. the discussion of the ditch in Chap. III.

228. (AIG 71)   Mortarium in white pipeclay fabric. Gillam 285. 320-370.

229. (AIG 607)   Colour-coat beaker in white fabric with dark grey slip. Hunting scene. Gillam 85. 180-220.

230. (AIG 111)   Dish in orange gritty fabric with flat rim; the core and patches on the exterior are grey. Park House ware: cf. Chap. II, p. 118.

231. (AIG 105)   Jar in BB fabric with large rim. Gillam 139. 150-250.

232. (AIG 117)   Jar in grey smooth fabric with groove above shoulder. Gillam 108. 80-130.

233. (AIG 132)   Jar in grey calcite-gritted fabric with internal groove for lid and pronounced shoulder. Gillam 163. 360-400.

234. (AIG 56)   Dish in BB fabric. Gillam 314. 220-360.

235. (AIG 38)   Dish with plain rim in BB fabric. Gillam 329. 190-340.

236. (AJG 112)   Mortarium in gritty buff fabric with black grits. Incised lines running round rim.

237. (AJG 150)   Mortarium in orange fabric with dark red slip on rim. Fabric and grit as Gillam 270 (Wilderspool product), but shape closer to Gillam 266. 180-220.

238. (AJG 606)   Flat-rimmed bowl in BB fabric. Resembles Gillam 306. 120-160.

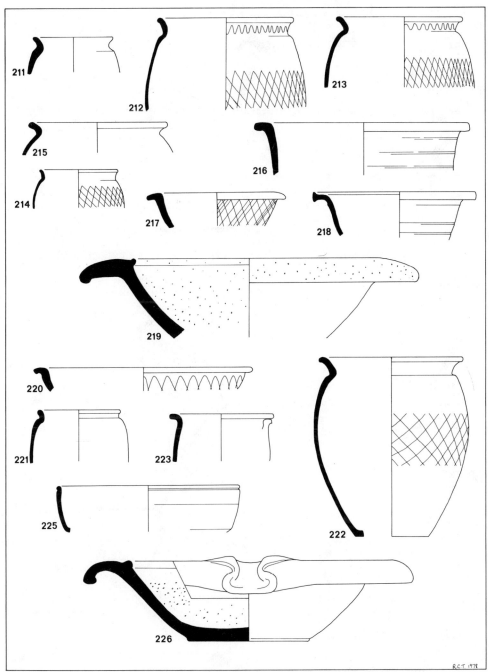

FIG. 106. – Watercrook: the fort. 211-9, coarse-ware from the rampart oven; 220-6, the guard-chamber, phase 3 (1:4).

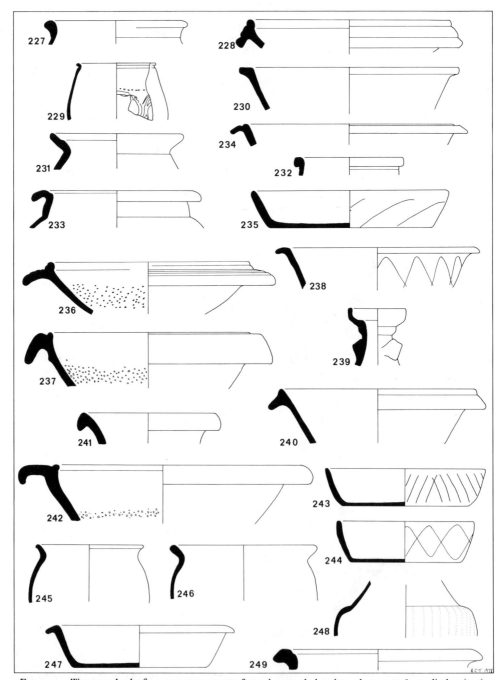

FIG. 107. – Watercrook: the fort. 227, coarse-ware from the guard-chamber, phase 3; 228-49, ditch 1 (1:4).

239. (AJG 89)   Flagon with one handle in pink fabric with traces of white slip.

240. (AJG 151)   Flanged bowl in grey smooth fabric.

241. (AJG 499)   Jar in light-grey fabric with orange surface.

242. (AJN 131)   Mortarium in buff gritty fabric with white-grey grits. Closest to Gillam 239, (80-110) but of a different fabric.

243. (AJN 187)   Dish with plain rim in BB fabric. Closest to Gillam 325. 90-130.

244. (AJN 162)   Dish with plain rim in BB fabric with large acute lattice design and curved sides. Closest in shape to Gillam 325. 90-130.

245. (AJN 174)   Jar in BB fabric with small lattice design. Cf. Gillam 116. 130-150.

246. (AJN 96)   Jar in BB fabric with wide rim. Gillam 145. 230-300.

247. (AJN 165)   Dish in BB fabric with flat rim. Gillam 309. 160-200.

248. (AJN 601)   Carinated beaker in orange-grey fabric with pale grey core. Traces of a dark greyish slip. Vertical rows of pinprick decoration.

249. (AQE 277)   Jar in grey calcite-gritted fabric.

250. (BAK 4)   Hammerhead mortarium in pipeclay fabric. Grey, brown and white grits. Closest to Gillam 279. 210-320, but this has black/red grits.

Ditch 1a (Fig. 108)

The samian consists exclusively of Hadrianic or earlier date but the few sherds of coarse ware would appear to take the date of the fill into the later second century.

251. (BBG 6)   Dish in buff-orange gritty fabric.

252. (BDS 21)   Mortarium in smooth orange-buff fabric with traces of white slip. No grits remaining. Similar in shape to Gillam 244. 110-150.

253. (BDS 7)   Jar in BB fabric. Gillam 135. 170-250.

Ditch 1b (Fig. 108)

254. (BBL 8)   Narrow-mouthed cup in colour-coat ware. White fabric with orange slip on the inside and dark brownon the outside. Type dated to c. 250-320.

255. (BBW 1)   Cup in smooth orange fabric.

256. (BBW 12)   Cup in orange gritty fabric with cornice rim.

257. (BBW 9)   Single-handled flagon in fairly smooth orange fabric. Shape and handle are closest to Gillam 17 (180-360), though the lip is different.

Palisade Trench (Fig. 108)

258. (AKZ 461)   Raetian-type mortarium with a grey slip and light-coloured grits. 180-250.

Ditch 2 (Figs 108, 109)

For detailed discussion of the chronology, cf. Chap. III. The lower part of the ditch appears to have been filled in the Hadrianic period while the top was finally levelled in the first half of the third century.

259. (AQB 99)   Jar in orange smooth fabric with grooves round body and hollow of neck.

260. (AQM 149)   Mortarium in buff hard fabric with light-coloured grits.

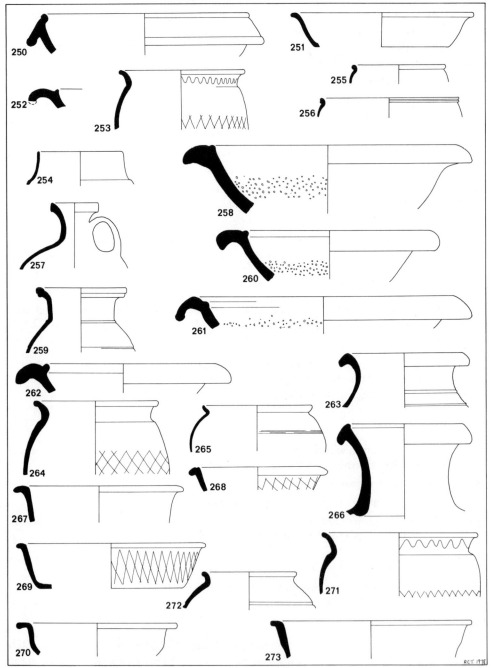

FIG. 108. – Watercrook: the fort. Coarse-ware: 250, ditch 1; 251-3, ditch 1a; 254-7, ditch 1b; 258, palisade trench; 259-73, ditch 2 (1:4).

261. (AQQ 133) Mortarium in orange-buff sandy fabric with white and grey grits.
262. (AQQ 140) Mortarium in orange-pink sandy fabric. No grits remaining.
263. (AQQ 144) Jar in smooth pale orange fabric with two grooves round body.
264. (AQR 495) Jar in BB fabric. Gillam 142. 190-280.
265. (AQR 602) Cup in orange-brown hard fabric. Mica-dusted. Grooves round shoulder.
266. (AQR 485) Narrow-mouthed jar in grey fabric with darker grey surface internally and black externally. Surface burnished on rim and round neck but not under rim. Gillam 30. 180-210.
267. (AQR 496) Bowl in BB fabric with flat rim. Gillam 219. 120-150.
268. (AQR 498) Bowl in BB fabric with grooved rim. Gillam 226. 220-250.
269. (AQR 497) Dish in BB fabric. Gillam 306. 120-160.
270. (AQT 163) Flat-rimmed bowl in smooth grey fabric.
271. (AQT 137) Jar in BB fabric, closest to Gillam 133. 160-220.
272. (AQT 156) Jar in buff gritty fabric, with dark grey slip and groove around body.
273. (AQZ 153) Bowl in BB fabric. Gillam 221. 120-210.
274. (AQZ 181) Flagon in pink sandy-textured fabric.
275. (AQZ 183) Dish with hooked rim in smooth grey-buff fabric with dark-grey core.

Ditch 3 (Fig. 109)

A third-century group.

276. (AJH 134) Mortarium in pipeclay fabric; closest to Gillam 280. 210-320.
277. (AJH 218) Hammerhead mortarium in white gritty fabric with ridged rim.
278. (AJH 91) Jar in orange soft fabric.
279. (AJH 139) Bowl in BB fabric with large acute angle lattice design. Closest to Gillam 236. 200-240.
280. (AJH 107) Jar in soft orange fabric with a slightly reeded rim.

Intervallum road (Fig. 109)

281. (AIQ 901) Jar in grey smooth matt fabric. First half second century.
282. (AIW 608) Dish in BB fabric with flat rim. Gillam 306. 120-160.

THE FORT: UNSTRATIFIED POTTERY (Figs 110-113)

Jars in grey fabrics.

283. (AJE 109) Grey sandy fabric. Gillam 103. 80-120.
284. (AHV 870) Soft, smooth grey fabric with two grooves around shoulder. Gillam 105. 80-120.
285. (AJO 492) Rough-cast jar in orange fabric with black slip. Cornice rim and two grooves around shoulder. 80-140.
286. (AIX 87) Grey fabric with darker exterior surface. Gillam 109. 90-130.

287. (BAM 830)   Smooth grey-buff fabric with groove round neck. Late first-early second century.

288. (BAO 806)   Dark grey slightly gritty fabric.

289. (AQO 159)   Smooth grey fabric.

290. (AQO 192)   Grey gritty fabric.

291. (AQN 127)   Grey fabric of a sandy texture.

292. (APE 16)   Grey fabric burnt to orange.

293. (AJO 90)   Light grey sandy fabric.

294. (APC 219)   Smooth dark grey fabric with band of incised decoration around body, consisting of horizontal and diagonal lines.

295. (AHV 281)   Smooth grey fabric.

Jars in black-burnished fabrics.

296. (AJO 483)   No lattice remaining. Gillam 122. 120-60.

297. (AJE 98)   With wavy line under rim. Gillam 122. 120-160.

298. (AHV 55)   Burnt to orange in places. Gillam 127. 130-70.

299. (AJO 154)   Gillam 130. 140-80.

300. (AIH 805)   Small acute lattice design. Gillam 132, 140-220.

301. (AIZ 804)   Gillam 133. 160-220.

302. (AHV 57)   Gillam 133. 160-220.

303. (AIF 47)   Closest to Gillam 135. 170-250.

304. (BAJ 2)   Closest to Gillam 142. 190-280.

305. (BAI 5)   Gillam 145. 230-330.

306. (AIU 45)   Smooth fabric but roughly made. Gillam 147. 148. Late third-early fourth century.

307. (AKF 244)   Gillam 147. 290-370.

Jars in calcite-gritted fabrics

308. (BCZ 808)   Dark fabric.

309. (AHN 801)   Black fabric, burnt to orange in places. Gillam 161. 370-400.

310. (AHN 802)   Grey-black fabric. Gillam 163. 360-400.

311. (BDL 809)   Black fabric.

312. (AIB 37)   Black fabric with three grooves round shoulder.

313. (AIH 24)   Black surface on the outside and grey on the inside. Groove for lid. Closest to Gillam 163. 360-400.

314. (AHF 1)   Black fabric with internal groove for lid. Gillam 163. 360-400.

315. (AHF 2)   Black fabric with internal groove. Late fourth century.

316. (AHF 4)   Black fabric with internal groove. Late fourth century.

317. (AHF 5)   Grey-black fabric with internal groove. Late fourth century.

318. (AHF 6)   Black fabric with internal groove. Late fourth century.

319. (AHF 7)   Grey fabric with internal groove. Late fourth century.

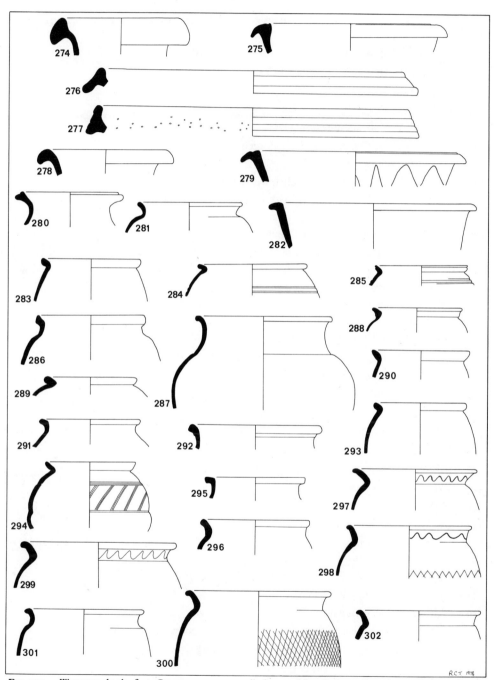

FIG. 109. – Watercrook: the fort. Coarse-ware: 274-5, ditch 2; 276-80, ditch 3; 281-2, *intervallum* road; 283-302, unstratified (1:4).

Jars in other fabrics.

320. (AQO 190) Coarse gritty fabric, light grey on the interior and orange-grey on the exterior, with black surface.

321. (APE 15) Pale orange gritty fabric with groove on shoulder.

322. (AQO 194) Orange-buff sandy fabric.

323. (AQO 193) Smooth buff fabric.

324. (AQO 121) Red-orange sandy fabric with groove round hollow of neck.

325. (BCN 807) Buff sandy-textured fabric.

326. (BAM 810) Buff smooth fabric, with grooves round shoulder.

Bowls and dishes in grey fabrics.

327. (BAM 816) Dish in dark grey fabric with chamfered base.

328. (BDL 818) Dish in grey fabric with grits incorporated though smooth. Plain rim. Gillam 330. 330-370.

329. (BBT 872) Flanged bowl in grey smooth fabric.

330. (BAJ 1) Flanged bowl in grey smooth fabric. Gillam 229. 350-400.

331. (AQO 179) Bowl in grey gritty fabric with reeded rim and grooves under rim and around body. Closest to Gillam 215. 80-125.

332. (AIX 95) Bowl with flat rim in grey fabric with darker grey smooth surface. Gillam 217. 110-130.

333. (BCN 817) Dish in pale grey smooth fabric with flat rim.

334. (AIL 825) Dish in smooth grey fabric with plain rim. Gillam 333. 350-400.

Bowls and dishes in black burnished fabrics.

335. (AJD 826) Dish with large lattice design. Gillam 306. 120-160.

336. (AIY 824) Dish with large acute lattice design. Gillam 306. 120-160.

337. (AIZ 58) Dish with large acute lattice design. Gillam 306. 120-160.

338. (AJE 110) Dish with large lattice design. Gillam 306. 120-160.

339. (AIU 46) Dish in black burnished fabric burnt to grey. Gillam 307. 120-160.

340. (AJE 85) Dish with large acute lattice design. Gillam 307. 120-160.

341. (AJE 92) Dish with small acute lattice design. Gillam 307. 120-160.

342. (AIH 821) Dish with chamfered base. Gillam 308. 130-180.

343. (AIL 822) Dish in good quality black burnished fabric with beaded rim and chambered base. Gillam 318. 160-200.

344. (AJE 86) Dish with plain rim. Gillam 327. 190-340.

345. (AJE 88) Bowl in greyish fabric.

346. (AJE 93) Dish with flat rim and acute lattice design.

347. (AIE 820) Dish with one wavy incised line around body.

348. (AKI 201) Worn dish with small acute lattice design.

349. (AJO 157) Small acute lattice design.

350. (AJN 170) Flanged bowl in black burnished fabric.

351. (AIY 823) Flanged bowl in black burnished fabric.

352. (AIC 23) Dish in good quality fabric with large acute lattice design.

FIG. 110. – Watercrook: the fort. Unstratified coarse-ware (1:4).

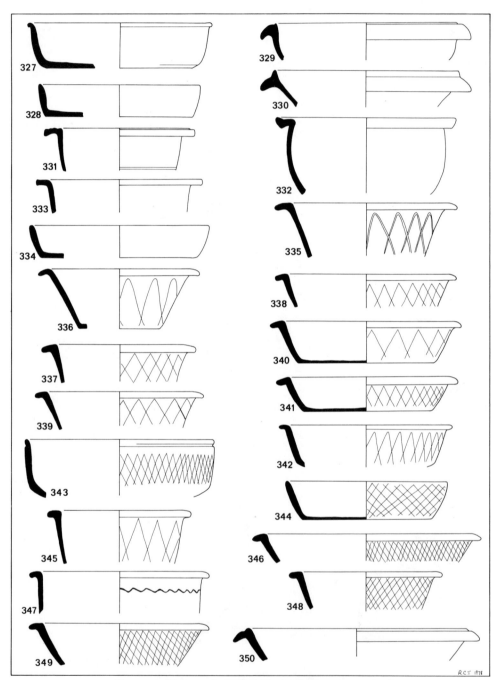

FIG. 111. – Watercrook: the fort. Unstratified coarse-ware (1:4).

Bowls and dishes in other fabrics.

353. (BAM 815)   Dish in light grey fairly smooth fabric.

354. (BAO 819)   Dish in buff gritty fabric, similar to above.

355. (APC 221)   Bowl with reeded rim in gritty fabric, orange burnt from grey.

356. (AJE 59)   Flanged bowl in orange sandy-textured fabric, reminiscent of Drag. form 38.

357. (BBA 873)   Bowl in orange-buff gritty fabric similar to Gillam 195 (140-200), reminiscent of Drag. form 40.

358. (BBT 814)   London Ware bowl. Black fabric with smooth surface decorated with incised lines, dots and concentric semi-circles (cf. also 94, *supra*).

Mortaria

359. (APE 14)   Buff sandy fabric. Gillam 240. 80-110.

360. (AQO 185)   Buff fabric with white and grey grits. Gillam 243. 100-140.

361. (AJE 94)   Poor-quality orange-red fabric with white grits. No slip remaining. Gillam 245. 110-160.

362. (AIC 22)   Fairly smooth orange-buff fabric, with traces of a cream slip. Light-coloured grits. Gillam 245. 110-160.

363. (BBD 812)   Sandy orange fabric with multi-coloured grits. Closest to Gillam 244. 110-150.

364. (AJD 54)   White fabric with black grits. Gillam 253. 140-180.

365. (AHX 813)   White fabric with traces of a darker slip and black grits. Gillam 283. 250-350.

366. (AIX 484)   Fine white fabric with black grits. Gillam 283. 250-350.

367. (AQO 518)   Coarse-cream fabric with white and grey grits. Second century.

368. (AIC 24)   Orange fabric with light-coloured grits. In shape, like Gillam 243, 245. 100-150.

369. (AQO 114)   Red smooth hard fabric with large grits.

370. (AQC 62)   Cream gritty fabric with grey-brown grits.

Flagons

371. (AQO 158)   Buff sandy-textured fabric.

372. (AQO 130)   Ring-neck flagon in smooth cream fabric. Closest to Gillam 4. 90-130.

373. (APW 272)   Orange smooth fabric. Gillam 6. 120-200.

374. (AHO 827)   Sandy grey fabric, very similar to Gillam 18 (350-400); this, however, is in a colour-coated fabric.

375. (BBC 829)   One-handled flagon in fairly smooth orange fabric with piecrust decoration on the rim.

376. (BBN 828)   One-handled flagon in orange sandy fabric with piecrust decoration on the rim.

377. (APE 11)   One-handled ring-neck flagon in orange sandy fabric. Closest to Gillam 4. 90-130.

378. (APE 12)   One-handled flagon in gritty orange fabric. Closest to Gillam 13. 80-130.

Cups and beakers.

379. (AQO 115)   Cup in orange-red fabric with buff slip.

380. (AIF 48)   Cup in smooth orange fabric with cornice rim.

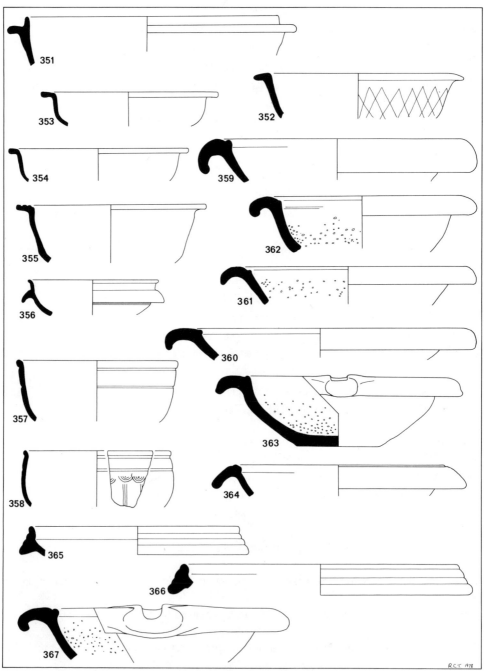

FIG. 112. — Watercrook: the fort. Unstratified coarse-ware (1:4).

Miscellaneous.

381. (BAJ 3) Colander in grey, fairly smooth fabric with a flat base. The holes occur only in the base.

382. (AHB 833) Fragment in soft orange fabric, slightly paler in colour on the interior surface, and with a grey core. This could be part of a face-vase. It has a circular impression above a linear one and incised lines around these, which may represent hair.

383. (BBE 832) Lid of cheese-press in grey fabric with darker grey smooth surface. It has regular rows of punched holes and one larger hole in the middle, surrounded by grooves.

384. (BAN 831) Probably a handle, in orange sandy fabric, decorated with incised lines and dots.

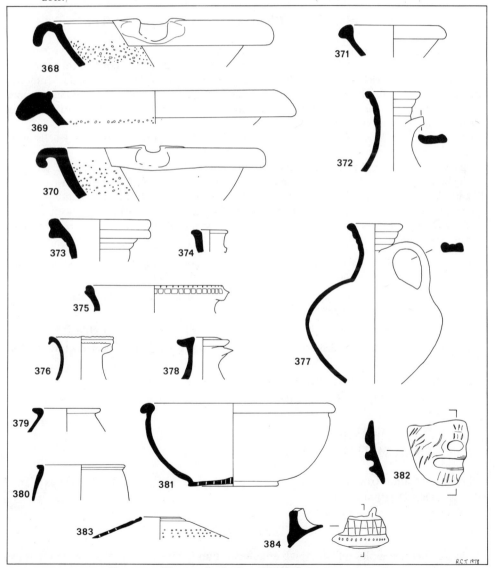

FIG. 113. – Watercrook: the fort. Unstratified coarse-ware (1:4).

(Fig. 123).

385.　(BBT 874)　A ring-base in a grey fabric with a smooth black surface. The base is stamped with an illiterate mark, of a type not uncommon on second-century coarse-wares of this class.

Beaker Culture sherds (not illustrated)

386.　(AQU)　Mr George Jobey kindly reports as follows:
Two abraded sherds, probably from the rim of an All-Over-Corded Beaker with a few lines of cord within the rim. Ditch 2.

MORTARIA STAMPS (Fig. 123) By K. F. HARTLEY

226. (BCT 13). Diam. *c.* 36 cm. An almost complete mortarium from unit 3 in the guard-chamber in smooth, cream fabric with red-brown trituration grit. When complete the retrograde stamp reads LOCCI.PRO for some such name as Loccius Probus or Loccius Proculus. Although only one die may be involved, most of his stamps show a bar at the top of the L, as in this example. The explanation for this is not certain but it may have resulted from a mistake in the original cutting of the die, which was blocked in, the filling falling out later.

Other stamps of his have been noted from Alcester; Aldborough; Ambleside; Benwell; Binchester; Cirencester; Kenchester; Leicester (2); Little Chester; Mancetter (5); Orton Longueville; Ribchester; Sawtry, Hunts.; Shenstone; South Shields; Thistleton, Rutland, and Wall in England; and in Scotland from Balmuildy (4); Bar Hill; Birrens; Mumrills; Newstead; Old Kilpatrick and Rough Castle. This potter's activity is dated primarily by the stamps at forts on the Antonine Wall, and his rim-forms fit with manufacture *c.* 135-165. He worked at Mancetter, where his activity overlapped with that of two other potters, Loccius Vibius and Iunius Loccius, to whom he was surely related.

The other mortarium stamps have already been fully published (in Potter 1976, 52-5), though not their contexts. They include:

1.　(ARG 512)　MARINVS. *c.* 70-110, Brockley Hill. From the foundation trench for the fence beside the north-east road, phase 1.

2.　(AHE 513)　ST N I. ? *c.* 140+, Norfolk. Close to the fort wall but unstratified.

3.　(AEG. ACG 514)　Trademark. Second century but pre-Antonine, Wilderspool. East *vicus*, phase 3.

4.　(AAA 10)　Trademark. *c.* 100-40, Wilderspool. East *vicus*, unstratified.

5.　(AIH 515)　Illegible two-line stamp. First half of the second century, Wilderspool. Fort, unstratified.

6.　(ABD 516)　MATUGENVS. 90-125, Brockley Hill. East *vicus*, phase 3.

7.　(ABE 517)　MATUGENVS. East *vicus*, phase 3.

For other stamps from the site, cf. North 1934, Fig. 1f; North and Hildyard 1945, 161: stamps L OCCIVIBI and VAS
SAN

AMPHORAE

No further examples of stamped amphorae handles were found apart from those published in Potter 1976, 55-6 by J. J. Paterson.

SAMIAN WARE (Figs 114-22) By Felicity Wild

The site as a whole, particularly the east *vicus*, produced a large quantity of samian ware, probably representing almost sixteen hundred vessels. The present report attempts a summary of the stratified groups in their capacity as dating vidence, following the arrangement observed in the body of the report. All the significant decorated sherds from stratified contexts have been listed. A selection of the unstratified decorated ware has been published in detail, to show the pieces of intrinsic interest and to demonstrate the range of wares occurring at the site throughout its occupation. The potters' stamps have all been listed alphabetically at the end of the report, with those from stratified groups cross-referenced under the relevant context.

The evidence of the samian suggests that the site was first occupied at some point during the decade 90-100. The conclusive feature is the scarcity of form 29, which ceased to be manufactured *c.* 85. The complete collection from the site contains only one example of this form (54 below) and a small rim sherd from another. Of the form 37 bowls which superseded them in popularity, nine are likely to have been fairly early examples of the form, dating from *c.* 75-95 or 100 (1, 26-7, 42-3, 55-8), and ten stamps on plain vessels fall within this date range (S11-2, S14, S16, S23-5, S32-4). The only early plain form present is form 15/17, of which there are fragments from fourteen examples, mostly the more spreading variant which continued throughout the first century. Allowing for a proportion of earlier material to enter any site already in the possession of the first settlers, it seems surprising that only two pieces from so large a collection were certainly manufactured before 90. Both at the fort and the east *vicus*, the groups which can be assigned to the earliest phase contain wares from Les Martres-de-Veyre, which were not reaching Britain before *c.* 100. These, however, clearly represent occupation debris rather than provide a *terminus post quem* for construction.

During the first century and early years of the second, the main source of supply was the South Gaulish potteries centering on La Graufesenque, which continued to export in quantity until *c.* 110. However, a little South Gaulish ware must have reached the site after this date, as witnessed by the stamp of the Hadrianic-early Antonine South Gaulish potter, Q.V.C., who probably worked at Montans. During the first quarter of the second century, a major supplier was the Central Gaulish pottery at Les Martres-de-Veyre. Wares from this source were reaching Watercrook during phase 1, and continued to do so until the early Antonine period. The later products of this pottery, which ceased manufacture by *c.* 160, are represented by the work of Cettus (79). The amount of decorated ware recovered from Les Martres-de-Veyre was quite small, although in all, these wares probably amount to *c.* 9% of the total from the site.

From *c.* 120, Lezoux becomes the main source of supply. The presence of two unusual pieces (66 and 67) suggest that some material may have been reaching the site from Lezoux before this date. The fabric of 66 is that normally associated with the pre-export period, as is the ovolo of 67, although here occurring on a fairly standard Lezoux fabric. Both these bowls are likely to have been made by potters at work over the period when regular export started.

From the early Antonine period, a steady trickle of samian was reaching the site from east Gaul. This probably amounts to about 5% of the total material from the site, which is about, or slightly higher than, the average from military sites on the west side of Britain. The wide range of date and origin of these pieces is interesting. In the early Antonine period, samian was reaching Watercrook from Lavoye (13), possibly from La Madeleine (the potter Lossa, S17), and from Rheinzabern (33, 53, 87-8). The later products of the Blickweiler potteries are represented (34), of mid- to late-Antonine date, and some of the later Rheinzabern products may have been reaching the site in the third century (12, 25). Two small sherds, badly burnt (35), are probably from the Argonne potteries. It thus appears that, even after the end of export from Lezoux at the end of the second century, some samian may have been reaching the site from East Gaul.

Note: I wish to express my grateful thanks to Mr B. R. Hartley and Miss Brenda Dickinson of Leeds University for providing me with the information on which my notes on the potters' stamps are based. The potter and die numbers are theirs (potter numbers in lower case Roman numerals to distinguish their numbering system from those of Stanfield and Simpson in Central Gaul and Ricken at Rheinzabern, both of whom use upper case Roman Numerals and will appear in their forthcoming *Index of Potters' Stamps on Samian Ware*. I must also express my gratitude to Mr Hartley for discussing with me a number of the more unusual decorated pieces, to which he alone has amassed parallels.

Abbreviations:

O: cf. Oswald 1936-7.
S & S: cf. Stanfield and Simpson 1958.
The Rheinzabern ovolos and details are from Ricken-Fischer 1963.

THE FORT

Phase 1

The only stratified material came from the foundation trench for the fence beside the north-east road, and was all South Gaulish and Flavian or Flavian-Trajanic, except for one fragment of form 18 or 18/31, which is in the fabric of the Central Gaulish pottery at Les Martres-de-Veyre. The presence of this piece suggests a deposition date after *c.* 100.

1. (ARC 2010, AQO 1358)   Form 67, South Gaulish. Two fragments showing scroll decoration with the long-necked bird (0·2257) in the lower concavity. Both form and decoration are typical of the Flavian period. A similar leaf was used by Vanderio (Knorr 1919, Taf. 80A, C) and by Iucundus, Sasmonus and Secundus (*ibid.*, textbild 9). The bird was used by various potters, including Vitalis (*ibid.*, Taf. 83M, where it occurs with a similar rosette spacefiller). Both rosette and butterfly binding occur on 20 below, which also shows affinities to the style of Vitalis. Flavian.

2. (BCF S343)   Form 37, South Gaulish. One fragment, with zonal decoration of festoons, slightly smaller and finer than those of Vitalis (Knorr 1919, Taf. 84G) and closer in size to those of Felix (Knorr 1952, Taf. 24D, E). The six-leafed pendant is probably that of Cosius Rufinus (Knorr 1919, Taf. 24B). The zonal decoration suggests that this is an early example of the form. *c.* 80-100.

3. (APH 2311)   Form 37, South Gaulish. Small fragment showing panel decoration in the style of the Flavian-Trajanic potters, with the gladiator (0·999) used by M. Crestio and Mercato. *c.* 90-110.

4. (BCF S293)   Form 37, South Gaulish. One fragment showing panel containing centaur (0·722) and fawn (0·646). Both types are common in the Flavian-Trajanic period, occurring, for example, at the Bregenz Cellar (Jacobs 1912, 8, 14, 21). *c.* 90-110.

5. (ARC 2018)   Form 37, South Gaulish. One fragment showing panel decoration with Diana and hind (0·104). *c.* 90-110.

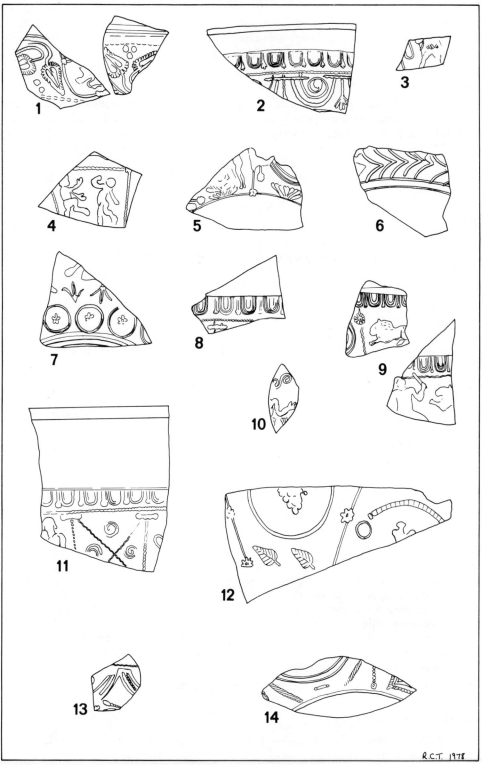

FIG. 114. – Watercrook: the samian (1:2).

Phase 2

The material from all the groups associated with the phase 2 structures was primarily of Hadrianic-early Antonine date, and nothing from them need be later than *c.* 150.

Fort wall construction trench

6.   (AIP 1115)   Form 37, Central Gaulish, slightly burnt. One fragment showing basal wreath of large chevrons used by X.6 (Rogers 1974, G. 325). The wide basal ridge was also used by him (S & S, pl. 75, 13, 19). *c.* 125-150.

7.   (AIP 478)   Form 37, Central Gaulish. One fragment in the style of the potter X.6, showing his trefoil and medallion with six-point rosette (S & S. pl. 75, 13). *c.* 125-150.

8.   (AIP 987)   Form 37, Central Gaulish, showing the ovolo used by Attianus and Austrus. *c.* 130-160.

Drain

9.   (AKJ 2361, 2319)   Form 37, Central Gaulish. Two fragments, from different bowls, both in the style of Geminus, showing his lion (0·1422) and the warrior (0·210). *c.* 120-140.

Rebuild of rampart

10.   (AJO 1527)   Form 37, Central Gaulish. One fragment showing Neptune (0·13) and the large S motif characteristic of X.6 and the Large S Potter. *c.* 125-150.

The rampart material also includes the stamps of Dagomarus, *c.* 125-140 (S13) and Quintilianus, *c.* 125-150 (S27).

Rampart oven

11.   (AJK 2055)   Form 37, Central Gaulish. One fragment in the style of the potter X.6. The ovolo and cross decoration appear on a bowl from Corbridge (S & S. pl. 74, 1). The prisoner (0·1146) was also used by him. *c.* 125-160.

Phase 3/4

North-east gate guard-chamber

This group contained material dating to the later Antonine period, including East Gaulish ware of probable third century date.

12.   (BAE S169-171, BBI S209, 210)   Form 37, East Gaulish. Five fragments in the style of Iulius I and Lupus of Rheinzabern. The medallion with grapes (Ricken-Fischer 1963, P. 164) was used by Lupus (Ricken 1948, Taf. 157, 7, 10, 11), as also was the leaf (P. 37) and beaded borders with rosette (0·48) (Ricken 1948, Taf. 159, 1, 3). The suppliant appears on work in the style of Iulius I and Lupus (*ibid.*, Taf. 160, 14). The small ovolo fragment probably shows Ricken's E.18, which occurs on a sherd from Rheinzabern in the style of the same potters, and probably comes from the same bowl. The bowl should probably be dated to the first half of the third century.

The stamp of Martius iv, *c.* 160-190 (S19) comes from these layers.

The ditches

The ditches all contain late Antonine and some possible third century material.

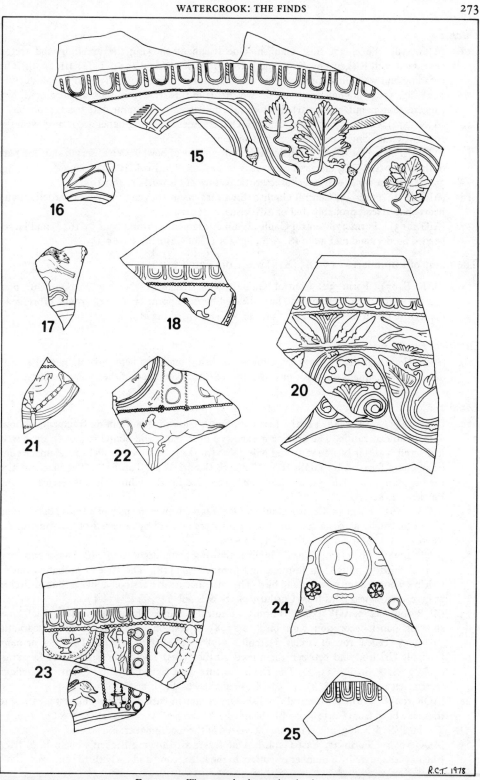

FIG. 115. – Watercrook: the samian (1:2).

Ditch 1

13. (AJG 878) Form 37, East Gaulish. One fragment showing the arcading and trefoil associated with Ricken's ovolos A and B from Lavoye (Ricken 1934, Taf. XIII, 20, 8). The arcading and wavy-line border appear on a sherd from Birrens with Ricken's ovolo A (Wld 1975, fig. 59, 99). The occurrence of two sherds in this style from the Saalburg earth-fort suggests that manufacture started before 140, and an early Antonine date seems probable.

14. (AJN 1273) Form 37, Central Gaulish. One fragment showing panel decoration with the rope twist and fringed cushion used by Cinnamus. *c.* 150-175.

15. (AJN) Form 37, Central Gaulish. Several fragments of bowl with leaf scroll, showing part of the stamp SEV∃RI, die 7a of Severus iv of Lezoux. The ovolo is his ovolo 2 (S. & S., fig. 37, 2). and the rope twist is a characteristic feature of his work. *c.* 160-195.

16. (AIG 823) Form 30, Central Gaulish. Small fragment showing festoon or medallion and heart-shaped leaf, probably that of Advocisus. *c.* 160-190.

17. (AIG 1103) Form 37, Central Gaulish. Small fragment showing boar (0·1642) and large-beaded borders and bud motif (S. & S., fig. 40, 11) of Casurius. *c.* 160-190.

The stamp of Lupinus, *c.* 155-185 (S18) was from Ditch 1.

18. (BAK S167) Form 37, Central Gaulish. One fragment showing festoon with bird (0·2239). The ovolo, festoon and large-beaded border appear on a sherd from Corbridge in the style of Casurius (S. & S., pl. 134, 31), who also used the bird. *c.* 160-190.

Ditch 1b

19. (BBL. *Not illustrated*) Form 37, Central Gaulish. Small fragment showing part of a large ovolo, either Cinnamus ovolo 1 or Casurius ovolo 1. Second half of the second century.

Ditch 2

20. (AQZ 1385, 1386, 1388, 1392) Form 37, South Gaulish. Four joining fragments of bowl with zonal decoration. The upper zone shows a bush motif and hound (0·1925); the lower, leaf-scroll with bird (0·2232A) and Nile goose (0·2244). A close parallel to the upper zone occurs on a form 29 by Vitalis from Windisch (Knorr 1919, Taf. 83E). The bird was also used by him (*ibid.*, Taf. 83, 21). The leaf is recorded for Biragillus, Flavius Germanus and Patricius. *c.* 80-100.

21. (AQR 2476) Form 37, Central Gaulish. One fragment showing part of a saltire decoration, placed unusually across a festoon. The motifs were all used by Drusus I of Les Martres-de-Veyre (S. & S. pl. 10, 121; 16, 197). *c.* 100-120.

22. (AQR 1098) Form 37, Central Gaulish, showing panel decoration with Diana and hind (0·106), bird (0·2295A) in festoon, and panther (0·1518). The style is probably that of Criciro, who used the panther and bird. The latter occurs in a festoon above a zone of circles, as here, on a signed bowl from Cardurnock (S. & S., pl. 117, 2). *c.* 135-170.

23. (AQR 1096, 2475, AQV 3568) Form 37, Central Gaulish. Three fragments of small bowl showing panel decoration with bird (0·2298) in festoon over hare (0·2116); caryatid (0·1199); vertical row of circles; Hercules (0·783). The style is that of Divixtus, or more probably Criciro, who between them used all the types. The ovolo is probably Divixtus' ovolo 2 (S. & S., fig. 33, 2). The festoon occurs on a signed bowl by Criciro at Ovilava (Karnitsch 1959, Taf. 58, 4). *c.* 150-180, or slightly earlier if by Criciro.

24. (AQR 1095) Form 37, Central Gaulish. One fragment with decoration almost identical to that on a bowl from Corbridge with the finisher's stamp of Aventinus II (S. & S., pl. 156, 3). The bust (S. & S., fig. 46, 4) is a characteristic of the mouldmaker. *c.* 160-190.

25. (AQQ 1072) Form 37, East Gaulish. One fragment showing Ricken's ovolo E.40 from Rheinzabern, used by a number of potters in the late second and early third centuries.

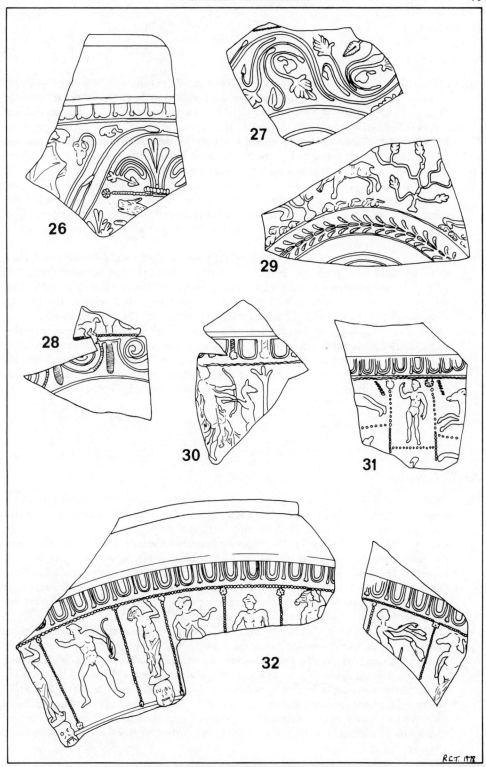

FIG. 116. – Watercrook: the samian (1:2).

Unstratified

South Gaulish

26. (APA 2187)   Form 37. One fragment with leaf-scroll decoration with hound (0·1994) and Nile geese (0·2244, 2286). The ovolo is worn, but is similar to the large rosette ovolo used by Frontinus and common at Pompeii and on first-century sites in Scotland. The smaller leaf occurs at Pompeii on bowls with this ovolo (Atkinson 1914, 42, 52), as do the Nile geese. An unpublished bowl from Gloucester shows a very similar decorative scheme, with geese and similar use of the four-leafed bud. Although that bowl shows a different ovolo, its style shows obvious similarities to that associated with the rosette ovolo. *c.* 75-90.

27. (AIX 876, AHZ)   Form 37. Two joining fragments, showing leaf-scroll with Nile geese (0·2244, 2286). The largest leaf was used by Frontinus (Knorr 1952, Taf. 25). A scroll with similar binding, Nile goose and small heart-shaped leaf occurs on an unpublished bowl from Gloucester which shows his large rosette ovolo. This is undoubtedly an early example of form 37, and may date *c.* 75-95.

28. (APG 72, 74, AQO 1470)   Form 37. Three fragments showing zonal decoration with plant motif and bird (0·2231A) over festoons with thick corded pendent between them. The pendent is similar to that of Germanus and his associates (Knorr 1952. Taf. 27B, 28E), though they normally used it with a leafed festoon. The ribbed festoon was used by Passienus (Knorr 1919, Taf. 63C) and Frontinus (Knorr 1952, Taf. 25A). *c.* 80-110.

29. (ARL 2551)   Form 37. Fragment showing decoration with trees and animals, including stag (0·1748). Similar trees were used by Germanus, and the stag occurs on work in his style. It also occurs with trees and the rock motif on bowls in the Bregenz Cellar deposit (Jacobs 1912, 3, 12) probably to be attributed to the style associated with Mascuus. The basal wreath motif occurs commonly on work in this style (Wild 1972, fig. 15A, D). *c.* 90-110.

Central Gaulish

30. (AHI 122, 124, AJY 1323)   Form 37. Three fragments, not joining, probably from the same bowl in the style of X.6, showing Diana and hind (0·106). The ovolo, bud and type occur on a bowl from Carzield (S. & S., pl. 76, 28). *c.* 125-150.

31. (AIH 360, ABU 731)   Form 37. Two fragments, one from the *vicus* (also unstratified), from the same bowl showing panel decoration with bear (0·1616), figure (0·633A) and stag (0·1781). The ovolo, guideline and wavy-line border were used by Bassus, an associate of Quintilianus (S. & S., pl. 73, 41). The bear, figure and rosette junction are all attested for the Quintilianus group. Although their normal border is a wavy line, bead rows sometimes occur, particularly with a basal row of quatrefoils (S. & S., pl. 70, 20). *c.* 125-150.

32. (AHI 636, 446, AJD 770, AAF 183)   Form 37. Several fragments, not all joining, showing panel decoration with, in order: Venus on mask (0·305); satyr (0·607); Venus; maenad (0·363); Pan (0·717); Venus. Other fragments also show maenad (0·354) and another, uncertain, dancing figure. The style is that of a potter, Paternus (Hartley's Paternus iv), whose cursive signature is known from bowls at Barnsley Park and Caerwent. The ovolo, borders with rosette junctions and frequent use of the Venus (0·305) are characteristic of his style. A sherd from Ovilava (Karnitsch 1959, Taf. 44, 5) showing the Venus and borders, should also be attributed to this potter. A Hadrianic-early Antonine date seems probable. *c.* 135-165.

East Gaulish

33. (AHI 635)   Form 37. One fragment showing Ricken's ovolo E.19 from Rheinzabern, the bird (his T. 248) and plant (P.103). All these features occur on a sherd from Rheinzabern in the style of Ianus or Ianuarius I. The presence of work in this potter's style in period 1a at Birdoswald suggests that he started work during the Hadrianic period, and an early Antonine date seems likely.

34. (AKF 1424, 1633)   Form 37. Two non-joining fragments in the style of the potter L.A.L. of Blickweiler. The type is his Venus (o.286A), and the ovolo and canopy are listed by Ricken (Ricken-Fischer 1963, E. 38, O. 3a). All these features occur together on an identical stamped bowl from Herapel (Klumbach 1933, 13). Antonine.

35. (AHI 199)   Form 37. Two small fragments in light orange fabric, badly burnt, with matt orange glaze. The decoration, with vertical leafed panel divisions ending in rosettes, suggests the products of the Argonne potteries (Chenet-Gaudron 1955, fig. 61L). Antonine.

EAST *VICUS*

The samian from the features assigned to phase I suggests occupation during the later Flavian and Trajanic periods. Most of the material is South Gaulish, but wares from Les Martres-de-Veyre are also present.

Wall trench A36

36. (AEP 2582)   Form 37, South Gaulish, showing panel decoration with part of small bird to l., and feet of large bird, probably a crane or cock, to r. The basal wreath and grass motif are typical of the Flavian-Trajanic period. *c.* 90-110.

The stamp of Iucundus ii, *c.* 75-95 (S16) comes from this group.

Pit A16

37. (AEE 2469)   Form 37, South Gaulish, showing basal wreath of Z-shaped gadroons. A similar wreath occurs on a bowl from Ovilava (Karnitsch 1959, Taf. 11, 3) attributed to M. Crestio or Pudens, and one of smaller gadroons on bowls in the style of Mercato (*ibid.*, Taf. 16, 3, 4). A zone of similar gadroons appears on a form 29 by Sasmonus (Knorr 1952, Taf. 53F). *c.* 80-110.

38. (AEE 2473, ABR 1839, 1838, 1856)   Form 37, South Gaulish. Six fragments from bowl with zonal decoration, showing triple festoon with birds (probably o.2248, 2296), central horizontal wreath, and bush, stags (o.1699, 1745) and tree motif with bird The style is that associated with Mercato. A similar upper zone occurs on bowls in his style from Ovilava (Karnitsch 1959, Taf. 14, 4-6). He also used the stags, basal wreath and similar bush. The stag, wreath and bush occur on another bowl attributed to the style of his slightly earlier associate Secundus (*ibid.*, Taf. 10, 7), who used the stags with a similar tree on a form 29 from Windisch (Knorr 1919, Taf. 74C). Probably *c.* 90-110, though in view of the parallels with Secundus, it could be slightly earlier.

39. (ADS 2157)   Form 37, South Gaulish, showing ovolo with rosette tongue and coarse-roped border typical of the Flavian-Trajanic period. The ovolo may be that used by Mercato (Knorr 1919, Textbild 47), which occurs with a saltire, as here, at Ovilava (Karnitsch 1959, Taf. 15, 57. *c.* 90-110.

40. (AEE 2285)   Form 37, Central Gaulish, showing the ovolo and border of Igocatus of Les Martres-de-Veyre. The type may be his Perseus (o.234). *c.* 100-120.

Lower fill of well A10

41.   (ACY 2672)   Form 37, South Gaulish, with poorly impressed triple-pronged ovolo and narrow decorated zone showing hares (0·2056, 2114) opposed across leaf tuft. The leaf tuft and basal wreath were used by Mercato (Knorr 1919, Taf. 57). An almost identical bowl was found at Northwich (Wild 1972, fig. 12, 2). *c.* 90-110.

Wall trench A37

42.   (ADA 2322, ACC 1448)   Form 37, South Gaulish. Two fragments (one unstratified) from bowl with zonal decoration showing hound (0·1927) and hare (0·2072) with bush, over festoons. An identical zone of festoons occurs on a form 29 by Vitalis from Mainz (Knorr 1919, Taf. 84G). The hare was also used by him (*ibid.*, Taf. 81A), probably with this hound. Another bowl by him from Mainz (*ibid.*, Taf. 84F) shows parallels to the upper zone, as does a bowl by Pudens (*ibid.*, Taf. 68). *c.* 75-100.

43.   (ADA 2073)   Form 37, South Gaulish. Small fragment with scroll decoration containing bud and spirals. The general scheme is similar to that of an unpublished bowl from Gloucester showing the large rosette ovolo of Frontinus. However, too little of the present bowl survives to attempt a close attribution. *c.* 75-100.

44.   (ADA 2061)   Form 37, South Gaulish, showing panel decoration with saltire and satyr (0·597) *c.* 90-110.

A22

A mainly South Gaulish, Flavian-Trajanic group, but including three fragments of Central Gaulish ware in the fabric of Les Martres-de-Veyre. One of these is a scrap of form 37 showing part of the inverted dolphins used by Drusus I in place of the ovolo (cf. S. & S. pl. 11, 133). These pieces are likely to be early Hadrianic at latest, and to date *c.* 100-120.

45.   (ACS 2703)   Form 37, South Gaulish, showing panel decoration with Peleus (0·883) and saltire. The buds in the saltire were used by a number of potters, but occur thus on a form 29 by Iucundus (Knorr 1919, Taf. 43E). However, the style of this bowl indicates a slightly later date, and a closer parallel is an unsigned bowl from Burladingen, showing the Peleus and saltire with a larger bud (*ibid.*, Taf. 99B). Probably *c.* 90-110.

Phase 2

Wall trench A46

46.   (AFL 2715)   Form 37, Central Gaulish. Small fragment showing the leaf used by Sacer (S. & S., Pl. 84, 14), *c.* 125-150.

A23 Hearth

47.   (ADM 2158)   Form 37, South Gaulish, showing panel decoration, probably with Minerva (0·137). *c.* 90-110.

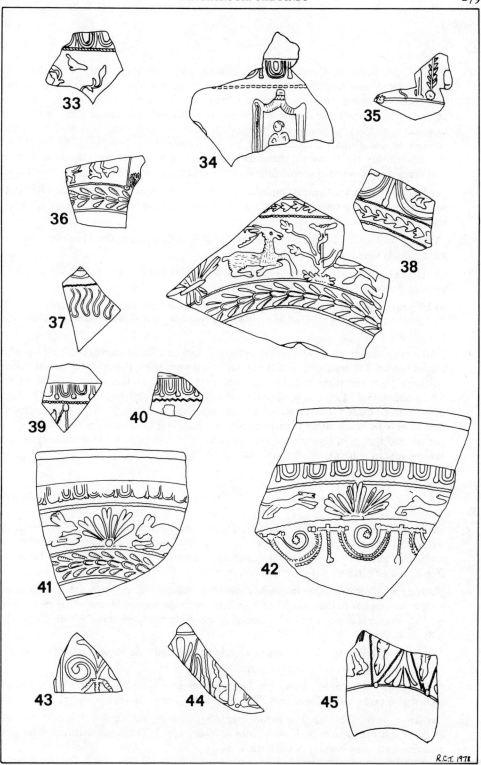

FIG. 117. — Watercrook: the samian (1:2).

R.C.T. 1978

Phase 3

A4

48. (AAH 679)   Form 37, Central Gaulish. One fragment, showing panel decoration with figure (0·583A) and horizontally ribbed column ending in a square box. The column, box and coarse wavy-line border are typical of the style of an anonymous potter who also commonly used small medallions. Several pieces in his style are known. Sherds from an identical bowl from Silchester and Ashfurlong, near Olney, Bucks., have been published (*Wolverton and District Archaeological Society Newsletter* 9, (1965), 7). A sherd from Ribchester (Mus. No. B100013) shows the medallion containing the box seen on this sherd. The potter's work shows links with Docilis, and a Hadrianic-early Antonine date is probable.

49. (AAH 432)   Form 37, Central Gaulish, with freestyle decoration showing goat (0·1849A) and small panther (probably 0·1553). The ovolo and pendent leaf were used by Albucius, who also used the panther. *c.* 150-180.

50. (AAH 522)   Form 37, Central Gaulish, in the style of Cinnamus. The Diana (0·111) and all the motifs were used by him. *c.* 150-175.

51. (AAH 524)   Form 37, Central Gaulish, showing Cinnamus' ovolo 1 and the head of a panther (probably 0·1507). *c.* 155-175.

52. (AAH 523)   Form 37, Central Gaulish, showing panel decoration with the warrior (0·141). The ovolo and motif are those of Advocisus. The type has been recorded on work in his style. *c.* 160-190.

53. (AAH 525)   Form 37, East Gaulish, showing Ricken's Rheinzabern ovolo E. 69 with corded border. The style is that of the potter who stamps IANUF, who used the dot-rosette (Ricken's 0·42) and triple medallion (Ricken 1948, Taf. 3, 4). Other sherds by him from Rheinzabern (*ibid.*, Taf. 2, 8, 9) show the same ovolo, border and diagonal lattice. The form of the potter's name is uncertain, but the apparent ligature of the SF in the stamp suggests that he may be Ianus rather than Ianuarius. He is among the earliest of the Rheinzabern potters, and a piece in his style has been recorded in period 1a at Birdoswald, suggesting a Hadrianic start to his career. Probably early Antonine.

Unstratified

South Gaulish

54. (ACN 2436, AEC 2177, 2178)   Form 29. Three fragments from lower zone with horizontal wreath of chevrons over panels with hare (0·2074) and hound (0·1923) divided by a panel of wavy lines and leaf tips. The panel decoration is identical to that on a bowl by Iucundus from Günzburg (Knorr 1919, Ta. 31D). *c.* 70-85.

55. (AEC 2179)   Form 37. One fragment showing medallion with cupid (0·436). The general style is very similar to that on a bowl from Pompeii in the style of Mommo (Atkinson 1914, 60). The corner leaf was used by M. Crestio on a bowl from Margidunum (Oswald 1948, pl. XXI, 1). *c.* 75-95.

56. (AEW 2675) Form 30. One fragment showing ovolo and tree in the style of Germanus (Karnitsch 1959, Taf. 5, 1; Jacobs 1912, 2). *c.* 75-95.

57. (AFR 2694, 2692, 2668)   Form 37. Three joining fragments in the style of Germanus, showing his ovolo, vine (Knorr 1919, Taf. 39R) and Bacchus (0·564). *c.* 75-95.

58. (ABE 652, 715)   Form 37. Two joining fragments showing leaf-scroll with hound (0·2014) in lower concavities over bush with ?lions (0·1397, 1472). The zonal decoration suggests that this is an early example of the form. *c.* 75-95.

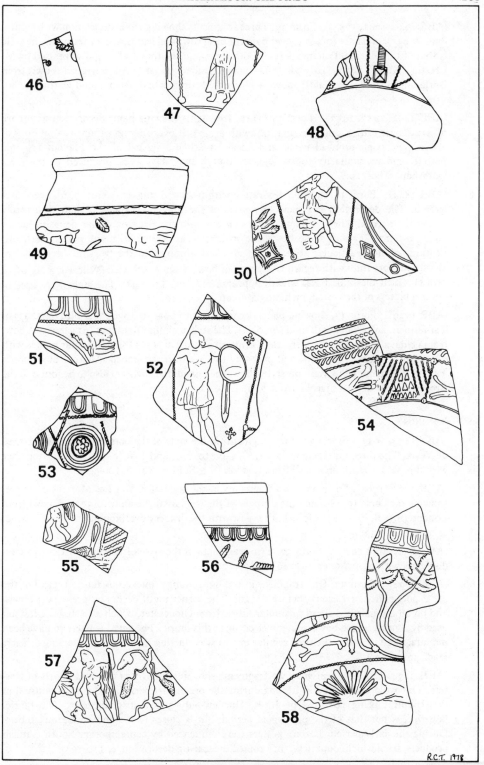

FIG. 118. – Watercrook: the samian (1:2).

59. (ABR 1640, 1641, 1755)   Form 37. Three fragments showing panel decoration with saltire, man (0·635), and hare (0·2074) over panel of bead rows and leaf tips, over festoon. The style is that of the Flavian-Trajanic period. Both types and the four-leafed bud were used by M. Crestio (Knorr 1919, Taf. 28C, D) among other potters. An unsigned bowl from Burladingen (*ibid.*, Taf. 99B) shows a saltire with similar bud, festoon and leaftips. *c.* 80-110.

60. (ABU 1454, 1457, 1453)   Form 37. Three fragments showing panel decoration with hare (0·2129) over saltire, and lion (0·1400) with grass tuft over festoon similar to that on (59) above. The triple-pronged ovolo and basal wreath are typical of the Flavian-Trajanic potters, and its similarity to 59 suggests that it may have been produced in the same workshop. *c.* 80-110.

61. (ABR 1854)   Form 37, showing decoration with trees and stags (0·1699, 1746), over basal wreath. The decoration is typical of potters of the Flavian-Trajanic period, who rarely signed their work. The tree motif occurs on bowls in the Bregenz Cellar deposit (Jacobs 1912, 3-5, 12). Two of these bowls are in a style associated with the potter Mascuus. Features of this particular style, which also has affinities to the work of Mercato, are discussed more fully with regard to a group of bowls from Northwich (Wild 1972, 64-6), on two of which the same basal wreath appears (*ibid.*, fig. 15, A,D). The stags were used by several potters of the period, including Mercato. *c.* 90-110.

62. (ABR 1439)   Form 37, showing panel decoration with boar (0·1670) over bird (0·2293) in leaf festoon, and Diana with hind (0·104B). The style is similar to that of (61) above. A bowl from Ovilava in the style of Mercato (Karnitsch 1959, Taf. 15, 3) shows similar panels with 0·2293 in festoon, grass tufts, and probably the same corner tendril. Another bowl (*ibid.*, Taf. 18, 6) attributed to Mascuus style, shows the Diana. Parallels are also to be found in the Bregenz Cellar deposit (Jacobs 1912, 7, 9). *c.* 90-110.

Central Gaulish

63. (ABU 1452, 1047)   Form 37. Two fragments in the style of the potter X.2 of Les Martres-de-Veyre. The three types, cupid (0·367A), satyr (0·718) and goat (0·1852), occur together with this basal wreath on a bowl from London (S & S, Pl. 7, 80). *c.* 100-120.

64. (ACK 1760, 1764). Form 37. Two fragments in the style of X.2 of Les Martres-de-Veyre, showing the cupid (0·389) and the drapery of the woman at the altar (0·322). A bowl from London (S & S, Pl. 7, 80) shows both types, with the drapery overlapping the cupid's wing, as here. *c.* 100-120.

65. (AFI 2632, AFH 2629)   Form 37. Two fragments in the style of Igocatus of Les Martres-de-Veyre, with his prisoner (0·1146). *c.* 100-120.

66. (AFR 2696)   Form 37. One fragment in the light orange, micaceous fabric typical of the pre-export period at Lezoux (before *c.* 120). The corner motif occurs on pre-export bowls, and on an unpublished sherd in similar fabric from Gloucester, which also shows a festoon used by Avitus, whose bowls sometimes occur in this fabric. The sherd is likely to have been manufactured at about the time regular export was starting, and to be of Trajanic or early Hadrianic date.

67. (AEH 2274, 2201)   Form 30. Two fragments showing hare (0·2115?) and panels of leaf-tips. The ovolo is one used at Lezoux during the pre-export period, and is very unusual in this country, being recorded by B. R. Hartley only once outside Lezoux. The fabric, however, is not that of the pre-export period, but is closer to a standard Lezoux fabric. During the early period, Lezoux potters were influenced by contemporary South Gaulish products, from which, doubtless, they copied the leaf-tip decoration. *c.* 110-125.

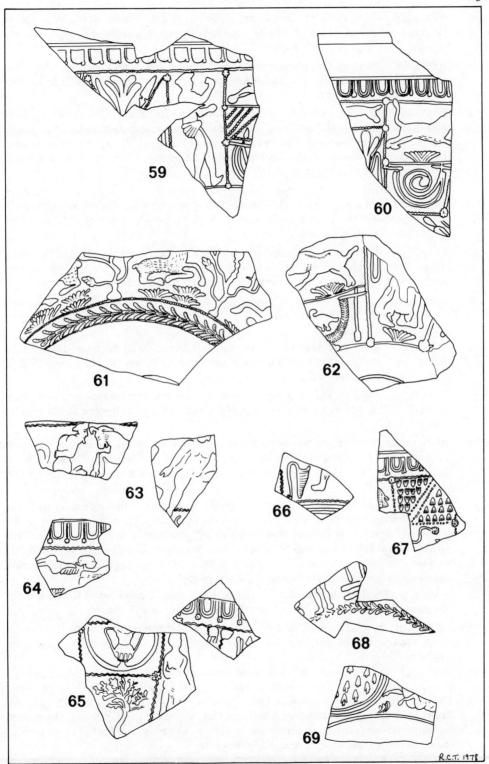

FIG. 119. — Watercrook: the samian (1:2).

68. (ACX 2226, 2229) Form 37. Two joining fragments in a light-coloured fabric, typical of the Hadrianic period, showing a basal wreath of chevrons, possibly that of Avitus and Vegetus (S & S, Fig. 14, 3). Hadrianic.

69. (AEG 2168) Form 37. One fragment in the style of the potter X.5, showing the edge of the type Luna in her chariot (0·117). The decoration is identical to that on bowls from London and Caersws (S & S, Pl. 67, 12). c. 125-145.

70. (ACD 1691, ACG, 1730, 1727) Form 37. At least three fragments of bowl, showing rivet-holes in rim. The ovolo is that of the Quintilianus group, who also used the bunch of grapes (S & S, Pl. 69, 9, by Ianuaris). The type is clearly a lizard (0·1531A). The guideline beneath the ovolo is just visible above the wavy-line border, a feature noted on other bowls by these potters (S & S, Pl. 70, 19; 73, 41; and 31 above). c. 125-150.

71. (ACD 1560, AEH 2252, ADJ 2257, 2259, 2262) Form 37. Two main sherds and three other pieces from a small bowl. The decoration is almost identical to that of a bowl from York in the style of the Quintilianus group (S & S. Pl. 71, 30) with a cursive signature below the decoration, probably of Ianuaris. c. 125-150.

72. (ACD 1559) Form 37. Two fragments of a bowl with the cursive signature of Drusus of Lezoux in the mould beneath the decoration. The types shown are the warrior (0·167); dancer (0·353); horse (probably 0·1903) in festoon over panther (0·1520). c. 125-150.

73. (AEH 2424, 2431 etc.) Form 37. Several fragments showing panel decoration with vine scroll and bear (0·1595) over panther (0·1499). The ovolo, vine scroll and panther were used by Drusus. c. 125-150.

74. (ACG 2027) Form 37. One fragment showing panel decoration in the style of Docilis, with cock (0·2361) and pigmy (0·698). The ram's horns (S & S, Pl. 92, 12) and column (S & S, Pl. 91, 1) were both used by him. c. 130-150.

75. (AEH 2375) Form 37. One fragment in the style of Docilis, who used the ovolo. The hare (0·2064) and festoons with concentric circles (S & S, Pl. 92, 15) both occur on bowls in his style. c. 130-150.

76. (ACD 1598, 1565) Form 37. Several fragments showing panel decoration with lion (0·1379), Pan (0·709A) and saltire ornament. The ovolo and general style are those of Paternus iv (see (32) above). The Pan, large bud and snake motif have all been attested on his work. c. 135-165.

77. (ABU 144) Form 37. One fragment showing the lower part of the decoration with lion (0·1422) leaftips and basal row of fine beads. Beneath the decoration are traces of the cursive CR signature of Criciro, who used both leaf and lion (S & S, Pl. 118, 15). Close parallels to this sherd can also be found among the bowls attributed by Stanfield and Simpson to "Donnaucus-Ioenalis" style (S & S, Pl. 44, 511; 46, 544), which suggests that this may be among Criciro's earlier products. c. 135-170.

78. (AAQ 300) Form 37, showing the cursive signature CR of Criciro beneath the decoration. The panels show his caryatid (0·1206) and Bacchus (0·566). c. 135-170.

79. (ACJ 2419, 1895) Form 37, in the fabric of Les Martres-de-Veyre. Two non-joining sherds, showing the characteristic small S and leaf of Cettus. The types are uncertain, but may be his Mercury (0·532) and Minerva (0·126B). Early Antonine.

80. (AAF 309) Form 37, showing freestyle decoration with cupid (0·420), bear (0·1627) and lion (0·1405). The style shows similarities to that of Cettus, who used the cupid and bear. The bear and lion occur together on a bowl in his style from London (S & S, Pl. 141, 16). None of Cettus' very characteristic details occur on the present sherd, although the general decorative scheme is similar to that on the bowl from Silchester (S & S, Pl. 141, 10), which shows the lion and possibly the bear. Early Antonine.

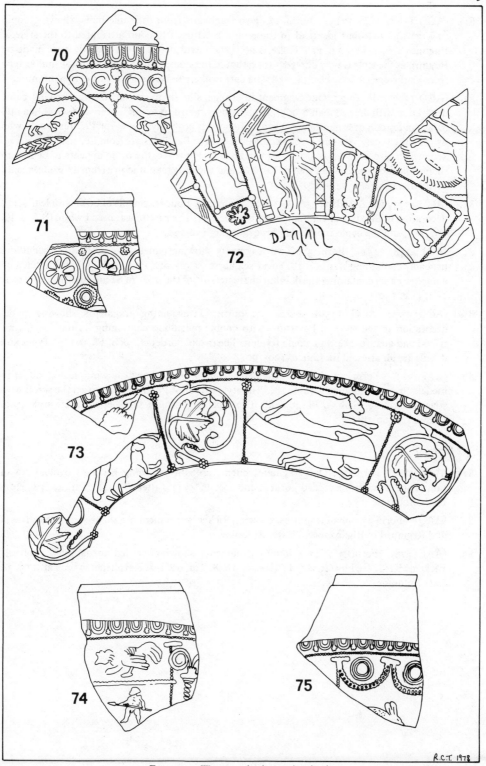

FIG. 120. — Watercrook: the samian (1:2).

81. (ACD 1562, ACG 1723)   Form 37. Two fragments from the same bowl, showing cupid (0·417) and gadroons identical to those on a bowl from London attributed to the style of Pugnus (S & S, Pl. 154, 17). There is no certain evidence that these bowls were made by Pugnus, as the style is very different from that of the stamped bowl with ovolo of similar type from Corbridge (S & S, Pl. 154, 13). The date is likely to be Hadrianic or early Antonine.

82. (ABD 1303)   Form 37. One fragment in orange, slightly micaceous fabric, showing panel decoration with draped man 0·905), medallion with bird (0·2239C) over vine scroll, sea bull (0·42) in festoon over panther (0·1520). The style is probably that of the Paullus group, who used all the types. The vine scroll occurs on a bowl in Paullus' style from Lezoux (S & S, Fig. 50), which also shows 0·905 and 0·42 in festoon. However, the ovolo appears to be new to them. The fabric also is not that of Lezoux, and suggests manufacture from a Lezoux mould at another centre. *c.* 145-180.

83. (ACD 1572, 1602, AAF 317, ACG 1850)   Form 37. Four fragments of bowl with leaf-scroll decoration in the style of Cinnamus or his associates. The rosette was used by him (S & S, Pl. 162, 60), and the ovolo is probably his ovolo 3. *c.* 150-170.

84. (ACJ 2448, 2451)   Form 37. Two fragments showing panel decoration with medallion, probably containing stag (0·1781) over sea horse (0·52), and Pan mask (0·1214) divided by a narrow panel containing the dolphin characteristic of the work of Secundus (Hartley 1961, 102, 4). *c.* 150-180.

85. (ACD 1577, ACG 1759)   Form 37, burnt. Two joining fragments showing panel decoration in the style of Paternus, with double medallion containing Triton (0·19), his tripod and goat (0·1843) in single festoon. The ovolo, borders (S & S, Pl. 104, 9), types and details are all attested for him. *c.* 160-190.

86. (AAF 327)   Form 37, burnt. Fragment from a small bowl showing leaf-scroll with medallion containing mask (0·1218). The style is that of Paternus, who used the scroll with striated binding (S & S, Pl. 104, 8). The type occurs on a small bowl in his style from Lezoux. *c.* 160-190.

East Gaulish

87. (AAF 310)   Form 37. One fragment, burnt, probably showing Ricken's ovolo E.19 of Ianu(arius) I, with his corded borders and rosette (0·41) (Ricken 1948, Taf. 4, 1, 5, etc.). Early Antonine.

88. (AAQ)   Form 37. Small fragment, showing Ricken's ornament 0·228, used by Ianu(arius) I and Reginus I of Rheinzabern. Early Antonine.

89. (AAF 178)   Form 37. Two joining fragments showing corded medallions, probably Ricken's K.52, used by Cerialis IV (Ricken 1948, Taf. 60, 1-2; Karnitsch 1959, Taf. 113, 3). Late Antonine.

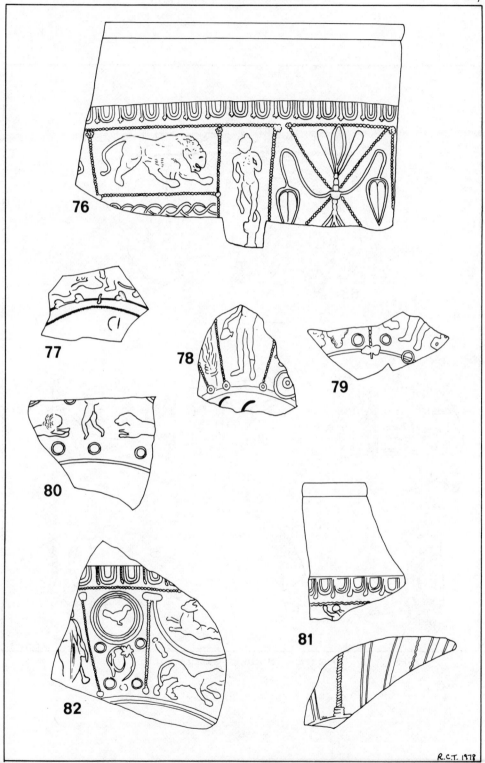

FIG. 121. – Watercrook: the samian (1:2).

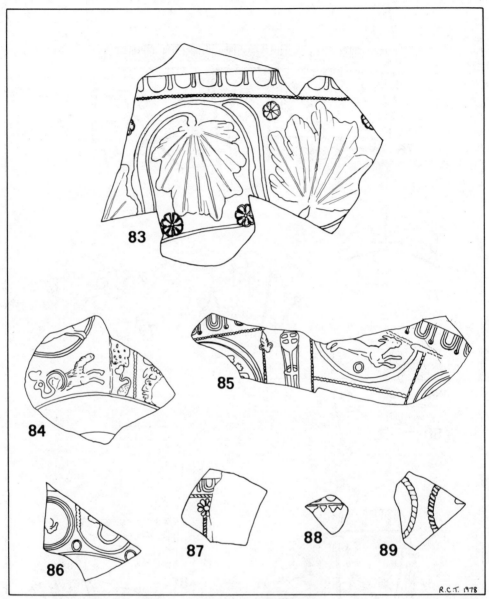

FIG. 122. – Watercrook: the samian (1:2).

SAMIAN STAMPS

S1.   ALB[VCIANI]   (AJD 729)   Form 33, Central Gaulish. Die 6e of Albucianus of Lezoux. The die, not itself recorded at Lezoux, occurs on the late Antonine forms 31R and 80, and at Arras, where it arrived after *c.* 170. *c.* 155-185.

S2.   APOLINARIS   (ACD 1575)   Form 27, Central Gaulish. Die 1a of Apolinaris, who probably worked at Les Martres-de-Veyre. This die occurs in the earth-fort at the Saalburg. *c.* 120-145.

S3.   [BALBINI.M   (ACJ 1884)   Form 18/31, Central Gaulish. Die 2a of Balbinus of Les Martres-de-Veyre. This curiously cut, but distinctive die, attributed fairly certainly to Balbinus, has been found at Les Martres, in the Hadrianic fire at London, and on form 15/17. *c.* 100-125.

S4.   BELINI[CCVSF]   (AAF 182)   Form 27, Central Gaulish. Die 5a of Beliniccus. This die has been recorded at Les Martres-de-Veyre, where the potter worked, but otherwise in no closely datable contexts. *c.* 110-130.

S5.   [BIGA].FEC   (ACG 1732)   Form 18/31, Central Gaulish. Die 1a. Although this die has not been recorded there, Biga worked at Lezoux. Other dies of his have been found in the earth-fort at the Saalburg and on Hadrian's Wall. *c.* 120-145.

S6.   [BV]CCIVS.F   (AHI 135)   Form 18/31, Central Gaulish. Die 1a. The die has been recorded at Lezoux, where Buccius presumably worked. It occurs on no closely datable sites, but was used mainly on the Hadrianic-early Antonine forms 18/31 and 18/31R. *c.* 125-155.

S7.   CERIA[LISF]   (AQN 1223)   Scrap, probably form 33a, South Gaulish. Almost certainly die 1a of Cerialis i, who presumably worked at La Graufesenque. No close dating evidence is available. Flavian.

S8.   [CIN]NAMVS   (AFE 2652)   Form 18/31, Central Gaulish. Die 6b of Cinnamus ii of Lezoux. This is one of the potter's early dies, and was found in a pit at Lezoux dating *c.* 135-140. *c.* 135-155.

S9.   CI.N.T.V.SS.A   (ACG 2026)   Form 18/31R, Central Gaulish. Die 1b. Other dies of Cintussa have been found at Lezoux, where he worked. This die occurs on the Hadrianic-early Antonine forms 27, 18/31 and 18/31R. *c.* 130-160.

S10.   [LLII]COO   (AHI 120)   Form 18/31. Central Gaulish. Die 12a of Cocillus of Lezoux, although this particular die has not been recorded there. There is no close dating evidence for this stamp. Probably *c.* 150-170.

S11.   CO[SRVF]   (ABP 812)   Form 27g, South Gaulish. This die of Cosius Rufinus of La Graufesenque has been found on Flavian sites, at Nijmegen (both in the fortress and the civil settlement Ulpia Noviomagus) and at York. Another die occurs at Camelon. *c.* 70-90.

S12.   OFCREST   (AAF 455)   Form 18, South Gaulish. Die 2a of Crestus of La Graufesenque. The work of this potter has been recorded at Carlisle and Corbridge. *c.* 75-100.

S13.   DAGOMA.   (AHV 442)   Form 18/31R, Central Gaulish. Die 13a. The die has been recorded at Lezoux, where Dagomarus worked, in the Birdoswald Alley, and in Hadrianic contexts in the Rhineland. *c.* 125-140.

S14.   [OF F]RONTNI   (APD 51)   Form 18, South Gaulish. Die 14a of Frontinus. The die is recorded at La Graufesenque, where he worked, and also at Corbridge. *c.* 75-100.

S15.   IOENALISF   (ACH 2276)   Form 27, Central Gaulish. Die 1a of Ioenalis of Les Martres-de-Veyre. The die has been recorded at Les Martres and in the second fire at London. *c.* 100-120.

S16.   OF IV[CVN]   (AEP 2581)   Form 18, South Gaulish. Die 5e of Iucundus ii. The die has been recorded at La Graufesenque, where he worked, at Catterick and Corbridge. *c.* 75-95.

S17.   LOSSΛ[FEC]   (BDW S406)   Form 18/31 or 31, East Gaulish. Die 1b of Lossa, whose work has only been recorded once in Britain, at Stanwix. His output was almost exclusively dishes, of forms 18/31 and 31, with one form 32 noted, but not seen, during the compilation of Hartley's new index of potters' stamps. Lossa is likely to have worked at one of the earlier East Gaulish factories, probably La Madeleine, in the period *c.* 130-160.

S18.   LVPINIM   (AIG 1161)   Form 33, Central Gaulish. Die 3b of Lupinus of Lezoux. This die occurs at Lezoux and on the late Antonine forms 31R, 79, 80 and 15/31. *c.* 155-185.

S19.   MA[RTIM]   (BAB S5, BAE S35-39)   Form 33, Central Gaulish. Die 1b of Martius iv. This is a stamp of the later Lezoux Martius, which occurs at Lezoux, and at sites on Hadrian's Wall, the Brougham cemetery and Malton. Although usually on form 33, it has been recorded on form 80. *c.* 160-190.

S20.   [PATE]RCLVSF   (AAF 458)   Form 18/31, Central Gaulish. Die 12a of Paterclus ii, which has been recorded at Les Martres-de-Veyre, where he worked, on form 15/17, and in the second fire of London. *c.* 100-125.

S21.   [PA]TER[CLO]   (ABR 1233)   Scrap, probably of form 18, Central Gaulish. Die 17a of Paterclus ii of Les Martres-de-Veyre. *c.* 100-125.

S22.   ꟼECV[IΛR.F]   (AIH 372)   Form 27, Central Gaulish. Die 5a of Peculiaris i of Lezoux. His work has been recorded at Corbridge, Wallsend and Newstead. This die is common on form 27, but sometimes occurs on forms 79 and 80. In view of its form, the present piece is likely to have been made in the earlier part of the date range, *c.* 140-170.

S23.   PEREGRI[Ʌ]   (ACX 1883)   Form 18, South Gaulish. Die 3a of Peregrinus i of La Graufesenque. The die occurs on form 29 and at Flavian foundations in Britain, at Ilkley, Corbridge, Camelon and Loudoun Hill. *c.* 75-100.

S24.   PER[EGRIΛ]   (APA 1410)   Form 15/17 or 18, South Gaulish, showing the same die, 3a of Peregrinus i. *c.* 75-100.

S25.   OFPONI   (ABR 1232)   Form 27, South Gaulish. Die 8g of Pontus of La Graufesenque. Although this die has not been recorded from La Graufesenque, it occurs in mid-Flavian contexts at Inchtuthil, Corbridge, Holt, Okarben and the Saalburg. *c.* 80-95.

S26.   Q.V.C   (AEH 2326)   Form 27g, South Gaulish. Die 1d of the potter who stamps his initials, presumably of the *tria nomina* Q(uintus) V(alerius) C(———). He probably worked at Montans, as his fabrics and distribution match those of the other Montans potters. His stamps occur in second-century contexts in Britain, and this die has been noted at Newstead. *c.* 120-150.

S27.   [QV]INTILIANI[M]   (AJO 1316)   Form 18/31, Central Gaulish. Die 1b of Quintilianus i. This die has been recorded at Lezoux, where he worked, and on Hadrian's Wall. His work has also been recorded from Antonine sites in Scotland, at Inveresk, Camelon and Birrens. *c.* 125-150.

S28.   RVFFI.M   (AHI 648)   Form 18/31R, Central Gaulish. Die 2a of Ruffus ii. The die has been recorded at Lezoux, where he worked, and on the Hadrianic-early Antonine form 27. It occurs in the Rhineland, on Hadrian's Wall and at Newstead. *c.* 130-155.

S29.   [OF SE]XCN   (AAF 456)   Form 27, South Gaulish. Die 4a of a potter Sex(tus?)-Canus, or possibly the *tria nomina* of a Roman citizen, as S26 above. The die has been found at La Graufesenque, where he worked; at Holt and Wilderspool in Britain; and at Butzbach and the Saalburg in Germany. *c.* 90-110.

S30. TIB[ERI.M] (ADG) Form 15/31, Central Gaulish. Die 1c of Tiberius ii of Lezoux, although this die has not been found there. It occurs mainly on dishes (form 18/31, 31, 18/31R) but occasionally on form 33. By contrast, die 1a and 1a' usually occur on form 27, and more rarely on form 33 and 80. There is no close site evidence for the dating of this stamp. *c.* 150-170.

S31. [VER]ECV (BBT S289) Form 27, South Gaulish. Die 8a of Verecundus ii. Although one stamp of this potter has been noted from Banassac, die 8a is common in Britain and was therefore almost certainly used at La Graufesenque. Although his most common stamp, the only dated context in which it appears is Chester. Another stamp is known on form 29 from Camelon. *c.* 75-100.

S32. OF.VIR[ILI] (BAA S184) Form 15/17 or 18, South Gaulish. Die 6c. This is a stamp of the La Graufesenque potter Virilis i, which has not yet been recorded from the kiln site. It occurs at many mid-Flavian foundations, including Corbridge and the Saalburg. Many examples of this die show a faint vertical vetween the V and the I, presumably from a scratch on the die. The Watercrook piece does not appear to have this, and may therefore be an early impression. *c.* 75-100.

S33. OE EΛ (ABR 1638) Form 27, South Gaulish, showing an apparently illiterate stamp. This stamp has been recorded on form 29 at La Graufesenque (Hermet 1934, Pl. 114, 15a) with C.I.SA- in the decoration. *c.* 70-90.

S34. [Ɔ]IIIIΛꟻ[O] Form 18, South Gaulish, showing illiterate stamp no. 43. This has been recorded at La Graufesenque, and at the Nijmegen fortress. *c.* 70-100.

226   **385**

FIG. 123. – Watercrook: mortarium stamp (1:1) and illiterate stamp (1:1) on the base of a black-ware vessel (1:2).

COINS By D. C. A. SHOTTER

THE EXCAVATIONS OF 1974

The coins from the excavations of 1974 have received full publication in the interim report (Potter 1976, 56-63); since the preparation of that report, however, treatment of the finds has revealed a further unstratified coin from site A (east *vicus*);

(SF 206)   AE barbarous imitation, Claudius II   A.D. 268-270
           (All detail illegible)

It has also been possible, following further treatment of the coins, to revise two identifications, as follows:

(a) Phase I (east *vicus* (SF 294): the *denarius* given as Neronian is in fact a coin of Caesar (46 B.C.; Crawford 1974, 467, 1b). The obverse has the head of Ceres right with the legend COS TERT DICT ITER; the reverse has priestly implements with the legend AVGVR PONT MAX M.

(b) Phases 3/4 (east *vicus*) (SF 231): the coin given as illegible is in fact a radiate copy, probably of Tetricus I.

(c) Phases 3/4 (east *vicus*) (SF 75): the coin given as a probable *as* of Antoninus is a worn *as* of Vespasian.

The coins from 1974 may thus be summarised:

Site A (east *vicus*)

Phase 1: Republican 1.

Phase 2: Republican 1, Vitellius 1, Vespasian 1, Domitian 2, Nerva 1, Trajan 8.

Phases 3/4: Nero 1, Domitian 1, Trajan 1, Antoninus Pius 2, Gallienus 1, Tetricus I 1, radiate copy 1.

Unstratified: Domitian 1, Septimius Severus 1, radiate copy 1, Claudius II, 1.

Site B (east angle of fort)

South end of site: Trajan 1.
Rampart (phase II): Trajan 1, Hadrian 1.
Oven: Illegible 1.
Construction trench for fort wall: Republican 1.
Ditch 1: Domitian 1, Trajan 2, Gallienus 1, Victorinus 1, radiate copy 1.
Ditch 3: Trajan 1.
Unstratified: Trajan 1, Severus Alexander 1, Illegible 1.

Site C (north-east exit from fort)

Beneath latest road-surface: Nerva 1, Trajan 1.
Ditch 2: Vespasian 1, Hadrian 1.
Unstratified: Vespasian 1, radiate copies 2.

THE EXCAVATIONS OF 1975

Nineteen coins were recovered in the excavations, ranging from the Trajanic period to a single coin of Constantine I (A.D. 320), the latest so far to come from excavations at the site.

Guard-chamber (phases 3-4) (5 coins)

1. (SF 396)   AE *sestertius*, Hadrian   A.D. 134-8
   Obv. HADRIANVS AVG COS III P P
   Rev. FELICITAS AVG S C   Wt 22·404 gms   (*RIC* 749)

2. (SF 363)   AE Radiate copy, Claudius II   A.D. 268-70
   Illegible
   Wt 0·704 gms

3. (SF 367)   AE radiate copy, Victorinus (?)   A.D. 269-71
   Illegible and fragmentary   Wt 0·342 gms

4. (SF 366)   AE radiate copy, Tetricus I (?)   A.D. 271-3
    Illegible and fragmentary   Wt 0·513 gms

5. (SF 374)   AE radiate copy, Victorinus   A.D. 269-71
    Rev. matchstick figure of *Hilaritas*   Wt 0·951 gms

Ditch 1 (5 coins)

6. (SF 461)   AE *antoninianus*, Claudius II   A.D. 268-70
    Obv. IMP C CLAVDIVS P F AVG
    Rev. LIBERTAS AVG   Wt 2·732 gms   (*RIC* 61)

7. (SF 469)   AE radiate copy   *c.* A.D. 270
    Illegible and fragmentary   Wt 0·859 gms

8. (SF 449)   AE Constantine I   A.D. 320
    Obv. CONSTANTINVS AVG
    Rev. D N CONSTANTINI MAX AVG;
    within wreath VOT XX; T̄SAVI   Wt 2·759 gms   (*RIC* VII, p. 510, No. 101)

9. (SF 376)   AE *antoninianus*, Victorinus   A.D. 269-71
    Obv. IMP C VICTORINVS P F AVG
    Rev. PIETAS AVG   Wt 2·933 gms   (*RIC* 57)

10. (SF 382)   AE radiate copy, Tetricus II   A.D. 271-3
    Rev. matchstick figure of *Pax*   Wt 1·032 gms

Foundation trench for fence beside north-east road (2 coins)

11. (SF 416)   AE radiate copy, Claudius II   A.D. 268-70
    Rev. matchstick figure of *Salus*   Wt 0·917 gms

12. (SF 458)   AE *antoninianus*, Tetricus I   A.D. 271-3
    Obv. IMP C TETRICVS P F AVG
    Rev. Illegible   Wt 1·420 gms

Unstratified (7 coins)

13. (SF 346)   AE *as*, Trajan   A.D. 98-117
    Illegible   Wt 6·894 gms

14. (SF 347)   AE *as*, Hadrian   A.D. 117-138
    Illegible and fragmentary   Wt 5·211 gms

15. (SF 354)   AR *denarius*, Antoninus Pius   A.D. 140-3
    Obv. ANTONINVS AVG PIVS P P TR P COS III
    Rev. AEQVITAS AVG   Wt 2·368 gms   (*RIC* 61)

16. (SF 344)   AR *denarius*, Antoninus Pius   A.D. 158-9
    Obv. ANTONINVS AVG PIVS P P TR P XXII
    Rev. FORTVNA OBSEQVENS COS IIII   Wt 3·407 gms   (*RIC* 286)

17. (SF 358)   AR *denarius*, Caracalla under Severus   A.D. 196-8
    Obv. M AVR ANTON CAES PONTIF
    Rev. PIETAS   Wt 2·618 gms   (*RIC* (Caracalla) 12)

18. (SF 343)   AE radiate copy, Victorinus (?)   A.D. 269-71
    Illegible   Wt 0·700 gms

19. (SF 352)   *antoninianus*, Tetricus I   A.D. 271-3
    Obv. IMP TETRICVS P F AVG
    Rev. LAETITIA AVG   Wt 1·453 gms   (*RIC* 86)

OTHER COINS FROM WATERCROOK

The interim report (Potter 1976, 62) provided a list of coins previously reported from Watercrook: to these should be added a small number of further coins:

(a) One each of Salonina (*RIC* 193, No. 16) and Constantine I (*RIC* VII, 170, No. 70) should be added to those recovered in North's excavations of 1931. These coins are listed in the accession records of Kendal Museum and were found after the close of North's excavation; the coins themselves have not been located but have been included in the statistical tables below.

(b) In the Lancashire River Unit's work which followed the 1974 and 1975 excavations, the following coins were recovered by various people from the site. They are now in Kendal Museum.

Vespasian: 3 coins (2 *sestertii* and 1 *as* – all illegible).
Domitian: 1 *sestertius* (illegible); 1 *denarius* (*RIC* 115)
Trajan: 1 *as* (illegible); 1 *sestertius* (*RIC* 667)
Hadrian: 1 *sestertius* (illegible)
Faustina I: 1 *as* (illegible)
Gratian: *LRBC* II, 523a.

DISCUSSION

The sample of Roman coins excavated or reliably reported from Watercrook stands at 100; four of these are illegible, although they can with certainty be assigned to the first or second centuries. Although too small to allow confidence that all of its trends are significant, the Watercrook sample is now one of the largest from Roman sites in north-west England.

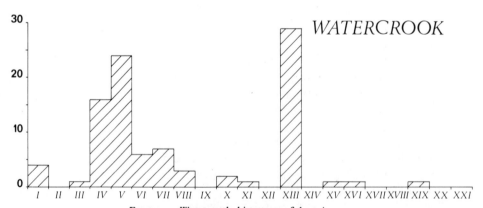

FIG. 124. – Watercrook: histogram of the coins.

The chronological distribution (Fig. 124) of these coins is shown in the following table:

Period		No. of coins	% of sample
I	(–A.D. 41)	4	4.17
II	(41-54)	—	—
III	(54-68)	1	1.04
IV	(68-96)	16	16.67
V	(96-117)	24	25.00
VI	(117-138)	6	6.25
VII	(138-161)	7	7.29
VIII	(161-180)	3	3.13
IX	(180-192)	—	—
X	(192-222)	2	2.08
XI	(222-235)	1	1.04
XII	(235-259)	—	—
XIII	(259-275)	29	30.21
XIV	(275-294)	—	—
XV	(294-307)	1	1.04
XVI	(307-330)	1	1.04
XVII	(330-348)	—	—
XVIII	(348-364)	—	—
XIX	(364-378)	2*	2.08
XX	(378-388)	—	—
XXI	(388-)	—	—

*including a coin of doubtful provenance, not listed elsewhere.

Chronological implications: the first century

The most obviously distinctive feature is the relationship between coins of the Flavian and Trajanic periods, in which the latter out-number the former by nearly two to one, and present a sharp contrast to such sites as Chester, Manchester and Ribchester, where the relationship is reversed. On the face of it the relationship between these two periods ought to offer a general indication of whether a site should be considered early or late Flavian – or later.

Clearly, however, there are factors besides the date of origin which will affect the relationship: for example, a break in occupation in the Trajanic period might be expected to have a greater effect on Flavian than on Trajanic coins: the former would presumably provide the bulk of coinage in circulation in Britain, at least in the early Trajanic period, and it may be, for example, that the best way to explain a closely parallel distribution of coins at Lancaster between the Flavian and Trajanic periods is in terms of a break within the Trajanic period; indeed, the Watercrook coin distribution would not preclude that phenomenon also. Just as clearly, later breaks will affect Flavian coinage less, although the composition of Antonine hoards suggests that Flavian coins still provided a significant proportion of the coins in circulation in the mid-second century. Sites in north-western England which most closely echo the Watercrook relationship are Maryport (Jarrett 1976, 48) and Wilderspool (report forthcoming).

Assessment of the degree of wear sustained by individual coins is harder for Watercrook, since corrosion of the bronze coins was generally very advanced. However, those coins of Vespasian where assessment was possible suggested a considerable degree of wear before loss. Similarly unsatisfactory as a guide is the amount of pre-Flavian coinage in evidence: the proportion for Watercrook is very similar to that at other north-western sites. In any case the numbers of coins involved are generally small. It may, however, be worth noticing that Watercrook has produced only one Republican coin, an issue of Caesar from the east *vicus* (discussed *supra*). There are also two very worn *denarii* of M. Antonius' legionary series from the excavations of 1974. The circulation pattern of Antonius' coins was markedly different from that of other Republican coinage. Further, there are only two pre-Flavian imperial issues, both *denarii*, which a study of hoards shows to be relatively long-lived.

The trend of these observations, therefore, is to argue against the Agricolan origin generally assumed for Watercrook (Birley 1957, 14), and to suggest instead a date later in the first century.

The second century

The high mark of Trajanic coins at Watercrook is followed by a much smaller Hadrianic proportion (6.25%); in absolute terms, however, the Hadrianic showing is closely similar to that of other north-western sites, and, in any case, so marked a proportion of Trajanic coins is hardly conceivable without supposing some occupation within the Hadrianic period. Strength is undiminished into the reign of Antoninus Pius, though the recent coins have exhibited a tendency to be issues from either early or late in the reign, which may leave a question mark over the state of Watercrook for Antoninus' middle years.

The latter part of the second century falls away sharply; this is a trend noted on all north-western sites (with the present exception of Ravenglass), and the reasons for it are at least partly monetary – a smaller volume of loss of bronze coins corresponding with the increasing significance of the *denarius* in an inflationary period. However, the drop at Watercrook is rather sharper than normal; indeed, only one certain coin of the period 161-192 (North 1932, 116) has been reported from Watercrook. This presents a *prima facie* case at least for a reduction in activity at sometime in the late second or early third century. That we should not postulate a break too early, however, would seem to be suggested by the strength of coins of Antoninus already noted.

Wear of coins of first and second centuries

Analysis of wear is hazardous in any circumstances, and it is necessary to exercise caution in its interpretation. It is of course impossible to pinpoint exactly from the numismatic evidence periods in which the fort may have been unoccupied, but it is worth noting that there are no certain coins issued between 112 and 134, nor between 143 and 155. If we turn, on the other hand, to periods of "cluster", we find evidence for one between *c.* 90 and 110 and another between *c.* 130 and 145. Thus, although this evidence does not provide a basis for assuming a break early in Trajan's reign, it would not be unreasonable to suppose that the fort may have lacked a garrison from the late Trajanic to the late Hadrianic period *and* that the occupation which appears to have re-opened in the 130s was shortlived. Although the coins cannot be used to provide a precise date for the end of this phase it would again not be unreasonable (as suggested in the discussion in Chap. III) to connect it with the Antonine occupation of Scotland. The resumption of the coin series with issues of the late 150s would further suggest that the fort regained a garrison at the end of the occupation of Scotland.

The period from 170 to 250 is notoriously difficult to interpret numismatically, and military sites in north-west England generally yield few coins from it. There are, however, from Watercrook no issues of the earlier second century whose state of wear would suggest them to be late second- or early third-century losses (Reece 1974, 87).

The third century

The first half of the third century is represented by three coins only – a worn *denarius* of 196-8, a relatively fresh coin of 206, and a very worn *denarius* of Alexander Severus. Again, care is required before conclusions too far-reaching are drawn from this; coins of 222-53 are poorly represented on all north-western sites, and the evidence of contemporary hoards suggests that they may have been slow in making an impact on coins in circulation. Coins of the preceding period (192-222) are also generally poorly represented with the exception of the two Hadrian's Wall forts of Castlesteads and Birdoswald. That this should not necessarily be taken to indicate an occupation-break is suggested by the fact that other sites exhibiting a similar trend of coin loss have epigraphic evidence attesting building and other activity during the period (*RIB* 581 – Manchester; 587, 590, 591 – Ribchester).

The mid-third century (253-275) represents a peak of coin loss at most north-western sites; Watercrook is here no exception, with 30% of the sample deriving from this period. The group, however, contains no coins earlier than Gallienus' sole reign, nor are there any coins of Postumus. The bulk of the recognisable coins are official issues or copies of the period 268-273 – a pattern which is to be observed in a number of hoards from the north-west (Hachensall Hall Farm and Worden in Lancashire, Agden in Cheshire: Shotter 1978). At the same time we should note the absence from Watercrook of coins of legitimate emperors after Tetricus and of Carausius. The former is a commonly observed phenomenon though the latter might suggest that the period of occupation in the mid-third century was relatively short.

A factor which slightly complicates the issue at Watercrook is the high incidence (68%) of very poor local imitations. There is no question of these coins having been part of a disturbed hoard, since they have have been reported from all sampled parts of the site, including North's excavations in 1931. That the imitations should be seen as the near-contemporaries of their prototypes is suggested by the fact that in the most recent excavations they have been found in the same groups as the prototype issues.

The fourth century

The majority of north-western sites display a distinctive pattern of coin loss during the fourth century, gradually falling through the century from a high peak in the 330s and 340s. The sample from Watercrook contrasts sharply with that pattern – two coins of Constantine I and one each of Gratian and Valens being the only fourth-century coins recorded from the site: of the two coins of Constantine I, one is said to have come from North's excavation of 1931, whilst the other – a very fresh coin of 320, minted at

Thessalonica – was recovered from the highest level of the fill of ditch 1 during the 1975 excavations. The coin of Gratian was recovered close to the 1975 excavations during the River Unit work in 1976.

On a total sample of nearly 100 coins, one would not expect the distribution to be badly untypical; it thus seems doubtful whether these fourth-century coins indicate a full-scale occupation at least of the sampled part of the site. It is worth noticing that the closest parallel in the north-west in its fourth-century coin loss is the site at Wilderspool; here after a break from the period of Gallienus, there are four Constantinian coins and no others from the fourth century.

Metals and denominations

	Period	Aurei	Denarii	Antoniniani etc.	Folles etc.	Sestertii	Dupondii	Asses
I	(-A.D. 41)	1	3	—	—	—	—	—
II	(41-54)	—	—	—	—	—	—	—
III	(54-68)	—	1	—	—	—	—	—
IV	(68-96)	1	3	—	—	5	3	3
V	(96-117)	—	3	—	—	6	9	6
VI	(117-138)	—	1	—	—	2	3	—
VII	(138-161)	—	3	—	—	1	2	1
VIII	(161-180)	—	1	—	—	—	—	2
IX	(180-192)	—	—	—	—	—	—	—
X	(192-222)	—	2	—	—	—	—	—
XI	(222-235)	—	1	—	—	—	—	—
XII	(235-259)	—	—	—	—	—	—	—
XIII	(259-275)	—	—	29	—	—	—	—
XIV	(275-294)	—	—	—	—	—	—	—
XV	(294-307)	—	—	—	1	—	—	—
XVI	(307-330)	—	—	—	1	—	—	—
XVII	(330-348)	—	—	—	—	—	—	—
XVIII	(348-364)	—	—	—	—	—	—	—
XIX	(364-378)	—	—	—	2	—	—	—
XX	(378-388)	—	—	—	—	—	—	—
XXI	(388-)	—	—	—	—	—	—	—
Illegible		—	—	—	—	2	—	2
	Totals	2	18	29	4	16	17	14
	%	2·00	18·00	29·00	4·00	16·00	17·00	14·00

Reece (1973, 232) has recently demonstrated the preponderance of the *denarius* in the pre-Flavian period and again in the later second century; the Watercrook sample demonstrates the absence of pre-Flavian *aes* denominations which itself argues against early Flavian occupation of the site. The growing preponderance of the *sestertius* among *aes* coins during the second century, however, is not marked, and it may be that the most convenient explanation of this is to be found in the considerable periods when the fort may have been without a garrison. It would of course be possible to argue on the basis of wear that a number of the Trajanic *sestertii* were in fact losses of the Antonine period.

The value of the total coin loss recorded for Watercrook is approximately three *aurei* (or 75% of the worth of any infantry man's annual pay (Breeze and Dobson 1976, 172 ff.), though it should be noted that this includes two actual *aureus* pieces, whose source may have been other than normal pay (for example, donatives) and which may therefore be regarded as untypical coins. We may, however, in tabular form, present loss-value of first and second-century coins at Watercrook in comparison with other sites in north-west England (periods I-IX):

Site	No. of coins lost			%			
		AV	AR	AE *sestertius*	*dupondii*	*asses*	Value
(a) *All coins*							
Watercrook	64	3·13	23·43	25·00	26·56	21·88	3 *aurei*
Lancaster	60	—	35·00	25·00	13·33	26·67	1·25 *aurei*
Ribchester	136	3·68	27·94	25·74	18·38	24·26	7 *aurei*
Ravenglass	15	6·67	20·00	46·66	6·67	20·00	1·25 *aurei*
(b) *Without aurei*							
Watercrook	62		24·19	25·81	27·42	22·58	1 *aureus*
Lancaster	60		35·00	25·00	13·33	26·67	1·25 *aurei*
Ribchester	131		29·01	26·72	19·08	25·19	2 *aurei*
Ravenglass	14		21·43	50·00	7·14	21·43	0·25 *aureus*

The proportion occupied by *sestertii* is relatively constant, with the exception of Ravenglass, where a high proportion (albeit on a small sample) is probably to be explained by the fort's late beginning – that is at a time when *dupondii* and *asses* had come to provide less of the currency in circulation. Beyond this, it is worth noting that Lancaster and Ribchester, two sites which were probably garrisoned by cavalry during the period, have higher proportions of *denarius*-loss than the other two. Other variable factors, such as occupation breaks, might be taken into account; for example, what would be the effect on the proportions of low denomination *aes* coins of the fort's *late* Flavian foundation and its probable Hadrianic break? Despite the problems, however, it may be that we have evidence in the pattern of coin loss to suggest that whereas Lancaster and Ribchester were cavalry forts, Watercrook and Ravenglass probably were not.

THE ANIMAL BONES By P. W. FIFIELD

There were 5785 mammal and bird bone fragments recovered from the excavations at Watercrook in 1974 and 1975. Unfortunately the bones were generally in a poor state of preservation. In most cases they were also in a fragmented condition, presumably the result of butchery. It is most likely that the animal bones represent the domestic refuse from the site. This being so, the animal bones from the Watercrook excavations provide us with direct information about the diet of the inhabitants of the fort and *vicus* and indirect information about the economy of the surrounding area.

The Species represented

Of the 5785 bone fragments recovered in the excavations, a total of 3774 was identifiable (65.2% of the total number of fragments). The remainder consisted of 1030 rib and vertebra fragments (17·8%) and 981 fragments (17·0%) which were either too small or too damaged to allow positive identification.

Only the stratified bone from the site has been included in this analysis and it has been divided into four main units:

(i) Flavian-Trajanic
(ii) Hadrianic/early Antonine
(iii) Antonine-late third century
(iv) Romano British. This category includes bone that is stratified in Roman levels but cannot be dated precisely.

In Table One the total number of bone fragments is given for each species. The term ovicaprid is used to refer to both sheep and goat species, as it is very difficult to differentiate between them in the case of most small fragments. Table Two shows the total number of bone fragments for the three main stock animals: cattle, ovicaprids and pigs.

Tables One and Two show that there were far more cattle bones in the sample than any other species. Indeed there are over twice as many cattle bones as all the rest of the species added together. However, there are several reasons why we cannot take these proportions at their face value as a simple guide to the diet and economy at the site. First, the faunal sample has been obtained from only part of the site. Second, the retrieval methods used in the excavation may have biased the faunal sample: as Payne (1972) has shown, ordinary recovery methods tend to produce a faunal sample biased towards the bones of the larger animals, as wet or dry sieving is needed to recover adequately the small bones of the smaller animals; since sieving techniques were not employed at Watercrook, it is possible that cattle (the larger bones) are somewhat over-represented in the sample, and sheep and pigs (the smaller bones) are under-represented. Table Three, showing the anatomical composition of the sample for the three main stock animals, illustrates the extent of the bias. The long bones – metapodials, mandibles and scapulae fragments – have clearly been recovered in greater numbers than the smaller bones such as astragali, carpals, tarsals and phalanges. There was only one sheep carpal bone recovered and no pig carpal bones in the sample. There were a great many individual teeth of all species in the faunal assemblage. Teeth, being made of the hardest substance in the body, have survived more abundantly than the mandibles and maxillae that once housed them.

A third reason for caution is the fact that we would probably expect a degree of lateral variation in the sample as it comes from a complex site, but this cannot be detected on the small Watercrook sample. For example the analysis of the faunal sample in Roman and medieval Exeter (Maltby 1977) revealed significant variations across the site in the samples from administrative, market, residential quarters and so on. In a large faunal sample, such differences might be detected between the fort and the *vicus* at Watercrook and within different quarters of the two sites. No significant differences however could be detected between the small samples from the various trenches excavated so far and I have therefore combined the individual samples for this analysis.

The fourth reason is that species proportions based on the simple count of identifiable fragments is not a very reliable calculation because a large fragile bone from one animal (like a cattle scapula) can break up into many fragments whereas the same bone from a smaller animal might well break up into fewer identifiable fragments. Therefore a more reliable indicator of species proportions is the calculation of the minimum number of individuals represented in a faunal sample. The minimum number is obtained by adding up the most abundant anatomical element present for each species in each phase. If, for example, there were six left mandibles and five right mandibles in one feature, then there would be a minimum number of six individuals present. Table Four shows the results of this analysis for the three main stock animals.

Although in Table Four cattle remain the dominant species, the proportions of the different animals have changed. The calculation of the minimum number of individuals has revealed, for example, that the pig is a far more significant component in the sample than the total number of pig bone fragments suggests. The ovicaprid and pig elements in the sample represent 46·3% of the individuals present compared with only 26·1% of the total bone fragments. It seems clear therefore that the smaller species were of greater importance in the economy and diet of the site than is indicated in the simple bone-fragment count, although the minimum number of individuals analysis does tend to over-emphasise minor species in small samples.

Cattle are by far the most important animal at Watercrook in terms of the edible meat they produced. In Table Five the minimum of individuals present on the site has been converted into the amount of total edible meat expected by each species. Cram's suggested figures of 498 lbs of edible meat for cattle, 60 lbs for sheep and 100 lbs for pigs have been used (Cram 1967). The figures again reveal that pig was more important in the economy than Tables One and Two indicate.

The relative ages of the different individuals in each species can be determined by examining the tooth eruption and epiphyseal fusion evidence. Absolute ageing, however, is much more difficult. Absolute ages are known for the dentition of fusion stages of modern domestic stock, but after two centuries of improvements in stock breeding, today's animals reach maturity at a much faster rate than those in the past. This being so it would be unwise to put definite ages to particular stages in development of a particular species. As a general guide, however, the ageing estimates made by Silver (1969) have been used in this discussion (Table Six).

The fusion evidence (Tables Eight, Nine) has been divided into various groups of different bones that fuse at about the same age. The percentages of unfused epiphyses are listed at the bottom of each group – these unfused bones belonged to animals slaughtered before reaching that particular age. The ageing estimate for any particular species at each stage of development is also included in the tables.

The tooth eruption evidence has been divided into the following stages of development:

Group 1. Deciduous teeth only present.
Group 2. Deciduous teeth and first molar present.
Group 3. Deciduous teeth with the first and second molars present.
Group 4. The first two molars are in wear and the third molar in eruption.
Group 5. All premolars and molars present.

As mentioned previously many of the teeth were found individually and their precise stage of eruption and wear was difficult or impossible to assess; they have not been included in the ageing analysis. The mortality data are integrated with the other information about the Watercrook animals in the species-by-species discussion below.

Cattle

Cattle were clearly the most abundant stock animal on the site. The cattle would have been well suited to the lush grassland pastures in the valley of the River Kent where the site is located. The species is a versatile one, producing a variety of different resources. Meat is the most obvious commodity produced and, as all parts of the animal are represented, it is likely that at least some and probably most of the animals were brought to the site on the hoof and slaughtered there.

The ageing evidence (Table Six) suggests that a large proportion of the animals had reached full maturity before being slaughtered, as they had all their teeth in wear and all their bone epiphyses fused. There are very few examples of young beasts in the sample. There was one tibia in the sample, which judging by its size came from a very young animal which had died at birth or very soon afterwards. Otherwise there are very few examples of animals killed before the distal epiphyses of the humerus had fused, and there was only one example of a mandible with only the milk teeth and one molar present. As there would be less meat value for animals of this age, it would have been unlikely to find large numbers slaughtered when immature.

A relatively high proportion of the cattle was killed before the fusion of the distal epiphyses of the metapodials and tibiae had occurred. According to Silver (1969) this would have been at about 2-3 years of age. These animals were probably young castrated males – bullocks – which were killed for their meat. What were the older cattle? In Fig. 125 I have plotted the maximum thickness at the distal fusion point of the metatarsal (vertical axis), against the maximum width of the distal epiphysis (horizontal axis). Clearly there are two groups of cattle of differing size, indicated by this figure, older than

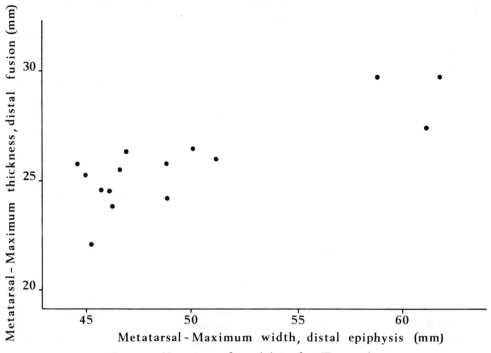

FIG. 125. – Measurements for cattle bones from Watercrook.

the young beef cattle (which with unfused metatarsals are not represented in the figure). The two groups are probably cows and bulls – the larger specimens representing the bulls and the smaller specimens the cows. The higher proportion of cows to bulls is to be expected as one bull can adequately service up to at least thirty cows. The importance of the milk produced by the cows is difficult to assess. It is impossible to estimate the amount of cow milk and other dairy products that was sent into the fort or *vicus* from the herds in the surrounding area. On the other hand the importance of the cow at the site suggests that dairy products were probably a common part of the dict of the community.

To summarise, therefore, the ageing data suggest that many cattle brought to the site were mature beasts. They had probably had a long working life either ploughing the land or producing milk and calves. At the same time, however, a certain amount of the meat was obtained from young bullocks slaughtered at about two to three years of age.

Ovicaprids

There are few clear differences between sheep and goat bones especially when most specimens consist of small splinters of bones. An attempt has been made to differentiate between them using horn cores and metapodials.

The sample contained a number of small horn-core fragments belonging to cattle, sheep and goats. Only twelve ovicaprid horn cores could be positively identified and out of these there were only two goat horns. The goat horn-core has a much flatter cross section than that of the sheep and can be identified reliably if a large enough fragment has survived.

A second method of distinguishing sheep from goats involved comparing the measurements obtained from the distal epiphyses of the metapodials. This method was devised by Gromova and successfully used by Hole *et al.* (1969). It is suggested that the outer articular condyle on the distal end of the metapodials is usually over 63% of the inner or medial condyle for sheep and under 63% for goats. When this test was applied to the metapodials in the Watercrook sample, all the specimens were placed in the sheep category (Table Seven).

The evidence therefore seems to indicate that although goats were present at the site, sheep were far more abundant. As the sheep has a greater economic potential than the goat, this is not surprising. Sheep yield three main resources – meat, dairy produce and wool – whereas goats only produce meat and milk; sheep would also have been far better adapted to the climate of northern England than goats.

It is difficult to reconstruct the age structure of the ovicaprid population because the sample is very small. Table Eight gives the ageing data that is available for the ovicaprids at the site.

In contrast to the data obtained for the cattle the ageing information for the sheep reveals that only a small proportion of the flock was kept until it had reached full maturity. Most animals seem to have been killed in their third year (using Silver's estimates). It is possible that many more older animals were kept for their fleeces on surrounding farms and were never sent to the fort and that only younger animals were sent as meat for the garrison.

A number of very young lambs was found in the sample. The percentages in the Romano-British column in Table Eight may well have been biased by the almost complete skeletons of three young lambs found in the construction trench of the fort wall. None of these individuals was likely to have been more than a few months old.

Pigs

It has been noted already that the percentage of pig-bone fragments in the total faunal assemblage probably does not reflect accurately the importance of the animal in the economy. Certainly the edible meat weight ratios suggest that pork formed a larger part of the diet of the inhabitants of the site than mutton. The pig is a useful animal as most parts of its body can be eaten, it is relatively easy to rear and it can be fed on almost anything that is edible. Pigs can be left to find their own food or pannage in any woodland or forest area. It is quite possible that some of these animals were kept in the fort or *vicus* itself.

Table Nine shows the limited ageing data for the pig that can be obtained in the sample. Most of the pigs seem to have been fattened up and slaughtered at a young age, possibly in their second year. Only a few individuals were kept to reach full maturity, presumably for breeding purposes.

Red deer

A total of 52 red deer fragments were found in the sample. All of them came from Phase 3 (Antonine-late third century) deposits. All but three of the fragments were antler fragments and the majority of these were found in the fill of various ditches. Many of the antler fragments had been sawn and cut, indicating evidence of some sort of antler industry on the site. As only one metatarsal, one first phalanx and one humerus fragment were recovered other than the pieces of antler, it is difficult to assess to what extent deer were eaten at the site. No other types of deer were found in the excavated sample.

Horse

Fragments of horse bone were found in all phases and in all the trenches at Watercrook. A large proportion of the horse sample consisted of tooth fragments, all from mature beasts. One pit inside the east *vicus* provided a complete set of lower teeth from an individual but the mandibles had not survived. The composition of the sample has made it impossible to tell whether these animals were eaten after they had reached the end of their working lives. It is certainly not unlikely that, like venison, they provided an occasional source of meat. Also, as in the case of the red deer fragments, most of the horse fragments were recovered from ditch-fill deposits. Presumably the horse was needed at Watercrook for both military and civilian purposes.

Dog

Several dog bones were found but they were too fragmentary to draw any conclusion about the size or breed of the Watercrook dogs. All but two of the fragments came from mature individuals. The two were scapulae fragments belonging to a small puppy certainly not more than six months old. These were recovered from site B, from the phase 3 occupation levels. As the total number of fragments suggests, there were no complete skeletons or evidence of definite burials of particular individuals. Similarly there was no evidence of butchery on any of the fragments, although there is no reason why dogs could not have been eaten by the inhabitants of the site.

Other species

Two hare metapodials, both from phase 3 features, were recovered. Presumably small game contributed occasionally to the diet of the people who lived on the site. With the River Kent in close proximity, it is not unreasonable to assume that fish formed some part in the local diet. Although no fish bones were recovered it is unlikely that this important resource would have been ignored completely; sieving may well produce evidence of fish bone at the site.

Birds

Only five out of the fourteen bird bones found in the sample could be positively identified. These all belonged to phase 3 deposits and were all domestic fowl bones. It is likely that poultry were kept throughout the Roman period and formed part of the diet of the local population; possibly other species such as geese and ducks were also reared by the inhabitants of the site.

Discussion

As has been emphasised throughout this report the extent to which definitive conclusions can be drawn is limited by the size of the sample. Whilst the analysis has shown that cattle, sheep and pigs played a significant part in the diet of the inhabitants of the site, it is difficult to assess the extent to which this picture of meat consumption at the site reflects the animal husbandry and farming strategy of the area as a whole.

The analysis also shows that most parts of the carcase are represented in the sample, rather than selected joints. One conclusion that can be drawn from this is that the animals were brought to the fort on the hoof to be slaughtered there, rather than butchered elsewhere and brought to the site as salted meat joints. However, the faunal sample on its own cannot tell us whether these animals were reared by the military themselves or by the native civilian population. Around the fort was an area of military land (the *territorium* or *prata*), which possibly extended for a considerable distance. Here much of the livestock could have been reared in peacetime. The animals could have been reared by the military, or possibly by civilians leasing the land. As there was a substantial *vicus* next to the fort, it is probable that the civilian population was involved with much of the stock keeping, Another source of meat for the fort was of course from the surrounding native settlements. This could take the form of requisitions or compulsory purchase at a fixed price (Davies 1971, 123). As I have argued above, the faunal sample suggests that young sheep were brought to the fort for the garrison, whereas the breeding population of sheep – primarily kept for wool – remained in the surrounding countryside. Old ewes and breeding rams would have been slaughtered and eaten in the countryside but clearly the military demanded younger, more tender, animals for their meat.

Whilst the available faunal sample tells us something about diet at Watercrook and hints that the stock economy of the area outside the fort we clearly need to know far more about the economic relationships between fort and *vicus* and between these and the surrounding native settlements. It is to be hoped that the Watercrook faunal sample discussed in this paper can be augmented by further material from the fort and the *vicus* and in particular by faunal samples from native settlements in the environs of the fort.

Note: the list of additional measurements of the Watercrook animal bones has been filed in typescript form in both Lancaster University Library and with the finds in Kendal Museum.

Table 1: *TOTAL NUMBER OF IDENTIFIABLE BONE FRAGMENTS RECOVERED*

Species	Phase 1		Phase 2		Phase 3		Romano-British		Total	
	No.	%	No.	%	No.	%	No.	%	No.	%
Cattle	328	68.5	408	68.5	1823	73.8	145	63.0	2704	71.6
Ovicaprid	94	19.6	136	22.8	372	15.1	52	22.6	654	17.3
Pig	40	8.3	47	7.9	195	7.9	23	10.0	305	8.1
Red Deer	0	0	0	0	52	2.1	0	0	52	1.4
Horse	15	3.1	1	0.2	13	0.5	2	0.9	31	0.8
Bird	2	0.4	2	0.3	6	0.2	4	1.7	14	0.4
Dog	0	0	2	0.3	6	0.2	4	1.7	12	0.3
Hare	0	0	0	0	2	0.1	0	0	2	0.1
Total	479		596		2469		230		3774	

Table 2: *TOTAL NUMBER OF IDENTIFIABLE BONE FRAGMENTS RECOVERED FOR THE PRINCIPAL STOCK SPECIES*

Species	Phase 1		Phase 2		Phase 3		Romano-British		Total	
	No.	%	No.	%	No.	%	No.	%	No.	%
Cattle	328	71.0	408	69.0	1823	76.3	145	65.9	2704	73.8
Ovicaprid	94	20.3	136	23.0	372	15.6	52	23.6	654	17.8
Pig	40	8.7	47	8.0	195	8.1	23	10.5	305	8.3
Total	462		591		2390		220		3663	

Table 3: COMPOSITION OF THE SAMPLE FOR THE THREE MAIN STOCK SPECIES

Bone	Phase 1			Phase 2			Phase 3			Romano-British			Total		
	C	O	P	C	O	P	C	O	P	C	O	P	C	O	P
Mandible	13	8	7	21	7	8	103	40	23	7	5	3	144	60	41
Maxilla	2	1	—	11	4	1	11	3	4	—	1	2	24	9	7
Tooth	44	5	6	88	19	11	292	64	48	84	17	9	508	105	74
Skull	17	2	—	37	6	2	68	27	25	4	2	—	126	37	27
Atlas	—	1	—	1	2	—	5	2	1	—	—	—	6	5	1
Axis	—	2	—	5	1	—	9	3	3	—	1	—	14	7	3
Scapula	32	11	2	41	10	2	194	24	9	12	1	—	279	46	13
Humerus	31	6	2	24	1	3	210	30	14	3	4	1	268	41	20
Radius	17	7	—	21	16	1	144	27	8	6	4	1	188	54	10
Ulna	4	1	4	9	2	—	40	2	8	2	1	1	55	6	12
Carpal	4	—	—	8	—	—	34	1	1	1	—	—	47	1	1
Metacarpal	32	8	4	23	10	3	77	30	13	3	3	—	135	51	20
Pelvis	13	3	2	14	8	1	68	8	11	7	—	—	102	19	15
Femur	20	8	4	19	20	6	124	30	6	3	1	—	166	59	16
Patella	1	—	—	1	—	—	2	—	—	—	—	—	4	—	—
Tibia	34	18	1	25	16	—	128	32	9	3	8	—	190	74	11
Fibula	—	—	2	—	—	1	1	—	—	—	—	—	1	—	4
Astragalus	3	—	—	2	1	1	36	6	2	—	—	—	41	7	3
Calcaneum	5	2	3	4	4	—	31	4	1	3	2	—	43	12	5
Navicular Cuboid	4	—	—	5	—	—	13	1	—	—	—	—	22	1	—
Tarsal	—	—	—	1	—	—	2	—	—	—	—	—	3	—	—
Metatarsal	28	10	1	12	6	4	115	28	3	3	1	1	158	45	9
First Phalanx	12	1	2	25	3	2	59	9	5	3	1	—	99	14	9
Second Phalanx	5	—	—	7	—	1	33	1	1	—	—	2	45	1	4
Third Phalanx	7	—	—	4	—	—	24	—	—	1	—	—	36	—	—
Total	328	94	40	408	136	47	1823	372	195	145	52	23	2704	654	305

C = Cattle　　O = Ovicaprid　　P = Pig

Table 4: MINIMUM NUMBERS OF INDIVIDUALS PRESENT

Species	Phase 1		Phase 2		Phase 3		Romano-British		Total	
	No.	%	No.	%	No.	%	No.	%	No.	%
Cattle	12	48.0	7	36.8	41	62.1	6	46.1	66	53.7
Ovicaprid	8	32.0	6	31.6	15	22.7	4	30.8	33	26.8
Pig	5	25.0	6	31.6	10	15.2	3	23.1	24	19.5
Total	25		19		66		13		123	

Table 5: EDIBLE MEAT WEIGHT TOTAL *(In Pounds)*

Species	Phase 1	Phase 2	Phase 3	Romano-British	Total
Cattle	5976	3486	20,418	2988	32,868
Ovicaprid	480	360	900	240	1,980
Pig	500	600	1,000	300	2,400

Table 6: AGEING DATA – CATTLE BONE FUSION EVIDENCE

Bone	Phase 1 NF.	Phase 1 F.	Phase 2 NF.	Phase 2 F.	Phase 3 NF.	Phase 3 F.	Romano-British NF.	Romano-British F.	Total NF.	Total F.
Scapula d	–	3	–	7	–	55	–	2	–	67
Humerus d	2	11	–	2	1	55	–	–	3	68
Radius p	–	7	–	11	–	66	–	2	–	86
% N.F.	8.7%		0%		0.6%		0%		1.3%	
0-18 months*										
Metacarpal d	4	1	1	1	7	16	–	–	12	18
Tibia d	1	7	–	5	7	26	–	1	8	39
Metatarsal d	1	9	–	1	5	23	1	–	7	33
% N.F.	21.4%		12.5%		22.6%		(50%)		22.1%	
24-36 months										
Calcaneum p	–	2	–	2	7	8	2	1	9	13
Femur p	3	4	2	4	4	24	–	1	9	33
% N.F.	33.3%		28.6%		26.8%		(50%)		29%	
36-42 months										
Humerus p	–	–	–	–	2	12	–	–	2	12
Radius d	–	–	1	3	6	18	–	2	7	23
Femur d	–	1	1	3	1	26	–	4	2	34
Tibia p	–	–	–	1	1	10	–	–	1	11
Ulna p	–	–	1	–	4	–	–	–	5	–
% N.F.	0%		30%		17.5%		0%		17.3%	
42-48 months										

NF – Epiphysis not fused   F – Epiphysis fused
p – Proximal Epiphysis   d – Distal Epiphysis
* Silver's estimates 1969 (252-3)

TOOTH ERUPTION EVIDENCE

	Phase 1	Phase 2	Phase 3	Romano-British	Total
Group 1	0	0	0	0	0
Group 2	0	0	1	0	1
Group 3	0	2	0	0	2
Group 4	1	0	4	1	6
Group 5	2	2	2	0	6

Table 7: SHEEP METAPODIAL MEASUREMENTS (IN MILLIMETRES)

Phase 3	Metacarpal $9.9 \div 14.4 \times 100 = 68.75\%$ (Sheep)
,,	,, $8.3 \div 12.0 \times 100 = 69.2\%$ (Sheep)
,,	,, $9.5 \div 11.9 \times 100 = 79.8\%$ (Sheep)
,,	,, $9.5 \div 13.8 \times 100 = 68.8\%$ (Sheep)
,,	,, $9.4 \div 13.6 \times 100 = 69.1\%$ (Sheep)
,,	Metatarsal $8.8 \div 13.4 \times 100 = 65.7\%$ (Sheep)
Romano-British	Metacarpal $9.6 \div 13.9 \times 100 = 69.0\%$ (Sheep)
,,	Metatarsal $9.6 \div 13.8 \times 100 = 69.1\%$ (Sheep)

Table 8: *AGEING DATA – OVICAPRIDS BONE FUSION EVIDENCE*

Bone	Phase 1		Phase 2		Phase 3		Romano-British		Total	
	NF.	F.	NF.	F.	NF.	F.	NF.	F.	NF.	F.
Scapula d	–	5	–	3	–	8	2	1	2	17
Humerus d	–	2	1	7	2	10	1	3	4	22
Radius p	1	1	–	5	–	5	3	–	4	11
% N.F. 0-10 months*	11·1%		6·25%		8%		60%		16·7%	
Metacarpal d	3	0	1	1	3	7	4	2	11	10
Tibia d	3	2	3	5	4	11	4	2	14	20
% N.F. 18-24 months	75%		40%		28%		75%		45·5%	
Metatarsal	–	1	–	1	1	3	3	–	4	5
% N.F. 20-28 months	0%		0%		25%		100%		44·4%	
Calcaneum p	–	1	–	4	1	2	3	–	4	7
Femur p	–	–	–	2	–	7	6	1	6	10
Ulna p	–	–	–	–	–	–	3	–	3	–
% N.F. 30-36 months	0%		0%		10%		92·3%		43·3%	
Humerus p	–	–	1	–	4	1	1	–	6	1
Radius d	-	1	1	3	–	–	–	1	1	5
Femur d	4	–	2	–	1	–	–	2	7	2
Tibia p	1	2	–	1	2	–	–	–	3	3
% N.F. 36-42 months	62·5%		50%		87·59%		25%		60·7%	

NF – Epiphysis not fused   F – Epiphysis fused
p – Proximal Epiphysis   d – Distal Epiphysis
*Silver's estimates (1969. 252-3)

TOOTH ERUPTION EVIDENCE

Group	Phase 1	Phase 2	Phase 3	Romano-British	Total
Group 1	1	1	1	0	3
Group 2	0	2	3	0	5
Group 3	0	2	2	2	6
Group 4	0	0	0	0	0
Group 5	0	1	1	1	3

Table 9: AGEING DATA – PIG BONE FUSION EVIDENCE

Bone	Phase 1 NF.	Phase 1 F.	Phase 2 NF.	Phase 2 F.	Phase 3 NF.	Phase 3 F.	Romano-British NF.	Romano-British F.	British NF.	British F.
Scapula d	–	1	–	2	–	6	–	–	–	9
Humerus d	–	1	1	1	–	1	–	–	1	3
Radius p	–	–	–	1	–	2	–	1	–	4
% N.F. 0-12 months*	0%		25%		0%		0%		5·9%	
Metacarpal d	2	1	–	–	2	1	–	–	4	2
Tibia d	1	–	–	–	1	2	–	1	2	3
Metatarsal d	–	–	1	–	2	1	–	–	3	1
% N.F. 24-27 months	75%		100%		62·5%		0%		64·3%	
Calcaneum p	–	–	–	–	1	–	1	–	2	–
% N.F. 24-30 months					(100%)		(100%)		(100%)	
Humerus p	–	–	–	–	1	2	–	–	1	2
Radius d	–	–	–	–	–	1	–	–	–	1
Ulna p	1	1	–	–	5	–	–	–	6	1
Tibia p	–	–	–	–	–	1	–	–	–	1
Femur p	–	–	–	–	–	1	–	–	–	1
Femur d	–	–	–	–	–	–	–	–	–	–
% N.F. 36-42 months	50%		–		54·5%		–		53·8%	

NF – Epiphysis not fused   F – Epiphysis fused
p – Proximal Epiphysis   d – Distal Epiphysis
*Silver's estimates.

TOOTH ERUPTION EVIDENCE

Group	Phase 1	Phase 2	Phase 3	Romano-British	Total
Group 1	–	–	–	–	–
Group 2	–	3	–	–	3
Group 3	1	–	2	2	5
Group 4	–	–	–	–	–
Group 5	2	–	–	–	2

BIBLIOGRAPHY

Atkinson, D., 1914. "A hoard of samian ware from Pompeii." *JRS* 4, 27-64.

Birley, E. B., 1955. "A Roman inscription from Watercrook". CW2 lv, 46-53.

—— 1957, "The Roman fort at Watercrook". CW2 lvii, 13-17.

Boon, G. C., 1966. "Roman window glass from Wales". *Journal of Glass Studies* 8, 41-7.

Boon, G. C. and Savory, H. N., 1975. "A silver trumpet brooch with relief decoration, parcel-gilt, from Carmarthen, and a note on the development of the type". *Ant. J.* 55, 41-61.

Brailsford, J. W., 1962. *Hod Hill, volume I. Antiquities from Hod Hill in the Durden Collection.* British Museum.

Breeze, D. and Dobson, B., 1976. *Hadrian's Wall.* Allen Lane, London.

Bulmer, W., 1938. "Dragonesque brooches and their development". *Ant. J.* 18, 146-53.

Bushe-Fox, J. P., 1932. *Third report on the excavations of the Roman fort at Richborough, Kent.* Research Report of the Society of Antiquaries of London, 10.

Charlesworth, D. 1959. "Roman glass in northern Britain". AA4 xxxvii, 33-58.

—— 1959a. "The Glass". *In* Daniels, C. M., *The Roman bath house at Red House, Corbridge,* AA4 xxxvii, 164-6.

—— 1961. "Roman jewellery found in Northumberland and Durham". AA4 xxxix, 1-36.

—— 1966. "Roman square bottles". *Journal of Glass Studies* 8, 26-40.

—— 1974. "The Glass". *In* Neal 1974, 203-6.

Chenet, G. and Gaudron, G., 1955. *La céramique sigillée d'Argonne des IIe et IIIe siècles.* Gallia Supplement VI.

Collingwood, R. G. and Richmond, I. A., 1969. *The Archaeology of Roman Britain,* Methuen.

Cram, C. L., 1967. "Report on the animal bones in the excavation at Hockwold-cum-Wilton, Norfolk. 1961-2". *Proc. Cambridge Antiquarian Society* 60, 75-80.

Crawford, M. H., 1974. Roman Republican Coinage. C.U.P.

Cunliffe, B. W. (ed.), 1968. *Fifth report on the excavations of the Roman fort at Richborough, Kent.* Research Report of the Society of Antiquaries of London, 23.

—— 1975. *Excavations at Portchester Castle, Vol. I, Roman.* Research Report of the Society of Antiquaries of London, 32. Thames and Hudson.

Curle, J., 1911. *A Roman frontier post and its people, the fort of Newstead in the parish of Melrose.* Glasgow.

Daniels, C. M., 1968. *"A hoard of iron and other materials from Corbridge".* AA4 xxxvi, 115-26.

Dameski, V., 1961. "A survey of glass vessels" (English summary). *Archeološki Vestnik.* Ljubljana, 68-70.

Davies, J. L., 1977. "Roman arrowheads from Dinorben and the *Sagittarii* of the Roman army". *Britannia* VIII, 257-70.

Davies, R. W., 1971. "The Roman military diet". *Britannia* II, 122-41.

Dopperfeld, O., 1966. *Römisches und Frankisches Glas in Köln.*

Faider-Feytmans, M., 1952. "Les verries du tumulus de Frizet". *Études d'histoire et d'archeologie Namuroises dédiés a Ferdinand Courtoy,* 71-81.

Feacham, R. W. de F., 1951. "Dragonesque fibulae". *Ant. J.,* 21, 32-44.

Fenelli, M., 1975a. *Le tredici are, votivi anatomici. Lavinium,* vol. II. Istituto di topografia antica dell'Università di Roma.

—— 1975b. "Contributo per lo studio del votivo anatomico: i votivi anatomici di Lavinio". *Archeologia Classica* 27, fasc. 2, 206-52.

Fowler, E., 1960, "The origins and development of the penannular brooch in Europe". *PPS* 26, 149-77.

Frere, S. S., 1972. *Verulamium excavations, vol. I.* Research Report of the Society of Antiquaries of London, 28.

Harden, D. B., 1959. "New light on Roman and early medieval window glass". *Glastechnische Berichte* 32K, 8, 8-16.

Harden, D. B. and Price, J., 1971. "The Glass". *In* Cunliffe, B., *Excavations at Fishbourne, II.* Research Report of the Society of Antiquaries of London, 27, 330-6.

Hartley, B. R., 1961. "The Samian ware". *In* Steer, K. A., *Excavations at Mumrills Roman Fort 1958-60.* PSAS 94, 100-10.

Hawkes, C. F. C. and Hull, M. R., 1947. *Camulodunum.* Research Report of the Society of Antiquaries of London, 14.

Henig, M., 1970. "The veneration of heroes in the Roman Army". *Britannia* I, 249-65.

—— 1977. "Death and the maiden: funerary symbolism in daily life". *In* Munby, M. and Henig, M. (eds.), *Roman Life and Art in Britain.* BAR 41, 347-66.

Hermet, F., 1934. *La Graufesenque (Condatomago).*

Hole, F. et al., 1969. (with Flannery, K. V. and Neeley, J. A.), *Prehistory of the Deh Luran Plain.* Memoirs of the Museum of Anthropology, University of Michigan, 1.

Hull, M. R., 1968. "The brooches". *In* Cunliffe, 1968, 74-93.

Jacobs, J., 1912. "Sigillatafunde aus einem römischen Keller zu Bregenz". *Jahrbuch für Altertumskunde,* VI.

Jacobi, L., 1897. *Das römer Kastell Saalburg bei Homburg vor der Höhe.* Reichs Limes Kommission, Homburg.

Jacobstahl, P., 1944. *Early Celtic Art.*

Jarrett, M. G., 1976. *Maryport, Cumbria: a Roman fort and its garrison.* CW Extra Series, 22. Kendal.

Jones, G. D. B. and Grealey, S., 1974. *Roman Manchester.* Altrincham.

Karnitsch, P., 1959. *Die Reliefsigillata von Ovilava.*

Kenyon, K. M., 1948. *Excavations at the Jewry Wall site, Leicester.* Research Report of the Society of Antiquaries of London, 15.

Kilbride-Jones, H. E., 1938. "Glass armlets in Britain". *PSAS* 55, 366-95.

Kleibrink, M. Maaskant, 1975. *Classification of Ancient Engraved Gems. A Study based on the Collection in the Royal Coin Cabinet, The Hague.* Leiden.

Klumbach, H. 1933. "Der Sigillata-Töpfer L.A.L." *Mainzer Zeitschrift,* 28, 60.

Knorr, R., 1919. *Töpfer und Fabriken verzierter Terra Sigillata des ersten Jahrunderts.*

—— 1952. *Terra-sigillata Gefässe des ersten Jahrhunderts mit Topfernamen.*

Liversidge, J., 1955. *Furniture in Roman Britain.*

—— 1973. *Britain in the Roman Empire.* Cardinal.

Lloyd-Morgan, G., 1977. "Mirrors in Roman Britain". *In* Munby, J. and Henig, M. (eds), *Roman Life and Art in Britain.* BAR 41, 231-52.

LRBC. Hill, P. V., Kent, J. P. C. and Carson, R. . G., *Late Roman Bronze Coinage.* London, 1960.

Maltby, J. M., 1977. *The animal bones from Roman Exeter.* Unpublished M.A. thesis, Sheffield University.

Manning, W. H., 1966. "A hoard of Romano-British ironwork from Brampton, Cumberland". CW2 lxvi, 1-36.

—— 1976. *Catalogue of Romano-British ironwork in the Museum of Antiquities, Newcastle upon Tyne.* Dept of Archaeology, University of Newcastle upon Tyne.

Maxwell, G. S., 1974. "Objects of glass". *In* Rae, A. and V., "The Roman fort at Cramond", *Britannia* V, 197-9.

Neal, D. S., 1974. *The excavation of the Roman villa in Gadebridge Park, Hemel Hempstead 1963-8.* Research Report of the Society of Antiquaries of London, 31.

North, O. H., 1932. "The Roman station at Watercrook." CW2 xxxii, 116-23.

—— 1934. "Finds from the Roman station at Watercrook." CW2 xxxiv, 35-40.

North, O. H and Hildyard, E. J. W., 1945. "Excavations at the Roman fort at Watercrook 1944." CW2 xxxxv, 148-62.

Oswald, F., 1936-37. *Index of figure types on Terra Sigillata.*

—— 1948. *The terra sigillata (samian ware) of Margidunum.*

Payne, S., 1972. "Partial recovery and sample bias; the results of some sieving experiments". *In* Higgs, E. S. (ed.), *Papers in Economic Prehistory,* C.U.P., 49-64.

Potter, T. W., 1976. "Excavations at Watercrook 1974; an interim report". CW2 lxxvi, 6-66.

—— 1976a. *A Faliscan town in South Etruria.* London, British School at Rome.

—— in press. "Scavi al santuario repubblicano a Ponte di Nona, Roma." *Notizie degli Scavi,* forthcoming.

Radley, J. et al. 1974. (with Tallis, J. H. and Switsur, V. R.), "The excavation of three 'narrow blade' Mesolithic sites in the southern Pennines, England". *PPS* 40. 1-19.

RCHM 1936. *An inventory of the historical monuments in Westmorland.* London, HMSO.

RCHM 1961. *Eburacum.* HMSO.

Reece, R., 1973. "Roman coinage in the western Empire." *Britannia* IV, 227-51.

—— 1974. "Numismatic aspects of Roman coin hoards in Britain". *In* Casey, P. J. and Reece, R. (eds), *Coins and the Archaeologist.* BAR 4, 78-94.

RIC Mattingly, H., Sydenham, E. A. and Sutherland, C. H. V., *The Roman Imperial Coinage.* London.

Ricken, H., 1934. "Die Bilderschüsseln der Kastelle Saalburg und Zugmantel". *Saalburg Jahrbuch* 8, 130-81.

—— 1948, *Die Bilderschüsseln der römischen Töpfer von Rheinzabern (Tafelband)*.

Ricken, H. and Fischer, C., 1963. *Die Bilderschüsseln der römischen Töpfer von Rheinzabern* (Textband).

Robertson, A., 1975. *Birrens (Blatobulgium)*. Constable, Edinburgh.

Robinson, R. 1975. *The Armour of Imperial Rome*. London.

Rogers, G. B., 1974. *Poteries Sigillées de la Gaule Centrale I*. Gallia Supplement 28.

Scarborough, J. 1969. *Roman Medicine*. Thames and Hudson, London.

Shotter, D. C. A., 1978. "Roman coin hoards in Lancashire". *Lancashire Archaeological Journal* 1. in press.

Silver, I. A., 1969. "The ageing of domestic animals". *In* Brothwell, D. and Higgs, E. S. (eds), *Science in Archaeology*. Thames and Hudson, 283-302.

Stanfield, F. A. and Simpson, G., 1958. *Central Gaulish Potters*.

Stevenson, R. B. K., 1956. "Native bangles and Roman glass". *PSAS* 88. 208-21.

Webster, G., 1969. *The Roman Imperial Army*. London.

Wheeler, R. E. M., 1932. (With Wheeler, T. V.), *Report on the excavations of the prehistoric, Roman and post-Roman site in Lydney Park, Gloucestershire*. Research Report of the Society of Antiquaries of London, 9.

—— 1943. *Maiden Castle, Dorset*. Research Report of the Society of Antiquaries of London, 12.

—— 1954. *The Stanwick fortifications*. Research Report of the Society of Antiquaries of London, 23.

Wild, F., 1972. "The Samian ware". *In* Jones, G. D. B., "Excavations at Northwich (Condate)". *Arch. J.* 128., 53-66.

Wild, F., 1975. "The Samian ware". *In* Robertson, 1975, 141-76.

Wild, J. P., 1970. "Button and loop fasteners in the Roman provinces". *Britannia* I, 137-55.

CHAPTER V

WATERCROOK AND RAVENGLASS: THE NAMES AND THE GARRISONS

By D. C. A. Shotter

DESPITE THE FACT that the excavations of 1974-78 represent the most extensive campaigns ever undertaken on these two sites, no clear evidence has come to light on the questions of the Roman name and garrison of either site; for the single piece of evidence referring to a unit of the army – the sealing from Ravenglass of *Cohors I Aelia Classica* (inv. 71) – offers no clue as to where that unit was garrisoned. Nonetheless, the excavations have contributed in a general way to the discussions in that they have provided clearer chronologies for the sites.

Discussions of the Roman names of sites in north-west England have been lengthy and frequent, although it has to be admitted that in the majority of cases we are still a long way from certainty. What is more it has recently been argued (Hassall 1976) that there is still a case for reconsideration even with some of the sites which have for a long time been thought to lie beyond the need for further controversy. Further uncertainty is also introduced into the discussion by the realisation that major sites may as yet await discovery. What, for example, would be the effect on the apparently secure sequence of names of sites on the Cumbrian coast of the discovery of new sites? The presence of a coin hoard at Braystones and of other Roman material in the area may indeed argue for a site between Ravenglass and Moresby.

A very small number of sites have names which are attested epigraphically – Chester probably (*Eph. Ep.* IX. 1274a, b), and Ribchester (*RIB* 583) – although Hassall (1976) has made a case for a further two, suggesting that Old Carlisle may be the Maglone or Magis of the Notitia Dignitatum (*OCC* 40. 28/29; cf. Vik (ani) Mag(lonenses) or Mag(enses) of *RIB* 899) and that Birdoswald may be Banna (cf. Venatores Banniess(es) of *RIB* 1905). Of these, however, the "re-naming" of Old Carlisle is not without difficulties, as Hassall admits; Vik Mag could be Vik(anorum) Mag(istri), and there is some reason to believe that the *Ala I Herculea,* placed by the Notitia (40.55) at Olenacum, is the *Ala Augusta* frequently attested epigraphically at Old Carlisle (*RIB* 894 etc.).

Besides the sites for whose names there is epigraphic evidence, there are sequences of names in other documents which it is reasonable to affix to certain sites; for example, the sequence of Lavatres, Verteris and Braboniaco occurs in the Notitia (40, 25-27): it appears to correspond to the reverse sequence in *Iter* V of the Antonine Itinerary (467, 4-5; 468, 1), and to indicate Bowes, Brough under Stainmore and Kirkby Thore.

It is hardly possible, therefore, on present evidence to expect to find precise identifications of the names of Watercrook and Ravenglass. This idea, however, seems to be an appropriate occasion to review the arguments which, since Haverfield (1915, 77-84), have identified Alone of *Iter* X of the Antonine Itinerary (481, 1-482, 4) and Alione of the Notitia Dignitatum (40, 53) with Watercrook. Similarly we should review the relationship between Clanoventa, Glannibanta, Cantiventi and Ravenglass. To this end, the evidence of the Antonine Itinerary, Notitia Dignitatum and the Ravenna Cosmography will be examined.

ANTONINE ITINERARY (Rivet 1970, 34-82)

Iter X is a route of 150 miles from Clanoventa to Mediolano; the intermediate posts are Galava, Alone, Galacum, Bremetonnaci, Coccio, Mamcunio and Condate. Of these sites, only Bremetonnaci (Ribchester) is certainly identified, although with exception of the vexed Coccio, which is usually taken as Wigan, but which involves a rather contorted route (Rivet 1970, 54), the route southwards from Ribchester is usually accepted as running to Whitchurch in Shropshire.

Northwards from Ribchester, however, the problems are considerable; Galacum must be presumed to be either Burrow in Lonsdale or Lancaster, both having been favoured at one time or another (Rivet 1970, 54; Leather 1972, RR/8-9). If Burrow in Lonsdale is preferred, then the distance between Galacum and Alone (19 miles) favours Low Borrow Bridge as Alone; on the other hand, with Lancaster as Galacum, Alone would appear to be Watercrook. If Alone is accepted as Watercrook then further stages to Ambleside (Galava) and Ravenglass (Clanoventa) would seem approximately appropriate.

This, however, leaves out of account an etymological argument which would regard the presence of an Alauna on the River Kent as most inappropriate. The sequence of names – Galacum, Alone, Galava – would suit a Lune valley route (Rivet 1970, 68 and 74); further, if we assumed a disturbance to the distances in the Itinerary which could have been occasioned by the similarity of the names, Galacum and Galava, then we might take the stage from Galava to Alone as 19 miles and Alone to Galacum as 12 miles. Thus from Ribchester the *Iter* would proceed northwards to Galacum (Lancaster), Alone (Burrow in Lonsdale), Galava (Low Borrow Bridge). The etymological propriety of assigning the name Alone to a Lune valley rather than a Kent valley site is strengthened by the dedication at Lancaster to the local deity, Ialonus Contrebis (*RIB* 600), which is apparently echoed at Burrow (*RIB* 610).

Proposals that Alone is either Burrow or Low Borrow Bridge cause problems for the remainder of the route northwards. Rivet noted that if Alone were Low Borrow Bridge, this would cause difficulties in continuing to identify Galava with Ambleside; a road-route from Low Borrow Bridge to Ambleside is not known, but it could hardly be as short as 12 miles. In any case, on the scheme for *Iter* X postulated here, with Low Borrow Bridge as Galava, Clanoventa can no longer be identified with Ravenglass.

The particular suitability of the identification of Clanoventa with Ravenglass has been etymological (Rivet 1970, 70); the form found in the Notitia is Glannibanta, which means the "field" or "market" by the "shore". As Rivet notes, however, the form in the Antonine Itinerary – *Clan* – means "clear" rather than "shore", hence weakening the suitability of Ravenglass. In terms of the distance involved (18 miles), a stage from Low Borrow Bridge to either Ambleside or Brougham seems possible. A stage to Brougham would appear more natural; at the same time, its position near the junction of the main north/south route and that over Stainmore would seem to justify the *-venta* element. On the other hand, the identification would disturb the accepted identification of Brougham as Brocavo of *Iter* V; although the verbal similarity of Brougham and Brocavo is accidental, the distances involved in the stages Verteris (Brough under Stainmore) – Brocavo (Brougham) – Luguvalis (Carlisle) are accurate enough to convince.

The suggested schemes for the northern section of *Iter* X may thus be summarised:

	Haverfield (1915)	Rivet (1970)	Leather (1972)	(above)
CLANOVENTA	Ravenglass	Ravenglass	Ravenglass	Brougham/Ambleside
GALAVA	Ambleside	Ambleside	Ambleside	Low Borrow Bridge
ALONE	Watercrook	Low Borrow Bridge	Watercrook	Burrow
GALACUM	Burrow	Burrow	Lancaster	Lancaster
BREMETONNACI	Ribchester	Ribchester	Ribchester	Ribchester

Thus, there seems to be a case for arguing that *Iter* X of the Antonine Itinerary contains the name of neither Watercrook nor Ravenglass.

NOTITIA DIGNITATUM

The problems raised by the document in general and the command of the *Dux Britanniarum* in particular are no less intractible than those of the Antonine Itinerary. As Jarrett puts it (1976, 16): "it is not possible to detect any logical geographical order, or an order of battle at any known date ...". The date of the document and its date(s) of reference have been frequently disputed (Bury 1920, 13; Ward 1973, 253; Breeze and Dobson 1976, 271; Mann 1976, 1); whilst a date very late in the fourth century is widely assumed, attempts have been made to assign an earlier date at least to the Wall sub-section of the Duke's command (Gillam 1949, 38), chiefly because, whilst the units in the main part of the Duke's command are largely *numeri* and *cunei*, those of the sub-section are *cohortes* and *alae* – in many cases those which are attested on third-century inscriptions.

Amongst the forts of the Duke's command is Alione, garrisoned by *Cohors III Nerviorum,* a unit which, as Birley observed (1957, 15), was a *cohors peditata*, and which is also attested at Vindolanda (*RIB* 1691). Frere (1974, 271) suggested that Alione should be identified with the Alauna of the Ravenna Cosmography (see below), which is usually placed at Maryport. Whilst Maryport's situation on the river Ellen provides an etymological propriety to the identification, Jarrett (1976, 16) has challenged it on the ground that the *Cohors III Nerviorum* was not a suitable unit to be placed in the garrison sequence at Maryport.

Similar problems are encountered in the case of other possible identifications of Alione, if we assume that it is the same site as Alone of the Antonine Itinerary. In the case of Watercrook, we have no archaeological evidence of the nature of the garrison at any time; too little is known of the fort's interior even to permit a guess as to whether it was cavalry or infantry. Further, the present state of our knowledge of the site leaves certain doubts about the nature of fourth-century occupation – the relevant period as far as concerns the Notitia. Although fourth-century material has come from the most recent excavations, its implication is not unequivocal, and the pattern of coin loss is quite unlike that of other military sites known to have been occupied in the fourth century. Thus to postulate the presence of a quingenary cohort at Watercrook between 300 and 400 is not without difficulties.

Nor are the problems dissipated by assuming Alione to be either Low Borrow Bridge or Burrow in Lonsdale; for, whilst evidence appears to exist in both cases for occupation into the later fourth century, Low Borrow Bridge at any rate at some time in its history appears to have been garrisoned by an *ala* (*RIB* 756; Birley 1947, 9). In the case of Burrow, there is no evidence at all of the garrison's nature.

The sub-section also includes an entry for Glannibanta, which, as we have seen, is usually taken to be the same site as Clanoventa of *Iter* X, and to be identified with Ravenglass. Although there are reasons to place Clanoventa elsewhere than at Ravenglass, it is still possible that Glannibanta is not to be identified with Clanoventa.

The problem of placing Glannibanta is exacerbated by the evident confusions in the western end of the line of Hadrian's Wall, which has been the subject of Hassall's recent discussion (1976): he has argued for a disturbance to the text which should be restored so that Birdoswald would become Banna, and Castlesteads, Amboglanna. Difficulties, however, remain; for, beyond Amboglanna, the Notitia lists Petrianis, Aballaba, Congavata, Axeloduno, Gabrosenti, Tunnocelo, Glannibanta.

The Rudge Cup and Amiens Skillet appear to run in the opposite direction – Maiae (presumably Bowness on Solway), Aballava (Burgh by Sands: Birley 1939, 210), Uxellodum, Camboglans, Banna. Hassall's argument against the omission of Stanwix is persuasive, thus presenting a good case for taking Uxellodum/Uxellodunum as Stanwix. The Notitia's Petrianae would therefore be either an alternative name for Stanwix, or (if we assume that Axeloduno is to be equated with Uxellodunum), a further textural corruption caused by dittography with the name of the unit.

Beyond Aballaba, our evidence for placing the Notitia's locations is very thin; Hassall (1976, 117 and note 49) has an ingenious suggestion for Congavata – *torquata,* a title of the *Ala Petriana*; Axeloduno may be Stanwix. However, the Notitia does not appear to mention Bowness on Solway; instead, the document lists Gabrosenti, Tunnocelo and Glannibanta, which are usually taken to be sites of the Cumberland coast system, terminating at Ravenglass. Although there is no proof in the Notitia that the identifications are correct, a few points should be made: first, the same sequence (in reverse order) recurs in the Ravenna Cosmography (see below). Secondly, the *Cohors II Thracum,* attested epigraphically at Moresby (*RIB* 797, 803-4), is placed at Gabrosenti, although we should note that *Cohors II Lingonum,* also attested at Moresby (*RIB* 798), is placed in the Notitia at Congavata. Thirdly, whilst there are apparently insufficient sites in the Notitia's sequence for all the coastal forts, the etymology of Glannibanta does suit Ravenglass. The Notitia's unit at the site – *Cohors I Morinorum* – is not attested at any other site in Britain, although it does appear in two diplomas (*CIL* XVI 48 and 69: Birley 1958, 27).

Thus, the Notitia does not advance the attempt to ascertain the Roman names of Watercrook and Ravenglass; although it does raise doubts as to whether Watercrook should be identified with Alione. In the case of Ravenglass, the Notitia's evidence is more equivocal; whilst Glannibanta has the etymological propriety for Ravenglass, the propriety is not exclusive: indeed it might be argued, particularly if the Notitia is not following the coastal line, that Tunnocelo with its cohort recruited from the fleet (*I Aelia Classica*) is a more suitable identification.

RAVENNA COSMOGRAPHY

The Ravenna Cosmography is a document of the seventh century, which apparently derives in part at any rate from a road map (Richmond and Crawford 1949, 5); the lists of names radiate from centres which are mentioned once and subsequently have to be understood at the commencement of each route for which they are the starting-point. Thus Manchester (Mautio) is the starting-point for two routes: one leads via Alicuna and Camulodono into the north-west terminating at Ravonia (probably Bravoniaco = Kirkby Thorc), whilst the other runs via Bresmetenaci Veteranorum (Ribchester) into west Yorkshire.

Of these, we are concerned mainly with the former, and it is clouded with uncertainties. It is possible, for example, that some of the names might refer to sites no longer known. Following Camulodono, the list gives the two similar names of Caluvio and Galluvio, which may be Galacum and Galava of *Iter* X; if so an equivalent for Alone is missing, although Alauna (usually identified in this case with Maryport) does figure later in the list.

After Galluvio come Medibogdo and Cantiventi; on the usual interpretation, these are Hardknott, which does not appear in *Iter* X or the Notitia, and Cantiventi which is equated with Clanoventa/Glannibanta, and taken as Ravenglass. If, however, we are placing Clanoventa in the eastern side of the Lake District, it is more likely to be Ambleside than Brougham, since there is hardly room to insert a site (Medibogdo) between Low Borrow Bridge and Brougham. It would not in fact be impossible for Galluvio (= Galava) to be Low Borrow Bridge, followed by Medibogdo as Watercrook (which is etymologically at least suited to the present topography of the site), and Cantiventi as Ambleside.

This would, however, again seem to disturb the apparently neat listing of the Cumberland coast sites between Ravenglass and Bowness, and in particular the propriety of siting Alauna on the Ellen river. In any case, we should perhaps exercise some caution before assuming that Cantiventi to Maio does represent the coastal sites, since this would involve the unusual repetition of a name (Maio: Breeze and Dobson 1976, 276), which appears a little later obviously in its context of Hadrian's Wall. Further whilst Olerica and Derventio, which come after Maio, may be Old Carlisle and Papcastle, this would involve a long jump to Kirkby Thore (if indeed that site is Ravonia/Bravoniaco).

We should probably admit that we cannot achieve any real certainty with this part of the Cosmography; it is possible, for instance, that, within the long list of names from Alicuna to Ravonia, there is a subsidiary break, as apparently happens in the next entry which proceeds from Ravonia (Kirkby Thore) first to Valteris (Verterae/Brough under Stainmore), and then to Bereda (Voreda/Old Penrith?). Thus if Caluvio is Galacum/Lancaster, the Cosmography might be tracing the Lune valley route to Low Borrow Bridge (Galluvio), thence returning to Lancaster to take the alternative northward route to Watercrook (Medibogdo?), and from there proceeding perhaps either to Ambleside or Brougham.

In any case, it is clear that, as with *Iter* X and the Notitia, it is not possible to pin down for certain the Roman names for Watercrook and Ravenglass: nor can we, therefore, use the evidence of the documents to add anything meaningful concerning the garrison patterns of the two forts.

The foregoing observations serve to illustrate how little we know as yet of the Roman occupation of north-west England. Indeed, as has recently been pointed out in another context (Potter 1976b, 183), the size of the studied sample of north-western sites is still exceedingly small; and in view of this it is extremely optimistic to expect to identify sites about most of which we know little or nothing, and for few of which we have anything even approximating to a clear chronology.

BIBLIOGRAPHY

Birley, E. B., 1939. "The Beaumont Inscription, the *Notitia Dignitatum* and the garrison of Hadrian's Wall". CW2 xxxix, 190-226.

—— 1947. "The Roman fort at Low Borrow Bridge". CW2 xxxxvii, 1-19.

—— 1955. "A Roman inscription from Watercrook". CW2 lv, 46-53.

—— 1957. "The Roman fort at Watercrook". CW2 lvii, 13-17.

—— 1958. "The Roman fort at Ravenglass". CW2 lviii, 14-30.

Breeze, D. J. and Dobson, B., 1976. *Hadrian's Wall*, Allen Lane, London.

Bury, J. B., 1920. "The Notitia Dignitatum". *JRS* 10, 131-54.

Frere, S. S., 1974. *Britannia* 2nd edition, Cardinal.

Gillam, J. P., 1949. "Also, Along the Line of the Wall". CW2 xxxxix, 38-58.

Hassall, M. W. C., 1976. "Britain in the *Notitia*" *in* Goodburn, R. and Bartholomew, P. (eds.), *Aspects of the Notitia Dignitatum* BAR 15, 103-17.

Haverfield, F. J., 1915. "The Romano-British Names of Ravenglass and Borrans". *Arch J.* 72, 77-84.

Jarrett, M. G., 1976. *Maryport, Cumbria: A Roman Fort and its Garrison.* Kendal.

Jones, G. D. B. and Shotter, D. C. A., 1978. *Lancaster Excavations 1971-75.* Manchester.

Leather, G. M., 1972. *Roman Lancaster, some Excavation Reports and some Observations.* Lancaster.

Mann, J. C., 1976. "What was the *Notitia Dignitatum* for?" *In* Goodburn, R. and Bartholomew, P. (eds.), *Aspects of the Notitia Dignitatum.* BAR 15, 1-9.

Potter, T. W., 1976a. "Excavations at Watercrook 1974". CW2 lxxvi, 6-66.

—— 1976b. "Recent Work in the North-West". *Current Archaeology* 53, 182-6.

Richmond, I. A. and Crawford, O. G. S., 1949. "The British Section of the *Ravenna Cosmography*". *Archaeologia* 93, 1-50.

Rivet, A. L. F., 1970. "The British Section of the *Antonine Itinerary*". *Britannia* I, 34-82.

Ward, J. H., 1973. "The British Sections of the *Notitia Dignitatum:* an Alternative Interpretation". *Britannia* IV, 253-63.

CHAPTER VI

THE ROMAN FORT AT BOWNESS ON SOLWAY

INTRODUCTION

THE FORT AT BOWNESS was, after Stanwix, the second largest on Hadrian's Wall and also the most westerly. It is likely to have held a milliary cohort and to have exercised responsibility not only for the western end of the curtain but also for part of the Cumberland coast defences. These consisted of a system of milefortlets and turrets, apparently linked by a palisade, that stretched for at least 23 miles down the coastal dunes of north-western Cumbria and probably further (Jones 1976; Potter 1977; Chap. VII). They were laid out in two sections, one based on the fort at Maryport and the other on the Anthorn peninsula; Moricambe bay, the estuary of the Rivers Wampool and Waver, provided the natural division between the two chains of defences. Presumably Bowness was the command centre for the Anthorn section, which terminated in the exceptionally large milefortlet at Cardurnock (Simpson and Hodgson 1947), while Maryport supervised the second stretch. The probability of a third section of coastal defences, south of St. Bees Head, is discussed in Chaps I and VII.

Bowness then was of exceptional strategic importance, as its size, 7 acres, implies. However, little is known either of its history or of its layout. Its probable name, *Maia*, is recorded on the Rudge Cup, the Amiens Skillet and in the Ravenna Cosmography, although the Notitia Dignitatum apparently omits Bowness. Epigraphically, the record is confined to five inscriptions (one attributed to Bowness, *RIB* 2056, comes from Kirkbride), three of which date to the third century. Two are altars, datable to 251-3; they were dedicated by Sulpicius Secundianus, described as *Trib(unus) coh(ortis)*, which makes it clear that the fort was garrisoned by infantry in this period (*RIB* 2057, 2058). The third is a building-inscription which may date to the reign of Caracalla (Birley 1961, 211). This meagre list demonstrates how little attention has been paid to Bowness in the past. The first methodical excavation was not undertaken until 1930, when Birley (1931) cut several sections across the defences and located the west gate, and this was followed in 1955 by trenching beyond the west gate (Daniels 1960). But it was not until 1973 that the first opportunity was taken to examine something of the interior (Potter 1975), by which time large parts of the site had come under development or suffered damage. Consequently it was important that when the present site, in the centre of Bowness, became scheduled for building, that a full excavation should be mounted. As Fig. 126 and Pl. XXIIa make clear it was one of the few large areas to survive without houses or outbuildings, while its position close to the *latera praetorii* also conferred special interest upon this field. In the event the buildings of the fort proved to be disappointingly preserved and the stratigraphy incomplete or damaged: but some useful evidence was recovered, emphasising that every effort needs to be made to save the remaining open areas from development. Indeed, some are already under threat as the process of infilling along the village street continues.

Before presenting the results of the 1976 excavations, it will, however, be useful to summarise the main conclusions from the work of 1973 (Potter 1975). Attention in this season was focused upon the west gate area, the *porta praetoria*. This was a brief campaign, arranged at short notice and confined to limited trenching under appalling weather conditions. Even so, it was demonstrated that the fort was initially provided with a turf rampart, only 4 m in width (Fig. 127) which was later cut back for the insertion of a stone wall, 1·40 m in width. Both the post-sockets for the timber gate and part of the north guard-chamber of the stone gate were identified; but there was no real dating evidence to indicate the period of the conversion into stone of this part of the fort. Behind the defences was the *intervallum* road, 8 m wide, and beyond that the remains of a narrow building, 3·45 m in width, with clay-and-cobble foundations (phase 2). Its form suggests

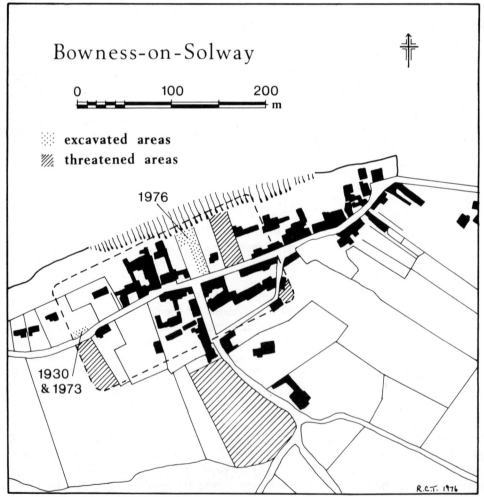

FIG. 126. – Bowness on Solway: plan of the fort showing excavated and threatened areas. Only modern houses constructed before 1960 are shown.

that it was a storehouse or stable rather than a barrack-block. However, it was probably not the first building on the site for its trenches cut through a spread of charcoal, sealing an earlier posthole (Potter 1975, Fig. 4), which implies an older phase with timber buildings that had been burnt down.

BOWNESS-ON-SOLWAY 1973

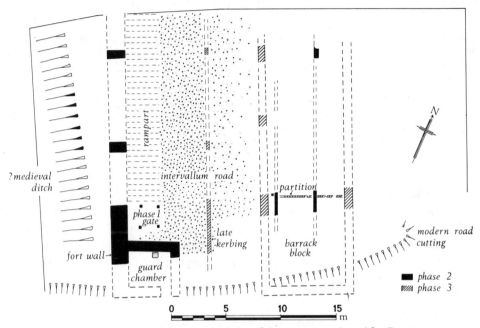

FIG. 127. – Bowness on Solway: general plan of the 1973 excavations. After Potter 1975.

The narrow building was subsequently demolished and a dump of clay laid over the site (phase 3). This provided a firm platform for a new building, also made with clay-and-cobble footings. This was 6·9 m in width inside the walls and yielded evidence for a timber partition. The internal width is narrow for a barrack but, when the unusual breadth of the walls is taken into account, does not fall far outside the normal range, and the building can probably be assumed to belong to soldiers' accommodation. Dating evidence was not very full but stratified pottery in the make-up layers certainly takes the period of construction into the third century and implies a *terminus ante quem* of *c.* 250, if not before. The early third century would be a likely context, given the volume of rebuilding on the frontier at this time. Occupation through the third and fourth centuries is attested by a scatter of pottery of this period, together with the addition of wooden structures to the east end of the barrack-block. Stone-packed postholes cut through the *intervallum* road may also indicate late Roman building activity. But late fourth-century material, normally abundant on sites occupied in that period (as we have seen at Ravenglass), was sparsely represented and, in conjunction with its absence from the area immediately beyond the west gate (Daniels 1960), may be taken to imply a very small garrison in the post-367 period. Interestingly, the 1976 excavations also yielded very little late Roman pottery, although there was a coin of Gratian (367-75). This suggests that the nucleus of late fourth-century occupation has yet to be found.

The excavations of 1973 provided, therefore, a skeleton history for this part of the fort, although little information concerning its plan. The 1976 excavations provided an opportunity to check this sequence and establish something of the layout of buildings in the central area of the fort. Unfortunately, spoil had to be dumped beside the excavations, restricting the area available to some 600 m² (about 60% of the field); since all the features proved to have been of timber this imposed considerable difficulties in interpretation, and undoubtedly limited the value of the excavation. Post-Roman disturbance was also extensive. However, it will undoubtedly be worthwhile, when the opportunity arises, to excavate the other remaining open areas within Bowness. The civilian buildings lining the south road outside the fort (clearly visible as shadow marks on Pl. XXIIa) also provide another obvious target.

The 1976 excavations took place over a period of some seven weeks between March and May. Day-to-day supervision was in the hands of Richard Turner and John Witherington and it is their report that furnishes the basis of the following account. They have also drawn up the plans and, with the assistance of Margaret Howard, studied the coarse pottery.

Acknowledgements

The composition of the team and the more general acknowledgements have already been made in the preface. Here we would like to thank the landowner, Mr R. Hudson, for permission to excavate; Mr B. Paisley, who allowed us to use his field for our huts; and our many friends in the village for their hospitality, especially Mr and Mrs P. Hunter and Mr and Mrs V. Telford.

THE 1976 EXCAVATIONS

By R. C. TURNER and J. H. S. WITHERINGTON

Prior to the start of the excavations the site was stripped of topsoil by machine and was then divided for the purpose of recording into five zones – A, B, C, D and E (Fig. 128). The machine also dug two trial-trenches to establish the level of the natural red clay, the one in zone A then being used as a sump during the wet-weather conditions that prevailed in the early stages of the excavation.

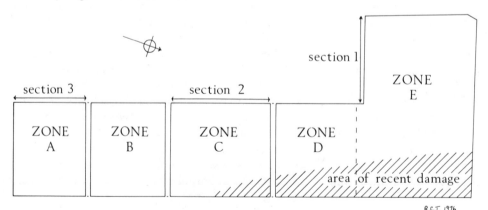

FIG. 128. – Bowness on Solway: plan showing the excavated areas and section lines.

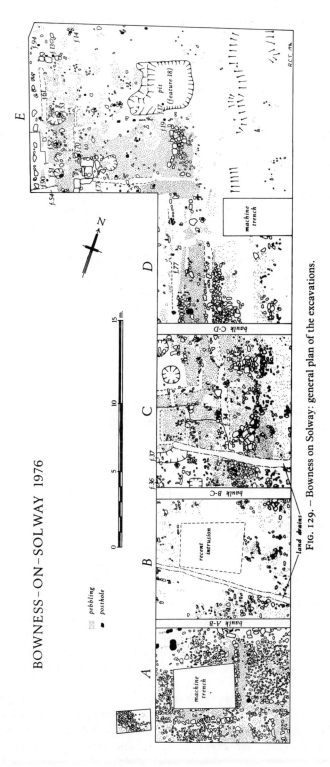

FIG. 129. — Bowness on Solway: general plan of the excavations.

The earliest archaeological evidence from the site is represented by two flints, one of them a Bronze Age arrowhead. The earliest Roman feature was a large pit (Figs 129, 130, feature 18) cut into the natural surface. It was 4 m wide, 3·6 m long and 1 m deep, with the sides cut not more than 20 degrees from the vertical (Pl. XXIIIa). Another shallower pit adjoined it on the south-west corner; it was 1 m wide, 1 m long and 20 cm deep. It was unclear whether or not these were two separate features, one cut by the other; but the fact that the two fills were similar, that joins were made between sherds from the two areas and that both features lay beneath the phase 1 buildings suggests that they belong to the same period.

The fill of the pit (Fig. 130) was a homogeneous layer, 60 cm deep, of damp brown-grey clayey material, containing charcoal and large stones (units 6 and 8) and separated only by a thin band of grey turfy material, 4 cm deep, 40 cm from the bottom (unit 7); sherds of the same pot were found both above and below this layer. From the fill came a large quantity of pottery: three samian vessels, fragmented when found but restored to form near-complete pots (Fig. 141), and a number of other pots in a similar state, the majority being black-burnished types (Fig. 137, Nos 1-11). These were distributed randomly over the whole fill of the pit and, although some areas produced larger concentrations than others, the finds did not form tip-lines down the sides of the pit. Other finds included iron, slag, tile and bone, as well as fragments of glass, lead and two small pieces of leather.

Section across clay pit

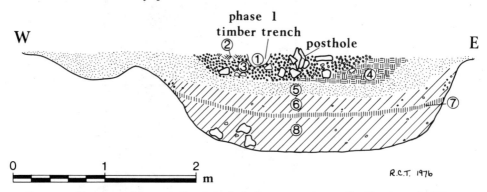

FIG. 130. – Bowness on Solway: section through the clay quarry pit preceding the phase 1 building.

The whole pit was sealed by a sterile layer of red clay, 15 cm deep (unit 5), over which were laid the structures for the first building phase. The homogeneous nature of the fill both above and below the grey turfy band suggests that a significant length of time cannot have elapsed between the depositions of the lower and upper fills. It did, however, remain open long enough for the fill to acquire debris from metal-working and large pieces of tile. This presumably represents the rubbish of the first building-work on the site, thrown into the pit along with excess turf from the levelling of the site. The pit may have originally been dug to provide clay for the northern rampart. Other patches of red clay in zone E just to the west of the pit, also sealed a pre-phase 1 layer; this did not seem extensive but yielded a Trajanic-Hadrianic jar (Fig. 138, No. 12) and a few other sherds.

Description of the Phases (Pls XXIIb, XXIIIb; Fig. 131)

Phases 1-3

These three phases cover the period of construction and use of one structure which occupied most of the excavated area. In general character and alignment this building remained the same throughout the three phases. The major walls were of timber, the uprights usually set into a sleeper-beam laid horizontally in a small trench or chocked up with large cobbles (Pl. XXIIIb). The partitions within the building were defined by lines of postholes, normally stone-packed and sometimes joined together by a narrow trench (see, for example, feature 73). The floors, where they have survived, were of rammed gravel and it is evident from the number of fragments found that the roof was tiled with *tegulae*. The building itself lay on a gentle slope falling towards the south-east corner, which became very wet after rain. The builders overcame this problem by levelling the floor of each room with a combination of turf and heavy stones to fill in the low side. The flooring was then laid over the top, creating a series of shallow steps up the site (Fig. 132, section 2). That this period could be divided into three phases became clear in zone C, which revealed three distinct superimposed Roman floor-levels, although without any intervening occupation debris. While on no other area of the site were three floor-levels preserved in this way, it is nevertheless evident from the number of partitions in zones D and E that some rebuilding took place during the course of the life of one of the structures. It is easiest to assume that the reflooring belonged to the same event. As a result features definitely assignable to phase 1 are described first and those belonging to phases 2 and 3 are described together.

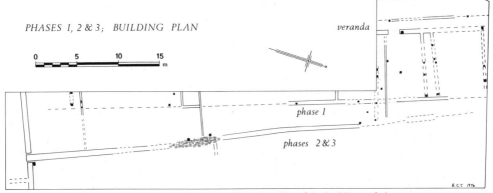

PHASES 1, 2 & 3; BUILDING PLAN

veranda

phase 1

phases 2 & 3

0 5 10 15
m

FIG. 131. – Bowness on Solway: interpretative plan of the buildings of phases 1-3.

Phase 1

The remains of this period comprise a long rectangular timber-framed building orientated north-south, measuring *c.* 57×8 m. The only major wall-line that was not re-used in later phases ran along the east side of the building. It was visible in the pit section (Fig. 130, unit 1) as a U-shaped trench, with a width of 30 cm and a depth of 12 cm, and to the south was a line of heavy cobbles, revetting the eastern edge (Pl. XXIIIa). This gave way to a trench running parallel to the west baulk of D (feature 77); over this part of its length the trench was edged with charcoal and measured 25 cm in width and 15 cm in depth. Because of medieval intrusions only a short length of the trench remained in zone C, where it in part underlay the later floor surfaces. In zone B no trace was left, but in zone A the wall-line included a large double posthole which was associated with another posthole forming a line perpendicular to the main wall. This latter posthole can be shown stratigraphically to relate to phase 1 (Fig. 132, section 3, unit 7).

The line of the west wall was only revealed in zone E. The interpretation is complicated by the fact that this wall appears to have been used throughout all three phases but yielded little or no evidence to suggest rebuilding or replacement. If, however, a sleeper-beam technique was employed, this may well have left little trace of reconstruction. As it is, the surviving indications are those of a shallow trench paved with flags along part of its floor (Fig. 132, section 1, unit 6). Other flagstones in this area may represent the threshold of a door.

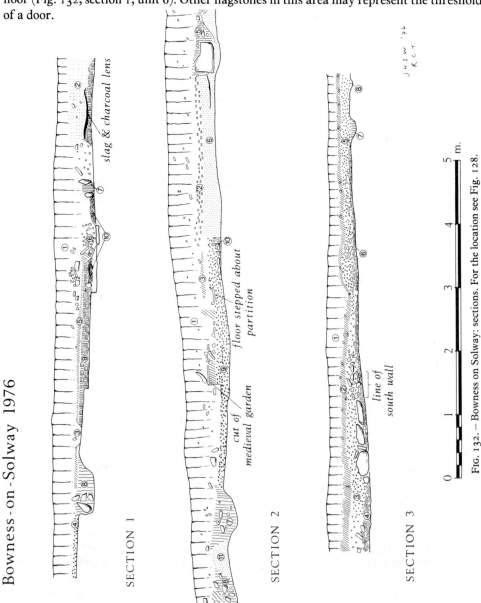

FIG. 132. – Bowness on Solway: sections. For the location see Fig. 128.

The likely position of the end-wall on the south side was located in zone A. It was marked by parallel lines of heavy cobbling, suggestive of a sleeper beam, chocked by stones. As with the west wall, there were no signs of replacement but it is again probable that this line continued to mark the end of the buildings of phases 2 and 3.

Several partitions within the building could be shown to belong to phase 1. We have already mentioned the posthole in zone A. In addition, in zone C, there was a shallow trench, 22 cm wide, which joined the east wall, and, in zone D, a narrow charcoal-lined trench, 12 cm wide, which ran into feature 77. In zone E no certain partitions of this phase could be shown to exist, although it would be plausible to suppose that at least some of the lines shown on Fig. 131 belong to this phase. From such meagre evidence, the number of partitions within the length of building present cannot be calculated exactly. There were, however, three phase 1 elements beneath the later veranda. They consisted of two stone-packed postholes (features 90 and 94), both supporting small posts 8 cm square, and a shallow trench (feature 61) running north from feature 90. This indicates that there was a veranda 2 m wide.

Phases 2 and 3

In these periods the east wall was shifted by between 2·5 and 4 m to the east, creating a much wider building. This wall showed wide variation in its construction and considerable deviation from a straight line. In zone A there was a sleeper-beam, resting on a bed of fine gravel and packed on either side by cobbles; these were notably larger along the western edge. The line could be traced across parts of zone B either as a line of packing or a soil mark. In zone C it was preserved only as two large stone-packed postholes, both set into the western edge of a dump of red clay. From here on northward the wall was represented by a trench cut into the old ground surface and lined or packed with large cobbles (Pl. XXIIIb). It had a width of up to 60 cm and a depth of 15 cm. This feature could not be traced in zone E. The south wall, on the other hand (which, as we saw above, followed the same alignment as that of phase 1), was of uniform construction with horizontal sleeper-beams resting on a bed of heavy cobbles and then chocked on either side with large stones. The beam was 50 cm wide.

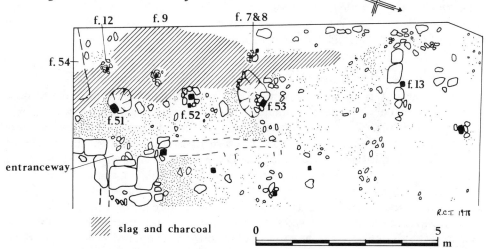

slag and charcoal

0   5

m

FIG. 133. – Bowness on Solway: detailed plan of zone E.

The west wall could only be traced over part of its length. In the south section of zone E the trench (Fig. 132, section 1, unit 6) rested on a line of sandstone flags, 40 cm wide and 5 cm thick. Immediately beyond its junction with a partition, feature 73, there was an entrance formed by three flags, set back from the wall. It was fronted by a worn door-sill, 80 cm long (Fig. 133). Nearby was a sandstone block with a pivot-hole. The wall continued with a large stone-packed posthole, feature 70, supporting a rectangular post, 10 cm by 12 cm, and was then visible as a shallow trench 40 cm wide. After a stretch of 3 m the trench was cut away by modern activity in the northern half of zone E. However, the base of a stone-packed posthole, feature 14, survived on the projected line of this wall.

Of the many internal partitions that were identified, only feature 73 joined the lines of the west and east walls. It survived as a shallow trench 20-35 cm wide, bounded by pebble floor surfaces. There were, however, traces of three other partitions in this area, spaced at intervals of 4, 1 and 4·7 m. These were built largely with stone-packed postholes. In the remainder of the site only two other partitions were found. One, in the centre of zone C, ran partly in a shallow trench and partly on a line of re-used sandstone blocks (Pl. XXIVa). The other, in the north-west corner of zone A, consisted of three stakes set in a shallow trench (Fig. 132, section 3, unit 8). The floors were made of gravel, normally laid on a heavy cobble foundation which varied in thickness so that the floor in each room was level. The veranda was on the same line as that of phase 1, but the uprights were set in a sleeper-beam laid in a shallow trench. The veranda was floored with gravel.

Some evidence was found to suggest the presence of further rooms beyond the east wall. This area of the site had been badly damaged by post-Roman intrusions which had cut away many structural traces. But one partition was located in zone C; it consisted of a short length of trench, 40 cm wide and 14 cm deep, which petered out after about a metre. In zone A, the sleeper-beam setting was outlined by cobble stones, marking the south wall of the building; it was found to continue to the most easterly limits of the excavated area. The beam, which was 40 cm wide, was slightly offset from the line of its neighbour. The junction between the south and east walls was reinforced by a large stone-packed posthole, set into the corner. In addition there were indications of a further wall-trench, packed with cobbles, extending from the south wall into the south-east angle of the excavated area. Despite the fact that the cobbled surface beyond the south wall superficially resembles a road-surface, it is nevertheless evident from the presence of this wall-trench that a part of the building did in fact extend over this area.

Phase 4 (Fig. 134, Pl. XXIVb)

The remains of this period were confined to a single building. In zone C the phase 3 floor had been cut by a number of postholes, set in a shallow trench, forming two sides of a rectangular building. All the postholes were stone-packed and supported rectangular posts varying in size from 8×10 cm to 5×8 cm. The corner post was 6×12 cm. The east side of the building continued northwards into zone D but the large number of post-sockets in that area (Fig. 134) made it difficult to establish where the building ended. It is probable that feature 55 formed part of the structure; 35 cm deep and stone-packed to support a post 12 cm square, it could even have been the corner. More important, however is the fact that it yielded one of the few pieces of fourth-century pottery from the whole site (Fig. 138, no. 31). It is unlikely that the east side of the building continued as far as feature 78 although it is on the same line; it was only 20 cm in diameter and the packing is small

BOWNESS-ON-SOLWAY 1976

Fourth-Century Building

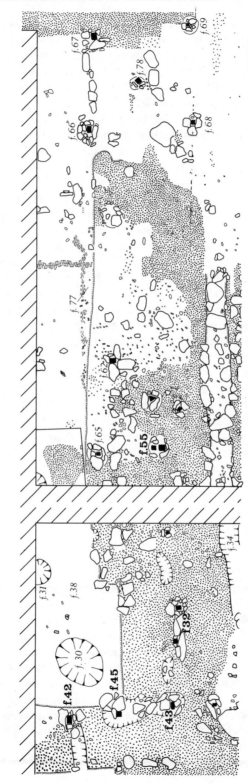

Fig. 134. — Bowness on Solway: plan of the fourth-century building, together with other features in zones C and D.

whereas, by comparison, the post-pits for the rest of the building were much larger (some over twice the size) and more substantially packed. This would imply that the building was *c.* 5 m in width. The floor of the building was largely cut away in phase 5 and there was no stratified dating evidence except for the sherd mentioned above. We can probably associate this building with the very few fourth-century sherds and the two fourth-century coins found in unstratified context. The function of the building can only be guessed but it may have housed part of the last garrison of the fort.

There are other features on the site which may be attributed to phase 4, but whether they should be regarded as contemporary with the zone C building is less certain. Three of them are post-pits cut through the latest surface of the veranda; feature 51 (75×65 cm) had a depth of 70 cm, and had been dug so that its diameter narrowed as its depth increased. The post-socket in the bottom in fact left a ledge in the cut so that only a few stones were needed to wedge the post (which measured 16×14 cm), into position. It was sealed by a layer, 7 cm deep, of redeposited red clay natural. The post-pit to the north of this, feature 52, was smaller: 60 cm in diameter and 30 cm deep. This was also stone-packed to support a post 10×8 cm in size. There were indications that this pit had been re-used, and that the third post-pit, cut through the veranda and in a line with the other two, had also been re-used. This pit, feature 53, measured approximately 1·35×0·85 m and had been dug to a depth of 50 cm. The lowest, and first, post-socket was stone- and clay-packed to support a post 10×8 cm. Its replacement was circular, *c.* 9 cm in diameter, and cut into the pit fill above and to one side of the first.

It is difficult to see what structure, or part of a structure, these posts would have supported. They form a line, which is possibly extended by the inclusion of feature 13, a shallow post-pit of an altogether different nature, 60 cm in diameter and 16 cm in depth, packed on the north side by red clay and on the south by two large stones. There is also a possible return in the form of feature 54, a wall-trench 20 cm wide running east-west along the south baulk of zone E. However, it is more likely to correspond with other features outside the excavated area than with those inside. It is furthermore noteworthy that there was an extensive scatter of slag and charcoal in this area (Fig. 133).

Phase 5

There was a long break in occupation between the late Roman period and the twelfth or thirteenth centuries. In the Middle Ages, the floors of phases 1-3 in zone C were partly cut away and replaced by a red-brown, clayey, charcoal-flecked fill, over which there was a layer of small cobbles which might have constituted the edge of the floor or path surface (Fig. 132, section 2, unit 2). Into this fill were cut two pits: feature 30 was 1·10 m in diameter and 35 cm deep, and contained a grey, charcoal-flecked fill, with a few sherds of green-glazed pottery. Feature 31 had a similar fill and measured 1·10×70×15 cm. Two other features were also cut into a red clayey fill at the south end of the zone: a small ditch, 75 cm wide and 30 cm deep, running in an east-west direction, and another pit. The largest medieval feature, however, was an area of dark garden-soil which had been cut through the floor-levels of the Roman building. It covered approximately 20 m² and was up to 20 cm in depth; it contained *c.* 100 green-glazed sherds, but no later material.

Post-medieval activity

Subsequently there has been a great deal of activity on the site, in places removing all traces of Roman occupation. Zone B, for example, was almost totally robbed of any archaeological features a generation ago (according to local sources) under the guise of an excavation. Recent field drains, too, have played their part in the destructive process but perhaps the greatest damage was done by the modern cut into the red-clay natural surface along the eastern half of the site.

Chronology of the Phases 1-3

In bringing together the evidence both of the structures and the finds, two limitations are immediately apparent. In the first place, the Roman structures have been badly disturbed in medieval and recent times, making the full recovery of the building-plan impossible and leaving little of the Roman material in stratified contexts. Secondly the volume of datable finds is very small considering the extent of the area investigated. Thus any conclusions must be tentative and are not necessarily true for the fort as a whole. Fortunately, the phase 1 building sealed a large and well dated pottery group, contained in a pit. The coarse-ware covers the range *c.* 120-180 with two vessels conventionally dated *c.* 140-180. The samian includes two Flavian-Trajanic vessels, and a much larger number dating to the Hadrianic – early Antonine period; the two latest vessels can be assigned to 125-150. From stratigraphic evidence, the pit would seem to be the work of the builders of the fort. The decision to move the forts onto the wall was taken during the

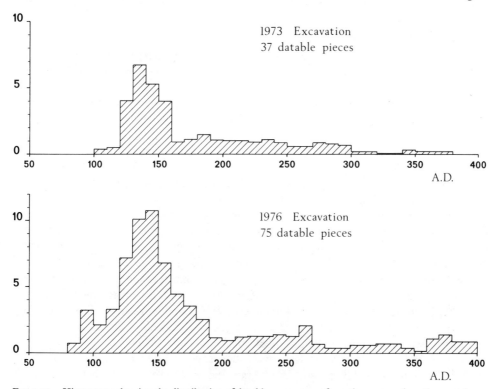

FIG. 135. – Histograms showing the distribution of datable coarse-ware from the 1973 and 1976 excavations.

building of the Wall and is thought to have been made before 125 (Breeze and Dobson 1976, 45). Taking the finds as a whole, they could be made to fit this date, though some years later would be more comfortable.

As a guide to the date of the later Roman phases, the assemblage of datable items from the whole site has been taken collectively to form the basis of Fig. 135. To construct this diagram each datable piece is given a score of one, which is equally divided among the decades of its stated range. The shape of the diagram should reflect the periods of activity on a site although distortion may be introduced by the many factors that affected the distribution of coarse-ware, samian and coins to sites in north Britain during the Roman period. Nevertheless certain conclusions can be made from the diagram itself, and by comparing it with those from other sites or other parts of the same site. The two excavations within the fort at Bowness have produced rather small samples of material and so the comparisons and conclusions remain subject to statistical variation.

The diagram shows that the majority of the 1976 material belongs to the period 120-180 and there is little doubt that the construction and use of the buildings of phases 1, 2 and 3 falls within this range. Phase 1, as we have seen, probably begins c. 125-135. The end of phase 3 is indicated by the sharp fall in the coarse-ware c. 180-190, corroborated by the near absence of later Antonine samian. It is impossible to define the chronological distinction between phases 1, 2 and 3 although it is tempting to fit them into the standard Hadrian's Wall model of periods Ia, Ib and II; but there are too few data to support or refute this hypothesis.

Interpretation of the Building

Any definitive interpretation of this building is excluded by the partial and fragmentary nature of the plan that was recovered. Substantial areas of the structure lay outside the excavated area and the constructional features that could be identified were mostly insubstantial and ill-defined. Our conclusions must be correspondingly tentative. At first sight the building might be regarded as a barrack-block, divided into a series of *contubernia*. On reflection, however, this does not seem plausible. Quite apart from the extraordinary dearth of domestic rubbish, the plan has many atypical features. Its overall dimensions were at least 57 m in length and 8 m (later 10·5 m) in width – which would make it much too long for a barrack-block, and, in the later phases, much too wide. It also lacks both the officer's quarters and the central wall, dividing the *contubernia* into an inner and outer room. Nor do the partition divisions correspond to the normal range of 3·5-4·5 m; in this building the intervals appear to average some 7 m, although there is little real regularity in the surviving pattern. Consequently we can probably assume that the remains are not those of a barrack-block but of another type of building.

The position of the site within the fort does suggest that it could have lain within the central range, possibly to the north-east of the *principia*. This gives scope for a wide variety of buildings, amongst them storehouses, stables and workshops. Store buildings tend to be long, narrow structures, without a veranda, while stables should yield evidence for drains, especially on such sloping, impermeable ground. A workshop also seems an unlikely interpretation, given the scarcity of industrial and domestic debris. One other possibility is that the building was part of a hospital, a structure that, where recognised, (e.g. Fendoch: Richmond and McIntyre 1938-9; Housesteads: Charlesworth 1976), normally lay within the central range; but suggested examples are usually not as large as this building at Bowness and customarily possess a courtyard or internal corridor. Consequently we cannot offer any certain interpretation of this structure, beyond emphasising that it is most unlikely to have been a barrack-block.

NOTES ON THE SECTIONS (Fig. 132)

The location of each section is shown on Fig. 128.

Section 1

1. Topsoil and subsoil.
2. Recent pebble and soil fill.
3. Phase 3 posthole, feature 22.
4. Phase 3 pebble surface.
5. Red clay layer, cut by phase 3 features.
6. Primary wall-**trench** of all phases of the building with rubble fill lying on red sandstone flag.
7. Phase 2 or 3 **posthole** with dark fill.
8. Large posthole with a yellow clay fill, feature 24; the stone packing belongs to phase 3, probably re-using an earlier pit.
9. Stony, yellow-brown clay layer, pre-phase 3.
10. Grey, turf-like material with a thin charcoal lens.

Section 2

1. Topsoil and subsoil.
2. Stone and soil layer, possibly a medieval surface.
3. Patches of red clay.
4. Patches of red clay.
5. Medieval pit with a stony fill, feature 31.
6. Soft, red-clay layer with a charcoal lens, feature 38; related to phase 4 or later.
7. Medieval ditch with a greasy dark fill, feature 37.
8. Medieval pit with a greasy dark fill, feature 36.
9. Phases 1, 2 and 3 gravel floors.
10. Timber-trench with a dark fill cut by unit 6, forming a partition of phase 1.
11. Layer similar in composition to unit 6, cut by medieval intrusions, units 7 and 8.

Section 3

1. Topsoil.
2. Post-medieval stony red clay, feature 5.
3. Surface lying on heavy cobble packing, relating to all Roman phases, feature 21.
4. Grey, charcoal-flecked, levelling layer.
5. Phases 1-3 cobble and pebble floor-surfaces, feature 48.
6. Red-clay layer.
7. Phase 1 posthole with brown fill.
8. Phase 2/3 timber-trench of partition.

Pit section, Feature 18 (Fig. 130)

1. Red clay packing of main wall-trench, phase 1.
2. Grey, turf-like material.
3. Iron-stained fine gravel.
4. Pea-grit and gravel fill.
5. Redeposited red-clay material used to seal the pit.
6. Saturated grey-brown clay mixed with some stone and charcoal.
7. Thin layer of grey clay.
8. Similar to unit 6, but with some heavier stone and some organic material.

THE FINDS

Small Objects (Fig. 136)

There is a remarkable dearth of metal and glass objects, given the extent of the excavated area: the contrast with a site like Ravenglass (where a similar size of excavation took place) is very striking. There are no more than 14 pieces of bronze, two of lead, one object of glass and only three iron instruments (apart from a comparatively small number of nails).

1. (SF 30)   A bronze harness-mount, with an attachment rivet on the back. The roundel was presumably intended to hold an enamelled design, all trace of which has disappeared. Phase 4.
2. (SF 38)   A bronze trefoil object with a fitting for a pin at the top, held by an iron rivet. The design on the face resembles an animal face. An unusual object, best explained as a brooch. Phase 0.
3. (SF 18)   Bronze terminal with an iron core. Unstratified.

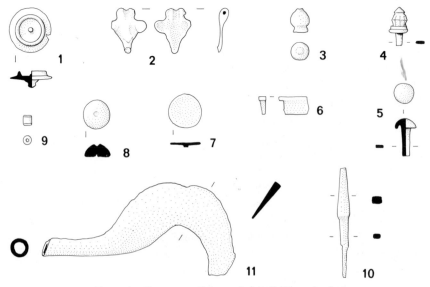

FIG. 136. – Bowness on Solway: the small objects (1:3).

4. (SF 28)   An elaborate bronze nail-head with a rectangular shank. The head is facetted and further decorated with two circular flat knobs on the facetted part. Unstratified.

5. (SF 17)   A bronze nail with a domed head and a rectangular shank. Unstratified.

6. (SF 24)   A bronze lock-bolt of common type. Unstratified.

7. (SF 22)   Flat-topped bronze stud. Unstratified. Two other examples were found.

8. (SF 13)   A lead weight in which the central perforation has only been partially drilled. Unstratified.

9. (SF 15)   A pale blue glass bead, with an incised line at both the top and bottom of the barrel. Unstratified.

10. (AR)   An iron artillery bolt-head. Unstratified.

11. (AQ)   A small reaping-hook with a socketed ferrule. Phase 3.

Not illustrated

Amongst the other finds were two small bronze rings, a single piece of folded lead and an iron ferrule, probably the lower part of a spearhead.

ROMAN AND MEDIEVAL POTTERY

Roman Coarse-Ware (Figs 137-9)

The excavations produced a useful sample of datable pottery, very little of it, however, from sealed deposits. The exception is the group from the pit (feature 18) which was sealed by the phase 1 wall-line of the main building. These vessels thus form an important closed Hadrianic group which is therefore described and illustrated separately from the other vessels (Fig. 137). From the rest of the pottery, a representative sample for illustration and description has been selected. It was noted that the black-burnished types all belonged to Gillam's hand-made category I, but two separate fabric divisions within this category are made here:

Fabric A: has a black surface with a brownish-black core; in texture, fairly close-bodied with a large amount of quartz-sand; it tends to favour the thinner-walled cooking-pots.

Fabric B: has a dark grey surface with a lighter core; in texture, generally more open-bodied than Fabric A and also contains much quartz sand. It is the commoner of the two fabrics.

As it was unclear whether the distinction between these two fabrics lay in the source of manufacture, the firing, or the degree of use to which the vessels had been put, a sherd of each fabric was submitted to Dr David Williams (Department of Archaeology, University of Southampton) who kindly sent the following comments: "a heavy mineral analysis was undertaken on two body-sherds from Early BB 1 cooking-pots. Both sherds produced assemblages characterised by a high tourmaline content, and agreed well with analyses on BB 1 vessels shown to have been made in the Wareham-Poole Harbour area of Dorset (Williams 1977, group I). A similar origin for the two samples from Bowness on Solway is likely. The variation in colour between the two sherds is probably due to uneven reducing conditions experienced in the firing. If it is correct to think of Dorset BB 1 being mostly fired in bonfires (Peacock 1973, 64), we should perhaps expect a greater variation in surface colours than is normal in kiln-fired products (Hodges 1964, 40). Certainly, much of the Dorset BB 1 seen by the writer is in fact dark grey rather than black."

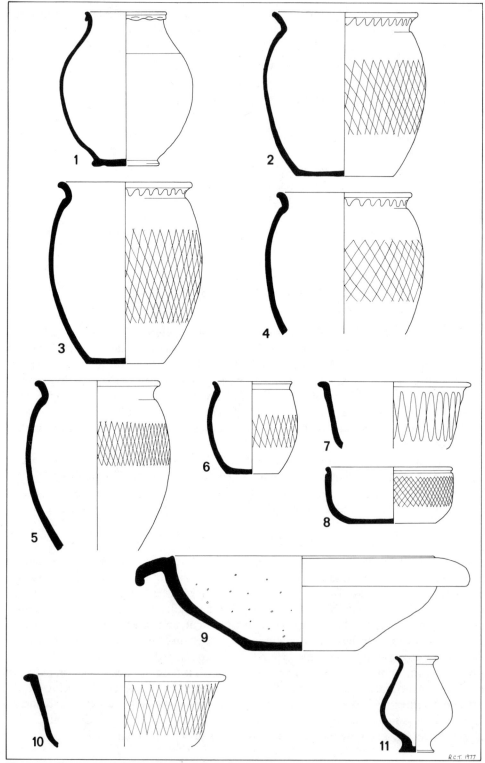

FIG. 137. – **Bowness** on Solway: coarse-ware from the clay quarry pit (F18) preceding the building of phase 1 (1:4).

Vessels from feature 18 (Fig. 137)

1. (DI 4)   Narrow-mouthed jar in a fine, orange-pink fabric with a frilled rim. Trajanic-Hadrianic.

2. (DI 7)   BB cooking-pot in Fabric A with scribed wavy lines on neck. Early to mid second century (see Gillam 1976, 63).

3. (DI 8)   BB cooking pot in Fabric A. Gillam 132. 120-180.

4. (DI 9)   BB cooking-pot in Fabric B. Closest to Gillam 125 or 118. 120-180/120-160.

5. (DK 1)   BB cooking-pot in Fabric B. Gillam 122. 120-160.

6. (DI 5)   BB beaker in Fabric B, perhaps a smaller version of Gillam 123. 120-160.

7. (DI 10)   BB bowl in Fabric A. Gillam 221. 140-180.

8. (DI 6)   BB bead-rim dish in Fabric A. Gillam 233. 125-160.

9. (DI 11)   Mortarium in an orange fabric with multicoloured grits; fabric and form typical of Docilis and Austinus. Gillam 247. 120-160.

10. (DL 1)   BB bowl in Fabric B. Gillam 221. 140-180.

11. (DL 2)   Miniature jar in a gritty orange fabric. Cf. Bushe-Fox 1916, 64, no. 84 for a parallel from Wroxeter, dated *c.* 90-130.

Vessel from other pre-phase 1 contexts (Fig. 138)

12. (DP 1)   Jar in a light-grey soapy fabric. Closest to Gillam 111. Trajanic/Hadrianic.

Vessels from other phases (Figs 138-9)

13. (DE 1)   Single-handled flagon, closest to Gillam 14. Incompletely fired grey fabric with an orange-red core. The mottled surface with a number of inclusions, a cracked interior surface and a dented exterior suggest that this may be a waster. Phase 2/3.

14. (BE 1)   Single-handled beaker in a brown-grey fabric. See Gillam 1976, 65, no. 26 for a parallel of mid-second century date. Phase 2/3.

15. (CA 1)   Small jar or beaker in a soft gritty fabric. Phase 4.

16. (AK 2)   Rough-cast beaker with a brown colour-coat on a smooth buff fabric. Unstratified.

17. (AQ 2)   BB beaker or jar form in Fabric A. Phase 2/3.

18. (DH 1)   Jar in a light-grey soapy fabric, similar to no. 12 above. Gillam 111. Trajanic/Hadrianic. Phase 1.

19. (AM 1)   Jar in a brick-red fabric with a dark grey core. Early second century. Phase 4.

20. (BH 2)   Wide-mouthed jar or bowl in a gritty buff fabric. Unstratified.

21. (BN 1)   BB cooking-pot in Fabric B. Gillam 118. 120-160. Phase 1.

22. (BQ 1)   BB cooking-pot in Fabric B. Gillam 127. 130-170. Phase 2/3.

23. (CM 1)   BB cooking-pot in Fabric B. Gillam 120. 120-140. Phase 2.

24. (DF 1)   BB cooking-pot in Fabric A. Closest to Gillam 122. 130-170. Phase 2/3.

25. (BA 2)   Cooking-pot in a slightly gritty dark grey fabric with lighter exterior surface. Unstratified.

26. (DB 1)   Jar in a grey fabric with a highly burnished black exterior surface and top of rim. The lower part of the inside of the rim is worn, suggesting the seating for a lid. Unstratified.

27. (AP 2)   Cooking-pot in a black calcite-gritted fabric. Gillam 163. 360-400. Unstratified.

28. (AX 3)   Cooking-pot in a black calcite-gritted fabric. Gillam 161. 300-370. Unstratified.

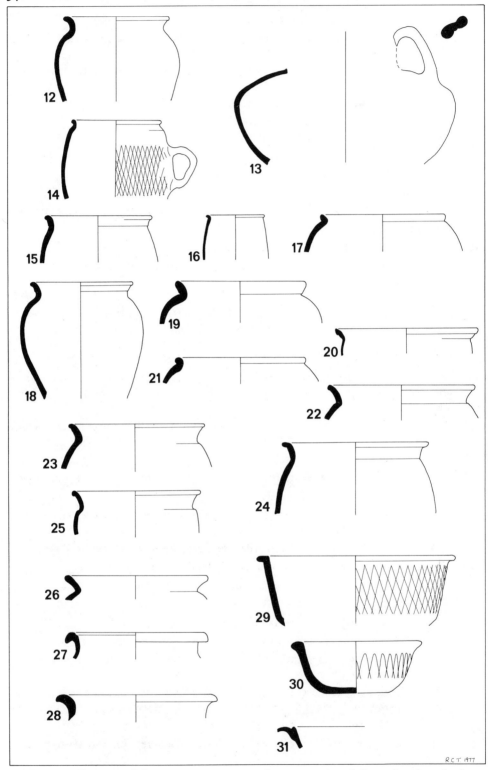

FIG. 138. – Bowness on Solway: coarse-ware. 12, pre-phase 1; 13-31, vessels from other phases (1:4).

29. (BT 1) BB bowl in Fabric B. Gillam 221. 140-180. Phase 1/2/3.

30. (BH 1) Small BB bowl in Fabric B. Closest to Gillam 219. 120-150. Unstratified.

31. (CC 1) Flanged bowl in a cream-coloured fabric with faint traces of a dark slip. A fourth-century type. Phase 4.

32. (BT 2) Mortarium in a white fabric with a darker cream-coloured slip. Stamp of VIATOR (Fig. 142). 110-160. Phase 1/2/3.

33. (BQ 2) Mortarium in a cream-coloured fabric with multi-coloured grits. Stamp reads DOC F (Fig. 142).

34. (AM 2) Mortarium in a white fabric. Gillam 288. 150-350. Phase 4.

35. (BB 1) Mortarium in a cream-coloured, dark-gritted fabric with traces of a buff slip. Gillam 282. 230-340. Phase 5.

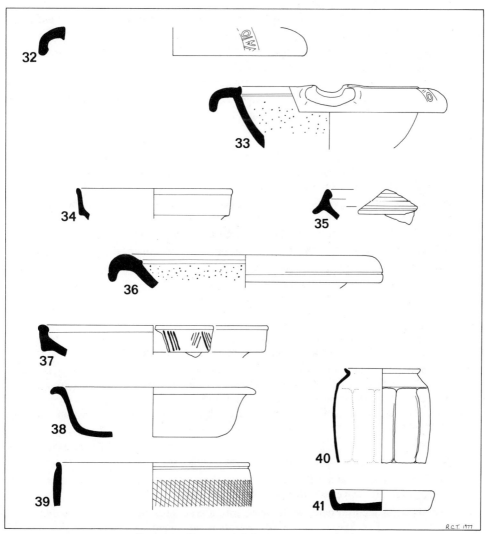

FIG. 139. – Bowness on Solway: coarse-ware (1:4).

36.   (AR 1)   Mortarium in a brick-red fabric with a grey core and multi-coloured grits. A mid second-century type. Unstratified.

37.   (BX 1)   Mortarium in a gritty cream-coloured fabric with traces of a darker slip. Brown linear decoration on rim. Gillam 289. 370-400. Unstratified.

38.   (AQ 1)   BB dish in Fabric B. Gillam 308, but without lattice decoration. 130-180. Phase 2/3.

39.   (AF 1)   BB bead-rim dish in Fabric B. Gillam 318. 160-200. Unstratified.

40.   (BE 1)   Fluted beaker in a smooth orange micaceous fabric. Phase 2/3.

41.   (BA 3)   Base of a lamp or shallow dish in a soapy orange fabric, possibly hand-made. Unstratified.

The Medieval Pottery (Fig. 140)

A total of 535 sherds of medieval pottery was found. The large majority of these came from the area of garden soil, cut into the Roman levels in the middle of the site, and the ditch and pits associated with it. Most of the material is fragmentary and few joins could be made, indicating that a large number of vessels is represented. Little work has been carried out on medieval pottery from the north-west and there are only three dated groups of pottery, two from Carlisle (Jope and Hodges 1955; Jarrett and Edwards 1964) and one from Kirkcudbright Castle (Dunning, Hodges and Jope 1958). Parallels have been taken from these reports.

Unglazed coarse-ware

1.   (BG M12)   A cooking-pot in a hard gritty pink fabric with an orange-brown exterior. Cf. Jope and Hodges 1955, 53, No. 92, which belongs to a thirteenth-century group.

2.   (AZ M90)   A cooking-pot in a finely gritted cream fabric. In shape corresponds to Jarrett and Edwards 1964, 50, No. 72.

3.   (AX M1)   A cooking-pot in a hard, coarsely gritted cream fabric.

4.   (AX M20)   A long-necked "beaker" in a soft finely gritted orange fabric.

5.   (AZ M89)   A cooking-pot in the same fabric as No. 1 similar to Jarrett and Edwards 1963, 53, No. 94. A thirteenth-century type.

Glazed wares

The vast majority of the sherds show traces of a glaze in a variety of shades of green and brown; but very few rims were found. Consequently only a small selection is illustrated.

6.   (AX M4)   A rim of a jug with a heavy strap handle, pinched on by thumb and forefinger. The fabric is hard, gritty and cream-coloured with a brown exterior. A light-green glaze has been applied to the outside of the jug, but only remains in patches. There is a description of the technique of production of these thirteenth-fourteenth-century vessels in Jope and Hodges 1955, 98, No. 25.

7.   (AX M162)   A handle in a similar fabric to no. 6 but with a grey core. The glaze is a darker green and is applied to the upper surface of the handle only.

8.   (AZ M85)   A small flat handle in a soft, orange fabric, decorated with wavy ridges down the upper surface. It is covered with a green and brown glaze.

9.   (AP M99)   A jug in a hard, white fabric with a grey core. The outside is covered with a brown glaze. Two lines of impressed decoration run round the body. The piece has the appearance of a waster.

10. (AZ M88) A small jug in the same fabric as No. 6 with a greeny-brown glaze. The neck has a line of impressed decoration.

11. (AX M78) The base of a large pitcher in an orange fabric with a grey core and an olive-green glaze on the exterior. The body and base have been pinched together, as have two other examples from this site. There is a discussion of this form in Dunning, Hodges and Jope 1958. This type dates to the late thirteenth-early fourteenth centuries.

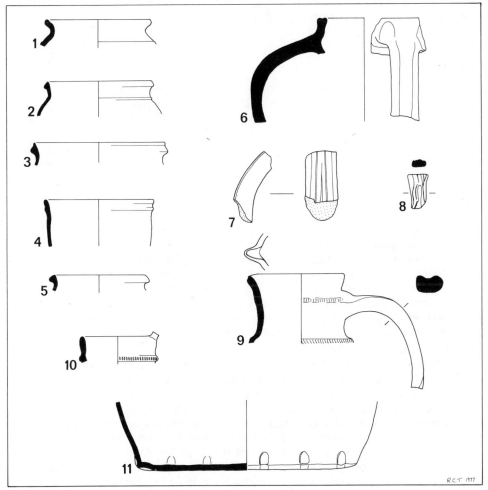

FIG. 140. – Bowness on Solway: medieval pottery (1:4).

SAMIAN WARE By FELICITY WILD

The pit group (feature 18)

The pit produced three almost complete vessels and a number of smaller sherds. The complete vessels were of form 33 and 37 (A and 1 below) and a large dish (diameter 29 cm) of form 36. The latter was of South Gaulish manufacture and Flavian-Trajanic date. The only other South Gaulish material from the group consisted of two sherds from late versions of form 15/17, also of Flavian-Trajanic date. The rest of the group was of Central Gaulish origin and Hadrianic-early Antonine date. Apart from the 33 and four 37s listed below, it included form 27, 18/31 and 18/31R. It contained nothing inconsistent with a date of deposition during the Hadrianic period.

Stamp

A   SERVILIO.OFI   (DI S270)   Form 33 (complete), Central Gaulish, showing die 1a of Servilio of Lezoux. This stamp occurs at Lezoux, and is otherwise only recorded on forms 18/31 and 27. Few stamps of Servilio have survived and none from a dated context, though the forms suggest a Hadrianic or early Antonine date.

Decorated ware

1. (DI S269)   Form 37 (complete), Central Gaulish, with mould stamp of Avitus iii of Lezoux among the decoration (Fig. 141). The decoration shows panels containing the Hercules (o·760) alternating with a vertical row of leaf buds between rows of chevrons. The Hercules panel is repeated six times round the bowl, in one case with the right arm and club compressed against the body, so as to fit in between widely spaced corner tendrils. All the details are attested on Avitus' style (*CGP*, Pl. 62, 6, 7; 63, 9). The die (9a) appears only to have been used on moulds, and is known on bowls of form 37 from Lezoux, Mears Ashby (Northants) and Paris. Although reading ΛVII, the associated styles of decoration make it clear that Avitus iii is in question, and presumably AVIT was intended. Both at Lezoux and in Britain, Avitus' work appears in both Hadrianic and early Antonine contexts, and a date *c.* 115-145 would fit the evidence.

2. (DK S262)   Form 37, Central Gaulish. Several fragments, some from the pit group, of a bowl showing leaf-scroll with birds (o·2315 and probably o·2252), and with Neptune (o·13) and Vulcan without tongs (o·66) in the lower concavity. The ovolo was used by the Sacer-Attianus group and later by Cinnamus at Vichy. The leaf-tip space filler was a characteristic feature of Attianus and of Cinnamus' associates, the Paullus group. All the types were later used by Cinnamus. However, as the bowl is in a normal Lezoux fabric, it seems more likely to have been the work of a predominantly Hadrianic predecessor than of Cinnamus himself. The leaf-scroll was used by Sacer and Attianus. The ovolo, leaf-tips and bird (o·2315) occur together on a bowl from Gloucester attributable to the Large S potter or Attianus. A date in the Hadrianic-early Antonine period seems certain; *c.* 125-150.

3. (DK S267)   Form 37, Central Gaulish. Small fragment showing the Large S motif characteristic of X.6 and the Large S potter; *c.* 125-150.

4. (DI S244)   Form 37, Central Gaulish. Small, worn fragment, which may have been partially trimmed to form a disc, showing the fore-quarters of an animal, probably a stag or hound. The exact type is not identifiable from Oswald, and although the coarseness of the piece suggests an Antonine date, a Hadrianic origin cannot altogether be ruled out.

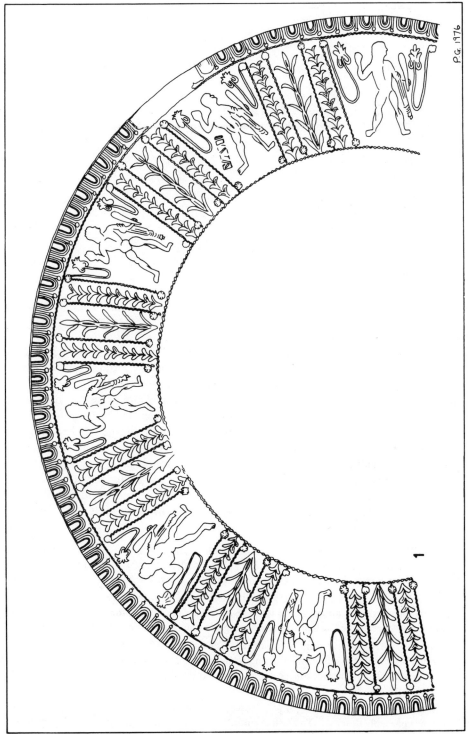

Fig. 141. – Bowness on Solway: samian vessel from the clay quarry pit preceding the building of phase 1 (1:2).

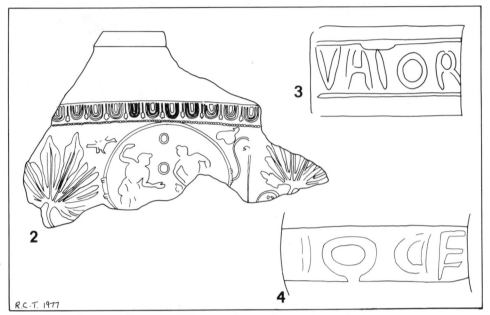

FIG. 142. – Bowness on Solway: samian vessel, 1:2 and mortaria stamps, 1:1.

Other samian from the site

A notable feature of the samian from the site as a whole is the small proportion of decorated ware. All the decorated sherds have been listed below, with the exception of two worn and featureless sherds of Antonine date. The greater proportion of the material is Central Gaulish and Hadrianic or early Antonine. Apart from those listed in the pit group, there are only three other South Gaulish sherds from the site. All are Flavian-Trajanic, and quite consistent with an initial occupation in the Hadrianic period. Although the decorated ware suggests that the import of samian to the site continued during the second half of the second century, the later Antonine plain forms (e.g. forms 79 and 80, 31R, the samian mortaria) appear to be absent. The one undoubtedly late piece is the East Gaulish sherd (12 below), though unfortunately the poor state of preservation makes a precise identification, and therefore a precise dating, impossible.

Stamps

B   [ANNI]OZF (BE S197)   Form 27, Central Gaulish, showing die 1b of Annius ii of Lezoux. This stamp is known in the Birdoswald Alley. It is usually on forms 18/31, 18/31R and 27, but one or two examples are on form 38, so some Antonine activity is likely *c.* 125-150.

C   CRAC VNA.F   (BE S192)   Form 18/31, Central Gaulish, showing die 2a of Cracuna i of Lezoux. This stamp appears in both pre-Antonine (Verulamium, period IIB) and early Antonine contexts (the Castleford pottery shop). It also occurs in Scotland. *c.* 130-160.

D   ERICI.M   (AH S57)   Form 18/31 or 31, Central Gaulish, showing die 1a of Ericus of Lezoux. This stamp occurs commonly on forms 18/31, 18/31R and 27, and is frequent in the Rhineland. Other stamps of this potter occur in Scotland and at Verulamium (period IID). *c.* 130-160.

E   Illiterate. (AF S49)   Form 18/31, Central Gaulish, showing part of the potter's stamp, which is probably illiterate. The dish is embedded in a lump of slaggy material. From the form, a Hadrianic—early Antonine date seems likely.

Decorated ware

5. (AR S146)   Form 37, South Gaulish. Small fragment with worn surface, showing panel decoration with coarse roped borders typical of the Flavian-Trajanic period. *c.* 90-110.

6. (AA S23)   Form 37, Central Gaulish. Small fragment, probably from a freestyle hunting scene, showing the rock motif (0·2155) without the snake, used as a filling ornament. This motif was used on bowls attributed to Donnaucus' style (*CGP*, Pl. 42. 487), and also on Donnaucus-Sacer style (*CGP*, Pl. 84, 3, where it occurs with animal types, as here). The fabric of this piece is probably that of Les Martres-de-Veyre, which suggests a date of *c.* 100-125.

7. (CO S236)   Form 37, Central Gaulish. Rim sherd showing the ovolo used at Les Martres-de-Veyre by the Donnaucus group, and at Lezoux by Attianus and Austrus. The fabric is probably that of Lezoux, suggesting a Hadrianic-early Antonine date.

8. (BA S218)   Form 37, Central Gaulish. Rim sherd, showing edge of ovolo, almost certainly Cinnamus' ovolo 2. *c.* 150-170.

9. (AN S62)   Form 37, Central Gaulish, showing panel decoration with astragalus borders and Pan (0·709). The type, borders, and astragalus were used by Paternus (cf. *CGP*, Pl. 104, 2).

10. (AA S42)   Form 37, Central Gaulish, showing poorly impressed ovolo, probably Advocisus' ovolo 1. *c.* 160-190.

11. (AE S75)   Form 37, Central Gaulish, showing panel decoration with large-beaded borders typical of the work of Doeccus and Casurius. At the base of the sherd is the edge of the Pan mask (0·1214), used by both potters. The upper type is uncertain, but also appears to be a mask. *c.* 160-190.

12. (AC S19)   Form 37, East Gaulish. A close identification of this very poorly preserved sherd is impossible, but the ovolo is probably closest to Ricken-Fischer's E.41 and the type to the tree P.4. Both features occur together on a mould in the style of the third-century Rheinzabern potter Primitivus IV (Ricken, Taf. 199,9). A late Antonine or early third-century date seems probable.

I should like to record my sincere thanks to Mr B. R. Hartley for supplying notes on the potters' stamps. The potter and die numbers are his, to appear in his forthcoming *Index of Potters' Stamps on Samian Ware*.

The following abbreviations have been used:

CGP: Stanfield and Simpson 1958.
O: Oswald 1936-37.
Ricken-Fischer: Ricken and Fischer 1963.
Ricken: Ricken 1948.

COINS By D. C. A. SHOTTER

None of the six coins from the 1976 excavation was recovered from a stratified context, and most of them were poorly preserved.

From material overlying the latest floor surface in Zone C

1. (SF 16; AX)   AE *as*   after A.D. 84
   Obv. IMP CAES DOMIT AVG GERM[
   Rev. Illegible
   Very worn   Wt. 8.251 gms

2. (SF 19; AX)   AE *antoninianus*   A.D. 260-8
   Legends illegible, but probably Postumus
   Very worn   Wt. 2·459 gms (clipped)

From material overlying cobbles in Zone A

3. (SF 9; AM)   AE 3   A.D. 367-75
   Obv. D N GRATIANVS AVGG AVG
   Rev. GLORIA NOVI SAECVLI OF|I
   $\overline{\text{CON}}$
   Fresh   Wt. 2·243 gms   *LRBC* II.517

4. (SF 21; AM)   AE
   Legends illegible, but probably fourth century
   Fragmentary   Wt. 0·936 gms

Zone E

5. (SF 36; DG)   AE *as*   A.D. 98-9
   Obv. IMP CAE]S NERVA TR[AIANVS AVG GERM P M
   Rev. S C (Pietas)
   Very worn and fragmentary   Wt. 4·245 gms   *RIC* 392

6. (SF 26; BE)   AE *dupondius*   A.D. 114-7
   Obv. IMP CAES NER TRAIANO OPTIMO AVG GER DAC PARTHICO P M TR P COS
   VI P P
   Rev. Illegible
   Wt. 10·466 gms

I have discussed elsewhere (in Potter 1975, 46-7) the meagre coin evidence from Bowness, consisting of a small second-century bronze hoard, and three second-century coins from the excavations of 1930 and 1973; the chief effects of the latest group of coins from the site are to strengthen further the showing of coins of the late first and second centuries, and to advance the latest-known coin from the site from the reign of Commodus to that of Gratian. For the latest coins from Hadrian's Wall sites and the significance of these coins, see Birley (1961, 259 ff.) and Kent (1951, 4-15).

The following abbreviations have been used:

LRBC: Carson, Hill and Kent 1960
RIC: Mattingly et al. 1923.

BIBLIOGRAPHY

Birley, E. B., 1931. "Three notes on Roman Cumberland: Bewcastle, Bowness-on-Solway, Petrianae". CW2 xxxi, 137-46.

—— 1961. *Research on Hadrian's Wall*. Kendal.

Breeze, D. J. and Dobson, B., 1976. *Hadrian's Wall*, London.

Bushe-Fox, J. P., 1916. *Third report on the Excavations at the Site of the Roman town at Wroxeter. Shropshire, 1914*. Research Report of the Society of Antiquaries of London, 4.

Carson, R. A. G., Hill, P. V. and Kent, J. P. C., 1960. *Late Roman Bronze Coinage*, London.

Charlesworth, D. "The hospital, Housesteads". AA5, iv, 18-30.

Daniels, C. M., 1960. "Excavations at Bowness on Solway, 1955". CW2 lx, 13-19.

Duff, H., 1939. "Roman remains at Bowness-on-Solway". CW2 xxxix, 327-29.

Dunning, G. C., Hodges, H. W. M. and Jope, E. M., 1958. "Kirkcudbright Castle, its pottery and ironwork". *PSAS* 91, 117-36.

Gillam, J. P., 1970. *Types of Roman coarse pottery in Northern England*, Newcastle.

—— 1976. "Coarse fumed ware in North Britain and beyond". *Glasgow Archaeological Journal* 4, 57-80.

Hodges, H., 1964. *Artifacts*. London.

Jarrett, M. G. and Edwards, B. J. N., 1964. "The medieval pottery from the excavations at Tullie House, Carlisle". CW2, lxiv, 41-57.

Jones, G. D. B., 1976. "The western extension of Hadrian's Wall: Bowness to Cardurnock". *Britannia* VII, 236-43.

Jope, E. M. and Hodges, H. W. M., 1955. "The medieval pottery from Castle Street". CW2 lv, 79-107.

Kent, J. P. C., 1951. "Coin Evidence and the evacuation of Hadrian's Wall". CW2 li, 4-15.

Mattingly, H., Sydenham, E. A., Sutherland, C. H. V. and Carson, R. A. G., 1923. *Roman Imperial Coinage*, London.

Oswald, F., 1936-37. *Index of Figure Types on Terra Sigillata*.

Peacock, D. P. S., 1973. "The black-burnished pottery industry in Dorset." *In* Detsicas, A. P. (ed.), *Current Research in Romano-British Coarse Pottery*. CBA Research Report 10, 63-65.

Potter, T. W., 1975. "Excavations at Bowness-on-Solway, 1973. CW2 lxxv, 29-57.

—— 1977. "The Biglands milefortlet and the Cumberland coast defences". *Britannia* VIII, 149-83.

RIB. Collingwood, R. G. and Wright, R. P. *The Roman Inscriptions of Britain I, Inscriptions on Stone*. 1965. Oxford.

Richmond, I. A. and McIntyre, J., 1938-9. "The Agricolan fort at Fendoch". *PSAS* 73, 34-154.

Ricken, H., 1948. *Die Bilderschüsseln der Römischen Töpfer von Rheinzabern*. Tafeln.

Ricken, H. and Fischer, C., 1963. *Die Bilderschüsseln der Römischen Töpfer von Rheinzabern*. Text.

Simpson, F. G. and Hodgson, K. S., 1947. "The Coastal milefortlet at Cardurnock". CW2 xxxxvii, 78-127.

Stanfield, J. A. and Simpson, G., 1958. *Central Gaulish Potters*.

Williams, D. F., 1977. "The Romano-British black-burnished industry: an essay on characterization by heavy mineral analysis". *In* Peacock, D. P. S. (ed.), *Pottery, early commerce and economics; characterization and trade on Roman and later ceramics*. London.

CHAPTER VII

SYNTHESIS: THE ROMAN OCCUPATION
OF THE NORTH-WEST

DATA AND METHOD

THE NORTH-WEST OF ENGLAND is by no means ripe for the detailed synthesis which, for instance, Jarrett (1969) was able to provide for Wales in his revision of Nash-Williams's *Roman Frontier in Wales*. There are good reasons for this. Most important is the fact that most sites have yet to yield anything like an adequate body of data. Taking the military sites of the hinterland of Cumbria, for example, we find that there has been no scientific investigation at all of the interiors of Beckfoot, Brougham, Old Carlisle or Old Penrith. A rather larger group has been subject to trial trenching, although the total examined for each site amounts to less than one per cent of the area within the defences; these include Barrock Fell, Brough under Stainmore, Burrow in Lonsdale, Burrow Walls, Caermote, Kirkbride, Low Borrow Bridge, Moresby, Park House, Troutbeck and Wreay Hall. Finally there are the sites where more extensive work has taken place. Amongst these we can now list Watercrook and Ravenglass, as well as Maryport (Jarrett 1976), Papcastle (Charlesworth 1965), Kirkby Thore (Charlesworth 1964) and more recently Carlisle; we should note, however, that at none of these sites has more than five per cent of the interior of the fort been properly studied. Indeed the average area examined is closer to two per cent. There has been quite large-scale clearance at Hardknott and Ambleside, but much of this was very early work and its value is commensurately less.

On the frontier itself the situation is not particularly different. With the exception of Birdoswald and Bewcastle, none of the forts has been treated to much more than small-scale trenching; Bowness, where some two per cent of the interior has now been examined, is an exception. Rather more data are available for the milecastles and turrets, especially for the stretch between MC48 (Poltross Burn) and T54a and for MC79. The Stanegate fortlet at Throp has also been studied, as have a number of Cumberland-coast milefortlets and turrets, although only MF5 (Cardurnock) and MF1 (Biglands) have seen large-scale work (Potter 1977).

If we take these sites together, it is clear that the overall sample is far too small to permit much in the way of generalisation. Indeed, experience at Biglands, Watercrook and elsewhere suggests that limited trenching can all too easily lead to erroneous deductions about the layout and chronological development of a site. Some of the lacunae in our knowledge can of course be filled from antiquarian descriptions and collections. The epigraphic record, for instance, is large, both for the Wall and for forts in the hinterland. Leaving aside the frontier sites, we have more than twenty inscriptions each from Carlisle, Old Carlisle and Maryport (which has over 70 examples); more than ten from Kirkby Thore and Brougham, and nearly thirty others, distributed between Ambleside, Beckfoot, Brough, Burrow Walls, Hardknott, Low Borrow Bridge, Moresby, Papcastle, Ravenglass and Watercrook. The overall total is in excess of 200 inscriptions, many of which contain crucial evidence for the identity and history of the garrisons; for building and repair work; and for other matters such as religious cults. On the other hand, it should be borne in mind that only a small proportion can be closely dated – 27 out of 204 for the sites listed above – and that conclusions drawn from their distribution (e.g. Fig. 147) must be correspondingly tentative. Even the Roman name for the majority of fort sites remains uncertain, as Hassall (1976) has recently underlined in a stimulating attempt to challenge some long-held tenets.

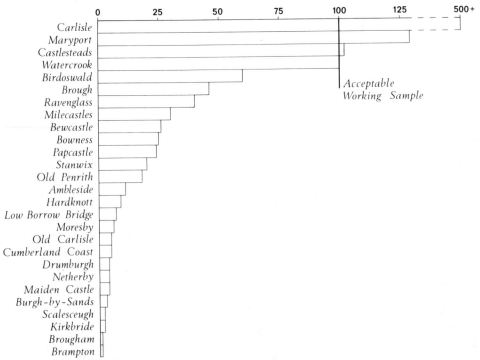

FIG. 143. – Histogram showing the number of coins (excluding hoards) from Roman sites in Cumbria. Work at Watercrook suggests that a sample of at least 100 coins is required from a fort of 3-4 acres to indicate the main trends in the pattern of occupation.

Given the paucity of dated inscriptions, the chronologies for individual sites have been built up partly on the basis of numismatic evidence and partly on studies of the pottery. Some of the judgements have undoubtedly been hasty. For example, an Agricolan origin for Ravenglass was suggested mainly because one first-century mortarium had been found on the beach below the fort platform. This is perhaps an extreme instance, but it is unquestionably true that chronologies have rarely been supported by an adequacy of evidence. Fig. 143 shows, for instance, the numerical distribution of coin finds (excluding hoards) from Roman sites in Cumbria. Only four of the 27 sites or groups of sites have yielded more than 100 coins, while just seven have produced over 30. The results from

Watercrook would indicate that a sample of at least 100 coins is necessary to reflect the main chronological patterns from a three to four acre fort. Smaller samples may suggest trends but in a statistical sense we cannot rely on the conclusions.

The interpretation of the pottery poses other sorts of problems. Since 1957, the basis of coarse-ware classification has been the corpus published by John Gillam, now in its third edition (1970). A full discussion of the chronology of individual types would not be appropriate here, but it is worth noting that the date-ranges are very closely tied to events on the frontier. Thus dates like 120, 140, 200 and 367 figure very prominently in the life-span of the coarse-ware vessels. In addition, it is clear that the variety and quantity of pottery in circulation show marked changes from period to period. Thus, in any average assemblage from a site occupied between c. 80 and 400, there are likely to be large numbers of vessels of the Flavian-Antonine period and many types of 360-400. By contrast, for the third century, where there were fewer variants and smaller quantities of pottery (most of them very long-lived forms) on the markets of northern England, we can expect to observe a falling-off in the overall distribution of finds. This is a feature readily visible on histograms from Ravenglass, Watercrook, Maryport and other sites (Figs 39, 63, 81, 143). The result is that the pottery statistics tend to divide the finds from a military site into the conventional Wall periods (Birley 1961, 263-5) and that they may well lead to quite false hypotheses about abandonment and reduced activity. Indeed, we have already seen something of these problems in previous chapters. At Watercrook, for example, the question of occupation between c. 220 and 270 remains unresolved, just as at Ravenglass it would have been difficult to decide upon the nature of third-century occupation without stratigraphic evidence. Yet both these sites have comparatively large samples of pottery and, in the case of Watercrook, a total of 100 coins.

The burden of these caveats, then, is to underline just how little we can say with certainty about the Roman occupation of north-west England. Our understanding of the history of known forts is still at a very preliminary stage and there are undoubtedly more new sites to be found. We are in a position to offer only tentative hypotheses about the history of the region and these now need rigorous testing in the form of large-scale work. Nevertheless, it may be useful to provide some brief discussion concerning the successive phases of military occupation, if only to help to frame some of the targets for future research.

NATIVE SETTLEMENTS (Fig. 144)

The stone-built native settlements preserved in the marginal pasture-land lining some of the Cumbrian valleys have been well known since the detailed survey in RCHM 1936. Some like Ewe Close and Severals were substantial villages which achieved considerable economic success. Others such as Eller Beck near Kirkby Lonsdale (Lowndes 1964) were modest farmsteads, exploiting the alluvium of the valley floor for arable and the adjacent uplands for grazing. In both cases small stock-compounds are found, while some of the larger sites are associated with extensive dyke systems, enclosing units of as much as 30 acres (Jones 1975). Whether the morphological distinction between varying forms of "enclosed" and "agglomerate" settlements advanced by Webster (1971) will prove to be meaningful in terms either of chronology or of agricultural policy is something that awaits proper excavated evidence. Most of the field-systems and habitation nuclei are not closely dated and appear to represent a complex palimpsest of features. What is not in doubt is that these sites, some of which have been demonstrated to have been in occupation during the Roman period, belong to a phase when the major valleys such as those of the Lune, Kent and Eden were the focus of an intensive and efficient agricultural system. Survey work in the Lune valley, for example, is beginning to demonstrate a pattern of settlement where each site exploited one of the low spurs that line the margins of the lower ground. Similarly, in the south-western part of Cumbria, known farms are distributed in an apparently regular way at the junction between the coastal plain and the lower fell slopes. There seems little doubt that this was a deliberate choice of position: the lowlands were best suited to arable, better-class grazing and woodland (for pannage), while the uplands provided summer pasture. It is worth observing, however, that cereals seem, on the evidence of pollen diagrams (Pennington 1970), to have been cultivated at higher altitudes than in the present day.

What has not been appreciated until recently is the density of these settlements. Most of the better-preserved stone-built sites have survived only because they are found on marginal land, barely touched by recent ploughing. Those on the lowest hill-slopes have been much more vulnerable to late medieval and modern agricultural development and have been largely obliterated. Even sherd-scatters are rare since the native sites seldom produce much in the way of finds. Thus, in the Ravenglass area, very extensive field walking by Mr Cherry has yielded remarkably little in the way of settlements below the 150 m contour. Similarly, in central and north Lancashire, the known sites are largely confined to the edges of the higher ground. That settlement did extend onto the lower contours has, however, now become apparent from the results of recent aerial survey. The upper Eden valley and its tributaries, for example, can be shown to contain a very considerable number of sites in the cultivated ground along the periphery of the alluvial floor (Higham and Jones 1975). One has recently been excavated at Crosshill Farm, near Penrith: it proved to comprise a circular enclosure, defended by a ditch and rampart. Inside was a circular house, occupied during the second century. This was subsequently replaced in the later Roman period by several rectangular buildings (Jones *in* Frere 1977, 377). Similarly, on the undulating eskers of the lowland to the south of the Solway, block-flying in the drought of 1974-5 yielded àn extraordinary concentration of settlement enclosures, field-systems and trackways (Higham and Jones 1975), reminiscent of the Roman landscape on the silt-lands of the Cambridgeshire Fens. Some of these sites cluster in the vicinity of forts such as Old Carlisle; but the overall distribution is more remarkable for the even way in which the sand and gravel ridges were exploited than for its focus upon the Roman military centres. A few of the farms have been tested by excavation (Blake 1959) and have disclosed evidence for timber buildings and a meagre level of Romanisation. On the other hand, the contemporaneity of many elements of this landscape has been put beyond doubt, a conclusion that is broadly confirmed by the result of pollen-analysis (Pennington 1970). It is interesting to note, however, that pollen diagrams, in conjunction with radio-carbon dates, indicates that deforestation of the Cumbrian lowlands was a feature of the late Roman and early medieval periods. It is perhaps too tempting to assume that the main stimulus to development was the presence of the Roman garrisons; in reality, factors like population-growth may prove to be more important elements in the explanation of this densely settled landscape.

The question of the relationship between the forts and their *territorium* has recently come under greater scrutiny. Using Polybius's figures (vi, 39, 13) of an allowance of 11

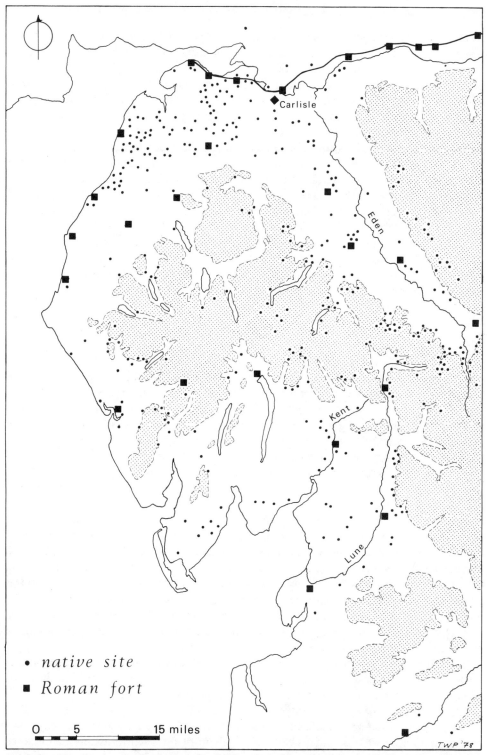

Fig. 144. – Map showing the distribution of probable and possible native sites, occupied in the Roman period, in Cumbria and northern Lancashire, together with the principal Roman forts. Stippled: land over 250 m. Sources: Higham and Jones 1975; Cumbria County Council records (courtesy of T. Clare); Lancashire Field Officer records (courtesy of A. C. H. Olivier).

bushels of wheat per soldier per year, Manning (1975) has suggested that a cultivated area of some 700 acres could have provided the grain requirement for an auxiliary fort with a quingenary cohort. Much of this ration must have been produced locally, presumably from the fertile alluvial plains that surround so many of the forts. Native sites, demonstrably occupied in the Roman period, lie very close to many of the forts (for example at Burrow in Lonsdale and Low Borrow Bridge) and their produce must have been partially directed at the needs of the garrison. Livestock, on the other hand, may not always have been reared locally. Fifield has shown in his study of the Watercrook bones that cattle were slaughtered mainly when mature, implying that they were brought to the site on the hoof. They may well have been raised on the grazing in the uplands to the east or north of the site. Pork, which from the meat-weight figures seems to have been of greater importance than mutton and lamb, also contributed to the diet. The pigs were no doubt reared in local woodlands, whose presence is attested by red-deer bones from the ditches of the fort. The military records from sites like Vindolanda (Bowman 1974) shows that livestock was often purchased, while Davies (1971) has demonstrated the fallacy of the view that the soldiers' diet was commonly vegetarian. Meat was in fact a very significant element, as both literary and archaeological evidence prove.

EARLY MILITARY OCCUPATION

It was for long thought that the Cumbrian region, or at least the Cumbrian coastal plain, came under direct Roman control during the governorship of Agricola. Flavian occupation was envisaged at Maryport, Papcastle, Caermote, Watercrook and elsewhere (Frere 1974, Fig. 3), indicating a network of forts on the pattern of Agricolan occupation in Scotland. The case began to crumble with Hartley's rejection of Ambleside as an Agricolan site (Hartley 1966, 12) and the eventual realisation that Maryport (Fig. 148) could not be dated this early (Jarrett 1976). In fact only two forts can be proved Agricolan, both as a result of very recent or current work (although there must be others). One is Lancaster, where excavation in 1975 on Castle Hill disclosed a turf rampart with, behind it, the *intervallum* road and timber-framed barracks of a hitherto unknown phase of building (Potter *in* Jones and Shotter 1978). Several sherds of samian form 29 were found in these levels which, with other finds, confirm that occupation dated to before *c.* 85. The other site is Carlisle, which is now yielding abundant evidence for an early-mid Flavian military presence, again dated by form 29s. Indeed, when the new data are set out, there may well be a compelling case for suggesting occupation as early as Petillius Cerealis, as has long been suggested. We may recall that there is good reason to suppose that the marching camps on the Stainmore Pass are earlier than Agricola (Richmond and McIntyre 1934; Hartley 1966, 11), and Carlisle would have been a logical objective for an army using this cross-country route.

Given the absence of proven Agricolan sites in the Lake District, we can assume that Agricola's line-of-march took him up the Lune valley from Lancaster, through the gorge at Tebay, and then onwards over Shap and down the Eden corridor. Burrow in Lonsdale (Hildyard 1954), Low Borrow Bridge (Hildyard and Gillam 1951) and the Eden valley forts have yet to yield any significant quantity of Flavian material and it is not clear how he may have secured this route; eventually a chain of forts will probably be disclosed although, as at Corbridge, these may not necessarily be found beneath the known sites.

The flat valley north of Tebay would, for example, be a likely setting for the precursor of Low Borrow Bridge; this strategically important site was commanded by a castle (Castle Howe) in medieval times. Another possibility is Park House, five miles south of Carlisle, where a single-period turf-and-timber fort (but interpreted by Higham and Jones (1975, 34) as a farmstead) has been located (Bellhouse 1954). It seems probable, however, that a strategy of containment was employed where forts straddled the major lines of communication; these were the tactics in north-east Scotland and initially those in Galloway too, and would have made good sense in an upland region like the Cumbrian massif with restricted east-west communications. Tacitus (*Agricola* 20) in fact notes that "when he had achieved sufficient by striking terror into the enemy, he turned to clemency and held out the allurements of peace. In this way many *civitates* which to that day had acted independently of each other gave hostages, laid aside their anger and allowed their territory to be demarcated by forts and garrisons (*praesidiis castellisque circumdatae*)". Presumably, then, a treaty was made with the Lakeland tribes, enforced by the presence of Roman garrisons along the main north-south corridor.

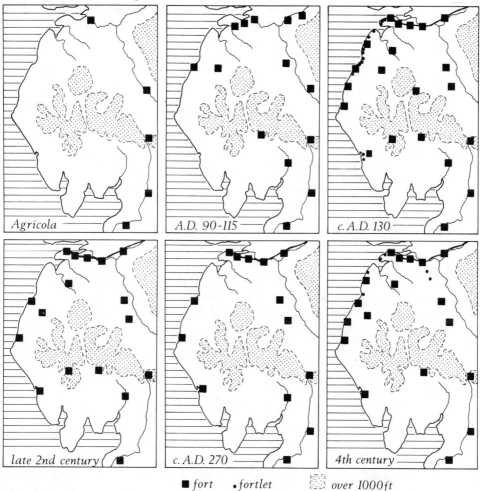

■ *fort*   • *fortlet*   ▦ *over 1000ft*

FIG. 145. – Successive phases in the Roman military occupation of Cumbria.

It was not until the late Flavian period, however, that the Romans brought this region under direct military control. It followed the first phases of the withdrawal from Scotland and, despite Tactitus's well known phrase, *perdomita Britannia et statim missa*, must have been seen as an important act of consolidation. The best dated site is Watercrook which on the evidence of samian and coins, is likely to have been founded in the 90s. Ambleside I, Caermote I (Bellhouse 1960), Kirkbride (Bellhouse and Richardson 1975) and Maryport (Jarrett 1976; Fig. 148) also appear to have been first occupied at this time, supplementing a chain of forts up the Lune-Eden valley corridor. How complete the known pattern may be is a matter of conjecture; but, given the rather sparse distribution, it is likely that other sites remain to be found. South-west Cumbria, for example, is one puzzling blank, especially since the known fort at Ravenglass was not founded until Hadrianic times. In fact, there are quite large quantities of Roman material from this region, especially the Cartmel and Furness peninsulae, which cannot be explained entirely by native settlement. Coins are particularly prolific (Shotter, forthcoming) and include a *denarius* of Otho from Urswick and a *sestertius* of Nero from Broughton. The other issues for which we have records all represent second to fourth-century emperors, but with six findspots in the Furness area and five round Cartmel, underline the strength of Roman penetration into this region. It would be most surprising if some of these finds do not reflect a military presence at one or more points along this fertile and vulnerable coastal belt.

The Trajanic period saw a perceptible strengthening of the network. Although the known fort at Ravenglass was not yet in occupation, the earliest phase at Hardknott may date to this period, since there are Trajanic forms amongst the pottery (Collingwood 1921). Building work is also attested at Lancaster (*RIB* 604), while to the north the frontier line settled upon the Stanegate, with forts at Kirkbride, Carlisle, Old Church, Brampton and Nether Denton; a newly discovered site to the south of Burgh-by-Sands also probably fits into this system. However, it is equally clear that the Flavian-Trajanic network did not exist for long before there was some modification. Several sites have yielded indications of a period of abandonment during this time, including Lancaster and Ambleside. Similarly there are grounds for suggesting a reduced garrison or break in occupation at Watercrook, Maryport, Caermote and Kirkby Thore. While we cannot assume a single date for these garrison movements, there are a number of likely historical contexts; amongst them is the probability of a call for reinforcements for Trajan's wars in Dacia in the early years of the second century, as well as hints of trouble at the time of Hadrian's accession (Frere 1974, 145-8). But the details of the archaeological evidence are still elusive and the individual fort-sequences unclear. Only when we come to the reorganisation of the frontier in Hadrian's reign (discussed below) is the full pattern of control in any way clear.

HADRIAN'S WALL AND THE SECOND CENTURY

The construction of a continuous *limes* between the Solway Firth and the Tyne estuary entailed a substantial re-deployment of troops. In the east and south Pennines the policy was largely directed at a reduction of the garrisons, with numerous forts being evacuated at this time (Hartley 1966). In contrast, west of the Pennines there was every effort to consolidate the Roman hold over the region by a programme of rebuilding, combined with the foundation of some new forts. Re-deployment of troops in the north-west is implied by the evacuation of Kirkbride (Bellhouse and Richardson 1975), of the Stanegate forts and fortlets, and possibly of Papcastle (Birley 1963); and by the laying out of new forts at Caermote (Bellhouse 1960), Kirkby Thore (Charlesworth 1964), Ambleside (Collingwood and Richmond 1969, 35), Hardknott (Wright 1965), Ravenglass, Watercrook (both late Hadrianic sites) and probably Old Carlisle (Birley 1951). The stone forts at Low Borrow Bridge (Hildyard and Gillam 1951) and Burrow in Lonsdale (Hildyard 1954) may also belong to Hadrian's reign. At the same time the curtain was extended down the vulnerable low-lying coastal plain of north-western Cumbria by the construction of a chain of milefortlets and turrets (Potter 1977) together with the forts of Beckfoot, Maryport, Burrow Walls and Moresby. As Jones (1976) has shown, this system was linked by a continuous palisade, an arrangement that is reminiscent of contemporary fortifications between the Rhine and Danube (Schönberger 1969), though that frontier across the *Agri Decumates* was much more substantially constructed.

Neither the full extent or the detailed chronology of the Cumbrian coastal defences has yet been worked out, however. The assumption that the milefortlets extended only as far as St Bees Head has now been shown to be implausible since the earliest military occupation of Ravenglass unquestionably takes the form of an early Hadrianic fortlet. Moreover, the likelihood of a similar site, one Roman mile to the south of Ravenglass fort (cf. Chap. I), implies a regular arrangement of fortlets and turrets as in north Cumbria. How far this system may have continued is unknown, but it would be surprising, given the topography of south-west Cumbria, if it was not carried on to Millom or even Barrow-in-Furness. It is a most striking indication of the enormous lengths to which the Romans were prepared to go to protect the western flanks of their frontiers from sea-borne attack. The Hadrianic *limes* in Britain was clearly much more elaborate than we have hitherto supposed.

That the coastal defence system underwent significant changes from the original blueprint is equally clear. In particular, the decision to add forts to the chain of milefortlets and turrets seems, as on the Wall, to have been a late one. At Ravenglass, as we saw in Chap. I, the fortlet was rebuilt as an auxiliary fort in late Hadrianic times; similarly an inscription from Moresby (*RIB* 801) shows that the fort there was not completed until after 128. In the hinterland of southern Cumbria, too, the decision to build stone forts may well have come in the 130s. While the building inscription from Hardknott cannot be more closely assigned than 117-138 (Wright 1965), it is nevertheless clear from our work at Watercrook that this fort was still under construction in the late 130s or early 140s. It could well be then that the forts of southern Cumbria were, in the main, a feature of late rather than early Hadrianic times.

Early in the 140s, frontier strategy changed with the building of the Antonine wall. As Hartley (1972) has shown, this had drastic repercussions upon the garrisons on Hadrian's Wall and in many parts of the hinterland. Many forts were completely evacuated or retained only on a care-and-maintenance basis. In the north-west of England it is still difficult, however, to estimate in detail the overall scale of the evacuation. At sites such as Biglands, the first milefortlet of the Cumberland coast chain (Potter 1977), the buildings were clearly demolished; the debris was then heaped up in the gateway and burnt. At Watercrook, too, it looks as though the fort wall was abandoned when only half-built and the site deserted. Elsewhere, the pattern is far from clear. Excavations on Castle Hill in

Lancaster indicated the demolition of structures about this time (Potter *in* Jones and Shotter 1978) and the numismatic evidence is in favour of a period of evacuation. But there are about fifteen samian stamps in Lancaster Museum which have parallels on the Antonine Wall and some of the coarse-ware from the site is also indicative of early Antonine occupation. Similarly, at Ribchester, Maryport, Ravenglass and Ambleside (Burkett 1977) a case can be made either for continuous occupation or for some activity in the early to mid Antonine period. Such evidence as we have suggests therefore that the withdrawal of troops from the north-west in the early 140s was not by any means total and that a substantial garrison may have been left in the region.

Even though the true size of the Antonine army in the north-west remains to be demonstrated, there is now a rather sharper focus upon the processes of the withdrawal from the Antonine wall. It has long been recognized that this divided into two principal phases: a short though total evacuation of the Forth-Clyde line in *c.* 155-8, traditionally explained by a Brigantian uprising, followed after a short reoccupation by the permanent abandonment of the Scottish frontier. Apart from some attempts to define a third phase of occupation upon the Antonine Wall (an idea now largely discredited: Frere 1974, 180 and fn.31), the debate has centred on the date of the final withdrawal. Despite some lingering doubts (e.g. Jarrett 1976, 18-19), the evidence does seem to converge upon *c.* 163 as the most appropriate termination for activity on the Antonine Wall. This is the conclusion from study of the samian and coins (Hartley 1972) and follows closely upon the death of Antoninus Pius in 161: it was very possibly imperial ambition that motivated the creation of this new frontier line, and Pius's death that brought about its abandonment.

In the north-west it is the frontier sites on the Hadrianic *limes* that best reflect these vicissitudes. Very clear evidence comes, for example, from the first milefortlet on the Cumberland coast, at Biglands House (Potter 1977). Here the Hadrianic fortlet was twice recommissioned (Fig. 146) after its initial demolition. Moreover, since the pottery and coins from the site terminate in the later second century, we can be sure that this sequence of rebuilding and evacuation took place between *c.* 140 and 180/200: it is reasonable to assume, therefore, that Biglands II corresponds with the brief re-occupation of Hadrian's Wall in *c.* 155-8 and that Biglands III marks the return to the Tyne-Solway *limes* in *c.* 163. Similarly, at Bowness on Solway, the terminal fort at the western end of the Wall, work in 1976 showed that there were three phases of timber buildings during the second century; here, too, it is tempting to interpret these in terms of frontier changes. The other sites of the Cumberland coast have yet to be examined with these questions in mind but it is already clear that many sites were evacuated *c.* 140 and subsequently re-occupied. At MF5, Cardurnock (Simpson and Hodgson 1947), for example, at least one Antonine phase was identified, while a number of other milefortlets (including MF16 and 22) and turrets (T12a, 12b, 15a, 16b) have also yielded explicit evidence for rebuilding in the mid to late second century (Potter 1977). Whether the whole Cumberland coast system of defences was revived after the abandonment of the Antonine Wall is not yet known: but it is now certain that parts of the chain were recommissioned, possibly as at Biglands on two separate occasions, reflecting the fluctuations in the frontier line between *c.* 155 and 165.

The effect of these changes on the hinterland of north-west England has still, as we indicated above, to be worked out. Watercrook was certainly re-occupied in the period *c.* 150-70, and in the governorship of Calpurnius Agricola (*c.* 163-6) building work (Fig. 147) is attested at Ribchester (*RIB* 589) and probably at Hardknott (*RIB* 793). Garrison

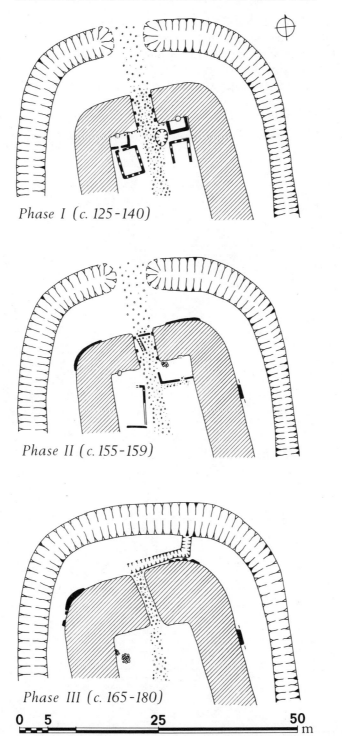

Phase I (c. 125-140)

Phase II (c. 155-159)

Phase III (c. 165-180)

FIG. 146. – Biglands milefortlet: the sequence of occupation (source: Potter 1977).

changes may well have initiated this work, the aim being to tighten the hold over this region. This military structure did not, however, remain unaltered for very long. By the early 180s there was once again campaigning in Scotland, under Ulpius Marcellus, provoked by attacks from north of the Wall (Dio 73, 8), and in 197 the removal of the Roman army in Britain to support the imperial ambitions of Clodius Albinus most

DATED INSCRIPTIONS A.D. 163 - 208

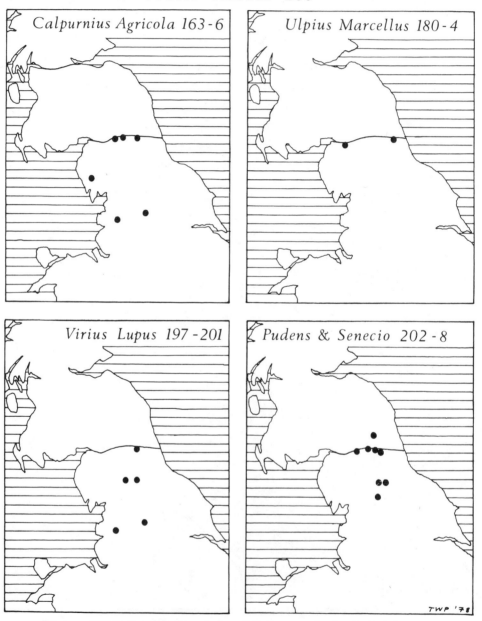

FIG. 147. – Distribution of dated inscriptions of the later second and early third centuries.

probably provided another opportunity for enemy attack. Virius Lupus, the successor of Albinus, was in fact forced to purchase peace from the northern tribes (Dio 76, 5, 4) and building inscriptions dating to his governorship (Fig. 147) show widespread repair work in the Pennine region. Trouble seems to have persisted into the early third century, although the building inscriptions of 202-8 cluster within the frontier region (Fig. 147), perhaps indicating a rather different focus for the attacks or at any rate progress made with defensive measures. Eventually Severus himself came to Britain, and was soon involved in extended campaigning in Scotland, which led to major administrative and military changes.

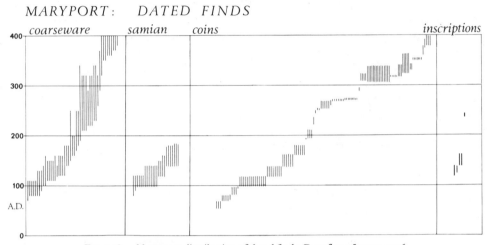

MARYPORT: DATED FINDS

FIG. 148. – Maryport: distribution of dated finds. Data from Jarrett 1976.

In the north-west of England, the events of this period have still to be properly measured in archaeological terms. That there were garrison changes at many sites during this period is well known from the epigraphic record and has already been given due emphasis (e.g. Frere 1974, 195). Similarly it is now evident that the Cumberland coast defences, except for some or all of the forts, were abandoned at some point between *c.* 180 and 200, matching the declining use of the milecastles and turrets on Hadrian's Wall. Given that a fort like Ravenglass could be successfully attacked and burnt, as we have seen in Chap. I, these small coastal sites must have seemed exceptionally vulnerable, as well as expensive in manpower. The move to create much more massive defences had as yet hardly begun but, even so, a system of turf-built milefortlets and small stone turrets may well have been thought superfluous by the late second century. For the rest there is comparatively little that we can say about this period. Ravenglass is the only north-western site where enemy attack is indicated by the evidence, underlining its vulnerability to sea-borne raids. The fort was immediately rebuilt, probably because it formed a harbour for a naval squadron. Other forts, however, appear to have been run down from early in the third century. Occupation lapsed over part of the interior of Bowness on Solway, the garrison at Lancaster may have been reduced and other sites, such as Watercrook and Hardknott, were probably evacuated. The impression is that, after the tumultuous events of *c.* 180-210, there came a long period of peace, when the north-west was controlled by a smaller and more thinly spread garrison.

THE THIRD AND FOURTH CENTURIES

We have already discussed the difficulties of recognising occupation in the first half of the third century: coins are comparatively rare and pottery of this period does not lend itself to close dating. Consequently it is difficult to estimate the precise course of events in this part of the third century. There is some help from epigraphy, however. Inscriptions dating to the reign of Severus Alexander (222-35) are known from Ribchester (*RIB* 587) and Old Penrith (*RIB* 919, 929), as well as from Chesters, Netherby, Chesterholm, South Shields, Great Chesters and High Rochester. The reigns of Gordian III (238-44) and Philip I (244-9) also saw widespread activity; there are inscriptions of this period from Ribchester (*RIB* 897, 9) and Old Penrith (*RIB* 915) and a new fort was founded at this time at Lanchester in County Durham, where the headquarters-building, armouries and a bath-building with a basilica required complete reconstruction (*RIB* 1091, 2). At Lancaster, too, a bath-house and basilica are described as *vetustate conlabsum (sic)*, their restoration belonging to the period 262-6 (*RIB* 605). These inscriptions may be taken therefore to demonstrate activity at a number of sites, possibly at some of them (Lancaster is a likely example) preceded by a period of desertion. On the other hand, a number of forts have yet to yield any convincing evidence of occupation at this time, amongst them Watercrook, Burrow in Lonsdale, Low Borrow Bridge, Kirkby Thore, Caermote, Ambleside, Hardknott, Beckfoot and Burrow Walls.

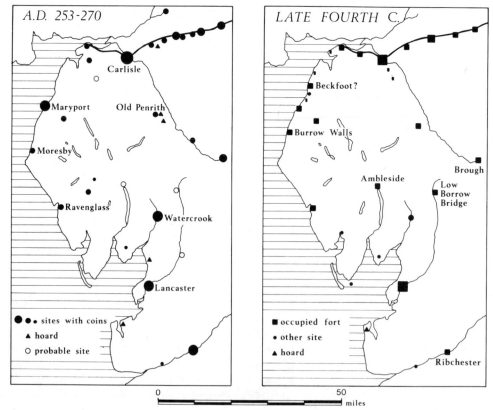

FIG. 149. – Distribution of Roman military sites and coin-finds in Cumbria and northern Lancashire in 253-70 and the late fourth century.

During the third quarter of the third century, however, there are hints of change in the situation. Interpretation is helped by the enormous abundance of contemporary coins: at Watercrook, for example, we have shown how the final accumulation in the east guard-chamber of the north-east gate can be assigned to the period between *c.* 265-90, on the basis of the numismatic evidence. The distribution and volume of the coins of this period is of some interest (Fig. 149). Whilst they are widespread (there being examples even from long-deserted sites like Kirkbride and Hardknott), the inland forts such as Low Borrow Bridge, Ambleside and Burrow in Lonsdale have so far yielded comparatively small collections. The sites along or accessible from the coast, on the other hand, have tended to produce a very much larger volume of finds, particularly from Maryport and Lancaster and, of the valley sites, from Watercrook and Ribchester. Given that Lancaster was under restoration in 262-6 (*RIB* 605) and that Watercrook was re-occupied in the same period, it may be that these finds should be viewed in the context of a reconstruction of some of the coastal defences (perhaps with a limited reoccupation of some sites in the hinterland). If so, it is tempting to relate this activity to the building programme of the Saxon Shore forts of south-eastern England (Johnson 1976, Johnston 1977), many of which may have been constructed as a response to the barbarian attacks on Gaul in 276 (Cunliffe 1977). Alternatively, a strengthening of the coastal and valley forts could be seen as the logical sequel to sea-borne attacks, which is the likeliest explanation for the numerous coin hoards of this period in Lancashire and Cumbria (Shotter 1978 and forthcoming). Indeed, as we have seen in Chap. I, the fort at Ravenglass was burnt down at some point in the later third or early fourth century, quite probably as the result of a raid from the sea, Whether this attack can be related specifically to the hiatus that ensued from Carausius's attempt to set up an independent empire is a matter of conjecture, but it does demonstrate how necessary coastal defences had become at this time.

Unfortunately, there is little evidence to show how these defences may have developed over the next few decades. An exception is Lancaster, where we know of the construction of a new fort. It is represented by the massive foundations of the Wery Wall, laid across an older bath-house. A deep V-shaped ditch was dug in front of the wall and the remains are known of at least one external tower. It would appear, therefore, that the Wery Wall forms part of a defensive arrangement that closely parallels the architecture of the Saxon Shore forts. The construction of the fort is not very precisely dated but a *terminus post quem* is provided by a coin of 326 from beneath the wall (Jones and Shotter 1978). This shows that the building work was substantially later than the main series of Saxon Shore forts, but it may be close in date to the fort of Pevensey. Caer Gybi on Anglesey may also have been built at this time and it is tempting to correlate this activity with the visit of Constans in 342 (Frere 1974, 387-9). In addition, there was a new coastal fort, constructed sometime in the first half of the fourth century, at Burrow Walls (Bellhouse 1955), while Maryport and Ravenglass were certainly in garrison, though their defences were apparently left unmodified. The impression, therefore, is of a strong chain of shore forts, probably with Lancaster as the command centre of the system in the north-west. Moreover, there is evidence that at least three of the second-century milefortlets along the Cumberland coast (MF5, 12, 20: Potter 1977) may also have been recommissioned sometime in the fourth century, further emphasising the importance that was attached to this line of defence.

In the hinterland of the north-west the details of the fourth-century network are much more obscure. Whilst we know that there was extensive rebuilding on Hadrian's Wall in the early fourth century and that several new forts were established in the north-east (Wilkes 1965; Frere 1974, 384), the extent to which this affected Cumbria is uncertain. That the garrison of the region was strengthened seems clear enough, for fourth-century material is common at numerous sites. But we still lack sufficient evidence to comment upon either the overall distribution or the individual history of the forts. Two small fortlets in the Eden valley were certainly occupied late in the fourth century – Wreay Hall (Bellhouse 1953) and Barrock Fell (Collingwood 1931) – and were probably intended to guard the main road to the south; but nothing is known either of their internal arrangements or of the size of the garrison. They may well belong to the Theodosian reconstruction that followed the Great Picts' War of 367-8 (Tomlin 1974). Late fourth-century pottery is also recorded from many of the forts (Fig. 149) but there is structural evidence from few sites and, as we have seen at Watercrook, such finds may not always indicate military activity. That many of the coastal forts remained in garrison in the period is certain from work at Lancaster, Ravenglass and Maryport, where we can reasonably suppose occupation down to the end of the fourth or the beginning of the fifth century. The prevalence of timber-framed buildings of this date is worthy of note, with examples from Ribchester, Ravenglass, Maryport, Bowness on Solway and a number of Wall forts; but their form seems to vary widely, from small irregularly constructed buildings, as at Bowness, to versions of the standard barrack-block, as at Ravenglass. Although the use of timber provides a common link, the disparities in architectural style emphasise the strong local traditions that emerged towards the end of the Roman period. Despite the indications that a widespread network of forts was maintained in the late fourth century, it is hard to envisage this as a unified military structure: the pattern seems to become increasingly that of a localised system of defence.

The latest stages in the history of the frontier region are, however, totally obscure. The evidence from the excavations of the latest levels of the military sites indicates only that the forts were evacuated without demolition or destruction of the buildings. We cannot provide a close date for this final abandonment although it is probably significant that few emerged as medieval foci. There was evidently a significant hiatus between the late Roman and early medieval periods but, until some of the centres of fifth- and sixth-century occupation are identified, we cannot hope to comment in any meaningful way upon this transition. Together with the acquisition of a fuller sample of Roman material, the discovery of sites that are transitional between late classical and medieval times must now provide a major target for north-western studies.

BIBLIOGRAPHY

Bellhouse, R. L., 1953. "A Roman post at Wreay Hall near Carlisle", CW2 liii, 49-51.

—— 1954. "A newly discovered Roman fort at Park House near Carlisle", CW2 liv, 9-16.

—— 1955. "The Roman fort at Burrow Walls near Workington", CW2 lv, 30-45.

—— 1960. "The Roman forts near Caermote", CW2 lx, 20-3.

Bellhouse, R. L. and Richardson, G. G. S., 1975. "The Roman site at Kirkbride, Cumberland", CW2 lxxv, 58-90.

Birley, E. B., 1951. "The Roman fort and settlement at Old Carlisle". CW2 li, 16-39.

—— 1961. Research on Hadrian's Wall. Kendal.

—— 1963. "Roman Papcastle", CW2 lxiii, 96-125.

Blake, B., 1959. "Excavations of native (Iron Age) sites in Cumberland, 1956-58", CW2 lix, 1-14.

Bowman, A. K., 1974. "Roman military records from Vindolanda". *Britannia* V, 360-78.

Burkett, M. E., 1977. "Rescue dig in Ambleside". CW2 lxxvii, 179-80.

Charlesworth, D. 1964. "Recent work at Kirkby Thore." CW2 lxiv. 63-75.

—— 1965. "Excavations at Papcastle 1961-2", CW2 lxv, 102-14.

Collingwood, R. G., 1921. "Explorations in the Roman fort at Ambleside (fourth year, 1920) and at other sites on the tenth Iter", CW2 xxi, 1-42.

—— 1931. "A Roman fortlet on Barrock Fell, near Low Hesket", CW2 xxxi, 111-18.

Collingwood, R. G. and Richmond, I. A., 1969. *The Archaeology of Roman Britain*. London, Methuen.

Cunliffe, B., 1977. "The Saxon Shore – some problems and misconceptions". *In* Johnston 1977, 1-6.

Davies, R. W., 1971. "The Roman military diet". *Britannia* II, 122-42.

Frere, S. S., 1974. *Britannia. A history of Roman Britain*. Cardinal.

—— 1977. "Roman Britain in 1976". *Britannia* VIII, 356-425.

Gillam, J. P., 1970. *Types of Roman coarse pottery in Northern England*. Newcastle.

Hartley, B. R., 1966. "Some problems of the military occupation of the north of England", *Northern History*, 1, 7-20,.

—— 1972. "The Roman occupations of Scotland: the evidence of samian ware". *Britannia* III, 1-55.

Hassall, M. W. C., 1976. "Britain in the Notitia". *In* Goodburn, R. and Bartholomew, P. (eds.), *Aspects of the Notitia Dignitatum*. British Archaeological Reports, Supplementary Series 15, 103-18.

Higham, N. J. and Jones, G. D. B., 1975. "Frontiers, forts and farmers: Cumbrian aerial survey 1974-5", *Arch. J.*, 132, 16-53.

Hildyard, E. J. W., 1954. "Excavations at Burrow in Lonsdale, 1952-53", CW2 liv, 66-101.

Hildyard, E. J. W. and Gillam, J. P., 1951. "Renewed excavation at Low Borrow Bridge", CW2 li, 40-66.

Jarrett, M. G., 1969. *The Roman frontier in Wales*. University of Wales. Revised edition of V. E. Nash-Williams's volume.

—— 1976. *Maryport, Cumbria: a Roman fort and its garrison*. CW2 Extra Series 22, Kendal.

Johnson, S., 1976. *The Roman Forts of the Saxon Shore*, London, Elek.

Johnston, D. E., 1976. (ed.) *The Saxon Shore*. CBA Research Report, 18.

Jones, G. D. B., 1975. "The North-Western interface". *In* Fowler, P. J. (ed.), *Recent work in Rural Archaeology*, 93-106. Moonraker Press.

—— 1976. "The western extension of Hadrian's Wall: Bowness to Cardurnock". *Britannia* VII, 236-43.

Jones, G. D. B. and Shotter, D. C. A., 1978. *Roman Lancaster*. In press.

Lowndes, R. A. C., 1964. "Excavation of a Romano-British farmstead at Eller Beck", CW2 lxiv, 6-13.

Manning, W. H., 1975. "Economic influences on land use in the military areas of the Highland Zone during the Roman period". *In* Evans, J. G., Limbrey, S., Cleere, H. (eds.), *The effect of man on the landscape: the Highland Zone*. CBA Research Report 11, 112-16.

Pennington, W., 1970. "Vegetation history in the north-west of England: a regional synthesis". *In* Walker, D. and West, R. G. (eds.), *Studies in the Vegetational History of the British Isles*, 41-79. C.U.P.

Potter, T. W., 1977. "The Biglands milefortlet and the Cumberland coast defences". *Britannia* VIII, 149-83.

RCHM 1936. *Westmorland*. Royal Commission on Historical Monuments (England). HMSO.

RIB. Collingwood, R. G. and Wright, R. P. *The Roman Inscriptions of Britain*, I, *Inscriptions on Stone*. 1965. Oxford.

Richmond, I. A. and McIntyre, J., 1934. "The Roman camps at Reycross and Crackenthorpe". CW2 xxxiv, 50-61.

Shotter, D. C. A., 1978. "Roman coin hoards from Lancashire". *Lancs Arch. J.* 1. In press.

—— forthcoming. "The Roman occupation of North-west England: the Coin Evidence". CW2 in preparation.

Schönberger, H. 1969. "The Roman Frontier in Germany: an archaeological survey". *JRS* 59, 144-97.

Simpson, F. G. and Hodgson, K. S., 1947. "The coastal mile-fortlet at Cardurnock", CW2 xxxxvii, 78-127.

Tomlin, R. S. O., 1974. "The date of the 'Barbarian Conspiracy' ", *Britannia* V, 303-9.

Webster, R. A., 1971. "A morphological study of Romano-British settlements in Westmorland", CW2 lxxi, 64-74.

Wright, R. P., 1965. "A Hadrianic building inscription from Hardknott", CW2 lxv, 169-75.

Wilkes, J. J., 1965. "Early fourth-century rebuilding in Hadrian's Wall forts". *In* Jarrett, M. G. and Dobson, B. (eds.), *Britain and Rome*, 114-38. Kendal.

INDEX

African red slip ware, 120

Agricola, 145, 152, 177, 352, 356-7; coin evidence, 296

agricultural evidence, 6, 34, 134-6, 354

ala Augusta, 315

ala I Herculea, 315

ala Sebosiana, 73-4

Alfenus Senecio, 34

Allectus, 40

Alone (Alione), 316-20

amber, 218

Ambleside, 5, 141, 147; early history, 177; name, 315-20; general history, 351 f.

amphora stamps, 122, 268

animal remains, *see* faunal remains

Antonine Itinerary 315, 316-7

Antonine Wall, 34, 153, 157, 160, 178-9, 297, 359

archers 222, 223

armlets 72, 232, 234

arrowheads, iron, 159, 160, 161, 193, 222-3; Bronze Age flint example, 326

Barburgh Mill, 25

Barnscar, 7

barrack-blocks, 19, 25-34, 145, 323, 334; sizes, 26-7; double median walls, 31

Barrock Fell, 351, 366

bath-house, 3, 143, 195

beads, 73, 218, 232-3, 337

Beaker pottery, 234, 268

Beckermet, 18

Beckfoot, 29, 46, 147, 351, 352, 359, 364

Bellhouse, R. L., 6

Benwell, 29

Bewcastle, 351

Biglands, 10, 351, 359, 360

Birdoswald, 297, 315, 318, 351

Birley, E. B., 5

Birrens, 31

black-burnished ware, analysis of, 337

bone, objects of, 72, 218-9

botanical analysis, Ravenglass, 133-6

Bowes, 315

Bowness on Solway, 45; name, 318-9; excavations at, 321-48

Brampton kilns, 35

Brantrake Moss, 6

Braughing, flooding at, 197

Braystones, 8, 315

breastwork of fortlet at Ravenglass, 17

Bronze Age occupation 6-7, 100, 234, 326

bronze, objects of 65-72, 206-17, 336-7

brooches, 35, 65-9, 206-12, 336

Brough under Stainmore, 75, 351, 352; *vicus* at, 194; name, 315-20

Brougham, 195, 351, 352; name, 315-20

Burgh by Sands, 318, 358

Burrow in Lonsdale, 139, 147, 351, 356, 359, 364; name, 315-20

Burrow Walls, 42, 46, 351, 352, 359, 364, 365

Caermote, 147, 351, 356, 358, 359, 364

cairns, 6, 7

calcite-gritted ware, 116-8

Calpurnius Agricola, 179, 360-2

Carausius, 40, 365

Cardean, 27, 31

Cardurnock, 10, 18, 321, 351, 360

Carlisle, 139, 195, 317, 351, 352, 356, 358; medieval pottery from, 342

Cartmel, 18, 139, 358

Carvoran, 21

Carzield, 25

Castlesteads, 297

cattle, 133, 300-3; stall, 183

cavalry, 27, 36, 147, 148; pay, 299

chalets as barrack-blocks, 45

Charlesworth, D. *The glass*, 99-100; *Glass, beads and armlets*, 230-34

Cherry, J., *Settlement evidence*, 6-9

Chester, 45, 295, 315

Chesters, 41, 75, 364

civitas Carvetiorum, 195

Clanoventa, see Glannibanta

claviculae, 155

Clodius Albinus, 33, 362-3

cohors I Aelia Classica, 41-2, 73-4, 315, 318

coins, Roman, 8, 102-5, 180, 291-9, 348, 352-3, 358

Collingwood, R. G., 3, 5, 143

Collingwood, W. G., 8, 143

Contrebis, 316

contubernia, 19, 25-7, 38

Corbridge, 18, 27, 33, 356

Crambeck pottery, 45, 116

Crosshill Farm, Penrith, 354

Cumbrian coast defences, 18, 29, 46, 139, 321, 359

Dalton, 141

defences, fort at Ravenglass, 14-16, 19-21; fort at Watercrook, 144-5, 150-6, 168-76

destruction deposits at Ravenglass, 33-4, 38, 40-1

Diana Veteranorum, 194

Dio, Cassius, 33, 194, 362, 363

ditches, *see* defences
Donaldson, A., *Botanical analysis*, 133-6
duodecim scripta, game of, 76

Eden valley, 139, 354, 358, 366
Ehenside Tarn, 8
Eller Beck, 14, 353
Eskdale, 1, 6
Eskmeals, 9, 18
Ewe Close, 353

Fair, M. C., 4, 6, 118
faunal remains, 133, 299-311, 356
fence beside road at Watercrook, 155-6
Fendoch, 25, 32, 334
Fenland, 197, 354
Fifield, P. W., *The animal bones*, 299-311
flint, objects of, 100, 234
flooding, 10, 148, 180, 195-8
fluvial history at Watercrook, 195-8
fortlets, 14-18
forts, sizes of, 146-7
Furness, 18, 139, 358

games, 36, 76-9
gaming board, 75, 78
gaming counters, 31, 33, 36, 72, 75-87, 220, 232
garrison history, north-western forts, 315-20
gates, 144, 156-64, 322
Gelligaer, 147
gemstones, 46, 97-8, 222
geophysical work at Watercrook, 146, 148
Glannibanta, 315-20
glass, objects of, 36, 99-100, 230-34
graffiti; on gaming counters, 76, 78-87; on pottery, 101-2, 236
granaries, 146, 147
grave, medieval, 47
Great Chesters, 45
Great Picts' War, 20, 41, 366

Hadrian's Wall, 5, 14, 18, 333, 358-63, 366; building of, 29; barracks, 27, 45, 366; second-century history, 34, 178-9, 358 f.; history in A.D. 180-207, 34; history in A.D. 296, 40-1; history in A.D. 367-8, 41; third-century coin evidence, 297; names at western end, 318; epigraphic evidence, 351-2; Wall periods, 353
Haltonchesters, 29, 33, 44
Haltwhistle Burn, 18
Hardknott, 1, 35, 147, 195, 319, 351, 352, 358, 359, 360, 364, 365; road at, 5-6, 18; Calpurnius Agricola inscription, 179
harness equipment, *see* horse equipment
Hartley, K, F. *Mortaria stamps*, 120-2, 268
Helm hillfort (Castlesteads), 141
helmet carrier, 67
Henig, M. *Gemstones*, 97-8
Herodian, 34
Heysham, St. Patrick's Chapel, 47
Hildyard, E. J. W, 143, 145
hillforts, 141

Hincaster, 139, 141-2
Hod Hill, 32
horse bones, 133, 183, 304
horse-equipment, 36, 46, 71, 148, 159, 161, 183, 212, 222, 224, 336; horse-shoes, 224
hospital, 334
Housesteads, 25, 334; chalets at, 95
Hyginus, 14

inscriptions, 101, 143, 236, 351-2, 364
intervallum road, 21, 23-5, 145, 152, 167, 323, 324
iron, objects of, 87-90, 220-9, 336-7
iron working; Eskmeals, 9; Ravenglass, 44, 89; Watercrook, 158, 174-5, 178, 183-4, 222; Bowness, 326; smithing hearths in the North-West, 183-4

jet, objects of, 218

Kendal, 139
Kent, river and valley, 139, 148, 195-8, 354
Kirkbride, 351, 358, 359, 365
Kirkby Lonsdale, 141
Kirkby Thore, 177, 315, 351, 352, 358, 359, 364

Lancaster, 6, 73-4, 139, 177, 194, 299, 356, 358, 359-60, 364-5, 366
Laus Pisonis, 77
lead, objects of, 73-4, 217, 336, 337
leather, objects of, 16, 90-1, 220, 326
Levens Park, 141-2
lime-kiln, post medieval, 195-6
Lockwood, H. *The coarse pottery* (with R. C. Turner), 106-18; *The coarse pottery*, 237-68
Lollius Urbicus, 178
Low Borrow Bridge, 139, 147, 185, 316 f., 351, 352, 356, 359, 364
Ludus Latrunculorum, game of, 77-9
Lune valley, 139, 141, 354, 356, 358

Manchester, 152, 184, 194, 236, 295, 297, 319
Martial, 77
Maryport, 21, 29, 45, 46, 147, 177, 295, 317-20, 321, 351, 352, 356, 358, 359, 360, 365, 366
medallion, eighteenth century, 47, 102
medieval pottery, 118, 342-3
Mesolithic flints, 100, 234
Middleton milestone, 139, 195
Middlewich, 184
milefortlets, 14, 18, 359, 360 f.
Moresby, 29, 73, 147, 318, 351, 352, 359
mortaria stamps, 120-2, 268, 341
Muncaster castle, 45, 105
Muncaster kilns *see* Park House kilns

nails, 87-9, 222, 228, 229
native settlement, 6-9, 141, 353-6
Neolithic flints, 100, 234
Nether Denton, 358
North, O. H., 143, 144, 145
Northwich, 184
Notitia Dignitatum, 42, 73, 317-8, 321

oculist's stamp, 218
Old Carlisle, 147, 183, 194-5, 315, 319, 351, 352, 354, 359
Old Church, Brampton, 358
Old Penrith, 182-3, 194, 319, 351, 364
Olivier, A. C. H. *The brooches*, 65-9, 206-12
ovens, 21-3, 96, 167-8, 190
Ovid, 77

palisade, 14, 16, 92-3, 172, 359
Papcastle, 147, 351, 356, 359
Park House kilns and pottery, 5-6, 23, 106, 118-20; tiles from, 23, 35
Park House, possible fort at, 351, 357
Pen Llystyn, 18, 27
pigs, 304, 356
Platorius Nepos, 29
pollen evidence, 6, 354
Poltross Burn, 351
Polybius, 354
pottery, coarse ware; from Ravenglass, 106-20; from Watercrook, 237-68; from Bowness, 337-42; histograms, 106, 162, 194, 333, 353. *See also* African red slip ware; amphora stamps; Beaker pottery; black-burnished ware; calcite-gritted ware; Crambeck ware; medieval pottery; mortaria stamps; Park House pottery; samian
praetorium, 148
principia, 146, 147-8

Quernmore (Lancaster), kilns at, 6, 35
querns, 8, 94, 183, 234

ramparts, 16, 20-1, 144-5, 150-3
Ravenglass; harbour, 1, 11, 42; topography of 1-5; early fortlet at, 14-18; excavations, 12-60; name and garrison, 315 f.
Ravenna Cosmography, 194, 319-20, 321
red deer, 168, 170, 304, 356
Red House, Corbridge, 28
Ribchester, 45, 152, 179, 194, 236, 295, 297, 299, 315, 360, 364, 365
roads, Roman; Ravenglass-Hardknott, 5-6; Lune valley, 139; Watercrook area, 139-41; Watercrook, north-east road, 164; Watercrook, east road, 185-7
Rudchester, 33, 44

samian, 28-9, 34-5, 123-33, 269-91, 344-7; histograms, 162
Saxon Shore forts, 365
Scalesceugh, 35
sealing, of lead, 73-4
Severals, 353
Severus, 33, 34, 179, 194, 363
sheep, 133, 303, 356
Shotter, D. C. A. *Lead sealing*, 74-5; *Graffiti*, 101-2; *Coins*, 102-5, 291-9, 348; *Epigraphy*, 236; *Watercrook and Ravenglass: the names and the garrisons*, 315-20
shoes, 90, 227
silver, objects of, 205

smithing hearth, 183-4
spearheads, 89, 223
spindle whorls, 9, 72, 73, 218
St. Bees Head, 18, 94, 359
Stanegate, 358-9
Stanwix, 318, 321
storehouses, 323, 334
surgical instruments, 160, 215

Tacitus, 152, 177, 356, 357
Tebay, 357
tent panel, 90; other possible fittings, 92, 220
terni lapilli, game of, 77
Theodosius, 41, 45, 366
Throp, 18, 351
tile, 96, 143, 220; possible tile stamp, 236; *see also*, Park House kilns and Quernmore
Trajan, 358
Troutbeck, 351
Tunnocelum, 42, 73, 318
Turner, R. C. *The identification of the game*, 76-9; *Querns*, 94-5, 234; *Flints*, 100, 234; *The coarse pottery* (with H. Lockwood), 106-18; *The 1976 excavations at Bowness* (with J. H. S. Witherington) 324-37; *Roman and medieval pottery* (with J. H. S. Witherington), 337-43
turrets, 321, 359

Ulpius Marcellus, 34, 362

Vegetius, 150
Vernon, Admiral, 47, 102
vicus; at Ravenglass, 1, 5; at Watercrook, 180-95; at Old Penrith and Old Carlisle, 183-4; history in third and fourth centuries, 194-5; economic evidence, 305
Vindolanda, 317, 356
Virius Lupus, 33, 34, 363
votive plaque, 21

Warborough Nook, 8
Wales, 21
Watercrook; setting, 139-43; previous work 143-5; plan 146-8; defences, 150-6; chronology 176-80; *vicus*, 180-95; name and garrison, 315-20
Walls Castle, Ravenglass (bath-house), 3
Wallsend, 44
whetstones, 75
Wild, F. *Samian Ware*, 123-33; 269-91, 344-7
Wilderspool, 184, 295
window panes, 41, 99, 230
Witherington, J. H. S. *The 1976 excavations at Bowness* (with R. C. Turner), 324-37; *Roman and medieval pottery* (with R. C. Turner), 337-43.
wood, objects of, 92-4
Wreay Hall, 351, 366

York, 78, 197

Plate Ia. – Ravenglass: aerial photograph taken at the end of the 1976 season. The estuary is to the left, the afforested part of the fort platform to the right.

Plate Ib. – The fort platform at Ravenglass seen from the estuary. The tide has nearly reached its highest average summer level.

PLATE IIa. – Ravenglass: general view of the 1976 excavation (trenches B, C, D) looking south.

PLATE IIb. – Ravenglass: ditch of the Hadrianic fortlet (phase 0). Note the metalling of the third-century minor street, sealing the peat fill formed by the demolished rampart. Scale divisions: 50 cm.

PLATE IIIa. – Ravenglass: part of a palisade stake in the cleaning-channel of the ditch of the Hadrianic fortlet (phase o). Scale divisions: 50 cm.

PLATE IIIb. – Ravenglass: palisade-trench of the Hadrianic fortlet (phase o) beneath the metalling of the minor street of the third and fourth centuries. Scale divisions: 50 cm.

PLATE IVa. – Ravenglass: the defences of the later fort.

PLATE IVb. – Ravenglass: the latest of the three ovens at the back of the rampart. Late third/early fourth centuries. Scale: 1 metre.

PLATE Va. – Ravenglass: an earlier tiled oven at the back of the rampart, with four tiles from a later rebuild still in position. Scale: 1 metre.

PLATE Vb. – Ravenglass: stone-lined drain of fourth-century date, along the south side of the *intervallum* road. Scale divisions: 50 cm.

PLATE VIa. – Ravenglass: trench B, looking west. Partially excavated are the wall-trenches of phase 1 (left) and 2. To the right is the cobbled veranda. Scale divisions: 50 cm.

PLATE VIb. – Ravenglass: wall-trenches towards the end of excavation in trench C, looking west. The trench to the left belongs to phase 1, while the two centre trenches represent the end-walls of barrack-blocks 4 and 5, of phase 2. The postholes are still later. Scale: 2 metres.

PLATE VIIa. – Ravenglass: trench C, looking west. The two end-walls of barrack-blocks 6 and 7 of phase 3, together with stone-packed postholes of phase 4. Arrowed: phase 3 hearths. Scale divisions: 50 cm.

PLATE VIIb. – Ravenglass: tile hearth in the inner room of barrack-block 7, phase 3. Scale: 30 cm.

PLATE VIIIa. – Ravenglass: trench B, looking north. The *intervallum* road and the stone-lined drain, together with building-trenches of phase 3, are shown. Scale: 2 m.

PLATE VIIIb. – Ravenglass: bag of gaming-counters, resting on burnt floor-boards and sealed by burnt daub. Scale: 10 cm.

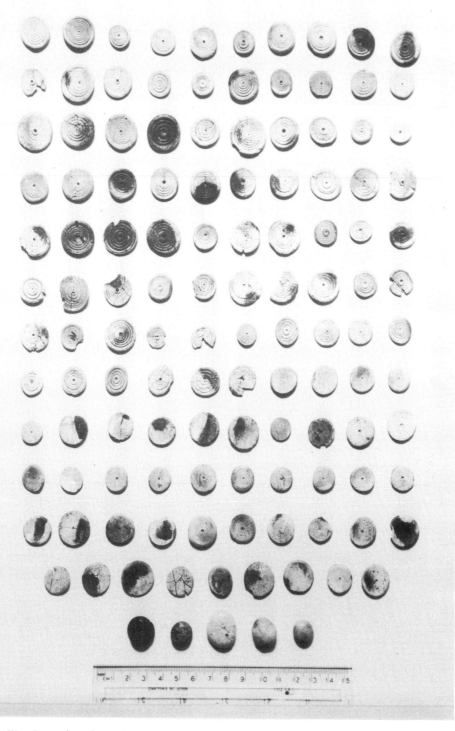

PLATE IX. – Ravenglass: the gaming-counters.

PLATE Xa. – Ravenglass: gemstones. Left, 111; Right, 112 (Photos: R. Wilkins, Institute of Archaeology, Oxford).

PLATE Xb. – Ravenglass: the bronze medallion of Admiral Vernon, 1739.

PLATE XI. – Watercrook: aerial photograph looking south-east, taken in 1949. Photo: J. K. St Joseph
(*Cambridge University Collection: copyright reserved*).

PLATE XIIa. – Watercrook: the east corner of the fort, looking south-east.

PLATE XIIb. – Watercrook: detail of the fort wall and rubble footing of phase 3, *c.* 150-70.

PLATE XIIIa. – Watercrook: the junction between the incomplete fort wall of phase 2 (right) and the fort wall of phase 3, looking south-west. In the foreground, the inner ditch, 1.

PLATE XIIIb. – Watercrook: the east guard-chamber, north-east gate, looking north.

PLATE XIVa. – Watercrook: detail showing the masonry of the north wall of the east guard-chamber, north-east gate. Scale: 40 cm.

PLATE XIVb. – Watercrook: the north-east gate showing the late blocking and the stone-lined drain.

PLATE XVa. – Watercrook: the north-east road, with successive surfaces.

PLATE XVb. – Watercrook: the inner ditch (1).

PLATE XVIa. – Watercrook: the inner ditch (1) at the east corner of the fort, showing the cleaning-channel and long inner edge.

PLATE XVIb. – Watercrook: palisade-trench on the berm between ditches 1 and 2, with stake impressions revealed as damp-marks.

PLATE XVIIa. – Watercrook: tips of iron slag and charcoal filling the lower part of ditch 2, and sealed by dumps of gravel and silt. Scales: 2 m.

PLATE XVIIb. – Watercrook: ditch 2 on the east side of the fort with, beyond, ditch 3.

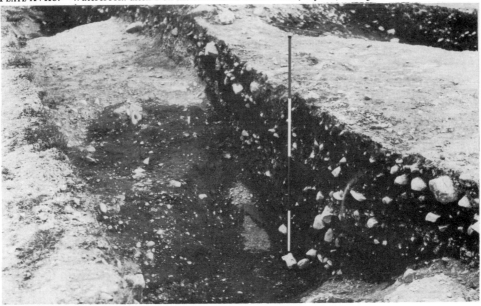

PLATE XVIIIa. – Watercrook: ditch 3, looking east, showing the original ditch and (foreground) the recut of phase 4.

PLATE XVIIIb. – Watercrook: lime-kiln set into alluvium beside the River Kent.

PLATE XIXa. – Watercrook: general view looking south-west, showing (foreground) the timber building of the north *vicus* and, beyond, the north-east gate.

PLATE XIXb. – Watercrook: stone-packed post-settings in a wall-trench of the north *vicus* building.

PLATE XXa. – Watercrook: the service road overlying ditch 1a, and running between ditch 1 and the north *vicus* building.

PLATE XXb. – Watercrook: east *vicus*, wall-trench and a line of stakes, perhaps representing a fence, cut into the subsoil.

Plate XXIa. – Watercrook: east *vicus*, section through the floors of the phase 3 building to the south of the road, showing nine successive surfaces.

Plate XXIb. – Watercrook: east *vicus*, section through the floors and occupation deposits. The scale rests on natural soil.

PLATE XXIIa. – Bowness on Solway: aerial view of the village, looking south a. *vicus* buildings facing the south road. b the 1976 excavations.

PLATE XXIIb. – Bowness on Solway at the end of excavation. The figures mark the line of the east wall of the phase 1 building.

PLATE XXIIIa. – Bowness on Solway: north part of the site showing the pit dug before the construction of the phase 1 buildings, together with other structural features.

PLATE XXIIIb. – Bowness on Solway: zone D, showing the east wall of the building of phases 2 and 3.

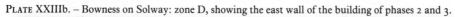

PLATE XXIVa. – Bowness on Solway: one of the timber sill-beam partitions, carried on two stone sill-plates and packed on the left side. Zone C, phases 2-3. Scale: 25 cm.

PLATE XXIVb. – Bowness on Solway: zone C, showing postholes of the fourth-century building (arrowed) together with the east wall of the phase 2-3 structure.